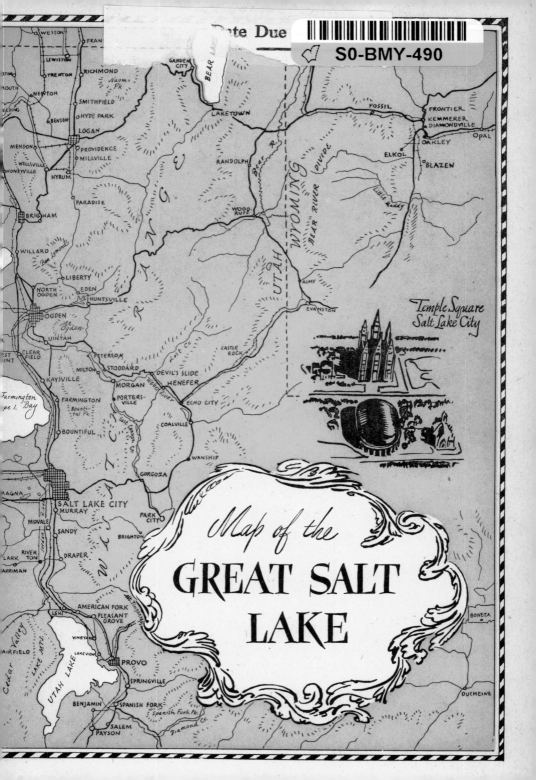

Map of the

GREAT SALT LAKE

Temple Square
Salt Lake City

THE GREAT SALT LAKE

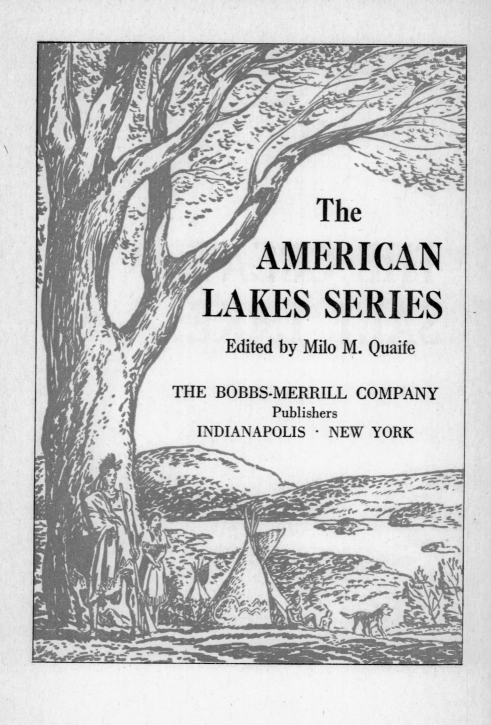

The
AMERICAN
LAKES SERIES

Edited by Milo M. Quaife

THE BOBBS-MERRILL COMPANY
Publishers
INDIANAPOLIS · NEW YORK

THE GREAT
SALT LAKE

DALE L. MORGAN

979.2
M828

First Edition

22941
ap '47

To

MAURICE AND LUCIE HOWE

EDITORIAL INTRODUCTION

BESIDE the Garonne River near the Spanish border of France lies the village of Lahontan, ancestral home of the Baron de Lahontan. Although it has existed for generations it finds a place in but few atlases or encyclopedias. Far to the westward, in the westerly portion of America's Great Basin lies prehistoric Lake Lahontan. In the earlier postglacial period it was almost as large as Lake Erie and several times as deep. Today its vestigial remains consist of a few shallow lakes and ponds scattered over the Nevada desert.

In the easterly portion of the Great Basin lies prehistoric Lake Bonneville, anciently almost as large as Lake Huron or Lake Michigan. All that remains of it today is shallow Great Salt Lake, near whose shore the metropolis of Mormondom was founded a century ago. If Lake Bonneville were to resume its ancient dimensions, Mormon Temple and Utah State Capitol would alike be buried hundreds of feet deep.

Curious indeed are the strands which make up the web of history. Baron Lahontan was a brilliant young Frenchman who came to Canada as an army officer in 1683. Although promotions and honors were repeatedly accorded him, a decade later, still in his twenties, he became a deserter, to live for the rest of his life an exile from his native land. Despite his erratic character he won enduring literary fame, and along with it a reputation as one of history's colossal hoaxers. In an otherwise excellent description of contemporary New France he incorporated a fictitious narrative of the pretended ascent of a fictitious Long River, a tributary of the Mississippi; on whose upper waters he encountered a fictitious tribe of natives who told him of a westward-flowing river which emptied by a mouth 2 leagues wide into a salt lake 900 leagues in circumference.

It seems highly improbable that Lahontan had obtained any actual information about the existence of the Great Salt Lake, and his fictional invention must be regarded as a marvelously lucky shot in the dark. In any event his *Nouveaux Voyages*, published at The Hague in 1703, contains the first recorded mention of the Salt Lake, and to it he owes the honor of having his name bestowed, almost three centuries later, on Pleistocenic Lake Lahontan.

Like Lahontan, Captain Bonneville never saw Great Salt Lake. Like his countryman of an earlier century, too, Bonneville was not overly careful about observing the standards of simple honesty. A graduate from West Point and a veteran army officer, under the pretense of conducting an exploring expedition he obtained an extended leave of absence from his military duties, only to devote his time and energy to a prolonged trading expedition. Overstaying his leave, he was cashiered from the army. Although he had ample opportunity to visit Great Salt Lake, he did not bother to do so, yet he strove, with some temporary success, to attach his name to it. Eventually this effort failed completely, but a generation later his name was given to the vastly greater geologic Lake Bonneville, and still later to the great Bonneville Dam.

In 1830 the Mormon Church was born as one among many obscure frontier sects. Despite the almost constant opposition of the gentile world it throve amazingly and in 1844 its capital city of Nauvoo was the metropolis of the state of Illinois. That year, however, the Prophet, Joseph Smith, was lynched by a gentile mob and the ensuing state of civil war between Saints and gentiles was only ended by the removal of the former to the isolated region of the Great Salt Lake.

Here were laid the foundations of the commonwealth of Utah just a century ago. For half this period the relations of the Saints with the gentile world continued stormy enough. The recent half-century of statehood, on the contrary, has been one of peaceful membership in the sisterhood of American states.

In the present volume Mr. Morgan relates the story of Great Salt Lake and its tributary area from the earliest geologic period to the present time. Necessarily, in doing so, he has supplied a summary narrative of the many exploring and trading expeditions, Spanish, British, and American, through whose combined activities the Great Basin was made known to the civilized world.

The ultimate test of the capacity of American historians for objectivity was once said to be furnished by the career of John Brown. We think, however, that the subject of Mormonism affords a more severe test. So controversial is it, indeed, that even yet almost everything in print on the subject reveals a marked pro or anti-Mormon bias. Although Mr. Morgan is a native of Salt Lake City and thoroughly informed about the stormy past of Mormonism, his readers will have extreme difficulty in detecting any trace of bias in his narrative. Despite his unfailing interest in the human background of his subject, he maintains throughout the highest standard of impartial scholarship.

Although still in his early thirties, Mr. Morgan has authored numerous monographs dealing with Mormonism and Utah; has edited the State Guide of the Utah Writer's Project; and has written *The Humboldt: Highroad of the West* for the Rivers of America Series. In prospect is a comprehensive history of Mormonism, for which he has been accumulating notes and data for nine years, and upon whose actual writing he will embark in the late fall of 1947. Readers of his present *Great Salt Lake* will entertain no doubt that in him Utah and Mormonism have found a competent and fair-minded historian.

M. M. QUAIFE
Detroit Public Library

TABLE OF CONTENTS

LIST OF ILLUSTRATIONS

LIST OF MAPS

THE GREAT SALT LAKE

Chapter 1

The Mountain Sea

GREAT SALT LAKE is unique among the great American lakes, arresting in its name, yet least known. Its name itself has an aura of the strange and the mysterious, but it resists those who would know it. Lake of paradoxes, in a country where water is life itself and land has little value without it, Great Salt Lake is an ironical joke of nature—water that is itself more desert than a desert.

Moody and withdrawn, the lake unites a haunting loveliness to a raw desolateness. Not many have achieved a sense of intimacy with it. It is intolerant of men and reluctant in submission to their uses. Defending itself with its own shallows, the lake is almost impossible of access except at its southeastern shore. Men have attempted to force it into the servitude of navigation; recalcitrantly it has withdrawn from their piers, leaving them high and dry, or has risen to inundate them entirely. Men have mined its waters of its salts; indifferently the lake has replaced the salts from its affluent waters and has remained unchanged.

The pervasive mystery clinging to the lake has found expression in a bizarre folklore. Gigantic Indians riding on elephants have lived upon its islands, and the mysterious white Indians, the Munchies, once dwelt there, too. Maelstroms have ravaged its surface, great vents have opened in its bottom to drain its water horribly into the bowels of the earth, and of course it was connected to the Pacific Ocean by subterranean passage. Appalling monsters have bellowed in its shallows and made forays upon its shores. Noxious vapors rising from its surface have brought instant death to birds flying above it, and its corrosive salts have burned the skin from swimmers rash enough to risk themselves in its waters.

All these tales one believes or not, at his pleasure. But other ideas about the lake are widely held. In the years of the "ox-team telegraph" rumors periodically swept the East that the lake had left its bed and sunk Great Salt Lake City in fifty feet of water. There still exists a tendency to wonder whether the Mormon country can

17

be quite safe from a lake so strangely removed from common experience. Such fears are hardly shared by those who dwell in its immense valley, but even they look upon the lake a little askance. It is regarded as given to irrational moods of violence, its navigation attended by unusual hazards. Its strangling brine is feared unreasonably, and swimmers are carefully indoctrinated in the technique of caring for themselves should the stinging salt splash into their eyes—suck a finger clean and wash the eyes with saliva.

Wholly apart from the folklore, the lake has an obstinate and fascinating identity of its own. It has its own history, a startling history. But also in three centuries it has been a part of the written history of men. Spaniards and mountain men sought it out; the Mormons fled to it for a promised land. Its salt waters and the blazing deserts of its making, lying athwart the American westering, forced trails and roads and railroads north and south around it. A barrier sea, fascinating and strange, implacable and wayward!

Visitors have called its waters bright emerald, grayish green and leaden gray; they have called them sapphire and turquoise and cobalt—and they have all been right. Its color varies with the time of day, the state of the weather, the season of the year, the vantage point from which it is seen. It can lie immobile in its mountain setting like a vast, green, light-filled mirror, or, lashed by a sudden storm, rise wrathful in its bed to assault boats and its shoreline with smashing four-foot waves. The wind is its only master. The wind drives it contemptuously about from one part to another of its shallow basin, piling up the water here, exposing the naked lake floor there, as if the basin itself were twisted and tilted under the surging green brine.

It lies at the bottom of three great north-south depressions which together comprise the valley of the Great Salt Lake. East of the lake the mighty rampart of the Wasatch Mountains, rising as high as eleven and twelve thousand feet above sea level, exacts from the prevailing westerly winds a tribute of rain and snow which created the lake and has maintained it. West of the Wasatch rises a lesser, parallel range, the Oquirrh, which dips beneath the lake at its southeastern shore to create its only good beaches. Farther north, this range rises intermittently as Antelope Island and the speck called Egg Island, then again as Frémont Island, and emerges finally as that long, rocky spine, the Promontory Mountains. A third parallel range, the Stansbury Mountains, falls off to a sand bar at the lake shore, lifts to create Stansbury Island and finally subsides into the water as two rocky crests called Carrington and Hat Islands. Along its west shore the lake is contained for much of its length by the Lakeside Mountains and Strongs Knob but then breaks free to the west for a few more miles to wash against the eastern base of the Terrace and Hog Mountains.

The lake is deepest in the sunken valley lying between the two island chains. In 1850 Captain Howard Stansbury found depths up to 36 feet between Carrington and Antelope Islands, as against an average depth of 13 feet. The depth is less today, for the lake in 1947 was approximately 4 feet lower than in Stansbury's time.

Roughly Great Salt Lake is 75 miles long by 50 wide, but its dimensions can rarely be stated with any precision. All its shores slope so gently that its shore line is subject to extraordinary fluctuation. A rise of a few feet in the lake level may change its contours amazingly and add hundreds of square miles to its surface area.

The shallowness of the lake's basin has been its primary defense against intruders. Save only for the southeastern beaches at the base of the Oquirrhs, it is everywhere bulwarked with mud morasses and salt marshes which have made it nearly inaccessible and have done much to preserve its atmosphere of desolate strangeness. From all but a very few it has withheld itself. There have been those who have gone out upon its waters to find it possessed of an unimaginable glory, a true splendor. But intimacy with the lake for most has been of a more remote kind.

Since 1903 the fills and trestles of the Lucin Cutoff have hurtled trains east and west across the lake, and the Southern Pacific's passengers have come to know something of its character. But a Pullman is insulated from reality. Carefully groomed upholstery, starched white pillows, obsequious porters and unwearying air conditioning do violence to the very nature of the lake.

Walk the salt-encrusted beaches of the southeastern shore and savor the sour, strange odor, half-stench yet alive and individual, that rises from the drying salt flats. Watch the heavy, unquiet water seeking the beach, while with harsh, untiring outcries the gray-and-white winged gulls wheel above you. This is a holiday hour; children play along the beaches; an old man floats on his back before

you, gently rising and falling in six inches of brine transparent above
the rippling lake floor; girls sun themselves on the sand; and a boat
with tall white sails is making for the boat harbor. But listen to the
gulls and stare out over the water. Behind you is the shoulder of the
smoky Oquirrhs, burnt umber and ocherous gray; in front of you,
far out, is deepening green water intercepted by a band of deep, dark
blue in which is set the low-lying gold-and-amethyst bulk of Antelope Island. To the west the high, bare silhouette of Stansbury
Island awaits the descending sun. The sunlight plays magically
with the water, spilling quicksilver on it the while it prepares the
stain of scarlet and gold which must see the sun to its setting. The
feel of the sun and the salt on your skin, the wide sweep of the open
sapphire sky, the strangely scented wind raucous with the screaming
of the gulls, the intermingled beauty and stripped ugliness of lake
and shore . . . in all these things is something of the experience of
Great Salt Lake.

There are other, more distant intuitions. Take US 89, the mountain highway, south from Ogden, follow it around the hillsides to the
mouth of the Weber, above the green-and-gold cove of Uintah, then
drive on around the shoulder of the Wasatch south toward Salt Lake
City. The highway climbs a long hill and curves gently amid the
orchards from which come Utah's surpassing peaches. All at once
the land to the west falls away and the Great Salt Lake spreads far in
the plain before you. There is the wide silver ribbon of beach beyond the green valley farmlands, the concentrate blue line of the lake,
and the warm-hued mass of Antelope hugging the dark band of
water. The lake lies immaculately alone under your sight—withdrawn and desolate, yet touched with a strange, compelling beauty.

Similarly, it is worth bumping and bouncing over the old road to
Promontory to go on a few miles beyond the gray, pyramidal Golden
Spike monument and experience the sudden shouting presence of
the northwestern arm of the lake. Except for the twisting, rutted
road and the unsteady line of dusty telephone poles, this is the lake
of history that lies abruptly under sight. The gray-green sage and
greasewood seem withdrawn and unfriendly, the darkly green
blotches of juniper immensely unrelated to human existence, the far
curve of lake shore new and undiscovered; you know that this is

how it always was, back to the time when the first immigrant company to California went this way.

This experience may be constantly repeated. The lake is too difficult to approach to be taken for granted; the tang of surprise and the shock of recognition are a part of its character.

Men have made themselves at home only along the southern and eastern shores of the lake. Except along the old route of the Central Pacific over the Promontory summit and around the north shore, which was finally abandoned in 1942, and along the Lucin Cutoff, with its service points and sidings, the northern and western shores of the lake are almost completely uninhabited. Kelton, the jumping-off spot for the Oregon and Idaho stages until a railroad was built to the Northwest, is the sole metropolis of all this vast area. It consists today of a single store, a red warehouse and a few buildings constructed of railroad ties, its sole reason for survival some outlying sheep and cattle ranches.

At the south shore of the lake small Mormon towns with their green farmlands and smoke-encrusted smelters give an accent of life to Tooele Valley, rimmed by the Oquirrh and Stansbury Mountains. But the Great Salt Lake country, expressed in terms of the people who live there, is the sloping plain stretching for over a hundred miles along the west face of the Wasatch Mountains and curving southward to include, by courtesy, Utah Valley.

This long, narrow strip of land, only 20 or 30 miles wide, has been called the Wasatch Oasis and comprises most of Utah's five richest and most populous counties—Utah, Salt Lake, Davis, Weber and Box Elder. Seven-tenths of the population of the entire state lives in this green oasis. Provo, (18,071 population) in Utah Valley is surrounded by a cluster of vigorous small towns. Salt Lake City (149,934 population), the state capital, wholly dominates Salt Lake Valley and is a regional metropolis as well, profoundly influencing life for hundreds of miles in all directions. The Davis Valley is a continuous wealth of green farms broken up into a succession of small towns. In the Weber Valley is Ogden (43,688 population), Utah's second largest city, and its chief rail center. Northernmost of these prosperous towns is Brigham City (5,641 population), at the head of Bear River Bay. Though the Wasatch Oasis is regarded as extending northeasterly into Cache Valley, where Logan (11,868 population) is Utah's fourth city, this area is more remote from the lake shores.

For all these cities the distance to salt water varies from five to twenty miles. Land adjacent to the lake is generally poor, alkaline and badly drained; the benchlands lying close under the mountains not only have richer soil but may be more readily irrigated by diversion canals which bring the waters of the canyon creeks to the land. The population has naturally concentrated itself on the higher land.

The lake has three great affluents—Bear River in the north, emptying into Bear River Bay; Weber River, with its delta some miles to the south; and Jordan River, emptying into the lake several miles northwest of Salt Lake City. Both the Bear and the Weber rise in the high Uinta Mountains 80 miles to the east, and after long and tortuous courses break through the Wasatch mountain wall to reach the lake. The Jordan drains fresh-water Utah Lake, which itself is principally fed by the Provo River, a stream rising within a few miles of the Weber and the Bear. Among Great Salt Lake's three primary affluents, the Bear is by far the most important, the waters of the Weber and the Jordan to a large extent having been diverted for irrigation purposes.

Great Salt Lake itself is the remnant of a vast inland sea which once rolled over most of western Utah and small areas of eastern Nevada and southern Idaho. Called Lake Bonneville, that prehistoric fresh-water lake was almost as big as Lake Michigan and far deeper. For a time it spilled over the rim of the Great Basin, north into the Snake, but as the climate changed, it shrank upon itself, breaking up into half a dozen smaller lakes. Great Salt Lake, Utah Lake, Rush Lake, Sevier Lake, and Little Salt Lake, far south in Utah, are all remnants of the ancient sea.

Through thousands of dry years, perhaps fluctuating widely in that time but in the long run receding, Great Salt Lake withdrew toward its present lake bed. Evaporation of its waters during all these years created a higher and higher concentration of the mineral salts its tributary waters had poured into its depths, and the withdrawal from the Pilot Range, at the Nevada border, formed a vast, level, salt-strewn desert like nothing else under the American sun, a poisoned earth where the old idea of the Great American Desert has taken final refuge.

The lake has been many times given up to death since men came to its shores. In the 80's the great geologist, Grove Karl Gilbert, predicted its early disappearance. Increasing diversion of its affluent waters for purposes of irrigation could have no other outcome, he reasoned. Antelope and Stansbury Islands would become permanently united with the mainland; the greater part of Bear River Bay and Farmington Bay would become dry; the deltas of the Bear and the Weber would join near Frémont Island, and the lake would make its last stand in the central depression west of Antelope Island.

Gilbert's reasoning was impeccable, but the lake has shown a great obstinacy in the matter. Although its level has exhibited a general downward trend, from time to time the lake has embarked on astonishing adventures.

Exact data have been kept on its fluctuations since 1874, and traditional data have been correlated for the quarter-century before that time to give a precise picture of its fluctuations. The lake level is calculated with reference to an arbitrary elevation designated as the "zero level." The present zero, on the Saltair gage, is at an elevation of 4,196.85 feet above sea level. This is used as the convenient standard of comparison, although there is another gage at Boat Harbor with the zero mark 10 feet lower. At the time of the Stansbury Survey in 1850 the lake was 4,201 feet above sea level. In the next 5 years it rose almost 4 feet higher, but at the end of the decade fell 5 feet. In 1862 it began a sudden, sharp climb, by 1868 rising nearly 12 feet, and in 1872 and 1873 rising 6 inches to its highest recorded mark. After 1875, however, it began to plummet, falling more than 10 feet in 9 years, and persuading Gilbert that it would soon dry up entirely. It rallied briefly in 1884-1885, rising to 4,207.5 feet, but it fell yearly thereafter until in 1905 it plumbed a depth almost a foot below zero on the Saltair gage. Gilbert's prophecies seemed on their way to rapid fulfilment when, under the stimulus of a succession of wet years, the lake started climbing again; in four years it climbed 8 feet, to a level 3 feet above Stansbury's mark of 1850. For 15 years the lake level remained fairly stable, but trending slightly upward until it reached the 4,205 mark. Then again, however, it dropped clear out of sight. In 1934 it struck zero on the Saltair gage, and kept going right on down, in 1935 reaching a low of 3.1 feet below zero.

However, the lake level promptly rose 2.5 feet, but drought in 1940 brought it down again to an all-time low, 3.2 feet below the zero level, or 4,193.55 feet above sea level. At this point stubbornly the lake again began to struggle upward, and in April 1946 for the first time since 1934 it rose above the zero level, climbing as high as .3 feet into the plus zone (4,197.15 feet) before relaxing back below the zero line, in the usual late summer fluctuation.

The lake fluctuates from month to month as from year to year. The level is always highest in the late spring, when the lake has been swelled by the spring runoff, and usually lowest in late November and December, when evaporation has got in its deadly work; this fluctuation during the year normally approximates about one foot, though in 1907 the lake actually gained about 3.5 feet, losing only about a foot of that amount during the months of adversity.

These fluctuations in the lake level directly follow upon conditions of precipitation. A series of wet or dry years will be followed by a corresponding increase or decrease in the size of the lake. It is said that the effect of wet or dry years in the lake's watershed is felt with diminishing effect for seven years.

Though irrigation has cut down the inflow of water, the lake has been more intimately responsive to general conditions of precipitation than to diversion by irrigation projects, and here rests the lake's case for survival: it cannot dry up until all its affluent waters have dried up, until a far-reaching climatic change has come about. And there may be as much reason to anticipate a cycle of wet years as of dry. So, far from disappearing, the lake may become as obnoxious a neighbor as it showed itself to be in 1924-1925, when it threatened to put the Lucin Cutoff out of business and flood the highway along its south shore. Or it may behave as it did in the 70's, when it flooded vast areas of low-lying meadowland and induced the Salt Lake County Commission to send out an exploring expedition to learn whether the rising waters could not be diverted westward to expend themselves in again flooding the long-dry Salt Desert.

This continuous fluctuation of the lake level has given the Great Salt Lake islands an adventurous history. Depending on the stage of the water, there are as many as 13 islands. In low water some are joined to the mainland or each other, and in high water some are inundated in whole or in part.

Antelope, the largest of the islands, is 15½ miles long by 5½ miles wide with an area of 23,175 acres. It rises abruptly from the water on its western shore but slopes gently toward the brine on its eastern side. Alone among the lake islands, it has been continuously inhabited since 1848, used for the grazing of sheep, cattle and horses. Antelope disappeared from it in the 70's, but a small herd of buffalo has been maintained there since the early 90's. In time of low water it is connected to the mainland by a sand bar over which cars may be driven, but visitors, whether by land or by water, are not encouraged by the owners, for fear of such fires as in 1945 destroyed thousands of acres of valuable grass.

Frémont Island, north of Antelope, is 5 miles long and 2 miles wide with an area of 2,945 acres. Though Frémont in 1843 described it as "simply a rocky hill, on which there is neither water nor trees of any kind," there is a seepage of brackish water near the waterline on the north coast, and two artesian wells provide an additional supply for the sheep which are pastured on the island.

Stansbury Island, west of Antelope, is usually a peninsula connected with the mainland, 11½ miles long and 5½ miles wide, with an area of 22,314 acres. Mountains rising 3,000 feet above the lake make it the most rugged of the islands. Like Antelope and Frémont, it is privately owned and used for grazing purposes.

Carrington Island, north of Stansbury, is a circular islet slightly more than 2 miles in diameter with an area of 1,767 acres. Although good roofing slate was early found on it, the island was never utilized until it was homesteaded by sheepmen in 1927.

Gunnison Island, the other principal island, in the northwestern part of the lake, is less than a mile long and has an area of only 155.06 acres. Like Bird (or Hat) Island, a 22-acre pile of granitic conglomerate, it is held under mineral patent for its guano deposits and is the largest of the 4 islands harboring bird rookeries.

Egg Island and White Rock, lying off the west coast of Antelope, are tiny islets also occupied by waterfowl, and like Dolphin and Cub Islands in the northwestern part of the lake, still public domain.

Mud Island, off the mouth of the Weber, is actually a 600-acre sandbar exposed only when the lake is low; another such sandbar is Badger Island, between Stansbury and Carrington Islands. Strongs Knob on the west shore with an area of 703 acres is normally a part of Strongsknob Mountain, severed from it only when the water is very high.

Although an island at no stage of the water, Promontory (almost universally miscalled Promontory Point), with its long, mountainous finger probing the heart of the lake, is a feature of the shore line as important as any of the islands; it, too, is privately owned in large part and is used as a range for livestock.

The Pacific Railroad in 1868 was tantalized by the idea of driving directly west across the lake but had to settle for a circuitous course to the north, and the Golden Spike was driven at the wind-blown summit of the Promontory Range on May 10, 1869. In 1902-1903, when the Union Pacific and its affiliated lines were engaged in straightening their routes, the opportunity was seized to build west across the lake during a time of low water, and the Lucin Cutoff resulted, slashing the distance to Lucin, far west in the Salt Desert, by 44 miles and eliminating the heavy grades over the Promontory.

The Cutoff drove a final spike into the hopes Salt Lake City had never been able to abandon, that it would get on the main line of the Union Pacific by adoption of "the only logical route" to the Pacific, around the south shore of the lake; the city was not entirely reconciled to the Cutoff until railroad lines down into the heart of Utah were completed to Los Angeles in 1905, giving Salt Lake City arterial connection with the Pacific Coast. In 1908 the old dream of a railroad around the south shore of the lake was finally realized when the Western Pacific was completed, giving the Denver & Rio Grande Western an outlet to San Francisco.

To construct the 102-mile Lucin Cutoff 3,000 men worked a year and a half. The cost was in excess of $8,000,000, and the job required hundreds of trainloads of rock and the timber from 38,000 trees. The arm across Bear River Bay to Promontory Point is 9 miles long, all of it rock fill except for 600 feet of pile trestle midway its length. From Promontory Point to Lakeside on the west shore of the lake is 20 miles. There are 4 miles of rock fill, then 20 miles of wooden trestle work, and a final 6 miles of fill at the west shore.

The salt water seems to preserve and harden the 100-foot pilings, but the Southern Pacific, the modern incarnation of the Central Pacific, must maintain a safety patrol at Saline, on the west shore of Promontory, to keep the rock fill under constant inspection, for storm waves exert an inconceivable battering force against the fill. For boatmen the Cutoff presents some problems, for clearance between bents of the trestles is not great, and passage is difficult if not impossible when waves are high. Moreover, when the lake level is high, vertical clearance is limited, and sailboats must dismast.

Like the railroad, the airlines chose the direct course westward. A flashing series of beacons guides planes east and west from the Salt Lake Airport across the low-lying salt water. The lake has never been hospitable to commercial boats, so its history is almost barren of dramatic shipwrecks, but since 1935 airplanes have periodically crashed in the heavy brine to provide the lake with derelicts of a different kind.

Most memorable of these crashes was the first, a two-motored Standard Oil Company of California plane on October 6, 1935. Three men lost their lives, and it required four months of intensive work to locate the plane; the oil company brought in Coast and Geodetic Survey officers familiar with hydrographic work, outfitted four search boats and carried on full scale surveying and dragging operations. Headlines were also made by the crash of an Army plane on August 31, 1937. One flier made the long swim to the highway west of Black Rock, frightening motorists with the specter of "a naked maniac" waving his arms at them, but his companion, after electing to stay with the ship in the stormy seas, swam for it too late. Search parties found his body two days later. On April 25, 1943, a B-25 bomber flying out of Sacramento crashed in the northwestern part of the lake, five men losing their lives, and a P-47 ship was wrecked off the west coast of Antelope on August 7, 1944, the pilot being killed. Early in May, 1946, a student pilot, stunting just off Black Rock, dipped his wing too low and paid with his life for his foolhardiness, plunging into the lake within 50 feet of two bathers.

More headlines have been made by crashing planes and by marooned boating parties than by drownings. Because the lake is feared for its strangeness and regarded as dangerous to swimmers and boatmen, its safety record is probably unapproached by any American lake of remotely comparable size. Among the few drownings perhaps the most celebrated was that of the Salt Lake merchant, J. D. Farmer, on August 6, 1882. His "semipetrified" body was not found till October 11, 1886.

Boating activity has periodically been attended by fatal mishaps; the earliest, perhaps, was that of three young men sailing out of Hooper in mid-June 1889. In general, however, boatmen are not flattered by the hue and cry that goes up in the newspapers when a boat does not get back to the boat harbor on schedule. The salt water sometimes splashes on the engines of outboard craft, putting them out of commission, and the high waves kicked up by storms are always regarded with respect, but a boat can ride out almost any storm if it is equipped with an anchor and scope of line and a means of bailing the boat. With a proper anchor overboard and the motor off or the sails furled, the bow of a boat will stay in the wind and withstand wind and waves. In fact, a boat with an anchor can come home safely without any other means of propulsion, simply by anchoring when the wind is unfavorable and lifting the anchor to drift with the wind when it is favorable. The prevailing winds, being westerly, will soon drift the boat to the inhabited eastern or southeastern shores of the lake, for in only a moderate wind a boat will drift a mile an hour.

During the 1930's more attention was attracted to the salt flats west of the lake than to Great Salt Lake itself, when the possibilities of the salt beds for racing automobiles were first fully realized. As early as 1911 W. D. Rishel had taken a big Packard to the salt to "open 'er up" to the terrific speed of 50 miles an hour. Thoroughly sold on the vast, salt plain as a speed course, Rishel three years later induced the speed demon, Teddy Tetzlaff, to take his Blitzen Benz to the salt flats. Tetzlaff broke all records with a mark of 141.73 miles an hour, but the American Automobile Association and the Automobile Club of America declined to recognize the feat.

The salt flats then lapsed back into oblivion, but after the Salt Lake daredevil, Ab Jenkins, became acquainted with the salt flats in 1925 by winning a race with an excursion train from Salt Lake City to Wendover, in which he traveled the newly completed Victory highway, he conceived the idea of turning the level expanse of salt to serious purposes of speed demonstration. In case of mishap a

driver had plenty of room to fight his car. The concretelike salt also had a cooling effect on tires, and its hardness insured that in case of a blowout the rim of the wheel would not dig into soft sand, as it had been known to do at Daytona Beach, Florida, hurling car and driver end over end. The only disadvantage was that the salt, always a little moist from the effect of solar evaporation upon the mud and water underlying it, furnished slightly less traction than a dry dirt, board or concrete track.

Jenkins made a 24-hour run on the salt beds in 1932, driving the entire time himself at an average 112.935 miles an hour, but he could get no official recognition, and it was a week before the Salt Lake City newspapers would condescend to notice the "stunt." The race course, a 10-mile circle, had been marked out by the Utah State Road Commission with 4-foot stakes, placed every 100 feet in holes made by driving a steel wedge into the salt. Jenkins says that the surface was so hard that at times the steel wedges bent like wax while they were being driven in. Twenty small oil flares lighted the course at night.

In 1933 AAA sanction was finally obtained, and in his 12-cylinder Pierce-Arrow Jenkins averaged 117.77 miles an hour for 24 hours and covered 3,000 miles in 25 hours, 30 minutes and 36.62 seconds. This was far in advance of anything it had been possible to do on European tracks and immediately attracted the attention of British drivers. When Jenkins' runs of 1934 shoved the 24-hour average up to 127.229 miles an hour, these drivers began making preparations to try their own luck on the Salt Desert.

For some time Sir Malcolm Campbell had been trying for a new record at Daytona Beach in his *Bluebird,* and in August 1935 he brought his car to the salt flats. His first trial, on September 3, brought him his coveted record of 301.13 miles an hour for the measured mile. Before Campbell's arrival, his fellow countryman, John Cobb, pushed Jenkins' 24-hour mark up to 134.85 miles an hour, though the Utah-born driver alone made a specialty of driving the entire run himself. Jenkins regained the record at 135.58 later in the summer, but the following year the English drivers, Cobb and George E. T. Eyston, returned to the competition. A summer of racing left the record in Jenkins' possession, but the 24-hour mark had been pushed up to 153.823 miles an hour. Under   stress of competition, all the cars were now being powered by airplane engines.

In 1937 Jenkins advanced his record for 24 hours to 157.27 miles per hour, and in 1939 he boosted it to a still higher figure, 161.18 miles per hour. Campbell retired from racing after his triumph in 1935, but his countrymen, Cobb and Eyston, embarked upon a competition between themselves for the one-mile record. In November 1937 Eyston covered the distance in his *Thunderbolt* at the speed of 311.42 miles an hour, and the next summer he shoved the record up to 347.49 miles. Cobb streaked over the course at a 350.25 pace, but this record lasted for just one day as Eyston promptly regained supremacy with a 357.5 figure. Cobb, however, had the last word. He returned to the Bonneville Salt Flats, as they had now been named, just before war broke out in the summer of 1939, and set the record, 368.9 miles an hour, which has since stood.

The rigorous testing given the British engines and the engineering genius that went into them bore rich dividends during the war when the gallant few of the RAF had to fight the Battle of Britain. It is the 24-hour endurance runs that primarily contribute to automotive engineering advances. The salt beds are a unique testing ground, a "speed laboratory," for making cars safer and better.

In this contrary fashion, by sharing its bed with a few lusty engineers and racing drivers, Great Salt Lake contrives a certain utility. But it seems more in character in other situations. In May 1939 it inveigled off course an Ogden resident herding sheep on Frémont Island. He had started for the mainland with horses and a two-wheeled cart along a narrow sand bar eight inches under water spanning island and shore. Though the way was marked at quarter-mile intervals with stakes, the herdsman, unused to "horse and wagon seamanship," wandered off his course and lost his horses in quicksand. He had to hike the six miles to shore and arrived in no very happy frame of mind.

That is rather more like the Great Salt Lake to which history has always had to accommodate itself. Always it has defied those who would use it. The most ambitious project of all, to dike it along its chain of islands—from the south shore to Antelope, from Antelope to Frémont, and from Frémont to Promontory, shutting the salt

L. Clyde Anderson

Sunset at Great Salt Lake, Stansbury Island in background.

Ute man and Ute woman (about 1871).

water into its western half and creating of its eastern reaches a fresh-water lake to provide industrial water—has threatened the very existence of the obstinate mountain sea. But even though the great French engineer, De Lesseps, builder of the Suez Canal, is said to have urged the practicability of the idea, and though intensive studies were made in 1935-1936 establishing its feasibility, the lake has a way of wriggling out of all such tight spots. Dr. Thomas C. Adams, who directed the engineering investigation, says that present public attitudes trend toward the feeling that it would be better to reserve such a development until other developments are made at higher levels on the affluent streams, where the water would be fresher and might be more economically developed.

Although there are a few scattered salt and sodium product refineries along its shores, and although potash has been mined from its Salt Desert, the mountain sea manages to maintain itself aloof from easy money-making. In the end you must take the lake on its own terms—refractory, obstinate, not to everyone's taste. Self-preoccupied, often sullen of mood, yet on occasion yielding itself up with an abandoned beauty that only the desert knows, it is a fit lake for a desert land.

Chapter 2

First Comers

No one knows when man first came to dwell in the immense valley of the Great Salt Lake. That puzzle is a part of the greater puzzle as to when man first came to live in the New World itself.

It was long believed that primitive man arrived in America only within the last few thousand years. But in 1926 at Folsom, New Mexico, chipped flint darts were found embedded in the bones of a prehistoric subspecies of bison; soon after at Lindenmeier, Colorado, was found a prehistoric campsite used by the Folsom people, and still another campsite was shortly found at Clovis, New Mexico. Challenged by such discoveries, archeologists soon were finding the characteristically chipped "Folsom points" the length and breadth of the great Mississippi Valley, from the Rockies to the Appalachians.

After a period of skepticism archeologists began seriously to postulate that perhaps 20,000 to 30,000 years ago the Folsom man had come to the American continent across Bering Straits, and moved southward down the great corridor of western Canada into the Great Plains. Though nothing else might be known of him, it could be assumed that he was the product of a long technological evolution; this was demonstrated in the craftsmanship required to shape his flint darts. Obviously a nomadic bison hunter, the Folsom man lived in no settled places, leaving no old habitations archeologists could dig out; with no farming implements or utensils for seed gathering except skin bags, he had no wealth of possessions to scatter about after the careless fashion of the human race, possessions to be found by the scientists of a far future day. While archeologists were still chewing on their new problem, fresh discoveries were made. In Yuma County, in eastern Colorado, flint points were found differing from the Folsom points so markedly as to be clearly the product of a different culture. Successive discoveries indicated that both Folsom and Yuman peoples had lived primarily on the eastern slopes of the Rockies, though scattered Folsom and Yuman points found in the Great Basin showed that these ancient hunters, or peoples kindred to them, had ranged through this region as well.

Still there was some question about the antiquity of Folsom and Yuman man. Archeologists disinclined to believe that either dated back to glacial times, so it was therefore a revolutionary discovery that was made in 1933 by Dr. M. R. Harrington at Gypsum Cave, in southern Nevada. Digging down through many layers of deposits in the floor of Gypsum Cave, down through the remains of relatively recent Indian cultures, Dr. Harrington came upon an amazing deposit—layers of what could be identified as the excrement of the extinct ground sloth, a glacial-age animal which had laired in this cave. And below this was found not only fossil remains of the sloth—wisps of coarse, yellowish hair, bones and claws—but charred pieces of wood, flint dart points, primitive ropes fashioned from twisted sinew and even short, painted wooden shafts, which possibly were primitive atlatls, spear throwers.

Here, at last, was triumphant evidence that man had been contemporary in America with glacial-age animals, that the history of man on this continent went back perhaps 25,000 years. However, the flint dart points in Gypsum Cave were as distinct from Folsom and Yuman points as these were from each other. And still another turn was given the puzzle when archeologists found in the Mohave country points of a fourth type, the Pinto.

Soon investigators were reporting the discovery of intermixed Yuman and Folsom points on the one hand, and Gypsum and Pinto points on the other. In such circumstances archeologists always set up a desperate yell for stratigraphy—for careful determination of the circumstances under which two cultures are found together and as to which lies deepest, so that something may be worked out in the way of relative chronology. Just such a cry went up, and before long a site discovered in southeastern Wyoming showed that the Folsom people had antedated the Yuman, however ancient the latter might prove to be.

The antiquity of such finds does not begin to compare with that of remains found in Asia, where protohuman skulls have been found to indicate that man existed perhaps so long as 400,000 years ago, nor have these finds lent any color of belief to the idea cherished by some that man originated in the New World rather than in the Old.

But the demonstrable time that man has dwelt in America was doubled, trebled or even quadrupled.

And there was now a starting place for working forward as well as backward. Archeology previously had labored patiently with the great Pueblo cultures of the Southwest, searching for clues as to their origins. The Pueblo peoples, so called because the sixteenth-century Spanish explorers found them living in settled villages, could be divided into five successive periods, which, with the help of a chronology based on annual tree rings counted in the timbers of their ruined buildings, could be dated back to about 800 A.D.

Obviously, however, the nomadic hunters who once had dwelt in the Southwest had not just suddenly built themselves immense, mud-walled villages and taken to raising maize, beans and squash. It had to be guessed that there had been an interim period when these Indians had built semipermanent buildings which they had occupied during the season maize was being cultivated, the rest of their time going for the age-old pursuit of game. This interim culture archeologists called the Basket Maker and it was accepted as a practical reality for years before actual remains were found to substantiate its existence. Ultimately the Basket Maker period was divided into two, Basket Maker I, of which very little is known even yet, and Basket Maker II, whose rock shelter and cave dwellings have been found in many places throughout the Southwest.

The chronology of the Pueblo and Basket Maker cultures together could be carried back to perhaps 500 A.D. But there the puzzle rests: what of the 10,000 year gulf between Folsom or even Yuman man and the Basket Maker I? It is not alone the interrelationships of Folsom, Yuman and Gypsum man, complicated by that other tantalizing culture, the Pinto, which has to be worked out. The relationship of all these to the Basket Maker has to be established.

In the midst of these puzzles the Great Salt Lake suddenly becomes interesting and important. Glacial and postglacial man must be sought out where he lived. His old campsites must be found on the banks of ancient riverbeds, or along the shores of ancient lakes. Areas of the Great Basin which now are the most arid of deserts were, in glacial times, green and inviting with forest and meadow. Hunters here could seek out the musk ox, the camel, the horse, even the mastodon and the mammoth; or, perhaps, harvest the seeds of the abundant grasses. The shores of old Lake Bonneville were undoubtedly many times visited by these lost races of men during the time when the lake was carving out caves along its shore line. When the lake level fell, as evaporation sucked up its waters, the caves that had been created were attractive places for men to shelter themselves from the inclement weather.

So the ancient caves of the Great Salt Lake region, like those of other old lakes in the Great Basin, offer inviting locations for determined new researches. Archeologists have dug in the caves along the shore lines of vanished Lake Lahontan in the western part of the Great Basin, in similar caves along the shores of old Lake Mohave in the southwestern reaches of the Great Basin, and they are digging now in the caves carved by old Lake Bonneville.

What is found in these caves will have a limited antiquity. The caves could not have been occupied before the recession of the Pleistocene lakes, which began perhaps 25,000 years ago. Older evidences will have to be searched for elsewhere; campsites must be found on ancient watercourses—a difficult job to begin with, and necessarily to be attended by much good luck if anything is recovered after so many thousands of years.

Still, the caves are a starting point; the archeologists as they dig patiently in one cave after another can work forward in time, hoping to learn of the relationships of one culture to another. Absolute dating of whatever is found is attended by many difficulties, with a wide range of possible error. Yet the resources that archeology brings to such tasks are surprising. There is always the fact of bedrock or its equivalent, the virgin gravels deposited by the ancient lake before its withdrawal from the cave. If human remains are shown in very close association with virgin deposits, with little intervening mud, dust or other sterile depositions, there is a high probability that the cave under investigation was occupied soon after its abandonment by the lake.

In 1930-1931 Dr. Julian H. Steward of the University of Utah carefully explored two caves on Promontory and another at the south shore of Great Salt Lake near Black Rock. In these caves he found remains of a new culture, which he labeled the Promontory. The Promontory people were evidently a race of bison hunters, nomads who entered the Salt Lake Basin from the north. The time these hunters invaded the region, in terms of the Basket Maker and Pueblo cultures, could not be established on the basis of these initial investigations, but just prior to the entrance of the United States into the second World War Elmer R. Smith of the University of Utah dug for an answer to the question in two caves at the south shore of the lake and two other caves in the Desert Mountains at the western rim of the Salt Desert. He discovered Pueblo and Promontory pottery intermingled—Pueblo deepest, Pueblo and Promontory associated, Promontory alone, and on top traces of recent Shoshonean culture.

The Promontory man, then, was no stage in the early evolution of the Folsom man; he was relatively a late-comer. When he invaded this country from the north, he found already living here the first Pueblo peoples. It is important that the relative chronology of the Promontory culture should thus have been fixed, for a mystery remains. Under the Promontory depositions in the caves he dug, Dr. Steward found scattered artifacts of a still older culture. The remains were too scanty to permit a very satisfactory guess as to the nature of the people they represented, but they bore nothing in common with the Pueblo remains which subsequently were found in association with the Promontory deposits, and it was a fair presumption that they antedated the Pueblo peoples. Dr. Steward hazards the suggestion that the people who left those scanty remains were the Salt Lake Basin contemporaries of the Basket Makers who were developing farther to the south and east. More digging in more caves will be necessary before archeologists can talk with confidence about these matters.

Nevertheless, the picture of ancient man in the Great Salt Lake region begins to take form. Though Folsom man, or a related culture, may once have lived in the vicinity of old Lake Bonneville, his presence there has not yet been established. Everywhere, not only in the Great Salt Lake country, a tremendous gap exists between Folsom man and the earliest Basket Makers. But perhaps about 500 A.D. the Basket Makers appeared in the Southwest with their revolutionary contribution toward a settled, or semisettled, agricultural life. Their contemporaries in the Salt Lake Basin were nomadic hunters of the immemorial kind, but by about 1000 A.D. the technological innovations of the Basket Makers had ripened into Pueblo I, and this culture had moved northward into the Salt Lake Basin.

These first Pueblo peoples in the Salt Lake country lived in pit houses, small adobe habitations in the form of a truncated cone, and had a pottery of poorer type than characterized peoples living farther south. To a greater extent than was usual, they combined hunting with agriculture; perhaps the difficulties of growing maize at a point so far north as the Great Salt Lake contributed to this continued dependence on hunting.

About 1000 A.D. the Pueblo peoples in the Southwest, in southern Utah and Colorado, and in New Mexico and Arizona, began to leave their small masonry houses to live in large, terraced pueblos of three or four stories, the beginning of the time of great cultural advances called Pueblo III or Great Pueblo. This was not, however, echoed in the Salt Lake country. Instead, the Pueblo people in the north began to abandon their habitations and migrate southward.

It is entirely possible that they were driven before the invading Promontory people, beginning about 1100 A.D., and the continued southward movement of the invaders may have been responsible for the ultimate abandonment of the great pueblo ruins still to be seen in southeastern Utah and adjacent Colorado and New Mexico. Archeologists are seeking now to establish whether the Promontory people could have been the ancestors of the Navaho, a fascinating idea to be worked on from both ends, tracing the Navaho backward and the Promontory people forward in time.

Archeologists maintain due reserve about this idea, but they are quite certain that the Promontory people had nothing in common with the Shoshonean peoples who occupied the Great Basin at the time white explorations began; their cultures are too dissimilar.

The Shoshonean culture seems first to have appeared in the western half of the Great Basin and to have spread eastward perhaps 500 or 600 years ago. In the course of their migrations the Shoshoni became differentiated as several peoples. One group, the Comanche, split off to penetrate as far south and east as the plains of central Texas. The Ute moved into western Colorado, northern New Mexico, and eastern Utah, occupying the mountainous area south of the Uinta Mountains and east of the west face of the Wasatch Mountains, including some fertile valleys at the base of the Wasatch, like Utah Valley. The Shoshoni proper, as they have been known in historic times, occupied western Wyoming, southern Idaho, northern

Utah and parts of northern Nevada and eastern Oregon. The Western Shoshoni occupied parts of western Utah and central and eastern Nevada. The Southern Paiute occupied western and southern Utah and southern Nevada, while the Northern Paiute occupied western Nevada up and down the long front of the Sierra Nevada.

The lives of all these peoples were shaped by the peculiar nature of the country they occupied. In contact with the Spanish frontier, the Ute and Comanche acquired horses which spread north to the Shoshoni and thence to the tribes of the Pacific Northwest. Horses revolutionized the lives of all these tribes, enabling them to become nomadic hunters on a scale hitherto undreamed of, and to associate in numbers and effect a close tribal organization such as had never been possible before. They were enabled to strike long distances for game; specifically, to invade the Great Plains in quest of buffalo. The Comanche so mastered the horse culture as to make themselves the terror of the southern Plains; their very name still has a blood-curdling ring. And the Shoshoni suddenly found themselves enabled to withstand the shock of the Siouan pressure upon their flank—withstand it and even expand out upon the Plains.

The horse, however, was of no service to the bands of Paiute and Western Shoshoni overspreading western and southern Utah and eastern and southern Nevada. Lacking buffalo, this desert region could not support a horse culture, and the best uses to which these Indians could have put horses would have been to eat them. The Indians here necessarily were hunters of small game and gatherers of seeds and roots. They lived on rabbits, gophers, ground squirrels, lizards, snakes, fish, insects of all sorts, seeds, edible plants and roots of every kind. These were the "Diggers" of America's literature of universal disgust, declared to represent man in his lowest state. Even in our own time writers have not been wanting to say that the Diggers "had no culture," or had "lost their culture," to the point of degenerating below the use of fire.

But this is mistaken. The life of the "Diggers" represents a necessary adjustment to the conditions of environment; theirs was a technology no less specialized than the techniques of living worked out by the Plains tribes. The desert country except in special situations would not allow large concentrations of population. The basis of social organization was normally the family, and the Western

Shoshoni, for example, knew nothing of tribal chiefs until intrusive white men acting for a remote "Great White Father" created a need for someone who could assume authority to act for a band or a whole "tribe." But within the small familial organization the Diggers had intricately developed techniques for living from season to season— for hunting antelope, for gathering seeds and piñon nuts, or for roasting and storing crickets and grasshoppers. An oyster and snail-eating race of white men could regard their staple diet with disfavor as shocking evidence of bestiality—but this would seem to be a matter of narrow prejudice.

Agriculture was almost entirely limited to the south. In the Sevier Valley the Pahvant Ute grew maize, beans and squashes, the name Corn Creek surviving to memorialize this accomplishment; and still farther south, in the Virgin River Valley the Southern Paiute subsisted primarily by cultivation of the soil, resorting even to irrigation.

The valley of the Great Salt Lake itself was strangely a neutral ground. Commonly the Ute did not go north beyond Utah Valley, while the Shoshoni regarded the Bear River as the southern limits of their territory. At some time early in the nineteenth century, however, a small band split off from the Utah Valley Ute to move north into the Salt Lake Valley and intermarry to some extent with their Shoshoni neighbors; this was Wanship's band, subsequently known favorably to both the mountain men and the Mormons. Another small band under the chief Gosip also established itself in Salt Lake Valley; little is known about this band or its chief, except that he died early in 1850.

In the valleys and among the mountains at the southwest shore of the lake dwelt four or more bands of Indians locally known in Utah history as the Goshoots or Goshutes (now authoritatively rendered "Gosiute") who seem to have been disliked and feared by their tribal neighbors, but modern ethnological research has found them indistinguishable from the Western Shoshoni who occupied eastern Nevada.

The various Indian bands the length and breadth of Utah occupied homelands with quite definite territorial boundaries, and well-understood rituals attended the entrance of members of one band into the homeland of another. Those failing to observe these social usages might be presumed enemies on whom the members of the individual bands could fall without ceremony. Warfare, however, was not common to the Utah Indians in prewhite times. The poverty of the environment made warfare a luxury overexpensive; the Indians were kept too busy finding food to go searching for trouble.

After the Ute acquired horses and learned that there was a market in New Mexico for Indian slaves, they made periodic incursions among the Southern Paiute, either trading for children, whose starving parents might be induced to sell, or simply kidnaping them; for this reason some of the southern bands were decimated by the time of the Mormon entrance into Utah.

Although the Northern or Plains Shoshoni enjoyed a bad reputation among the fur traders in the first few years of white penetration of their country, about 1830 they mended their ways and ever after were known above almost any other Indians as the white man's friends. Influential in the maintenance of such relations was the great chief Washakie, who came to power in the 1840's.

The Ute, by contrast, were somewhat temperamental neighbors, particularly after the chief Walker (anglicized from Wakara) made his mark about 1840. Walker, whose name meant "Yellow," seems to have been born about 1808 on the Spanish Fork River in Utah Valley. He rose to eminence, so Theodore Talbot was informed in 1843, through being such a good trader, trafficking with the whites and reselling profitably to his people. About the same time he began levying a polite blackmail on the caravans traversing the Spanish Trail to California, and in 1845, with a growing taste for plunder, he conducted a memorable horse raid upon the southern California ranchos. Frémont, who encountered him while coming up through Utah in the spring of 1844, gave him a romantic write-up which insured his prestige among the whites and his literary immortality, but until the early 1850's he was a lesser chief, owning as a superior his half-brother, Sowiette. After the Mormon migration to Utah, Walker had an equable interview with Brigham Young and was baptized into the Church and even ordained an elder, after the Mormon fashion of the time. He encouraged the Mormon settlements in Sanpete and Little Salt Lake Valleys, but in 1853 he fell out with his white brethren over their interference with his Indian slaving and briefly went to war.

Since the Mormons regarded the Indians as the "Lamanites," who had been cursed with a dark skin as told in the *Book of Mormon,* but who were destined to be redeemed and become a "white and delightsome people," they exhibited a generally kind attitude toward them. Brigham Young never tired of reiterating that it was cheaper to feed than to fight the Indians, and he declined to go to war with Walker, arranging instead a council of peace on the Sevier River the following spring. Walker died in January 1855, accompanied to the spirit world by 12 or 15 of his best horses and by 2 squaws and 2 slave children, sacrificed by his tribesmen.

The one other Indian war of note in Utah was fought out in central Utah in 1865-1868, when the Ute chief, Black Hawk, carried on a harassing guerilla warfare. In this case the Mormons had no choice but to fight, and a number of small skirmishes took place before a treaty of peace was negotiated.

The notoriety of being war chiefs fell principally to Walker and Black Hawk; other chiefs in Ute history have been celebrated for their peaceful ways. Wanship in Salt Lake Valley received the Mormon intruders amicably in the summer of 1847, and ultimately a Mormon town was named in his honor. Sowiette, during his years of power, was consistently friendly. In central Utah the Pahvant chief, Kanosh, was celebrated for his good will toward the Mormons, and Kanarra and Tutsegabits, Southern Paiute chiefs, had the same reputation.

Inevitably the Indians were dispossessed of their homelands. Though Brigham Young at one time advocated their entire removal from Utah to some likely location—say the Snake River or the Sierra Nevada, where the government could care for them better and remove them from proximity to the whites—he about-faced to show himself consistently the Indians' friend, urging his Saints to dwell among them, do them good, teach them to farm and graze livestock, and even to intermarry with them. He dispatched missions to seek after their welfare, the most celebrated being the Southern Indian Mission to the Santa Clara Valley in 1854, but others going to Fort Limhi in Idaho, Las Vegas and Carson Valley in Nevada, Fort Supply in Wyoming and the Elk Mountains in eastern Utah. Yet all such earnest gestures of friendship could not prevent the inevitable tragedy of dispossession. The spread of Mormon settlement deprived all the Indians of their best lands, and they moved sadly in the end to reservations. There are 10 of these in the state today administered by the federal government, and 2 others administered by the Church; the most important of the 12 is the Uinta-Ouray reservation in the Uinta Basin, where the remnants of the Ute are gathered.

What did these Indians make of the Great Salt Lake? No doubt it was accepted without wonder as simply another fact of nature. One name for the lake, as recorded by Lieutenant J. W. Gunnison in the fall of 1849, was "Ah oop pah." Probably this name came from a Ute informant, but Gunnison neglected to give its significance, and the Ute vocabularies available now suggest nothing more plausible than Ah oomp (pine) + pah (water), an unlikely translation, for the shores of the lake are not forested. Dr. Ralph V. Chamberlin's investigations among the Gosiute have yielded two names for the lake, "Piá-pa" (great water) and "Titsa-pa" (bad water).

The successive white explorers of Great Salt Lake flattered themselves that they were first to navigate the salt waters, and particularly that they were first to visit the islands. But flint arrowheads have been found on Frémont and an Indian burial on Gunnison. During the Stansbury survey of 1850 the surveyors were put to some inconvenience when Indians swam to Carrington Island and helped themselves to the red cloth used to cover the triangulation station. Antelope Island is a case all its own, for by 1840 a son of Wanship had taken up his residence and established a recognized claim of which Frémont, in the course of his exploration of 1845, was obliged to take grave cognizance. How or when this claim was relinquished to the Mormons does not appear, though it may be that this son was identical with the son of Wanship, called Jim, who early in 1848 was killed in a brush with the Utah Valley Utes.

Interesting Gosiute names for most of the islands have been gathered by Dr. Chamberlin. Antelope is "Pa'ri-bi-na" (elk place; elk breeding place). Stansbury is "Ya'ban-go-a" or "Yan-go-a" (meaning not clear). Frémont is "Mo'ko-mom-bite" (from "Mom-bite" meaning owl). Hat or Bird Island is "Pa'u-hna" (sea gull settlement or breeding place). In listing personal names of the Gosiute, Dr. Chamberlin was told of "Pa'wi-noi-tsi," a man spoken of in tradition who a very long time ago had built a vessel and navigated the lake; his name itself signified the feat, for "pa" means water, and "wi'a-no" to travel or ride. But this Indian of the long ago is otherwise lost to our history.

For Indians as for whites, the Great Salt Lake was essentially a desert of water. In a country where salt was common, its brines had little of interest or significance for them, and it gave them as food only the brine shrimp and the larvae and pupae of the brine flies which were washed up on the shore, together with such waterfowl as could be trapped or shot out of the air. To the poverty of their lives the lake brought only another poverty, another challenge in their agelong struggle to survive.

Chapter 3

Makers of Legends

───

I<small>T WAS</small> a wonderful journey on which the Baron Lahontan set out in September 1688. Or, if the journey itself was in any way unremarkable, assuredly the tale of it was not. As he set out from Michilimackinac, the Baron was equipped with a formidable apparatus of exploration, complete with soldiers and huntsmen and "new Canows loaded with Provisions and Ammunition, and such Commodities as are proper for the Savages." He crossed Lake Michigan and by way of Green Bay and the Wisconsin River made his way to the great Mississippi. There was little of note in this, perhaps, but as the Baron journeyed along the Mississippi he came upon a marvel hitherto unguessed, the Long River.

This new and wonderful river was the least of his discoveries, for after a voyage up it requiring 48 days, he arrived at the villages of the Gnacsitares. The chief of this nation received the Frenchmen coldly, but eventually he condescended to see the voyageurs, bringing with him not only 400 of his own subjects but four *Mozeemlek savages*—slaves of appearance so singular that the Baron, so he said, mistook them for Spaniards. They wore clothes, had thick bushy beards, and their hair hung down under their ears. Their complexion was swarthy, their address civil and submissive, their mien grave, and their carriage engaging. They came from a country far to the west, beyond a ridge of mountains six leagues broad, "and so high that one must cast an infinity of Windings and Turnings before he can cross 'em."

The Mozeemlek country clearly was a most extraordinary one. Their principal river emptied itself into a Salt Lake 300 leagues in circumference, and its lower course was "adorn'd with six noble Cities, surrounded with Stone cemented with fat Earth." The houses of these cities had no roofs, being open above, like a platform. Nor was it enough that there should be six such noble cities; there were also "above an hundred Towns, great and small, round that sort of Sea, upon which they navigate with such Boats as you see drawn in

44

[my] Map." The people of that far country made "Stuffs," copper axes and other manufactures of such kind as the Baron's interpreters could not give him to understand, as being altogether unacquainted with such things. The people about that salt lake called themselves Tahuglauk, and were "as numerous as the Leaves of Trees."

Fascinated by the reports of such marvels, the Baron questioned the Mozeemleks closely, but all of importance he could learn was that the great river of their nation "runs all along westward, and that the salt Lake into which it falls is three hundred Leagues in Circumference, and thirty in breadth, its Mouth stretching a great way to the Southward."

Long River, Mozeemlek, Tahuglauk and all, it was a gorgeous yarn that the Baron published at The Hague in 1703. In the presence of a glowing myth, it has always been difficult to be content with noonday facts, and the Baron's readers wanted to believe him. They still want to believe him; they go on searching for reasons not to disbelieve him. Were there not Pueblo villages in the Southwest, bearded Indians in Utah, a Colorado river of the West and, above all, a mountain sea? History, geography and archeology are impertinent to question the Baron closely.

Worthier legends are the heritage from Spanish adventuring, for however the stories are colored, they have the authority of the honest experience that went into their making.

In 1540 the conquistador Francisco Vásquez de Coronado marched north from Mexico in search of the fabled Seven Cities of Cibola. While resting at Zuñi he dispatched one of his captains, García Lópéz de Cárdenas, to explore the desert lands to the north. Cárdenas made his way to the southern rim of the Grand Canyon but could find no way down to the bright waters of the Colorado glinting in the canyon depths and turned back to Zuñi. It was a dry and terrible land he had seen, and through two centuries explorers were content to leave it to itself.

Lack of information only stimulated the geographers, who wanted to think that somewhere in the trackless north was a lake of Copalla from which the ancient Aztecs had come, and a color of belief came into such ideas after the Spanish colonization of New Mexico in 1598. The provinces to the north were divided as two, Quivira and Teguayo. Quivira was the realm of great plains spreading eastward from the Rockies, which during the next two centuries became the scene of very considerable Spanish activity, as far north as the North Platte. But that other province, northwest of Santa Fe, remained almost wholly unknown. On his Colorado River expedition of 1604-1606, Juan de Oñate learned from the Indians that the source of the stream was 160 leagues to the northwest, and this remote northern land was called by the name of Teguayo when in 1678 Governor Peñalosa unavailingly proposed to explore it. Little was known of Teguayo except that it was peopled by many different tribes of Indians, but a captive who claimed to have escaped from Teguayo said that during two years' captivity he had seen a large lake on the shores of which dwelt many people.

Was this that mysterious northern lake from which the Aztecs had come in antiquity? For a century and a half, Lake Teguayo might vie with the lake of the Tahuglauk for the credence of the map makers.

There are never any finalities in history. Back of the beginning is always the shadowy intuition of other beginnings, and monolithic facts which stand up rebellious and alone. In 1938, in the wall of the Colorado's Glen Canyon, Charles Kelly found carved a strange date: 1642. The inscription has all the appearance of genuineness. If genuine, who carved it? A forgotten Spanish adventurer 134 years before Escalante?

In this realm of the nameless and the unknown there is the French enigma, too; the question whether trader or voyageur too obscure to be caught in history's wide net may not have penetrated anywhere before any other. As early as 1706 the Spanish found traces of French trading activities in eastern Colorado, and who may say whether such traders did not drift among the Indians from one tribe to another as far west as the desert valleys beyond the Rockies? No tradition of such far wandering got back to the French settlements in upper Louisiana, however. At late as 1794, when *La Compagnie de Commerce pour la Découverte des Nations du haut du Missouri* began exploratory operations up the Missouri with the idea of ultimately extending its trade all the way to the Pacific, there was no certain information as to the nature of the country at the headwaters of the Missouri even—nothing but a rumor from the Indians concerning Great Falls.

Except for another of history's stubborn monoliths, one would have to relegate to the cloudland of dream and mere possibility all ideas of original discovery by the French in the Unknown Land which the Spaniards had called Teguayo. The traveler, Jules Remy, opens a door upon possibility. On the occasion of his visit to Great Salt Lake City in 1855, eight years after its founding, Remy remarked that what little had been known of the region before the coming of the Mormons was owed to the accounts of some Canadian trappers, and he added to his narrative a cryptic footnote: "There is still to be seen, in a naturally-formed cave in the mountains about the Salt Lake, an inscription in French almost obliterated, but in it the name of 'Lecarne, 17 . . .' is still legible." Was this hearsay only, something invented out of Gallic pride, or something Remy saw himself? In pioneer times a well-known cave was situated at the southern extremity of Great Salt Lake, and it is not altogether impossible that an inscription was carved upon its walls. But, unluckily, that cave has been buried under the slag dumps of the Garfield smelters, and it may be a millennium or two before anyone gets into it again.

From all such shining intangibles history has to turn to everyday certainties, to journals and maps which may be taken in hand and assessed with calipers and the calendar. In the struggle with the Unknown Land, it is the expedition of the two Franciscan priests, Silvestre Velez de Escalante and Francisco Atanasio Dominguez, that first gives comfort to history. Yet these priests were themselves makers of enduring legends.

By 1776, as the fruits of 11 years of desultory exploration north from Santa Fe, a considerable knowledge of southwestern Colorado had been gained. By 1776, also, the settlement of California had so far progressed that six missions had been established. With a view to extending the explorations so as to find an overland route to connect Santa Fe with the new settlements in California, the two devout Franciscan friars, Escalante and Dominguez, sought the sanction of the government for an expedition of discovery.

Escalante had come to New Mexico in 1768. His duties required wide travel in New Mexico, Arizona and Sonora, and in the spring of 1775 he made some preliminary reconnaissance of a possible route to Monterey, venturing as far west as the Hopi towns in Arizona. The idea of seeking an overland route farther to the north, through the lands of the "Yutas," he first advanced in October 1775. Such a route, he conjectured, might be easier and more direct than one south of the Colorado. Moreover, there was some rumor of Spaniards dwelling beyond the Colorado, perhaps descendants of shipwrecked sailors who had gone inland and settled in the country of the Yutas. It was not least among the advantages of the proposed exploration that discovery of these people "would be very useful to the Religion and to the Crown, either to prevent any invasion of our kingdom if they are strangers, or to unite them with us if they are Spaniards as the Indians say."

The Governor lent financial support and backing, and accordingly, with a small escort of 10 soldiers including the retired captain of militia, Don Bernardo de Miera y Pacheco, who was the map maker for the party, the two friars on July 29, 1776, set out from Santa Fe.

Two members of the little party of exploration on several occasions had traveled north as far as the Gunnison River, and it was with some assurance that the priests and their escort rode north into Colorado. The Spaniards were not entirely ignorant of the nature of the country to which they were going, for a month after the journey began, Escalante made mention of a "Yuta" band among whom were "some Timpangotzis [Utah Valley] Indians through whose land we intended to pass."

At the villages of some "Yutas" on the North Fork of the Gunnison they found two Timpangotzis Indians whom they persuaded to guide them. Setting out again on September 2 in a course generally north and west, they crossed the Grand and White Rivers, and arrived on September 13 at a stream to which they gave a name very soon to become central in the legendry of the West—the San Buenaventura (St. Goodventure). It was the Green River. Crossing to its west bank, near present Jensen, Utah, they followed the Duchesne and Strawberry Rivers through the Uinta Basin, and by way of Diamond Creek and Spanish Fork Canyon on September 23, 1776, emerged into "the lake and vast valley of Nuestra Señora de la Merced de los Timpanogotzis"—Utah Valley.

On all sides tremulous columns of smoke cried out the alarm of the Yutas at their arrival. Perhaps, the priests surmised, they were mistaken for Comanche. The guide, Silvestre, rode off to allay any fears, and soon the warlike preparations changed to earnest expressions of peace and affection. To the people who gathered from the various camps in the valley, the priests explained that one of the main reasons for their coming was to seek the salvation of the Indians' souls. If they received the Law of God, Fathers would come to teach them, and Spaniards to live among them, men who would instruct them how to plant and raise cattle. By such means they would become possessed of food and clothing like the Spaniards, and the Spanish king "would look upon them as his own children and would care for them as if they were his own people."

The Indians gave tokens of friendship, and it was with glad hearts that the Spanish company, on the third morning, turned southward in quest of Monterey. With them they took a report of this far country—a report from which the world might gain its first knowledge of an actual salt lake beyond the Rocky Mountains. The Timpanogotzis Lake, the Indians had told them, was joined to the north with another lake stretching for many leagues, a lake with waters "harmful or extremely salty, wherefore the Timpanois Indians assure us that anybody getting a part of his body wet, instantly feels a severe itching around the wet part." Around this lake lived a populous and peaceful tribe whose name, Puaguampe, signified witch doctors, or wizards. They spoke the Comanche language, fed on grasses and drank from springs of good water found around the salt lake. Their huts were built of dry grass and roofed with earth. They were not enemies of the Utah Valley Indians, so the priests heard, but because on one occasion they approached and killed a man, they were not considered as neutral as before.

Had the friars yielded to curiosity and gone north another fifty miles to the low-lying expanse of Great Salt Lake, history could pigeonhole the lake within a comfortable finality, "discovered in 1776 by the Spanish priests, Dominguez and Escalante." In turning south with no more than the report of the lake's existence, they gave history something priceless, a page forever left blank to the imagination, to myth and dream.

The southward journey made its own contribution to the legendry of this land. Four days after resuming their journey, the little company rode up to the banks of a river which appeared from the name given it by the Indians to be the San Buenaventura. Escalante was frankly doubtful, for if it were indeed the Buenaventura, the river flowed less water here than where they had crossed it higher up, nor had the guide Silvestre intimated that the San Buenaventura flowed near his home.

No such doubts troubled the map maker, Don Bernardo de Miera. With vigorous strokes of his pen he joined the two rivers as one, and made this river to flow into a brackish lake of indefinite extent, a lake to which he gave his own name.

It was the Sevier River and Lake the explorers had reached, and here they came upon the race of bearded Indians of whom the rumor had reached even so far as Santa Fe. These Indians, who spoke the Yuta language, were found indeed to possess thicker beards than Indians of Utah Valley and in their features they resembled the Spaniards "more than they resemble any of the other Indians so far known in America." The devout priests had come upon a curious sort of substantiation for a part of the tale of the redoubtable Baron Lahontan.

These bearded Indians told the Spaniards of Sevier Lake, and further informed them, erroneously, that after leaving the lake the river followed a westerly course. But there was no word of Monterey, nor indication that the Indians had ever heard of white men in the west, and the country was unpromising for water. The little company continued its journey southward in the face of a freezing wind on which the snow began to blow. For two days they were snowbound, and even after they prayed the intercession of the Virgin Mary, it remained freezing cold.

Plainly it was time to reconsider the advisability of trying to reach Monterey. An immense distance to the west was still to be traversed, yet they had found no likely route, and the mountain passes would be filling with snow. To go on would be at the risk of their lives, by starvation as well as by freezing. And, mark well, if they went on to Monterey, they could not return to Santa Fe before June. What, then, of their promises to the Yutas? Would the Indians not be frustrated in their hopes or even consider that they had been deliberately deceived? Finally, there was the consideration that a new and shorter route might be found to Santa Fe, and that other Indians before unknown might be discovered . . . The two priests decided on returning to Santa Fe.

Don Bernardo de Miera, however, had built up great hopes of honor and profit to accrue to him from reaching Monterey overland. Sullen and caustic by turns, as they recommenced the journey, he argued that Monterey could be no more than eight days' travel to the west. What a fiasco, to give up now! He found willing ears, and after three days the party was rife with dissension. First imploring divine mercy and the intervention of their patron saints, the priests proposed that the decision be left to the will of God, that they cast lots to determine whether to return to Santa Fe or make the effort to reach Monterey. All agreed, as Escalante wrote, "like Christians, and with fervent devotion recited the third part of the rosary, while we recited the Penitential Psalms with the litanies and the other prayers which follow. Concluding our prayers, we cast lots, and it came out in favor of Cosnina. We all accepted this, thanks be to God, willingly and joyfully."

So they made their hard way back to Santa Fe through the Colorado badlands, completing their epic journey on January 2, 1777.

No one will ever know for what reasons, but the promised mission was never sent to the Yutas. It was obscure traders only who, as the years went by, went in the track of the padres to the Yuta country—obscure necessarily, because such trading expeditions were forbidden by law, and violation was punishable by imprisonment and confiscation of goods. The first white man who ever looked upon Great Salt Lake—first, perhaps, even to taste its bitter waters—may have weighed in his mind, against the pains and penalties of the law, a distinction of discovery . . . and found the distinction outweighed in the balances. During the half-century after Escalante, only the most shadowy glimpses may be had of Spanish adventuring in the Great Basin. A Spanish document of 1805 records vaguely an expedition into the Yuta country of a Yuta interpreter named Manuel Mestas, who sought to recover stolen horses, and a more detailed account has survived of a party of seven men under Mauricio Arze and Lagos Garcia who traveled in 1813 to the lake of Timpanogos. According to its story, this company displeased the Timpanogos

Yutas by refusing to buy slaves, and after a fight in which eight horses and a mule were killed, made its escape south to the "Rio Sebero." There the party encountered the bearded Indians seen by Escalante a generation before. Again meeting a hostile reception, they took the road to the Colorado. The chief Guasache waited on the road to trade with them, as was his custom. Again the reluctance of the Spaniards to buy slaves offended the Indians, but, profiting by their earlier experience, the traders bought 12 slaves so as to proceed in peace, and thus, after an absence of almost four months, they came back to Abiquiu in July.

The implication of such fragmentary documents is that the trail to and from the Yuta country was well known, but no real information as to the activity of the Spanish traders in the far north has come to light. It is to the journals of Lewis and Clark that one must turn for indications that by 1805 the Spanish traders had extended their operations up through the valley of the Great Salt Lake as far north as the Bear.

Meriwether Lewis reached the anxiously sought camp of the Lemhi Shoshoni, in central Idaho, on August 13, 1805. Among many other things of interest he learned that the Shoshoni possessed horses with Spanish brands, a bridle bit, and other articles significant of contact with traders. This evidence of intercourse with the Spaniards Sergeant John Ordway soon documented in his journal—"it is only by their acc^t 8 day travel to the South to the Spanish country." Eight days' hard travel southward on horseback would be a journey very nearly to Bear River, the southern boundary of the Shoshoni country. If one may infer from that an acquaintance by the Spanish traders with the entire valley of the Great Salt Lake, one may also infer that not many ventured north of the Yuta country at this date, for Private Joseph Whitehouse, who likewise made note of the eight-day southward journey to the Spanish country, added in his own journal, "but these Indians git but little trade amongst them."

So the expedition of the great captains holds up a dim mirror to reflect the northern limits of Spanish adventuring and offer a tantalizing half glimpse of Spanish traders in the valley of the Great Salt Lake in the first years of the century, men dead to history whose names might have been writ in large letters. The captains themselves at Lemhi had reached their farthest south. After turning north to the Bitterroot Valley, they went on west across the mountains to the Columbia and the sea. Next year they came home in triumph, bringing America the heritage of a known and named land, though there remained, beyond the farthest southward reach of their map, a *terra incognita*—the Spanish Country.

The homeward-bound captains, as they floated down the Missouri, encountered a first embodiment of the forces and the enterprise that would finally reveal fully that unknown land. In August 1806 near the Mandan villages they met two American trappers, Joseph Dickson and Forest Hancock, who, as Sergeant Ordway noted, "were from the Ellynoise country, and have gathered a great deal of peltry since they have been out about 2 years and have carshed the most of it in the ground they tells us that they are determined to Stay up this river and go to the head where the beaver is plenty and trap and hunt untill they make a fortune before they return." Private John Colter, though he had been away from home two years, was given permission to join these trappers. So he was caught up on the first wave of a tide washing west upon the "Shining Mountains."

The tide was one difficult to resist. After a year of adventure, spent perhaps on the Yellowstone, in the summer of 1807 Colter came down river again, only to meet with the second wave of that westward-setting tide, the party with which Manuel Lisa was instituting organized fur trade in the Louisiana Purchase. Colter turned back, once again, into the West. He had already spent an adventurous three years in the mountains, and it was three years more before he saw St. Louis again.

Lisa's party built a post at the confluence of the Yellowstone and the Big Horn, and it was from this fort, later in the year, that Colter made the lone southward journey which gave Colter's Hell, a luminous prescience of Yellowstone Park, to American folklore. More significant was the enterprise of Andrew Henry in the fall of 1810. The relentless Blackfeet forced the abandonment of the post at the mouth of the Big Horn, but Henry did not at once retreat from the north country; his men penetrated south as far as Wind River, and across the continental divide to Henrys Fork of the Snake, where was built the first American post beyond the Rockies. Though Henry abandoned that fort in the spring and returned to St. Louis, his venture bore immediate fruit. The company of overland Astorians under Wilson Price Hunt, which came up the Missouri in May 1811, learned from several of Henry's men that there existed a better route for crossing the mountains than Lewis and Clark had found— a route south toward the headwaters of the Platte and Yellowstone.

The Astorians sold their boats to Lisa and bought horses for the overland journey. Crossing South Dakota and central Wyoming, they surmounted the continental divide by Union Pass and the Tetons by Teton Pass, arriving early in October at Henry's deserted establishment on the Snake. Here four trappers were detached, John Hoback, Jacob Reznor, Edward Robinson and Martin H. Cass, and they were joined by Joseph Miller, who in irritation had resigned his partnership in the Astorian enterprise. The rest of the company, after building canoes, began the dangerous voyage down the Snake. At Caldron Linn, after the drowning of one of the party, the journey was resumed by land. Beyond the Boise River, however, Hell's Canyon obstructed their course along the Snake even by land, and most of the now-starving company turned west across the formidable mountains of eastern Oregon to reach the Columbia. The fragmented party thence straggled down the river to Astoria.

Lewis and Clark had been first to look upon the Snake, but only for a short distance above its confluence with the Columbia. The Astorians had followed its entire course in the long arc through southern Idaho, and to that extent they had made known the country, almost as far south as the Spanish possessions.

The work of exploration and legendmaking was continued by a detachment of Astor's men which promptly set out back across the continent. Saluted by the cannon of the fort, the returning Astorians, an "express" under Robert Stuart, left Astoria on June 29, 1812. The six men journeyed up the Columbia and then retraced the route of the previous year's party across the mountains. As they traveled south along the west bank of the Snake, they fell in with an Indian who had guided the westbound Astorians over Teton Pass the preceding fall. From this Indian history gets its first intimation of a fateful fact of geography, South Pass—" a shorter trace to the South than that by which Mr. Hunt had traversed the R Mountains."

Eight days later Stuart's little company astonishingly came upon an almost naked white man fishing in the Snake. It was John Hoback, from whom Wilson Price Hunt's party had parted, far up-stream, in October. Out of the willows a moment later came Miller, Robinson and Reznor; Cass, they said, had villainously deserted them in the spring with one of their two remaining horses.

The tale of their wanderings was strange, with a legend-breeding geography. They had, Robert Stuart wrote, "on leaving the Party at Henry's Fort last Fall, gone 200 miles South, where they made that season's Hunt on a River which must discharge itself into the Ocean to the Southard of the Columbia—From thence they steered 200 more due East where they found about Sixty lodges of Arapa-hays . . . who robbed them of several horses as well as the greater part of their clothing &c—they then left them & continued their journey 50 miles, where they wintered, and early in the Spring were overtaken by the same Rascals, who then robbed them of all their Horses & almost every thing else—They with half of the ammuni-tion left purchased of them two of their own Horses and after travelling about 930 miles in which they suffered greatly by Hunger, thirst & fatigue, met us almost in a state of nature without even a single animal to carry their Baggage."

These four wanderers clearly had reached Bear River, a stream Stuart was soon to reach himself at its great bend and call Miller's River, but how far they explored the Bear there is no way of know-ing, except that, from Stuart's understanding of their travels, they could hardly have gone so far south as to the salt waters of the inland sea.

Stuart regaled his "half famished friends with the best our small pittance of luxuries could afford," and then the small company, now numbering 10 men, set out again, eastward along the Snake. But the spell that the flowering mountain valleys, the spreading sage plains, and darkly forested peaks had laid upon John Colter's heart and which they were to lay upon the hearts of uncounted mountain men, was too much for Hoback, Reznor and Robinson to resist. At Caldron Linn, half-naked as they were, they announced their pur-pose to stay and make a two-year hunt in the country below Henry's Fort. Thus, as would happen again and again before the era of the mountain men ended, they made the West forever their own. Six-teen months later, with others of the Astorians, they were killed by the Snakes in camp near the mouth of the Boise.

One of the four wanderers, Joseph Miller, chose to join with Stuart, his "curiosity and desire of travelling thro' the Indian countries being," as Stuart drily observed, "fully satisfied." With Miller as their uncertain guide, the little company continued east along the Snake to the Portneuf, up that river, and over the divide to Bear River, a route familiar in reverse to thousands of later travelers of the Oregon Trail. On Saturday, September 12, the Astorians passed the Bear Lake outlet, where "the mountains receded to a great distance and a beautiful low Plain occupied the intervening space," but they had no intimation of the existence of the blue mountain lake soon to be famous in the annals of the fur trade, and chose to follow the Bear proper because the "south Branch" seemed out of their course.

They had an Indian lodge trail to follow, but on this very day they fell in with a party of Crows, adroit thieves whose idea it was to trade horses for gunpowder with the amply justified expectation that they could promptly steal the horses back. Smoke signals gave frank warning that the trail up the Bear was full of hazard, so on September 13, 1812, the returning Astorians left the river for a course more easterly. Miller had led them to expect a river in this direction, but they could find nothing of it, and with the sharp peril from the Indians, it seemed best to move north and retrace across the mountains the route of 1811. Catastrophe overtook them on September 19. They could have no doubt it was the Crows they had met on Bear River who swept suddenly upon the camp, yelling, to stampede every horse—and "once those creatures take fright," Stuart lamented, "nothing short of broken necks can stop their progress."

The seven men, left afoot, tightened their belts and set out for home. "We have food enough for one meal," Stuart wrote gamely, "and rely with confidence on the inscrutable ways of Providence to send in our road wherewith to subsist on from day to day."

It was a reliance not misplaced. Their courageous purpose took them over Teton Pass, down into Jackson's Hole, up the Hoback River and over the divide into the valley of "Spanish River"—the Green—on a course generally east, but trending to the south. This route, on September 21-22, 1812, took them southeastward through that great open plain which has become one of the great names in American history—South Pass. They are the first white men known to have traversed it. Beyond the Pass they fell upon a "Branch" soon to become known as the Sweetwater, and from this point in their long, hard journey down the Platte their every footprint marked out the future Oregon Trail. On April 13 they reached the Oto village on the lower Platte and from two traders obtained a skin canoe enabling them to go on by water. On April 30, 1813, "a little before sunset we reached the Town of Saint Louis all in the most perfect health after a voyage of ten months from Astoria during which time we had the peculiar good fortune to have suffered in one instance only by want of provisions."

Robert Stuart's party was within the physical bounds of the Great Basin for seven days only, and any knowledge they would have of the Great Salt Lake would come from the explorations of others—ten, twenty and thirty years after their time. But they brought back to the frontier settlements not only their own ragged selves but the stuff of a newly fascinating legend. The legend of the West itself was implicit in their confident word of a road across the backbone of the continent. Immediately on their arrival, the *Missouri Gazette* published a long account of their experiences, and in that account was a significant summation:

"By information received from these gentlemen, it appears that a journey across the continent of North America, might be performed with a waggon, there being no obstruction in the wheel rout that any person would dare to call a mountain, in addition to its being much the most direct and short one to go from this place to the mouth of the Columbia river. Any future party who may undertake this journey, and are tolerably acquainted with the different places, where it would be necessary to lay up a small stock of provisions, would not be impeded, as in all probability they would not meet with an Indian to interrupt their progress; although on the other [Lewis and Clark] route more north, there are almost insurmountable barriers."

The *Gazette* might thus instruct Americans as to their destiny and find willing echoes in the most influential journals of the day. But for the moment destiny must wait. From the traders at the Oto village Stuart had gotten the first intimation why—"the Americans and English were at logger-heads." The War of 1812 had been in progress very nearly a year, and within a few months it proved the climactic disaster in a succession of catastrophes that had befallen the Astorian venture; Astoria fell into the hands of the great North West Company of Canada, which had reached the Columbia almost simultaneously with the Americans.

In terms of United States history and the westward movement, the extinction of Astoria constitutes a full stop, an area of dead energies where much had promised. But in the larger terms of American history, as of dramatic discovery in the Great Salt Lake country, much was gained by establishment of a British flank in Oregon: The Nor' Westers contributed their own chapter of uncertainty and conjecture to the tale of the Unknown Land.

Donald Mackenzie, who had come overland with the Astorians, remained for a time as a Nor' Wester. A tub of a man, aboil with inexhaustible energies, he took upon himself the job of leading the brigades which in 1816 the Company resolved to send into the unexplored country "south and west toward California and the mountains." Mackenzie located Fort Nez Percé near the confluence of the Columbia and the Snake, and from this post in 1818 took a party 25-days' journey south and east, penetrating finally to a rich beaver country beyond the Snake to what was termed, elusively, "the Spanish waters." But the Indians in that region were inclined to be hostile; Mackenzie swung north in a wide circuit to the headwaters of the Snake and thence west again back to Fort Nez Percé.

He remained at the fort only seven days before setting out again for the south, resolved, "should the natives prove peaceably inclined and the trapping get on smoothly among them, to spend part of the winter in examining the country further south," at which time he was anxious also to have an interview with the principal chiefs of the Snake (or Shoshoni) nation, not having hitherto seen them. While on this journey Mackenzie wrote Alexander Ross, a fellow Astorian who likewise was now a Nor' Wester, a letter with a tantalizing date line, "Black Bears Lake, September 10, 1819." He had almost certainly reached Bear Lake; he may even have given it its name. But it is unlikely that he went much farther south.

In 1820-1821 Mackenzie took a third expedition to the Snake Country, but it is impossible to say precisely where he went. This was the last of the great brigade leader's expeditions, for he returned east next year. Whether an expedition was kept in the field in 1821-1822 is not clear, but in 1822-1823 a party was fitted out for the Snake Country under Finan Macdonald, and this company apparently returned again as far south as Bear River. Yet again no one may say where the trappers penetrated except that they, being "at its Sources," presumed it to be "the Spanish River or Rio Collorado," and the presumption must be that no one descended the Bear so far as the immense salt lake into which it gives up its waters.

The adventuring of Mackenzie and Macdonald is the British bequest to the legendry of the Great Salt Lake country, a legendry in which all things are forever possible and Frenchman, Spaniard, Briton and American are the heroes of any dream. Positive discovery, now swiftly to follow, must deal with a strange heritage of mystery and myth with which the legendmakers of three centuries had cloaked the unknown.

Chapter 4

Rendezvous with History

BARON ALEXANDER VON HUMBOLDT was one of the foremost scientists of his time. At the beginning of the nineteenth century he journeyed to Mexico, returning to Europe to write a *Political Essay upon the Kingdom of New Spain* that was crammed with information about the antiquities and the geography of western America. Heir to all the Spanish adventurings, he brought them into the purview of organized knowledge. He drew upon both the manuscript journal of Escalante and the map of Miera, and his own map of interior western America, published in 1808, left a 40-year impress on American cartography.

Humboldt's geography of the northern Spanish dominion was compounded equally of fact and myth. On his manuscript map, Don Bernardo de Miera had depicted a Laguna de los Timpan[o]gos (Utah Lake) connected with a more northerly lake unnamed and of indefinite extent, fed from the east by a Rio de los Yamparicas (the Weber; or possibly the Bear) and drained from the west by an unnamed river of large size. Except for that western outlet, a fancy of his own, Miera's cartography was entirely sound. His map of the country to the south, however, had the grave defect of uniting the Sevier River with the Green as the "Rio de San Buenaventura." The brackish lake into which the Sevier discharged (Sevier Lake) he named Laguna de Miera, indicating at the same time another eastern affluent, the Rio Salado. The western limits of the Laguna de Miera he made no attempt to define.

All this information Humboldt faithfully incorporated into his map, except that he made the Rio de los Yamparicas a western rather than an eastern affluent of unnamed Great Salt Lake, and except that he gave no name to the vaguely defined Sevier Lake. From Humboldt's map these features, with other details derived from the Escalante journal itself, went immediately into the maps of western America. To the Humboldt conception was added only the ideas derived from the map William Clark published in 1814. Ascending the Columbia in 1806, Lewis and Clark had learned of a large affluent, the Willamette, heading far in the south. After a brief reconnaissance William Clark had "perfectly satisfyed" himself of the size and magnitude of this river, which evidently watered "that vast tract of Country between the western range of mountains and those on the sea coast and as far S. as the Waters of Callifornia about Lat^d. 37 North." Named the Multnomah, the river was shown on Clark's map as extending far to the south and east, roughly paralleling the course of the Snake.

These were the sources of the myths. The cartographers quickly combined the unnamed Great Salt Lake and Utah Lake into a single body of water, which sometimes was left unnamed but usually was styled the Timpanogos. This lake was represented at first as drained by a single outlet, the Multnomah. At the same time Miera's conception of a R. Buenaventura and a R. Salado draining into an unnamed lake was faithfully followed—the cartographers, like John Melish in 1816, tentatively draining that lake with a "Supposed course of a river between the Buenaventura and the Bay of San Francisco which will probably be the communication from the Arkansaw to the Pacific Ocean." Melish was satisfied with a single outlet for his unnamed Timpanogos, and so was John Robinson in 1819, but Robinson would have no truck with the Multnomah; instead he drained his Timpanogos by a Timpanogos River flowing into the Bay of San Francisco. There was a notable lack of agreement about which of the two lakes, Timpanogos or Salado, should have the honor of debouching into the Bay of San Francisco; thus Thompson in his *New General Atlas* of 1820 gave back the Multnomah to Lake Timpanogos and scrupulously depicted (Miera's) "Salt Lake" with its affluents, the Buenaventura and Salado, but firmly echoed Melish's conception of a Buenaventura continuing on to San Francisco Bay. In the same year the French map maker, Brué, reintroduced an old idea into the mapping of the Great Basin. His Timpanogos was more than orthodox, with a river at its head creditably resembling the Bear, and with Humboldt's imaginary western affluent, the R. Yamparicas. But he tentatively joined the Timpanogos with the southern lake, and this latter he boldly called *"L. Teguayo ou Sale."*

Thus at a stroke the early Spanish conception of a Lake Teguayo returned to history. Next year the German cartographer Weiland

The mythical lakes and rivers of the pre-exploration West, based on the map by D. H. Vance in Anthony Finley's *New American Atlas* (1826).

Soda Springs at Bear River on the Oregon Trail (about 1870), now submerged by the Soda Springs Reservoir.

Devil's Gate, Weber Canyon (1870), after a passage had been blasted for the Pacific Railroad.

adopted Brué's idea of a *"Sale oder Tegujo See"*; and, as Lake Timpanogos was now sagging from having to carry on its shoulders the
idea of the true Great Salt Lake, he stood that lake again firmly on
end.

Gradually the Multnomah was contracted from out of the Timpanogos area, but in 1826 a fresh innovation captured the map
makers. The Vance map of that year depicted not only a Timpanogos draining from the southwest tip of Lake Timpanogos, arriving
at the Pacific between Cape Mendocino and the Bay of San Francisco, but also a "R. los Mongos," which flowed directly west to the
Pacific south of Cape Orford.

With these staple ingredients the mappers of the mythological
drafted their maps for the next twenty years, each according to his
fancy. Least subject to aberration was the representation of Sevier
Lake in the south; piously the cartographers supplied it with its
affluents, the Buenaventura and the Salado, and no less piously they
drained it by a real or tentative Buenaventura flowing to the Pacific.
The only details subject to vagary were the name of the lake and the
point where its outlet reached the Pacific. The lake itself was called
Salt Lake, Lake Salado, Lake Teguayo, or, once in a while, Lake
Buenaventura. Concerning the outlet of this lake the cartographers
could not make up their minds. Now and then the Buenaventura
was made to flow to San Francisco Bay, but this idea in its purity lost
its appeal. The conclusion finally worked out was that the Buenaventura flowed into the Pacific south of Monterey, but the river had a
new identity by the time it reached the ocean, being alternatively
called the San Felipe or the Carmelo, the former name drawn from
the explorations of Father Francisco Garcés in California's Tulare
Valley in 1776 and perhaps originally applied to the Kern River,
but now come to be a confused conception of the Salinas River.

The idea of the Buenaventura River became, finally, the most
stubborn of the myths. It lasted longest, died hardest and left the
most enduring impress on history—this because ultimately it became
identified with the Sacramento. In the face of actual exploration
now to reveal the Unknown Land the idea of the Rio de los Mongos,
the Timpanogos and the Multnomah died quickly. But the Buenaventura as an idea transferred itself first to Great Salt Lake and then
at last to a river almost without source conceived to gather itself in

the desert Unknown, carve asunder the Sierras and flow to San Francisco Bay.

What the maps might say did not much concern the *engagés* and the free trappers. But to the brigade leaders and captains who hungered after fame and sought not furs alone among the spinal ranges, twisting canyons and sage-sown valleys beyond the Rockies the maps presented puzzling problems. Discovery was a complex combination of unlearning and learning; and the learning was complicated because the mountain men soon showed themselves in their own right prolific makers of myths and legends, among which exact geographers might venture at their peril.

The opening up of the West had to wait upon the Treaty of Ghent, ending the War of 1812; the fur trade could not flourish while the British intrigued among the tribes of the upper Mississippi and Missouri. Slowly interest reawakened, and by 1817 the St. Louis press was urging that a powerful company be established to prosecute the fur trade to the "White Capped Mountains, and along Jefferson's, Madison's, and Gallatin's rivers." Giving point to such arguments, within a few weeks Manuel Lisa came down the Missouri from his fort near the mouth of the Platte with a cargo of furs valued at some $35,000.

That kind of business was worth looking into. By 1821 numerous parties of traders and trappers were operating in the upper Missouri country. And as a fillip to enterprise, in that year revolution in Mexico opened Santa Fe to American trade.

Among the Missourians aroused by these developments on the western frontier was Virginia-born William Henry Ashley, who had come to Missouri not long before Lewis and Clark returned from the Pacific. Rapidly, he became not only a "gentleman of credit" but one of political and military eminence. In Andrew Henry, who had taken up lead mining after retiring from the mountains in 1811, Ashley found a natural partner. Early in 1822 with a gratifying fanfare of publicity the two men launched their first expedition to the mountains. Their advertisement in the *Missouri Gazette,* February 13, 1822, which called for 100 "enterprising young men" to ascend the Missouri to its source, "there to be employed for one, two or three years," has been called the most famous of all want ads. It peremptorily summoned to their destiny a group of continental explorers as remarkable as any America has known.

Among those who now or soon thereafter joined the Ashley enterprises was Jedediah Smith, a young New Yorker of stern Methodist conscience, humorless yet compassionate, driven resistlessly to exploration of far places. There was William Sublette, known as Cut Face to the Indians from a slash along his chin, a tall, blond, blue-eyed, Roman-nosed fellow, able Indian fighter and energetic bourgeois. Thomas Fitzpatrick was fully the equal of Sublette and a man of finer grain; a large-framed, ruddy-faced man whose hair turned gray after a terrible experience with the Blackfeet, to the Indians known as White Hair or as Broken Hand, from a hand injured in the bursting of his rifle. Jim Bridger, "Old Gabe," or, as the Crows called him, "the Blanket Chief," was spare of frame but powerful, gray-eyed and brown-haired, ill-educated but with a mind receptive to a limitless knowledge of the West and sauced by a shrewd native wit. Jim Clyman, laconic and drily witty, writer of rude poetry and natural leader in dangerous country; Moses (Black) Harris, swarthy fellow with a large capacity for wondrous lies— as Clyman said, "A free and easy kind of soul Especially with a Belly full"; Hugh Glass, he of the terrible adventure with the grizzly, described as "bold, daring, reckless & excentric to a high degree"; Mike Fink, the last of the river men, of undying fame in our folklore for the end he met on this expedition; Jim Beckwourth, the "Enemy of Horses," mulatto of ferocious courage and infinite talent for living and telling extravagant lies. . . . They compose a great company.

Scores of others, of hardly less renown, joined them within the next few years. Joe Walker, six-foot Tennessean, dark and bearded, one of the bravest and most skillful in a company where courage and skill were everyday commonplaces; Joe Meek, cousin of future President James K. Polk, exuberant daredevil and wit; Kit Carson, squat, deep-chested and broad-shouldered, with sandy hair, flat features and a relentless energy; Old Bill Williams, gaunt and red-headed, with shambling gait and unbounded eccentricity of speech

and manner.... No catalogue can name them all. They made the
West their own and, like their country's destiny, different because
of them.

In the spring of 1822 Andrew Henry established his base at the
mouth of the Yellowstone and dispatched parties up the affluents of
that river and the Missouri. Ashley brought him reinforcements
later in the summer and in March 1823 set out from St. Louis with
still another group of men—a crew of such extraordinary character
that Jim Clyman dismissed Falstaff's Battalion as "genteel in comparison." But there was no luck for Ashley on the Missouri. The
Indians who had driven the Americans from the upper Missouri a
decade ago now again began to stalk the trappers with diabolical
success. Four of Henry's men were slaughtered by the Blackfeet
near the mouth of Smith's River; seven of the Missouri Fur Company's trappers were ambushed by the same tribe on the Yellowstone;
and the Assiniboin ran off fifty of Henry's horses—all in a matter of
weeks. The culminating disaster befell Ashley himself. As he
reached the Dakota country at the end of May, the Arikara fell
treacherously upon his company. Thirteen were killed and almost
as many wounded. They withdrew down the river a distance to
lick their wounds and summon help. A punitive force under Colonel
Henry Leavenworth came up from Fort Atkinson near old Council
Bluffs, and this was reinforced by Henry and some of his men, a
detachment of Missouri Fur Company trappers and a large contingent of Sioux. A three-day battle was somewhat inconclusive, but
the Missouri highroad was reopened.

Taking 13 men, Andrew Henry turned back up the river toward
his post on the Yellowstone, from which he would dispatch parties
southwest into the mountains. The remainder of the Ashley force,
save only those who returned down river with Ashley himself, obtained horses and late in September 1823 started directly overland
from Fort Kiowa toward the mountains. They were commanded by
24-year-old Jedediah Smith, who so soon had won his spurs, and
notably among their number were Fitzpatrick, Clyman and William
Sublette.

As Henry's men worked slowly southward up the Yellowstone
toward the continent's intricate vertebral ranges, Jedediah took his
company across South Dakota, through the badlands west of the

Cheyenne River and into the Black Hills. It was here they came upon the grove of petrified trees famous in mountain lore—that "putrified forest with putrified birds on the branches a-singin' putrified songs." In this country young Jedediah had his cruel initiation to the West; a grizzly's fangs ripped bare his whole skull, almost to the crown of his head.

Though Jedediah bore to the end of his short life the scars of this savage encounter, within two weeks he was sufficiently recovered that they could move slowly westward again. In February, after vainly endeavoring to cross the snowy mountains north of the Wind River range, they tried a new route farther south. Thus they struck upon the Sweetwater and in March made the epic rediscovery of South Pass.

Through the pass they went on as far as Green River, splitting up into small parties which trapped throughout the spring. In June they turned back toward the Sweetwater, the appointed place of rendezvous.

That rendezvous established a famous precedent and a famous institution. Heretofore trappers had operated from fixed posts, to which they returned with their furs to trade for supplies, but after 1824 supplies were brought instead to places of rendezvous, in annual caravans which came up from the Missouri frontier. Rendezvous was the year's summing up for all the adventuring and far wandering. Here the coups were counted, the lies exchanged, the horses raced, the whisky drunk and the year's business done. The rendezvous severed the bonds that held the mountain men to home, and they stayed in the mountains, growing into a race apart. To the red man's life, which they adopted, they added an appalling efficiency and a cold ferocity which made a dozen of the Fur Brigade a match for anything they might anywhere encounter. They took squaws from among the tribes and roamed the West, imprinting upon their minds the intricate desert immensities and the infinite wisdom of survival in a land where God himself was often careless whether men survived. Now and then they might take the back trail, but their hearts yearned for the blazing stars and the clean wind off the sage or down the piney canyons, for the unleashed freedom the mountain-desert alone could give them.

Late that first summer Fitzpatrick got some furs down out of the mountains, not enough to excite Ashley, but a foretaste of things to come. It was a greater wealth than fur that Fitzpatrick brought from the mountains. The promise of the Missouri had never been anything but a surly assurance of trouble. Now the Missouri could be abandoned to its snag-filled, turbid channels and the deadly Blackfeet infesting its headwaters. The rolling brown Platte down whose valley Fitzpatrick had come was, to be sure, useless for any kind of navigation. But the returning Astorians 11 years before had descended its valley talking of it as a road, and now it could be seen as an immense natural highroad to the mountains—and to all that lay beyond.

The river craft that had served America well—flatboats, keelboats, canoes, pirogues, rafts—might be exchanged for riding animals and pack mules, for wagons and prairie schooners. Water could cease to have the significance of transportation and become, bitterly representative of all the West, something to open the dry throat of the wayfarer, existence itself. And also the West could now be discovered to the nation's mind. For all the heroic journeying of Lewis and Clark and the Astorians, the Pacific Coast had been an infinitely far island of the sea. Now it became continent's end. Oregon promptly became something more than a political abstraction; California was entangled in the American destiny beyond extrication. And the idea of South Pass was erected against the western horizon like a beacon for a church not even conceived yet soon to be in search of sanctuary.

From their first brief rendezvous on the Sweetwater in the summer of 1824 Ashley's men turned back to the mountains, to the thousand fascinating questions of where creek or river ran, what might lie over the next divide or at the end of a canyon. But South Pass by no means was the only avenue to the West's wealth of beaver. Other parties of trappers spread through all the mountain country, south out of the Oregon country and northwest across the mountain deserts from Taos.

Etienne Provost had been one quick to take the trail to Santa Fe after Mexico flung open the gates of trade. Concerning his partner, LeClerc, little is known, not even his first name with certainty, though possibly he was the onetime Astorian, François LeClerc. Provost and LeClerc began trapping out of Taos, possibly in the fall of 1823, and by the end of the next year, perhaps following in general the route of Escalante half a century before, they reached the southern slopes of the Uinta Mountains in eastern Utah, separated from Ashley's men in the upper Green River Valley only by the high wall of the Uintas.

The details of Provost's adventuring have only recently begun to emerge into view, and its impossible to say how far north and west he ranged in this fall of 1824. There is a great deal more than a probability that he got as far west as Utah Valley and the valley of the Great Salt Lake itself; he may have been first among the American trappers to see that darkly low-lying salt sea with its amethystine islands and tall, flanking ranges. But history has no certainties about Provost, only elusive glimpses of him. It was apparently in the autumn of 1824, in the valley of the Great Salt Lake, that his party was treacherously set upon while smoking the peace pipe with a band of Snakes. Seven men were slain and the survivors, including Etienne himself, necessarily fled to the Uinta Basin where, at the mouth of White River, LeClerc and the rest of the party were wintering. This was hardly a propitious introduction to the Great Salt Lake country, but in the spring Provost rode again in that direction.

Meantime Ashley's men were ranging widely from their base in the upper valley of the Green. The larger of the detachments, under William Sublette, crossed the divide to the valley of the Bear, and, perhaps following the long northern sweep of that stream to Soda Springs and so on south, they reached what they called Willow Valley, soon to be renamed Cache Valley. Here, only a few miles above the gates through which Bear River plunges down into the valley of the Great Salt Lake, the trappers went into winter quarters. When argument arose as to the course of the river on which they were encamped, the trappers backed up their opinions with hard cash, and young Jim Bridger was saddled with the job of deciding the wager. Accompanied by several others, Bridger followed the river down through its canyon until the lake in its misty immensity spread out before him. Going on to its shores, the little party of mountain men dismounted to drink, only to choke on the unexpected brine. "Hell," Bridger ejaculated, "we are on the shores of the Pacific!" Even at an altitude of 4,200 feet above sea level, that was an illusion not immediately dispelled.

Bridger's claims as first discoverer were backed up in 1857 by an old comrade, Samuel Tullock, yet the persistent mystery shrouding all the early history of Great Salt Lake has resisted such definite claims to discovery. Myth and history together have proposed other discoverers among the ranks of the mountain men, including even Bridger's later partner, Louis Vasquez. In October 1858 the Salt Lake correspondent of the San Francisco *Daily Evening Bulletin* came away from an interview with Vasquez with the idea that in the fall of 1822 (*sic*) Vasquez had wintered with a party of trappers in Cache Valley and had been forced by an eight-foot fall of snow to hunt a better valley. Descending Bear River, the story went, Vasquez in company with several others rode into Great Salt Lake Valley and so discovered the lake, at first taking it to be an arm of the Pacific. "They found the valley free from snow, and well filled with herds of buffalo. Returning to their party, they guided them over into this valley, when they divided—one party under Weber, wintering on the river which now bears his name; the other party wintering on Bear river, near its mouth." Though this account is specific in its details, the context establishes its events as of 1825-1826, not 1824-1825, and Vasquez is known to have been not in the mountains but in St. Louis during that historic first winter.*

The claims for Vasquez led to a further ramification in the tale of discovery. They came to the ears of W. Marshall Anderson, who had known Vasquez in the mountains in 1834, and he hastened to state in the *National Intelligencer* of February 25, 1860, the prior rights of Etienne Provost, to whom alone belonged, he said, "the credit of having discovered and made known the existence and whereabouts of that inland sea." Nothing but this most elusive tradition has supported the claims of Etienne Provost until late years.

Claims of discovery, however, have been registered for still other men. On July 4, 1897, the *Salt Lake Tribune* published a letter from a resident of Bellevue, Iowa, concerning his acquaintance 40 years before with a onetime Danish sea captain, John H. Weber. This man

---

* This account of Vasquez has escaped the attention of historians of the fur trade. It is found in the *Bulletin* for October 29, 1858.

assertedly had gone to the mountains in the spring of 1822 as a partner with Ashley and Henry. "The Captain told me more than once of his discovery of Salt Lake in 1823. He called it a great boon to them, as salt was plentiful around the border of the lake, and for some time before they had used gunpowder on their meat, which was principally buffalo. . . . Captain Weber was also the discoverer of Weber Canyon and Weber River, both of which bear his name. . . . In the autumn of 1827 [he] returned to St. Louis; in 1832 he removed to Galena, Illinois . . . a few years later he came to Bellevue, Iowa, where he died in February, 1859." In this letter there are many inaccuracies, yet the existence of a person by this name is attested not only by the name of Weber River but by the interview with Vasquez in 1858. Perhaps the multiplicity of the claims of discovery proceeds in some part from misunderstanding. Reminiscences of trappers intended only to describe their own first experience of the lake may have become in the ears of their auditors narratives of outright discovery.

Complex as it is, in this puzzle there are still other involutions.

Late in the summer of 1824 Jedediah Smith separated from William Sublette's company and with a small party of six men struck northwesterly across the Green River Valley into Jackson's Hole. Then, like the westbound Astorians 13 years before, he crossed the great Tetons and descended into the valley of the Snake. Andrew Henry had been in this country in 1810, and the men of the North West Company had crossed and recrossed it since 1818; perhaps Jedediah and his six men were not surprised to fall in with a dozen tatterdemalion Iroquois trappers, a detachment of the Hudson's Bay Company's first Snake Country Expedition. But that encounter was symbolic. British trappers, too, had their dramatic part to play in the revelation of the Great Salt Lake country.

The Hudson's Bay Company Snake Country Expeditions became a famous institution. The first of them had been taken south from Flathead Post by Alexander Ross in February 1824. They had trapped their way to the headwaters of the Salmon River, and, with some misgivings since the Iroquois were notoriously unreliable, Ross had dispatched a party of 12 Iroquois to trap the country farther east and south. The misgivings were only too well founded; the Iroquois neglected their trapping, traded away their goods to the Indians for trivialities, were duly pillaged and, when the Americans under Smith stumbled over them, were ragged and destitute.

With the Americans in company the disgraced Iroquois returned to the Salmon River in October. Ross regarded them with a jaundiced eye, for they had not only squandered four months in the field but had arrived actually in debt to the Americans. Moreover, Ross was disposed to view the Americans with suspicion, taking them rather to be "spies" than trappers; he was not pleased to hear that the quarter was "swarming with trappers who next season are to penetrate the Snake country with a Major Henry at their head, the same gentleman who fifteen years ago wintered on Snake River."

His unwelcome visitors evinced a disposition to accompany him, and Ross took them with him in turning back from the Snake country to Flathead Post. On arrival there toward the end of November, he was handed a letter from Governor George Simpson appointing him in charge of the post and naming the energetic Peter Skene Ogden to the command of the Snake Expedition.

In Ogden a striking personality entered the history of the Great Salt Lake country. He was born in Quebec in 1794 of old loyalist American stock. His father had intended him for a clergyman or a lawyer, but the great West seized upon his imagination, and at the age of 17 he entered the service of the North West Company. During the bitter warfare between that firm and the Hudson's Bay Company he served his employers so well that when the courts took a hand and began to find indictments, he was among those for whom the North West Company found pressing assignments in its inaccessible Columbia Department. After the fur wars ended with the merger of the two companies in 1821, he was left at loose ends. But when Governor George Simpson came to the Columbia Department in the fall of 1824, determined to end the shameful mismanagement, wasteful extravagance and constant dissension which had made the department not only a moral disgrace but, and more stingingly, a financial liability, he settled upon Ogden to revitalize the Snake Country Expedition.

Dangerous and unrewarding except in hardship, it was not a popular post, but to win the eye of the governor counted for a great deal. Ogden swiftly made his preparations for departure. Thoroughly out of patience with Ross for bringing the Americans into the heart of the Oregon country, Ogden nevertheless took them south with him—perhaps as the most expedient means of getting rid of them. Ross said farewell to them on December 20, impressed with the proportions of the effort that was to be made, "the most formidable party that has ever set out for the Snakes," with 2 gentlemen, 2 interpreters, 71 men and lads, 364 beaver traps, and 372 horses.

In the valor of his ignorance Governor Simpson designed that the Expedition should proceed "direct for the heart of the Snake Country towards the Banks of the Spanish River or Rio Colorado pass the Winter & Spring there and hunt their way out by the Umpqua and Wilhamet Rivers to Fort George [the successor to Astoria] next summer." These plans reflected two geographical misconceptions, that the Colorado (i.e., Green) was identical with the Bear, and that the Umpqua and Willamette extended so far into the interior as to head near that river.

Ogden made first for the sources of the Missouri, trapping with some success as he went, though 18 horses were stolen by the Blackfeet. The going was very hard as the southward journey continued, the snow and cold taking a heavy toll of the horses, and for 20 days after reaching the Salmon River in March the party was unequal to the hazard of crossing the mountains. On March 20 they got across the divide, though the snow had drifted three and four feet deep, and they reached the Snake on April 2. Blackfeet, however, were prowling in the vicinity, and within three days a man was killed at his traps.

Ogden had now to learn like Ross before him that in this country it was one thing to command and another thing altogether to enforce commands; he had to exert all his powers of persuasion before he could induce his men to go on south with him. They began the ascent of the Blackfoot River, but on April 23 another war party ran off 20 more horses.

The freemen and *engagés* became openly mutinous, and it was only by a mixture of threats and promises that Ogden again got his party moving south. Crossing the divide, they reached the Bear on May 5, perhaps near Soda Springs.

With unalloyed pleasure Ogden here parted from Jedediah Smith. The seven Americans ascended the river in search of their compatriots while the Hudson's Bay Company men went on down the stream. This river, Ogden remarked, was "supposed by Mr. Bourdon who visited in 1818 and subsequently Mr. Finan McDonald who were at its Sources to be the Spanish River or Rio Collorado, but it is not." It was another river system entirely. Trapping as he went, Ogden followed this river southward, at one of its forks learning from a band of Snakes that a party of 50 Americans had wintered there but had returned home early in the spring without taking many beaver.

As it had been for Bridger a few months before, Bear River became for Ogden the highroad to discovery. On May 20, 1825, he found that the river "discharged into a large Lake of 100 Miles in length"—the earliest known description of Great Salt Lake by one who had seen it. But misfortune which had closely stalked Ogden throughout the winter overtook him here in the proportions of disaster; his explorations were abruptly ended; and he fled the Great Salt Lake country to avert a complete debacle.

Three days after he reached the shores of the salt lake, Ogden was surprised to fall in with "a party of 15 Canadians and Spanjards." From their leader, Etienne Provost, Ogden was amazed to hear that they had come from a "Spanish" settlement "called *Taas* distant about 100 miles from St Fe." which was supplied with goods brought overland in wagons from St. Louis. Trappers were swarming from everywhere. Indeed, before nightfall still another party of American trappers, to the number of 25 or 30, rode up brazenly with 12 or 15 of Ogden's Iroquois. The Americans—among whom, Ogden observed with a bitter imprecation on the head of Alexander Ross, were some of the seven who had come south with him from Flathead Post—encamped a hundred yards away. At once they hoisted their country's flag, and bellowed to the British trappers that as they were in United States Territory, whether indebted or engaged, all were now free.

On this bristling note the situation rested until morning. The

American, Gardner, then swaggered to Ogden's tent. The British trappers were in United States territory, he blustered. Britain had ceded all its rights to this country, and as Ogden had no license to trade or trap, he should get out.

Ogden coldly looked the American over. "When we receive orders from the British Government to abandon the country, we shall obey."

Gardner strode off but only to harangue Ogden's trappers, whose surly mood for months had verged on open rebellion. When Ogden angrily followed the American into an Iroquois lodge, one of his own Indians turned on him. All the Iroquois including himself, the rebel burst out, had long wished for an opportunity to join the Americans. "If we did not the last three years, it was owing to our bad luck in not meeting them, but now we go, and all you can say or do cannot prevent us." And here was Gardner, intolerably virtuous: "You have had these men too long in your service and have most shamefully imposed on them, treating them as *slaves* selling them goods at high prices and giving them nothing for their furs." Yes, the Iroquois shouted, it was all true! As for the gentlemen of the company, they were "the greatest villains in the world, and if they were here I would shoot them, but as for you, sir, you have dealt fair with us all. We have now been five years in your service, the longer we remain the more indebted we become although we give 150 beaver a year, we are now in a free country and have friends to support us, and go we will!"

The Iroquois made off with their furs, shouting the most galling obscenities, and the Americans boisterously welcomed them. Only in his two gentlemen, William Kittson and Thomas McKay, was Ogden able to place any confidence, but the support of these was enough to prevent the entire pillaging of his party. Twenty-one men made off to the Americans, and two more deserted when at daylight the next morning Ogden gave orders to raise camp. This "most formidable party that had ever set out for the Snakes" was reduced to barely 20 men, and of the allegiance even of these Ogden could not be certain. He had to get out of this vicinity or risk losing everything.

He could not escape, however, without having to hear through the triumphant Gardner: "You shall shortly see us in the Columbia and this Fall at the Flat heads and Kootenais, as we are determined you shall no longer remain in our Territory!" Ogden replied shortly, "When we receive orders from our own Government we shall withdraw, but not before." Gardner howled a last word after him: "Our troops will reach the Columbia this fall and make you!"

Ogden was convinced that the Americans had been trying to goad him into firing on them, whereupon they would have had an excuse for making an end to his whole party. The importance of this whole episode, however, was not its nearness to land piracy but its significance as revolution. A bad situation had grown up in the Columbia Department by which the Hudson's Bay Company trappers were assessed too much for their supplies and paid too little for their furs. After Ogden's report of his debacle, sweeping changes were made in the rate structure and the Snake Country Expedition was made into an instrument for sweeping the country of its furs—an instrument so efficient that the threatened invasion of the lower Columbia by American trappers was forever forestalled.

That, however, was the work of the next half-dozen years. In this spring of 1825 Ogden rode north out of the Great Salt Lake Valley with bitter feelings, damning Alex Ross for ever having brought the seven Americans to Flathead Post, apprehensive lest he fall in with other American parties and lose the 3,000 beaver he still possessed, certainly in no mood to explore west of the salt lake for the sources of the Umpqua and the Willamette (he might thereby open a new road to Fort George for the convenience of the Americans).

Ogden found his way north to the Snake, which he reached on June 5 by a route different from his outbound trail—very likely up the Bear and over the divide to Marsh Creek and the Portneuf. Thence, several times alarmed by reports that parties of Americans were in his vicinity, he made his way back to Flathead Post via the sources of the Missouri.

Where that promising expedition of 1825 met with disaster it is not yet possible to say except that it evidently occurred within three-days' travel from the point where he came upon Great Salt Lake. The likelihood is strong that the locale was the lovely mountain valley above the city of Ogden, which from the time of the Fur Brigade has been known as Ogdens Hole.

Ashley himself set out for the mountains in November 1824,

leaving Fort Atkinson with 25 men, 50 pack horses and, significantly, a wagon and teams. The initial part of his route, up the Platte to its forks, anticipated the route the Mormons adopted 22 years later, and much of his route after arriving at the Front Range in northern Colorado subsequently became known first as the Cherokee Trail and then as the Overland Stage Route. He crossed the continental divide by that high desert upland, Bridger's Pass, and went northwesterly to come upon the Big Sandy, an important affluent of the Green. Eager for further explorations, Ashley selected six men to build two boats and embark with him on a voyage down the Green, while he split up the rest of his party in three detachments, to trap in as many directions.

Ashley himself descended the Green as far as Desolation Canyon, appalled by the red rock country through which the river flowed, with its "lofty mountains heaped together in the greatest disorder, exhibiting a surface as barren as can be imagined." Turning back, he purchased a few horses from some friendly "Eutau" Indians, and ascended the Duchesne to its remote headwaters. Crossing the Uintas in the vicinity of Bald Mountain, Ashley fell upon the headwaters of the Bear. Familiar reflex of the day's geography, he called this river the "Beaunaventura." From this stream Ashley made his way directly to the place of rendezvous on Henrys Fork.

Including the Hudson's Bay Company deserters, there were 120 men at the rendezvous. For a year they had been scattered in small detachments throughout the Green, Snake, Bear and Great Salt Lake valleys; the record of their wanderings would be priceless in our history. Although Ashley's curiosity was aroused by reports of a "Grand lake or Beaunaventura," particularly because the Indians were understood to say that a river flowed out of its western side into an unknown country, he must be a businessman first and solicitous of the tender feelings of his creditors in St. Louis. With an escort of 50 men, including young Jedediah Smith, on July 2, 1825, he left the rendezvous to find a navigable point on the Big Horn from which to float his furs down to St. Louis. Hereafter furs would go out by land on pack mules, but this last time the Missouri river system might be used. And the thing was done in style, if Jim Beckwourth may be believed. They arrived in St. Louis with a full grown grizzly in tow, and the redoubtable Jim led it through the streets and chained it to the apple tree of the quaking Major Thomas Biddle, a fearsome token of the general's esteem.

A man in quest of a reputation as well as wealth, and shrewd in the uses of publicity, Ashley was not long back from the mountains before he drafted for General Henry Atkinson of the War Department a letter descriptive of his experiences. His account of the Great Salt Lake country reflects in some degree the experiences of his men and exhibits the state of knowledge concerning the salt lake in July 1825. Some of his hunters, he said, had crossed to this region in the summer of 1824 and wintered on and near the borders of the lake. "They had not explored the lake sufficiently to judge correctly of its extent, but from their own observations and information collected from Indians, they supposed it to be about eighty miles long by fifty broad. They represented it as a beautiful sheet of water deep, transparent, and a little brackish, though in this latter quality the accounts differ; some insist that it is not brackish." (This uncertainty as to the salinity of the lake has been attributed to the saltiness of Bear River Bay, which varies with the flood stage of Bear River.)

Though Ashley might thus answer his responsibility to geography, he was not the man to be equally responsible to history. There was no naming of names in his narrative, save only that of Jedediah Smith, and though Ashley must have been well aware of their extent, Etienne Provost's explorations were totally neglected.

What Ashley had to say to the War Department he was more than willing to repeat to the press, and on March 11, 1826, the *Missouri Advocate* printed the momentous news of a "NEW ROUTE *to the Pacific Ocean, discovered by* GENL. WILLIAM H. ASHLEY, *during his late Expedition to the Rocky Mountains."*

"*The route* proposed, after leaving St. Louis and passing generally on the north side of the Missouri river, strikes the river Platte a short distance above its junction with the Missouri; then pursues the waters of the Platte to their sources, and in continuation, crosses the head waters, of what Gen. Ashley believes to be, the Rio Colorado of the West, and strikes for the first time, a ridge, or single connecting chain of mountains running from north to south. This, however, presents no difficulty, as a wide gap is found, apparently prepared for the purpose of a passage. After passing this gap, the route proposed, falls directly on a river, called by Gen. Ashley, the Buenaventura, and runs with that river to the Pacific Ocean."

The description rings down the corridors of history, a prescience of the Oregon Trail, though the idea that the Buenaventura ran to the sea was unfounded. At the same time the *Advocate* gave itself the distinction of being first to publicize the existence of the great lake in the mountains:

"Gen. A. . . . fell upon what he supposed to be, the sources of the Buenaventura and represents those branches, as bold streams, from twenty to fifty yards wide, forming a junction a few miles below where he crossed them, and then empties into a large lake, (called Grand Lake,) represented by the Indians as being 40 or 50 miles wide, and sixty or seventy miles long—This information is strengthened, by that of the white hunters, who have explored parts of the Lake. The Indians represent, that at the extreme west end of this Lake, a large river flows out, and runs in a westwardly direction. Gen. A. when on those waters, at first thought it probable they were the sources of the Multnomah; but the account given by the Indians, supported by the opinion of some men belonging to the Hudson Bay Company, confirms him in the belief, that they are the head waters of the river represented as the Buenaventura. To the north and northwest from Grand Lake, the country is represented as abounding in SALT."

Though this information was in some degree inexact, both as to the lake and as to a road to the Pacific, and though it exhibited the confusion of the explorers in trying to liberate themselves from the tyranny in which the map makers still held them, it was the fruit of personal investigation and experience, a strong white light of reality beginning now at last to penetrate into what had been so long the province of myth and dream.

Chapter 5

The Lure of Far Places

Tantalizingly fragmentary is the information about the first exploration of Great Salt Lake by the mountain men. Though reluctant for reasons of his own to believe that such an exploration ever was made, Captain Bonneville told Washington Irving that four men were said to have been sent in a skin canoe to circumnavigate the lake and that they suffered excessively from thirst, "the water of the lake being extremely salt, and there being no fresh streams running into it." Still later, writing what he knew of the discovery of the lake, Robert Campbell advised Lieutenant G. K. Warren that in the spring of 1826 four men went around it in skin boats to learn whether any streams containing beaver were to be found emptying into it, "but returned with indifferent success." Campbell himself had gone to the mountains that spring with an Ashley company, and on arriving at Cache Valley, he had "found the party just returned from their exploration of the lake"; he remembered their report that it had no outlet.

Warren Ferris, who came to the mountains in 1830, heard something about that adventure, too, saying it was accomplished by four men in a small boat who were absent on the expedition 40 days, and who "on their return reported that for several days they found no fresh water on its western shore, and nearly perished from the want of that necessary article. They ascertained that it had no visible outlet, and stated as their opinion that it was two hundred miles long and one hundred broad, but this was doubtless a gross exaggeration."

A single contemporary reference to that lonely and undeniably hazardous exploration has survived, a story printed in the *Missouri Herald* of November 8, 1826, soon after Ashley arrived back from the mountains. After characterizing the "Great Lake" as a most remarkable body of water previously unknown unless from vague accounts, and describing it as estimated to be 100 miles long and 60 or 80 wide, the *Herald* went on to say that it had been "coasted last spring by a party of gen. Ashley's men in canoes, who were occupied four and twenty days, in making its circuit." These men, the newspaper said, "did not exactly ascertain its outlet, but passed a place where they supposed that it must have been."

The ambiguity of that supposition has often been found amusing, yet it is an interesting corroborative detail. The opening along the western lake shore north of Strongs Knob, across which the lake retreated from the Salt Desert in prehistoric times, may have seemed a likely outlet, while the shallows would have prevented exact reconnaissance except at the cost of great exertion on the part of the voyagers.

Who were the mountain men venturesome enough to "go to sea"? History has yielded up more details about their identity than about their experiences. The capable Jim Clyman, traveling east from California in 1846, was so startled at the extent to which the lake had shrunk that he remarked to his journal, almost involuntarily: "this lake like all the rest of this wide spread Sterility has nearly wasted away one half of its surface since 1825 [*sic*] when I floated around it in my Bull Boate." Louis Vasquez would seem to have been one of Clyman's companions on that voyage, for as he told his story in 1858, he "built a boat, and circumnavigated this sheet of brine, for the purpose of finding out definitely whether it was an arm of the sea or not, and thus discovered that it was in reality merely a large inland lake, without an outlet." Henry G. Fraeb is also declared to have been a member of the exploring party— this on the authority of an unpublished letter by Warren Ferris written from 30 to 50 years after. It is to be remembered, also, that the expansive old mountain man, Black Harris, told the westbound Mormons in 1847 "that he had travelled the whole circumference of the lake, and that there was no outlet to it."

By way of making the story more complex, two days after Harris talked to the Mormons, Jim Bridger told them that some of his men had been around the salt lake. "They went out hunting and had their horses stolen by the Indians. They then went around the lake in canoes hunting beaver and were three months going around it. They said it was 550 miles around it." Possibly the episode described by Bridger was one of later date; if so, it may be that Black Harris was a member of this party, not that of 1826.

Whoever did the actual exploring, the pack trains brought from the mountains in the fall of 1826 a new and more ample knowledge of the salt lake. Ashley's advices to the *Missouri Herald* barely anticipated in print the extraordinary letter written by Daniel Potts to his brother in Philadelphia, a letter which, as promptly published in the Philadelphia *Gazette and Public Advertiser* on November 14, 1826, first applied to Great Salt Lake its name in history:

"The Great Salt Lake lies in a circular form from N. E. to N. W. the larger circle being to S: it is about 400 miles in circumference, and has no discharge or outlet, it is generally shallow near the beach, and has several islands, which rise like pyramids from its surface. The Western part of the Lake is so saturated with salt, as not to dissolve any more when thrown into it. The country on the S. W. and N. W. is very barren, bearing but little more than wild sage and short grass. The S. E. and E. are fertile, especially near the outlet of the Utaw Lake and Weber's river. The former is about 30 yards wide at its mouth, the latter from 50 to 60, and very deep. This river rises to the E. in the Utaw mountains, and in its course passes through three mountains, to where it enters the lake. . . ."

As if it were a loadstone, the Great Salt Lake had drawn the Fur Brigade to itself from the far corners of the West. Now the immense mountain lake released the mountain men to even wider wanderings.

Ashley came to the rendezvous of 1826 feeling the tug of new destinies. His partner Henry had retired, discouraged, from the fur trade in the fall of 1824, but Ashley had reaped the rewards of persistence. The packs of fur he had taken down in 1825 and the packs he would take down this year had delivered him out of the hands of his creditors and left him, besides, a comfortable fortune. Governor Simpson of the Hudson's Bay Company might look down his nose at Ashley as a militia general who had been "a Farmer a Shopkeeper, a Miner and latterly an Indian Trader," dismissing him as having gained "merely a little eclat by his trapping speculations, notwithstanding all the bombast that appeared in the American NewsPapers of 1824, 1825 & 1826 in regard to their 'enterprizing Countryman.'" But eclat was the kind of thing on which a politician thrived, and Ashley in the summer of 1826 was ready to sell out to his three lieutenants, Smith, Jackson and Sublette.

Simpson's verdict on his American antagonist stood, in any event, too close within the flat perspective of the pound sterling. Ashley perhaps had originally no conscious purpose of exploration, and his discoveries would not long have awaited other hands. Nevertheless, the expeditions that he financed or led himself had a crystallizing effect on American life. The issues were understood clearly, as early as the fall of 1826, and the newspapers could state them. Overland expeditions, in large bodies, might now be made to that remote region beyond the mountains "without the necessity of transporting provisions for man or beast. . . . Wagons and carriages could go with ease as far as general Ashley went. . . . the elevation is exceedingly small where the passage of the mountains was effected—so small as hardly to affect the rate of going of the caravan, and forming at the most, an angle of three degrees, being two degrees less than the steepest ascent on the Cumberland road."

Jedediah Smith went down to St. Louis with Ashley in the summer of 1825, and returned with him to the mountains in the spring of 1826. At the rendezvous on the site of Ogden, above the long blue line of the lake, he and William Sublette and David E. Jackson came to final agreement with Ashley. The farewells were said at last. Beckwourth, at least, remembered the general kindly, "a man of untiring energy and perseverance, cheerfully enduring every toil and privation with his men . . . no difficulty dejected him; kind and generous in his disposition, he was loved equally by all." Ashley returned to St. Louis the friend and business agent of the three young fur traders, and he would have come to the mountains a final time the next year had he not fallen ill at the frontier. In 1829 he ran unsuccessfully for the Senate, but in 1831 he won a by-election to fill a vacancy in the House and he was twice returned to office by the Missouri electorate. In 1836 he ran for governor but was defeated by Lilburn W. Boggs. He died of pneumonia on March 26, 1838, just as the slow fire he had lighted in American history was beginning to blaze up along the western sky line.

Like Ashley, Etienne Provost left the mountains in 1826. The previous year his partner LeClerc had been killed by Indians enroute in from Santa Fe, and Etienne was content to join the expanding American Fur Company. He had ventured greatly and was always respected as a partisan, but he sank into slow obscurity and he died in 1850 in St. Louis, all but unknown, all but unmourned. The Robidou brothers, who like Provost had adopted Taos as a base of operations, were more persistent and would leave a more tangible impress upon the history of the intermontane country. But for a time after Ashley's withdrawal from the fur trade Smith, Jackson & Sublette were the sole inheritors to a wilderness empire.

Jackson was vested with the responsibilities of the resident partner, and Sublette was given the supply and transport job. But to Jedediah Smith, and his scarred young head must have lifted to the thought, fell the task of purposeful discovery.

The central mystery was the country south and west of the Great Salt Lake. The idea of the Buenaventura was not easy to dismiss. The maps had a compulsive fascination, and though Great Salt Lake was proved to have no outlet, there were still vague and contradictory stories heard from the Indians about a westward-flowing river. Even Peter Skene Ogden, who did not venture south of the Snake watershed for three and a half years after his debacle of 1825, heard rumors of such a country, rich in beaver. A party of 30 Americans in the early spring of 1826 had skirted the Great Salt Lake to the north in search of rumored rivers rich in furs, but had found such hard going that they had retreated, half starved, north to the Snake. What the sun-scorched, thirsty lake explorers had to say about its malignant western shore was also calculated to give pause to discoverers. . . .

So with his 17 men Jedediah rode south. At the Sevier they separated from the route of the Spanish padres, going up the river rather than down it toward its lake. Beyond Utah Valley no more signs of buffalo were seen, though now and then an antelope or a mountain sheep fled their unexpected presence. Toward the headwaters of the Sevier they turned west into the mountains, ascending Clear Creek and crossing over into the valley of "Lost River," the Beaver. The earth was here burnt to a reddish hue, and under the darkly blue September skies its color deepened into reluctant vermilion as they climbed toward the south rim of the Great Basin. Junipers scarred the red hills, their green so somber as to seem black, and the dusty silver-green of sagebrush flowed everywhere, until the eye wearied of it, a strange, parched country.

But as they descended stony Black Canyon to the Virgin River, they found a country still more strange. To the east the mountains were breaking up, so that now and then they glimpsed the tops of far red buttes which were like the earth itself set afire, and the vegetation was beginning to change, much of it thorned and armored against the furnace dryness. They reached a river, the Virgin, whose waters ran southwest, a rusted brightness along the red earth. This river Jedediah called in honor of his President, the Adams, following it through a difficult canyon and on to its mouth in a river which, though vastly larger and altogether changed, Jedediah could recognize: "the Seedskeeder" or Green—the Colorado.

The party followed the river down four days, through a wasteland extraordinarily barren, rocky and mountainous, until its valley widened into a strip of land timbered and fertile, where dwelt "a nation of Indians who called themselves *Ammuchabas*"—the Mohave. The company of mountain men rested among the Mohave 15 days, fortunately being able to buy some horses—stolen from the outlying California ranchos—to replace those lost in the deserts. With two Indians who consented to guide them, they then struck west across the blistering desert to that "Inconstant River"—the Mohave—which flowed fitfully in the gray waste, unreasonably appearing and disappearing. The American adventurers followed that river to its head and by the Mohave Trail crossed the mountains into San Bernardino Valley.

At the Mission San Gabriel the Americans were generously received, but it was not altogether auspicious that they had ridden in out of the unknown upon obviously stolen horses, and the displeasure of the California officials hedged Jedediah about until, by the intervention of some American sea captains then at San Diego, he was given sanction to return as he had come. Rejoining his men with supplies, he took the back trail. But the unknown was too powerful a lure, and Jedediah turned north in search of the Buenaventura.

The quest for the fabled river was unavailing. The tremendous mountain range on their right opened to no great eastern river and it grew ever higher the farther north they went. In May the Americans reached the stream since called the Rio de los Americanos, and

here they turned abruptly east into Mount Joseph, as Jedediah denominated the mighty Sierra. Twice they were defeated by the
snows. As it was imperative that Jedediah get across the mountains
to the rendezvous with Jackson and Sublette, he established his men
in a permanent camp on the Stanislaus. Taking wiry Robert Evans
and the stalwart blacksmith, Silas Gobel, together with seven horses
and two mules on which were loaded hay and provisions, Jedediah
made a final endeavor the third week in May.

Although the snow in Sonora Pass was from four to eight feet
deep, the spring sun had packed it hard, and in eight days the three
men got over the frowning heights, though at the cost of two horses
and one mule. The journey after they came down out of the snows,
however, was like a nightmare itself, the days a burning succession
of endless, dry, sandy valleys and barren, rocky hills, with vegetation
scant and the lack of water a constant fear to dry the lips and shrivel
the belly. It seemed incredible that the occasional scrawny, naked
Indians they saw could find any subsistence in this wasteland. One
horse gave out, then another; they fed on the starved flesh and always
kept plodding northeastward, sustained by the hope that each succeeding day would open the low-lying salt lake to view.

By June 22 they had crossed central Nevada and reached the Deep
Creek Mountains, camping on a creek almost at what would one
day be the Utah state line. "The Country in the vicinity," Jedediah
wrote in his journal, "so much resembled that on the south side of
the Salt Lake that for a while I was induced to believe that I was near
that place. During the day I saw a good many Antelope, but could
not kill any. I however, killed 2 hares which, when cooked at night
we found much better than horse meat." In the two days following
they walked 75 treadmill miles northeast, now and then finding
water in salt springs, but on the second afternoon having to take
refuge from the sun in holes dug in the sand. "Our sleep," Jedediah
recorded, "was not repose, for tormented nature made us dream of
things we had not and for the want of which it then seemed possible,
and even probable, that we might perish in the desert unheard of and
unpitied." In this moment values took their proper perspective. His
dreams "were not of Gold or ambitious honors, but of my distant,
quiet home, of murmuring brooks, of Cooling Cascades." The three
wayfarers aroused and stumbled on through the night, the murmur

of falling waters still sounding in their ears, the apprehension that they might never live to hear that sound in reality weighing heavily upon them.

The sun arose upon this desolate waste which had no end; it gleamed upon the sterile salt with a cruel brilliance, "insuportably tormenting." At ten o'clock in the morning Evans gave out. Jedediah and Gobel could only lay him in the shadow of a small juniper and go on in hopes of finding water. Only if they found it soon could Evans be saved, but they left him "with feelings only known to those who have been in the same situation." And three miles farther on they reached water. Groaning with pleasure, Gobel plunged into it bodily, and Jedediah began pouring the water down reckless of consequences. But then, filling a kettle and taking some meat, the young captain turned back for Evans.

Hope filled them again. Next day they went another 10 miles to some brackish springs where they found a family of Indians who spoke a Shoshonean tongue. These Indians could give no information about the salt lake, but in the evening the gaunt Jedediah discovered from a height what he thought to be a large body of water. In the morning they traveled north another 10 miles, and as they rounded the ridge which formed the eastern boundary of the valley, Jedediah's heart leaped to the sight of water extending far to the north and east. "The Salt Lake, a joyful sight, was spread before us." Was it possible, said Jedediah's companions in suffering, that they were so near the end of their troubles? Jedediah wrote in his journal:

"For myself, I durst scarcely believe that it was really the Big Salt Lake that I saw. It was indeed a most cheering view, for although we were some distance from the depo, yet we knew we would soon be in a country where we would find game and water, which were to us objects of the greatest importance and those which would contribute more than any others to our comfort and happiness.

"Those who may chance to read this at a distance from the scene may perhaps be surprised that the sight of this lake surrounded by a wilderness of More than 2000 Miles diameter excited in me those feelings known to the traveler, who, after long and perilous journeying, comes again in view of his home. But so it was with me for I had traveled so much in the vicinity of the Salt Lake that it had become my home of the wilderness."

They turned east along the south shore of the lake and encamped after another 15 miles. The next day they traveled another 20 miles to reach "the outlet of the Uta Lake," and had to build a raft of cane grass on which to bear their things. Jedediah first swam across, leading his horse and the one remaining mule. Then, placing their things upon the raft, he took a cord in his mouth and swam before while Gobel and Evans, neither of them very good swimmers, swam behind. The current was strong and swept them a considerable distance; "it was with great difficulty that I was enabled to reach the shore," Jedediah wrote, "as I was verry much strangled."

All were exhausted and worn down, but sustained now by the hope that the ordeal was nearly finished. Next day Jedediah got a shot at a bear, wounding it badly but failing to kill it, so that they must eat that night the last of their horse meat, talking a little of the probability of their sufferings being soon at an end but only a little, "for men suffering from hunger never talk much, but rather bear their sorrows in moody silence, which is much preferable to fruitless complaints."

In the morning Jedediah killed a deer. They cooked it and feasted on it for two hours; in his tough wilderness philosophy Jedediah could reflect, "So much do we make our estimation of happiness by a contrast with our situation that we were as much pleased with our fat venison on the bank of the Salt Lake as we would have been in the possession of all the Luxuries and enjoyments of a civilized life in other circumstances." So with a longer stride they made their way to rendezvous in Bear Lake Valley, arriving in midafternoon of July 3, 1827. "My arrival," Jedediah says briefly, "caused a considerable bustle in camp, for myself and party had been given up as lost. A small Cannon brought up from St. Louis was loaded and fired for a salute."

To a man who had come through such sharp perils, through weeks of hunger, thirst and grinding fatigue after months of wandering, the cannon might be accepted without surprise, with no sense of wonder or prescience. But the cannon had come on a wheeled carriage, the first wheeled vehicle to cross the continental divide. In 1824 Ashley had started from Fort Atkinson with a wagon and teams, but the wagon had been abandoned somewhere along the way. This four-pound cannon of 1827 left its wheeled track up the long valley of the Platte and the Sweetwater, across South Pass and the valley of the Green into the valley of the Bear. Soon, now, there would be wagons to cut that track deeply into the western earth.

Booming out over the blue waters of the lovely mountain lake, the cannon sounded not only as welcome to the lost who were returned, but also as alarum and farewell. As though it echoed in faraway Santa Fe, complaint was made to Mexico City the following year over the establishment of a fort for the beaver trade four days beyond Lake Timpanogos. If the arm of Mexican authority had been able to reach into this far province, however, after 1828 it would have found little on which to lay its hand. Though the history of the American fur trade has been rife with legends of a fur traders' fort built in the Great Salt Lake country, placed now at Sevier Lake, now at Utah Lake, now at Great Salt Lake on the site of Ogden and now at Bear Lake or in the Bear Valley, in reality the "American fur depot" or "the American post at Salt Lake" disappeared into thin air whenever the pack mules were loaded and the trappers climbed aboard their horses.

To General William Clark in St. Louis, Jedediah wrote from Bear Lake a long letter descriptive of his year's explorations, a letter which the general gave to the *Missouri Republican* and set at once to its corrective labors with the world's geographers. The letter must go to St. Louis in lieu of the explorer himself, for Jedediah had much unfinished business on the Pacific Coast.

So on July 13 with 18 men he again rode south, going from the head of Bear Lake southeasterly to the Bear, and then southwest to the Weber, which he followed till it turned sharply east into the mountains. Crossing Kamas Prairie to the Provo, he followed that river down through its canyons to Utah Lake. Here he traded with a large band of Ute, obtaining two horses and then continued on in his track of the year before.

At the Mohave villages he was again received kindly, but the kindliness was a mask for treachery. The Mohave fell upon his party at the moment of crossing the Colorado, and the ten on the bank behind including the valiant Gobel were slaughtered in a sudden terrible onslaught.

For weapons the 9 survivors had only 5 guns, and the rude lances they could make by tying their knives to light poles. Jedediah, realistically appraising the possibilities, thought they were finished. Their horses gone, they could not turn back or well go forward, and for provisions they had only 15 pounds of dried meat. Even if they did not die under Indian war clubs it seemed impossible that they could get across the salt plain to the Mohave River. Ahead there were other difficulties. If they escaped all the immediate perils, on rejoining the company awaiting them in central California, they should have to go to the coast for supplies and answer for a second trespass upon the soil of California.

But courage, intelligence and energy—what a later generation of Americans calls, simply, guts—sometimes could be enough. After Jedediah's sharpshooting mountain men picked off two of the Mohave, the Indians kept their distance, and the little company could strike off into the desert westward. Though they suffered from thirst, they found water when they had to have it, eventually reaching the river which, inconstant as it might be, yet was constant enough to see them through to the mountains.

This was, however, a fated expedition. Jedediah might rejoin the members of his expedition of 1826 and after long interrogation, a period in "the Callibose" and interminable negotiation, receive the necessary permission to purchase supplies and take his men north out of California. But all through the long journey up the east bank of the "Buenaventura," as Jedediah called the Sacramento River, disaster flew above them on its black wings. Reaching the area of present Red Bluff, where the Sierra was bending to the west as though to enclose the sources of the Buenaventura, Jedediah elected to strike off northwest toward the sea. If there had been any purpose of returning direct to rendezvous, Jedediah here gave it up. And so the 19 men made their difficult way to the sea and up the Oregon coast to the river of the Umpqua.

On the morning of July 14, 1828, with 2 of his men Jedediah left camp to look out a way, encouraged by word from the Indians that the worst of their difficulties was over, that after they got up the Umpqua 15 or 20 miles they should have good traveling to "the

Wel Hammett or Multinomah," and thus to the Hudson's Bay
Company post on the Columbia. During his absence the Umpqua
fell on his men as ferociously as had the Mohave, and of them all
Arthur Black alone escaped to make his perilous way to Fort Vancouver. The returning Jedediah himself was fired on by the Umpqua
and together with his two followers put to flight.

The Hudson's Bay Company received the refugees courteously
and during the autumn sent an expedition south to recover Jedediah's
furs and equipment. After wintering at the fort, in the spring of
1829 he ascended the Columbia to Fort Colville. From there he made
his way south to rejoin his associates on Henrys Fork of the Snake.
Though he trapped in the mountains for another year, he returned
no more to the Utah country.

When he came from the mountains in the fall of 1830, Jedediah had
been from home almost five years. And it was nearly eight years since,
as an exuberant youth of twenty-three, he had joined with Ashley.
He bore the scars of the savage life he had lived, no less upon his
mind than upon his flesh. He could feel himself fortunate in some
respects, unfortunate in others. His mountain years had made him
reasonably affluent, and he had satisfied the devouring longing to
know, to make known what had been unknown. He could anticipate the satisfaction of publishing his journals and his maps, making
the world different because he had lived. But in him was an emptiness. "Oh when," he wrote his brother Ralph, "shall I be under the
care of a Christian Church? I have need of your Prayers, I wish our
Society to bear me up before a Throne of Grace." His mind returned
restlessly to such thoughts: "I entangle myself altogether too much
in things of time—I must depend entirely upon the Mercy of that
being, who is abundant in Goodness & will not cast off any, who
call, sincerely, upon him; again I say, pray for me My Brother—
& may he, before whoom not a Sparrow falls, without notice, bring
us, in his own good time, together again."

But he had been too long brother to death and disaster. Jedediah
spent the winter of 1830-1831 visiting with his family and friends,
but in the spring perhaps the old lust to see and to know seized him
again; he acquiesced in the plans of his old partners for a trading
expedition to Santa Fe. On the Cimarron plain in May, as he
searched for water, he was attacked by 15 or 20 Comanche—"they

succeeded in alarming his animal not daring to fire on him so long as they kept face to face," his brother Austin wrote sorrowfully to their father. "So soon as his horse turned they fired, and wounded him in the shoulder he then fired his gun, and killed their head Chief it is supposed they then *rushed* upon him, and despatched him—Such my farther [sic] is the fate of him who you loved."

It was more than Jedediah's blood that soaked the Cimarron sands. A knowledge, an energy and a passion flowed out with that blood, and American history was different because of their passing. Fires through the years consumed most of his journals and maps, and his discoveries leaked into the world's knowledge of itself uncertainly, indirectly and late, while he himself was nearly forgotten. In our own time, however, the name of Jedediah Smith has taken on its rightful stature, and the heroic measure of his accomplishment stands for all to see. His was the rediscovery of South Pass, but that is almost indistinguishable in the achievements of Ashley's great company of mountain men. Jedediah's great explorations were those made from the two rendezvous in the Great Salt Lake country. He found a way to southern California, the first to go all the way from St. Louis to the California coast. He was first to travel the length of California and Oregon, from San Diego to Fort Vancouver on the Columbia, and he was first to cross the breadth as well as the length of the Great Basin. Had he lived, he would have revolutionized American understanding of the West, but even in death he could not be altogether defeated—his hard-won knowledge survived in the minds of the mountain men.

A labor of primary exploration remained. In the fall of 1828 Peter Skene Ogden took his fourth Snake Expedition into a part of southeastern Oregon before unknown, and by way of Quin River and the Little Humboldt he rode south to discovery of a new river. Ogden called it Unknown River, unable to conceive where it flowed, but it came to be called by his own name and by a name, "Mary River," to honor an Indian wife with whom trapper fancy in the course of time endowed him. Years after, Frémont would rename this river the Humboldt. Ogden, now in the Great Basin for the first time since the spring of 1825, explored down his Unknown River a distance, then turned east toward its headwaters with death and hunger in his party. His Indian guide informed him on December 18, 1828, that they were "near the Utas Country not far distant from Salt Lake," and the day after Christmas Ogden had, as he wrote in his journal, "a distant view of great Salt Lake, heavy fogs around it." On December 28 when his company had been three days without food, he sent eight hunters ahead and could validate the verdict of Jedediah Smith—"Here we are at the end of Great Salt Lake having this season explored one half of the north side of it and can safely assert as the Americans have of the south side that it is a barren country destitute of everything." The hunters sent in advance fortunately killed a buffalo, and the third day of the new year was kept as a feast. During the last weeks of the winter he trapped the Malad, the Portneuf and the Bear, and then in late March he split his party, sending half to Fort Nez Percé through the Snake Valley while he took fourteen men to revisit his Unknown River.

"Ogden's track" of this spring is another piece in the complex mosaic of western discovery, for it was the inception of a tomorrow in history—a trail established from the headwaters of the Raft to upper Goose Creek, and thence to Thousand Springs Valley and the Humboldt. The Americans in 1826 had traversed some part of that trail, but with insufficient southing to discover the West's desert river, that river route from the Great Salt Lake country to the Sierras. Ogden trapped all down the long course of his Unknown River, finding at the end of May that it spread in a large lake—the Sink of the Humboldt. In the face of a hostile demonstration by the Indians, he turned back to Fort Nez Percé but with the promise that these Indians would see him again.

Next fall he took a company south again, extending his trails, as he said, "by far greater distance to the Gulph of California." The record of that expedition would be the worthy parallel to that of Jedediah's California exploration of 1826, but on his return to the Columbia, Ogden's boat overturned in a whirlpool, with the loss of nine men and his journals and maps. History may only conjecture that he went south along the eastern face of the Sierras to the Mohave country, thence down the Colorado to the Gulf of California. Returning, he adopted a route like Jedediah's of 1828, up the central valleys of California, thence to Fort Vancouver.

Ogden and Smith—they are the two great names in the primordial exploration of the Great Basin. Smith left the mountains in 1830 and was slain next year. Ogden came back from his California expedition in the summer of 1830 to the welcome news that his long service as a brigade leader was over. He continued in the service of the Hudson's Bay Company for many years, and in 1847 he succored the survivors of the Whitman massacre. He died at Oregon City in 1854.

The Snake Expedition in Ogden's hands had been a worthy instrument of empire. At the cost of such physical privation that he felt a convict at Botany Bay to be a gentleman of ease by comparison, he had trapped the Snake Country ruthlessly, so stripping it of furs that the Americans were walled out of Oregon until missionary zeal and land hunger should bring immigrants overland. . . . Yet the immigrants would come in the end, an inundation to dismay the Company and unsettle Ogden's last years. They were the inheritors to Jedediah Smith's America.

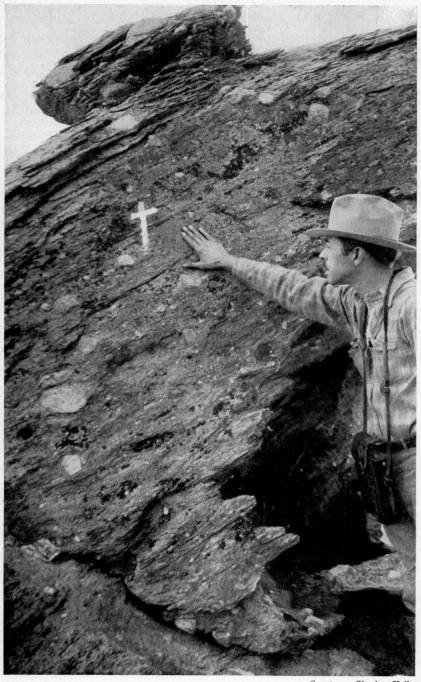

The Kit Carson Cross on Frémont Island, carved in 1843.

Charles Kelly

The Donner-Reed trail across the Salt Desert, still visible a century after.

Chapter 6

Era of the Mountain Men

I**N OUR** history the mountain men are strangely compelling figures. Though the routine of mountain life was often dull, the work hard and frequently profitless, subject at all times to a ruthless exploitation by the traders, a romance remains. It is not alone that mountain life was footloose and free, or that it balanced on the knife-edge of danger and death. Through most of the West, the mountain men were firstcomers. Their everyday life is our irrecoverable history—who first saw this stream or lake, who first encamped in this valley, who first surmounted this pass. Jedediah Smith's integrity of purpose could withstand all adversity and bring him finally into the clear light of history, but most mountain men have survived in our knowledge by accident and good fortune.

The first quick wealth of fur was stripped from the Utah country in the four years after Great Salt Lake was discovered, and after 1828 the annual rendezvous, that center of gravity for mountain life, moved northerly toward the dangerous country of the Blackfeet. During its four-year heyday the Great Salt Lake country was roamed from one end to the other. There were stark desert wastes which repelled the wandering seekers after fur, the wastelands of dead Lake Bonneville and the red rock labyrinths of the Colorado plateau. But where streams flowed with a promise of beaver, or even where springs could be found dependably spaced to sustain a trail, the mountain men quickly found their way.

The first penetration of the Utah country had been from the north, the east and the southeast, as the trappers came down out of Oregon, over South Pass or up from Taos. But the Fur Brigade had ventured west into New Mexico, Sonora and Arizona, trapping the tributaries of the Rio Grande and the Colorado. Jedediah Smith barely anticipated them in penetrating to California, and on his second trip intersected the eastbound trail of some company of now nameless adventurers. The Utah country became an oasis in long journeys, jumping-off-place before desert *jornadas* or haven at the end of them.

All the country along the west front of the Wasatch was certainly known by the time Smith, Jackson & Sublette left the mountains in 1830. All the circuitous valley of the Sevier had been trapped, and mountain men had even, on occasion, become entangled in the red rock chaos of the upper Virgin. They had trapped all the mountain creeks of the Wasatch and the Uintas, the upper and middle valleys of the Green, the valley of the Grand—now called the Colorado—and the three Parks of the Rockies. Imperceptibly the unknown became the known.

This erosion of the mysteries progressed in the south as well. Ewing Young in the fall of 1829 took a party, including the youthful Christopher Carson, to California from New Mexico by a route south of the Colorado, crossing at the Mohave villages and following Jedediah Smith's old trail to the coast. Almost at the same time Antonio Armijo took a company of 60 Mexicans west from Abiquiu in an expedition of discovery rivaling that of Jedediah Smith for the part it played in the establishment of a transcontinental trail.

Armijo followed trails through northern New Mexico and Arizona familiar since Escalante's time to reach the Crossing of the Fathers on December 6, 1829. From this point he struck more westerly across the jumbled vermilion deserts to arrive on December 19 at what he called the "Ravine of the Foul Water," the sulphur-tainted East Fork of the Virgin. Next day he reached what he mistakenly called "Rio Severo," the Virgin, and went on to encamp near the site of St. George. A three-day exploration up the rugged canyon of the Santa Clara River persuaded him to call this stream, which to Jedediah Smith had been Corn Creek, the "River of the Badlands." As he found no route to the west more promising, like Jedediah he continued with his company on down the Virgin to its mouth in the Colorado, where he arrived on the first day of the new year.

In his party was one Rafael Rivera, who the previous year had come east from California and knew something of the lower Colorado, though Rivera apparently had gone east by way of the Gila. Rivera with other scouts was sent out ahead; more zealous than they, he continued on when they turned back, and for seven days Armijo had to worry about what had happened to him. Armijo descended the Colorado three days, unhappy about the rough road he must follow, and then halted and sent out searching parties for his missing scout. On January 7 Rivera rode triumphantly back into camp, announcing that he had gone clear down to the Mohave villages and found the ford by which he had crossed to Sonora the previous year.

Armijo's party was then at the mouth of Vegas Wash. Here the Colorado, baffled in its sweep to the west, plunges straight south. Although the river could be followed down to the Mohave villages and a known trail, Armijo's purpose was exploration. Accordingly he ascended Vegas Wash into Vegas Valley—and now his expedition becomes important to history, for west of Las Vegas he found the desert route which was the key section of the Spanish Trail. He rode west around the Spring Mountains, and apparently by way of the brackish springs known subsequently as Resting Springs came to the bitter waters of the Amargosa, a stream he called the "River of the Payuches," for "a settlement of tranquil people" he found there. He traveled down the river two days, but when it began to bend west and north toward Death Valley, he turned south up a wash to Salt Springs. From here he had to push out into one of the most dreaded of the Mohave *jornadas,* encamping the first night without water and reaching Bitter Springs, which he hailed as the "Lagoon of the Miracle," on the second day. Without pausing, he pushed on into the desert and on the third day reached the haven of the Mohave.

The labor of exploration was over, but there remained a five-day journey up the river, marked by hardship laconically noted: "We ate a horse." And again, "We ate a mule belonging to don Miguel Valdes." On the last day of the year the party arrived safe at Mission San Gabriel. They rested two months and then retraced their route—as Armijo says, "without any adventure other than the loss of worn out horses and mules, until I entered the settlement of the Navajos, among whom I experienced losses of animals which were stolen from me: and I arrived in this province of Xemey [Jemez], to-day the 25th of April, 1830."

Armijo had partially wrenched the trail to California from its dependence on the Colorado; after him, there remained only one primary labor of trailfinding, that part of the trail between Las Vegas and the Virgin.

Except through the Vegas and Mohave deserts, the "old Spanish Trail" was not narrowly confined. Through the broken red rock deserts and the high mountain chains of southeastern and central Utah many variant trails were marked out. Six months after Armijo returned to New Mexico, Ewing Young's partner, William Wolfskill, left Taos with a company of trappers bound for the central valleys of California. Wolfskill took the now-familiar trail up through western Colorado, turning west to cross that river below the mouth of the Dolores, not far above present Moab in Utah. Still other variants of the "Spanish Trail" subsequently would come up from the south past Moab to join with the Wolfskill trail at this point. Wolfskill went on to the Green and apparently gained "Pleasant" or Sevier Valley by Castle Valley and Salina Canyon. The details of his itinerary are not clear, but perhaps he turned up the Sevier and crossed the Wasatch Mountains to the Little Salt Lake via Frémont Pass—a route that soon became a standard variant of the Spanish Trail. Reaching the Virgin, Wolfskill's company went on to California by Jedediah Smith's old trail.

The details of these wanderings, with all the complex variations in the trailfinding, make up a theme too complex for this book, and one for which the facts are still fragmentary and sought after, a challenge to historians. But these adventurings accomplished something immediately important. It was quickly discovered that manufactured goods conveyed on pack mules from New Mexico commanded a good sale in California, while the large California mules were prized in the markets of New Mexico. Annual caravans began to move both ways along the Spanish trails, through Utah. It was a trade which lured even the trappers. Jedediah Smith's old partner, David E. Jackson, entered into the business on arriving in Santa Fe in 1831. Two of Jedediah's brothers joined with him, and before long, others of the mountain men entered upon this trade, or wandered along the caravan trails to settle down in the California sunshine.

While these mule paths were being developed in the south as the highroads of a modest commerce, an involved competition in the north was redefining the whole character of the fur trade.

In 1827 Joshua Pilcher took an expedition to the mountains as the last gasp of the old Missouri Fur Company, which had had so redoubtable a history since Lisa's time, but 1830 was really the year of decisive change. Smith, Jackson & Sublette sold out to Jim

Bridger, Thomas Fitzpatrick, Milton G. Sublette, Henry G. Fraeb and Baptiste Gervais, styling themselves the Rocky Mountain Fur Company, and in the same year the American Fur Company expanded its operations to the mountains. Heavy trapping since 1824 had stripped the West of much of its fur, and the reduced area that could be trapped was crisscrossed not only by these two great companies but by four other firms which by 1832 had entered the field.

Among the latter, the most important were the enterprises of the New England ice-merchant, Nathaniel J. Wyeth, and of the regular Army officer, Captain Benjamin Louis Eulalie de Bonneville. Wyeth had hoped to establish a fur-trading and salmon-exporting venture in Oregon. His party broke up enroute across the continent, however, and the vessel he had sent around the Horn with trading goods was lost at sea. In 1833 he headed eastward from the Columbia, seeking some scheme to retrieve his fortunes. In the Salmon River country he encountered a party of Captain Bonneville's trappers, and a dazzling idea occurred to him. Why not propose to the bald "booshway" a joint trapping venture into the country lying west of Great Salt Lake, an expedition to go all the way to the Bay of San Francisco? On June 22 he broached just such a proposition to Bonneville.

Bonneville had come up the Plains the year before, about ten days behind Wyeth. Son of a French *émigré,* the bald-headed little captain was a West Pointer on leave of absence from the Seventh Regiment. His venture into the fur trade was designed to have a certain military significance; he engaged to provide the War Department with information about the country and the Indians beyond the Rocky Mountains.

By taking 20 wagons to the mountains, Bonneville followed the example of William Sublette, who in 1830 had showed that the thing could be done. The idea seemed eminently practical. Transporting the baggage in wagons would save the delay occasioned by packing and unpacking the horses and mules every morning and evening. Fewer horses would be required; they could be more easily defended; and on the prairies the wagons themselves might serve as an excellent fortification in the event of attack.

William Sublette had gone only to Wind River, but Captain Bonneville took his own wagons over South Pass itself, and on to the Green, where he built a log fort which the disrespectful free trappers promptly denominated "Fort Nonsense." The captain wintered on the Salmon and was enroute back to his caches when Nathaniel Wyeth crossed his trail.

All of Bonneville's activities in the mountains are attended by a certain ambiguity, so that in everything it is impossible to know to what degree he was actuated by monetary or by military motives. Wyeth's proposition, first broached in the letter of June 22 and thrashed out personally on July 4, was calculated to appeal to motives of whatever kind. Bonneville was to provide nine men to accompany Wyeth and his two *engagés,* and he was also to provide most of the trapping and trading equipment. Wyeth would lead the party, and they would equally divide the furs obtained. Thus, as Wyeth wrote his associates, he should "make a hunt, and probably reach to near the Spanish settlement of St. Francisco and on my return obtain last years deposites of furs &c. All this if I do not loose my scalp."

Wyeth announced these plans in letters written to friends and relatives on July 4, when he advised them they would not see him for another year. But overnight something happened to the arrangement, and the New Englander changed his mind. Either Bonneville backed out of the proposition with a view to an enterprise of his own or, and quite as probably, Wyeth decided to play for higher stakes— go east and return to the mountains next year with a new outfit. Bonneville knew a good idea when he saw one, however, and the expedition he fitted out for California on his own hook has played a famous part in the annals of Great Salt Lake.

In the tale of Captain Bonneville's adventures that Washington Irving gave to the world in 1837, the expedition sent out from the 1833 rendezvous under the capable Joe Walker was explained as having been designed to satisfy a passion the captain felt for authentic information about the mysterious Great Salt Lake. Its valley being no longer so frequented as it had been, mountain legend was beginning to work anew upon the lake. To have it properly explored and its secrets revealed, so Irving writes, was "the grand scheme" of the year. Moreover, there seemed some prospect that such an exploration would be attended with great profit, from the numerous beaver streams said to fringe the lake. All this being the case, it was with a proper sense of public outrage that Bonneville admitted that a party sent to explore the lake had, in some strange fashion, turned up in California.

It may be that the captain's public indignation at the miscarriage of his cherished lake expedition was not unrelated to the delicacy of his situation as an army officer who had undertaken to dispatch a company on a mission of clear trespass upon foreign soil; if there was leeway for doubt as to whether Great Salt Lake was in Mexican or United States territory, there was none whatever as to coastal California. A miscarriage of plans in consequence of the misbehavior of willful subordinates could be viewed in a more lenient light than could a purposeful trespass. Whatever Bonneville's motives, it is evident he was well aware that California, not Great Salt Lake, was Walker's destination.

For such an expedition there was no trouble getting recruits: stories were already beginning to be told about California. Forty signed up at once, all that Bonneville's resources enabled him to equip. Among those who engaged to go were Zenas Leonard and George Nidever. The previous year they had been with Black Harris' company of free trappers which had got into this very country; they had then had a look at the salt lake which in retrospect would possess such burning interest for Bonneville.

Zenas Leonard, for one, could have satisfied the captain's curiosity about the lake in every essential particular. Indeed, if Bonneville had a very real interest in the lake, a few years later he would have found it profitable to read Leonard's narrative of his travels. The Big Salt Lake, Leonard wrote in 1839, was fed by the Bear and "Weabers river," two streams "about the same size, say from two to three hundred yards wide, & from three to four hundred miles long.—They run South Parallel with each other, and empty into the Big Salt Lake on the Nor[t]h side, at no great distance apart." This lake was surrounded on the north by "a mountainous & broken country, and on the South & West by a barren, sandy plain, in a manner incapable of vegetation. There is also a hill or peak near the centre of it so high that the snow remains on it the greater part of the year. The water is of such a brackish nature that only part of it freezes in the coldest weather of the winter season. Its briny substance prevents all vegeta-

tion within a considerable distance of the margin of the lake. The
Bear and Weabers rivers are the principal streams by which it is fed.
In the Spring of the year, when the snow and ice melts and runs
down off the mountains, this lake rises very high, on account of it
having no outlet: and in the fall, or latter part of summer it sinks—
leaving salt one and two inches thick on some part of its shores. . . .
The rivers which empty into this lake abound with many kinds of
fish, such as trout, cat-fish, and others suitable for hook and line,
particularly at their mouths. Where the country is low, and small
streams empties into them, the dams of the beaver causes the water
to overflow its banks, and makes a swampy, marshy country for miles
round. People trapping on these streams are compelled to construct
canoes of Bull and buffaloe skins, in order to visit their traps." This
was, on the whole, competent observation, though the size of the lake
was exaggerated, the Stansbury Island was not too well described
and the Jordan River was left out of account.

But California, not the mountain sea, was the object of the bald
booshway's interest. Walker said good-by to him on July 24, 1833.
Zenas Leonard thought Joe Walker "well calculated to undertake a
business of this kind," hardened to wilderness hardship, understanding the character of the Indians very well, kind and affable to his men
yet able to command, and delighting in the exploration of unknown
regions. The 40 men comprising the party, reinforced apparently by
a group of free trappers, were advised by some wandering Bannock
to lay by a stock of buffalo meat, buffalo being never found where
they were going. Having jerked the meat, they set out along the
north shore of the lake with the intention of striking for Ogden's
River—the Humboldt—when they reached its western extremity.
The country was poor, almost without game, and it got poorer as
they left the lake and took a westerly course "into the most extensive
& barren plains" Leonard had ever seen—the northern reaches of the
Salt Desert. Indian footpaths led them to infrequent brackish springs
and ultimately they came upon a little encampment of Shoshoni
apparently better off and more enterprising than most in this desert
country. They listened to the plans of the whites, grimacing and
nodding. One of them, a veritable Indian Odysseus, could talk of
the country west.

After journeying southwest for many days, he said, they should come to a high mountain covered with snow the whole year round (the Ruby Mountains), on each side of which would be found the head of a large river (the Humboldt and Franklin Rivers), descending into sandy plains to form innumerable small lakes and sink into the earth and disappear. Still farther down they would come to a tremendous mountain (the Sierra Nevada) across which he had never traveled. In all this space there was no game, and near the big mountain would be found a tribe of poor Indians (perhaps the Washo) who probably would not be friendly.

This was a far knowledge to find in a little brown man who must have traveled this distance on foot. And it was a dependable knowledge, as the company learned with the passing days. Gratefully they saw the abrupt mass of the Rubies rise along the western sky to guide them to the river that must be their trail into the west.

All were glad to see the last of the country lying west of the lake. Zenas Leonard thought it most like an absolute desert of any land he had yet seen—"so dry and sandy that there is scarcely any vegetation to be found—not even a spear of grass, except around the springs. The water in some of these springs, too, is so salt that it is impossible to drink it. The Indians say that it never rains, only in the spring of the year. Everything here seems to declare that, here man shall not dwell."

Down the Humboldt—"Barren River," they called it—they made their way toward California. Little beaver sign was seen; the Indians of this country were not prosperous in appearance. Tempers frayed, and when traps were stolen, the mountain men began making targets of the red men. Walker administered a tongue-lashing to the offenders but the damage was done. Smoke signals before and behind marked their progress down the sullen river, and when they reached the swampy meadows above the sink of the Humboldt, the Indians made so hostile a demonstration that Walker decided it was policy to teach them a lesson.

A number of the men had never been engaged in any fighting with the Indians and were anxious to try their skill. Thirty-two of them surrounded a defiant band numbering perhaps a hundred and shot down three dozen Indians. Screaming, the rest fled in all directions into the tall grass. Leonard, who had engaged in this slaughter, reviewed it with a realistic eye. Though the spectacle might revolt the heart of the philanthropist, in a country swarming with hostile savages, it was hardheaded policy to strike a decisive blow.

The barren river they had followed so far spread into a green-scummed lake. The later immigrant road went along the east shore of that lake and after a desert crossing ascended the canyon of the Truckee, but the trappers built rafts of rushes, crossed the river above its mouth and made southward for the Carson Sink. The high rampart of the Sierra Nevada forbade them entry into the central valleys of California, and Walker rode ever farther south, hunting like Jedediah Smith before him for the legendary Buenaventura. But there was no Buenaventura, and the necessity of crossing the mountains before snow enveloped the passes drove them up into the precipitous canyons. They were three exhausting weeks getting over the mountains, but they found a hard way down to the San Joaquin Valley along the rim of Yosemite. The green valleys into which they rode teemed with game, but, to Walker's bitter disappointment, there were no buffalo.

Walker rode on to Monterey, more fortunate than Jedediah Smith in his reception. He and his men were given passports, and hospitality was showered upon them, with horse races, bullfights, bear-baitings, fandangos, and ripe-fleshed *señoritas* vying for their attention.

It was a perhaps reluctant but sizeable expedition that took the back trail in February—54 men, 340 horses, "and for provisions, 47 beef, and 30 dogs, together with a considerable portion of flour, Indian corn, beans, some groceries, and a few other articles necessary on such an expedition." They had no stomach for another crossing of the Sierras in these latitudes and rode south up the San Joaquin Valley, determined to go as far south as the Spanish Trail, if necessary. Luckily a band of Indians informed them of a practicable trail across the mountains. Two volunteered to guide them, and in four days, as Leonard says, they "landed safely on the opposite side of the mountain, in a temperate climate, and among tolerable pasture, which latter was equally as gratifying to our horses as the former was to the men." The mountain pass thereafter was to be called by Walker's name, and the known fact of its existence encouraged some of the earliest of the California immigrants to attempt new Western trails.

Once across the mountains, the company rode north in search of their outbound trail. Impatience to reach it led to an all but disastrous attempt at a cutoff; they turned back none too soon, leaving 64 horses, 10 cattle and 15 dogs to bleach their bones in the desert wastes. That experience was never forgotten in the mountains. Until Frémont's time, a decade after, the mountain men were content to leave intact within the wall of their desert defenses the dry mysteries of the central Great Basin.

Walker's company came at last into their old trail. Crossing the Carson Desert to "Battle Lakes," they found the Indians in ugly temper. With a cold ferocity they again fell upon the red men, slaughtering 14. Then in triumph they rode up the Humboldt to its head and, very likely by the route through Thousand Springs Valley, Goose Creek, and Raft River that thousands of forty-niners tramped just 15 years later, they made their way to the Snake. A few days later they rejoined Bonneville in the Bear River Valley.

What did Bonneville make of all this? Irving pictures his mind as a medley of outrage, grief and disgust for the atrocities committed and the miscarriage of his plans.

"The failure of this expedition was a blow to his pride, and a still greater blow to his purse. The Great Salt Lake still remained unexplored; at the same time, the means which had been furnished so liberally to fit out this favorite expedition, had all been squandered at Monterey; and the peltries, also, which had been collected on the way. He would have but scanty returns, therefore, to make this year, to his associates in the United States; and there was great danger of their becoming disheartened, and abandoning the enterprise."

It is a curious passage in one of the classics of our literature, strongly colored by the captain's complex motives; it does less than justice to one of the really significant adventures in the era of the fur trade. Bonneville's devouring interest in the Great Salt Lake was never in evidence while he was in the mountains; he traveled so near it as the old site of rendezvous at Bear Lake without exhibiting enough curiosity to spend a couple of days in riding over to its shores. When he drafted maps for Irving's account of his adventures, however, he plastered his name on the lake, and years later wrote sulkily to Lieutenant Warren, "It was from my explorations and those of my party alone that it was ascertained that this lake had no outlet; that the California Range basined all the waters of its eastern slope without further outlet. It was for this reason that Mr. W. Irving named the Salt Lake after me, and he believed I was fairly entitled to it."

His map, it is true, dispensed with that old illusion, the Buenaventura, but Bonneville's published adventures had nothing so cogent to say about the farther West as the unpretentious narrative of Zenas Leonard, which was at pains to explain:

"This desert [the Great Basin itself] which had presented such an insurmountable barrier to our route, is bounded on the east by the Rocky mountains, on the west by the Calafornia mountain, on the North by the Columbia river, and on the south by the Red, or Colorado river. . . . There are numerous small rivers rising in either mountain, winding their way far towards the centre of the plain, where they are emptied into lakes or reservoirs, and the water sinks in the sand. . . . The Calafornia mountain extends from the Columbia to the Colorado river, running parallel with the coast about 150 miles distant, and 12 or 15 hundred miles in length with its peaks perpetually covered with eternal snows. There is a large number of water courses descending from this mountain on either side—those on the east side stretching out into the plain, and those on the west flow generally in a straight course until they empty into the Pacific; but in no place is there a water course through the mountain."

Bonneville's pretensions met with no favor among his mountain contemporaries. Warren Ferris, who like Bonneville left the mountains in 1835, commented scornfully on the attempt made to rename the salt lake, "from no other reason that I can learn, but to gratify the silly conceit of a Captain Bonnyville. . . . There is no more justice or propriety in calling the lake after that gentleman, than after any other one of the many persons who in the course of their fur hunting expeditions have passed in its vicinity. He neither discovered, or explored it, nor has he done any thing else to entitle him to the honour of giving it his name, and the foolish vanity that has been his only inducement for seeking to change the appellation by which it has been known . . . can reflect no credit upon him."

Advertising, even self-advertising, nonetheless is potent; when geologists 40 years later cast about for a name for the ancestral Great Salt Lake, they settled on that of the bald booshway. Bonneville lived out the remainder of his years in the semiobscurity of professional army service, but his name has been immortalized in our culture.

Wyeth returned to the wars in the spring of 1834 on the basis of a contract with the Rocky Mountain Fur Company, which seemed to offer advantages on both sides. The Company would get out from under the thumb of their previous suppliers, Sublette & Campbell, and Wyeth would re-establish his fortunes.

It did not, however, work out so easily as that. Sublette & Campbell were not at all minded to give up their lucrative hold on the mountain business, and they stood a chance of disrupting Wyeth's deal, for his contract had provided that either party could abrogate it by payment of a forfeit.

A race to the mountains resulted. Sublette & Campbell kept a slender lead as far as the confluence of the Laramie and the Platte, and as this site had long suggested itself as a likely one for a trading post, Sublette & Campbell divided their force. While Sublette raced ahead with the best animals and a part of the trading goods, Campbell stayed behind to supervise the building of a fort. This fort, commenced June 1, 1834, was formally christened Fort William, but the authority of history spoke otherwise, and the post so built was that resounding force in Western history, Fort Laramie.

More heavily burdened than his rivals, Wyeth had to plod on to the rendezvous with such speed as he could make. Arriving there, he saw his worst fears realized. On behalf of the partners, Fitzpatrick told him that they would pay the forfeit rather than accept the goods.

Wyeth was not consoled by Fitzpatrick's explanation, nor much inclined to believe it, but Broken Hand told him the bitter truth: The fur business had taken a disastrous turn; there had been no worse year since Ashley came to the mountains. Fraeb and Gervais had decided to leave the partnership, and though Bridger and Fitzpatrick were disposed to carry on in a new partnership with Milton Sublette, they had elected to come to terms with the American Fur Company. They agreed at this rendezvous that hereafter they should receive their supplies from the great company and make over to it all their furs. The American Fur Company's partisan, Lucien Fontenelle, took this triumphant news from the mountains that fall.

Black change everywhere clouded the future, and even the new partnership would survive only another year. It was not simply that beaver were disappearing. Astor himself the previous summer had seen in London an ominous portent—"It appears that they make hats of silk in place of beaver"—and had set about withdrawing from the business which for so many years he had cherished like an only child.

The unlucky Wyeth pondered which way to turn. He had intended establishing a line of interior posts, sooner or later. Why not make a beginning now? On the Snake, somewhere near the mouth of the Portneuf, he would establish a trading post of his own. Without delay he did just this, naming it in honor of one of his backers, Henry Hall.

Fort Hall! It is another great name in Western history. On August 5, 1834, the fort was completed. So, Wyeth wrote his uncle, they "manufactured a magnificent flag from some unbleached sheeting a little red flannel and a few blue patches, saluted it with damaged powder and wet it in vilanous alcohol, and . . . it makes, I do assure you, a very respectable appearance amid the dry and desolate regions of central America. Its Bastions stand a terror to the sculking Indian and a beacon of saf[e]ty to the fugitive hunter."

Wyeth also envisioned locating a post in the vicinity of the Great Salt Lake. But bad luck pursued him, all his resources had to go into strengthening Fort Hall, and a year later he had to admit himself beaten: "Our salmon fishing has not succeeded. Half a cargo only obtained. Our people are sick and dying off like rotten sheep of bilious disorders." Nevertheless, to his wife he wrote gently, "Keep up good spirits my dear wife for I expect when I come home to stop there and altho I shall be poor yet we can always live." He returned to New England and found in ice exporting the success he had vainly sought in the mountains. But he is remembered for the conspicuous achievement represented even in his failures. He had courage, energy, imagination, dry humor and comfortable human failings, and he left the West an honorable heritage.

The last five years of the era of fur are years of slow disintegration. Imperceptibly the emphasis shifted from trapping to trafficking with the Indian tribes for buffalo robes. There were always free trappers to seek out the horizons, but the Fur Brigade began to break up. In 1835 Fitzpatrick, Bridger and Milton Sublette gave up the ghost and took service with the American Fur Company. Bonneville left the mountains; Wyeth followed next year; and in 1837 Fort Hall was taken over by the Hudson's Bay Company, the farthest British outpost.

A new processional began, of personalities strange in the mountain tradition. In 1834 five Methodist missionaries to the Flathead, including Jason and Daniel Lee, were escorted to the mountains by Wyeth. Next year the Presbyterian missionaries, Samuel Parker and Marcus Whitman, made an exploratory journey to rendezvous, Parker going on to Oregon and Whitman returning east. In 1836 Whitman with his wife Narcissa and Henry Harmon Spalding with his wife Eliza embarked upon a still more historic journey. Mrs. Whitman and Mrs. Spalding were the first white women to cross South Pass, and the first to appear at rendezvous, where they created a sensation among the trappers. The determined Whitman had brought a wagon as far as the rendezvous on Horse Creek, and he was set on taking it all the way to the Columbia. The struggle with that wagon is a small epic in itself. By the route that subsequently became known as the Greenwood or Sublette Cutoff, it was hauled by main force over the Bear River Divide and on to Fort Hall.

Even there Whitman was not prepared to give up. If he couldn't take a wagon beyond that point, he would at any rate take a pair of wheels, fashioned as a rude cart. In his valiant way, Marcus Whitman imprinted the track of wheels upon the earth all the way to Fort Boise before he abandoned his purpose.

Two years later rendezvous saw another group of these missionaries. The white women visited with the squaws of the mountain men but were fascinated and disturbed by the antics of the trappers who, as Mary Richardson Walker gravely noted in her journal, "halloed, danced, fired and acted as strangely as they could," waving Blackfeet scalps and blowing on tin horns, a music "accompanied by an inarticulate sound of the voice." Mary heard that many of the mountain men tried to act as much like Indians as they could and would be glad if they really were red men.

The pulse of the fur trade beat ever more slow, uncertain and weak. The last great rendezvous was that of 1838 at the confluence of the Popo Agie and the Wind. The onetime Wyeth man, Osborne Russell, now an independent trapper, observed the dismay among the trappers occasioned by the rumor that the company intended to bring no more supplies to the Rocky Mountains. Many left the brigade to wander individually about the country and did not appear at the rendezvous which, after all, was held in 1839 at Horse Creek once more. Signs of the end in that year were plain to everyone. Even the unaccustomed eyes of the missionary, Asahel Munger, could see that the business was breaking up. In the mountain men was a new sullenness and a new criminal violence. Munger witnessed an attempted horse theft and observed simply, "The men are most of them out of business and know not what to do."

A technological revolution had overturned the mountain men's world. Fort Laramie and Fort Hall had been true outcroppings of the future in the free and reckless present. Fixed posts like them throughout the 30's freckled the high plains. The Sioux, Cheyenne, Arapaho and Crows had not figured in the lives of the Fur Brigade except as hazards, but trade with these tribes became the mainstay of the fur companies. Buffalo robes, however, were no production of the transmontane country. Buffalo had been plentiful in the valleys of the Snake and the Great Salt Lake in the 20's and even in the early 30's, notwithstanding Jim Bridger's tale that they all died in the tremendous snows of 1830-1831 and were rolled into the pickling vat of the salt lake to be preserved for mountain larders. But the westward range of the buffalo retracted into the east each year, and by 1840 the mountain men ceased expecting to find buffalo west of South Pass.

The corruption of liquor had also come into the fur trade. Rotgut spread like a poison into the trade, productive of enormous profits and complete debauchery. Moreover, in 1838 smallpox came up the Missouri from the States to decimate whole nations of Indians.

Era of dissolution! Final rendezvous was held in 1840, sad ghost of yesteryear's forgathering. It was alone notable because the Jesuit priest, Father Pierre-Jean De Smet, enroute to the Flathead country, celebrated at Horse Creek the first mass ever said beyond the mountains, and because wagons brought to this rendezvous by three

Protestant missionaries and Joel Walker, brother of Joe, were taken by a little party of mountain men all the way to Whitman's post at Waiilatpu, a wheeled track at last made to the Columbia.

During this era of breakup and change the Great Salt Lake is like a scenic backdrop, illumined only now and then by the spotlight of some itinerant adventurer. Trappers of all the companies wintered occasionally in Cache Valley and wandered over into the greater valley. In the late spring of 1835 Jim Bridger had a party of trappers near the mouth of the Bear, and if the memory of Isaac Rose may be trusted, Old Gabe engaged in a curious sequel to his discovery of the lake a dozen years before. The lake islands attracted Bridger's attention, and one day, Rose says, he ascended a small hill and surveyed the largest of them with a telescope. As he saw signs of small streams, Old Gabe decided beaver might be found there. The Indians could give no information of the islands and did not know of any trappers who had ever visited them. Bridger decided to go a-voyaging. His men constructed two rude rafts, and loading these with traps and provisions, they commenced poling out into the lake. The clear emerald water deepened under them and made the poles useless. At the same time a wind sprang up, alarming them with the prospect of being swept far out into the lake. For two or three miles they drifted helplessly, looking longingly back at the low shore, but eventually the water shoaled. Hastily they poled the rafts back to dry land, having had their fill of salt water navigation. . . . It is a curious story and perhaps it really happened, though bullboats, not rafts, were the mountain men's usual style.

Chiefly significant for the history of the lake were not these vagrant visits by occasional trappers but the breakdown of the fur trade and the establishment of posts around the far periphery of the lake. Fort Hall was there rocklike in the north, truly a stone Wyeth had rolled into the garden of his competitors, backed up as it now was by the resources of the Hudson's Bay Company. There was no Fort Bridger until 1841, but Antoine Robidou in the winter of 1837-1838 built a post in the Uinta Basin, and up the Green some distance, in Browns Hole, Philip Thompson, William Craig and William Sinclair located still a third fort, formally christened Fort Davy Crockett, in memory of late events in Texas, but more familiarly known to the trappers as Fort Misery, "the meanest fort in the West."

All these posts served the same purpose that had been served by rendezvous. Small parties of trappers could operate from them in all directions, returning at intervals to trade for supplies. But something irreparable was gone from the mountain men's world, a preoccupation, an excitement, a meaning to existence.

Joe Meek relates that in the late summer of 1840 Doc Newell sent word he wanted to see him, and soon Meek rendezvoused with his old comrade at Fort Hall. "Major," said Newell, "we're done with this life in the mountains—done with wading in beaver-dams, and freezing or starving alternately—done with Indian trading and Indian fighting. The fur trade is dead in the Rocky Mountains, and it is no place for us now, if ever it was. We are young yet, and have life before us. We cannot waste it here; we cannot or will not return to the States. Let's go down to the Willamette and take farms."

"I'll go where you do," said Joe Meek, "what suits you suits me."

They set off for the Columbia together. It is somehow symbolical that they made their way there pushing and hauling on the four wagons that had been brought to Fort Hall. The door they closed upon the past opened a portal for the future.

Chapter 7

Shadows Before

OSBORNE RUSSELL came to the mountains with Wyeth in 1834. He helped build Fort Hall and remained to learn the complicated business of being a mountain man. When his period of service with Wyeth ran out in the late fall of 1835, feeling himself independent of the world and no longer a greenhorn, he joined Bridger's brigade.

Thereafter, for three years, he roamed the hazardous land of the Blackfeet as that last frontier of the fur country was stripped of its furs. By the time of the last great rendezvous of 1838 he saw what the future portended, but although it was with only the meagerest of success that he trapped the Snake and Yellowstone country in the two years following, he could not bring himself to acknowledge that the old life was gone.

One by one his friends left the mountains. He had a last hunt with Joe Meek before the Major set out for the Willamette, but he would not follow Meek's example, not at once. As though he had a mission to perform for history, late in the fall of 1840 he packed up his possibles and rode south toward the Great Salt Lake country.

In Cache Valley he came upon a few French Canadians and half-breeds wintering at a Snake village, and contentedly he settled down with them, accompanying them when, in mid-December, they all moved down into the valley of the great lake.

They first set up their lodges on the Weber below its confluence with the Ogden, but soon moved up on the benchland to the future site of Ogden itself. It was a beautiful country, the sloping plain under the high wall of the Wasatch, and there was game in great plenty, for the elk had left the mountains to winter among the thickets along the river banks. The weeks went by pleasantly, marked by a Christmas feast, by hunts for elk or big horn in the mountains. Time had no urgency, no reality except the slow progression of the seasons marked by the occasional entries in the journal he was keeping.

In late February Russell roused himself to ride south to Salt Lake Valley to trade for furs at the Ute encampment. His journal, as he rode south along the shore of the salt lake, was conscientious in its observation of the country, and he saw clearly with what little labor and expense the numerous fine springs and streams here could be made to irrigate the lovely, fertile valley.

Wanship, a tall, dark-skinned Indian thin of visage and with piercing eye, welcomed Russell into his lodge, ordered his horses taken care of and passed around the big pipe. Gravely he asked the news—where the white man had come from, where he was going, for what purpose, how and for whom. As gravely Russell returned his answers, after which Wanship gave him an extract, so the mountain man said, of all he had seen, heard and done for ten years past.

When supper was over, Wanship's women retired from the lodge and the principal men assembled to smoke and hear the news. The evening passed pleasantly until midnight, when the assemblage broke up, the women returned and all retired to their blankets.

White purposes were working to grind this life into dust, but in the first days of March 1841 Russell rode freehearted about the valley with the Ute, hunting the northward-flying wild ducks and geese that filled the air with their harsh, plaintive crying. Was there not, the mountain man wondered, a happiness in ignorance that knowledge and science destroyed? Here was a people contented and happy.

"If a Eutaw had eight or ten good horses, a rifle and ammunition, he was contented. If he brought a deer at night from the hunt, joy beamed in the faces of his wife and children and if he returned empty a frown was not seen on the faces of his companions. The buffalo had long since left the shores of these lakes and the hostile Blackfeet had not left a footprint here for many years."

Russell sought what could be learned about the southern extremity of the salt lake. The Indians could tell him hardly more than their grandfathers had told Father Escalante, that it was "a sterile, barren, mountainous country, inhabited by a race of depraved and hostile savages who poisoned their arrows and hindered the exploring of the country."

Having obtained all the furs he could, at the end of March Russell prepared for the return to Fort Hall. Just before his departure, Wanship's son came in. With his family he had passed the winter on Antelope Island, going to and from island and shore on a 12-foot raft of bulrushes. There were large numbers of antelope on the island, and though there was no wood, wild sage served for fuel. Wanship's eyes awakened. He could remember a time, he said to the white man, when the buffalo had passed from the mainland to the island without swimming. The depth of the waters was yearly increasing.

Russell rode back north. To the unaccustomed eyes of white settlers soon to come, Salt Lake Valley might desolate the heart with its barrenness, but to the mountain man in this spring of 1841 it was luxuriantly beautiful. The spring grass "had sprung up to the height of six inches, intermingled with various kinds of flowers in full bloom. The shores of the lake were swarming with water fowl of every species that inhabit inland lakes." Rejoining his winter comrades on April 2 at Bear River, he went on to Fort Hall.

For a few additional weeks he trapped about the fort. In mid-June the Presbyterian missionary, John S. Griffin, with his wife and child arrived from the Columbia. Russell conducted them to Green River. But rendezvous was a thing of the dead past: no one was there to take them to the States. The missionary decided to retrace his way to the Columbia, and Russell escorted him back to the fort.

They arrived August 8, 1841. Four days later the mountain man was startled by the appearance of the short, dark Jesuit priest, Father De Smet, who rode in from the east accompanied by a young Flathead convert. The following day no fewer than 16 Oregon immigrants together with seven more Catholics, the whole guided by Thomas Fitzpatrick, drove their wagons up to the Hudson's Bay Company's post.

With them came four dusty horsemen calling anxiously for information. They were members of an immigrant company that three days ago had separated from these travelers at Soda Springs to break a road for their wagons down Bear River toward the salt lake.

Somebody tell them, the four horsemen demanded, *how could you get to California from the Great Salt Lake?*

It was now 17 years since the rediscovery of South Pass. In that time a varied company of adventurers had yielded to the long American compulsion *to go West*—men in search of fortune, men consecrated to the service of God, men in quest of health or adventure, men exulting in youth's springtime *Wanderjahre,* men intoxicated with novelty or far places or their own freedom. Trail dust had eddied up about them, graying their hair and clothes and their sun-roughened faces, settling thick upon the blanket rolls of the horsemen and blowing stiflingly about the grinding wheels and weathered canvas of their wagons.

During all those 17 years desire had freshened on the winds blowing from the Rockies. Oregon first captured the nation's imagination, but in 1840 the rising enthusiasm along the Missouri frontier was energized rather by a glowing vision of California. Men listened spellbound to returned travelers like the Robidou brothers, who talked of sunlit pastoral paradises and had an overwhelming answer to the first question that any Missourian asked about a new country: in all of California only one man was ever known to have had chills and fever and he was a matter of such wonderment that the people of Monterey went 18 miles into the country to see him shake. Moreover, the "Spanish" authorities were friendly, the people the most hospitable on the globe; you could travel all over California and it would cost you nothing for horses or feed. Even the Indians were friendly.

During the summer and fall of 1840 men in western Missouri enrolled by the score in the "Western Emigration Society." But second thoughts set in, and when spring rolled around, it was a very slender company that assembled at the rendezvous on the Kansas River.

In this company, moreover, two minds prevailed about the route. Some wanted to go with the Santa Fe traders to New Mexico, and then by the caravan trail to California, while others wanted to take wagons west up the Platte and over South Pass to Fort Hall. Nobody had any clear idea how California might be reached from that point, but there were old maps showing a great interior lake drained by two rivers which flowed to the Pacific; it might be possible to build canoes and float the rest of the way to the coast. The best information was contradictory; the rivers might not be navigable, might not even exist. Still there was encouraging word from Dr. John Marsh, now resident in California, whose letters directed immigrants to bear southwesterly from Fort Hall to the Snowy Mountains. Here they could find a pass and reach the San Joaquin River, which would lead them to Marsh's rancho at the foot of Mount Diablo near San Francisco Bay.

In the end, a small pack company joined the New Mexican traders and took the trail to Santa Fe, but the majority, more significant for the history both of the Great Salt Lake country and the West, took the problematical northern route over South Pass.

It was not too encouraging a group that rendezvoused on the Kansas River. Wagons straggled up only one by one, and nobody knew where to go, or anything about plains management. John Bartleson, elected captain because he threatened that otherwise he and the six with him would not go, was as ignorant as any. So, when word came that the famous mountain man, Thomas Fitzpatrick, was coming up behind, guiding a company of Catholic missionaries, the Bartleson party waited humbly for the privilege of going with him.

By May 18, since all but the wagon of Joseph B. Chiles had come up to the encampment on the Kansas River, the travelers launched upon their journey. Five days out they were overtaken by Chiles, and on May 26 by a final arrival, the eccentric 64-year-old Methodist preacher, Joseph Williams. Fifteen wagons and 4 Red River carts carried their belongings; they had horses, mules and oxen but no cows. Including the 11 men in the Catholic contingent, there were 66 men in the company, at least 5 women, and a scattering of children. Among them were schoolteachers and mountain men, Indian missionaries and Kentucky backwoodsmen, pleasure seekers and farmers, an absconder, a future candidate for the presidency. . . . and a woman bravely insisting, "Where my husband goes I can go, I can better stand the hardships of the journey than the anxieties for an absent husband."

The pattern of their trail life was a pattern for the life of all the thousands of immigrants to come. Dissension over the rate of travel, breakdown of wagons and endless spading at stream crossings, wonderment at the visage of mountain men who surely had never seen razor, water, soap, or brush, a wedding in the company, a fatal accident, a scare by Cheyenne, a sudden furious hailstorm, buffalo in numbers beyond imagining, dust and wind and sun, more dust and more sun intolerable in a sky of brass, the great landmarks of the plains: Chimney Rock, Scotts Bluff, Independence Rock, the perpetual slow climb toward South Pass while the listless horizons and the monotonous creaking of the wagon wheels whipsawed the nerves . . . the journals of a generation of Americans assent to this experience.

South Pass was surmounted July 18, and the company slowly descended the Sandy toward the Green. Men sent out to search for the trappers found no one at the old rendezvous, but a score of the die-hards captained by Bridger's partner, Henry Fraeb, were overtaken on their way to the buffalo country, and they returned to trade buckskin clothing and peltry for merchandise, not excluding a villainous alcohol loosely called whisky, which some of the forehanded immigrants had brought along. The mountain men were a rough-looking set, young "Cheyenne" Dawson thought, and he observed curiously that they had contracted many Indian customs, "such as eating every time they were invited, without regard to previous meals, and making the squaws do all the camp work, even to saddling their horses."

This meager rendezvous broke up on July 25, 1841. The pleasure seekers in the party, half a dozen in all, turned back toward the States. The immigrants and the Catholic missionaries moved on up Hams Fork and the Little Muddy toward the Bear River Divide. And Fraeb took his mountain men on toward the buffalo country, his string all but played out. . . . Within a few weeks Bridger and Fraeb decided to build a trading post of their own. They selected a site on the Green between the mouths of Blacks Fork and Henrys Fork. While Bridger began putting up the first ramshackle sheds, Fraeb traveled east a few miles and set about the job of making meat. A war party of Sioux and Cheyenne pounced upon his company, and though the Indians were fought off in a desperate battle waged throughout a long August day, Fraeb was one of the whites whose stick went under. The fort commenced under such dark auspices was relocated three times in three years, situated finally some distance up Blacks Fork: this was Fort Bridger.

The dividing ridge was crossed at the head of the Little Muddy, and the wagons—now reduced to 13, because Chiles had sold his at Green River and another had been abandoned there—began the descent of Bridgers Creek toward the Bear. This route was adopted also by the wagons of the four succeeding immigrations, though after 1845 the favored route was the Greenwood or Sublette Cutoff farther north. John Bidwell thought theirs "a most difficult route," but they accomplished a full 20-mile day's journey to reach the Bear River bottoms, whence they began the long, circuitous pull down the Bear Valley, at first north and then more westerly. West of Thomas Fork the mountains closed in upon the river and John Bidwell was sure no person would ever believe wagons had passed these "huge eminences of nature," unless he had seen it with his own eyes. But the view was worth it—rugged summits of almost every shape were fantastically sculptured against the western sky; to the south lay a beautiful little lake; and through the valley bottom the river meandered among dark green willows and scattering cottonwoods to disappear among hills empurpled by the evening.

That distant blue lake, Fitzpatrick could tell them in memory of all that had gone from the West, was Sweet Lake, the Little Lake—Bear Lake. They were within three days' journey of Soda Springs, where the Bear would swing abruptly south toward the Salt Lake and bring immigrants and missionaries to the parting of the ways.

During those three hot August days the immigrants besieged the Broken Hand with all the questions that anxiety could formulate. Everyone knew that without the steadying influence of his judgment and experience, his plains craft and wisdom of survival, they could well have been blotted out by the immense, indifferent plains. What they knew about taking care of themselves they had learned from his teaching and the force of his example. Beyond Soda Springs they would be on their own.

And he could tell them nothing about the country west of the salt lake, nothing except that mountain men from time to time had gotten into that region in search of beaver. The only helpful suggestion he had was that they might be able to find someone at Fort Hall who could give them information.

Hard decision was upon them. The moment came on reaching Soda Springs August 10. Only 32 men, including Benjamin Kelsey with his valiant wife and baby, had heart for the purpose that had brought them so far. The remaining 16, including the 4 other families, decided for Oregon. The little company drew asunder: 9 wagons to go down the Bear, 3 to go with the 4 missionary carts and wagon over the mountains to Fort Hall.

Father De Smet said his farewells first, as he set out ahead of the others, accompanied only by a young Flathead convert, at nightfall on August 10. The genial little Jesuit had enjoyed his companions and the journey; they remembered him with affection and respect the rest of their lives, and regretfully said good-by to him. A certain legend has obtained currency about the father, that in this year 1841 he personally explored the valley of the Great Salt Lake; monuments, even, have been erected in commemoration of this idea. But this August passage through the hot, dusty valley of the Bear was Father De Smet's nearest approach to the great lake. He rode off through the gathering darkness north toward Fort Hall, and he would never be so near the salt lake again.

Bartleson and 3 others were delegated to make the trip to Fort Hall for information, the rest of the California party turning down the Bear to go slowly ahead with the wagons until the others should overtake them. So on August 13 the 4 men dismounted before the Hudson's Bay Company post demanding information, any information from anybody, about how to go where they were going.

There was little enough that anybody could tell them. Even Osborne Russell, who had now lived 7 years in the mountains, had no useful advice. All that Bartleson could learn was that somewhere west of Great Salt Lake he could come upon a desert river called Marys River which would guide him as far as the California Mountains. But he must take care about finding this river. If the immigrants strayed too far south, they would get into a parched wasteland without grass; if they got too far north, they would get into a broken country with terrible canyons where they might wander about in helpless bewilderment and perish.

The four seekers swallowed on this information and said the last good-bys. Fitzpatrick was taking the Catholics up Henrys Fork of the Snake and on to the field of their labors in the Flathead country. The little band of Oregon-bound immigrants was preparing to abandon their three wagons and pack on to the Columbia. Still with them was the Reverend Mr. Williams. Excitable, eccentric, disapproving of the Universalists, deists and worse in whose company he traveled, given to much singing of hymns, determined prejudices against traveling on the Sabbath, and long, rambling arguments on theology, there was yet in him an extraordinary energy undiminished by his advanced years—a devout and fearless man who had not hesitated to set out alone into the formidable plains and who would not hesitate before any other dictate of his will. . . . To them all Bartleson and his three companions said farewell, with that mingled sorrow and apprehension which must always attend the breakup of the immigrant's world. Loading their packhorses with the provisions which were almost the only fruits of their journey to Fort Hall, the Californians took the back trail for the Bear.

Meanwhile the wagons had set out down Bear River, with the idea of going on to Cache Valley to recruit the stock while awaiting the return of the party that had gone to Fort Hall. The valley had never hindered the mountain men and their pack animals, but getting wagons through was a wearing business. They had first to cross a scorched brown lava plain, and then to force their way through a hilly country beset at every step by the interminable sagebrush, which continually resisted the wagons and occasionally overturned those more lightly laden. They encamped the second night some 20 miles down the river, near the mouth of Cottonwood Creek. The river here armored itself with surly lava canyons, so they struck southwesterly across the hills, the sudden ridges and ravines which entrapped them forcing them to journey to almost every point of the compass; the road was, as John Bidwell observed, "uncommonly broken." Diagonally they descended Battle Creek into the north end of Cache Valley, but they were incapable of knowing they had reached their contemplated encampment, and still seeking it, they continued along the western foothills of the valley. Indian fires blazing in the mountains filled the air with a baffling haze which the eye could not penetrate and which enwrapped them in a smoky unreality. The immigrants thought this smoke boiling up from the hills an alarmed intelligence of their movements, though the Indians in the mountains, who were resorting to their seasonal mode of harvesting crickets and grasshoppers for a winter food supply, quite likely knew nothing of this significant penetration of their country.

Southwest of present Clarkston the nine wagons pulled up over the shoulder of Black Butte, and on August 17, 1841, jolted down through the acrid haze into the Great Salt Lake Valley. Bear River was directly to the south, but they could not see it, and their descent into the valley was abruptly halted by what Bidwell called "a deep salt creek"—the Malad River some 20 miles above its confluence with the Bear. To cross this brackish river they had to search some distance upstream for a ford. They then turned south, hoping soon to reach the Bear, but had to encamp in the vicinity of present Fielding, suffering with thirst, for the water of the Malad was so salt they could not drink it.

At sunup they got the wagons moving again, hoping soon for fresh water for the animals and themselves, but as the sun mounted mercilessly into the skies they could see nothing before them but spreading arid plains glimmering with heat and salt, which became at last white as snow, hard-baked in the sun, with no green thing growing anywhere upon them. The smoky red sun tantalized them with mirages; half-believing, half-doubting, they saw timber on the plain and lunged on only to have the green trees tremble in the shimmering air and then vanish altogether. In desperation they turned east, and in five miles came to the Bear, approximately at the site of Corinne. But even along the Bear the desert earth was grudging. Though there was a green plentitude of grass, it was so salt the animals could hardly eat it, the salt glittering upon its blades like an arrogant frost.

Buffeted by the sun, they remained here all day on August 20, sending two men to explore the country and learn if Cache Valley was much farther ahead. The scouts returned to report that the wagons were within ten miles of where the river emptied into the Great Salt Lake itself. John Bidwell reflected bitterly in his journal, "This is the fruit of having no pilot—we passed through cash valley, where we intended to stop and did not know it."

Western trails and explorations, 1841-1846.

Besieged by salt, they felt no interest in the ramous lake. On the following morning they turned northwest, completing the ironical triangle they had traced on this salt plain. To notify those who had gone to Fort Hall which way to follow, they left a paper on a pole at the intersection with their southbound trail. Resuming the journey, they moved on a few more miles to camp west of present Tremonton, finding grass and water which, Bidwell adjudged, "answered our purpose very well, though both were salt."

Early next morning one of the four who had gone to Fort Hall arrived in camp alone. He had been left behind by the others when his loaded packhorse was unable to keep pace. He had seen the paper at the intersection and come on straight to camp. His disgusted comrades did not arrive until late in the day, after making the weary round of the triangle. There was no travel that day, Sunday, but they rolled west again on the twenty-third, past springs and salt plains into an upland pocked with the demoniacal sage. During the afternoon they climbed toward the summit of the Promontory Range, all unaware that less than three decades later a Pacific Railroad would lay its last rails in their footsteps. Beyond the Promontory summit, just at evening, the juniper-clad hills fell away and they shouted to the sunset splendor of Spring Bay, the northwestern extremity of Great Salt Lake.

But they could find little water, their cattle strayed far in search of it, and they were late getting started next morning. Ten miles took them to Monument Point at the north end of the lake, where numerous deep, clear springs poured forth their abundant waters. Salt was everywhere. The grass that grew in small clumps on the plain was laden with it; the salt formed on the stalks and blades in lumps from the size of a pea to that of a hen's egg, very white, strong and pure. The little company spent all the day of August 25 at this oasis but next day resumed the struggle with the sage—"or rather," John Bidwell cried out in his journal, "it ought to be called, wormwood, and which I believe will grow without water or soil." Neither the aridity nor the barrenness of the plain over which they traveled could relieve them of the everlasting sagebrush. Its scent drifted heavily upon the air, and its muscular branches never ceased to wrestle with the wagons.

For, stubbornly, they carried the wagons on, across this country where wagons had never gone before. Whether up stony ridges or down steep-banked ravines, through marshes or across sage plains, a way was forced for the wagons, and the mark of those wagon wheels was the mark of the future imprinted upon this land.

They found no water, that day they rolled on west from the springs at the lake shore. In desperation the company turned north along an Indian trail, knowing that in this country all trails must lead to water. Long after nightfall they pulled on, but they were forced to make a dry camp. Daylight showed a glint of green ahead; they rolled on another five miles and reached a spring with its riches in grass, at the southeastern extremity of the Raft River Mountains.

It was now evident enough that they must explore a way to Marys River. They were all a little frightened by the warnings given them at Fort Hall, and the promise of death and destruction hung heavy on the desert air they breathed. It was decided that the company should remain here for a few days recruiting the livestock while Bartleson and Charlie Hopper rode on west to search out a way to the desert river which must be their salvation and guide.

The two scouts were gone a long time. Those left in camp did a little unsuccessful hunting, traded with the Indians for horses and serviceberries . . . and felt rise within them that dreadful urgency to be doing, to be getting somewhere, to *go on*. It was impossible to rest with a high heart; the unknown weighed too heavily upon them. And what if something had happened to Bartleson and Hopper?

After a week it was decided to start moving on by slow stages. The oxen were yoked to the wagons and they rolled slowly west through Park Valley. Five days later the two dust-covered scouts rode into camp, grinning with their good news. They had found, five days' journey to the west, a river which must be Marys River. Wagons could not be taken the route they had gone, but it seemed likely a route could be found more to the south.

The course chosen would carry them along the rim of the Salt Desert. Seven years before, Joe Walker's California-bound company had rounded the shoulder of the lake, only to carom into a more westerly course. Now a company of innocents could struggle with their wagons in this country.

On the first day they got the wagons along 15 miles, but they encamped without water, a warning they heeded. A second 15 miles, due west this time, brought them to water at Owl Springs. Benjamin Kelsey bowed to the logic of necessity, coldly clear in the parching light reflected from this white desert floor: he decided to abandon his wagons. Packing his 19-year old wife Nancy on a horse with their baby, and putting the more valuable of their belongings on their other horses, he set out again, driving their failing oxen before them. That day the company accomplished another 12 miles, and the following day, September 13, they reached a milestone in western history, the first immigrant arrival at Pilot Peak. Four years later Frémont would reach this critical watering place after a venturesome southern crossing of the Salt Desert; in 1846 immigrant companies would come in out of that desert as though to salvation itself.

The Bartleson party, however, moved on south and west around the shoulder of the Pilot Range. They covered 25 hard miles, but after nightfall the exhausted animals could go no farther and they had to halt waterless in the center of arid Steptoe Valley. Soon after sunup they started moving again, climbing up through a gap in the Toano Range and roping the wagons down into the high, dry plain of Gosiute Valley. Through the smoky air they could make out the lofty peaks of the Pequop Mountains. Pressing on westerly, they reached after 15 miles travel some abundant springs with their green, attendant grasses. And barely in time. Hour by hour their animals had visibly failed.

So here at the base of the Pequops the rest of the wagons must remain. They had come a long, toilsome and honorable journey, across the width of three future states, Nebraska, Wyoming and Utah, to this derelict finish in eastern Nevada. Their trail from the Missouri River to Soda Springs would be bitten deep into the earth by thousands of wagons to come. Their route down the Bear and around the shoulder of the Great Salt Lake would not again be used, but in five years other immigrants would come from Pilot Peak to these springs, and burn these historic wagons in their campfires, an offering to the inscrutable gods presiding over the Western trails.

The abandonment of the wagons had its own strange ceremoniousness. While they were looking over their property deciding what could be taken on in packs, an old Indian, like a patron spirit of this desert immensity, came down out of the mountains. The whites understood his signs to mean that he had dreamed of their coming,

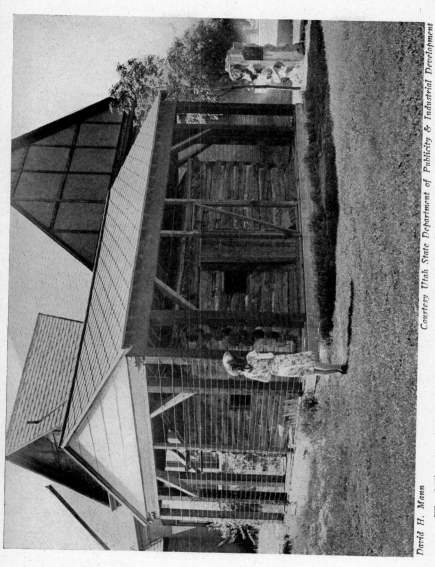

Courtesy Utah State Department of Publicity & Industrial Development

The Miles Goodyear Cabin, built 1844-45, the first permanent white residence in Utah.

W. H. Jackson

Courtesy, U. S. Geological Survey

The Hayden Survey at the upper crossing of the North Platte on the Oregon Trail, 1871.

and that in the dream he had been instructed to descend into the plains on the east side of the mountains, where he would find strange men who would give him a great many things. He passed about from mess to mess, his wrinkled face a mask of pleasure, and the whites began to make him presents—pieces of iron, castoff clothing. Whenever he received anything he thought useful, John Bidwell says, "he paused, and looking steadfastly at the sun, addressed him in a loud voice, marking out his course in the sky, as he advanced in his invocation, which took him about 2 minutes to perform—as he received quite a number of articles, it took him a considerable part of the day to repeat his blessings." On the second day, the preparations complete, they left the brown patriarch standing amid his new wealth and still circumscribing the heavens—"the happiest, richest, most religious man" Cheyenne Dawson saw during all the rest of his life.

They turned the southern shoulder of the Pequops, crossed Independence Valley to the south end of the East Humboldt Mountains, and rounded these mountains into Ruby Valley. Here turning north, they crossed the Ruby Mountains by Secret Pass, and camped delightedly on a stream running to the northwest, Secret Creek. This brought them on September 24 to a larger stream, the East Fork of the Humboldt, and though alarmed by the consistent northwestern course of the Humboldt, which seemed to deny that it could be the indispensable Marys River, they followed it down through its succession of canyons and finally, to their inexpressible relief, on October 2 saw it turn to the southwest at its Big Bend. Game was scarce; one by one the oxen were eaten, and thus gradually the journey dispossessed them. They followed the Humboldt to its sink, crossed over to the Carson River, and, reaching the Walker River, struggled up into the Sierras, fortunately crossing the heights at the head of the Stanislaus in advance of the paralyzing winter snows. They had their share of thirsting and starving, so that even the entrails of coyotes could afford them banquets, and Bartleson could talk feelingly of the privilege of eating out of the troughs with his hogs if ever he saw Missouri again. But down out of the Sierras they found their way, and on November 4 reached Marsh's rancho at the foot of Mount Diablo.

The journey stripped them almost to nakedness. But they had

always found the resources of will to go on. Cheyenne Dawson never forgot looking back once and seeing Nancy Kelsey following resolutely after him down a precipitous path, her child in her arms, barefooted and leading her horse. Heroic woman who would not be left behind, she was the first white woman to see the Great Salt Lake and first to cross the Sierras. Only by a few weeks was she second to Joel Walker's wife, who had come down from Oregon after the overland journey of the previous year, as the first white woman to cross the continent to California. Nancy had not faltered, and the men were not outmatched.

In the spring John Bidwell sent his journal back east as instruction for those who might follow where he and his fellows had led. Those who came with him, he reported, were in many instances well pleased with the country, but others among them were so sick of it they could not look at it; people regarded California as either the garden of the world or the most desolate place of Creation. But all those who had come West in search of health had found what they sought. If he were to come to California again, he thought, he would come not with wagons but with pack animals. On second thought, it might be advantageous to come by sea, as you could bring useful things like plows and wagons. A good American wagon might be worth $200 or $300 in this country.

Bidwell's second thoughts must fall upon deaf ears. Plows and wagons would come, and they would come overland.

On September 15, 1841, the same day the Bartleson party admitted defeat and abandoned their wagons under the high wall of the Pequops, Osborne Russell left Fort Hall for the valley of the Great Salt Lake "to hunt a few more beaver." The sign of the immigrant marked the land, yet still he could not bring himself to give up the free life which now for seven years had been his. Meek and Newell had gone on to Oregon a year ago, and dozens of others had disappeared, but there were two comrades to ride south up the Blackfoot with him. Hunting beaver and antelope alternately, they worked their slow way down the Bear, and in the last week of October arrived at its mouth in Great Salt Lake. The salt plain where the immigrants had traced their profitless triangle in August impressed

Russell so that he particularly described it in his journal. But he was rebelliously silent about the wagon tracks.

On November 5 the three trappers turned back to Fort Hall. From there they revisited the sources of the Portneuf. But change was beyond denial or restoration. In 1836 large bands of buffalo could be seen in almost every little valley on the small branches of the Portneuf. Now the only traces of them still to be seen were the scattered bones of those that had been killed. The trails they had so deeply indented over the years were overgrown with grass and weeds. It was time, Russell and his companions agreed, for the white man to leave the mountains, now that beaver and game had nearly disappeared.

Late in December they came back to the fort to spend the winter. In the spring Russell and Alfred Shutes were drawn back once more to the Great Salt Lake Valley. Through April and May they feasted on wild fowl and eggs at the mouth of the Bear, and they caught a few beaver. But this was farewell. At the end of May the two old comrades rode back to Fort Hall. The third week of June they reached the parting of the ways. Joseph Williams, who had spent a restless winter at the mission station in the Willamette Valley, had set his face toward the rising sun in April, undismayed even by the prospect that he might have to travel alone. James Ross and Edward Rogers, his westbound comrades of the year before, had joined with him, and the three men had turned up at Fort Hall in mid-June.

It was 16 years since Alfred Shutes had seen his native Green Mountains, and the arrival of the little party from the West decided him to revisit Vermont. He and Russell shook hands in good-by. There was nothing left for Osborne Russell in the mountains any longer. Straightening himself in the saddle, he too set out for the Willamette—the Willamette and the enclosed life of the farm.

Chapter 8

Connecticut Yankee and Cavalier

O N A May day in 1836 as Marcus Whitman was hastening
north to reach Council Bluffs before the caravan of the
American Fur Company should set out for the mountains,
he stumbled upon a boy alone in the prairie. A thin, spare youngster
who looked perhaps 16 years old, with flaxen hair and light blue
eyes, the boy wore an old straw hat, a ragged fustian coat, scarcely
half a shirt and badly worn buckskin pants. He had only one
moccasin, and though he carried an old rifle, his powder horn was
empty.

The night's rain had soaked him to the skin, and he had eaten
nothing for two days. But he could grin still. Asking no other
favors, he would appreciate it, he said, if the missionaries could spare
a little ammunition. With that he could kill some game, and he
thought he'd get along. Like themselves, he was making for the post
at the old Council Bluffs.

A little appalled by this kind of resolution in one so young, Whitman supplied the boy with such stores as he wanted and tried to
persuade him to turn back to the frontier. He would not be persuaded; he made a counterproposition. If the missionaries would
allow him to accompany them to Council Bluffs, he would assist
them all he could along the way. It was so agreed, and he gave them
his name: he was Miles Goodyear.

The undersized boy was older than he looked. He had been born
in Connecticut February 24, 1817, next to youngest of six brothers
and sisters. Both father and mother died before his fifth birthday,
and the children were scattered. When ten years old, Miles was
bound out for six years to a farmer of North Haven, and that experience as a bound boy fired him with a passion for freedom that drove
him West when his period of service ended. In 1834 he began drifting
west toward the frontier, and two years later he had reached the
jumping-off place.

Whitman furnished him with a horse and found that he made a
130

useful hand. In the end, Miles went with the missionaries all the way to the mountains. At rendezvous he might have abandoned them and attached himself to some roving band of free trappers, but he chose to go on toward Oregon—perhaps from promise of reward, perhaps out of a reluctance to break the associations that had grown up along the trail. But the terrible job of manhandling Whitman's wagon across the Bear River Divide wore his patience threadbare, and when the good doctor proposed dragging that wagon on to the Columbia, he and young Goodyear came to the parting of the ways.

The missionaries took Miles's desertion from their number with good grace, furnishing him with a couple of horses and the best outfit they could provide. Impressed with the boy's intensity of purpose, the missionary William Gray summed him up: "His idea of liberty was unlimited. Restraint and obedience to others was what he did not like at home; he would try his fortune in the mountains; he did not care for missionaries, Hudson's Bay men, nor Indians; he was determined to be his own man."

During three years he served out his mountain apprenticeship, living among the tribes or attaching himself to small parties of mountain men while he learned the minute lore of survival. By 1839, grown to man's stature, he could himself trade and trap out of Fort Hall with equipment furnished by the Hudson's Bay Company. The Snakes came to know him as *Inca Pompe,* the redhead, and the Bannock as *Mooritza,* the red deer; Connecticut became a memory stern, uncompromising and remote. In the course of time he took a squaw to wife. Tradition is that she was a daughter of Peteetneet, chief of a Ute band located in Utah Valley. She bore him two husky youngsters, a boy and a girl.

With his squaw he was at Fort Hall on the June day of 1842 when Joseph Williams and his two companions rode in, homeward bound from the Columbia. Alf Shutes came in with Osborne Russell and suddenly made up his mind to revisit his native Vermont which he had not seen in 16 years. Miles elected to accompany the little party for a distance along the trail, and a Frenchman with his squaw came also.

The six men and the two squaws left the fort June 21, 1842. Osborne Russell rode with them as far as Ross's Fork, separating

from them next morning to hunt and dry elk meat to see him through
to the Willamette. The others rode on to Soda Springs by way of
the Portneuf. As they rode up the Bear, Shutes described to the old
preacher the great valley lying to the south where he had hunted
with Russell in the spring. Perhaps Miles Goodyear already knew
that country. Or perhaps the tales to which he listened now first
struck fire from his imagination. It seems certain, however, that the
venerable Williams questioned Shutes with the greater eagerness.
Fresh from his inspection of the mission stations in Oregon, the
preacher wrote in his journal with delight that:

"the Eutaw Indians wish to have a missionary to come and settle
amongst them, and to learn them to raise grain. I am of the opinion,
that on the east side of Big Salt Lake . . . would be a great place to
establish a mission, and well calculated for raising all kinds of grain.
It is good, rich land, a well watered and healthy country. Fish and
fowls are very plenty. A beautiful prairie, about one hundred miles
long, lies between the lake and the mountain. The plains are covered
with green grass all winter, and well calculated for raising stock.
Some pines on the mountains, and cottonwood along the creeks and
rivers that flow into the lake. There is plenty of salt on the edges of
the lake. It is about two hundred and fifty miles in circumference,
and lies in 40° north latitude."

On June 27 the little company reached the old site of rendezvous
on Green River. No one was there. Undecided what to do, reluctant
to ride the direct trail east in the face of Fraeb's fate of the preceding
August, a story that had grown with the telling in the mountains,
they finally headed southwest for Bridger's new fort. But Bridger,
it developed, had left for the States with his furs a month before;
nothing was to be seen there except three little, starved dogs and the
grave of an Indian woman killed by the Cheyenne. Though the
experienced Shutes began to have grave misgivings and talked of
turning back, Williams' invincible faith and ignorance prevailed.
They decided to cross the Uinta Mountains to Robidou's fort and go
on to the States by way of Taos and the Santa Fe Trail.

The guide who took them by a rough road across the high Uintas
was, Williams says in his curious language, "the wife of one of the
Frenchmen." More than likely she was Miles Goodyear's squaw.

Imperturbably she managed her two children, "one tied to a board, and hung to the horn of a saddle, and the other in a blanket, tied to her back." The way was very laborious, but she brought them across the summit to one of the Uintas' serene mountain lakes. Here they camped for two days because, Williams says, identifying one of his "Frenchmen" at the last moment, "Mr. Miles and his squaw were both taken sick."

The impatient Shutes set off by himself for Fort Wintey. Rogers and Ross wanted to follow. Williams argued against profaning the Sabbath by travel, but finally he gave in, taking a certain gloomy satisfaction in the fact that they got lost and were three days reaching the fort.

At the post Williams had to wait nearly three weeks on Robidou's pleasure before he could set out for New Mexico. He improved the time by preaching to the mountain men, but they were singularly hardened souls; virtue was not in them; and he was glad to depart for a more Christian country.

At the mountain lake Miles Goodyear and the Frenchman had been left with their squaws to shift for themselves. It is to be doubted whether they cared much; the rigorous Williams conscience must have been uncomfortable to live with. In their own good time they moved on down the south slopes of the Uintas to Robidou's post, and they lazed about the fort till its owner returned in October with a fresh supply of trading goods.

Miles had not yet left Fort Wintey when, at the end of October, Marcus Whitman himself rode down out of the mountains with a single companion. It was now six years since Miles had parted with the doctor at Fort Hall, and he must have wondered what pressing necessity could have induced the missionary to undertake a winter journey to the States. It is not likely that Whitman talked about the dissensions among the missionaries which had made this famous "ride" necessary, but he consented to carry to the States the first word Miles had sent home since setting out for the mountains.

Writing to his younger brother, Andrew, Miles had little to say of his adventures, and nothing at all of his Indian wife and family. But he had much to say of the freedom he had sought and found. He had not made his fortune, he added, though he had property, horses, beaver and $2,500. If fortune favored him and his life was spared, in a few years he might come home. He dated the letter "Frontier of Mexico, Rocky Mountains, Nov. 1, 1842," and instructed that letters could be written to him at Independence, directed in care of Dr. Whitman, missionary to the west of the Rocky Mountains.

So the bound boy become mountain man bridged six years in time and thousands of miles in space by the purpose of a worried missionary. Marcus Whitman, who had brought him to the mountains, took down from the mountains this word of the far-wanderer, word which after four years would bring Andy Goodyear west in search of his lost brother.

In Miles Goodyear's story there are many gaps, and he vanishes from history for nine months after that chance encounter with Marcus Whitman. Where he spent the winter and spring of 1843 is uncertain. He next turns up at Fort Bridger in late July next year with his wife, his two youngsters, and a half-breed named LeMeuse.

Sixty lodges of Snakes were encamped in the thick willows below the fort, and one day, at a time when most of the men were out on an antelope surround, a raiding party of Arapaho and Cheyenne pounced on the horses of whites and Indians alike. The herd was stampeded into a full gallop, and while the main force of the raiders rode shouting behind in a crescent formation, a rear guard "made snake" along the line—zigzagging back and forth to keep pursuers from breaking through.

The five or six Snakes in camp, together with two white men, Uncle Jack Robinson and Miles Goodyear, galloped in furious pursuit. Three miles out, the returning Snake hunters ran into the marauders, but one who tried to head them was speared without ceremony. The squaws and boys rushed out from camp with guns, however, and every moment, as the chase lengthened, more armed Snakes joined the pursuit. In three or four miles they were able to turn back their own horses, but the Arapaho and Cheyenne continued in full flight with the 50 animals belonging to the fort.

In the very forefront of the chase Goodyear came up with the rearmost of the raiders, dinning the Indian insults into their ears: "You're dead men, every one of you! We'll kill you and eat you—dogs, we'll eat you!"

One of the Cheyenne leaped from his exhausted horse to continue the flight on foot, but as Goodyear thundered up he turned at bay. Fortunately his gun missed fire, and a Snake pounding up behind instantly drove an arrow into his heart. White man and red flashed past without slackening pace, and in the end six or eight Arapaho were shot out of their saddles—a heavy price to pay for 50 horses.

Inca Pompe had borne himself well in the fight, and he further ingratiated himself with the Snakes by cutting his lodge in two in respect for the Snake who had died. Altogether, in mountain estimation, it was the great event of the summer, and the holidaying members of Sir William Drummond Stewart's excursion party, which reached the mountains early in August, looked over the onetime Connecticut bound boy with a lively curiosity. The newspaperman, Matt Field, was much taken with the redheaded mountain man. But an attendant spectacle he found grist for his diary fully as fascinating: "Saw a fat squaw with a broad, glazed leather St. Louis fireman's belt around her waist, marked 'Central' in large gold letters! This was the squaw of Miles!" If this picture of Goodyear's partner in bliss does violence to romantic ideas of a lissome Indian belle, at least it pays tribute to Miles's talents as a good provider.

Meantime those routed Cheyenne and Arapaho had crossed the trail of one whose adventures in the Great Salt Lake country for several years were to be strangely intertangled with Miles Goodyear's. On the morning of August 5 while Lieutenant John Charles Frémont's exploring expedition was busy drying buffalo meat in the upper valley of the North Platte, some seventy mounted Indians charged down upon them out of the low hills. Seeing in time the reception preparing for them, they broke off in mid-career. More cautiously, then, they trotted up for a parley, explaining blandly that they had charged upon the camp in the belief that the whites were hostile Indians, and that they had discovered their mistake only at the moment of attack. While it was policy to receive this excuse as true, Frémont was fully persuaded that only their alertness and favorable position had saved his party from the loss of their horses, if not of their lives. These Indians, he explained in his published *Report,* "had been on a war party, and had been defeated, and were consequentiy in the state of mind which aggravates their innate thirst for plunder and blood."

At this moment of small crisis Frémont was two months along a trail destined to take him the length and breadth of the West. This was his second expedition, and his greatest. The previous year, in furtherance of the objectives of the Oregon bloc in Congress, Frémont had been sent on an expedition of reconnaissance to South Pass. The expedition had been a dazzling success, and he had been given an assignment more ambitious still, the making of a "connected survey" all the way to the Columbia.

He had set out from the Missouri frontier late in May, impressed by the extraordinarily animated and populous spectacle of the immigrant road; it was none too soon for a reconnaissance of the West. But Frémont could regard his party as itself something of a spectacle, with its 12 carts, each drawn by 2 mules, carrying the camp equipage and provisions, with its light covered wagon mounted on good springs, in which the instruments were conveyed, and with its 12-pound brass howitzer. The personnel of the party, moreover, was a singular combination of American, French, German, Canadian, Indian and Negro, while its language was something to defy transcription, a combination of all these tongues with a generous admixture of Spanish and mountain argot.

On the third day out, at the crossing of the Kansas, he veered from the Oregon road to travel west, first up the southern bank of the Kansas and then up the Republican Fork. Two weeks of almost constant rain so slowed them that he divided his party, leaving Thomas Fitzpatrick and 25 men to bring on the heavy baggage, while with 15 men, the howitzer, and the instrument wagon, he himself galloped on ahead to St. Vrain's Fort on the South Platte.

He reached the fort on the Fourth of July, his animals much worn down. He had had the intention of crossing the Rockies by the headwaters of the Arkansas and striking diagonally for the Great Salt Lake, thence north to a rendezvous with Fitzpatrick on the Snake. But after riding south to Pueblo, he found it impossible to obtain mules, and he learned, as well, that the Ute were committing hostile acts in northern New Mexico. While he hesitated for a course of action, up the Arkansas from Bent's Fort came Kit Carson to pay his respects.

Carson had been Frémont's guide in 1842, but the idyl of their friendship had been disturbed by an incident on the outbound trail. Frémont had been insistent on going beyond Fort Laramie despite the threatening aspect of the Sioux, and Carson had remarked frankly that not all the party would see the fort again; he had even made his will. Upon the timorous members of the party this act had a devastating effect, and Frémont had his troubles carrying through his project. A certain coolness had thereafter prevailed, and at Fort Laramie on the inbound journey Carson had separated from the party to return to his wife in Santa Fe. Now, however, delighted to see him again, Frémont proposed that the squat little mountain man join his expedition as a hunter. Carson assenting, Frémont dispatched him down the Arkansas 75 miles to Bent's Fort to buy what mules he could and bring them across country to St. Vrain's, where Frémont would meet him as well as Fitzpatrick.

By July 23 everybody was at the rendezvous on the South Platte, and Frémont could start west again. He had not at all given up his purpose of finding a new route across the continental divide, so he sent Fitzpatrick north to Fort Laramie with the heavy baggage, instructed to proceed west on the Oregon Trail, while he himself took 17 men directly west into the mountains. With him he took the instrument wagon and the howitzer.

So, by way of the Cache la Poudre, the Laramie Plains and the shoulder of the Medicine Bow Mountains, Frémont came into the valley of the North Platte and that touchy rendezvous with the Indians against whom Goodyear had so signally distinguished himself.

From that Indian rencontre, Frémont turned north; the rough and barren plateauland which here roofed the continental divide gave no encouragement to his plans for keeping south of the known road and over South Pass, and accordingly he regained the Oregon Trail 20 miles west of Devil's Gate.

The trail to Oregon was, Frémont saw at a glance, no longer a mere trail. It was a veritable road that wound west amid the red hills, beaten by so many feet that the Sioux could gravely wonder whether any whites were left in the east, and talk about going thence to occupy that country. The wagons of the year's great Oregon immigration had so pulverized the soil that the hoofs of the horses and pack mules flung up a choking dust cloud, through which Frémont pressed on as rapidly as possible. Fort Bridger he by-passed a mile or two to the north; and reaching the Little Muddy on August 19, he dispatched Carson and one other as an express to Fort Hall to pick up whatever provisions he could obtain. Following more slowly with the rest of his party, Frémont reached the Bear River bottoms early on August 21.

The young officer felt himself now treading storied ground. He had reached the principal tributary of Great Salt Lake, around which, as he remarked, "the vague and superstitious accounts of the trappers had thrown a delightful obscurity, which we anticipated pleasure in dispelling, but which, in the mean time, left a crowded field for the exercise of our imagination." The wonders related were not the less agreeable because highly exaggerated. Some of his mountain men were firmly convinced that somewhere on the surface of the lake was a terrible whirlpool, through which the lake waters found their way to the ocean by subterranean passage, and there were other campfire tales of such character that Frémont's mind "had become tolerably well filled with their indefinite pictures, and insensibly colored with their romantic descriptions, which, in the pleasure of excitement, I was well disposed to believe, and half expected to realize." These were romantic fancies, but he had a cold scientific purpose to serve. No instrumental observations or geographical survey of any description had ever been made in the vicinity of the salt lake. Even at the cost of a considerable southward detour, he must see the lake, float out upon its salt waters, and explore its islands.

Frémont left the Oregon road at Soda Springs. For a few miles he took the Bartleson route south down the west bank of the Bear, but then he elected to cross the river above its burnt lava canyon, nooning the second day on Whisky Creek and encamping that night on Trout Creek. Next day he took his instrument wagon and howitzer back across the river, up over a steep divide, and down Battle Creek, again on the Bartleson route. He encamped that night near the site of Preston, Idaho, but on the west side of the river. It was a hungry camp, as provisions were low and there was almost no game.

Though the Bartleson party had taken its vexed way down through Cache Valley almost to the Gates of the Bear, Frémont's attention was attracted by an Indian trail running up Weston Creek. It turned out to be an excellent route for pack animals, but something less than that for wagons, and occasionally they had to hack a way through the underbrush. Next day, patiently following the Indian trail, the party descended Deep Creek, and on the morning of the second day reached what had been Salt Creek to John Bidwell and was now "Roseaux, or Reed river [the Malad]," to the young topographical engineer. Carson still had not overtaken them, and hungrily they wondered what was keeping him, as they headed south down the Malad. Indians they met were themselves so starved that when they drew aside their blankets to display their lean and bony figures, Frémont had no heart to traffic with them for their small stock of roots and seeds.

On the night of September 1 they encamped in the marshland just above the mouth of the Malad. The lake they sought could not be far off, but there was no elevated point from which they could see it. Next morning Frémont dug into his equipage for what promised to be a useful contraption, an India rubber boat 18 feet long. In form it somewhat resembled a bark canoe, but its sides were formed by two airtight cylinders 18 inches in diameter, these connecting with others which formed the bow and the stern. When inflated, the boat could accommodate five or six men and a good deal of baggage. With its aid the camp equipage was ferried across the Bear, after which Frémont took Basil Lajeunesse into the boat and set out down the river, intending to rejoin the party at the night encampment.

The idea was no good. The river wound here, there and everywhere, and the boat moved erratically in the water. Finally Frémont gave up. Paddling to shore, he and Lajeunesse cached the boat, and footed it after their fellows. It was a long chase, for it was sundown at the end of a 15-mile hike before they overtook the others.

Lajeunesse went back on horseback to retrieve the boat. On his return next day the explorers resumed the southward journey but another three miles brought them to the delta of the Bear. Still the tall rushes and canes prevented seeing what they had come so far to view, though it was obvious that a long arm of the lake stretched up to cut them off from the mountainous "island" (actually, the Promontory) to the west. However, waterfowl were plentiful, and they ate well that night. Next morning Carson and his companion rode into camp with a little flour and a few other light provisions. The immigration, they reported, had almost exhausted the resources of Fort Hall, and very little in the way of supplies could be had.

The day was spent finding a fording place, one finally being located five miles up the Bear. Next morning, a dozen miles to the south, an isolated butte—Little Mountain—lifted in promise of their long-sought view of the lake. They set out toward it, but this obstinate lake resisted them to the end; deepening mud forced them to make for higher ground at the base of the Wasatch Mountains. After nooning on Willard Creek, they found better going along a broad and plainly beaten Indian trail which brought them around the base of Ben Lomond into the Weber Valley. At the hot springs here, the Indian trail turned east to evade the sloughs and marshland then occupying what is now the lower part of the city of Ogden. Thinking the trail was making for the slash in the mountains from which the Ogden River bursts, Frémont left it and made direct for the Weber. On the following morning, September 6, 1843, the little company of explorers rode once more for Little Mountain, reaching it without difficulty and ascending it a little breathlessly for what might be revealed to sight.

They were not disappointed. The great lake spread far to the horizon, contained dark and blue by gleaming white beaches of salt sand. To travelers so long shut up among mountain ranges, there was something sublime in so vast an expanse of silent waters. Several large islands lifted their rocky crests above the waves, but it was impossible to tell whether they were timbered or not; blotches upon them might be either woodland or naked dark rock. And as if reluctant to yield itself to the profanation of sight, the lake swathed itself almost at once in a sudden furious storm.

No closer location promising a campsite, Frémont rode to the last groves of trees on the Weber. Here a full day was spent preparing for a voyage of exploration. The party being much too large for the available supply of provisions, seven men were sent north to await Fitzpatrick's coming at Fort Hall. The others repaired the India rubber boat and inflated it in readiness for the morrow's adventure.

The lake party consisted of Frémont himself, Charles Preuss, Kit Carson, Baptiste Bernier and Basil Lajeunesse. François Badeau, Baptiste Derosier, and Frémont's free colored servant, Jacob Dodson, remained in camp to preside over the destinies of the horses, the howitzer and the instrument wagon. The sun went down in a brilliant sky of orange and green, and after dark they listened to deep-toned choruses of frogs, looking into the camp fire and talking low of the wonders dwelling in tomorrow. Perhaps the large islands were tangled wildernesses of trees and shrubbery, teeming with game of every description, with clear streams and springs of fresh water. These were fancies agreeable to contemplate. But there were other previsions, unsettling to think about. The boat, hastily built for them, had been pasted together in a very insecure manner, and there was a clear element of danger in the contemplated voyage, even if whirlpools and other mysterious perils were discounted.

At sunrise they embarked on the Weber. The voyage down the river was uneventful except for the discovery that two of the cylinders leaked so badly as to require one of the crew constantly at the bellows. They encamped for the night at the outlet of the Weber, dining on waterfowl that had fallen to their guns during the day. Next morning, September 9, they had a struggle to get over the shallow bar at the river's mouth, and had to strip and drag the boat through the shallows, stirring up from the fetid mud a stench from which they were all happy, after a mile of this noisome labor, to escape. Crossing a small black ridge on the bottom, they suddenly found the water salt and clear above a deepening sand floor. All sprang aboard. They were tempted to steer for the Promontory, which loomed ahead like a mountainous island, but Frémont finally declared for a smaller island to the south. They paddled gaily at first, but the bottom dropped down into the emerald waters, down beyond reach of their paddles, and their *chansons* died away in the painful realization that the craft bearing them out upon this strange sea was, after all "a frail batteau of gum cloth distended with air, and with pasted seams." The day was very calm, but there was a considerable swell. Patches of foam on the surface, slowly drifting south, indicated a current and raised anew the question of the whirl-pool.

Carson sighted something suspicious lacing the low shore of the oncoming island, and the paddles were lifted from the water so that Frémont might employ his telescope. What Carson had seen was caps of waves that were beginning to break under the force of a strong breeze that was coming up the lake. They pulled for the island, during a long time seeming scarcely to approach it, for though the boat rode the waves like a water bird, it was extremely slow. They had reached the halfway mark when two of the divisions between the cylinders gave way, and the bellows had to be used constantly to keep in a sufficient quantity of air. All of them flinched a little, for though the intensely green water was incredibly beauti-ful, the mark of its strangeness was on them—the film of white salt that dried upon them from the spray of their passage. Gradually, however, they worked across the rough open channel into smoother waters under the lee of the island, and about noon they reached shore, approaching with great care so that the sharp rocks might not cut holes in their boat.

The island proved altogether inhospitable, mocking their bountiful anticipations. It boasted neither water nor trees; it was simply a rocky hill 12 or 13 miles in circumference, rising 800 feet above the surface of the water. But the summit offered a commanding view from which Frémont sketched the lake's features. Beyond the reach of the eye, he felt the tug of mystery. Dared he risk exploring further? The snow cresting the peaks spoke of the lateness of the season. Could he take the responsibility of hazarding the lives of the party by extended explorations in a frail linen craft so insecurely cemented with India rubber? Romantic though he was, Frémont was a wilderness captain of ability: his lake explorations were finished.

The night was necessarily spent on the island. Driftwood fed their fire, and they had water, foresightedly brought from the main-land. The night was one of a kind not known in a long time, when they might lay aside their arms and sleep in perfect security. They awakened midway of the night to a strange, booming roar to which the island trembled. In a desert country they listened to an ocean surf!

In the morning the surf was still breaking heavily on the shore, and the lake was dark and agitated, so they made haste to be off. Frémont had accidentally left on the summit of the island the brass cover to the object end of his telescope, "and as it will probably remain there undisturbed by Indians," he commented, "it will furnish matter of speculation to some future traveller."

Though he had taken pains to comment on the lost object end of his telescope, Frémont inexplicably neglected to comment on something of more permanent interest left to commemorate his visit—a cross carved on a wind-and-water hewn rock at the island's summit. Here was real "matter of speculation" for a later generation; there were those to wonder whether the cross did not evidence the wanderings of Spanish padres in forgotten eras. In our own time, however, a narrative by Kit Carson has come to light to explain this mystery. They found on the island, Carson says, nothing of any great importance. "There were no springs and it was perfectly barren. We ascended the mountain and under a shelving rock cut a large cross which is there to this day." A hundred years after, the cross is still there. It may have been carved by Carson himself, recently a convert to the Roman Catholic church, or by one of the more characteristically religious French Canadians in the party. Frémont in 1842 had innocently cut a cross on Independence Rock, an act of which such damaging capital was made during the Presidential race of 1856 that it was perhaps fortunate his journal of this second expedition afforded bigotry no additional ammunition.

From this island, which Frémont named Disappointment Island but which Stansbury later named for him, the voyagers pulled for shore. A strong gale was blowing almost directly offshore, and in the heavy seas the frail boat threatened to tear apart. The wind was rising with the sun, and to make any headway at all required the efforts of every man in the party. There was danger that they would be blown into the open reaches beyond the island. "Pull for your lives!" Frémont called to his men, "if we do not arrive on shore before the storm commences, we will surely all perish!" The men pulled with a will, one pumping constantly at the bellows, and just before noon they thankfully reached shallow water immediately under Little Mountain. Landing on a low mud bar, they carried the baggage a quarter of a mile to higher ground. Preuss and Lajeunesse set off on foot for camp nine miles away while Frémont busied himself with observations. By the time the horses arrived, late in the afternoon, the gale had become so wrathful that a man could scarcely stand before it, and the waters were pounding high upon the shore. Thankful to be on dry land, mindful of what it would have meant to ride out such a storm in such a craft as theirs, they hastily loaded the equipage on the horses, and made for camp, arriving just in time to escape a thunderstorm that was blackening the whole sky. The anxious men in camp gave vent to their relief by firing the howitzer in booming welcome.

They remained in camp a day to boil down the bucket of salt water brought from the lake and then, on September 12, headed for Fort Hall. Their provisions were so far reduced that they must feed on yampa and kamas roots and on gulls shot by Carson. The "mournful" diet effectively dampened the men's spirits—"there was rarely an oath to be heard in the camp—not even a solitary *enfant de garce.*" By the fourteenth the men were so woebegone that Frémont gave them permission to kill a fat young horse, which quickly restored them to gaiety and good humor. Preuss and Frémont, certain civilized prejudices still remaining, preferred to starve a little longer, "feeling as much saddened as if a crime had been committed." The following night all were rejoiced to have Baptiste Tabeau gallop into camp with news that Fitzpatrick had come down from Fort Hall to meet them and was close at hand with flour, rice and dried meat, and even a little butter. Riding on north, up the Malad and down the Bannock, on September 18 they reached the Snake plain and Fort Hall.

Frémont here sent back to the States 11 of his men, and with the rest set out for the Columbia, arriving late in October to complete his "connected survey." Briefly vacillating as to whether he should charter a small brig and go home via the Isthmus of Panama or return overland by the head of the Missouri, he ended by doing neither. Instead he struck south, a long and hazardous journey that took him along the east base of the Sierras in baffled search for that old myth, the Buenaventura, and then over the Sierras themselves by a desperate winter crossing, the howitzer being abandoned in the snow. Half-starved, half-naked, they reached the haven of Sutter's Fort and by Sutter were re-equipped for the homeward journey.

It was a long and hard journey, south up the valley of the San Joaquin, across the Tehachapi Mountains by Oak Creek Pass, south again to strike the Spanish Trail where it came out of Cajon Pass, and by this *road,* as it seemed to them, down the Mohave River, across the Mohave and Vegas Deserts, up the Virgin and the Santa Clara and into the Great Basin again at its South Rim. A man was killed by the Paiute on the Virgin and another by his own carelessness in handling a gun, as they came up the long chain of the Utah valleys, but with all their adventures the rest came safely to Utah Valley on May 25, 1844.

In arriving at Utah Lake they had completed an immense circuit of 12° diameter north and south, and 10° east and west. In the eight months since they had left the Great Salt Lake they had covered 3,500 miles, and had seen a large part of Oregon and California, from the Rockies to the Pacific. There was no longer any question of a Buenaventura, that almost indestructible myth.

But more than that, they had established that there existed a great interior drainage area which could be called the Great Basin. Walled in from the sea by mountains or by deserts, it had its own lake and river systems, its own intricacy of valleys and mountain ranges. The contents of this Great Basin had yet to be examined. "That it is peopled," Frémont reflected, "we know; but miserably and sparsely. From all that I heard and saw, I should say that humanity here appeared in its lowest form, and in its most elementary state. Dispersed in single families; without firearms; eating seeds and insects; digging roots, (and hence their name,)—such is the condition of the greater part. Others are a degree higher, and live in communities upon some lake or river that supplies fish, and from which they repulse the miserable *Digger.*" It seemed to him that the whole idea of such a desert and such a people excited Asiatic rather than American ideas. In America such things were new and strange, unknown and unsuspected—and discredited when related.

It was a gloomy view of the Great Basin, yet in it he found some relieving light. In the Utah Valley itself the lake plain was in great part fertile, watered by a delta of prettily timbered streams. "This would be an excellent locality for stock farms; it is generally covered with good bunch grass, and would abundantly produce the ordinary grains." And he could say substantially the same thing about the Bear River Valley.

Strangely, now that he was again so near the Great Salt Lake, Frémont neglected to ride the few additional miles north that would have made clear the relationship of the salt lake to the fresh-water lake on which he was encamped. He heard that the two lakes were connected, that Utah Lake was "the southern limb" of the Great Salt Lake. One salt and one fresh: here was a problem requiring to be settled. But he did not attempt to settle it; instead he headed east up Spanish Fork Canyon, and the map that would result from his long journeys would oddly depict the two lakes as joined by a long, narrow strait. Over a year must elapse before he could return to these lake valleys and clear up the confusion in his mind.

The rest of the eastward journey was by way of Fort Wintey, Browns Hole, the Little Snake, the Three Parks of the Rockies and the Arkansas. He reached Bent's Fort on July 1, and Independence on the last day of July. Six days later the party broke up in St. Louis.

Frémont came home to triumph unalloyed. His report graphically opened the West to popular understanding and made him a newspaper hero as well. His adventures were reprinted far and wide, with boundless pride and satisfaction. *Niles' Register* was no more than expressing the national sentiment when it gave Frémont its accolade as one of the nation's "most amiable, talented, and enterprising sons."

This is merited praise. Frémont has always deserved well of his countrymen for his graphic reports on the West. He did a hard job. He made the West neighbor to the nation's mind; it has ever since been familiar in American thinking as it never was before.

Yet the values shift and blur as one looks steadily at Frémont's achievement, as one sees him standing there proud in the flooding light of a nation's concentrated attention. Out of the blur another picture emerges, a picture of a young man buying a set of plow irons. . . .

Let John Minto tell the story. An Oregon immigrant, at Fort Bridger in late August 1844 he saw a trade in progress. One of the parties to that trade was another Oregon immigrant who had exchanged one of his cows and his plow irons for some flour brought from Taos. The other party to the trade, Minto noted curiously, was a man five feet nine or ten inches in height, strongly framed in breast and shoulders, with light-brown hair flaxy at the ends, his eyes steel blue or gray—a man very different from the general sort on show about the fort. He talked quietly to the immigrant as he received the various parts of the plow—it was pretty late in the season for them to get to Oregon.

"I was in the country about Salt Lake last fall," he offered. "I think it would be a good country to settle in."

While he was talking and tying up the plow irons, a passer-by stopped to ask curiously what he was going to do with them. "Why," he said, "I'm going to try farming a little."

John Minto rode on toward Fort Hall. But the fellow stuck in his mind. Half a century later he had not forgotten what he had said or how he looked. . . .

A small incident to remember, perhaps, but one fortunately recalled. For Utah's first citizen was ready to enter upon a new future. On the rolling plain above the Great Salt Lake, at the confluence of the Weber and the Ogden within sight of the grove of trees from which Frémont had started on his exploration of the lake, Miles Goodyear was embarking on the adventure of settling down.

Chapter 9

The Barrier Land

THE editor of the Independence *Western Expositor* in September 1845 watched the dust settle in the streets of the flourishing frontier town and went around to his office to write a story about something that struck him as newsworthy. He had just parted from a redheaded mountain man named Miles Goodyear, who with a small company of six or eight men was packing to the mountains goods he had just bought in St. Louis. A little bemused by what he had heard of this fellow's plans, the editor outlined them in some detail.

The mountain man, he said, proposed building on the plains "a kind of a fort, and cultivating a portion of ground, more as an experiment than anything else, and if possible make it a sort of *half way house* between this and Oregon and California, where the companies may stop and refresh themselves, and obtain re supplies, for he expects to have the coming summer all kinds of vegetables and plenty of Indian corn and wheat, which they may pound up or grind into flour and meal. . . ." It was an interesting and novel conception; though something of the kind had once been attempted at Fort Laramie, nothing had come of it for lack of rain. "Success to him!" the *Expositor* said warmly.

Was this the flowering of Goodyear's transaction with the Oregon immigrant the previous year? It is impossible to say what he did with his time until he turned up on the frontier in the summer of '45 for the first time in nine years. He may have built that primitive cabin of cottonwood logs which came to have that resplendent name, "Fort Buenaventura." Or it may be that that cabin was built in the winter of 1845-1846, though there seems some reason to doubt that the location on the Ogden site would have commended itself as "a half-way house" until the great events of 1846. But if Goodyear in the fall of '45 had an idea of locating elsewhere than in the wooded bottoms of the Weber under the magnificent bastions of the Wasatch destiny decreed otherwise; within the year he would be drawn to that valley above the far brightness that was the Great Salt Lake.

Even as he hastened to completion his exciting *Report,* Frémont found himself caught up in the nation's swirling expansionist energies. Polk was elected President in the fall of 1844 on a platform that boldly looked to the annexation of Texas and the acquisition of California, and a third Frémont expedition had a highly expedient interest. The new venture was, Frémont says, to be "directed to that section of the Rocky Mountains which gives rise to the Arkansas River, the Rio Grande del Norte of the Gulf of Mexico, and the Great Salt Lake and its interesting region," with the survey to be extended west and southwest to the great ranges of the Cascade Mountains and the Sierra Nevada. In arranging the expedition "the eventualities of war were taken into consideration."

So here was John Charles Frémont, brevetted captain for his earlier exploits, back in St. Louis in June of 1845, drumming up 50 good riflemen and packers. Carson was laboring at a ranching venture on the Cimarron, but word from Frémont was enough, and north he came to join the party at Bent's.

The route taken to the Great Salt Lake was the one given up in 1843—up the Arkansas to the Royal Gorge, thence into the mountains north and west to strike upon the river higher up, over the divide to the basin of the upper Colorado and then over another divide to the valley of White River. Old Bill Williams was picked up during the crossing of the Rockies, and Joe Walker in the valley of the White. That river was descended to the Green, and then this powerful force for exploration—or war—struck west up the Duchesne, across to the headwaters of the Provo, and down that foaming mountain river to the serene silver mirror of Utah Lake, which was reached October 10. Two days later, encamping on "Hughes' Creek" (Dry Creek) near the outlet of this lake, Frémont could see that Utah was not, as he had termed it, a southern limb of the salt lake; it occupied its own valley perhaps a hundred feet above the level of the salt sea, and was joined with it not by a strait but by a turbid, northward-flowing river.

On the thirteenth he rode 40 miles north to an encampment on what he called "Station Creek," present-day City Creek at the very heart of the future Salt Lake City.

The Indians of Wanship's band told the captain that at this season of low water the largest of the lake islands could be reached on horseback. Taking Carson and a few others with him, Frémont splashed across the shallows south of the Jordan's mouth to explore this island. The water nowhere reached above the saddle girths, but the floor of the lake was a singular sheet of salt resembling softening ice, into which the horses' feet sank to the fetlocks. Two days were spent exploring the island. Grass and water were found, and antelope in considerable numbers. Some of these were killed, "and, in memory of the grateful supply of food they furnished," Frémont gave their name to the island.

When they returned to the shore, an Indian—Wanship's son, very likely—made bitter complaint about the game brought from the island. It was his, he said. *All* the antelope on the island belonged to him; they were all he had to live on, and the white captain must settle with him for this wrong done him. Frémont was a man ever tender enough of his own dignity, but this "imaginary claim" struck him as amusing. However, he directed that a bale be unpacked. From it he drew a red cloth, a knife and tobacco until the Indian expressed himself satisfied, nodding and grunting his approval of each article laid down.

Fascinated by the mountain sea, Frémont slowly moved on around its southern shore, camping at the base of the Oquirrhs on October 21 and at the abundant springs at the site of Grantsville on the twenty-third. The lake's waters were a saturation of salt almost beyond belief. The spray left salt on everything it touched, and plants and bushes, blown by the wind upon the salt flats bordering the lake, were encrusted with crystallized salt an inch thick. And it was a dead sea as truly as that of Palestine. No fish or animal life of any kind could be found in it, although the waters washed an evil-smelling scum in upon the lake shores, plainly the larvae of winged insects.

On October 25 Frémont rode around the north end of the Stansbury Mountains and turned his back on the lake to make for the springs in Skull Valley at present Iosepa. The obligation to be in California for whatever great events might transpire was exerting its powerful pull. But to strike for California from this jumping-off place was serious business: Frémont had reached the verge of the Salt Desert itself.

Old Bill Williams, for one, would have no part of this implacable desert of salt. A man who knew his own mind and who listened when it had something to say to him, Old Bill turned his back on such goddam foolishness and on October 27 set out for fairer parts. Next summer he turned up, his usual picturesque self, at Fort Bridger. But Frémont, determined to penetrate this desert which until now had withstood even the mountain men, attacked his problem with the accumulated trail wisdom of four years.

From the summit of the Cedar Mountains, 15 miles west of the springs in Skull Valley, the October sunshine gave a clear view of the naked, desolate plain that extended almost to the edge of sight. Closer at hand it was pocked with sage, but in the remote distance it was a vast emptiness of sterile white. On the far northwestern horizon, however, a snow-capped mountain peak glistened faintly in the sun. All the logic of experience said that at the base of such a peak water must be found.

Frémont rested his animals at the springs for four days, and on the evening of the fourth day launched Carson, Auguste Archambeau, Lucien Maxwell and Basil Lajeunesse out into the desert. If they found water or grass, they were to make a smoke, and he would bring the entire party in their track. Watching patiently with his telescope, Frémont at last saw a far column of smoke push up into the sky.

Therefore, he set out with his company two hours before sundown on the twenty-ninth. Nightfall made of the world a sinister presence horizonless yet close, eerie and soundless. His Indian guide was frightened out of his senses, so demoralized as to be utterly useless, so Frémont gave him his wage and allowed him to scuttle off into the darkness. The company rode on some miles farther and then halted, making fires of sagebrush to signal Carson's party. Just before daybreak the jingling of spurs announced the welcome return of Archambeau. The scouts had found water, he reported, and grass and wood in abundance.

At sunrise the party resumed the nerve-racking journey. The going was miry from recent rains; ten mules and several horses gave out and had to be left to die, but the company itself in the afternoon of the thirtieth reached the beacon peak. "To the friendly mountain," Frémont writes, "I gave the name of Pilot Peak," a name it bears still. The animals, pretty well done in, were turned loose without any fear they would stray from grass and water.

So Frémont, who more than two years before had parted company with the Bartleson trail, had come to it again. To this same haven the immigrants of 1841 had brought their wagons south down the desert's rim. Frémont had forgotten it when, years later, he wrote his *Memoirs,* but the wagon trail must have stood out in this desert like the National Road. The explorer chose, however, not to follow the wagon trace when, after a day's rest, he took the trail again. The Bartleson party, after circling the shoulder of the Pilot Range, had pulled north to cross the Toano Range by Silver Zone Pass. Frémont instead rode directly west to cross the mountains by the shortest route for a pack company. Beyond the summit he descended to springs at the base of the Pequops, about a dozen miles south of the springs where lay the skeletons of the wagons that had been abandoned to the prayerful Indian four years before.

Here, at Whitton Springs, Frémont divided his party. The larger detachment, with Theodore Talbot in charge and Walker as guide, he instructed to strike for Marys River and the known immigrant road. With 15 men he himself intended to take a desert route to the south. Walker's Lake, at the east base of the Sierras, was named as the place of rendezvous.

By the same route the Bartleson company had followed, Frémont took his detachment south around Spruce Mountain and west into Ruby Valley. The immigrants of 1841 had ridden northwest up this valley, over Secret Pass and down to the desert river that was their hope and salvation, but Frémont reached Ruby Valley south of the marsh dignified later with the name of Franklin Lake, and struck at once into the Rubies up a steep Indian trail over Harrison Pass. Descending into the broad valley of the Humboldt's South Fork, he encamped, perhaps on Twin Creek. From this camp, "using just such passes as the mountains gave," Frémont rode south to the head of the valley of the South Fork, over Chokup Pass into Diamond

Valley, and again south as far as the Devils Gate in the mountains northwest of present Eureka. Turning west across Antelope Valley and skirting the Monitor Range, he moved briefly south down Monitor Valley and over the low summit of the Toquima Range into Big Smoky Valley. The high Toiyabe Mountains forced him south down this valley another 70 miles, but he was then able to cross two low ranges and descend into Soda Springs Valley near present Sodaville. Here turning north, within three days he was encamped on the east shore of Walker's Lake awaiting the arrival of Talbot and Walker.

Meantime Walker had taken Talbot's detachment up over the Pequops, down into Independence Valley, over the shoulder of the East Humboldt Mountains into Ruby Valley, and like the Bartleson company of 1841, across Secret Pass into the valley of the Humboldt. The wagon road, now clearly marked by the immigrations of three years, led them clear to the sink of the Humboldt, whence they left it to strike south for Walker's Lake. Four days after Frémont, they reached the rendezvous on November 28.

California was now not far off. Frémont sent Talbot and Walker south around the Sierras by Walker's Pass, and with his own 15 men he rode north to gain the immigrant road up the Truckee. He reached the summit on December 4, thankful to find the pass still open, and arrived safely at Sutter's six days later.

Elated with his accomplishments, drawing a deep breath before plunging into the troubled seas of California affairs, Frémont wrote his wife that he had traversed the whole of the Great Basin, a country "hitherto wholly unexplored, and never before visited by a white man," and that by the route he had explored he could ride in 35 days from the *Fontaine qui Bouit* to Sutter's, while "for wagons, the road is decidedly better." In the same mood of elation he could tell United States Consul Thomas Larkin that his route, previously supposed a desert, was 800 or 900 miles shorter than the traveled road—and far preferable, "not only on account of the less distance, but . . . less mountainous, with good pasturage and well watered."

These were hardly responsible judgments. They were so colored by hope and desire as to border on dangerous nonsense. And now over the Sierras came just the man to seize on dangerous nonsense and exploit it to the full.

Lansford W. Hastings was a young Ohio lawyer with a restless eye for the main chance, who in 1842 made the overland journey to Oregon. Dissatisfied with that country, he had moved on to California, where he readily grasped the tremendous possibilities open to an adventurer who could gather about himself a military force. Returning east in 1844, he published a glowing book to lure immigrants to the sunny valleys of California.

In mid-August of 1845, with nine men, he again set out for the Pacific. The singular luck that attended all his ventures kept the passes open, and he arrived safely at Sutter's on Christmas Day. Sutter looked at the clouds piling up on the mountains and shook his head. Had they been delayed by so much as a day, he said soberly, they should have been cut off by the snow.

But things had worked out fine, and Hastings was not one to trouble himself with might-have-beens; already his mind was ranging back along the trail. His rhapsodic book must certainly produce an effect on the immigration of 1846, and the reports of Frémont's new route challenged his imagination. He had been so well assured that such a route was practicable that in his book he had unhesitatingly pronounced the most direct route to California to be one that would leave the Oregon route "about two hundred miles east from Fort Hall; thence bearing west southwest, to the Salt lake; and thence continuing down to the bay of St. Francisco." Here was confirmation of all his ideas, and a new argument he could bring to bear on the 1846 immigration.

Among those who traveled east with Hastings in April was Jim Clyman. It was now more than 20 years since Clyman had crossed South Pass with Jedediah Smith, and 20 years this spring since he had explored Great Salt Lake. He had gone east in 1827, first engaging in farming and merchandising in Illinois, at which time he had served shoulder to shoulder with Abe Lincoln as a private in the Black Hawk War, and then in pioneering Wisconsin. Troubled by a cough, he had embarked on a tour for his health, and on an impulse had gone to Oregon with the immigration of 1844. Next summer he had ridden south to California, and now he was turning again to the rising sun, struck with the April beauty of the California countryside, but homesick for Milwaukee.

The eastbound company got under way on April 23, 1846, numbering in all 19 men and boys, 3 women and 2 children. They met with some difficulty in forcing a way through the Sierras, but made good time up the long valley of the Humboldt. However, the river valley was extraordinarily parched, with so little grass for the numerous horses that on May 16 Hastings, his man Hudspeth, their Indian servant, Clyman, and 5 others struck out ahead.

On May 21 they spotted the new trail from the salt lake Hastings had been watching for. Encamping, they argued their course all that evening and throughout the next morning. The experienced Clyman was dubious, thinking the new route "very little nearer and not so good a road as that by fort Hall," but Hastings finally had his way, and late in the afternoon of the twenty-second they headed for the low gap in the hills southeast that was Secret Pass. The trail took them up and down a succession of mountain ranges, and on the fourth day, from the summit of the Toano Range, Clyman sighted the great salt plain lying to the east.

On May 28, heartened to think that if they could follow Frémont's trail they would not have more than 20 miles without water, they struck out southeasterly across the glittering Salt Desert. Surely, Clyman thought, this was the most desolate country on the whole globe with not one spear of vegetation. They had to camp without water, and even when they reached the Cedar Mountains they found no water until they descended its eastern slope to strike upon a brackish spring at its base. Wiping his sun-darkened face on his sleeve, Clyman swore; they had ridden 20 hours to cross this desert, and they had been 30 hours without water. Hastings, however, was delighted. Even if it had been a hard drive, they had made astonishingly good time.

Next day they rounded the Stansbury Range; the Great Salt Lake was in full view to their left. As they circled its southern shore, Clyman was struck with the extent to which the lake had wasted away since he had floated around it. They encamped for the night at the springs breaking out at the foot of the Oquirrhs, inveigling some Ute Indians into camp and receiving from them the disquieting news that the Ute and the Snakes were at war, and that the Snakes had lately killed two white men. On June 2 one of the Indians guided them to the ford of the Jordan, which was so full with the spring runoff that several packs carried by their small mules were soaked. While they halted to dry the baggage, Jim Clyman looked over Salt Lake Valley, impressed with what he saw. The mountains surrounding this valley, he wrote in his journal, were "picturesque and many places beautifull being high and near the base smoothe and well set in a short nutericious grass." But he had some doubts whether the valley was moist enough for the growing of grain.

Getting under way again, they headed up the rugged gorge of Parleys Canyon and thence northeast up Mountain Dell Creek "into a high ruged mountain not verry rocky but awfull brushy"—history's first description of Big Mountain. Descending Little Dutch Hollow into East Canyon, they followed it down until it narrowed into "a rough looking Kenyon," whereupon they bore off to the east up the small brook running down Dixie Hollow; the weather was cold and disagreeable, and no game had been seen; Clyman found it "difficult to determin what the few natives that inhabit this region subsist on," though serviceberries and chokeberries were blooming.

On June 4 they rode down Little East Canyon to its mouth in the Weber River, just above Devils Slide. Turning up the green, open valley of the Weber, they crossed it at the mouth of Echo and headed into that narrow, red-bluffed canyon, having to pick their way with care over its floor, "completely Strewn over with the boulder which have fallen from time to time from the cliffs above." Living things existed in this country, first a "Lonesome looking poor grisly Bear" and then summer songsters chirping among the willows. So they headed on northeasterly, down into the valley of the Bear, up Sulphur Spring Creek and over the farther divide to intercept the Oregon road running northwest from Fort Bridger. Turning about from northeast to southeast, now knowing where they were, they headed for the fort.

Bridger's post, however, to their alarmed disappointment, was completely deserted. The signs indicated that Bridger had taken his whole company northwest toward the lower part of the Bear a month or more ago. What should they do, so small a party in a country where Snakes and Sioux alike were hostile? After long debate they turned back upon their trail with the idea of intercepting the company expected from Oregon. That party, it soon developed, had already passed by. But, to their immense relief, the rear detachment of their own company, which had made the journey around by Fort Hall, came up along the trail. So, happily reunited, they all rode on east, crossing South Pass on June 18 and five days later encountering at the North Platte the welcome white tops of the 11 wagons in the forefront of the year's immigration.

Somewhere along the trail Hastings and Hudspeth, with their *vaquero,* separated from those bound for the States to drift back toward Fort Bridger. When wide-eyed young John McBride encountered them on the morning of July 3, they were encamped about 20 miles east of South Pass. A boy of 14, McBride had met in his father's home such personages as James Frazier, one of Lewis and Clark's men, but he was greatly impressed with Hastings, already notable to him as the author of an impressive *Emigrants' Guide.* Hastings, "a tall, fine-looking man, with light brown hair and beard, dressed in a suit of elegant pattern made of buckskin, handsomely embroidered and trimmed at the collar and openings, with plucked beaver fur," seemed an ideal example of the mountaineer. Hudspeth made a more doubtful impression, "a coarse, profane creature, who seemed to feel that loud swearing was the best title to public favor." Hastings talked to them about California so ardently that, though he gained no recruits for his new route, a dozen members of the McBride company eventually made for California instead of Oregon, and all of them took the southern trail by Fort Bridger in preference to the Greenwood Cutoff.

As the immigration rolled past, Hastings hammered at his theme. California was the garden spot of the world. It was true that there might be opposition from the California government to their entrance into that paradise. But if the immigrants concentrated their strength, if they went by the route he had himself explored, which was so much easier and shorter than the old road, they would have nothing to fear.

Among those who came inquiring to Hastings' encampment at Fort Bridger was a small pack party led by William H. Russell, with whom traveled Edwin Bryant, a Massachusetts-born Kentuckian who

like many another was on the trail in search of better health. They
reached the Hastings encampment just before midnight on July 17.
Their mules needed rest, so the company decided to laze around the
fort a few days. Bryant was not much impressed with Fort Bridger—
it amounted to nothing but a few miserable log cabins, rudely constructed and bearing only the faintest resemblance to habitable
houses. Yet the valley in which it was situated was remarkably
beautiful, and it afforded a most interesting spectacle, with circles of
white-tented wagons in every direction, the smoke of campfires
drifting on the air with a pungence to delight the nostrils, oxen
grazing contentedly on the rich green grass, and immigrants min-
gling with dark-faced mountain men and numerous Snake braves.

Hastings by now had a considerable following who were waiting
patiently to be started off to his promised land. Bryant had grave
doubts about the new cutoff, but as his eight companions wanted to
try it, Bryant decided that, being mounted on mules and having no
families, they could risk explorations.

At the fort he saw that most eccentric of all the mountain men,
Old Bill Williams. Engaging in a shooting match, Old Bill was
knocked galley-west when his gun burst. It looked like Old Bill was
done for, but they poured some whisky into him and Old Bill presently was sitting up wagging his gaunt red head: "Wagh! Since I
come to these-here mountains, I been wounded a hundred times and
struck by lightnin' twice, and no goddam mean gun can kill me!"
Also at the fort was Joe Walker, driving east four or five hundred
California horses. Walker was full of interesting yarns. He had left
Frémont the day before that headstrong cavalier had taken himself
up on the Gavilán Peak near Monterey to breathe fiery defiance upon
all the constituted authorities of California. A few days later, Walker
said, Frémont had thought it all over and come back down from his
embattled peak. When last heard of, the captain had been heading
north for Oregon, not yet ready to revolutionize California. Walker
expressed no good opinion of the new cutoff south of the salt lake.

Walker's high regard for the valley of the Great Salt Lake itself,
however, had already given rise to another small episode of striking
interest in the history of this mountain country. A week or so before,
here at the fort, he had been hailed by his old friend, John McBride's
father. Walker had been moved to ask them: if what they were

Courtesy, John D. Thornley

The Mormon Temple under construction, about 1880.

The Lion House, President Young's office and the Bee Hive House as they were in Brigham Young's day looking for was a place to take up farms, why didn't they settle in the great valley of the mountain sea? That valley had, he said, a mild climate, fertile soil, abundant timber for a settlement, and it would natura'ly become a center for the Indian and fur trade. Cache Valley was fine, too—a summer paradise—but cold in winter and on the whole less inviting than the greater valley below. Moreover, Salt Lake Valley had the special advantage that no Indians occupied it to dispute for the land with new residents. And horses could readily be obtained from California to trade with the immigration.

All these arguments, coming from such a source, made an impression. The idea for a day or two was the talk of the camp, but the women of the company had the final say; to think of halting in this wilderness a thousand miles from anywhere made their blood run cold. Nevertheless, the men were sufficiently curious that when they reached Soda Springs some of them rode south down the Bear to view the salt lake and its immense valley. John McBride rode with them, excited to see the wagon tracks made by the Bartleson company five years before. Long afterward he remembered his first view of the Great Salt Lake, "sea, river, plain and mountain wrought by nature into one grand panorama, with a cloudless sky and glorious sunlight over all. Words can never recall to me the sensations of that hour. It seemed a sufficient pleasure to have lived to look upon and enjoy such a scene." The third night they encamped at the confluence of the Ogden and the Weber, curiously noting here a cabin built of cottonwood logs. The occupant, they heard, just now was up in the Yellowstone country. The little party of sight-seers followed the Indian trail south, lingering a moment to examine the hot springs at the north end of Salt Lake Valley, and then rising in their saddles at the sudden sweeping panorama of the valley itself. A creek, soon to be called City Creek, ran south in the valley toward the Utah Outlet, and green columns of cottonwood gracefully marked the courses of other creeks in this valley. Grass grew four feet high in places. . . . The boy John McBride looked up at the awe-inspiring peaks looming over the valley to the southeast, at the promising canyon mouths that opened into the mountains. There was a splendor of wildness that tugged at his youthful imagination, but he was too young to rebel against adult decisions, and he turned back with the little party to rejoin the wagons at Fort Hall.

Back at Fort Bridger Hastings was at last ready to start his wagons rolling. His problem was simplified to some extent in that wagons had already been taken to the Bear Valley by a route south of the Oregon road. In 1843 the California-bound Chiles party had been short of meat, and before setting out for California, Joe Walker had led them southwest from Fort Bridger to the upper Bear, where they could hunt deer and elk. The eight wagons in this company had left a plain trail up over Bridger Bench to the Big Muddy, on into Pioneer Hollow past a curious copperas spring, up over a high divide and down into the valley of Sulphur Creek just above its mouth in the Bear. Walker had taken the Chiles wagons straight down the Bear Valley, but there would be little difficulty fording the river and climbing the hills to the head of Echo Canyon. With so much of his route plain as daylight Hastings shoved off on July 20.

The Bryant-Russell party got off a few hours in advance of Hastings, accompanied by three men from the wagon train and by Hastings' man, Hudspeth, who would guide them as far as the Salt Desert. On their mules they took a course more northerly than the wagons traveled with Hastings, crossing the divide near Altamont, descending into Stone Creek Valley and following the creek to its mouth in the Bear a few miles south of the site of Evanston. Mountain flowers were blooming along the way—the sudden red of wild geraniums, the tranquil blue of wild flax and a more startling yellow blossom boldly flaunted by an unfamiliar shrub. On the third morning they forded the Bear and plunged into the canyoned country beyond. Hudspeth was not content to go the way he had come east; this was a reconnaissance for a still better road through the mountains. Coming into the narrow, grassy valley of Saleratus Creek, they followed up it a dozen miles southwest and then crossed a divide into the narrow canyon of Lost Creek. Descending this stream, on the twenty-third they reached the triangular, rolling valley of Croyden, just above where Lost Creek flows into the Weber.

The Weber gave no promise of a passage west, unless they were willing to descend the rocky channel itself, so they rode patiently up out of the northeast corner of Croyden Valley to gain the Weber a little higher up. They had now reached familiar ground, for the red slash in the mountains to the south was Little East Canyon, down

Trails and routes through the Great Salt Lake country, 1841-1846.

which Hudspeth had ridden with Hastings and Clyman seven weeks before. Hudspeth, however, was determined to find a passage down the Weber itself, so he turned down the river. But the canyon proved absolutely impassable. Baffled, they sought information from a Ute encampment several miles upstream.

Their chief informant was an extraordinarily comical fellow who began by shaking hands, proceeded to embraces and ended by dancing about in a very ecstasy of delight. He examined all the baggage with great curiosity, tried on several blankets with much satisfaction and finally was willing to listen to questions. By signs he advised them to go southwest until they struck water, and then go northwest. But this was in some part the very route by which Hudspeth had come east, and he was more interested in advice from another of the Indians—to return to the triangular valley and then pass through the mountains parallel to the Weber.

Accordingly they rode back to Croyden Valley and made another effort to get through. Toward sundown, bedeviled and despairing, they had to give up. Without axes to clear the trail there was no way to get through except down the rocky river bed itself, an unhappy prospect with the snow still melting in the mountains. They camped that night in the little valley, and the next morning, July 24, started this search for a trail all over again. By now Hudspeth was willing to take the old trail up Little East Canyon. They rode up the canyon to its head and descended Dixie Hollow to the stream of which the Indian had told them—present-day East Canyon. Once again the mountains walled them in, for the creek led them straight into another impassable canyon—the narrows where the East Canyon dam has since been built. An Indian trail high on the mountainside was their salvation. It took them a breathless five miles down the stream, and then the canyon opened into a lovely green valley. They encamped for the night at the site of Morgan, and stayed there all next day to give their worn animals a chance to recruit.

While they rested, the unresting Hudspeth rode on down the lower canyon of the Weber, returning in the afternoon to report it practicable though difficult. Thereupon, while the pack party resumed its journey down the Weber, he and two of the immigrants turned back up the river in determined search of some way to take wagons through that canyon.

Bryant himself went on down the Weber, "compelled, as heretofore, to climb along the side of the precipitous mountains, frequently passing under, and sometimes scaling, immense overhanging masses and projections of rock." In midafternoon he and his comrades scrambled past the formidable Devils Gate just above the mouth of the canyon and hailed the broad, open valley of the Great Salt Lake, safely enlarged at last from "this natural prisonhouse." For a more extensive view of the great valley Bryant climbed up the mountainside. In the sunset the lake surface was a mirror of fire, set in pure white where the lake had receded from its salt shores—a magnificent sight, though the breeze sweeping in from the lake brought an odor strong and offensive. Nearer at hand, the Weber wound through the valley to yield up its waters to the lake. Trees lined its margin, and Bryant failed to make out among them the Goodyear cabin.

Two days were spent in camp, fishing for the large, gamy trout in which the river abounded and searching in the ravines for sweet serviceberries. On the third morning Hudspeth and his two young men got back into camp. They had forced a way through the upper canyon of the Weber, and six miles farther up had met Hastings' 40 wagons pulling out of Echo Canyon. The wagons had made good time to that point, and Hudspeth thought that, by making a road in the bed of the Weber at places and cutting out the timber and brush in other places, its canyons would be practicable. Bryant confessed to some misgivings. The difficulties to be encountered on this new route would begin at the upper canyon of the Weber, and he feared they would be serious indeed.

As they got aboard their mules and moved slowly south along the east shore of the lake, they were again impressed by the unutterable splendor of the sunset, the surface of the lake varying in tint from crimson to a pale scarlet—an ocean of flame that extended north and south as far as they could see, its white beaches setting off the color with brilliance like freshly fallen snow. On July 30 they passed the hot springs into Salt Lake Valley and encamped on City Creek where Frémont had camped the preceding fall. The last day of July they crossed the Utah Outlet without difficulty and made for the southeastern extremity of the salt lake. The encampment for the night was on Willow Creek, the site of Grantsville. Next day, in-

stead of making the long circuit north around the Stansbury Range,
they took an Indian trail up the creek, reaching the head of the
canyon by a hard climb and then descending the western slope to
encamp on a faint stream flowing from the hills—Kanaka Creek.
They were somewhat south of the springs at Iosepa, but the following day, after crossing Skull Valley, they came into the Frémont
trail. The Cedar Mountains, below which they encamped, seemed
dead; a few dwarf junipers alone attested the stubborn effort of the
land to fructify. They found some moist sand in a ravine near by and
by digging were able to obtain a scant supply of salty, sulphurous
water. A dense, smoky vapor filled the valley, concealing the summits of the distant mountains, and the fading sunlight had an un-
earthly quality, coloring the brown, barren land in tones even more
dismal and gloomy than normal. All of the party felt a dark apprehension, and an attendant eagerness to have the desert crossing over
and done with.

Long before dawn the little company rolled out of their blankets.
The smoky moon was a strange red ball hung in a lurid sky, giving
just sufficient light to display Skull Valley's frightful barrenness, its
solemn desolation. There was, Bryant wrote in his journal with a
feeling of oppression, "no voice of animal, no hum of insect, disturbing the tomb-like solemnity. All was silence and death." The winds
themselves seemed stagnant and paralyzed. It was a relief to have
the moon sink behind the high wall of the mountains and give over
the world to their breakfast fires.

As dawn grayed the sky, Hudspeth led them up into the mountains. Frémont had gone directly across the summit from the
spring, but what came to be called Hastings Pass, five miles to the
north, seemed more promising for wagons. At the summit Hudspeth pointed out the course they must follow, northwest across the
desert to Pilot Peak; the peak, however, could not be made out in
the smoky air, and they would have to find and follow the Frémont
trail. Hudspeth here must turn back to meet Hastings and the wagon
train; he swung his long arms, shouting his last advice: "Now, boys,
put spurs to your mules and ride like hell!" The advice was superfluous—water was 75 miles away.

After some search they found the Frémont trail at the base of the
mountains, and then with more confidence they trotted west, cross-

ing a low ridge where for the first time they could see the full immensity of the vast desert plain. As far as the eye could reach, it was snowy white, resembling "a scene of wintry frosts and icy desolation. Not a shrub or object of any kind rose above the surface for the eye to rest upon," a scene to excite mingled emotions of admiration and apprehension. A little beyond, they exclaimed with dismay. A narrow depression in the plain, five miles wide, so perfectly displayed the wavy and frothy appearance of surging water that Russell and Bryant alike cried out that they had taken the wrong course and struck an arm of the Great Salt Lake. As they anxiously sought for a way around this obstacle, another member of the party pointed out that the rushing waters were motionless and made no sound. They continued across this arm of dry lake bed and on through an ashy earth in which the mules sank to their knees, to their bellies even, creating a dust like a dense and bitter fog that hung above them.

As the sun rose in the sky, extraordinary mirages lured them on all sides, lakes dotted with islands and bordered by groves of green trees inviting them to tranquil refreshment; these gave way to beautiful villas surrounded by gardens, parks and stately avenues, and these in turn to a vast city with marble edifices studded with domes, spires and turreted towers, which rose along the horizon of the plain. No words, Bryant felt, could convey the character of this white desert. The whole distant view around "seemed like the creations of a sublime and gorgeous dream, or the effect of enchantment."

Toward noon they reached the flat plain—vast, white, uniformly level and utterly destitute of any evidence that any living thing had ever existed. They paused for a few moments to rest their mules and moisten their mouths and throats with a scant supply of brackish coffee brought in an empty powder keg. The mules faced about, wanting to take the back trail; their masters sympathized, but wrenched their heads west again. In the afternoon a salt storm nearly blinded them; they choked upon salt, and the very air they breathed was bitter with it. As the storm subsided, the most extraordinary mirage of the extraordinary day arrested their attention. Another party was discerned marching upon the plain. At first it was thought to be a small party of Indians, then as it multiplied it was guessed to be Frémont, returning east with all his force. Finally the truth became clear—the obscured atmosphere was giving back to them a phantom reflection of their own passage.

Late in the afternoon a low range of mountains rising in their path gave them the brief hope that they were reaching Pilot Peak. But this was Silver Island, and they still had more than a dozen miles to cover. It was 10:00 P.M. before they reached the life-giving springs at the base of the Pilot Range. Animals and men alike were exhausted. They had been 17 hours on the trail and had come 75 miles.

A day was required to get into condition to travel, but on August 5 they got started again, west on Frémont's trail, and on August 9 they reached the valley of the Humboldt in advance of all the year's immigration save for two energetic wagons. It was August 17, near the sink of the Humboldt, before they overtook these two wagons. They were driven by John Craig and Larkin Stanley, two Missourians who had left Fort Bridger three days after the pack party, and who considered themselves to be some two weeks in advance of all other California-bound trains. Craig and Stanley generously furnished the Russell-Bryant party with flour and bacon, and the nine men pushed on ahead with their pack mules, crossing the summit August 26 and reaching Sutter's the first day of September.

It had been a long, hard journey.

It was a journey that must be longer and harder for those on the trail behind.

Hastings made good time in bringing his 40 wagons to the mouth of Echo. Notwithstanding the job of road building he had to do, he got over the ground from Fort Bridger in seven days. The trail was easy, down the Weber and around through Croyden Valley, but then began the struggle with the lower canyons of the Weber. It required seven days to force a way through—at times in the streambed, three times by rigging windlasses to lift the wagons bodily over obstructions. The rope broke once near the windlass, and the men had to let go of the wagon and oxen or be themselves dragged to death. During a heart-stopping moment the oxen struggled for their lives, and then the wagon hurled them over the 75-foot precipice. The men stared a long time before returning to the labor, and everybody mopped his brow in relief when they pulled out of the canyon onto the open benchland at its mouth. That was accomplished about the 4th of August; it had required 16 days to come this far from Fort Bridger.

Behind the Hastings party, meantime, was coming another immigrant company. This second company to take the Hastings' Cutoff has been virtually unknown. Little is yet known of it except what may be conjectured from a remarkable map drafted by one of its members, T. H. Jefferson. Published in New York in 1849, this map depicts on four sheets the entire road traveled to California by its maker. Its occasionally dated campsites indicate that the wagon company with which Jefferson traveled reached Fort Bridger about July 24 and pulled on west over the new cutoff three days later. Jefferson's party reached the mouth of Echo Canyon in five days. Through the canyons of the Weber they made almost unbelievably good time. Two days got them from Echo to the Morgan meadows, and another two days brought them through the terrific lower canyon. On the night of August 4 on the very heels of Hastings they emerged into the Great Salt Lake Valley. But their animals had doubtless taken a beating, and next day they were able to go on only a mile or two while Hastings pulled ahead with the other wagons. Very likely they had to recruit all day on the sixth, as well. Anxious not to be left behind, they set out the next day determined to overtake the wagons ahead, and a stiff 32-mile drive south into Salt Lake Valley, and on west across the Utah Outlet, brought them that night into Hastings' camp on the shore of the salt lake.

Thus augmented, perhaps 26 wagons having been added to the original 40, Hastings' train made only a short nine-mile drive on August 8, encamping in Tooele Valley just beyond a singular rock formation which is now known as Adobe Rock, but which comes down in the heroic literature of this year as "Black Rock," a name since applied to a lesser prominence on the lake shore a few miles to the east.

Long after nightfall the camp sentinels roused to the sound of hoofs on the back trail. Three men rode into the firelight, their horses staggering with exhaustion. They introduced themselves, James Frazier Reed, William Pike and Charles T. Stanton, and demanded to see Hastings. They had come from a company of 20 wagons left in the Weber Valley just above the upper canyon. They wanted advice on how to get through the mountains. . . . Come to receive a pronouncement upon their destiny, they were the vanguard of the most tragically famous of all immigrant companies, the Donner party.

The story of the Donner tragedy is one of the most oft-told, as it is one of the most eloquently told, tales in the history of the West. The climactic drama of sacrifice, starvation, cannibalism and heroic endeavor in the Sierra snows I will not retell here. But some of the links in the chain of disastrous causation, the struggle with Utah's barrier land, have a unique significance for the history of this land.

Properly speaking, it was the Donner-Reed party, for though George Donner was accorded a nominal captaincy at the Little Sandy, James Frazier Reed, his Illinois neighbor, was its dominant personality. They had reached Fort Bridger July 28, eight days after Hastings' departure. But only the day before, Jefferson's company had pulled west along the new trail, and Bridger and Vasquez encouraged stragglers with the word that the new route saved 350 or 400 miles over the old. There was, or was thought to be, one stretch of 40 miles without water, but Hastings and his party were out ahead hunting for water, and it might be possible to avoid that desert.

Unconscious of the grim role history had reserved for them, on July 31 the Donner wagons took the trail west from Fort Bridger. They were seven days getting over the mountains to the Weber where, on August 6, they found in a cleft stick at the side of the road a note from Hastings himself. It advised that anyone following behind should not attempt the terrible canyons but should follow the pack trail over the mountains. The description of the route to be followed was, however, so altogether vague that the immigrants stared at each other in consternation. It seemed wise to ride after Hastings and demand more definite information. Leaving the wagons encamped on the banks of the Weber, on the morning of August 7 Reed, Stanton and Pike set out on the wagon trail. Hastings turned out to be a very long, very hard, two-day journey ahead, and they were very nearly at the limit of their endurance when they overtook him.

Stanton and Pike were in no shape to take the back trail at once, but Reed, after obtaining a fresh horse, set out on the morning of

August 9 with Hastings. The wagon train remained in camp until Hastings should rejoin them, though a part of the company moved on across Tooele Valley to the more abundant water and feed at what they called "Hastings' Wells"—the springs at Grantsville. There was the more reason for stopping in that John Hargrave, who had taken cold during the strenuous descent of the Weber, lay in one of the wagons, dying of pneumonia.

Hastings and Reed reached the site of Salt Lake City after a wearying day's ride, encamping that night in a canyon presumably Parleys. The distance was farther than Hastings had bargained for, and he told Reed that in the morning he would have to return to the wagon train. But on the morning of the tenth he climbed with Reed to a summit and explained as best he could the route over which Reed must bring the wagons—a route Hastings was now prepared to believe superior to that through the Weber canyons. Reed, who had a look at the Weber route, was fully persuaded that any other must be preferable. The two men then parted. Reed found an Indian trail to follow north and east—the same trail Clyman and Hastings had followed east two months before. Reed reached the anxious party the same night. After he explained what he had learned, it was unanimously voted to make the new road over the mountains instead of attempting the road down the bed of the Weber.

The pull up Little East Canyon began the following morning. It was hard work, cutting out the underbrush and digging out the road; the labor was the harder in that they had barely twenty able-bodied men for the work. But that first day they moved the wagons up six miles to the divide and encamped at the head of Dixie Hollow. For two and a half miles, the next morning, the road was fairly easy, but then the ravine narrowed, choked up by an almost impenetrable growth of willows. They labored several hours at a road down this ravine, then in desperation adopted a route high along the canyonside, sideling and dangerous but enabling them, on the third day, to reach East Canyon itself. Hudspeth had taken Bryant and his fellows down this canyon to the meadows at Morgan, but even if the lower canyon of the Weber had not debarred this route to them, there was no possibility of taking wagons down the creek. The Indian trail on the mountainside was out of the question, and as for the canyon bottom itself, the creek not only raced between narrow rock walls but actually plunged under a tremendous boulder in its bed, which absolutely blocked the way for wagons. They must go up this creek, following the blaze-marks Reed had made.

It took eight days of the most backbreaking labor to bring the wagons eight miles up this creek and the additional four miles to the summit of Big Mountain. Thirteen times the road writhed back and forth across the creek, and the canyon bottom was a nightmare of willows and scrub oak. There was one consolation only in the midst of all this labor. On the sixth day, as they moved yard by yard up the canyon they were overtaken by the three final wagons to take the Hastings' Cutoff, the Graves family.

There were four able-bodied men among the thirteen newcomers, and they set to work with a will. On August 21 the company reached the 7,445-foot summit of Big Mountain, and from this pass could catch a far glimpse of the Great Salt Lake Valley. Encouraged, they descended the steep western side of the pass into Mountain Dell Canyon and followed it down into the open meadows of Parleys Park. Their troubles, they supposed, were over; they had but to follow Parleys Creek down to the flatlands of Salt Lake Valley.

During all this time they had had to worry about what had happened to Stanton and Pike. The camp here hailed their return. The two men had, Virginia Reed Murphy wrote later, "suffered greatly on account of the exhaustion of their horses and had come near perishing." They were bearers of fresh bad news. It was utterly impossible, they said, for wagons to be taken through the rocky gorge of Parleys. There was a single alternative only, to make a sharp, steep climb north over a divide into another canyon and then descend that canyon to the lake valley.

So the wagons were hauled up Little Mountain and roped down the steep declivity into Emigration Canyon. Even so, it required a full week to cut a road through the tangled brush in the valley bottom, and it was August 29 before they reached the mouth of this canyon.

Even here, for a few more rods, they must chop at willows to reach the open valley, and oh God, how unutterably tired they were of cutting out willows! Rather than face even one more day of such labor, they chose to pull their wagons up an incredibly steep hill on the south side of the creek, at the very mouth of the canyon. Almost every yoke in the train was required to pull each wagon up that slope, says Virginia Reed Murphy; one who stands at its base today finds it almost beyond belief that any number of oxen could have taken wagons up that hill.

But at the summit of Donner Hill they were rewarded by the sudden spectacle of the great lake. A gently rolling valley perhaps 30 miles long and 20 miles across stretched wide before them. To the northwest the waters of the salt lake glistened in the sun like polished steel, a brightness to give them renewed hope and courage. That night, August 29, 1846, they encamped on the site of Salt Lake City. Next morning at the ford of the Jordan the wagons intersected the welcome trail of the Hastings wagons. They had fallen weeks behind, but now, at last, there was a plain trail to follow.

Hastings got back from the trip with Reed perhaps at sundown August 12. During the next two days the company swung around the end of the Stansbury Range to the springs in Skull Valley, and here made preparations for the Salt Desert crossing. Hastings belittled the desert as one of perhaps 40 miles, but the immigrants made careful preparation for the ordeal, filling all their vessels with water and cutting grass to take with them. Before nightfall on August 15 the 66 wagons launched out upon the long drive.

They traveled throughout the night, stopping only now and then to give the stock a little grass. Dawn revealed around them an illimitable salt plain, white as snow. The stock was showing signs of fatigue, but a little grass and water revived the animals as a cup of coffee and a cold snack revived the immigrants. Hastings encouraged them to think they would reach water by noon. But at noon they seemed to have made no progress at all toward the far peak, and the fierce August sun had lighted the fires of hell upon this plain. As the sun sank in the sky, the oxen began to give out or, crazed by thirst, to run heavily about, unmanageable, until exhaustion dropped them dead upon the salt. All through the afternoon wagons were abandoned. The oxen that could travel were taken out of the yoke and driven along; those that would not stir under any persuasion, not even the whip, had to be left to die.

Sundown relieved them, at least, of the unbearable glare. Hourly hoping for water and grass, they kept on going throughout that night, but dawn of the second day came up and still they had not reached the promised springs. Between dawn and noon more oxen were lost than in all the other hours since the crossing began, but at noon water and grass were reached at last—barely in time for their salvation. Forty miles! The desert had been double that.

Complete disaster had been very close, and for perhaps five days the immigrants recuperated in camp at Pilot Peak. The men went 30 miles back into the desert to rescue some of the stock, and the abandoned wagons were brought in. But short of their destination they could never rest for long. The immigrants got moving again, encouraged to see the Bartleson track. On the twenty-third they made a short drive south along the base of Pilot Peak; and on the twenty-fourth a long, dry drive, over the Toano Range, through Silver Zone Pass, and across Gosiute Valley brought them to what they called Relief Springs.

The ruins of the Bartleson wagons here were a grim assurance that their troubles by no means were over. The remains of the old wagons were burned in their campfires during a day of rest and then, once again, they took up the journey. Fifteen miles south took them to a warm spring, and from this point, instead of rounding the southern end of the Pequops, as had the Bartleson party and Frémont himself, the wagons were taken southwest very nearly by the trail Talbot's party had taken the year before. Three moderately hard drives brought them into the lush green meadows they called the Valley of Fountains—the north end of Ruby Valley—under the high, snow-crested Rubies.

By the pack trail up over Secret Pass they were now only two days' travel from the headwaters of the Humboldt, but instead Hastings turned south along the Rubies, searching for a more suitable pass. This was not necessarily, as has sometimes been suggested, Hastings' incurable penchant for new cutoffs. Secret Pass, for wagons, was all but impassable, with miry bottoms, rocky ravines and a formidable growth of willows all the way down Secret Creek. The alternative route, however, was long and circuitous, almost 60 miles of southing to be made before they could round the Rubies. It was September 8 before they reached the junction with the traveled road down the Humboldt. Hastings, as he considered, had done his duty by those who had entrusted their welfare to him. He presently set out in advance of the wagons, crossing the Sierras at the end of September and coming down into the California valleys to the jolting news that war existed between the United States and Mexico and that there would, notwithstanding all his labors and ambitions, never be a Republic of California.

And still the Donner party on the trail behind struggled on toward its rendezvous with the snow. The southeastern shore of the salt lake was reached late in the afternoon of August 30. They had left Fort Bridger 11 days after Hastings; they were now 23 days behind. John Hargrave of Hastings' company had died in this locality and now, strangely, there was a death in the rear company. On the afternoon of the thirty-first Luke Halloran, a waif Tamsen Donner had taken into her wagon at Fort Bridger, died of consumption, and all the day of September 1 was spent in interring him beside John Hargrave. The two were the first immigrants whose bodies were committed to Utah soil.

On September 2 the company rolled on to the springs which had been Hastings' Wells to the advance company and which were Twenty Wells to them. On the following day they swung around the mountains to the springs in Skull Valley. A board caught at their attention, a message obviously left for them. But, whether pecked by birds or torn by Indians, the message lay in scraps upon the ground.

Tamsen Donner was a woman of resource; she gathered the scraps and pieced them together so that the message emerged. It warned of two days and two nights of hard driving before they could reach water and grass.

So, as Hastings' company had done, the immigrants gathered grass and filled all their vessels with water before setting out into the desert at daylight on September 5. But their livestock was in far worse shape than Hastings' had been; in every way they were more poorly prepared for the dry drive. It was a hell into which they tramped. The first to reach the springs did so on the morning of the fourth day, abandoning their wagons 20 miles out. Reed went ahead seeking water for the company; his men mismanaged his cattle, and, crazed with thirst, they stampeded off into the night, never to be recovered. All of them were hard hit by the desert crossing, but Reed most of all, two of his wagons left to disintegrate on the desert during a hundred years. . . .

The struggle with the barrier land, so far from uniting them, had racked them with desperate resentments, furious angers, corrosive jealousies and a numbing, voiceless fear born of the realization that by far they were the lastcomers on the trail. The passions lying so near the surface broke free in an altercation on the Humboldt, when Reed killed one of the Graves party. He was banished from the company and went on ahead—ironically becoming, in the end, the most powerful force in the effort to succor them. Soon one of the company was left behind to die; still another, it could be suspected, was murdered for his money. Drawing in upon themselves with a mindless single instinct for self-preservation, they climbed into the Sierras. Snow paralyzed the world, and so they came to their rendezvous with destiny. . . . Eighty-seven came down out of Emigration Canyon into Salt Lake Valley on that hot day in the last week of August. Only 47 reached California alive.

There remains a word to be said about Miles Goodyear. At Fort Bridger on July 31 James Frazier Reed had written home an interesting morsel of news. "There are two gentlemen here—one of them an Englishman of the name of Wills, and the other a yankee named Miles—who will leave here in a few days to settle at some favorable point on the Salt Lake, which in a short time will be a fine place for emigrants to recruit their teams, by exchanging broken down oxen for good teams."

The mountain man Wells, so the record would indicate, was a man with something of a green thumb, Utah's first agriculturalist. Had Hastings' Cutoff been all the advertising said it was, had the California immigration been pulled south from the Fort Hall road on the basis of a triumphant demonstration in 1846, had not the time now become full for the harried Mormons, Fort Buenaventura might have resounded in Western history like Fort Laramie, Fort Bridger and Fort Hall. But destiny had other arrangements in view.

Leaving Wells in charge of his fort, in the late fall Goodyear rode to California by the Spanish Trail to dispose of deer skins he had collected in the mountains. He arrived at a fortunate time, his trails crossing at last with those of Frémont. That energetic fellow had marched a California Battalion south to subdue the native Californians, and by the time of Goodyear's arrival, he was sorely in need of something with which to clothe his nearly naked soldiery. The redheaded mountain man sold his skins and then moved north to Sutter's, buying horses as he went. Sutter recorded his arrival at the fort on May 22, miscalling him "Myers" but noting that he was going with a band of horses "to the big salt lake, his new established trading post." There was no large party going east this spring, but four men were preparing to take the trail, one of them John Craig of Ray County, Missouri, he whom Edwin Bryant had overtaken so far down the Humboldt the preceding August. With his partner, Stanley, he had enlisted in Frémont's California Battalion, but Stanley had died on the march south, and now Craig was going home.

The seven men rode east into the snow and up over the summit which men now for all time must know as Donner Pass. Down past the grisly cabins from which the Donners had been evacuated they drove their horses, down the Truckee, across the desert to the Humboldt and up that river toward home. They had a brush with the Indians in which Miles was wounded slightly, and they elected to try the new cutoff. The passage of the Salt Desert was forever hard and dangerous: five of the horses gave out and had to be left. But they came up around the lake and drove up over the Wasatch Mountains to the Bear River.

They reached the Bear on the afternoon of July 10, 1847. As they busied themselves about their campfire they roused to the sound of horses' hoofs. Four men rode slowly into their camp, watchful and curious. Goodyear straightened as they dismounted and introduced themselves. As they spoke, a recognition roused in his mind. Rumor had been busy on the trail: they were Mormons.

So the past and the future were joined at last. On the banks of the Bear on this July day of 1847, one world coalesced in another. A people tough, enduring, and stubborn had come to possess themselves of this mountain land and forever change its face.

Chapter 10

This Is the Place

BRIGHAM YOUNG succeeded to the leadership of the Mormon Church in August 1844 at a critical time. The murder of Joseph Smith and his brother Hyrum late in June had shocked and alarmed even its instigators, and the threat of civil war in Illinois between Mormons and anti-Mormons had subsided, but the fight for control of the church, together with the centrifugal force of ambitious projects the prophet had had on foot at the time of his death, bade fair to rend the church apart.

The Mormons could not maintain themselves in Illinois indefinitely. Passions had been aroused, of such violence that if the Mormons did not depart on their own initiative, they would certainly be expelled by force of arms, precisely as had happened in Missouri in 1838-1839. The same realization had come to Joseph Smith in the months immediately preceding his death, but the Mormon prophet had been incapable of formulating realistic plans for dealing with the emergency; he sought the sanction of Congress for raising an army of 100,000 men to occupy Oregon, and simultaneously he instituted negotiations with the Republic of Texas for a strip of land along the Mexican border whereon the Mormons might establish a government of their own.

But if Brigham Young understood that the Saints must evacuate Nauvoo, he also understood that it could not be done at once. Nauvoo was the trump card in the fight for control of the church. It was the City of Joseph. It was the City where the temple was being erected in obedience to the revelation of God. It was the heart and brain of the far-flung missionary activity. Nauvoo could not be abandoned except at the hazard of losing control of the energies it radiated. But standing fast in Nauvoo presented serious difficulties. Aside from pretenders to the leadership, Brigham had to cope with stubborn souls within the church like Lyman Wight and James Emmett, who regarded it as their mandate from the prophet to carry out his plans relating to Texas and Oregon.

176

It was impolitic to interfere with either Wight or Emmett, for Brigham had at first to feel his way in the authority he was establishing over the church. But he made of the incidents what capital he could by dwelling on the need for union, promising that no one should prosper who sought to divide the Saints, and publicly reflecting on the courage of those who fled Nauvoo during a time when they might think it imperiled.

As a justification for clinging to Nauvoo, Brigham Young put redoubled energy into the completion of the temple. But the ground was rapidly being cut from beneath his feet. Repeal of the Nauvoo charter by the Illinois legislature stripped the Mormons in law if not in fact of their resources for defense. Facing up to the inevitable necessity, the Mormon leader cast about for means to remove the church from Illinois.

He began by taking up Joseph Smith's "great western measure"— to the extent, at least, of addressing letters to President Polk and the governors of the several States asking their advice and support. He got a reply only from the governor of Arkansas, who largely agreed with views earlier expressed by Governor Thomas Ford of Illinois, that the Mormons would do well to migrate to some unoccupied country, particularly Oregon or California. Ford had thought California offered possibilities for "the prettiest enterprise that has been undertaken in modern times," and he had boldly suggested that the Mormons "go out there, take possession of and conquer a portion of the vacant country, and establish an independent government of your own subject only to the laws of nations."

Military conquest, however, was serious business. Brigham's mind was trending rather, as he told Hosea Stout in March 1845, toward "settling the interior of the country between the head waters of the Arkansas and the head waters of the Colorado of the West."

By late summer of 1845 the need for a decision was pressing. Fortunately, two important books descriptive of the farther West reached print during the summer—the graphic works of Hastings and Frémont. On the basis of Frémont's authoritative advices it was possible to settle upon a tentative objective for the Saints. On August 28, 1845, Brigham Young met with his council in Nauvoo and agreed that 3,000 able-bodied men should be got off in the spring for Upper California. This program evidently being found too ambitious, it was shortly modified by a decision that the company be one of 1,500 men. The Great Salt Lake Valley was named as their destination.

During September the anti-Mormons began to fall upon the outlying Mormon settlements, stoning and burning isolated farmhouses and harrying the terrified Saints into Nauvoo. With a posse of Mormons, the sheriff of Hancock County struck right and left at the night riders, but this only fanned the passions to a hotter flame. To a mediatory committee from Quincy, who came inquiring as to the intentions of the Mormons, Brigham said shortly that plans had already been set on foot for the removal of the Saints as soon as grass should grow and water run in the spring.

But the anti-Mormons granted no surcease; constables and marshals periodically searched Nauvoo to seize the Mormon leaders. Hoping that the Saints would be given some peace if the leaders left Nauvoo, at the end of January Brigham decided to start moving across the Mississippi. However, he had not reckoned with his people; prepared or not, be the cost in suffering what it might, the Saints must come also. Through February and March they poured across the river to the snowy Iowa shore by the hundreds and by the thousands.

On March 9, by then 55 miles west from Nauvoo, Brigham wrote his brother that none of the Twelve need be expected to return very soon. Nauvoo was no place for him again, not until the American nation had been scourged by the hand of Almighty God. "Do not think, Brother Joseph, I hate to leave my house and home. No, far from that. I am so free from bondage at this time that Nauvoo looks like a prison to me."

Yet he was as certainly imprisoned by the immense responsibilities of the emigration which moved around him. The Mormons were migrating not as individuals or families but as a whole people. Those who traveled before traveled upon the resources of those who stayed behind, and they must make provision for those behind to come after. In Nauvoo alone there were possibly 15,000 Saints, and how many more there were throughout the world no man could say. All across Iowa, as the spring sun thawed the prairies, the Saints wrestled with their future, building the roads and the bridges, halting companies of the Saints at strategic locations to put in crops for harvesting by brethren yet to take the trail. And the people on whom this labor fell were cold, hungry, badly clothed and worse housed, frightened by their own helplessness and the blank face of the future, alarmed lest the Missourians fall upon them, distrustful even of their leaders, afraid of being abandoned along the way.

At no time during the spring could the emigration be sufficiently disentangled from the necessities of the moment to get a company off toward the Rockies. On May 21, barely halfway across Iowa, Heber C. Kimball bluntly put the issue to the Camp of Israel. At their present rate of travel, it would take them years to reach the mountains. The Twelve had brought out provisions for a year, but they had fed it to the brethren who had come without supplies, and the energies of their animals had been expended in double-teaming the wagons of those who must otherwise be left behind. Unless the people let the Twelve go to find a place of gathering, the Church would be scattered.

Those who could not outfit themselves for the further journey agreed to remain behind and put in crops. But the fears could not be dispelled. Those fears followed the Twelve westward along the trail, an anxious mistrust, a corroding doubt. Brigham had continually to exhort his Saints, often in the most caustic language: they were hedging up their own way by the course they were pursuing. He could safely prophesy, he said, that the Saints would not cross the mountains this season, and that was what many of the brethren wished; they would rather go to hell than be left behind.

It was June 14 before the advance companies reached the swirling, brown Missouri near Council Bluffs. As the wagons formed in a hollow square on the east bank of the river, Brigham faced up to realities. There was no possibility that the Saints could carry on to the mountains the disjointed movement they had in progress all the length of Iowa. Any who set out into the plains must be fully provisioned, and the organization of Israel into its divisions of 100, 50 and 10 must be certain and disciplined, the companies compact and tight.

On June 28 Brigham proposed that forthwith a company without families be dispatched to the Bear River Valley in the Great Basin. The motion was unanimously voted, and scores of volunteers stepped forward. With his weary knowledge Brigham looked them over. He was aware, he said, that all that men and hell could invent to hedge up the way of the camp would be hatched up.

"If the church is blown to the four winds and never gathered again, remember I have told you how, when, and where to gather, and if you do not go now, remember and bear me witness in the day of judgment. When God tells a man what to do, he admits of no argument, and I want no arguments, and if you will go, I will warrant you safety in so doing."

There were no longer any doubts in his mind where he should locate the Saints. He had not discouraged the public talk that Vancouver Island was his destination, but he had no idea of settling there. Oregon? It was already peopled by thousands of emigrant Missourians, and he had no stomach for more border warfare. There remained only California. The Saints had come out of Nauvoo singing:

"The upper California, O that's the land for me—
It lies between the mountains and the great Pacific sea.
The Saints can be protected there, and enjoy their liberty
In upper California, O that's the land for me."

But notwithstanding he had permitted Sam Brannan to take a shipload of colonists to California by sea (they had sailed from New York on February 4, the same day the first wagons crossed the Mississippi), Brigham was interested in only so much of Upper California as lay east of the Sierra Nevada. To western California there was the insuperable objection that settlers, Mexican and American, already were in possession. Above all things the Saints must now come as first settlers to whatever land they occupied. Never again must there be "old settlers" to mobilize public sentiment for their expulsion. In the light of these necessities and of the information to be had from the books of Frémont and Hastings, the Saints could have one destination only—the valleys lying along the eastern rim of the Great Basin.

The Mormons had first come into the horizon of President Polk's mind, so far as his diary shows, on January 30, 1846, when he received a letter from Governor Ford about the intended emigration of the Saints from Illinois. At that time Polk had taken an aloof attitude, being, he said, no more disposed to interfere with the Mormons than with the Baptists or any other sect. Immediately following the declaration of war against Mexico, however, as he began to contemplate a military expedition to take California, the Mormons were brought forcibly back to his attention. On May 25, as he discussed his California project with Governor Archibald Yell of Arkansas and ex-Postmaster General Amos Kendall, he learned that an agent of the Mormons had arrived in Washington seeking aid from the Government for the emigration of the Saints. All of a sudden the Mormons were deserving of political attention. If, in a hostile mood, they turned up in California at some delicate moment in the progress of the conquest, they might throw all plans out of joint. It was expedient to do something generous for the Mormons. War made it desirable. War also made it possible.

On June 2 the California expedition was, as Polk noted in his diary, "definitively settled" in a meeting of the cabinet. It was also decided that the Mormon problem should be disposed of by authorizing Colonel Stephen W. Kearny, to whom command of the California force was being given, "to receive into service as volunteers a few hundred of the Mormons who are now on their way to California, with a view to conciliate them, attach them to our country, & prevent them from taking part against us."

So, in the last week of June, along the trail through Iowa rode Captain James Allen, U.S.A., with an offer to muster four or five companies of Mormons into government service for the war against Mexico. Brigham Young saw instantly that this was nothing less than Divine Providence interposing in behalf of the Saints. His people must make a distinction, he announced to them, "between this action of the general government, and our former oppressions in Missouri and Illinois." The only question to be settled was whether it was prudent for the Saints to enlist and defend their country.

"Suppose we were admitted into the Union as a State and the government did not call on us, we would feel ourselves neglected. Let the Mormons be the first men to set their feet on the soil of California. Capt. Allen has assumed the responsibility of saying that we may locate at Grand Island, until we can prosecute our journey. This is the first offer we have ever had from the Government to benefit us."

Raising a Mormon Battalion in this year, 1846, was not to be accomplished by the mere desire of Brigham Young. At this particular moment the rank and file had no very amiable feelings toward the United States. Though, for example, Henry W. Bigler agreed to volunteer, "It was against my feelings, and against the feelings of my brethren . . . when we called to mind the mobbings and drivings, the killing of our leaders, the burning of our homes and forcing us to leave the States and Uncle Sam take no notice of it and then to call on us to help fight his battles." Others talked about this unparalleled effort of the government to enslave the Saints to fight its battles.

Was this indeed a bondage into which it was desired to deliver the Saints? A year later, relieved of his present anxieties and able to afford the characteristic American luxury of damning the government, Brigham could say so. But now the Mormon Battalion was salvation; it was gospel. There were serious disadvantages in parting with some of the strongest and most active men in the Camp of Israel, and real sacrifices were involved on the part of the men themselves. But far outweighing these considerations was the fact that a considerable portion of the camp would be transported to California and there released with arms and accouterments after a year's service, that from their service an immediate cash income would flow into the camp to finance the further westward migration of the Camp of Israel, that government sanction could now be obtained for wintering in the Indian territory, and that the battalion would vindicate the Saints before American public opinion.

Brigham sent his lieutenants back along the trail through Iowa to harangue the Saints, and went himself as far as Mount Pisgah. Returning, on July 13 he laid down the law to his people: "If we want the privilege of going where we can worship God according to the dictates of our conscience, we must raise the Battalion." If there were not young men enough willing to enlist, he promised, "we will take the old men; and if there are not enough, we will take the women."

And he had a final hardheaded gospel for the Saints. They had lived near so many old settlers who could always say, "Get out," that he was thankful for the privilege of going to settle a new country. They were going to march to California; if the country should ultimately come under the government of the United States, the Saints would be the old settlers, and it would be their privilege in turn to say, "Get out!" If they refused this opportunity what would they do? "If you won't go," he threatened, "I will go and leave you."

By July 18 he had his full five companies, 526 men. They were exhorted to righteousness and promised their reward. Brigham assured them "that they would have no fighting to do"; he told them "we should go into the Great Basin, which is the place to build Temples; and where our strongholds should be against mobs," and advised them that they would probably be disbanded "about eight hundred miles from the place where we shall locate." Three days later, to the lilting strains of "The Girl I Left Behind Me," the battalion took up its march for Fort Leavenworth and Santa Fe.

Notwithstanding the battalion's drain upon the energies of the Camp of Israel, Brigham hoped throughout July that a company might yet be sent over the mountains this year and that the camp itself might be got as far west as the head of Grand Island, 200 miles up the Platte.

By the time the battalion departed, it had become obvious that the resources of the camp were unequal to such an effort. Accordingly, it was resolved that the main body of the camp should move up the Missouri a few miles to a wintering site, with a small company only to go on to Grand Island. Bishop George Miller was to make the year's only effort to cross the mountains. But by the beginning of August it had become apparent that even this lesser effort was beyond the capabilities of the camp. Bishop Miller, who had got as far as the Pawnee mission station on the Loup Fork, 110 miles west, and who was fuming at the inability of the Twelve to make up their minds what they wanted to do, was ordered to winter at that point with as many of his company as could be sustained there; the balance he might permit to go on to Grand Island. Perhaps twenty or thirty wagons could be allowed to go on as far as Fort Laramie, but there was to be no attempt to cross the mountains this fall. On August 4 even these permissions were revoked.

"According to the best knowledge we have, we are now disposed to recall our recommendation of making Fort Laramie or the island this winter, for there is danger of the [prairie] fires cutting off supplies for your stock, and we would like to have you so near us that we may visit each other occasionally through the winter."

Miller discovered that it was impracticable to winter at Grand Island, and therefore, risking the displeasure of the Twelve, he accepted the invitation of a Ponca chief to go north to the Running Water (Niobrara) River. Here his company settled down until spring while the main Camp of Israel dug in at what has ever since been famous as Winter Quarters, at the site of Florence, a present-day suburb of Omaha, Nebraska.

Still a third company of Saints had to reconcile itself to a winter encampment remote from the promised land. During the spring, when the hope had been high that the Mormons would get over the mountains, a small company of Saints from Mississippi and Illinois had headed west in the midst of the year's Oregon and California immigration, expecting to unite with the Camp of Israel along the trail. In all they numbered 43 persons with 19 wagons. They could learn nothing of the main body of the Saints, but they continued dubiously on up the Platte. On July 2 they met Jim Clyman's party making for the States, and were dismayed to hear that no Mormons were on the trail ahead. After much debate they continued on as far as Fort Bernard, a few miles below Fort Laramie. There an Indian trader, John Richard, told them that the best place to winter would be the head of the Arkansas. He was himself going to Pueblo with two ox teams, and they gratefully accepted his offer to let them come along. They started south on July 10, traveling in reverse the road Fitzpatrick had taken with Frémont's baggage in 1843, and reached St. Vrain's July 27. From this point on there was a wagon road, and without any difficulty they reached Pueblo on August 7. The mountain men here received them kindly and offered to let them have supplies and corn for their labor.

The encampment of the Saints at Pueblo was enlarged when the Mormon Battalion swung past toward Santa Fe. Fathers, mothers, wives and children had gone with many of the men, and the pace had told on them. On September 16 at the Cimarron crossing of the Arkansas these families, numbering 12 or 15, were separated from

Important Mormon trails.

the battalion and sent under escort up the Arkansas to Pueblo. They were soon joined by a great many of their brethren, for Philip St. George Cooke, named by Kearny to command the battalion after the death of Allen, ruthlessly weeded out the sick and the infirm and sent them in two detachments, under Captain James Brown and Lieutenant William M. Willis, to winter likewise at Pueblo. Fully a third of the battalion comprised what has become known as the "Sick Detachment."

These, then, were the threads Brigham Young had to weave into the fabric of his plans for 1847: the Mormon Battalion itself, making the long, arduous march through New Mexico and Arizona to southern California (where they arrived late in January); the Sick Detachment and the "Mississippi Saints" at Pueblo; Miller's company on the Running Water; and the Camp of Israel at Winter Quarters.

On November 19 Brigham Young had a visitor, one who came floating down the Missouri past the Mormon encampment, "Mr. Smith Catholic priest and missionary to the black feet Indians." It was Father De Smet returning to St. Louis after five years in the mountains, and Brigham questioned him with interest. A few days later two trappers turned up in camp—mountain men who cast a long shadow over the winter's planning.

Of the two, Justin Grosclaude was much the more interesting. A native of Switzerland and educated in France, he had been for 16 years in the service of the American Fur Company and spoke most of the Indian languages east of the Rockies. For $200 he volunteered to guide the Mormons over the mountains next spring; for $200 additional, the other mountain man, Cardinal, would go along as a hunter. Grosclaude gave a long and interesting account of the sources of the Yellowstone, and with a pencil obligingly sketched "a map of the country west of the Missouri and north of Puncah above the yellow stone." On November 26 the two trappers moved up the Missouri toward the Ponca villages without any definite engagement having been made, but with a half understanding that the Saints might engage them in the spring.

All this information Brigham kept revolving in his mind. What he wanted was a halfway station along the general line of the route to the Great Basin, a likely place where an advance company might put in crops to support the migrations to follow, exactly as they had done in Iowa. But where to locate it?

On December 12 he had a discussion with the Indian agent and with Logan Fontenelle, half-breed son of the mountain man, Lucien B. Fontenelle. What were the prospects of raising grain at the head of the Yellowstone? And what of the road to the mountains by way of the Running Water?

Young Fontenelle was dubious about the prospects for grain, the soil being too sandy and clayey; he also expressed the opinion that the Platte road was superior to that up the Running Water. Brigham's mind was half made up, however, and he was the more confirmed in his ideas on December 17 when he received a letter from Miller's camp describing an attempted exploration west to Laramie by three of that company. The men had had to return after traveling a hundred miles up the Running Water, for buffalo had swept the route clear of grass. But so far as they had gone they were favorably impressed with that road.

In a Christmas council agreement was reached on the plans for 1847. Three hundred pioneers were to be sent off before winter broke; they were to proceed to the head of the Running Water, sustaining their teams on the rushes as they traveled up the river. When grass began to grow on the plains they were to proceed to the foot of the mountains and put in a crop. Each of the Apostles was to raise a company which would follow after the pioneers as soon as grass should rise at winter quarters, the total number being limited to those who could subsist on the crop put in by the pioneers.

It was not contemplated that any considerable body of the church membership should cross the mountains in 1847. They were to pause, as the location was spelled out in a letter sent to England in January, "at the foot of the mountains somewhere in the region of Yellow Stone river, perhaps at the fork of Tongue river, say two days ride north of the Oregon road, and a week's travel west of Fort Laramie."

On January 14 Brigham Young brought forth "the Word and Will of the Lord." His only revelation, it did not touch upon location, but with respect to the immigration it codified the thinking and the experience of all these weary months.

But if revelation could give the force of divine sanction to the plans for the year, it could not alter human capability. The resources of the Camp of Israel were unequal to getting off an advance company by March 15, and it developed that the Saints on the Running Water were insufficiently provisioned to join with the pioneers in a journey up the Running Water. Decision was made to take the road up the Platte instead, and the Saints at Ponca were instructed to come south to Winter Quarters.

Once again plans had to be adjusted to that deadly factor, capability. On March 6, when it became evident that it would be impossible to get the pioneer party off by the fifteenth, E. T. Benson had raised the question whether it would not be desirable for the Pioneers to go all the way to the final location, with no effort to put in crops at a halfway place. Brigham rejected this suggestion, but by March 22 he had to bow to necessity. The expedient he hit upon was that the Pioneers should go all the way and find the resting place for the Saints, with none permitted to follow them this year except those able to sustain themselves until an 1848 crop could be harvested in the Great Basin.

As preparations for departure were being made, Bishop Miller raised for the last time the ghost of Texas, an idea he could not bring himself to give up. Brigham told him flatly that under no circumstances would the Saints go to Texas; the bishop's views "were wild and visionary"; when the Saints moved hence it would be to the Great Basin, where they would soon form "a nucleus of strength and power sufficient to cope with mobs." The rebellious Miller took his family on south toward Texas. Ultimately, convinced by the claims of James J. Strang, he joined the ill-starred Mormon colony Strang established on Beaver Island in Lake Michigan.

So the Pioneers set forth to find an abiding place for the Saints. There were 12 times 12 men on setting out, but one turned back because of illness. Three women went also. The story is that Lorenzo Young refused to go without his wife Harriet, and that Brigham and Heber C. Kimball then took each a wife. Polygamy had not yet been publicly avowed, and in the rolls of the immigration the women were discreetly called by their maiden names, Clarissa Decker and Ellen Sanders. Clarissa was the 19-year-old daughter of Harriet by an earlier marriage, and the only two chil-

dren who went were Harriet's sons. Altogether, the pioneer party
was composed of 148 persons, 72 wagons, 93 horses, 52 mules, 66
oxen, 19 cows, 17 dogs and an unspecified number of chickens.

The Pioneers have a unique heroic stature in Utah's history; they
have become central within a special mythology, so that their essential
humanness has become lost in the clouds of glory they trail. Among
them were future governors and bank presidents; among them also
were future horse thieves, bogus-passers and murderers. Three of
their number were blacks, and half a dozen or more were not members of the church. There were skillful mechanics and men all
thumbs, dead shots and men capable of shooting down the animals
of the camp itself, sunny natures and perpetual grouches, men of the
most pious and men of the most profane disposition—in short, a representative selection of the human race.

The West into which they journeyed was something less than a
trackless wilderness. The route they followed—to the Elkhorn,
across to the Loup, up that river and then up the Platte itself—had
been trodden uncounted times since Ashley hauled his wagon toward
the mountains in 1824. The carts of the fur traders had beaten a
plain trail; Marcus Whitman's wagons had gone to the mountains
by this road in 1836; and it was just three years since the Stevens-
Townsend-Murphy party, first to get wagons over the Sierras to California, had rolled west by this route, and immigrants had again gone
this way in 1845.

Upon his Camp of Israel Brigham imposed a discipline which
became the foundation for all Mormon migration to follow. It was
a discipline to which the Oregon and California immigrants would
never have submitted, and for the lack of which they paid a corresponding penalty in hardship and waste effort—a discipline possible
only because it was backed up by an authority founded in God. The
new state of things was a grateful relief from the recurring disorder
of the migration across Iowa, and eight days out Brigham could tell
the camp that he was well pleased with their proceedings, that he
had no doubt the Lord had led them and would continue to lead
them if they were faithful.

A month's westering, however, frayed this discipline at the edges.
Dice made their appearance in camp, and cards, checkers and domi-
noes; there were nightly mock trials with a broad humor at which
the camp could roar, dancing in the firelight to the sweet voices of

the fiddles. On May 29 an angry Brigham brought the camp up short. Inasmuch as the Saints were beyond the power of the gentiles, he said:

"we are beyond their reach, we are beyond their power, we are beyond their grasp, and what has the devil now to work upon? Upon the spirits of men in this camp, and if you do not open your hearts so that the Spirit of God can enter your hearts and teach you the right way, I know that you are a ruined people and will be destroyed and that without remedy, and unless there is a change and a different course of conduct, a different spirit to what is now in this camp, I go no further. . . . Suppose the angels had witnessed the hoe down the other evening, and listened to the haw haws, would they not be ashamed of it? . . . Now let every man repent of his weakness, of his follies, of his meanness, and every kind of wickedness, and stop your swearing and profane language, for it is in this camp and I know it, and have known it. . . . I now tell you, if you don't stop it you shall be cursed by the Almighty and shall dwindle away and be damned."

When the wagons began to roll again, William Clayton observed with satisfaction, "No loud laughter was heard, no swearing, no quarreling, no profane language, no hard speeches to man or beast, and it truly seemed as though the cloud had burst and we had emerged into a new element, a new atmosphere, and a new society." This chastening of Israel was not alone a milestone in the westward progress of the Pioneers. Brigham had addressed them with an assurance and authority never again absent in his relations with the Saints. One of the peculiar geniuses in American history in the directness and the efficiency with which he grappled with the desert, here on the banks of the North Platte he took a long step ahead in forging the Saints into an instrument suited to his hand.

As the miles lengthened from Winter Quarters, Brigham neglected no chance for information about the farther West. Some fresh reports concerning the Great Basin had come to him in February, when two men of the Sick Detachment of the battalion had completed a hazardous midwinter journey from Pueblo. The Saints wintering at

W. H. Jackson   *Courtesy U. S. Geological Survey*

The Burg on the Bear, Corinne in 1869.

Russell Lee, Farm Security Administration   *Courtesy, Library of Congress*

Morgan Valley between the two canyons of the Weber, 1941.

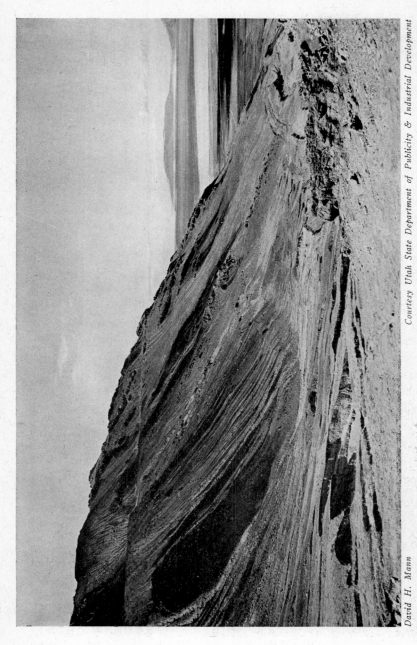

The ancient levels of Lake Bonneville carved on the northeastern slopes of the Oquirrh Mountains; in background, Great Salt Lake.

Pueblo had learned from the mountain men much that was interesting about the Great Salt Lake Valley; buffalo, elk, deer, antelope, mountain sheep and goats, grizzly bear, beaver and geese were reported in great abundance and salt in great plenty in the vicinity of the salt lake and Bear River Valley. It was even said that in a ridge of mountains running through the lake large quantities of precious minerals were found.

On May 4 the Pioneers saw three wagons descending the opposite bank of the river, traders making for Council Bluffs. One of the traders came splashing across the two-mile-wide Platte, and he could give them advice about roads. That on the other side of the river was good, he said, and more traveled. But after some debate it was decided to keep the north bank of the Platte all the way to Fort Laramie, for the reason that, as Clayton remarked, "we are making a road for thousands of saints to follow, and they cannot ford the river when the snow melts from the mountains."

On arriving at Fort Laramie June 2, the Saints found awaiting them some of the Saints from Pueblo, who two weeks earlier had come on in advance of their brethren. There were seventeen in all, including a mountain man, Lewis B. Myers, who had joined with them at Pueblo.

Detaching four men to meet and guide the brethren coming up from the south, Brigham started on with the rest, taking the long-established trail up the right bank of the North Platte.

Now that they had crossed the river, they had plenty of company. Five hundred wagons were reported on the trail ahead of them, destined mostly for Oregon, and numerous companies traveled near and behind them, some of them Missourians whom the Saints regarded with a fear and suspicion fully reciprocated. On June 9 the Pioneers met ten mountain men making for Fort Laramie and from one of these travelers got the first far intimation of Miles Goodyear's establishment: they heard that there was a man making a farm in the Bear River Valley.

The upper ferry of the Platte was reached on June 12, and it required a full week to get the wagons across the river. So much in demand was the ferry service, with the Oregon and California immigrants coming up behind, that when the company went on, nine men were detailed to stay behind and operate the ferry.

On the night of June 26 the Pioneers encamped just short of South Pass. Orson Pratt went on across the divide, searching for the place of highest elevation. At Pacific Springs, four miles beyond the summit, he encountered eight men eastbound from Oregon. With them was the experienced mountain man, Black Harris, who had come east with a view to hiring out as guide to some company bound for Oregon. He had copies of the *Oregon Spectator,* the first newspaper published on the Pacific Coast, and a single issue of Sam Brannan's *California Star.* Brannan, it appeared, had reached California with his shipload of colonists at the end of the preceding July, but his paper was secular indeed, with not so much as a word of the brethren, so the Saints laid the sheet by in disappointment. Harris spent all the next day with the Camp of Israel, trading his peltries and giving out information. The information was extremely discouraging. The Bear River Valley, he said, was destitute of timber and the soil was sandy, growing nothing but wild sage. Cache Valley got his grudging approval—tolerably well timbered and a good place to winter cattle.

Harris left the Saints on the morning of the twenty-eighth. They moved on past the junction of the Greenwood Cutoff and the Fort Bridger road, taking the more southerly route. In midafternoon they encountered Jim Bridger, whom they instantly identified as the most widely traveled man in all this region. Old Gabe, enroute to Laramie, stopped off for a talk.

It was a bewildering knowledge to tap, ranging easily over the entire West. Bridger mentioned the man who had newly opened the farm in "Bear River Valley"—the soil, he thought, was good and likely to produce corn except that the excessively cold nights might prevent its growth. But it was the valley of Utah Lake that came most luminously through his discussion. There was timber there and plenty of good grass, with little sage; he had seen no grapes, but berries and cherries were abundant. The Ute inhabiting this region were a bad people; if they caught a man alone, they were sure to rob and abuse him, if not to murder him, though parties of men were in no danger. Harris' gloomy ideas he rejected out of hand; Harris knew nothing of that section. He talked of the bare red rock country through which the Green cut its way, of the Mohave Desert, of the Hopi Indians, of copper mines in Arizona, of lead and silver mines east of the mountains, of wild flax, juniper berries and persimmons, of fish, corn, wheat and pumpkins, of north and south California, of promised lands: the West itself was Bridger's paradise. William Clayton's head whirled when he put away his notebooks: "we shall know more about things and have a better understanding when we have seen the country ourselves."

Separating from Bridger next morning, the Saints moved on southwest to the Green. On the afternoon of June 30, as they were preparing to cross the river, Sam Brannan rode into camp. With only three companions he had crossed the Sierras and made the perilous journey east up the Humboldt and on to Fort Hall. Leaving one of his little company there, he had come on with the other two to meet the Twelve—and bring them on to California.

His reception was not too cordial. Brigham had no intention of going on to the valley of California. Slapping the mosquitoes that were devouring him piecemeal, he said so. As he wrote to the Saints on the trail behind: "our destination is the Great Basin, or Salt Lake for the present, at least, to examine the country."

That letter was entrusted to 5 brethren designated to go back and guide the main companies from Winter Quarters. In the very moment of their departure, 13 battalion boys came riding up in advance of the Sick Detachment. One of them turned back with the 5 guides, but the other 12 joined the Camp of Israel.

Many of those in the camp, from the time of crossing the Green, suffered from the ailment that has come down familiarly in Mormon history as "mountain fever." In some this may have been the physical nausea consequent upon adjustment to high altitudes: in others it may have been a kind of tick fever. None died of it but many were violently ill.

The Saints reached Fort Bridger July 7. While some of the brethren traded rifles and clothing for buckskins, a council decided that Sergeant Tom Williams and Sam Brannan should turn back to meet the Sick Detachment. The battalion boys had received neither their discharge nor any pay since May 1, and Brannan could pilot a small company to San Francisco to collect the arrearages. With the departure of these two men, the Pioneers were reduced to the final number that entered Salt Lake Valley—147 men, 9 women and 2 children.

West of Fort Bridger Hastings' new route was found pretty rough and "but dimly seen." Even so, the company made good time up Bridger Bench, down across the valley of the Big Muddy and southwest through Pioneer Hollow. On the afternoon of the tenth they got over the high summit of the Bear River divide, 942½ miles from Winter Quarters, and descended the western slope to encamp on Sulphur Creek not far above its mouth in the Bear. They had been nearly three months on the trail, and now at last they were entering the Great Basin.

While Orson Pratt was wandering about geologizing, he saw a smoke curling into the air two miles downstream. Four men rode over to investigate, approaching warily lest it be an Indian encampment. It was, instead, the encampment of the redheaded mountain man, Miles Goodyear.

Goodyear accompanied the four Mormons back to camp. William Clayton inspected him with mingled approval and suspicion. "He is the man who is making a farm in the Bear River valley. He says it is yet seventy-five miles to his place, although we are now within two miles of Bear River. His report of the valley is more favorable than some we have heard but we have an idea he is anxious to have us make a road to his place through selfish motives."

Here, almost on the banks of the Bear, there was a perplexing fork in the trail. One wagon track swung southerly, one northerly. (Hastings seems to have taken the southerly route with at least part of his wagons, but Jefferson's company following behind, and probably the Donner party as well, had chosen the northern road. The two trails came together again at the head of Echo Canyon.) Goodyear recommended that the Mormons take the northern road, and several of the Saints rode with him to examine this route. "They represent it," observed William Clayton on their return, "as being bad enough, but we are satisfied it leads too far out of our course to be tempted to try it."

This dictum on what the Saints would do was premature. It seemed advisable, so that none might have occasion to murmur at the Twelve thereafter, to let the camp vote as to which road to take. The camp voted for Goodyear's route.

By the time the vote was taken, however, the mountain man had gone about his business. Learning that the Oregon immigration this year for the most part was taking the Greenwood Cutoff, he separated from Craig and the others bound for the States and with his two Indian helpers set out down the Bear to intercept the immigration that must be the market for his horses.

Soon after the Bear was crossed, Brigham Young was violently stricken with mountain fever. His wagon was halted, and a few others stayed to keep him company, while the camp itself was ordered on under the direction of Orson Pratt. During the evening Brigham was insensible and raving, but by morning he was improved. It did not seem advisable for him to travel, and Pratt was instructed to take 23 wagons and 42 men "and endeavour to find Mr. Reid's route across the mountains."

Having descended "Red Fork," (Echo Canyon), Pratt arrived in the open valley of the Weber at nightfall of the second day. On July 15 he crossed the Weber, and a six-mile pull down the left bank brought him to the Weber's formidable upper canyon. Pratt and John Brown rode some five miles down the immigrant road, back across the Weber, around through Croyden Valley and into the Weber Canyon itself, returning fully convinced that "Reid's route across the mountains" was the only practicable one.

It took some hunting, for grass had overgrown the road, but late in the afternoon the Donner-Reed trail was discovered. Next morning they started up Little East Canyon. Notwithstanding the 23 wagons that had gone through the year before, it required the labor of a dozen men with axes and spades to make the road reasonably passable. They got up over the divide and encamped for the night in Dixie Hollow. The journey on the seventeenth, first down into East Canyon and then up that canyon, was the hardest kind of work, and it was in vain that Pratt searched for a more feasible route; he was disposed to doff his hat to those travelers of 1846, and the immense labor they had expended in cutting a road up the brush-choked canyon bottom.

Since the eighteenth was Sunday, the Saints remained in camp, but next day Pratt and Brown set out to examine the country ahead. The road brought them to the pass over Big Mountain. On foot they ascended Big Mountain itself. Mountains rolled and twisted under their sight, but a few miles to the southwest they could see "an extensive level prairie" which they thought must be near the salt lake. Coming back down the peak, they rode on down the western slope of Big Mountain into Mountain Dell Canyon. The "prairie" they had seen was Parleys Park; the lake was by no means near yet, for beyond the mountain glen the creek plunged "through a very high mountain, where we judged it impossible for wagons to pass [Parleys Canyon]." Patient search disclosed the way the 1846 wagons had gone, north over a steep divide, Little Mountain, and down into a narrow canyon which henceforth should be known as Emigration Canyon. The two men now returned to camp. By dint of enormous labor expended on the road, the wagons meanwhile had moved 6¼ miles up East Canyon. On July 20 Pratt's 23 wagons patiently worked their way through to Parleys Park, and the night's encampment was on ground now inundated by the waters of Mountain Dell Reservoir.

The wagons behind had been slowly working their way west and south through the canyons. On the afternoon of the eighteenth Heber C. Kimball proposed to the camp that as Brigham was still ill, all except 8 or 10 wagons should go on ahead the following day, find a good place, and begin to plant potatoes and other crops, for summer was far advanced. Next day, accordingly, Erastus Snow, Willard Richards and George A. Smith took the main body of the Pioneers south up into the mountains from the Weber Valley, and during the evening of July 20 Richards and Smith wrote instructions to Pratt. Brigham, they said, had given them his views concerning a stopping place in the basin, saying that he felt inclined not to crowd upon the Ute until the Saints had a chance to get acquainted with them. Hence, it would be better to bear toward the region of the salt lake—and find a good place for their seeds, depositing these as speedily as possible, regardless of a future location. The time for planting was fully come, and it was important to do everything possible to facilitate the potato crop, no matter where it was planted.

"The president thinks the Utes may feel a little tenacious about their choice lands on the Utah we had better keep further north towards the Salt Lake, which is more of a warlike or neutral ground, and by so doing we should be less likely to be disturbed and also have a chance to form an acquaintance with the Utes, and having done our planting shall select a site for our location at our leisure."

Tucking this letter into his pocket, early on July 21 Erastus Snow set out to find Orson Pratt. He overtook him and his company at the foot of Little Mountain. Leaving the wagons to make their own way over the ridge to Emigration Canyon, the two men rode ahead. At the mouth of Emigration they were struck by the exceedingly steep and dangerous hill up which the Donner wagons had gone in preference to hewing out even one more willow, but they climbed this hill and, Erastus Snow wrote, "involuntarily, both at the same instant, uttered a shout of joy at finding it to be the very place of our destination." The open valley lay outstretched before them, and in the distance the broad waters of the Great Salt Lake glistened in the sunbeams.

Exultant, they descended into the valley, going a circuit of some ten or twelve miles before returning, long after nightfall, to camp. Next morning, while the wagons cut their way through those last few willows at the mouth of Emigration Canyon, Pratt, Snow, Brown and four others set out upon a more extended exploration, going as far as the warm and hot springs at the north end of the valley. Obviously the alluvial land fanning out from the canyon mouths was richest; near the Utah Outlet the land was poor and alkaline, unfit for agricultural purposes. Not less important than the promise of the land was the abundance of creeks and springs. Little sage-brush grew east of the river; there was mile upon mile of green and luxuriant grass. Also, an omen for the future, "We found the drier places swarming with very large crickets, about the size of a man's thumb."

The more humble members of the camp, descending the bench-land southwesterly toward the evening's encampment, which was made where Mill Creek is intersected by present State Street, had somewhat mingled feelings about this valley to which they had come from so far. They were impressed with the serene, summery weather, the beautifully transparent sky and the numerous trout-filled brooks flowing from the mountains; only the lack of timber seemed a draw-back to what William Clayton characteristically called "one of the most beautiful valleys and pleasant places for a home for the Saints which could be found." Notwithstanding the seeming aridity, the Saints could live here and do well while they did right, he thought. Yet also the Saints felt a sense of desolation and infinite remoteness; the wide, empty valley was filled with a loneliness in which a whole people might disappear like a stone dropped in still waters.

All of the company, except those who had stayed behind to attend Brigham Young, reached the floor of Salt Lake Valley on July 22. That night in the encampment on Mill Creek it was decided to move north four miles to the place recommended for putting in the potatoes. Next morning they rolled north up the future State Street, to the south fork of City Creek, drawing up their wagons on the south bank of the brook, a few yards south of what was soon to become Third South Street. It was a beautiful situation, with City Creek tumbling out of its canyon to divide just above the future North Temple and State Streets into two sparkling brooks, one running almost directly west toward the river, the other running south for a distance until it too turned west. The sun was hot and the hills were dry around them, but to the southeast the Cottonwood peaks gave majesty to the hour.

Orson Pratt summoned the assembled Saints to prayer: they had been two years striving to reach this great valley, he said, and they had been greatly blessed in their journey. Obediently the Saints dedicated the land and themselves unto the Lord, asking that rain be sent to make the earth fruitful. Willard Richards then exhorted them to throw aside all selfishness and work with all their might. "The temporal salvation of our families, our posterity, and the nations of the earth depends upon the integrity of our conduct," he reminded them, and they received his words in soberness.

Five men were appointed a committee to locate a ground for plowing, and at 11:30 A.M. they reported the staking off of a plot for potatoes. Plows were immediately set to work. The brethren had prayed for rain, but it has always been a fundamental Mormon precept that the Lord helps those who help themselves; some of the company were sent to dam the creek so that its water might be thrown upon the dry land. The dam was not finished this day, however, and the plows had rather a rough time with the baked earth; several were broken during the afternoon.

Though racked by days of mountain fever, Brigham Young was

feeling much better on the morning of July 24, 1847, and Wilford Woodruff bundled him into his carriage for the last stage of the thousand-mile journey. Late in the morning the carriage pulled up out of the canyon bottom on to the high benchland overlooking the valley. "President Young," Wilford Woodruff made note in his journal, "expressed his full satisfaction in the appearance of the valley as a resting place for the Saints, and was amply repaid for his journey." Thirty-three years later, in the emotional fervor of Mormonism's fifty-year jubilee, Woodruff had a more dramatic tale to tell. While gazing on the scene before them, he said, Brigham Young "was enwrapped in vision for several minutes. He had seen the valley before in vision, and upon this occasion he saw the future glory of Zion and of Israel, as they would be, planted in the valleys of these mountains. When the vision had passed, he said: 'It is enough. This is the right place, drive on.'" Brigham's own journal entry for this day was content to say prosaically that after crossing Emigration Canyon Creek eighteen times he emerged from the canyon and encamped with the main body at 2:00 P.M.

Acceptance of Salt Lake Valley as the gathering place for the Saints had to develop through several days, and meanwhile the camp was kept vigorously at work. By the afternoon of the twenty-fourth all the potatoes were in the ground, and a good many of them watered. The plowing went faster after the water had been "conducted over the ground," and on Sunday morning, July 25, many of the brethren got corn, beans and peas in.

On this Sunday both forenoon and afternoon meetings were held. By the close of the afternoon session Brigham was feeling strong enough to address his Saints. Those who did not like the look and custom of the Saints, he said, were at liberty to go where they pleased, but if they remained with the Mormons, they must obey the laws sanctioned by them. No more work must be done on the Sabbath. As soon as a place of permanent location was selected, a city should be laid out by the compass and chain. There should be no buying and selling of land; a man should have measured off to him what he could till. Every man should have his inheritance to cultivate as he pleased, but if he would retain that inheritance, he must be industrious.

It was contemplated that several of the Twelve should make a northern tour of exploration up the valley of the Great Salt Lake on Monday, July 26, but Brigham was not well enough, and the idea was finally abandoned. The Twelve did, however, take an excursion west to the salt lake on July 27. Just as they were starting, Amasa Lyman and Sam Brannan rode down out of Emigration Canyon to report that the Sick Detachment of the battalion and the Mississippi Saints would arrive at the Pioneer camp within two days. Lyman and Brannan joined the party going to the lake. The Donner road took them west to the lake shore, and they had, Erastus Snow recorded in his journal, "a fine bathing frolic. The water was warm and very clear, and so salt that no fish can live in it. The waters of the ocean bear no comparison to those of the lake, and those who could not swim at all floated upon the surface like a cork, and found it out of their power to sink. When we dressed ourselves we found our hair and skin perfectly coated with fine salt."

They explored as far as Tooele Valley, which impressed them as too dry to be suitable for a location of the Saints, and returned to camp next day. That evening, decision crystallized at last. The brethren were assembled on the future Temple Block, comfortable in their shirt sleeves, seated on the ground and watching the immense white moon come up over the shadowed mountains. Brigham allowed those who had been out in various directions to relate what they had seen, then he put the question to his Saints.

"Shall we look further or make a location upon this spot and lay out and build a city? We were the pioneers of the church and our business was to seek for a suitable location for the church. The question is, shall this be the spot or shall we look further?"

A motion was made to locate here. Norton Jacob seconded the motion, saying that if they went south toward the Utah Lake, they would find the country occupied by the Indians, whereas this valley was unoccupied. Erastus Snow pointed out that all who had been out exploring had returned satisfied with their location; also, the Lord had led them directly to it.

Brigham Young desired the camp, if this was their feeling, to manifest it by saying aye. In a deep-toned chorus they gave the word back to him. Brigham said:

"Then the feelings of the Twelve are the same and I know that as a general thing the minds of the brethren are like this: If the Lord should say by revelation this is the spot, they would be entirely satisfied if it was on a barren rock. Well, I know it is the spot, and we have come here according to the suggestions and direction of Joseph Smith, who was martyred. The word of the Lord was to go to that valley, and the best place you can find in it is the spot. Well, I prayed that He would lead us directly to the spot which He has done. For, after searching, we can find no better."

There was voiced at this moment a lonely dissent. William Vance spoke up to say that his feelings had been different from his brethren, though perhaps he was wrong; he felt that the Saints should go farther—perhaps to the other side of the lake.

Patiently Brigham replied that Brother William had a perfect right to his views.

"But if we were on the other side of the lake, we should not have the benefit of the warm north and west winds from the lake. I knew this spot was the one as soon as I saw it. Up there on that table ground we shall erect the standard of freedom."

The Twelve was nominated to be a committee to lay out the city "and apportion the inheritance." In accepting that responsibility, Brigham Young's mind and words ranged across the years, foreshadowing a long labor of city building, foreshadowing social customs, habits of thinking, a way of life. Brigham's quiet voice sounding in the moonlight, rising a little with emphasis when his feelings held him, gave to the Saints the lineaments of their future:

"We propose to have the temple lot contain forty acres and to include the ground we are now on. What do you say to that? All right. That the streets will be 88 feet wide and sidewalks 20 feet wide. The lots to contain 1¼ acres, and eight lots in a block. The houses invariably to be set in the center of the lot 20 feet back from the street and with no shops or other buildings on the corner of the streets. Neither will they be filled with cattle, horses, and hogs, nor children, for they will have yards and places separated for recreation, and we will have a city clean and in order. No one will be allowed to divide his lot or sell off a corner, but when improved, it may be right for him to sell the whole lot or his inheritance in the country and go to some other place, for many other places will be built up. A man may live here with us and worship what God he pleases or none at all, but he must not blaspheme the God of Israel nor damn old Jo Smith or his religion, for we will salt him down in the lake. We do not intend to have any trade or commerce with the gentile world. For so long as we buy of them, we are in a degree dependent on them. The Kingdom of God cannot rise independent of the gentile nations until we produce, manufacture and make every article of use, convenience or necessity among our own people. We shall have elders abroad among all nations and until we can obtain and collect the raw material for our manufacturers, it will be their business to gather in such things as may be needed. So we shall need no commerce with the nations. I am determined to cut every thread of this kind and live free and independent, untrammeled by any of their detestable customs and practices."

Norton Jacob painstakingly recorded in his journal these words from the fountainhead of authority. At the end he had only this to say: "At a late hour the meeting broke up." But as he stowed his journal away in his pocket, he stowed away the promise of destiny for a whole people. Here in its proper environment had been revealed the mind of Brigham Young. In the image of that mind a people could be fashioned, and now they would be.

Chapter 11

Founding an Empire

Iℕ ᴛʜᴇ first eight days that the Pioneers labored at the foundations of the Kingdom of God, they broke one lot of 35 acres and planted two-thirds of it with buckwheat, corn, oats and other grains, planted an eight-acre lot with corn, potatoes and beans, and planted four acres of another lot with garden seed. And by the last day of July three acres of corn showed green shoots two inches above the ground, and beans and potatoes were also up.

This was proof, William Clayton reflected, not only of the fertility of the soil but of the industry of the Saints, who had simultaneously made a road to the timber, hauled and sawed timber for a boat and made and repaired thirteen plows and three harrows.

Housing was a problem for which fortunately they had fresh and newly expert advice. The Sick Detachment of the battalion had marched down out of the canyons behind their fifes and side drum on July 29. With them came the Mississippi Saints. After their winter at Pueblo they were full of sage advice about building houses of adobe—bricks of dried mud. Adobe was all the more acceptable as a building material because of the scarcity of timber, which was one of the most pressing among the anxieties of the Saints. No one liked the prospect of wintering in wagons, and it was agreed to put up houses in the form of a stockade.

On August 2 the survey of the city was commenced and an adobe yard laid out. It was voted that the stockade be built on the public square now known as Pioneer Park, and through August the camp labored to enclose the 10-acre fort. Some few meanwhile were instructed to continue the exploration of the surrounding country; and the mountain man Lewis B. Myers, who was his own boss, explored at his pleasure.

On August 2 Myers came back from a reconnaissance of Utah Valley with an optimistic report on the timber, which he thought might be floated down the Utah Outlet to the pioneer camp. On August 4 several others rode south to look into this matter; they returned next day echoing Myers' praise, but less sanguine about its timber supply.

Captain James Brown, who had been busy outfitting himself for a trip to California to collect the balance of the battalion pay, got off August 9, taking with him Sam Brannan as his pilot.

A little group of explorers rode north with Brown. Lewis Myers, with a single companion, turned up the Weber to inspect Hastings' route; he liked the look of the timber in the canyon, but thought it very bad for a road and more roundabout than the route through the mountains. A larger detachment, including John Brown, J. C. Little and W. W. Willis, rode as far north as Bear River before separating from the California-bound men to explore Cache Valley.

What everybody wanted to hear about was Goodyear's post on the Weber. It consisted, John Brown reported, of some log buildings and corrals stockaded with pickets. The establishment had a herd of cattle, horses and goats, and a small vegetable garden. Exceedingly important was the question whether these high mountain valleys would grow corn, and Goodyear's tiny corn patch, tended throughout the summer by the English mountain man, Captain Wells, was an object of inquiry for every traveler who came down from the north.

A skiff had been under construction since July 29. On August 11 the craft was completed and launched in City Creek to soak. Albert Carrington put it on wheels and set out for Utah Lake to fish and explore the country. He had not reckoned, however, on the steep hill at the Point of the Mountain. It was evident that they had neither men nor teams enough to get the boat back up the hill if it were taken down into the southern valley, nor could it be run through the canyon of the Utah Outlet. Accordingly it was launched just below the canyon, and while two of the men turned back toward camp with the teams, Carrington and the other two floated back to Emigrant Ford in the new boat.

The new city was named "Great Salt Lake City of the Great Basin, North America." In official usage the "Great" in the city's name persisted until in 1868 it was eliminated by legislative enactment.

At the suggestion of Heber C. Kimball the Utah Outlet was renamed the Western Jordan. This was a name which struck the fancy of the Saints though "Western" promptly fell into disuse.

Brigham Young gave City Creek, Red Butte and Mill Creek their names, but Canyon Creek and Big Canyon Creek were less fortunate suggestions, the former subsequently becoming known instead as Emigration Canyon and the latter, after Parley Pratt built a road through it in 1849-1850, as Parleys Canyon.

In genesis, it was a respectable city in which the Pioneers convened late in August. It was staked off in 135 blocks, each of ten acres and subdivided into eight lots. The streets were eight rods wide, and there were three public squares in various parts of the city, in addition to the ten-acre Temple block. The stockade was rising fast, and the crops were growing finely. A beginning had been made, a place of gathering for the hundreds of families westbound along the trail.

The principal business of the August conference was the establishment of a government to rule until the heads of the church should return a year hence. "I move that there be a president to preside over this place," Brigham Young proposed. The motion was seconded and carried. "That all other officers that are necessary be appointed for this place." When this too was carried, Brigham told the assemblage that it was the right of the Twelve to nominate the officers. "We wish to know who is coming in the next company. If Uncle John Smith comes, it is our minds that he preside."

The Saints were exhorted to faithfulness and industry. "I want to engage 50,000 bushels of wheat and other grain in proportion," Brigham told them. "I will pay you 50 cents per bushel for corn, $1.25 for wheat and 25 cents for oats. Why not? I bring glass for you and you raise grain for me." He urged upon them the wisdom of fencing the city and the farm lands so that the Indians could not get in and so that the crops might be protected from the livestock. Heber C. Kimball talked to them in his familiar, earthy vein: "You should throw away selfishness for it is of hell, and I say in the name of Jesus away with it to hell! . . . Call upon God and we shall increase here. Away with the spirit of alienation and let us be united."

Ever since August 2 companies had been taking the back trail. Each, before departing, made the excursion to the extraordinary salt lake lying along the western sky line. Norton Jacob visited the lake on August 10, bathing in "the most beautiful water I ever saw," and made note of a new enterprise here on the lake shore: "Five of our men were here making salt and with three kettles, can make forty bushels per day and just as white as the Liverpool salt and just as fine." Four days later it was William Clayton's turn to visit the lake—and many others on August 24 made the holiday excursion to the lake as a necessary preliminary to departure.

Early on August 26 the last of the homeward-bound Pioneers began the long pull up the benchland toward the mouth of Emigration Canyon. For those who were staying behind, it was a lonesome experience to see the worn canvas of the wagon tops glint briefly in the morning sunshine and disappear into the canyon above the incipient city. Those who went carried with them a sense of achievement for all that had been done. But Brigham's wife Clarissa, who remained behind, swallowed a lump in her throat: "I felt very lonesome after you left," she wrote her husband, "it seemed to me that I was a lone child, though in a pleasant land."

Welcome indeed was a courier who rode into the valley on August 31 with news of the oncoming immigration, but it was September 19 before the first wagons wound down the canyons into Salt Lake Valley. The last companies arrived October 8.

Brigham had met his people just west of South Pass on September 5. In council with the Twelve and the officers of the camp he had nominated a president, a high council and a marshal for Great Salt Lake City, and for the guidance of his Saints he had dictated a long epistle. The Pioneers had fulfilled the mission on which they were sent, he said, by selecting a beautiful site for a city, one destined to be a place of refuge for the hungry soul. The officers nominated to preside over them should "observe those principles which have been instituted in the Stakes of Zion for the government of the Church," and pass such laws and ordinances as should be necessary for the peace and prosperity of the city, "though we trust few or none will be necessary; for you have had line upon line and precept upon precept, and know what is right."

More brethren had taken the trail than had been thought possible, so that it would be necessary to enlarge the fort commenced by the Pioneers. They were instructed how the cattle should be cared for, how the land should be used, what fences should be built. They were urged to plant their crops as early as possible, so that it might be learned whether grain could be matured before summer drought made irrigation necessary. If irrigation was requisite, City Creek would yield an abundance of water, and since in wisdom they should prepare for all eventualities, they should make ready "pools, vats, tubs, reservoirs, and ditches at the highest points of land in your field or fields that may be filled during the night and be drawn off to any point you may find necessary, through a tight and permanent gate prepared for that purpose." They should be careful in preserving the timber; they should put saw and gristmills in operation as quickly as possible, but should be careful not to contaminate the waters of City Creek. The fall was the best time to secure the year's stock of salt from the Salt Lake, "and we recommend that you procure good timber and erect a substantial bridge over the Western Jordan (Utah Outlet) before the water rises, which will give you easy access to the Lake which is a pleasant place of resort and its water very healthy for bathing."

This remarkable letter did not neglect its duty of exhortation: "Your present location is designed to you for a city of refuge, a place of rest; therefore see to it that ye pollute not your inheritance, for if you do, you might expect that the judgement of heaven will be poured out upon you." Any person who did not belong to the church but who loved the principles of peace and good society was at liberty to settle among them, "but it is not your privilege to let any one tarry amongst you, to corrupt the morals of the people; and it is the duty of the council to see that good and wholesome laws are enforced against all such, and to institute any office and call any officer to put down or remove such nuisances, if necessity shall require, which we hope may never be." It was recommended that all Saints arriving at Great Salt Lake City "follow our example and be baptised for the remission of sins," and so, leaving the follies of the gentiles, begin anew in the service of the Heavenly Father. This epistle they should make their oracle and guide; if they did so, they would be blessed and the spirit of the Lord would rest down upon them and their souls be filled with light and knowledge while their hearts rejoiced; yea, then would the riches of heaven and earth be multiplied unto them.

The thronging Saints inundated the infant city. The cattle and horses of the newcomers trampled down the light fences and destroyed the crops without ceremony, save only the potatoes—and the tops even of these were eaten smooth to the ground. Anxious for housing, the Saints piled into the stockade as they arrived, and the accommodations proved entirely inadequate. Two more blocks on the south were set aside for an extension of the Old Fort and construction began at once. "Considering all the circumstances," John Smith, the patriarch, wrote to Brigham on October 14, "great union and harmony prevail in our midst and a determination to receive the epistle of your quorum as the standard, and to uphold the established authorities."

Early in October the High Council in the valley was given something serious to think about. John Young reported that four men had gone north to Goodyear's post with their families and could not be regarded as being in good faith. Forthwith, the marshal was ordered to bring back the runaways, and on October 11 he reported that the dissatisfied Saints had promised to return, though with an ill grace; they had roundly cursed the authorities and told the marshal in plain words that they "did not like so much bondage." The dissidents took their time about returning, and on October 24 the marshal was told to take nine men and escort them back to the encampment of the Saints. Ten days later he reported that he had done so.

The whole episode was disquieting, and Henry G. Sherwood recollected Brigham's advice that Goodyear should be bought out, if possible. The mountain man's establishment 40 miles away might become a haven for apostates, a soil to nurture conflicts and mobs. Moreover, if Goodyear were bought out, the Saints would become the Old Settlers, long a baneful phrase in Mormon history but one which might now be put to use. Sherwood brought up the matter before the High Council, and on November 9 a committee was appointed to see whether the means could be raised. Two days later they reported their lack of success. But by a happy stroke of fortune on November 16 Captain James Brown rode into the Old Fort, returned from his journey to California. In his saddlebags jingled nearly $5,000 in gold. A year ago on the Missouri River the battalion pay had proved the salvation of the Saints, and now again it would be instrumental in building up the Kingdom.

By a strange coincidence Goodyear turned up in town the same day Brown got back from California. With him was his brother Andrew, to whom Miles had written the letter Marcus Whitman took from the mountains in the fall of 1842. After five years the younger brother had journeyed to the Rockies in search of the wanderer, arriving at Miles's post on November 13. The mountain man did not recognize his brother at first, but Andrew knew Miles at once by the familiar tones of his voice and by his red hair, which hung down on his shoulders. So the Goodyear brothers had ridden down to the Mormon city to see the sights—and, perhaps, investigate the market for real estate.

The High Council promptly authorized Henry G. Sherwood and Captain Brown to purchase Goodyear's property if it could be obtained on fair terms, and on November 25 the transaction was consummated. For $1,950 the far-wandering Connecticut Yankee sold out all his rights to the place on the Weber. Miles Goodyear was freed to pursue his lucky star under other skies, and the Saints had become, beyond any question, the Old Settlers of this country. Both had reason to be pleased.

At the end of November Parley P. Pratt asked permission from the High Council to raise a company of 20 men and go south to Utah Lake to fish and make a claim and trade with the Indians. Finally the High Council authorized him to take a company of volunteers, mostly men without families, and go ahead and make a location in Utah Valley if he could effect a treaty.

The skiff built in the summer was put back upon wheels, and early in December Pratt had the pleasure of launching it into the bright waters of the fresh-water lake. "We sailed up and down the lake shore on the western side for many miles," his *Autobiography* says, "but had only poor success in fishing. We, however, caught a few samples of mountain trout and other fish." Such ill-success was surprising, for Utah Lake in early times teemed with fish. Discouraged by the outcome of the venture, after a day or so the company hauled the skiff back home. The Great Salt Lake itself still awaited exploration, but that could not be attempted until spring.

At Christmas time Miles and Andrew Goodyear rode back into town. After disposing of Fort Buenaventura they had ridden over to Henrys Fork to pick up Andrew's baggage, and now they were enroute to southern California by the Spanish Trail. Five dissatisfied Saints elected to go with them. The High Council at first ruled that they could not go, and sent the marshal to bring them back, but on mature reflection the authorities changed their minds. The little party, numbering ten in all, rode on to California. Next year Miles drove east 200 horses, driving them all the way to the Missouri frontier, and in the summer of 1849 he came back across the continent, stopping off briefly at his old post on the Weber before going on to California. He and Andrew located a rich claim on the headwaters of the Yuba, but Miles contracted a fever and died on November 12, 1849. Almost his last words, the grieving Andrew wrote home, were those he wished inscribed on his tombstone: *"The mountaineer's grave. He sleeps near the western ocean's wave."*

Fortunately that first winter in Salt Lake Valley was open and warm. It was impossible to provide adequate housing for all, and there could have been much suffering. But housing was not the only problem; though all had been instructed to bring provisions for a year and a half, supplies disappeared more rapidly than had been thought possible; and many members of the battalion were without food of any kind. Many went on rations as early as the fall of 1847. Although his faith "did not fail one particle," Dr. Priddy Meeks found it "a solemn time" when his family's provisions began to give out, and like many another he lived on rose haws, sego lilies, hawks, coyotes and everything else remotely edible.

By the beginning of March 1848, 871 acres had been sown to winter wheat and much of it was up and looking thrifty; 423 houses had been built for the 1,671 inhabitants of the infant city; and 2 gristmills and 4 sawmills were either in operation or under construction. Wanship's band in Salt Lake Valley had accepted their new white neighbors with a good spirit. Some cattle were run off by the Indians around Utah Lake, but the chief whipped the offenders and promised that they would do better. The vernal equinox brought cold weather and heavy snows. Some of the houses, as Isaac C. Haight remarked in his journal, were flat-roofed and leaked very badly, making it unpleasant for the occupants, and throughout April the winter wheat seemed to offer only a discouraging prospect of a crop. Still, he wrote, "we trust in the Lord who has brought us here and believe that He will sustain us and not permit us to perish."

Albert Carrington had missed out on his contemplated August voyage on Utah Lake, but on April 19, 1848, he and five others, Thomas J. Thurston, Joseph Mount, Madison D. Hambleton, Jedediah M. Grant and William W. Potter, launched the skiff in the Jordan at the North Temple ford for an exploration of Great Salt Lake itself. Fashioned from 5 fir planks, the boat was 15 feet 4 inches long and 4 feet 4 inches wide, sufficiently large for the 6 men and their baggage.

The first afternoon they wound 15 miles down the Jordan, finding the channel good and the current strong. A mud hen was blown out of the air next morning, and the skiff was christened the *Mud Hen.* They rowed downstream another two miles, and then the Jordan spread out without leaving any channel. Resignedly the crew climbed out and hauled the boat 4 miles across the shallows. Not a living thing was discovered in the water, though waterfowl flew about in great abundance.

Finally reaching deeper water, the crew got back into the boat to steer for Antelope Island, called by the Mormon explorers "Porpoise Island," for a creature one of the brethren from the city had sworn he saw in the lake. The water soon shoaled, and they had another half-mile pull across a bar. Then the water deepened, but a mile and a half or so off the island the water again shoaled, and the *Mud Hen* struck bottom. At a distance they could discern several Indian ponies and three Indians, but nobody felt like undertaking the long hike to shore for a closer investigation; they chose to veer off into deeper water. When finally they made for shore again, they got to within a hundred yards of a beach before striking bottom. Shouldering the loading, they splashed ashore through the fiery waters of the sunset, encamping on the east side of the island some six miles from its northern point.

Next morning they had a closer look at the island. It was covered with good grasses, bunch grass prevailing. There was an abundance of starchroot, many sunflowers and rosebushes, some sage, a few serviceberry bushes, a few willows and some shrubbery in the ravines. A few antelope tracks, a lone antelope and two sage hens were seen.

Altogether, the island struck them as an excellent place for grazing livestock. A number of brackish springs broke out in the belt of land between the main shore and the beach, and while the resulting bed, slimy and rather oozy, was unpleasant for boatmen to cope with, the springs would be excellent for stock.

Returning to the skiff, they moved north in the lee of the island. A few miles short of the northernmost point, a narrow, pebbly beach invited them. They waded ashore and filled their keg at a large spring of cold mineral water before making for the small, triangular island Frémont had explored in 1843.

Four hundred yards off Frémont they ran aground and again had to wade ashore over a tufa bed full of holes and short channels. On the island they found onions, starchroot and wild parsnips in profusion, together with some sage and greasewood and much fine bunch grass. Finding also plenty of blue heron and goose eggs, they made off with 150 of them. Albert Carrington's lively curiosity extended to souvenir hunting as well as to geologizing, and he made a determined but fruitless search for the object-end of Frémont's telescope. After casting about for a suitable name, the explorers named this island, for the shape of its summit, "Castle Island"—a name which stuck for many years. Going again aboard the *Mud Hen,* they sailed to the northern extremity of the island and toward sunset made a landing on a narrow, rocky beach. The greatest depth of water found during the day was 10½ feet, while the average depth was about 6 feet.

On the fourth day they ran west by north for "a high point of land," Promontory Point. Three of the crew landed to explore, while the other three coasted on north. The land party found a number of dwarf junipers and two springs of good, pure water, with many other springs of more brackish taste. There was the usual fine bunch grass, and scattered onions and starchroots. To regain the boat the three men had to wade three-fourths of a mile through knee-deep mud and water. They were now in Bear River Bay, and here, off the outlets of the Weber and the Bear, the lake water freshened so much that it answered fairly well for drinking purposes.

At nightfall they turned west again in search of a campsite. Characteristically, the water shoaled very soon. For a mile and a half they dragged the skiff over the shallows. Then, disgusted, they left it and splashed the final mile to shore, camping on the Promontory at a long, high ledge of basalt, from the base of which issued numerous brackish springs. In the morning, April 23, they climbed the mountain heights to examine the lay of the land with their spy glass. They discovered, Albert Carrington says, that they were north of the outlet of the Weber, which flowed into the lake in a wide, shallow channel; they also saw that their boat was as far north as it could go in this bay, which "from the shallowness of the water and the extensive mud flats on the east, north and west sides of it," they named Mud Bay [Bear River Bay]. They were glad enough to turn south again, but they had to haul the *Mud Hen* three miles through the shallows before reaching eight inches of water. All clambered aboard, and with a spanking breeze in their favor sailed smartly down the east coast of Frémont Island to a landing in a fine rock harbor on the west coast of Antelope. In seven hours they had sailed 42 miles without shipping so much as a half-pint of water.

To the west loomed the peninsula soon to become known as Stansbury Island; but which they called Dome Island, from a fine dome near its center. They were disinclined to investigate the western half of the lake as they had the eastern half, and on the morning of the twenty-fourth they steered for the salt works at the south shore of the lake. Seeing no one there, on rounding Antelope Island they bore easterly for home. They soon got into shoal water and when within a mile and a half of land, ran aground. Each man taking his gun and provisions, they waded ashore and hiked back to the city. Worn out by their struggles to navigate the salt waters, Madison Hambleton suggested what his companions regarded as "a very appropriate and characteristic name for the Lake, viz, The briny shallow in contradistinction to 'the briny deep.'"

The *Mud Hen* itself had a final utility in the making of the West. A year later one of the lake explorers, Thomas Jefferson Thurston, hauled the boat north to Bear River for ferrying purposes. To the *Mud Hen* the forty-niners who traveled by way of Great Salt Lake City owed their dry-shod passage of the Bear.

A series of frosts during May kept striking at the crops, and as early as May 22 John Taylor noted that in some districts crickets and other insects were "very destructive to the rising vegetation," though he took comfort in the fact that their ravages were not such as to create any general alarm. On May 28 there was another heavy frost. Isaac C. Haight walked among the gardens to survey them in discouragement. Beans, cucumbers, melons, pumpkins and squash had all been killed; and in his journal he made a further note: "Corn hurt some and some wheat killed and the crickets are injuring the crops."

Eliza R. Snow added in her own journal, "This morning's frost in unison with the ravages of the crickets for a few days past, produces many sighs & occasionally some long faces with those that for the moment forget that they are Saints." By June 4 the combination of frosts and crickets was creating open alarm. The crickets appeared to be eating the heads off the grain as fast as it headed out, and the prospects for grain did not seem bright. Many of the Saints were beginning to think of leaving the valley for fear of starvation, Isaac Haight observed; but he was comforted to think that the Lord who brought them here was able to sustain them even if their crops failed, for the Earth was the Lord's and the fulness thereof.

Surely it was a miracle, the coming of the gulls. This was the way of it, as Priddy Meeks remembered it:

"Apostle Rich stood in an open wagon and preached out of doors. It was a beautiful day and a very salom one to. While preaching he says, brotherin we do not want you to part with your wagons and teams for we might need them intimateing that he did not know but we might have to leave. . . . At that instant I heard the voice of fowels flying over head that I was not acquainted with. I looked up and saw a flock of seven gulls. In a few minutes there was another larger flock passed over. They came faster and more of them until the heavens were darkened with them and lit down in the valley till the earth was black with them and they would eat crickets and throw them up again. A little before sundown they left for Salt Lake. . . . In the morning they came back again and continued that course until they had devoured the crickets and then left Sinedie and never returned. I guess this circumstance changed our feeling considerable for the better."

The Sea Gull Monument in Salt Lake City's Temple Square commemorates that miracle. It must be remarked, however, that, in writing to Brigham Young on June 9 in the midst of these events, the authorities in the valley noted only, "the crickets have done a considerable damage to both wheat and corn, which has discouraged some, but there is plenty left if we can save it for a few days. The sea gulls have come in large flocks from the lake and sweep the crickets as they go; it seems the hand of the Lord is in our favor."

At the time, the colonists exhibited a thorough matter-of-factness about the miracle. Those keeping intermittent daily journals did not mention the gulls, not even the zealously poetic Eliza R. Snow, and on June 21 all that the authorities had to add on the subject was that the crickets were "still quite numerous and busy eating, but between the gulls our efforts and the growth of crops we shall raise much grain in spite of them."

As the months went by, the story of the gulls took on a different aspect. When the war of the gulls and the crickets was renewed for a time in the spring of 1849, it could be seen to be as plainly "a miracle in behalf of this people," as was the sending of the quails in the camp of the Israelites.

This idea has pleased the Saints. It is equally out of gratitude and the hunger for miracle that the white-winged sea gulls today wheel across the Utah skies with their sharp, shrill cry, protected alike by taboo and written law. The crickets are long gone; when swine and fowl were allowed to run at large and when irrigation ditches became moats to entrap and drown them, they soon disappeared. The sea gulls still sweep in from the lake to follow behind the plow and the harrow, to pilfer from orchards, or to feed upon scraps from school children's lunches. Brazenly self-assertive, greedy and ill-mannered, the sea gulls yet are enshrined in an idea that will not be allowed to die.

Harvesting began late in July; the wheat looked better than expected, though it was very short in consequence of not being irrigated in season. By August 1 most of it had been cut and some of it was very good. The first harvest feast was celebrated in the valley on August 10 with songs of praise and thanksgiving, music and dancing, the firing of cannon and the shout of *"Hosannah to God and the Lamb, forever and ever!"* This harvest feast has never again been celebrated; ever since, the pioneer fiesta has taken place on July

24, the anniversary of Brigham Young's arrival in Salt Lake Valley.

Messengers from the oncoming immigration began reaching the valley early in August. Most of the Saints arrived in late September and early October. Brigham Young himself reached the valley on September 20. He had departed Winter Quarters on May 26, leaving, as he wrote in his journal, his houses, mills and the furniture he had acquired during his sojourn there, the fifth time he had left his home and property since he embraced the gospel of Jesus Christ. Once again only, and then as an offering only, would this sacrifice be required of him. He had brought his people to a final refuge, and he could take satisfaction in their rejoicing. "Thus ends this long and tedious journey from the land of our enemies," Hosea Stout characteristically wrote in his journal, "& I feel free and happy that I have escaped from their midst."

The destinies of the Saints, however, were bound up with some of the most violent energies that have exploded in American life. Some of the battalion boys, laboring at a mill for John A. Sutter on the South Fork of the American River, had been present in January when James Marshall brought from the millrace flecks of a dully gleaming metal. They had themselves dug the yellow metal from the streambeds. Four of their number, William and Nathan Hawks, Sanford Jacobs and Richard Slater, had left San Francisco on April 1 as an express to carry east Sam Brannan's *California Star* heralding the news. They had gone via Great Salt Lake City, pushing on from there July 9 and passing the westbound Saints west of Laramie on July 27. Their news, however, created not a ripple of interest either in the valley or in the Camp of Israel; the Saints were principally interested to hear that those of Brannan's company who had settled on the San Joaquin had vacated in favor of the mosquitoes.

It was a different matter entirely when a large detachment of returning battalion members reached Great Salt Lake City on September 28. Among their number were some who, like James S. Brown, Azariah Smith and Henry W. Bigler, had been on the ground when Marshall made his discovery. All had dug gold themselves, and knew the richness of the find. . . . It was impossible for Brigham to foresee the madness that would seize upon the States this fall as reports from California flooded in; it was impossible to foresee the tide of immigration that would roll west within the year. But he must have felt a certain disquiet as he pondered the news. Already there were those who felt restless and insecure in the valleys of the mountains. And he could reflect, again, that the Saints had always been equal to adversity: were they able also to cope with prosperity?

Those incoming battalion members had completed a labor of trainfinding in the region of the Great Salt Lake. Early in July 1848 Parley P. Pratt had made the preliminary reconnaissance for his Golden Pass route through the Wasatch, though this route required much work and was not used until 1850. But more important was the route north around Great Salt Lake which intersected the Fort Hall road to California at City of Rocks. Samuel Hensley, en route back to California with ten men after testifying in the Frémont court-martial, early in August had attempted to take Hastings' Cutoff. He had found the going so miry, however, that he had turned back to the Mormon city and instead gone north around the lake. It was a much "nearer" route he pioneered, and when he met the eastbound battalion boys far down the Humboldt, he gave them a waybill of his road. The homing soldiers were more than willing to try Hensley's cutoff, and their wagons cut around the north shore of the lake a track which was nothing less than a road; almost at once it became known as the Salt Lake Road or the Salt Lake Cutoff. Though longer than Hastings' Cutoff, it was less hazardous, and at all seasons of the year it afforded grass and good water. With the finding of this road the immigrant trails about the Great Salt Lake were complete, save only the cutoff James Hudspeth found in June 1849 from the bend of the Bear to Raft River, a little north of City of Rocks. The network of trails was ready, a stage for a spectacular drama in American history.

The Saints who poured into Salt Lake Valley in the fall of 1848 boosted the population to nearly 5,000. The pressures of this population burst the bounds of the city at once. Although an addition was made to the plat of Great Salt Lake City, there was a serious question about the sufficiency of the water supply for a city of such proportions, when every man must be a farmer. The next step logically was to lay off cities north and south.

Expansion northward had already begun. The Davis Valley had been used for herding purposes in the fall of 1847, when Peregrine Sessions located on the site of Bountiful, Thomas Grover on the site of Centerville, and Hector Haight on the site of Farmington. Still farther north was Brownsville, Goodyear's old "Fort Buenaventura"; Captain Brown had taken possession of the fort early in January. This expansion northward, however, was in the direction of the Oregon Trail and gentile corruption; Brigham looked more interestedly toward the south. A few of the Saints he located in this fall of 1848 between the Cottonwood creeks, ten miles south. But this was a mere temporizing with the destiny of the Saints. Brigham had larger plans developing in his mind.

It was not enough merely to occupy the chain of narrow valleys in the vicinity of the Great Salt Lake. There was, Brigham saw clearly, nothing less than an empire at stake, all the lands from the Rockies to the Sierra Nevada, and from the Oregon Territory south to the Colorado—uncounted thousands of square miles. As rapidly as he could find the resources, he meant to pre-empt that empire, occupy all the fertile valleys and forestall the gentiles. Access to the sea might be important. Accordingly, as a first step in his plans for the upbuilding of the Kingdom of God, Brigham directed Amasa Lyman to take a company of 20 men, find a road to the Gulf of California, and there locate a site for a settlement.

Before that should be done, however, Brigham saw the necessity of instituting important changes in the order of the Kingdom. He must be enabled to select the men he wanted. The Mormon Battalion had painfully exhibited the deficiencies of the volunteer system; he had had to plead and cajole to get his men; he had had insufficient control over them after enrolling them; and he had had to explain and justify himself when things did not go altogether according to plan. All this was violative of proper order. To the congregation in Great Salt Lake City on November 26, 1848, Brigham announced the shape he proposed to give the future.

The new order of things meant that men might be called at any time for any purpose, that it was equally a mission whether a man went to preach the gospel in South Africa or to colonize a desert outpost. A man's life belonged to the church; when he was "called," his standing in the priesthood was at stake, and his hope of salvation.

He might have lived ten years in one place, broken the earth and made it blossom, but if he was "called" for a mission of colonization, he must sell out and go. It was not enough that he should leave his property and go; where a man's wealth was, there his heart was also, and a man must serve God with a whole heart.

Thus foreshadowed on this cold November Sunday was a method of warfare with the desert, a technique of colonization. By it the Saints were made into an instrument by which the Kingdom might be builded as the Lord God, through his servant Brigham, should require, and the instrument was one that God's vicegerent would show to be admirably suited to his hand.

It is one of history's small ironies that the California expedition never got off. Next spring, instead, Amasa Lyman was designated to carry to the Saints in California an epistle warning, among other things, against letting a little shining dust, or filthy lucre, lead them astray. The Saints were also reminded that they had it in their power to do much good by forwarding their tithing and donations: their offerings were "now needed by the poor Saints, and the Lord has put it into your power to help them, and your stewardship will be required at your hands; and as you give, so it will be given unto you."

The restlessness in the valley was heightened by the excessive severity of the weather, as compared with the first winter. Most of the winter the ground was covered with snow; the wind at times seemed to blow a hurricane, and there were those, like Thomas Bullock, who awakened each morning disposed to thank God that they had not frozen to death during the night. The cattle experienced great difficulty in finding forage, and the herdsmen had to range at great distances from the city, exposing the cattle to annoying depredations by the Indians in Utah Valley. The harvest of 1848 had fallen below expectations, and the immigrants of that fall, like those of the preceding year, had come with insufficient provisions. By mid-December some price controls had become necessary, and the High Council decided that beef should be sold at 2½ cents per pound on foot and 3 or 3½ cents per pound over the butcher's counter. Since this price control was purely voluntary, however, it was of very little effect, and by February the owners of beef cattle were declining to sell at any price unless payment was made in gold coin or dust.

In the same sermon in which he raked down the gold-hungry, Brigham dressed down the profiteers, telling the butchers that as there were many who had beef to sell and would not take paper money, they should go and kill fat cattle anyhow, paying the owners a fair price for them; they might commence with his, so that nobody should have reason to murmur. The people need not be afraid of starving, he told them; there was plenty of provisions for all. A committee should go among them and make an estimate of provisions, and those who had a surplus should impart to those who had not; again, they might begin with him.

Beef promptly returned to the market, and the committee on breadstuffs soon reported that there was in the valley about three-fourths of a pound per person per day for the next five months. Although this would make for lean rations, the amount would see the Saints through to early harvest, and Brigham promised unreservedly that the harvest would be a bountiful one.

While Brigham labored to get the community functioning smoothly within the framework of a dependable discipline, he also turned his attention to the problem of a civil government. At the time of the pioneer journey in 1847 the Great Basin had been Mexican territory, but the land had been ceded by Mexico in the Treaty of Guadalupe Hidalgo. By the time Brigham had left the frontier for the last time, in May, it had become reasonably certain that the treaty would be ratified by the Congresses of the two nations. Late in the fall news of the ratification reached the valley. The necessity therefore had arisen to work out a government within the framework of the American Constitution. If the Saints took the initiative, they might get a government suited to their desires. If they waited, one might be imposed upon them, and they might well be fearful lest such a government fall into the hands of their enemies.

In December 1848 a memorial to Congress for a territorial government was drafted, and the gathering of signatures commenced. By the time it was sent east in May, the petition was 22 feet long and bore 2,270 signatures. The memorial proposed that the new territory should include all the country between Oregon and Mexico and between the Rockies and the Sierra Nevada, plus a strip of the southern California seacoast.

In the valley itself the Saints could not wait for Congress to provide a government. There was the problem of the obstreperous minority who exhibited a disinclination to submit to the rule of the High Council, and there was also some question about the legality of action taken against the Indian cattle thieves in Utah Valley, four of whom were killed at the beginning of March in a sharp encounter at Battle Creek. A provisional government more conformable to American political ideas than an ecclesiastical government was clearly called for. Accordingly, the High Council on March 4, 1849, voted that the marshal give notice of a public meeting at the Old Fort on March 12 "for the purpose of electing and appointing officers for the government of the people in the valley of the G.S.L. and vicinity, until the petition of the people be granted by the United States for a Territorial Government."

In actuality, the election was a plebiscite, the Council settling upon the names of those who were to be nominated for office, and the people sanctioning these names by unanimous vote. Brigham Young was elected governor, Willard Richards secretary and Heber C. Kimball chief justice; these three men already comprised the First Presidency of the Church. Two associate justices, a marshal, an attorney-general, an assessor and collector, a treasurer and a supervisor of roads were also elected. The bishops of the 19 wards were elected magistrates, while beyond the bounds of the valley additional magistrates were elected for Weber River (Ogden), North Cottonwood (Farmington), North Mill Canyon (Bountiful), South Cottonwood (Murray), Big Cottonwood and Mill Creek precincts.

Early in the summer this provisional government was transformed as the provisional State of Deseret. The General Assembly of the provisional state assembled in July in accordance with a constitution meanwhile drafted, and elected a delegate to take to Congress a memorial asking for outright statehood in preference to territorial status. It was this memorial rather than the one requesting a territorial government that was finally presented to Congress. Similar memorials were presented from California and New Mexico, but only California was granted statehood, the rest of the Mexican Cession being set off as the territories of Utah and New Mexico.

Although the boundaries of Deseret were cut down and nothing came of the covetous desire of the Saints for their outlet to the sea, Utah was still a territory of extraordinary size, extending all the way from the Rocky Mountains to the Sierra Nevada. And they were more fortunate than most new territories in job-hungry Washington; their own Brigham Young was named governor.

That outcome of the fight for statehood was, however, a year and a half in the future as the Saints, in the spring of 1849, commenced what must be the critical year in making the high desert valleys yield a sufficient sustenance. As a foretaste of the future, a colonizing mission under John S. Higbee late in March was dispatched to Utah Valley to build Fort Utah (other missions would go to Sanpete Valley in November and to Little Salt Lake Valley a year later). But in Salt Lake Valley the Saints began removing from the forts to their city lots, and began working in their gardens. Those who had the most virulent cases of the "yellow fever," as the gold hunger was called, rode north toward the California trail as soon as the grass showed green, but the great majority of the brethren labored at their fields of corn and wheat and their garden plots.

Throughout the spring provisions were scant; Priddy Meeks says in his quaint fashion that "the valley from a human standpoint presented nothing better than extreme suffering if not starvation," with the Saints scattering hither and thither, and eating whatever they could get. "And while all this was going on it looked like there was a splendid chance for going naked."

But God was looking out for his own. Just about the time Priddy's potatoes were in the best condition for "grabling," the gold diggers arrived in Great Salt Lake City, "nearly perished for vegetables," and not caring about the price, with plenty of dry groceries to trade. Very soon, Priddy and many another Saint was laying in "goods, bacon, tea, coffee and sugar besides many other articles," becoming "not only rich but well to live as regards groceries."

The first forty-niners arrived June 16, a pack mule company under Captain G. R. Paul, and the first companies with wagons came along six days later. Thereafter the immigrants came in by the thousands; before the summer was over, perhaps 10,000 passed through the valley, exchanging their worn stock for fresh, and their dry groceries and manufactured articles for milk, butter and fresh vegetables.

David H. Mann

Courtesy Utah State Department of Publicity & Industrial Development

The Lucin Cutoff seen from Little Mountain; in background, the Promontory and Promontory Point.

D. Eldon Beck   The Mormon struggle with the red rock desert typified at Fruita, Utah.

Goods sold cheaper in the Mormon city than their first cost price at the Missouri River.

Brigham Young watched them come and go throughout the summer, bidding the Saints be mindful that iron and coal had made England great, while gold had corrupted Spain, telling them that there was more delusion, the people on this continent were more perfectly crazy, than had ever been the case since the days of Columbus. Gold had ridded the community of its most miserable elements; the Saints were being sifted. "There is no effect without a cause," he moralized. "The Lord revolutionizes the world at his pleasure. He takes up one kingdom and sets down another. He will cause that gold mine to be a destruction to the nation that has cast us out, and that measure will be pressed down and running over, and then the cry will be 'Measure unto them double for what they have done unto my Saints.'" Yea, these very days had been prophesied by the leaders of the Saints for 18 years. "God Almighty will give the United States a pill that will puke them to death, and that is worse than lobelia. I am prophet enough to prophesy the downfall of the government that has driven us out. . . . Wo to the United States! I see them going to Death and destruction. I see them greedy after death and destruction."

He meditated on this image of the future and lifted his voice again to the Saints. "Our duty is to let our light shine, to hand out the words of eternal life and save those that can be saved."

Chapter 12

Stansbury's Survey

WITH the mail that got in from the States on July 1, 1849, came late numbers of the St. Louis *Republican*. In the issue of May 9 an article struck the eye of the Saints, and they folded the unwieldy sheet to read this news with close attention. So the story read, the government was sending an expedition to make "a trigonometrical and nautical survey of the Great Salt and Utah Lakes, and the surrounding country lying in the northern portion of Upper California."

Why this sudden interest in the Great Salt Lake? Was the purpose of this expedition exploration only? The Regiment of Mounted Riflemen was traveling overland to Oregon this year, and there were reports that a fort was to be built in the Bear River Valley, or perhaps near Fort Hall. Were these coincidences only?

Word of Captain Howard Stansbury's expedition filtered along the trail ahead of him. On July 12 he had arrived at Fort Laramie. On August 11 he had reached Fort Bridger. . . . Finally, on August 24, with the tail end of the California immigration, the government wagons jounced down into Salt Lake Valley. Here was the fact. Whatever the expedition boded would now become clear.

Stansbury himself had remained behind at Fort Bridger to await Bridger's pleasure in exploring a possible new route from the fort to the valley of the Great Salt Lake. Lieutenant J. W. Gunnison brought the wagons on to the Mormon city. On setting out from Fort Leavenworth, Gunnison had been ill with a fever, but he had persisted in coming, even though during much of the journey he had to travel flat on his back in one of the wagons. So when, from the summit of Big Mountain on August 22, he got his first glimpse of "the Salt Lake valley & of the Great Basin of California," he felt that he had reached a turning point in life. Only a short time before, he had been prostrate with fever and its consequences, and now by

224

the mercy of Providence he was well enough to attend to the duties of conducting the train and to ride nearly all day on horseback.

Immediately on his arrival the young topographical engineer went looking for Brigham Young. He was unsuccessful, but next morning a chance acquaintance introduced him to Bishop Joseph L. Heywood. Brigham Young was found at a neighbor's, and Gunnison was taken over to see him. The Mormon leader came out and, as Gunnison made careful note in his journal:

"we had a few moment's talk about our 'Survey' & parted to all appearance as good friends as before. Under much apparent indifference he showed anxiety—& I hear from various sources that our survey is regarded with great jealousy—and have had warning that secret means would be used to prevent any maps being made of the valley—even that our lives are in danger, as a hint from *the one man* [who] could take them."

Here was disquieting news for Stansbury when he rode into camp six days later. A man of forthright impulses, the captain went to see Brigham Young at once. It was a fortunate interview; the two men liked each other on sight. As soon, Stansbury subsequently wrote in his *Report,* as the true object of the expedition was fully understood, he was informed that the authorities were much pleased that the exploration was to be made; that they had themselves contemplated something of the kind and that they would cheerfully furnish any assistance they could. The captain was delighted with this reception, for he understood all too well that a program of "masterly inactivity" could limit his operations to the point of making it impossible to do his job.

The job was a novel one, anyway. Stansbury had been occupied with the construction of lighthouses on the coast of Florida when, at the end of March, his services were requisitioned to survey routes to and from the valley of the Great Salt Lake and to make a correct survey of the lake itself, not neglecting soundings, "so that its capacity for Navigation and transportation of supplies may be known." He got to work at once. Gunnison was assigned the job of triangulating Salt Lake and Utah Valleys, and the highly recommended Albert Carrington was hired to assist him, while Stansbury himself set out for Fort Hall to reconnoiter a wagon road and pick up supplies. He intended to return with a pack mule party via the west shore of Great Salt Lake to get a better idea of the problems its survey would entail.

His road north was the same Frémont had taken in 1843, up the Malad to its head, over the divide to Rattlesnake Creek, down to the Bannock and to the Snake a few miles below Fort Hall; it became for many years the standard road north and south. On October 9 the supply train arrived, and Stansbury turned south again. At the crossing of the Bear on October 19 he separated from his provision wagons, sending them on to Great Salt Lake City under Lieutenant George M. Howland, who had been detached from the Mounted Rifles to assist in the fall surveys. His own party of seven men, including his geologist, Dr. James Blake, and his guide, Auguste Archambeau, who four years earlier had crossed the salt desert with Frémont, then embarked on the "circumambulation" of the lake. They had 16 mules, 3 India rubber bags and a 5-gallon keg for packing water, a small tent without poles, a wall tent fly, provisions and blankets.

Stansbury was frankly advised that his expedition of reconnaissance was somewhat hazardous at this season of the year when water was extremely scarce. He wrote in his journal, "I was credibly informed that numbers of trappers & others had repeatedly tried the circuit & had failed being obliged to return with the loss of most of their animals." But he determined to make the attempt at least.

They had trouble crossing the deep, narrow Malad, and as a foretaste of troubles to come bivouacked on the ground, since poles for pitching the tents were unobtainable. Next morning they rode west four miles on the Salt Lake Road toward City of Rocks, and then turned sharply south to double the lofty Promontory. All day they rode south, covering some 22 miles, and when they halted for the night, it was on a small stream so bitterly salt as to be almost unfit to drink.

Stansbury was not a man who ever willingly traveled on a Sunday, but this was no place to observe the Sabbath; he was about to find, in fact, that this region was no respecter whatever of Sabbaths. Next morning he resumed the journey down the east side of the

Promontory, and toward noon reached a spring of at least tolerable water, where he could halt for the day.

On Monday, late in the afternoon, the party doubled the point of the Promontory. Though the immense numbers of waterfowl made a profound impression, with thousands of acres literally covered with wild geese, ducks and beautiful white swans, the scenery was depressing, the bleak shores of the lake treeless and naked. From the tip of the Promontory, Frémont Island rose boldly to the south and its aspect, which had induced the Mormon explorers of 1848 to name it Castle Island, induced Stansbury to think of naming it Coffin Island. The view, however, began to seem more interesting as they began the journey back up the western side of the Promontory. Stansbury wrote in his journal:

"The Western limit of the lake was lost in the dreamy mist which seemed to cover it as with a thin indistinct veil, which would not suffer you to define any object with precision, whilst it half revealed the whole, leaving the rest to the exercise of the imagination. The water to the west appears to be bold & very deep, & enough has already been seen to convince me of the absolute necessity of a large sail boat from which to supply the different surveying parties on the shore with water & provisions. Wood here there is absolutely none. Not enough to put up the necessary [triangulation] stations."

Timber for the stations would in most instances have to be transported by water, as would supplies of fresh water. He began to realize what an immense job he had taken on: "I fear my force will not be sufficient to complete it next year."

He could not but be impressed by the utter desolation of this country he had come so far to explore; it seemed "barren desolate & forlorn to the last degree. The silence of the grave seems to hang over it. Not the note of a bird, nor the chirp of an insect to be heard." There was difficulty, too, in obtaining water for the animals.

They found the going close to the lake miry, and often had to keep at a respectful distance from it. Indeed, after they rounded the head of Spring Bay this reconnaissance ceased to be one of the lake proper and became a reconnaissance of the Salt Desert; when they headed south again, they were a good deal west of the lake itself, though the desert in some lights was hardly distinguishable from the salt waters of the lake, with islandlike mountains lifting deceptively from the plain.

Water of every kind disappeared as they rode southwesterly into the Salt Desert. Even the lake itself vanished and they could see no signs of it in any direction; at the end of the second day's journey it became a serious point to find water for the mules, who had been without it all that time. In the miry going the mules began to give out, and on Sunday, October 28, Stansbury faced up to the fact that the lives of all their animals depended on finding water next day. He turned west across a salt plain level as a floor, staggered to realize that this field of solid salt was at least 10 miles long and 7 wide. But water, not salt, was their obsessive interest. Thankfully, during Monday afternoon, they reached a running stream at the foot of the Pilot Range. The mules had been giving out throughout the afternoon, and another half-dozen miles would have finished them.

Archambeau pointed out where Frémont had encamped four years before. It was, he said, a 70-mile desert they would have to cross in retracing Frémont's trail to the south end of the lake. So they remained in camp three full days to recruit the mules. On the third day Archambeau's mule was run off by some Indians. The only wonder, Stansbury thought wryly, was that more were not stolen; who would have thought to set a guard in such a place?

On November 3, after filling the keg and India rubber bags with water, and loading the mules with all the grass they could carry, they moved south a couple of miles along the foot of Pilot Peak to intersect Hastings' Cutoff, and on the "road from Mormon City," as Stansbury called it, set out to cross the Salt Desert again.

There might now be a beaten track across that desert, but its passage could never be easy. They plodded on until midnight, a recent rain having transformed the level plain into a quagmire. Dense clouds obscured the moon and threatened more rain. They passed four wagons and one cart "with innumerable articles of clothing, tools chests trunks books &c yokes, chains, & some half dozen dead oxen," probably sad remains of the Donner party, for the forty-niners had not taken Hastings' Cutoff. Encamping finally, they warmed themselves around a fire fed by a part of an ox yoke, the remains of a barrel and part of an old wagon bed. The mules were given two pint cups of water apiece, and some of the grass packed from Pilot Peak.

The night was windy and cold, and even after sunrise it blew as though the very devil were in it, so that "great coats leggings & all appliances were put in reqn to keep in the animal heat." Since the wood was exhausted, they went without breakfast until they reached a ridge, in the shelter of which a tiny fire boiled their coffee. With cold bacon and bread, that was their only meal of the day. The last of the water was given to the mules, and just at nightfall they reached the western slope of the Cedar Mountains.

Large fires soon were blazing, but everyone was too exhausted to care about eating, and all rolled into their blankets. During the night it snowed and by morning the hills were white around them. As it was Sunday, and all were stiff beyond endurance, they remained in camp throughout the day. Next morning, however, they followed the Hastings road across Hastings Pass into Skull Valley, heartened by some green grass growing in a spring, the first they had seen since leaving Bear River. Their difficulties were now over; they moved on into Tooele Valley and east across Salt Lake Valley to the city of the Saints.

Obviously, Stansbury reflected, the Salt Desert had at one time been a part of the lake itself, and a rise of but a few feet in the lake level would flood the low, saline plain to the foot of the Pilot Range. Denuded of vegetation except for infrequent patches of greasewood and sage, it seemed utterly worthless as a place of human habitation.

He could foresee only one valuable use for the desert: "its extent, and perfectly level surface, would furnish a desirable space on which to measure a degree of the meridian."

Meanwhile Gunnison had proceeded with the surveying operations. On September 20 he rode with Carrington to the south shore of the lake, making, he remarked slyly, quite an incident in the expedition: "having been a month in the vicinity & not having seen it, the existence of the Salt Lake might well have been doubted— now the reality is Known." He bathed in the clear, bright waters, finding the reports of their buoyancy in no wise exaggerated.

Albert Carrington was dispatched to survey the mouth of the Jordan, and the Mormon convert from Wales, Dan Jones, was hired to build a yawl for carrying on the exploration of the lake in the spring. The measuring of the base line was attended with considerable difficulty, what with haze, smoke, wind and mud. A momentary excitement aroused his men over a discovery of "gold" in a coarse mud in which they labored, but it turned out to be of no nobler kind than shining mica and pyrites. Gunnison's men got drunk occasionally, indulged in fistfights, and were sometimes insolent amid all the hard work. Some citizens made off with the theodolite, but it was fortunately recovered through the good offices of Brigham Young. On October 31 Gunnison admitted to himself that even with the help of Howland the survey was progressing very slowly—

"the consequence of misapprehension of directions by some & want of experience in all the workmen—The days are short & when a little cold it is hard starting out the party in the mornings. The current of the river is so strong & channel so crooked that we are obliged to transport the boat on a wagon & use it for crossing the stream only—We are now fairly in Utah valley & hope success for next month."

There was plenty of trouble even after the work in Utah Valley began. Rain made the work harder, and the camp was overrun by Ute begging for food. Howland, working on the shore line, found it marshy, filled with deep sloughs and springs which impeded progress on foot, while the tall reeds made it difficult to sight with the compass. Some of the beef cattle turned up missing, and to reclaim them from unsaintly Saints, Howland had to ride after the colonizing mission to Sanpete Valley, which had just passed by. It was November 18 before Stansbury arrived in camp. The work was prosecuted vigorously until December 4, but really wintry weather then set in and the party returned to Great Salt Lake City to take up winter quarters.

The season passed not unpleasantly. Late in December Archambeau and two others were dispatched to the Uinta Basin to trade for horses which they were to take over to Fort Bridger, bringing them to the Mormon city in the spring. The rest of the party remained in Great Salt Lake City; their quarters consisted, Stansbury says, "of a small unfurnished house of unburnt brick or adobe, unplastered, and roofed with boards loosely nailed on, which, every time it stormed, admitted so much water as called into requisition all the pans and buckets in the establishment."

The friendly relations with the Saints continued. Stansbury commented on the high tone of morals and the habitual observance of good order and decorum in the community, and Gunnison remarked in his journal on "the very happy social state enjoyed by this community—being so much of one mind & always speaking to each other in terms of brotherhood."

The advice and assistance of the two officers was sought when, at the beginning of February, the Saints found it necessary to do something about the Indians in Utah Valley. Having an eye to the security of his own work still remaining to be done, Stansbury strongly urged that appropriate action be taken and placed arms and ammunition, tents and camp equipage at the disposal of the Mormon authorities, at the same time granting leave to Lieutenant Howland to go along as adjutant and give the militia some professional advice. His geologist, Dr. James Blake, likewise went along in the capacity of surgeon.

The "Fort Utah War" was soon over. Lieutenant Howland, recalled to duty with the Mounted Riflemen, brought news of its successful progress on his return to the city February 14, and the troops themselves came back on the twentieth. They had lost one of their number but had slaughtered several dozen of the Ute in a series of skirmishes which permanently broke the power of this tribe in Utah Valley and opened the way for a great expansion of colonizing activity.

Toward the end of March the weather began to moderate, and on April 3 the topographical engineers broke up their winter quarters to embark upon an adventurous spring on and about the salt lake.

As the best way of beginning his job, Stansbury intended to make a reconnaissance of the entire lake by water, during which he would erect triangulation stations upon prominent points about the shores and islands, thus enabling him to cover the whole surface with a series of triangles by which he might verify the work. He also intended establishing on the eastern shore of Antelope Island a small depot which might be supplied by land, the water over the Antelope Island bar not being high enough to impede travel to and from the mainland. On April 3, therefore, Albert Carrington was started for the island with the teams while Stansbury and Gunnison boarded their new yawl in the Jordan and began to work it down the river toward the lake.

They reached the bar at the mouth of the Jordan on April 4 and spent six vexatious hours in ice-cold water getting their boat over the bar at the river's mouth. They arrived at the camp on Antelope at dark, chilled and hungry after a six-hour pull in the teeth of a raw wind, glad to see the fires of Carrington's party blazing on the beach.

On April 5 Gunnison put up a station on Antelope Island, and the next morning Stansbury loaded most of the party into the boat for a similar labor on Frémont Island—a work attended with great labor, for the heavy poles had to be hauled up slopes frequently exceeding a 45° angle. Stansbury wrote in his *Report* that from the highest table of the island:

"rises an oblong rocky eminence, resembling, from some points of view, ruins of an ancient castle, whence it had received from the Mormons its name of 'Castle Island.' Frémont called it 'Disappointment Island.' I deemed it but due, however, to the first adventurous explorer of this distant region to name it after him who first set foot upon its shores, and have therefore called it *Frémont Island*."

The island was found to be 14 miles in circumference, possessing neither water nor timber. If it were possible to obtain water by boring, the captain thought, the island would be wonderfully adapted to use as a range for sheep and goats, since security from Indians and coyotes would be complete.

On the return trip to Antelope the wind was favorable, and they spread their sails to the breeze. Though the boat was heavy, it moved along "in all the dignity and complaisance of a first-rate craft, persuaded that no other of equal pretensions had ever floated on the bosom of the solitary waters." A name was requisite, and finally the party settled upon the *Salicornia,* or *Flower of Salt Lake.* But this was too fancy, and she became instead the *Sally.* The yawl was unequal to all the demands that must be made upon her; so three of the men were sent to the south end of the lake to fetch from there a flat-bottomed skiff. It was brought into camp on Sunday, April 7, and thenceforth to the end of the survey the lordly yawl and the humble, unnamed skiff were worked together.

On reaching Antelope Island, Carrington was dispatched to the city to bring out some needed things and the new hand, John Hudson, who during the first week had remained at the expedition's quarters in town.

Hudson has been unknown, hitherto, in the annals of the expedition. He was, from the internal evidence of his brief journal, an Englishman. It is possible that he was the J. Hudson who traveled from New York in the summer of 1849 with the Colony Guard, a company of forty-niners which broke up along the trail. Some of the guard went on to California by the Humboldt route, others joined with the party which, in search of a cutoff, opened the history of Death Valley, and some—including J. Hudson?—may have wintered in the Mormon city. Having a perceptive hand and eye, Hudson was hired in the capacity of artist—"draughtsman" on the payroll. On the march west to Utah the expedition had been accompanied by a young man of artistic talents, F. R. Grist, upon whose sketches were based many of the lithographs that illustrate the published *Report,* and all its art work has been attributed to him. Grist, however went north in February with Howland, and the lively views of lake scenery that illustrate Stansbury's *Report* originate, in reality, in the work that Hudson did during the spring of 1850.

Hudson's journal glows with sudden appreciations, whether for the "shiny mud" of the shallows, or for the "clear oily flame" of the sage and greasewood burned in campfires. Tumultuously heaped-up sunset clouds could compose for him a landscape so glowing "as might warm into enthusiasm even a peeper through a theodolite." He could talk about "the al fresco bed" of a night's encampment on the sandy shores of the lake, or, on finding a crow's egg in a heron's nest, decide that these birds, "so far as a community of houses &c are followers of Fourier." He could go for a swim in the lake with Carrington, and return "as salt & dry as a pickled herring" only to find "dinner over & the water all drank . . . the usual fate of day dreamers." He was entirely capable of writing off 24 hours in his journal in this saucy fashion: "Nil. Followed the example of old Pope Gregory & skipped a day." And he could comment on the preposterous shallowness of the lake: "we had a hearty laugh at the circumstance of the anchor of the yaul being above water." He had at all times an artist's eye and an artist's enthusiasms, a feeling for the mood of a landscape, a ranging fancy and a picturesque sense of humor. Except for this excerpt of his life, preserved with the journals of the Stansbury expedition, he seems to be blotted out of our history. And the loss is ours.

The uncelebrated hero of the expedition, however, is Albert Carrington. As Stansbury was the only one in the party who knew anything about sailing a boat, he had to take on his own shoulders the job of supplying the camp. Exhausting as that labor was, it did not compare with the arduous work of superintending the chain line which was Carrington's responsibility; it is said that he was rheumatic the rest of his life from the hardships and exposures that attended his work on this survey.

While Carrington was in town fetching Hudson and the supplies, Stansbury sailed for the western islands. Great difficulty was experienced in weathering the north point of Antelope, the wind being very high and the crew raw and awkward. They succeeded, finally, but only after carrying away the step of the foremast. Around the point they stopped to repair the damage, and before going on, placed a pole station on the small rocky island off the tip of Antelope. From this islet, which was covered with wild birds, they made off with 76 heron eggs; and this tiny island ever since has been Egg Island.

They then set sail for an island 20 miles west, soon to be named for Carrington, but reached it only after considerable difficulty. The strong wind carried away the step of one of the masts a second time, and the men were quite seasick, since none of them were accustomed to the water. They got their station up before nightfall, however, and next morning went on to an islet five miles to the north which, after a fancied resemblance, they called Quaker Hat Island. The name was soon shortened to Quaker Island but was changed later to Hat Island, a name that still endures, though an alternative name, Bird Island, has come into general use in recent years. The islet at that time evidently had no nesting birds.

From Hat Island they sailed to Frémont Island, having forgotten to clothe its station on their first visit. There was no wind, and the men had a weary row of it. In the late afternoon, when they left Frémont for Antelope, they again had to take to the oars, and they arrived in camp long after dark, worn out. In the two-day voyage among the islands they had seen nothing that promised much, except an abundance of roofing slate. But that, Stansbury thought, was something: with timber scarce and difficult of access, shingles last year in Great Salt Lake City had cost $10 a thousand

In crisscrossing the lake they had made soundings as they went, and the greatest depth located was 33 feet, between Hat Island and Frémont. Usually, they found the lake only five or six feet deep, and sometimes only a few inches. The depth of any part of the lake, they were now beginning to realize, depended to a remarkable extent on the wind. If it was blowing in one direction, large stretches of the bottom might be high and dry; if it was blowing in the opposite direction, they might sail even with the yawl over that same section of the lake bottom. And if the shallowness of this briny sea did not occasion sufficient difficulty, Stansbury reflected, "The prodigious distances between objects & the time occupied in passing from on[e] to another proves a serious impediment. Our boat is heavy & lumbersome, & moves like a log."

The encampment on Antelope Island was broken up on the morning of April 12, and the camp equipage and provisions were loaded on the boats for removal to a new base somewhere on the east shore of the Promontory. Bear River Bay being notoriously shallow, Stansbury was anxious that this part of the survey be completed as early as possible. After vainly seeking a place to land, they were forced to leave the yawl and trek a mile to shore through the heavy mud, carrying their provisions and equipage on their shoulders. Fortunately a spring was located near by; the country was not often so obliging.

Next morning the survey of the east shore of the Promontory was begun, Carrington and Stansbury running the chain line. With four of the men Gunnison went off in the skiff to reconnoiter the mouth of the Bear. This was an arduous, four-day job, and before Gunnison's party got back, they ran into trouble. They finished their job late in the afternoon of the sixteenth and were dragging the skiff west through the shallows of the eastern shore when a sudden violent gale beat upon them, accompanied by thunder, lightning, hail and furious rain. They endeavored to make their way with four men wading by the side of the skiff, but the powerful gale drifted them off course. Gunnison described their straits in his journal:

"The spray dashed over boat & men, the rain & hail came in torrents & the wind drove it home & soon all were wet to the skin. The mists shut down upon us & we could see but a few steps around us. It was nearly sunset & growing dark. The men became bewildered & despairing of reaching camp, declared they could not survive till morning. The snow began to fall more freely & the air more chill. The two men at the stern said that we were changing the course as soon as the order to move was again given; and soon declared that those at the bow leading had changed entirely around. To convince all that I knew the position of the locality, we opened the instrument box & set free the needle."

But it was growing too dark to read the needle. They turned back for the mud flat, fortunately coming into their track of the day before and following it some distance back. Finally they turned up the skiff, and Gunnison ripped out the bottom boards to keep them out of the mud, which was four inches deep. By this time the men were too benumbed to do much for themselves, and Gunnison herded them into "a *bunch* using the skiff for a shield against the fierce North snowstorm."

In a few hours there was a lull, and Gunnison directed the men to stand on the boards until the skiff was thrown down. Pulling out the two boards which partially covered the bottom, he then prepared, as he said, for a night's lodging:

"When the platform was made over the Knee & cross timbers eked out with thwart boards & pieces the best we could in the dark; and laid with the softest side down, that is the side with least sticky mud on it determined by feeling, particularly with a sore hand from which the bandages had got loose, I placed two men 'edge wise' & crawled down by the side of them. The boat was not wide enough for three to lay on their backs, nor draw up their knees in the approved way of 'spooning it'—Then the two extra men, for there were five of us, were laid on the lower three, so as to break joints, bringing their heads up to our arms.

"We had a bit of an old sail along, which in turning up the skiff had been well trampled in the mud—this was to be the night canopy, & had been dragged up one side & now stretched over us. The snow continued and though our bodies felt cold enough for congealing water there was warmth enough rising to melt the snow on the sail & let it trickle through to our evident discomfort. The cloth kept the cold blasts of wind from us, still we were a little disposed to find fault with it when it struck our hands or faces as it left so much greasy plaster upon them."

The snow ceased toward midnight, but the wind howled over them until daylight. Nearly frozen to death, they thanked God for the first pale streaks of dawn. Almost cheerfully they jumped into the icy mud and pushed the boat a couple of miles to water deep enough to float it. Two hours later they reached camp. Stansbury, who had kept fires burning all night and who had periodically fired guns to guide them in, had hot coffee and dry clothes awaiting them.

Even under these circumstances, Gunnison and his men could only be given a half-hour's nap, for it was necessary to move camp. But the boats ran aground southeast of Promontory, and at nightfall they had to make for Frémont Island. The water gave out entirely, and they had to be content with a small sip of coffee. Since the men were tired after much rowing and wading in the cold wind and water, only one tent was pitched, Stansbury says—for "Mr. G, who had had enough of sleeping out the night previous." The wind which had risen during the night whipped up some very respectable waves on the island beach, and the captain, as he lay in his blankets, perhaps had a homesick moment, for these waves, he wrote in his journal, "altho they did not 'make our island tremble,' reminded many of us of scenes far away, when far more extended billows paid their tribute to the strand."

Next morning they sailed for the western shore of the Promontory, going without breakfast for there was still no water. After carrying their things to shore and hiking two miles for water, the men had their fill of work. Since some were quite unwell from their previous exertions, and all were jaded, stiff and sore, Stansbury gave everybody the rest of the day off.

It rained that night and promised more in the morning, but Stansbury and Gunnison set out for Black Rock, leaving Carrington to proceed with the chain line. It was to be Gunnison's job now to survey the land east of the lake as far north as Bear River.

Enroute, they put up another triangulation station on the island which had been called Dome Island, but which by common consent was now being called Stansbury Island. After this business was attended to, the two officers proceeded on to Black Rock and thence into the City. At once they were entangled in affairs which never got into the captain's official *Report*.

When Stansbury was ordered on his western duty, he cast about for competent scientific assistance, for neither he nor Gunnison had any adequate knowledge of geology. In St. Louis he hired a physician recently come from England, Dr. James Blake, and in Blake's hands he placed the responsibility for attending to the scientific collections and making the geological notes. They got along well on the journey west, and Blake accompanied Lieutenant Howland on the expedition sent against the Ute by the Mormon authorities. On that expedition he had carried his collecting enthusiasm to such lengths as to hire Abner Blackburn and James Orr to cut off the heads of the slain Indians and pack them in a box he might ship back to Washington. Since Blake had expressed the wish to wind up some work, he had been left in the city when the spring surveys opened.

Now, however, the captain was painfully surprised to learn that Blake had departed their house, carrying off "all the mineralogical & botanical specimens, those of natural history, the meteorological Register & in fact every thing he could lay his hands on, books, fishing lines, hooks, paper &c &c leaving a note for me saying that he had left the party & carried these things off with him to secure his pay." To add insult to injury, Stansbury heard that the doctor had boasted that such had long been his intention, and that he had only waited until after the merchant, Livingston, had departed for the States, carrying a draft for $300 Stansbury had made out in his favor.

Furious, Stansbury dispatched an express to overtake Livingston with an order countermanding payment of the draft, and then took his troubles to Brigham Young. He found Brigham very soured in his feelings on Blake. The doctor had, it developed, submitted a bill for his services on the Utah expedition. The Mormon president advised the captain to go before one of the Mormon justices of the peace and obtain a search warrant to recover his property. Stansbury did so at once, and the property was finally recovered, though not without some digging in Blake's garden. By no means was this the last of this affair, however. Esquire W. Farr ruled that when Blake should make his report, as he had agreed in St. Louis to do, the captain should be liable for moneys due the doctor. Blake made such a report early in June, and when Stansbury returned it as being wholly inadequate, haled him before the courts of Deseret on a suit to collect $1,436 for services rendered.

After argument the case was nonsuited on the grounds that Blake had previously obtained a judgment from the justice of the peace for what was due him. Blake returned to the legal wars again next day, but Esquire Farr, in the lower court, decided that, as the terms of contract had not been complied with, there was no cause of action.

Stansbury heard the decision with great satisfaction; as he wrote in his journal, "Expect he will get tired before long." The fuming Blake soon went off to California. He settled in Sacramento, eventually acquiring a certain note as a man of medicine and consulting geologist. But not without a final effort to obtain his just dues. In the fall of 1850, and again in April 1852 he made an effort to collect his salary by writing to the Secretary of War some letters in which he had very hard things to say about the captain, not omitting to call him a habitual drunkard. Stansbury wrote stiff rebuttals to both letters, and the Secretary of War eventually advised Blake to save his breath, as he would not order payment of the sum claimed. In the light of all this controversy it is not strange that, save for an anonymous mention or two, Blake vanished from Stansbury's published *Report*, nor that Stansbury had a kind word to say for the Mormon courts of justice.

After that first legal skirmish with Blake Stansbury placed his property in the Mormon mint and returned to his proper labors.

The wind was blowing too violently to make it advisable to sail from Black Rock at once, and Stansbury used the time to experiment with the brining properties of the lake waters. Suspending a piece of fresh beef from a cord, he immersed it in the lake for something over twelve hours, by which time the meat was found to be, he said, "tolerably well cured." It was a useful discovery; henceforth, when they wished to preserve beef, they had only to pack it into barrels and fill the barrels with lake water. Meats put up in this manner, Stansbury believed, would remain sound and good as long as if prepared by orthodox methods; it was advisable, however, to mix fresh water with the salt, as too long immersion in the natural brine changed the character of the meat from corned beef to what sailors knew as "salt junk."

By sundown the wind had died enough so that it seemed practicable to sail for Promontory. The weather was clear but extremely cold, and as none of the men knew anything about managing a boat, Stansbury ordered them to wrap themselves in blankets and get some sleep while he steered north. By sunrise they were off the campsite on the Promontory. And none too soon, for the captain was in a state of near collapse from the effect of the cold and from sitting so long in one position without exercise. His men led him to his tent and put him to bed almost frozen, heaping on him all the bed clothes they could find, including the India rubber tent carpet. For half an hour Stansbury thought he would die, his vitals were so cold, but the buffalo skins began to heat him and he fell asleep until afternoon.

With his accustomed energy Carrington had surveyed Frémont Island during Stansbury's absence and carried the chain line far up the Promontory shore. The next two weeks were spent bringing the chain line to the head of Spring Bay. The days were lengthening, and the peculiar beauty of the lake in hourly changing aspect wrung the hearts of all the men. Yet there were discomforts, too, not only the frequent trouble getting water and the difficult exertions attendant on moving the chain line over the hostile terrain but the appearance of gnats in countless numbers. Stansbury was fully persuaded that "if old Father Job had been afflicted with the incessant attacks of these persevering & sanguinary varmints the record of his wonderful patience would have been marvelously curtailed for they irritated the skin, inflamed the blood, tried the patience and occupied both hands and all the attentions in resisting their unceasing onslaught."

Beginning May 11 troubles of a different kind beset the camp. The captain had begun the day by dressing down the cook, Henry Standish, for being late with breakfast. That gentleman, being independent in the historic tradition of his craft, announced that Stansbury could get himself another cook, as of that moment, and that he was going to take himself to more appreciative parts. Remonstrating with Henry (a "Mexican Negro," Stansbury had earlier described him) for threatening to leave him in a situation where help could not be obtained, the captain said flatly that if he went, it must be without any help from the Corps of Topographical Engineers.

Although he might be 70 miles from the nearest settlement, no self-respecting cook could listen to such language. While the officers of the camp entertained the delusion that all had been settled, Henry went to the boat, got his bundle and set out for the settlements. Immediately the other hands commenced getting their own traps. For a moment the situation had explosive potentialities. Carrington went to talk to the men, and Stansbury and Hudson began taking down the tents, "fully expecting," Hudson says, "a sail to Black Rock." The captain sent for his pistols, "& the arrival of a brace of Colts made the odds in our favor." It was Carrington who smoothed things out. The hands, he found, had "gone off in a tangent thinking the Captn had discharged the mulatto cook Henry to go a long distance on foot & alone, without provisions—when in fact he had quit himself voluntarily after the best of treatment, for cause unknown to us."

Very shortly the hands began to feel foolish, and soon they were offering their humble apologies. "The men thought to frighten me into their measures but they found themselves so entirely mistaken that I do not think they will again attempt it," Stansbury summed up in his journal, "Mr Carrington & Hudson stood by me like men, & I feel much indebted to them for their firmness." But he had a kind word for the hands: they showed themselves, he thought, heartily ashamed of the part they had taken, and endeavored by assiduity to atone for it.

So the incident closed, and Stansbury did not reopen it in his published *Report,* not even to the extent of mentioning it. One yearns after a fuller knowledge of the embattled cook, his travels back to the Weber settlements and what became of him. "To thine own self be true" was an ideal in which Henry failed not, even on a far shore of Great Salt Lake, and history does well to keep track of such men.

Lugging by hand all the bedding, tents, provisions and water to and from the boats, was no small labor; the gnats took every advantage of the hands' being otherwise occupied than with repelling them; they were all but intolerable. Having to cope with the eternal shallowness of the lake made further inroads on the patience of the party; practically never was it possible to get the boats reasonably close to shore. And even when ashore, there was a multitude of difficulties. Timber was absolutely unobtainable, and the necessary stations often had to be built of small stones, the gathering of which was itself a labor of some proportions, after which making the stations stand up was a job to try their patience all over again.

Altogether, Stansbury could write in his journal with some feeling of the privations undergone by the boat party under his charge, and by the shore party under Carrington, saying that the progress of the survey was by no means commensurate to the fatigue and exposure suffered.

When they were reduced to a diet of hard bread and wiggle-tail water, Stansbury sailed to Black Rock for supplies. Swallowing his disappointment at having to remain behind, Hudson reflected how fortunate it was that the dirt was not dirty, i.e., that it was pure white sand which easily rubbed off when dry, for it had been long since he had enjoyed the luxury of a wash, water costing too much in labor to obtain to be used for any but necessary culinary operations. Carrington's labors continued to be hardly short of heroic.

The smoky condition of the atmosphere made it almost impossible to carry on his work, and he was tormented by badly inflamed eyes, the pain of which was not made more tolerable by the swarming gnats and mosquitoes. Although Stansbury was greatly pleased with the labors of the men, Carrington had a more jaundiced view of them, finding little energy in them except when they were prodded like children.

The survey had progressed down the west coast of the lake as far as the spit of land they called Dolphin Island, and here on May 28 Stansbury rejoined them with fresh provisions. Knowing their straits, he had forgone his usual scruples about Sunday, and the yawl had been rowed all the way from Antelope. En route, the boat underwent some pounding on a rocky bottom, and it was necessary to haul it into the shallows, overturn it and caulk, pitch and paint the seams. Although none of the men had tried their hand at this before, the operation was entirely successful. On the last day of May the yawl was put back into the water and the party set sail for Gunnison Island.

The island had not yet been so named: they were calling it Pelican Island, in honor of a capture made when building a station May 8. After the deadly labors in the shallows and the unending fight with the midges, this trip to Gunnison Island was like a holiday excursion. Hudson thought it one of the most enjoyable voyages he had made on the lake, with the sapphire water twelve to sixteen feet deep under them and masses of white cloud piled up against the blue sky, "shaped into gigantic torsos, or thrones fit for the Gods." He was much taken with the picturesque escarpments of the island itself, and its sandy cove with shores literally covered with pelicans and gulls—there were whole battalions of the pelicans to watch them with haughty suspicion.

Most of the party disembarked for the survey of the island, but Archambeau, who had just lately brought in from Fort Bridger the horses purchased last winter from the Uinta Ute, and who had come in the yawl with Stansbury, was dispatched to the Promontory for water. Although a storm was apparently building up, Stansbury had no fears for the *Sally* even in inexperienced hands, the boat being too heavy and her sails too small to be endangered by any wind. But the skiff, which had set out from Gunnison Island at the same time as the yawl, had not arrived even at nightfall, and Stansbury began to worry about it and its crew.

Neither of the boats appeared next morning, and it was obvious that a storm was going to strike at any time. In the middle of the afternoon the returning yawl was at last descried, and Stansbury with some anxiety alternately watched it and the blackening sky, having little confidence in the nautical skill of those aboard the boat, and conscious that those on the island had no means of getting away and no water to remain there if anything happened to the boats. It was a satisfaction, just before the storm struck, to see the sails were furled, the masts taken down and the boat brought to anchor; in these circumstances, nothing much could befall the yawl, even in the semihurricane now howling upon them.

But what of the skiff? Straining his eyes before the weather blotted out visibility entirely, Stansbury thought he made out the skiff in tow of the yawl, but he could not be certain. There was an uncomfortable hour while the storm raged. The *Sally* could then again be seen offshore; she hoisted sail and soon moved into anchorage. She had the crew of the skiff aboard, but the doubled one-inch towrope had parted, and she had lost the small boat in the storm. Stansbury put down the facts in his journal:

"They had as we had hoped descried the skiff in the storm of yesterday, & had steered for her & picked her up. The men were without their coats or bedding, exposed to the pelting of the hail storm, cold, sea sick, almost frozen & nearly scared to death. Had they not been discovered by the yawl, they w^d have suffered intensely if not perished as they had nothing to eat, & their skiff half full of water, which had come over the side. Had they used ordinary diligence in the morning they might easily have reached the I long before the storm commenced."

Though glad to know they were safe, he was dismayed by the loss of the skiff and unable to see how they could finish their job without it. His principal hope was that the wind, which had now changed direction, might shift it back again by morning.

After sunrise, from the summit of the island, they luckily made out the skiff floating on the water four or five miles to the south, so the captain soon rounded up the runaway craft.

In two more days the survey of "Pelican Island" and the adjacent "Cygnet" islet was completed. Their stock of water being reduced to less than a day's supply, Stansbury had to make the best of feeling unwell and sail 25 miles to the Promontory to refill the kegs. Returning, he broke up the camp on the island and tackled the problem of extending the line of survey down the west shore.

The laborious southward progress of the chain line was interrupted on June 12 when, as Stansbury was moving camp, he saw on the sand flat an old Indian with his squaw and papoose. Landing to inquire about the prospect for water, he discovered that this was an old fellow he had encountered in Skull Valley the preceding fall after the crossing of the Salt Desert, and who had promised to bring in a "give-out" mule in exchange for a blanket. None of his questions now elicited any information about that mule, and Stansbury strongly suspected that it had provided a large part of this little family's winter food supply. The old man and his wife were entirely naked except for breech cloths and tattered moccasins. A buckskin strap over the woman's shoulders supported the youngster on her back. The baby, Stansbury observed:

"was about 4 years old, a fine looking intelligent child & as fat as butter. The mother seemed to evince much affection for it, & was very much pleased when I threw around its shoulders a piece of scarlet flannel, which had been torn of[f] a station by the wind. We gave them something to eat & what was more welcome I suspect than all the rest a pan of water which they drank with great avidity."

The following day the party had the misfortune to carry away the foremast in the step, doubly a misfortune because no timber was available to repair the damage. But as far as the chain line was concerned, the day was a big success, for when the men returned to camp at sunset the line had reached a point south of Promontory Point. They had seen enough of the northern shores of the lake, as Hudson remarked in his journal; "we gladly turn our back upon Tophet & hail the outlines of Antelope, Stansbury & Carrington Islands & south we are but a few miles from Tuilia Valley & the residence of our fellow men."

On June 14 Stansbury established a camp some miles south for the benefit of the shore party, and prepared to sail for Antelope

Island to bring back a beef and water. By now he had had sufficient experience of "the Briny Shallow," but there were additional lessons in store. With a fresh west wind he sailed gaily on the direct course between Carrington and Stansbury Islands only to ground on an extensive sand bar that seemed to stretch all the way from one island to the other. He tried again, going north around Carrington this time, only to find himself once more embayed in the cul-de-sac of an extensive sand bar that seemed to stretch indefinitely west from the island. There was nothing for it but to skirt the bar until he could find a way around it, but night was approaching, a wind ahead was rising fast, and deep black clouds were darkening the tumultuous waters. With their heavy, flat-bottomed boat, rowing against a head wind in what even Stansbury regarded as a very respectable sea was hard work, but it was work or anchor, as there was no good shore to which they might retreat.

Toward ten o'clock they finally rounded the bar, having been forced to make a circuit of some ten miles out of their course. The wind continuing fair, Stansbury sent the crew to their blankets and continued at the helm himself all night. A part of the shoal, he judged, was a hard reef against which a northwest wind dashed the waves with great violence; the roar of the waves reminded him strongly of "the iron bound coast of N England or the heave of the sea upon the coral reef of Florida." Except for grounding on the tail of a sand bar extending southward from Hat Island, which they surmounted by shoving the boat over with handspikes, the night's voyage was uneventful. After a time the skies began to clear, and the stars appeared, shining with extraordinary brilliance. Huddling in two greatcoats, Stansbury reflected that this was the third night he had spent in this way, guiding his little boat over the dark and heavy waters of the lake. Nothing, he thought, could be more striking than the deep and total silence of this lake. "Save the dashing of the waves against the shore absolutely nothing is heard. Not the jumping of a fish the chirp of an insect, nor any of the least thing betokening life, unless it be that very rarely a solitary gull is disturbed in his midnight rumination & flys screaming away. All is stillness & solitude profound."

At the base camp on Antelope Stansbury was surprised and pleased to encounter his energetic second-in-command. Gunnison had finished the survey of the eastern side of the lake, carried the chain line six miles west of Black Rock on the south shore and was now engaged in surveying Antelope. Gunnison had had plenty of trouble, for, as the lake party had reason to know, this had been an extraordinarily rainy spring after a cold and snowy winter, and all the creeks flowing from the mountains had been in flood. Captain James Brown's toll bridges across the Weber and Ogden rivers had been carried away, and Gunnison had had to fashion a bullboat and ferry both streams. On June 2, back in Great Salt Lake City en route to the south shore of the lake, he had gone to Sunday meeting. The preaching, he observed drily in his journal, was Mormonism. "Indeed nearly all the sermons I've heard were the same; the greatness of Mormonism; the work of the 'latter days'; the knowing it to be true and it is to be rolled forth." He was himself a man religiously inclined, but at times the Saints bored him, and he turned not unreluctantly to his professional duties.

With the entire party at hand the remaining work on the lake survey did not take long. While Gunnison wound up the chaining of Antelope Island and then returned to the south shore of the lake to survey Tooele and Rush Valleys, Stansbury sailed to rejoin Carrington, getting there on the sixteenth in the midst of another storm. During the two days following Carrington Island was surveyed, and on the nineteenth Carrington rowed over to Hat Island to give it his attention while Hudson remained with the captain on the larger island to rebuild the station. It was evident that Indians had swum to the island and torn down the original station for the sake of the red flannel that clothed it. Feeling that a repetition of this offense must be prevented, the irrepressible Hudson occupied himself by drawing on the canvas a depiction of an American in the act of shooting the thief as he was denuding the station of its cloth. This, he explained, "was an hieroglyphical warning that such a fate would be theirs if they persisted in similar depredations."

On June 20 the party moved on to Stansbury Island. Hudson regarded it favorably—the most picturesque of the islands and inferior in size only to Antelope. As it was "luxuriantly covered with flowers, various grasses wild barley &c. & is eminently fitted for the location of a numerous herd of cattle," he rightly guessed that it would very soon be utilized for grazing purposes.

On Saturday night, June 22, Stansbury lighted a beacon fire and saw Gunnison's welcome return beacon flickering at Black Rock, so the next morning he fitted out the skiff with four oars and set out for Black Rock. He started two hours after sunrise, expecting to get there in a couple of hours, but notwithstanding all his experience and constant frustration in estimating distances, it required seven hours to reach Black Rock. His meditative assistant he found "discussing the spiritual wife doctrine with Charley Whites wife" (the Whites at this time were operating a salt boiling business at the beach here). Gunnison was nearly out of supplies, but yielded up 20 pounds of flour and a little tea. A storm blew up on the return trip, and Stansbury was quick to take refuge on shore. This storm, like most, was of short duration, and a little after dark he arrived back at camp.

Now the end was near for all these arduous labors. On June 27 Hudson recorded in his journal, "The chaining of the G.S.L. was at length over & both Officers & Men were devoutly thankful for its consummation." They all piled into the boats and made for Antelope Island. Here they found Gunnison's camp; he had finished his part of the job, and had gone to town looking for the captain. The work was all done, except for the triangulation. With most of the men, whom he paid off without further ceremony, Stansbury set out for the city. The Mormon town in the valley of the Great Salt Lake might disappoint many among the forty-niners who looked for more impressive things, but after so much of solitude, it was beautiful to Stansbury's eye.

The first half of July was spent in a final tiring labor, taking observations at the numerous triangulation stations scattered around the lake and upon its islands, but this work was finished on July 16. In his *Report* Stansbury wrote of his final leave-taking of this singular lake.

"The difficulty of finding water fit for the ordinary purposes of life—the necessity of transporting, by means totally inadequate, every pound of provisions and every drop of water needed for the daily consumption of a large party of men—the unavoidable distance of our depot, and the barren, savage inhospitality of the region we were obliged to traverse, have made this survey one of unusually arduous and protracted toil. But the salubrity of the climate is such that, notwithstanding our constant exposure to the vicissitudes of the elements, a large portion of the time without the protection of tents, not a man was seriously unwell, and most of the party were in the uninterrupted enjoyment of robust health."

He did well and uncomplainingly a difficult job, and he topped it off with a *Report* which has had a deservedly high reputation in the annals of American exploration. It is right that Stansbury should be remembered in history for this expedition to the valley of the Great Salt Lake, beyond any other professional contribution of his life. He returned east to a quiet life in charge of harbor surveys and construction on the Great Lakes. From retirement he was called back to service as a mustering and disbursing officer during the Civil War, and he died in service at Madison, Wisconsin, on April 17, 1863. It was the honorable reputation of the Corps of Topographical Engineers, at a time when the United States Army was not too highly regarded by the generality of the American people, to be known as "the working men of the Army." Howard Stansbury was a working man to the end, and the record of his exploration and survey of the Great Salt Lake shows it.

Chapter 13

Backwater

Two years before Stansbury, the Mormon explorers had been impressed by the possibilities of Antelope Island as an unfenced range for livestock, and their reports made an impression upon their brethren, who otherwise concerned themselves with the lake only to the extent of wondering whether its islands might not afford herbs valuable in the ministrations of the community's botanic doctors.

The result, even before Stansbury's explorations were formally inaugurated, was that the lake was bound up in the current of Mormon affairs in a peculiar fashion which lasted throughout the fifties.

In locating his church a thousand miles from anywhere Brigham Young stamped upon it both a character and a sustained theme of endeavor which ever since have been integral in its identity. "Gathering to Zion" became for the Saints a kind of Pilgrim's Progress— an affirmation of faith, an assumption of responsibility, and an ordeal undergone to evidence fitness to enter into the community of Saints. But also the gathering of the chosen was a paramount responsibility for the church itself.

There were two distinct stages in the gathering of Israel. There was, initially, the labor of reuniting those who had migrated from Nauvoo, expending themselves in the first westward surge of the church. This period ended with the great immigration of 1852. Thereafter, until the completion of the Pacific Railroad, the energies of the church were directed toward bringing across the plains the converts of its far-flung missionary system. Ways and means were continually pondered for making more efficient the system of immigration.

In particular, the church felt the enormous responsibility that was theirs for helping the poor. The wealthy among the Saints could provide their own "fit-outs" and make their own way to Zion, though always in the organized companies that were the hall-

mark of Mormon immigration. But the immigration of the poor
and the humble required the organized effort of the church itself.

The idea of a "Perpetual Fund to gather the poor" was first presented by Brigham Young to the congregation in Great Salt Lake
City on September 9, 1849, when it was voted that such a fund be
instituted. At the semiannual conference in October, the authorities
returned to the subject. "Most of you are aware," Heber C. Kimball
told them, "of the covenant made by the Saints in the Temple in
Nauvoo, that we would not cease our exertions until we had
brought the poor to this valley, or those that wanted to come. We
are here, and are healthy and have plenty to eat, drink, and to do,
and I prophesy you shall never have less while you live. Shall we
fulfil that covenant, or shall we not?"

The vote was unanimous to raise a fund for the purpose. The
fund was to be raised by voluntary donations; loans would be made
to deserving converts; and when the loans had been repaid after
the arrival in Utah, the fund would be restored. Thus it could be
used in perpetuity for the gathering of the poor. Making the appropriations from the fund in the form of a loan rather than a gift was
calculated, Brigham Young pointed out, to make "the honest in
heart rejoice, for they love to labor, and be independent by their
labors, and not live on the charity of their friends."

About $5,000 was raised during the first year, and the first Perpet-
ual Emigrating Fund companies arrived in the valley in late August
1850. It became necessary, however, to find some better expedient
for raising funds than donations.

The first step in this direction was taken in November 1849 when
the High Council, in one of its last legislative actions, passed an
ordinance providing that cattle left in the estray pound one month
should be sold for the benefit of the P.E.F. In consequence of this
action, and of the fact that many donations were in the form of
livestock rather than cash, the Perpetual Emigrating Company very
soon began to require a herd ground for its property. The islands in
Great Salt Lake were reserved for that purpose, and on September
14, 1850, the legislature of the State of Deseret, in formally incorporating the Perpetual Emigrating Company, validated this action
by providing that "The Islands in the Great Salt Lake, known as
Stansbury's Island and Antelope Island, are hereby reserved and

appropriated for the exclusive use and benefit of said Company, for the keeping of stock, &c."

Herding on Antelope Island had begun as early as the fall of 1848. In his journal Benjamin Ashby says that "Brothers Noble, Garr and Thurston took a ranch on Antelope Island just as winter commenced. Old Father Stump, old bear hunter Abe Garr, George Thurston and I, drove their cattle over. These were the first that were driven to the island. We were three days on the road. Towards night we crossed the lake, which was dry most of the way. About a fourth of a mile from the island, we got into soft mud, and the wagon stuck. I got off my horse, took off the bridle, threw it into the wagon, and endeavored to get the wagon out, but without avail. So it was left, and we made our way to the shore, where we camped in the snow."

When Fielding Garr moved the church stock to the island in the fall of 1849, Stump was still living there, and he remained for some years, building a house of juniper posts, set upright and covered with a dirt roof, at the head of a small, open canyon under a steep mountain wall. The old man, it is said, ultimately drove his horses and cattle to a secluded spot in Cache Valley, where a Ute squaw one day crept up behind him and cut his throat.

Garr built a corral and a house known for more than half a century as "the old church house." John Hudson of Stansbury's party, in April 1850 was favorably impressed with the island as a ranch, considering that it made "a fine grazing ground & could fresh water be found for the purpose of irrigation would be a desirable location for farms as judging from the luxuriant bunch grass, small grains would grow with but little culture." The previous fall Stansbury had left his animals in the care of a herdsman at Tooele, on the south shore of the lake, but, hearing some dubious tales about the fellow and liking the looks of Garr—who was, moreover, a bonded herdsman—on April 20 he ordered that his stock be driven to the island, where Garr kept it in good order until the topographical engineers left for the States.

Fielding Garr remained in charge of the church stock on the island until his death in 1855. Briant Stringham then took over the job, retaining the responsibility until his own death in 1871. Although the island had been set aside for the use of the Perpetual

Emigrating Company, no fine distinctions were drawn; it was used not only for the church stock but also, if occasion required, for that belonging personally to Brigham Young and Heber C. Kimball.

The history of the lake, during the first years after Stansbury completed his survey, was, very nearly, the placid life of the herdsmen about its shores and upon its principal island. From Stansbury Island clear around to Promontory licensed herdsmen watched over the stock of the several communities and of the merchants who were beginning to establish stores in Great Salt Lake City. Cattle and horses were the essential medium of exchange, for many of the Saints saw no cash from one year's end to the next. Horses, which might be traded to emigrants, and cattle, which might be trailed to beef markets in California, were almost the only exportable products of the Territory. Livestock could be moved over the immigrant trails only during the summer months when feed was good, so herd grounds were of prime economic importance.

Though Antelope Island was almost unrivaled as a herd ground, one of its prime advantages, its isolation, in the winter of 1853 began to pose a serious problem. The lake level had been steadily rising since Stansbury completed his survey, and it was becoming more and more difficult to ford the bar between the island and the mainland. There was a very real possibility that the water would rise so high as to make the island inaccessible. Therefore, in the spring of 1854 Brigham Young ordered the building of a boat adequate for the ferrying of the church stock.

This boat was launched in the Jordan River on June 30, 1854. The *Mud·Hen,* in which the lake had been explored in 1848, was a simple skiff, and Stansbury's flat-bottomed yawl, the *Sally,* had been not much more pretentious. It is not known what ultimately happened to either of these boats, but neither would have been of much service for ferrying stock. A 45-foot craft, the new vessel was much the most imposing of any that had been built for use on the lake, and it exemplified Brigham Young's characteristic willingness to try anything once, particularly if it had some mechanical novelty. On the occasion of her launching, when he appropriately christened her the *Timely Gull,* he commented that she was "designed for a stern wheel to be propelled by horses working a tread-mill." He evidently had some idea of converting her into a steamboat, for

Milo Andrus, who went east that fall in the interests of the church, made it known in St. Louis that he would take back to Utah the engine and fixtures, saying that the boat had already been built, and only awaited the machinery to be put into operation. The observant young English traveler, William Chandless, who came to Utah the next summer, heard that "it was in contemplation to start a small steamer on Salt Lake, that in high water might run up the Jordan near the city and connect it with the most northern settlements; or even up Bear River, if emigration should come by a more northerly route than at present." But he thought that the expense and difficulty involved in importing machinery "must render such a scheme, even if otherwise practicable, quite visionary, until the Mormons have extended their ironworks; machinery, if imported, could be applied to fifty more useful purposes." Brigham Young must have found himself of the same mind, for in 1856 the *Timely Gull* was finally fitted out as a sailboat.

It was fortunate that the boat was ready for use by the early fall of 1854. Even during the spring, the lake had been so high as to swim a horse on the Antelope bar, and cattle taken off the island at that time had to swim the greater portion of the way. Spring brought astonishing floods, raising the Jordan to levels higher than had ever been known, and by fall, had it not been for the *Timely Gull,* the stock on the island would have been marooned.

That would in other years have been simply an inconvenience, but during the fall of 1854 and the spring and summer of 1855 it could have been a tragedy, for the island shared in the general devastation when a visitation by grasshoppers hit the Mormon settlements.

There were two years of warfare with the grasshoppers; they came in clouds that darkened the sun, scourging the earth of everything green and giving the farms and the towns a strange, wintry aspect. Anson Call, a settler at Bountiful, has left a typical account of this locust visitation. They appeared suddenly from over the mountains, late one afternoon. The air seemed full of them, and, as he put it, they "covered him up," a dark, moving mass on buildings, garden and fields. The air rasping with the sound of their flight, the grasshoppers came over the mountains from the east, and as they landed, all in one direction, the wheat disappeared from view under them.

Ruins of the Wenner home on Frémont Island, 1943.

Blanche Wenner and John E. Jones at the Wenner burial plot, 1943.

Snowville in Curlew Valley north of Great Salt Lake. Inner lands are irrigated from Deep Creek; outer are dry-farmed. Note ancient beach of Lake Bonneville on mountains.

Irrigating alfalfa. Water may be taken from irrigation canals only at certain hours and for limited times.

The following morning, as irrationally as they had come, they arose in a cloud and continued their flight west across Great Salt Lake. It was like an intervention of Providence in behalf of the Saints, for whether by a shift of the wind or because the water from on high looked like inviting green fields, they were precipitated by the millions into the lake. Thereafter they were washed in immense windrows upon the beaches. There was a single windrow, it is said, which extended from the mouth of the Jordan for 70 miles north. For a long time an intolerable stench pervaded the whole eastern lake shore.

Anson Call was more fortunate than most, because, when relieved of the weight of the insects, his wheat lifted from the ground. The underside of the heads had not been destroyed, and he was able to gather a third of a crop. The grasshoppers returned again and again during the sixties, and that windrow of rotting grasshoppers along its shore became almost a characteristic feature of the lake.

Great Salt Lake was no moat to protect the islands from the winged hosts as it might have protected them from crickets. By the fall of 1854 the grasshoppers had wrought such havoc that it became essential to remove some of the stock lest all of it perish of starvation.

In October 1854 Brigham Young, Heber C. Kimball and others voyaged to the island in the *Timely Gull* and ferried to the mainland over 500 head of cattle. With the rest of the church cattle, numbering some two thousand head in all, these were taken to new herd grounds near Utah Lake. The following year, with the grasshopper devastations even worse, most of these cattle were driven north to Cache Valley, the first faint beginnings of colonization for that area.

The horses, being good rustlers, were left on Antelope to fend for themselves. From this time forth Antelope Island became noted for its horses. At all times a believer in blooded stock, Brigham Young bought the best stallions and brood mares he could find, and turned them loose on the island. By 1860, Solomon Kimball says, there were almost a thousand head of horses on the island, nearly as wild as deer, though Briant Stringham made it a point to corral every horse on the island at least once a year, branding them, handling them and generally looking them over. The horses that came off the island had an unequaled reputation in the territory.

There were, Solomon says, two reasons for this, their superior blood, and the effect of the environment. They became:

"nimble, wiry, and sure-footed by continually traveling over the rough trails of the island from the time they were foaled until they were grown. It became second nature to them to climb over the rugged mountainsides, and to jump up and down precipitous places four or five feet high. The speed which they could make while traveling over such places was simply marvelous. They neither stumbled nor fell, no matter how rough the country nor how fast they went. They were naturally of a kind disposition, and as gentle as lambs, after having been handled a few times. But with all of their perfections they had a weakness that made many a man's face turn red with anger; they loved their island home, and it was hard to wean them from it. When a favorable opportunity presented itself, during the summer months, they would take the nearest cut to the island, swimming the lake wherever they happened to come to it, and keep going until they reached their destination. Lot Smith's favorite saddle horse played this trick on him several times, even taking the saddle with him on one occasion."

The sharpening competition for the herd grounds led the territorial legislature, beginning in the winter of 1854-1855, to make a series of grants of rights to herd grounds. Stansbury and Antelope Islands were granted to Brigham Young in behalf of the Perpetual Emigrating Company. Frémont Island was granted to Phineas H. Young, Albert P. Rockwood and Jesse Hobson, and the Promontory was granted to the apostle, Lorenzo Snow. Over a three-year period 32 of these grants were made, including four along the lake shore between Tooele Valley and the mouth of the Jordan. Until they were repealed in 1860, these grazing grants controlled by far the greatest proportion of the territory's desirable herd grounds.

But even possession of such resources could not suffice to save the church stock in the disastrous "hard winter" of 1855-1856. The devastations by grasshoppers were followed by one of the worst winters on record. The snow everywhere piled up three and four feet deep on the level. Of the church herds in Cache Valley, numbering some 2,600 head, it is said that 2,300 died. The same thing happened through all the valleys south. Enough are said to have died on the flat plains west of Ogden to stretch from that city to Great

Salt Lake—a ten-mile distance—if they could have been laid end to end. One herdsman saved a part of his stock only by feeding them the boiled flesh of others that died. Heber C. Kimball and Brigham Young were fortunate in that they had put their sheep on Antelope Island in the fall; like the horses, these came through the winter almost without loss, since the animals were able to range on the more mountainous portions of the island where the wind blew away the snow. It is said that antelope, which were still found on the island as late as 1870, were on many occasions saved from starvation through the ability of the horses to paw the snow off the grass; they followed humbly behind and ate what the horses left.

Although the map name, Antelope Island, triumphed in the end, its appropriation to the uses of the church led to its being called Church Island, a name which persisted a half century and more. The other islands also came to have familiar names; from 1848 on, Frémont was often called Castle Island, sometimes known also as Miller's Island, for Henry W. Miller, Davis County settler who utilized it in the sixties for herding purposes. Similarly, Stansbury Island was called Kimball's Island, from the range uses to which it was put by Heber C. Kimball and his sons.

Church Island was visited by the authorities every year or two for a holiday outing. The *Timely Gull* came to grief late in 1858 when a gale swept it from its moorings at Black Rock and piled it up on the island; the wreckage was visible for many years. Fortunately, however, after the high stage reached in the late summer of 1854 the lake level began to fall, going down each year till 1862, when it began the longest sustained rise in its recorded history. Until then, it was possible to use the Antelope Island bar without swimming the horses, and wagons could cross to the island. Late in 1859 Brigham Young and his intimates had a typical holiday excursion to the island, one that has been described by Solomon Kimball. The Mormon president took all the church clerks with him; during the three-day outing they spent their time boating, bathing and climbing to the topmost peaks, and it amused Solomon in after years to recall the scenes around the evening campfires:

"the high-toned clerks . . . sitting around these fires broiling T-bone and tenderloin steaks, which they had fastened to the ends of long, sharp sticks. Then with bread and butter in one hand and their meat in the other, with plenty of good milk on the side, they ate their suppers with a relish that would have made the kings and noblemen of the earth look on with envy."

In all these years after Stansbury's departure, the lake lay like a backwater in the history of the people who dwelt upon its shores. Yet significant eddies of that history reached the backwater throughout this time.

That tantalizing problem of a better route to California, south of the lake, continued to preoccupy men who traveled the western trails. Samuel Hensley, with seven men, had made an unsuccessful effort to cross the Salt Desert in 1848 before pioneering, instead, the Salt Lake Road north of the lake. An obscure reference in a Mormon journal makes it seem likely that a small detachment of returning battalion members came east via Hastings' Cutoff early in the fall of 1848. But none are known to have crossed the Salt Desert the following year except Stansbury's pack party, perhaps because reports of the new road north of the lake attracted that way all who were making for the Humboldt.

In 1850 the forty-niners took renewed heart, and during July and August many pack parties traversed the hazardous desert trail to Pilot Peak. It is in this year alone that any fatalities are recorded in the crossing of the Salt Desert. Even these deaths were by cholera, and the victims were buried on the lower slopes of Pilot Peak.

The rising demand for a Pacific Railroad brought the next interesting travelers back to the Salt Desert country. In the spring of 1853 the government dispatched a series of expeditions to reconnoiter railroad routes, and command of one of these was given to Lieutenant—now Captain—John W. Gunnison, who on the basis of his work with Stansbury had established an enviable reputation in the Corps of Topographical Engineers. Gunnison took a southern route across the Rockies to reach Green River at the crossing of the old Spanish Trail—present-day Greenriver. Roughly he paralleled the Spanish Trail into Castle Valley and across the Wasatch Mountains to the valley of the Sevier River. He then carried his reconnaissance west and south almost to Sevier Lake, and by October 26 was on the verge of turning north with his sixty-odd men, as he had done four years before, to take up winter quarters in Great Salt Lake City, when his luck ran out.

Some immigrants trailing sheep to California had shot down three Pahvant Ute, and the angered Indians, characteristically wreaking vengeance on the first white party they fell upon, slaughtered the captain, six of his men, and his Mormon guide. Among the slain was John Bellows, like Gunnison a veteran of the Stansbury expedition.

The massacre was a misfortune not only for the government, which lost one of its most capable officers, but for the Mormon community, which was promptly accused by its irresponsible enemies of having instigated the deed; the suspicions engendered were not without effect in the ultimate breakdown of relations between the Mormons and the federal government.

Following the massacre Gunnison's second-in-command, Lieutenant E. G. Beckwith, brought the remainder of the party on to Great Salt Lake City. In the spring of 1854 he headed west to finish Gunnison's job. The project was to find a new route to the Sink of the Humboldt south of the Great Salt Lake and south of the existing road down the Humboldt Valley. Beckwith passed around the lake into Skull Valley, impressed with the effect of a tide caused by the wind, which piled up the water on the beach.

Stansbury had already reported on the Hastings road as far as Pilot Peak, so Beckwith turned southwest across the Cedar Mountains, using a pass still called by his name, and then crossed the southern reaches of the Salt Desert, reaching Ruby Valley by way of Granite Mountain, Fish Springs and Ibapah, Gosiute and Independence Valleys. A reconnaissance convinced him of the impracticality of Secret Pass for any but pack parties, so he followed the old Hastings trail south around the Rubies to the head of the Humboldt's South Fork. Thence he struck on westerly across a succession of ranges which he rapidly realized made a railroad entirely impracticable, and reached the Humboldt finally at Lassen's Meadows. From there he headed westerly across the Sierras into California.

This effort at trailfinding had a prompt echo the succeeding fall. Lieutenant Colonel E. J. Steptoe, enroute to California with some infantry and artillery detachments, was ordered to winter at Great Salt Lake City and see what he could do about rounding up the Pahvant Indians who had slain Gunnison. He exhibited interest in the possibility of taking his force on to Benicia by a route south of the lake, and he hired Oliver and Clark Allan Huntington to try to find such a trail to Carson Valley. The adventures of the Huntingtons I have described in *The Humboldt;* they had their share of danger and hard times. Although they discovered a "desert route," it was a dry one, and none but scattered pack parties ever attempted it.

So the Great Salt Lake lay aside from main-traveled trails, and overland immigrants who moved east or west through Utah knew the lake only as a far color on the horizon, unless they were sufficiently curious to make a bathing excursion from Great Salt Lake City to the Black Rock beach.

Chapter 14

Sound and Fury

THE Mormons were not fortunate in the first territorial officials that Washington saddled on them. Those officials did not begin arriving in the territory until June 1851, and it was midsummer before most of them had reached their posts, but by September Mormons and officials had had a falling out.

Two of the federal judges, the territorial secretary and one of the Indian subagents promptly returned east with the tale of their grievances, a tale that lacked for nothing in its reflections upon the loyalty and the morality of the Saints. Although these officials have never been regarded as justified in deserting their posts, there was a sufficient color of truth to their accusations to give the Saints some uncomfortable moments.

The occasion for the falling-out was some injudicious remarks by Judge Perry C. Brocchus, which the Saints interpreted as a direct insult aimed at their womenfolk. Some very harsh language that resulted convinced the officials their lives would be endangered if they remained at their posts, and this, added to some collisions in the performance of their official duties, persuaded them to leave Utah. It was impolitic on Brocchus' part to lecture the Saints as to their morals, but it was also impolitic on the part of the Mormons to live in polygamy without publicly sanctioning the doctrine.

Plural marriage had been sanctioned by revelation since 1843; that it had not been publicly espoused as late as the summer of 1851 may have owed somewhat to political considerations; the Saints wanted to raise no extraneous issues while they were engaged in getting the best kind of government they could wangle from Washington, officered to the maximum extent possible by their own leaders. Had it not been for the imbroglio with the federal officers, it is possible that plural marriage as a church doctrine would have been admitted in the fall of 1851 rather than a year later. The need for getting the church on firmer ground with respect to plural marriage had become patent; polygamy among the Mormons was becoming an open secret, for it had been reported by numerous forty-niners and was about to become the subject of philosophical discussion in the books of Stansbury and Gunnison.

Apart from polygamy there were other aspects of Mormon thinking which jarred upon the minds of those who had but an imperfect sympathy with the Saints; they were given to much extravagant language which could be, and frequently was, interpreted to show that hostile attitudes bordering on downright disloyalty were prevalent among them. They swore by the Constitution and regarded themselves as its only true defenders, but they were disposed to write off the government that ruled under the Constitution as a seasoned aggregation of damned rascals, and they were fully persuaded that God would not long delay in wreaking vengeance upon the United States for the outrages that had been visited upon his Saints.

The Mormons counterattacked the "runaway officials" in Washington, and the result was about a draw, for while the objectionable officials were replaced by others more to the taste of the Saints, they were promptly given other posts by the government. But in this fashion the political history of the Saints got off on the wrong foot, and that old bugbear, "the Mormon problem," reappeared in American life. It was now a problem infinitely more complex than it had ever been before. Hitherto, the Saints had always been minorities in the political subdivisions of the Union. In Utah they had, if not precisely a government of their own, certainly the means of creating one if their territorial status were converted into statehood. From being an internal affair of the states the "Mormon problem" now could become, on an instant's notice, an affair involving the federal government itself.

The interrelationships of the Saints and the government operated necessarily in an atmosphere of mutual suspicion. A succession of often rascally federal officials did the government no good in the estimation of the Saints, while a good deal of social intransigence and irritating self-righteousness on the part of the Mormons did not improve them in the estimation of those outside their fellowship. A constant social and political friction in the territory, and an acrimonious debate in the public press, in the forums of Congress and in the nation's churches over the moral and political issues rep-

esented in Mormonism gave the fifties a resounding character all
heir own.

The situation rapidly deteriorated after the summer of 1855.
udge W. W. Drummond (who brought his mistress to Utah in the
guise of a wife) launched a wholesale assault upon the Mormon
courts as being founded in ignorance, and he discovered an ally in
udge George P. Stiles, who had at one time been a Saint in good
tanding but who had, as the Mormons saw it, gone lusting after
trange gods. The surveyor general for the territory and the principal Indian agent embroiled themselves with the Mormons in the
lischarge of their duties, and the territorial secretary, Almon W.
Babbitt, notwithstanding his fellowship in the church, had to be
ooked upon with an extremely jaundiced eye.

On the Mormon side the situation was complicated by the
preaching of a crusade of reformation. Beginning early in the fall
of 1856, the Saints were exhorted to confess their sins and be rebap-
ized, and the elders went about from home to home catechizing
he Saints. The entire legislature was required to repent its sins
und be baptized before being allowed to proceed with its business,
nd in general there was an outburst of preaching on the subject.

Judge Drummond made off to Carson Valley in the spring of
856, going on to California and subsequently to the States to
oose his blasts against the Saints. Babbitt was killed by Indians on
he plains the same summer, and voices were not lacking to swear
hat he, like Gunnison, had really been slain by the Saints. And a
new turbulence in Great Salt Lake City grew apace through the
all of 1856 and the early winter of 1857.

Among those caught up in these surging times was Thomas S.
Williams. Though in our own day he wears the pioneer halo, Tom
was something of a hard case. Abner Blackburn says of him in his
Mormon Battalion days that he "made his brag that he had stolen
rom a hen on her roost to a steamboat engine," and this was not
mere boasting. William Chandless, almost ten years later, heard
hat he had possessed the reputation of a master in the art of
tealing:

'indeed, he had raised stealing to the level of one of the fine arts.
While at Nauvoo, he stole, one Sunday, the whole machinery of a

small sawmill, and sunk it in the Mississippi till all search was given over; a yoke of cattle he concealed in a hollow haystack, but the necessity of an opening to take in water gave the stack some queer look that betrayed him; above all, as a horse thief he was not second even to an Indian."

This spacious life Tom gave up early in the fifties to set himself up as one of Great Salt Lake City's most prosperous merchants. He branched out to the law, and before long was one of the shining ornaments of the Utah bar. Prosperity made him self-willed, however, and by the autumn of 1856 Brother Thomas and the church came to the parting of the ways; on November 16 he was formally excommunicated. This must at the time have seemed to him a mere incident. Like everybody else, just then he was engrossed in the bitter quarreling going on in the local courts. Hosea Stout, himself a member of the bar, had to record some of the fruits of the conflict in his journal on December 29: "Last night the Law library of Judge Stiles & T. S. Williams was broken open and the books and papers thereof taken away. A privy near by was filled with books a few thousand shingles and laths added and the concern set on fire and consumed."

This act of rowdyism had grave consequences, for it was reported in Washington that the records of the territorial courts had been burned with Stiles's private papers, and this ugly report had much to do with the ultimate decision to send a military force to Utah. The rowdyism was all too general. Stout had to note in his journal on January 14 that on the previous night the house of Henry Jarvis, a merchant excommunicated at the same time as Williams, had been broken into and his family driven out, "the House set on fire in two or three places and he beaten and drove off and hell played generally."

Such hooliganism was not alone the fruit of the reformation in progress this winter, though the aroused religious passions contributed to the tensions; a struggle was going on in the courts over the jurisdiction of the territorial, as distinguished from the federal, courts. There had developed an anomaly in the law which was not resolved until Congress in 1874 passed the Poland bill to limit the jurisdiction of the Mormon courts. A succession of federal judges, beginning with Drummond, attacked the Mormon judicial system. Each time the issue reached the point of crisis, however, the judges backed away from it. Drummond did so at Fillmore in the winter of 1855-1856, and Stiles did so again at Great Salt Lake City the next winter. The crisis in Stiles's court came in February 1857 with a tempestuous demonstration by some of the Mormon attorneys. Tom Williams resigned his membership in the Utah bar and made angry preparations to take his family east.

This deterioration of a Saint in good standing threatened ruin to a promising romance. Williams' young daughter, Caroline, had fallen in love with Heber C. Kimball's son, David, and the two had planned to be married. Now, however, Tom not only absolutely forbade the marriage, but prepared to take his daughter east. The young couple was determined not to be thwarted, even when Caroline's father placed trusted guards over her to watch her night and day. Just before the hour of departure, she seized upon an unguarded moment to dart out of the back door and into a carriage that was waiting for her. Before the guards had fairly missed her, Solomon Kimball says:

"she and her intended were hurled over to Judge Elias Smith's office and were made husband and wife for all time. They then jumped into the carriage, drawn by two fiery steeds, and accompanied by four mounted guards, composed of Joseph A. Young, Heber P. Kimball, Quince Knowlton and Brigham Young, Jr., they made a dash for Antelope Island, reaching their destination in less than three hours."

Back in town Tom Williams blew straight up into the air. In his journal on April 14 Hosea Stout made space for the juicy news:

"T. S. Williams' daughter Caroline Eloped to parts unknown last night He blames Prest H. C. Kimball and thinks David Kimball has got her and threatens to kill President Kimball. The police arrested Williams for Breach of the Peace He rages and raves like a mad man. To night I was out nearly all night on guard."

The party making for the States was leaving, and Williams had not the remotest idea where to look for his runaway daughter. He had to make the best of things, and next day Stout wrote with finality, "To day T. S. Williams Judge Stiles Genl Burr and P. K. Dotson with nearly all the gentile and apostate Scurf in this community left for the States."

On the island the honeymooners luxuriated in each other, the sweets of marriage all the sweeter for having been come by over such difficulties. Not a living soul, says Solomon Kimball, knew where they were, except those who had aided them in their elopement, until they returned from their hiding place when Caroline's father was far on his journey to the States.

The incident has a proper ironic aftermath for, as a result of the elopement, in the annual reunions of the Kimball clan T. S. Williams is revered among the pioneer fathers. Tom came back to Utah with the army in 1858, proving himself then quite as intractable a character as he had been before. Eventually, early in 1860, with a single companion he was killed by Indians on the Mohave, enroute to California on business. Though he died unregenerate, genealogy has taken him in hand, and it is assured that Tom Williams will not be forgotten.

That company of embittered officials and apostate Saints that made for the States in April 1857 might be dismissed by such good Saints as Hosea Stout with the Cavalier remark that "the fire of the reformation is burning many out who flee from the Territory afraid of their lives This is scriptural. 'The wicked flee when no man pursue' and so with an apostate Mormon he always believes his life in danger and flees accordingly."

But it was not so easy as that to disengage the Saints from their difficulties. The bitter reports brought east by those who departed Great Salt Lake City were a last straw. Characterizing the Mormons as being in open rebellion, the government ordered a sizeable military force to Utah to re-establish the supremacy of the law.

This was, the Saints told themselves when the news reached them late in July, no more than they had looked for during 10 full years. Missouri had tried to crush them, and Illinois; now the federal government would try its hand. But Brigham had promised them, 10 long years ago, that if they were given 10 years to establish themselves in the tops of the mountains, all hell should never prevail over them again. They were the children of God, secure in his keeping. Let armies come against them: God would smite them with pestilence and storms. And if other than scriptural injunctions were in order, then remember what had been said at Lexington in 1775: "If they mean to have a war, let it begin *here.*"

Put your trust in God, but keep your powder dry; so also the favorite Mormon precept, "The Lord helps those who help themselves." Taking full advantage of the government's administrative slip in failing to advise him that he had been superseded in office, Brigham Young in his capacity as governor chose to regard the troops advancing west as a mere mob, and on September 15, 1857, issued his famous proclamation: *"Citizens of Utah*—We are invaded by a hostile force. . . ." He declared martial law, mustered the Utah militia to resist the entrance of the troops and out into the Wyoming plains dispatched raiders under Lot Smith with orders to harass the westward-moving army in every way short of bloodshed.

In the end, the Saints were able to see the overruling hand of providence in everything that resulted. The services of supply for the Utah Expedition proved something less than adequate, particularly when Lot Smith and his men burned some of the supply trains. Winter closed down, and the troops had to bivouac at "Camp Scott," near the charred remains of Fort Bridger. Keeping a high tone with the Army, Brigham Young sent the federal forces a dispatch advising them that they might winter on the Green River or one of its forks, but if they did so, they must deliver up all their arms and ammunition to the Mormon quartermaster general and must return east early in the spring. Then, if they desired provisions, he would furnish these upon proper application. Exploded Captain Jesse Gove, "The old idiot! Did you ever see such impudence, such braggadocio? We will show him on which side of his bread the butter should be spread."

The Saints fortified the canyons of the Wasatch, and patrols kept an eye on the troops throughout the winter. By spring it had become clear that the Army would survive to enter Salt Lake Valley, nor did it any longer suit the purposes of the Saints to fight. Brigham Young resolved, instead, upon a heroic gesture to win the sympathies and support of the civilized world. Remembering the example of the Russians at Moscow in 1812, he would evacuate his cities and put them to the torch rather than submit to "Gentile oppression."

No one will ever know how serious Brigham Young was in this purpose. He sent exploring expeditions into the desert country of southeastern Nevada in vain search for fertile valleys to which the Saints might flee, and he could appear to threaten guerrilla warfare, a fanatical resistance far more savage and unrelenting than any Indian warfare could ever be. But there was no environment sufficiently hostile to defeat military expeditions that was also gracious enough to receive whole peoples into its recesses. Ultimately, if sufficiently hard pressed, Brigham might have been willing to attempt a removal beyond the continental bounds of the United States. But it was worth while to see what a gesture, carried out with the most deadly seriousness, could accomplish in shaping American public opinion.

As it turned out, Brigham was vouchsafed two strings for his bow. That old friend of the Saints, Colonel Thomas L. Kane, late in 1857 went to see President Buchanan to learn whether some peaceful solution of the Utah difficulty could be found. It is not clear whether Buchanan gave him any satisfaction, but Kane traveled to California by way of Panama and rode north to Great Salt Lake City by the Southern Road, arriving late in February 1858. After conferences with Brigham Young, he went on to Camp Scott in March. The Army officers gave him a hostile reception, this "nincompoop of a Mr. Col. Kane," but the new Utah governor, Alfred Cumming, who shared a dislike for the military which was general in the America of his time, agreed to accompany him into the Mormon city to see what could be worked out.

Cumming has not been too kindly remembered in Utah history. The gentiles resented his pacific attitude toward the Mormons and have always impugned his motives; the Saints resented him as the successor to their own Brigham Young, gossiped maliciously about his personal faults and were ungracious about his kindnesses. But he was a man of great patience, having a hard fund of common sense, an ability to turn a deaf ear to insult when policy required, and an understanding that the Mormons could be moved only through their own leaders. He soon satisfied himself that the

territorial records had not been burned after all—thus disposing of
one of the most serious bones of contention—and decided that the
temper of the Saints was not disloyal beyond reasonable bounds.
The people of Utah, he reported to Washington, were disposed to
accept his authority, and the "rebellion" might be considered at an
end.

Neither Brigham Young nor the Army could let the "Utah War"
fizzle out so easily. Brigham went right on gathering his people
out of the northern settlements with the threat to burn them to the
ground if the Army proved hostile, and Brevet Brigadier General
Albert Sidney Johnston, commanding the Utah forces, went right
on making his preparations to march his army into the central
valleys of Utah. In mid-June the Army left Camp Scott and on
June 26 marched through the silent, deserted city of the Saints.
With thousands of his people Brigham Young was south in Utah
Valley waiting on the result. The Army camped beyond the Jordan,
and after a few days moved south to the site chosen for the military
post in Cedar Valley west of Utah Lake.

By July 1 it was apparent that the war was over, and the majority
of the Saints turned homeward. "The Move" ever since has been
a high-water mark in the Saints' memory of their history—a triumphant demonstration of their solidarity, a vindication of their
religious convictions, and, in the sequel, a victory over the forces
of evil.

But if, in the sequel, the entrance of the Army into Utah and the
garrisoning of Camp Floyd was made to seem for the Saints a
triumph unalloyed, it could not be swallowed at the time without
a bitterness that lingered on the tongue. For mysterious reasons of
his own, the Lord had not prevented for more than a season an
invasion by the armies of their enemies. That force-in-being at
Camp Floyd subtly conditioned all Mormon thinking, and the
Mormon mind would never again be quite so intransigent. Their
future might be of their own making, but it could not be seen, after
the coming of the Army in the summer of 1858, as *wholly* of their
making.

Numerous special correspondents had journeyed to Utah to report
to the great papers of the country the outcome of this most dramatic

occurrence in the internal affairs of the nation since Andy Jackson all but came to blows with South Carolina. Deprived of their war, many of them turned to sight-seeing, and Great Salt Lake ever since has been prominent on the itinerary of transcontinental sight-seers. The dutiful correspondents applauded the lake scenery as "rough, harsh, grand," and evaluated the lake finally as certainly "one of the most marvellous bodies of water in the world."

During most of the first year after the Army located at Camp Floyd, all such excursions were left to the gentiles. Brigham Young maintained his own principle of nonintercourse, rarely venturing out from the walls about his property on South Temple Street. There were battles to be fought, but of such nature as must be fought by his lieutenants in the courts. Chief Justice D. R. Eckles announced that although President Buchanan had officially pardoned the Mormons, the pardon must be validated by his court. Another of the justices, Charles Sinclair, through the early winter of 1858-1859 heard an interminable contempt action brought against James Ferguson for the baiting of Judge Stiles in his court in February 1857. Ferguson offered to resign from the bar but was refused. He then asked the court, as Hosea Stout put it, "to give Judgement against *pro confesso* which was refused also." There being no help for it, Ferguson elected to fight the case, and with such skill and purpose that he eventually won a unanimous verdict from the mixed gentile-Mormon jury which sat on his case.

The most serious war in the courts was fought out, not in Great Salt Lake City, but in Provo, 40 miles south, late in the winter. Surrounding himself with an escort of troops from Camp Floyd, Judge John Cradlebaugh made a determined effort to dig into some grave crimes committed in Utah during the two proceding years. Seeing his purpose as not so much the ventilation of individual crimes as an assault upon the church itself, the Mormons fought him all along the line and were fortunate in enlisting the sympathies of Governor Cumming, who denied the necessity for the escort, decried its being quartered in the vicinity of Provo and took exception to the troops' being called under civil process other than that initiated through his own office. Johnston's instructions had been ambiguous, and he declined to yield. The dispute was referred to Washington; Cumming's authority was officially upheld;

and the power of the judges to make requisition upon Johnston for troops, either as escort or as *posse comitatus,* was nullified.

As Cradlebaugh, meantime, had found his Mormon grand jury disinclined to go along with him in the matter of finding indictments, he had angrily discharged it "as an evidently useless appendage of a court of justice," and had gone south to investigate the bloody Mountain Meadows Massacre of September 1857 in which upwards of 140 emigrants from Arkansas had been treacherously slain. This foray by Cradlebaugh was broken up by the summons for the troops to return to Camp Floyd, and his activities for all practical purposes came to a halt. He went on west to Carson Valley, still in his capacity as judge, to become involved in the tangled political affairs of the incipient territory of Nevada. Nevada ultimately sent him to Congress, where he engaged in philippics against the Mormons, but the second judicial crusade against the Mormon hegemony came to its effective end with Cradlebaugh's departure.

To Camp Floyd, not far behind the Army, in the summer of 1858 came Captain J. H. Simpson of the Corps of Topographical Engineers. Simpson was a formidably capable officer; exploring was his business. He was set to work without delay, first to locate a new road from Camp Floyd to Fort Bridger, and then to locate one from Camp Floyd west to Carson Valley.

Simpson did both jobs with his accustomed efficiency. Early in the fall of 1858 he located a route up Provo Canyon to Kamas Prairie, over into the valley of the Weber, down that river a distance and then up Chalk Creek Canyon, a little to the south of Echo, to strike the Bear south of the established immigrant road. Returning to Camp Floyd, he made some preliminary explorations 44 miles west, and then in the spring explored a new route all the way to Genoa in Carson Valley, well to the south of the Humboldt trail. Returning, he took a route still more southerly. His return route was even shorter than his outbound trail, but it was the latter which was adopted by the mail and stage lines and over which, after April 1860, the Pony Express rode.

The pioneering of the Overland Trail was a more lasting accomplishment of the Utah Expedition than its invasion of the valleys of Zion. Johnston himself was transferred to other responsibilities in

April 1860. He had kept strictly to himself at Camp Floyd, neither interfering with nor associating with the Saints in any way, and on his departure they gave him their accolade, "an officer and a gentleman," though they have never been able to forgo ironic reflections on the fact that he, chosen to suppress the "rebellious Mormons," should have died for the South on the bloody field of Shiloh. Soon after Johnston departed, the War Department reduced the size of the garrison at Camp Floyd to 10 companies. Fort Sumter was fired on in April following, and in July 1861 the post (by now renamed Camp Crittenden) was evacuated.

It was that ultimate evacuation that made clear to the Saints how the Dispenser of Events all the time had had an eye to their welfare. Over $4,000,000 worth of public property was sold for a song, realizing at auction only about $100,000. Many of Utah's family fortunes originated in the auction sales on the dusty grounds of Camp Crittenden in that hot July of 1861. And in this fashion, Saints like William Clayton could reflect comfortably, had ended "the great Buchanan expedition, costing the Government millions, and accomplishing nothing, except making the Saints comparatively rich, and improving the circumstances of the People of Utah." It was a moral they delighted to preach, and the Saints dinned it into the ears of their countrymen:

"Among the many lessons taught the people of this generation respecting the utter futility of any attempt on [the gentiles'] part to injure or retard the progress of the Church . . . there are none . . . that stand out so prominently before the world as that resulting from the sending of the United States' army to Utah."

Governor John W. Dawson reached town on the mail stage early in December 1861. Lincoln's designate to succeed Alfred Cumming, Dawson at once aroused the ire of the Saints by calling for a $40,000 contribution in taxes for the prosecution of the war against the rebellious Southern states, and by vetoing an act of the territorial legislature calling for a constitutional convention.

The Saints had only to take one good look at this Indiana fop to know that they wanted no part of him. His proposals of taxation were preposterous; did he imagine that the federal government would, as the territory had to, accept payment of taxes in kind? Could a war be prosecuted with adobe bricks, wheat and oats, cattle hides, fur caps and horseshoes? And if the territory waited upon the invitation of Congress to call a constitutional convention, it might wait a hundred years.

So when, about Christmas time, it began to be rumored around town that the governor had made grossly improper proposals to Tom Williams' widow, the Saints figuratively licked their chops. Rumor succeeded juicy rumor—that Sister Williams had raised the fire shovel on the governor, that he had offered her $3,000 not to expose him, that she had made affidavit to Brigham Young and that this affidavit was to be sent to Washington, that the governor had threatened to shoot T. B. H. Stenhouse if he published anything about the matter in the *News,* that the governor was sick and confined to his quarters. (And well he might be sick, the Saints reflected, if the governor had learned of their "mountain law" governing such matters; two men had been shot and killed in 1851, with the full approbation of the community, for just such transgressions.)

Nobody was surprised, then, to hear that Dawson had found it expedient to take the mail stage east out of Great Salt Lake City at 3:00 P.M. on December 31. Everybody could have wished that the Dawson affair had ended with the ripe odor of his departure. Six young Mormon rowdies, however, took it upon themselves to avenge the sullied honor of their townsfolk and followed the mail coach east to the station at Mountain Dell. With the connivance of the driver, they fell upon Dawson and beat him to within an inch of his life. For good measure, they plundered the coach of all his belongings.

Nobody had any sympathy for Dawson, but some decent respect for the law had to be observed, all the more so because the beating administered the governor robbed the Saints of moral force in the noise they could make in Washington over the political scum sent to govern them. So the sheriff told his deputies to get to work and lay the perpetrators by the heels.

Most of the young hellions were taken without difficulty, but Lot Huntington and Moroni Clawson, with a companion, hightailed it out of town. They failed to reckon with the Overland Telegraph, completed the preceding October, and they were soon run to earth near Fish Springs, on the southern rim of the Salt Desert. Huntington was killed, and the posse took the other two in charge.

These two prisoners made another break for freedom on arriving in Great Salt Lake City. The police shot them down on the street. This happened on Friday morning, January 17, 1862. It was barely three weeks since the Dawson scandal broke.

Notwithstanding the lurid character of all these events, there was nothing particularly remarkable about them. The surge and sway of political rough-and-tumble, the rascality of the gentile officials, the rowdyism of the Mormons—all these are elements of a social relationship that were constantly being repeated in one context or another. The Dawson affair had been unusual in its ramifications, including the almost irrelevant killing of three men, and those ramifications had extended beyond all reasonable bounds. The story had run down, and there was every reason to regard it as finished.

But it was not finished. The killing of 'Rone Clawson set on foot a whole new series of events. And now the story could become aberrant, something totally removed from the predictable operation of cause and effect. In ceasing to be the Dawson affair and becoming the Jean Baptiste affair, the story ceases to be typical and becomes unique. And in so doing, it provides Great Salt Lake with the strangest episode in its whole history.

No one claimed 'Rone Clawson's body, so it was buried at the expense of the county in the bare, windswept cemetery up on the north bench. Henry Heath, a member of the city police force, troubled by a sense of the amenities that should not be lacking in the burial even of a desperado, purchased clothes for Clawson at his own expense. No pauper, he thought, ever had better or cleaner burial clothing.

So, a week later, on a visit to the little settlement of Willow Creek (now Draper) at the south end of Salt Lake Valley, Heath was astonished at being indignantly accosted by George Clawson, 'Rone's brother. George had had 'Rone's remains exhumed and removed to Willow Creek, and on opening the grave had found the body entirely naked. He accused Heath of having buried his brother in that condition and was deaf to all protestations to the contrary.

Angry and upset, Heath rode back to town. Finally he went to unburden himself to the probate judge, Elias Smith. The judge told him to take three or four men and look into the case right away.

The policemen went first to the residence of Sexton J. C. Little for his ideas about how it could have happened that Clawson's body had been stripped of its clothing. The dumfounded sexton had no suggestions to offer, so, at a loss for a likely lead, they trooped up to Third Avenue to have a talk with the gravedigger, Jean Baptiste. The gravedigger was not at home, but his wife readily admitted them to the house.

The woman's mind was so feeble that it was difficult to get any intelligent answers out of her. But as the men talked at her, the curiosity of one of them was aroused by numerous boxes lying about the room. Idly he poked into one of the boxes, when an oath brought them all staring over his shoulder. The box was filled with burial robes. All the boxes were filled with burial robes.

Appalled by their discovery, the policemen set out for the cemetery. None of them knew much about Jean Baptiste. One had heard that he was an Italian who had come from Venice. Another had heard that he was not an Italian but a Frenchman, and another that although he was of French origin, he had come from Australia. A nondescript little man, he had come to Great Salt Lake City half a dozen years before to sink into the obscurity of his job in the cemetery; "John the Baptist," he was usually called.

The gravedigger was found at work in the snowy cemetery. A small and shrunken fellow, he paused in his labor with the frozen earth to watch them come up. At Heath's bitter accusation he fell upon his knees, calling upon God to witness his innocence. Heath took him by the throat and shook him like a rat; it required only a moment to choke a confession from him. For years he had been robbing the dead.

Not entirely able to comprehend this horror, the policemen stared at him. He began to beg piteously for his life, and finally they laid rough hands upon him and kicked and cuffed him to the city jail.

The news spread around town with cyclonic fury. Hundreds thronged to the county courthouse to examine the clothing brought from Baptiste's home. Although torn, some of the items could be identified. . . . The police locked Baptiste in the farthest recesses of the jail. Had they not, Judge Elias Smith wrote in his journal, "the populace would have torn him to pieces, such was the excitement produced by the unheard of occurrence."

Late the following afternoon Baptiste was placed flat in a wagon bed, covered with a blanket to screen him from view and taken back to the cemetery. The Mormon annalist says:

"He only admitted identifying about a dozen graves that he had robbed, the names of which the police made a note of, but it was very evident that he wilfully lied, as about 60 pairs of children's shoes and small clothes were found in his house—about a dozen men's shoes, garments and many parts of suits of females. He has robbed children and women's graves principally. Reports run that he has robbed nearly 300 graves."

The policeman, Albert Dewey, puzzled over this strange prisoner. Baptiste had used his victims' coffins for kindling wood, and had hoarded the clothes of the dead as a miser might hoard gold. Though he greatly feared death, he had no fear of the dead, and had prowled about among the graves at night to divest the dead of their apparel with no more concern than if he were eating his dinner: "Altogether he was a freak of human nature that I could not understand. Robbing the dead was a mania with him and he made it a business."

What could be done with such a monster? On Saturday, February 1, Baptiste was brought from his cell, and Judge Smith, so he wrote in his journal, heard Baptiste's statements "as to how he came to engage in the business of robbing the dead, and his confession as to the extent to which he had carried on the operation. According to his acknowledgments he had robbed many graves, but how many—he could not or would not tell."

Throughout the next week Jean Baptiste was kept in jail. The court record is absolutely silent about him; the personal journal of the judge is the sole indication that Baptiste ever received a judicial hearing, least of all a trial. But it is evident that for his own safety Baptiste could not have been freed on bail, even had he possessed friends to provide it. The public excitement, even a week later, was so intense that Brigham Young found it necessary to reckon with it in one of his discourses.

If the Saints wished to know what he thought of this matter, Brigham said, searching for words to comfort his people:

"I answer, I am unable to think so low as to get at such a mean, contemptible, damnable trick. I have three sisters in the grave yard in this city, and two wives and several children, besides other connection and near relatives. I have not been to open any of their graves to see whether they were robbed, and I do not mean to do so. I gave them as good a burial as I could; and in burying our dead, we all have made everything as agreeable and comfortable as we could to the eye and taste of the people in their various capacities, according to the best of our judgments; we have done our duty in this particular, and I for one am satisfied. I will defy any thief there is on the earth or in hell to rob a Saint of one blessing . . . when the resurrection takes place, the Saints will come forth with all the glory, beauty and excellence of resurrected Saints, clothed as they were when they were laid away."

They might do as they pleased with regard to taking up their friends, he said.

"If I should undertake to do anything of the kind, I should clothe them completely and then lay them away again. And if you are afraid of their being robbed again, put them in your gardens, where you can watch them by day and night until you are pretty sure that the clothing is rotted, and then lay them away in the burying ground. I would let my friends lay and sleep in peace."

Ultimately, the police put all the soiled burial clothing in a large box and buried it in a single grave in the cemetery. But it was not so easy to dispose of Jean Baptiste.

What to do with him? Brigham Young in that sermon of February 9 had pondered this question.

"To hang a man for such a deed would not satisfy my feelings. What shall we do with him. Shoot him? No, that would do no good to anybody but himself. Would you imprison him during life? That would do nobody any good. What I would do with him came to me quickly after I heard of the circumstance. . . . I would make him a fugitive and a vagabond upon the earth. This would be my sentence, but probably the people will not want this done."

The policeman Henry Heath remembered in after years that Baptiste was kept in the jail three weeks. More probably, it was three months. In the end Brigham Young's suggestion was followed—after a more vengeful fashion.

"It meant death to him," the policeman Albert Dewey says, "to turn him loose in the community—death that he deserved and in any country would have received. But he was such a hateful object that the sooner and further away he got from sight without being put under ground himself, the better every one would feel. So, to give him a chance for his life, to save him in reality from an exasperated public, it was decided to banish him, and a well-stocked island in the great Salt Lake was chosen for his future home."

So far in the case of Jean Baptiste the record is recoverable. But with his banishment to a desolate island in the Great Salt Lake, mystery overclouds the details.

He was placed in a wagon and taken from the jail to Antelope Island, across the Antelope bar. All accounts agree as to that. Since, if left on Antelope, he could have waded right back to shore again, arrangements were made with two Davis County stockmen, Henry and Dan Miller, to convey him in their boat to Frémont Island and there maroon him. (The Millers for some time had been using this island for their stock; it was becoming quite generally known as Miller Island.) The grave robber actually was conveyed to Frémont Island and left there. The stories agree as to that, also.

But other details are uncertain and disputed. A contemporary record says that his ears were cut off and that he was branded "Grave robber" on his forehead. It may be that a ball and chain was fastened to his ankle to prevent him from swimming to freedom. The policemen who took him to Antelope, however, 30 years later swore up and down that Baptiste had never been shackled with ball and chain, and they swore also that the branding had been a matter only of tattooing with indelible ink. The question of mutilation was not raised.

Albert Dewey says that the Miller brothers had erected on the island a shanty they kept stocked with provisions. Calling at the island three weeks after the banishment, they found that Baptiste had helped himself liberally to their provisions and was getting along well enough, but another trip to the island three weeks later disclosed the fact that the exile had flown. Dewey puts it:

"The roof and part of the sides of the cabin had been torn off. A part of the carcass of a three year old heifer was lying on the ground a short distance away, and a portion of the hide near by, cut into thongs. It was evident that with the tools found in the cabin, Baptiste had killed the heifer, built a raft from the logs and timber of the shanty and with this had made his escape from the island."

In some part, Dewey's tale is borne out by a contemporary notation by the church annalist in Great Salt Lake City, under date of August 4, 1862: "Today Dan Miller who had been over to the island lately reported that John the Baptist had gone. He had killed a two year old heifer and it is supposed that with two or three slabs which were on the island he had made a canoe and escaped."

With that journal entry Jean Baptiste vanishes altogether from the realm of ascertainable fact. He simply disappears. Yet his disappearance has left behind it a whole train of provocative possibilities.

About 1890 near the mouth of the Jordan River a party of duck hunters found, protruding from the mud, a human skull. They made search for the rest of the skeleton, but without success. However, late in March 1893 another hunter discovered a skeleton in the vicinity. The arm and leg bones were there, and the ribs and vertebrae, but no skull. "Around the leg bones," so the Salt Lake *Herald* reported, "was an iron clamp, and in attempting to lift this up a chain was found attached, necessitating a little digging up of the ground, and there, attached, to the chain, was an iron ball."

The *Herald* had an enterprising reporter who, more or less inaccurately, wrote up the long-forgotten story of the exiled grave robber on the theory that the find undoubtedly was the skeleton of Jean Baptiste:

"In his wandering around the island he no doubt became crazed from hunger, fear and cold, and falling into the briny water of the lake, was drowned or strangled. The winds coursing down the eastern side of the lake are almost invariably from the northwest, and at times little less than a hurricane, and it can be readily perceived that from the point where the bones were found that the body could have easily been carried thither, where the sand covered it up and where it has lain since until the receding waters of the lake washed away the covering and the remains were found."

This was a fascinating but also a sensational explanation as to what had become of Jean Baptiste, and it nettled the *Deseret News*. Denying that the skeleton could have been that of Baptiste, insisting that it must have been the skeleton of one or another of those who at various times had escaped from the territorial penitentiary, the newspaper set its own reporter to digging into the buried history. He was able to turn up the two policemen, Henry Heath and Albert Dewey, and in its issue of May 27, 1893, the *News* told their story.

In many respects the two policemen confirmed and amplified the known record. But on two things they were insistent: Baptiste had never been branded except with indelible ink, and "Steel nor iron shackles were never put on his limbs and there is absolutely no truth in the statement that he was turned loose on the island with a ball and chain on." "There was no ball and chain or shackles or gyves of any kind on his limbs. He was absolutely untrammeled." Consequently, as the lately discovered skeleton had been shackled, it could not have been the remains of Jean Baptiste.

Perhaps the policemen told the whole truth as to what was done with Jean Baptiste. And yet the whole thing had been a good deal more than irregular. Baptiste was dealt with by what must be described as lynch law and the fact that it was done by officers of the law only underlines this awkward fact. The policemen who were interviewed in 1893 had every incentive to put as kind an interpretation as possible on the part they had taken in the marooning of Jean Baptiste. There is something too forbearing about the attitudes they profess to have held toward their prisoner. To brand his forehead with his infamy and cut off his ears, as the matter-of-fact contemporary record indicates was done, accords much better with the sense of bitter outrage that prevailed in 1862 than to think he was simply turned loose on a desert island to shift for himself.

And yet, if there were tools on the island, if Jean Baptiste was able to demolish a hut and escape on a raft constructed of its parts, how was it that he was unable to free himself of his irons?

Still again, if the shackled bones found near the mouth of the Jordan were *not* the last earthly remains of Jean Baptiste, what became of him? There is no possibility that he died on the island; it is too small and over the years has been tramped by too many feet. His body would have been found. If he drowned in attempting to escape, it seems once more inevitable that his body must have been found—unless, indeed, he drowned in deep water and sank with the weight of his irons. But that raises anew the difficult question of the irons.

If, despite everything, Jean Baptiste ultimately escaped, where did he vanish to? Even if his ears were not cut off, even if his forehead was branded with ink only, how could he have found anonymity anywhere? This question was hardly answered by the *News.*

"The general belief is that he made his escape to the mainland on the north, somewhere near the Promontory; and it was reported some time afterwards on what would seem to be unquestioned authority that he was seen in a Montana mining camp and on being closely questioned by one who recognized him, confessed to being Jean Baptiste and related how he made his escape. Another rumor is that he joined himself to a west bound emigrant train, went to the coast where he lived for some time before coming to Utah, then left San Francisco, where he feared he would be recognized and made his way into southern California, where it is understood he died."

But, the *News* acknowledged, no one of whom it had been able to hear knew anything positively about Jean Baptiste since he had been left on the island in the lake.

A half century after, that summing up by the *News* still stands. The grave robber has vanished into unhappy legend, and none of history's resources of inquiry can drag out of the depths of time the answer to what became of him.

The whole episode is almost unparalleled in Mormon history. The *Deseret News* of 1862 had absolutely nothing to say of Jean Baptiste—nothing but the stenographic report of Brigham's sermon. The *News* had much to say of the Dawson scandal, the Dawson beating and the killing of Huntington and Clawson—no distaste for the sensational prevented an allusion to the affair of Jean Baptiste. What of the people who thronged the courthouse; what of the furor that gripped the city? How was it that a newspaper could pass such matters by?

And how is it that Jean Baptiste could be jailed—for weeks, admittedly; for months, almost for a certainty—and leave no trace in the criminal records? How could he be given a judicial hearing and leave not so much as a shadow upon the records of the court? (I have vainly searched the records of Salt Lake County; they afford minute details of the trial of Dawson's assailants, and other operations of the judicial machinery of 1862, but yield up no word of Baptiste.) And who, finally, could take upon himself the responsibility for sentencing a man, without trial, to be marooned upon a desert island?

Even when these puzzles are laid aside, the mystery attendant upon the entire affair of Jean Baptiste is wholly remarkable. For the Mormons have had enemies, both bitter and unscrupulous, during the whole course of their history, enemies who have delighted to seize upon real or imagined irregularities of which the Saints have been guilty, to make all the lurid capital possible to be made from them. Yet the strange case of Jean Baptiste is one they have left almost wholly aside.

Folklore and history alike have turned their face from Jean Baptiste. His story itself has almost sunk from sight. He is a presence on a lost page of history, the only specter of the Great Salt Lake.

Chapter 15

Wooden and Iron Horses

Young men whose whiskers grew red from their chins have singularly stamped the history of Utah. Redheaded Miles Goodyear was "Utah's First Citizen" in the years before the Mormons came, and Patrick Edward Connor, with whiskers as fiery as befitted a son of County Kerry, won himself the accolade, "First Gentile of Utah." Goodyear gave way at once before the Mormons, but Connor made it his business to come squarely to grips with the Saints, and there has never been any possibility that he, like Goodyear, might fade into the limbo of uncertain legend.

Connor first fills the eye of history on the blood-soaked Mexican battlefield of Buena Vista, when General Wool rode up to demand of him what had become of his men. Pointing with his wounded hand at the bodies strewn upon the field, young Captain Connor rebuked his superior: "General. There!"

After the war Connor's explosive energy took him to California in the high tide of the gold rush. No man to pan gold for day wages, soon he was cutting piling at Humboldt Bay; he chartered two brigs and himself piloted them in and out of the bay. This work soon bored him, perhaps, for when the celebrated marauder, Joaquin Murrieta, set the gold fields by the ears, Connor joined the select California Rangers who hunted him down, decapitated him, and publicly exhibited his head, after the fashion of the time. In 1854 Connor married and settled down at Stockton. "Settled down," however, is a figure of speech only, for he engaged in the contracting business and served as postmaster, secretary of the State Fair, treasurer of the San Joaquin Agricultural Society, captain of the Anniversary Guards, captain of the Stockton Blues, captain of the Union Guard, and Adjutant General of the Second Brigade. Here was just the man to be precipitated into the tangled destinies of the Mormons.

In August 1861 Connor was commissioned colonel of the Third California Infantry, and like his regiment, held high hopes of winning glory on the eastern battlefields. But while training was still in progress, in March 1862, the Shoshoni began to raid the Overland Trail east of Fort Bridger, and the chances of the regiment for action against Johnny Reb went glimmering. It was as "Soldiers of the Overland" that history would have to remember them.

The march east began in August 1862. Being stationed in Utah suited Connor's men not at all, and as the alkali dust bellied up behind them, they voiced their shame and indignation in the exact language their frustration required. Nor did they vent their feelings in griping only; their offer of $30,000 to the War Department for the privilege of going to the Potomac to be shot at was eloquent of their state of mind.

But patriotism, however ebullient, must be overruled by considerations of national policy, and the command must keep on marching into the sunrise. So, in the dusty splendor of their brass-buttoned blue uniforms, Connor's men comforted themselves with the idea that maybe they would end up fighting the Mormons. Dark suspicions were entertained about the loyalty of the Saints, anyway. The best that could be said about the Mormon attitude toward the war was that they wished as much bad luck to the South as to the North. If they were not overtly treasonable, nobody could suspect them of patriotic enthusiasm for the war. It was reported, indeed, that the Saints presumptuously proclaimed that God was dealing with the people of the United States for their maltreatment of his chosen ones.

Hence, as the regiment marched east, it muttered and scowled and promised to wipe the earth with the Saints if the opportunity should offer. Connor fully shared in the attitude of his men. He left his troops at Ruby Valley, going ahead in civilian clothes via the Overland Stage to look out a likely place to establish his command. On his return he wrote his superior,

"It will be impossible for me to describe what I saw and heard in Salt Lake, so as to make you realize the enormity of Mormonism; suffice it, that I found them a community of traitors, murderers, fanatics, and whores. The people publicly rejoice at reverses to our arms, and thank God that the American Government is gone, as they term it, while their prophet and bishops preach treason from the pulpit. The Federal officers are entirely powerless, and talk in whispers, for fear of being overheard by Brigham's spies. . . . I have a difficult and dangerous task before me."

The idea of relocating at Camp Crittenden he gave short shrift:

"I found another location, which I like better. . . . It is on a plateau about three miles from Salt Lake City, in the vicinity of good timber and sawmills, and at a point where hay, grain, and other produce can be purchased cheaper than at Fort Crittenden. It is also a point which commands the city, and where one thousand troops would be more efficient than three thousand on the other side of the Jordan. If the General decides that I shall locate there, I intend to quietly intrench my position, and then say to the Saints of Utah, enough of your treason; but if it is intended that I shall merely protect the overland mail and permit the Mormons to act and utter treason, then I had as well locate at Crittenden."

Connor was given free rein, and early in October he marched his force east from Ruby Valley. On the night of October 18 they encamped just west of the Jordan, and rumor ran wild through the camp that the Mormons would resist the crossing of the river, that the chief of the Danites was riding through the streets of Great Salt Lake City offering to bet $500 that the Army would not succeed in the crossing; it was reported also that the colonel had vowed that he would cross the Jordan if hell yawned below.

As it turned out not a solitary individual awaited them on the eastern bank. Wrote the San Francisco *Bulletin's* correspondent, almost regretfully, "It was a magnificent place for a fight, too."

On the morning of October 20, 1862, Connor's boys in blue resumed their line of march toward Great Salt Lake City, wondering just where they were going to locate, not unmindful after all of their colonel's boldness in marching them into the very heart of the Mormon domain. The objections of the Mormon leaders to close proximity of soldiers and citizens were well known and of long standing; there had been trouble with Steptoe's men in 1854-1855, and much friction with Johnston's command in 1858-1861. If things did come to fighting, the 750 men of the command and the thousands of Saints, it required a sanguine soul to anticipate any better outcome than that they would be avenged by their government in the end.

As they marched into the city behind their brass band, they found every street crossing occupied by spectators; and onlookers crowded the windows, doors and roofs all along the line of march. All was deadly silent; "not a cheer, not a jeer" greeted them. Were these manifestations of loyalty? The troops found it hard to think so.

In front of the mansion of the new governor, Stephen S. Harding, Connor's command heard the governor's formal welcome and then marched eastward toward the bench above the city. The chosen location was one on the sloping benchland just north of Red Butte Creek. In honor of the "Little Giant," Connor named this post Camp Douglas.

It was Indians, after all, with whom the Soldiers of the Overland did their fighting. The baptism of fire came in January in Cache Valley. A band of Shoshoni had been plaguing the immigrant road and the northern Mormon settlements. Connor marched through bitter winter weather to fall upon this refractory band. In the Battle of Bear River he slaughtered perhaps three hundred of the red men, and though the Mormons deplored this barbarity of the federal soldiery, the action brought a final peace to that region. The battle also brought Connor his brigadier general's star, and two year later the honor of dealing with the plains Indians when hostilities with the Sioux broke out in the Powder River country.

Once his command was established in Great Salt Lake City, Connor addressed himself to the Mormon problem. What was needed was a large influx of gentiles. Sheer weight of numbers could break down the tight Mormon economy and overturn the close-knit Mormon society. Agriculture did not promise much for revolutionary purposes, since the Mormons already held the most fruitful lands for hundreds of miles in all directions; and there was no visible economic base for a significant expansion of trade. But the Mormon position did have one vulnerable flank. Brigham Young had thrown his influence against prospecting for precious metals. No one knew what the territory might contain in the way of mineral resources. If a rich strike could be made somewhere,

L. Clyde Anderson

Boating on Great Salt Lake, Antelope Island in background.

David H. Mann

Winter playground at Snow Basin, in the Wasatch Mountains east of Ogden.

L. Clyde Anderson

Bathers floating on Great Salt Lake, borne up by the dense salt water.

another gold rush might settle the Mormon problem out of hand. Connor turned his California Volunteers loose to prospect the Mormon country.

Promising strikes were made at once. The territory's first mining district, the West Mountain District (covering the eastern slopes of the Oquirrh Mountains) was organized in the summer of 1863, and the organization of other districts followed rapidly. In June 1864 the first gentile town in Utah was laid out in Rush Valley, named Stockton for Connor's California home. Near this town Connor built the Pioneer Smelting Works, the first important smelter in Utah.

In Great Salt Lake City the Saints jeered at the "poor miserable diggers," inhabiting the bench above the city, but they had to acknowledge the tangible nature of this new commercial bustle. Already the New Jerusalem had come far from its pioneer beginnings. The trees which had been planted along the naked streets now threw blue masses of shade upon the walks, and the weathered adobe houses on their neat rectangular lots, snugly framed by their gardens, fruit trees and flowers, justified and ennobled these years of toil. But there were significant departures from the pioneer plan. The merchants had taken East Temple Street to themselves, and everybody now called it Main Street. During the era of Johnston's army it had acquired a dubious fame as Whisky Street, but it was now re-establishing its respectability, and the Saints freely availed themselves of its flourishing mercantile establishments, blacksmith shops, butcher shops, saddleries, tanneries—and even, on regrettable occasion, its city-operated liquor store.

The mining activity, combined with the lucrative new freighting business with the gold camps of Idaho and Montana, inaugurated in Great Salt Lake City the architectural era of bigger and better things. In the spring of 1864 William Jennings erected at the corner of First South and Main Streets his imposing Eagle Emporium. A three-story stone structure, it quite took the shine off the ramshackle adobes and the wooden false fronts of the competition. Across the street W. S. Godbe was impelled to put up something of comparable splendor, and, among others, the Walker brothers promptly followed the example set them.

The four Walker brothers are central figures in the economic warfare which shook the Utah valleys during the last half of this decade. They had migrated to Utah in 1852 with their mother, a widowed Mormon convert. They had nominally been members of the church, and like the most pious Saints with whom they rubbed elbows, paid their tithing and maintained their fellowship. After a period of apprenticeship they seized the opportunity provided by the sale of the government stores at the abandonment of Camp Crittenden. They went into business for themselves and won an immediate and resounding success.

The brothers have a certain celebrity in the history of Great Salt Lake, for to them belongs, seemingly, the distinction of launching in Great Salt Lake the first boat designed for the pure joy of sailing the salt waters. Unfortunately, almost nothing is known about their craft, described simply as "a lonesome pleasure yacht" that was maintained for some years. It may, however, have been this boat which was requisitioned for service on the great occasion of Schuyler Colfax's visit to Utah in June of 1865. As Speaker of the House, Colfax was lavishly entertained by Saints and gentiles alike. Colfax's party visited the lake, bathed in its salt water and, as the journalist Albert D. Richardson writes, "took sail in a little sloop, which we all found enjoyable except Mr. Colfax, who suffered greatly from sea-sickness." If this was the craft built by the Walker brothers, Richardson's is the only thing like a description of it, and it is not known what became of it. The Walkers may have sold it, for very soon after the Colfax visit they had a war to fight quite sufficient to engross all their energies, physical and financial.

Brigham Young had never been entirely able to reconcile himself to the gentile merchants. They had been welcome in the beginning, when there was such a desperate need of goods from the States. But the inundation of the forty-niners, who had all but given away their property in their haste to get on to California, established a standard of values beside which all the merchants thereafter must look like the most conscienceless of profiteers. Nor was this distortion in financial perspective the only reason for looking at the merchants with a jealous eye. It did violence to Brigham's sense of the fitness of things that outsiders should live off the labors of the Saints.

When everything good had been said about the gentile merchants, the fact remained that their only interest in the Saints was to make money out of them. They had no obvious interest in the upbuilding of Zion, paid no tithing and evinced no disposition to be saved. It did violence, again, to Brigham's every economic instinct to see the Saints dependent on the *outside* for anything whatever. It was plain to him that the only way the Saints could hope to become a rich people was to make themselves wholly independent. If they impoverished themselves to buy things that couldn't be provided within the territory, they would forever be the slaves of the gentiles.

All through the fifties he had carried on an intermittent campaign in pursuit of his economic ideas, preaching home industry and retrenchment, even attempting to abate the eternal feminine pursuit of fashion with a simple "Deseret costume" which the women could wear day in and day out the whole year through. He was utterly vanquished in that battle, even in his own home; it was of no avail even to denounce his wives from the pulpit. But he preached the Word of Wisdom to eliminate the dependence of the Saints on tea, coffee and tobacco; he urged the building up of a sheep and woolen manufacturing industry; and, to grow cotton, in 1861 he sent a colonizing mission to the Virgin River Valley.

The impact of Connor and boom times upon this perpetual struggle to render the Saints self-sufficient was irritating at best. The mines were an ever-present threat to Mormon hegemony, and in Great Salt Lake City the gentiles were waxing fat and sassy. They had their own paper, the exceedingly plain-spoken *Daily Union Vedette;* they were obviously enriching themselves at the expense of the Saints; and they gave aid and comfort to the apostates from the Mormon faith. It could be said, indeed, with more than a color of truth, that they were creating a race of apostates, for, as an example, in 1863 the Walker brothers declined to pay tithing any longer. (It is said that they offered to donate an equivalent amount direct to the poor, but this was received by the church as an intolerable affront.)

The problem of freeing the Saints from economic bondage occupied Brigham Young and his advisors throughout the period of Connor's occupation. The need was accentuated by the currency inflation occasioned by the war, and in the summer of 1864 a farm price convention was held to put price floors under the staple agricultural commodities. This idea broadened, and soon the Saints were being exhorted to control the trade and traffic of the mountains by organizing their own marketing co-operatives. By the fall of 1866 a semiorganized boycott had made itself felt, and the gentile merchants formally proposed to Brigham Young that as it was evidently his desire to force all to leave the territory who did not belong to the Mormon faith, with the Saints being intimidated and coerced from trading with any not of their faith, the church should buy out the merchants. The suggested basis was: "first—the payment of our outstanding accounts owing us by members of your church; secondly—all of our goods, merchandise, chattels, houses, improvements, etc., to be taken at a cash valuation, and we to make a deduction of twenty-five per cent from total amount."

Upon this proposition Brigham Young poured a stinging scorn: "If you could make such sales as you propose, you would make more money than any merchants have ever done in this country, and we, as merchants, would like to find purchasers upon the same basis." As for withdrawing from the territory, the gentile merchants might go or stay; it was all one to him. And, he took pains to point out, "every man who had dealt fairly and honestly, and confined his attention to his legitimate business, whatever his creed has been, has found friendship in us." It was only "avowed enemies of this community," he said, to which the Saints took exception.

The gentile merchants stuck it out because they couldn't get away, and if they were saved in the end, it was not by the Saints but by the Pacific Railroad.

The coming of the railroad, for the Mormon country as for all the West, marks the end of an era. With small exception, overland travel had been an affair of the summer months, when grass grew on the plains and in the mountains, and when the passes were clear of snow. The world closed down each winter in a stasis broken only by the warm spring sun, and Zion was compartmented within the confines of its own vast distances. All of that was changed with the coming of the railroad, the isolation in time and space broken down forever.

But there were other significant effects of the building of the railroad. The economy of the territory was overturned at a stroke. Every industry, every commercial undertaking, had to reckon the changed factor of freight charges in its equation of cost. Many kinds of home manufacturing enterprises were doomed at once, unable to compete with goods shipped in from outside. The effects of the railroad extended as far away as the Virgin Valley, where the cotton missionaries labored hopelessly and stubbornly. But the railroad also made its influence immediately felt in another fashion: complex ores it had not been feasible to mine could now be shipped as far as Liverpool for profitable reduction.

Not all of this could be foreseen by the Saints, and it was as much the evolution of their economic thinking as a means of armoring themselves against the impact of the railroad that they embarked in the fall of 1868 upon the organization of co-operative stores. That impulse toward co-operative endeavor, which had been an intermittent force in Mormon life since 1831, had a final flowering in 1874, when the aging Brigham Young organized the semicommunistic United Order of Enoch. Except in a few isolated communities, however, the United Order was short-lived, and in the end it could not survive even in the outlands. Champion of American industrialism, the railroad triumphed finally over even so stubborn an antagonist as the Lion of the Lord. Not all Brigham's labors and exhortations and hopes could avail against its pulverizing force.

For years before its coming it was the hope of objective observers that the railroad would have the effect upon Mormon society which in the long run it actually did have. But the process was expected to be rather precipitate, the overthrow of the Mormons to be a matter of months. The Saints laughed at all such hopes that breaking down their isolation would be their undoing; it was a poor church, they scoffed, that could not stand one railroad, and they pointed out that since 1854 they had regularly petitioned Congress for just such a railroad.

They wanted it to come by way of Salt Lake City. But this meant that it must be routed around the south shore of Great Salt Lake, and the engineers of neither the Central Pacific, building east, nor the Union Pacific, building west, could see it that way; both agreed, finally, that the best route lay north of the lake. However, before the Union Pacific committed itself finally to this opinion, it contributed an interesting and now virtually forgotten chapter to the history of the Great Salt Lake.

In 1868, as in 1902, when the Lucin Cutoff was finally built, it was obvious that the most direct route west from Ogden was straight across Great Salt Lake. Not only was it most direct; it also had the advantage of avoiding the burdensome pull up over the Promontory summit. But sending the Pacific Railroad "to sea" was a conception novel and perhaps hazardous as well. Was it advisable? Was it even feasible? In June 1868 F. C. Hodges was told to find out.

The big question was the depth of the lake. Hodges examined Stansbury's map and frowned. West of Promontory Point the map showed soundings as deep as 34 feet. It was clearly out of the question to build all the way across the lake. But between Promontory Point and the eastern shore, Stansbury showed a maximum depth of 10 feet. Hodges thought this over. Perhaps he could run the line across Bear River Bay to the tip of the Point, then up the west side of Promontory to the head of Spring Bay and on west by the same route that would be followed if the road ran entirely north of the lake. Though this might save no distance, if it avoided the heavy grades that would be necessary to cross the Promontory summit, such a line would be well worth the trouble its building might occasion.

Before coming to any conclusions, however, it would be necessary to sound the lake along the line to Promontory. The lake had been rising for six years, and without question it was well above the level of Stansbury's survey. Hodges obtained a boat and pushed out from the eastern shore. The boat was not caulked very well, and the heavy water soon shook the caulking out of the bottom, so that Hodges was finally thankful to get back to shore without having to swim for it, all the more so when he discovered, on reaching shore again, that his topographer could not swim a stroke. The voyage was productive of information—but information Hodges shook his head over. He had found 22 feet of water where Stansbury had found 10. It was hardly imaginable that they could venture upon a rock fill of such proportions.

Still, the job was only half done. The reconnaissance of the west shore of Promontory might reveal compensating features. Reading Stansbury's *Report,* Hodges was disposed to think that he would do well to follow the example of the topographical engineer 18 years before and arrange for supplying his party by water. The sailboat he called into service, the *Star of the West,* has no other known claim to fame. Her owner, a Mr. (John B.?) Meredith, joined the party, whether for the adventure or for his hire.

Hodges' persistence was all to no purpose, for the lake very quickly gave him a demonstration that it had absolutely no idea of countenancing a railroad at this time of its life. The boat had no sooner landed the reconnaissance party on Promontory and rounded the Point for the rendezvous at Storm Bay than it came to grief.

That unlucky night of June 13, 1868, all the crew slept on shore, but their provisions were left on the boat. The wind was blowing comfortably off shore and everything seemed shipshape when they went to bed. During the night, however, the wind veered around, and by morning it was blowing a furious gale from the westsouthwest. The sudden waves boomed in on the shore, and the men threw off their blankets to stand on the beach and stare through the gray morning light at the little boat wrenching at her cables offshore.

Hodges had no faith whatever in those cables and offered a substantial reward to anyone who could reach the boat and keep her from being blown ashore. No one who tried it, however, could keep his feet in the smashing surf. One of the party, bolder than the rest, tried to swim it but the waves simply hurled him back into the arms of his comrades, half-strangled by the brine. So they were reduced to staring impotently, hour after hour, while the anxious Meredith swore that he had never seen such a storm on the lake. After five hours of it, the boat lost her anchor stock. She was immediately swept in and broken on the rocks.

The men scrambled to salvage what they could of her cargo and struggled to save the boat herself, but the bottom of the *Star of the West* was stove in beyond repair. The *Deseret News* late in June finished the sad tale:

"She sank and remains at anchor and waterlogged in Storm Bay. Mr. Meredith started for Kaysville, to procure assistance, to get her home and hauled up for repairs; and he feels confident of soon having her again 'plowing' the Lake. The surveying party proceeded on Wednesday, the 17th, to Musquito Springs, over an almost impassable road, the most of the day being spent in making the distance—two miles. Next day they reached Railroad Springs, six miles further, over a similar road; and they were at Salvation Springs, all well, on the 21st."

So the Saints must resign themselves to the inevitable and let the railroad go wherever the engineers saw fit to take it. In fact, they would undertake to help it get there. Brigham Young liked nothing that he heard of the hell-roaring construction camps moving west toward Zion; it would be better for the Saints to do the work. Besides, they could use the money. Several of the apostles contracted to build the Central Pacific grades from Humboldt Wells to Ogden, and Brigham himself took the contract to build the grades for the Union Pacific through the notoriously impassable gorges of the Weber.

All of a sudden there was a boom in the market for lumber, and in its wake Great Salt Lake for the first time began to commend itself for commercial navigation. Connor launched a schooner, the *Pioneer;* and not content with that, late in 1868 he gave the lake its first steamboat, the *Kate Connor,* which was promptly set to transporting railroad ties and telegraph poles from the south shore of the lake. Connor had retired from the Army in the summer of 1866 when his California Volunteers were mustered out of service. Now a citizen of Stockton, the town of his founding, he could envision a profitable shipping business between the mines and the new railroad, and in the spring of 1869 he launched a third boat, the 100-ton schooner *Pluribustah;* Utah's First Gentile was in a fair way to have a veritable fleet in operation on the mountain sea.

The Union Pacific had been ambitious of reaching Ogden by the end of 1868, but it was March 1869 before the tracklayers burst through the canyons of the Weber. On the afternoon of March 8 the first locomotive steamed into Ogden, greeted by the banner, "Hail to the High Way of Nations! Utah Bids You Welcome!" The "soul-enlivening strains" from a brass band were punctuated at intervals by the roar of artillery, and there was oratory in great plenty. Among the many speakers, the apostle F. D. Richards pointed out that those who had said the Mormons did not wish a railroad to pass through their country were now confounded. "Our labors along the line," he declared, "especially through Echo and Weber Kanyons, are a standing and irrefutable testimony of our great desire and anxiety to see the completion of this, the greatest undertaking ever designed by human skill and wisdom."

A labor of road building remained. The Union Pacific swept on north to round Great Salt Lake in its headlong race to meet the Central Pacific. The great incentive was, of course, the federal bounty for each mile of track laid, which included not only cash subsidies and other bonuses but grants of land a mile square, alternating checkerboard fashion for 20 miles back on either side of the tracks. The grading gangs of the two railroads, working alongside each other west of Ogden, laid aside their shovels to employ their pick handles on each other; and the boisterous Union Pacific Irishmen and the tough Central Pacific coolies took turns blowing each other sky high with judiciously planted explosive charges.

All this jockeying for advantage, pursued in Washington as well as on the railroad right of way, ended in April, when it was formally stipulated that the junction should take place at Promontory. The tracklaying was completed, except for the final ceremonious lengths, on April 29, 1869. For 11 days the construction workers cooled their heels at Promontory, and then on May 10, 1869, with all the great personages present, the Golden Spike joined the two halves of the continent.

The two railroads paid off their subcontractors mostly in railroad bonds, but they evidenced a willingness to pay some of their debts in rails and rolling stock. The situation was made to order for the Saints to build a railroad of their own, and only a week after the ceremony at Promontory, ground was broken for the Utah Central at Ogden. By September tracklaying began, and on January 10, 1870, before 15,000 of his Saints, Brigham Young drove the last spike at Salt Lake City.

The building of this line to connect Salt Lake City with the Pacific Railroad, peculiarly a Mormon enterprise, was attended with a characteristic Mormon enterprise on Great Salt Lake. Possessing neither steamboats nor schooners, the Saints contrived to make the lake serve them as it had served the gentile contractors.

John A. Bevan tells the story in his unpublished reminiscences. William Jennings of Salt Lake and Thomas Lee of Tooele took a contract to furnish several thousand ties, cut mostly from Dry and Pine Canyons on the east side of Tooele Valley. The ties were cut and hewed in the mountains during the winter of 1868-1869, hauled down the canyons on bobsleds, and carried to the lakeshore in wagons. For convenience in hauling, they were hauled in double length—2 ties in one 16-foot stick. On being unloaded from the wagons, they were built into a large raft, about 300 feet long and 16 feet wide. The center of the raft was built up, but a 4-foot run-way was left on each side for the men to walk on. Each man, Bevan says, had a pole about 12 feet long with an iron spike in one end to stick into the bottom; the other end was against a small board on his breast which he pushed on.

"We would go to the front end—a man opposite each other—sit the pole down through the water in the mud then walk along the runway to hind end pushing as hard as we could. Our faces were to the west while the raft was going East. There was probably about from 18 to 20 men on the raft. We stayed on it night and day—had a camp-fire on it fixed with rocks and dirt."

The raft sounds unimaginably clumsy, but it did the job. Bill Fisher and Sam Lee superintended the polemen, one on the lake side, the other on the land side. When they were getting into shallow water, Sam would cry out, "Head 'er out, Fisher, we're getting too shallow!" and when the water deepened uncomfortably, Fisher would cry out, "Head 'er in, Sam, we're getting too deep!" Thus the raft was poled along the shore for 30 miles. They were 3 days and nights on the job, getting to the shore below Farmington in the afternoon of the third day. Bevan says:

"We drove the raft as hard as we could to within a rod or two of the shore, then swung the rear end around forming a sort of corrall in which we unloaded the ties and worked them to the shore where they were doged together endwise and hauled out with horses, loaded on to wagons and hauled up on the grade about ¾ of a mile away. I was not sea sick while on the water but when I stepped onto the land, it seemed to roll and pitch as the raft had done, and it made me very sea-sick. It took us several days to tear the raft to pieces and get the ties to the grade, but when we did get done, we came back home by way of Salt Lake City with the teams that went over there to haul the ties. We were gone about a month from home."

Nothing like it had ever been seen on the lake. Nothing like it has been seen since . . . but that is how pioneering is done.

Stockton had had five years to live up to its distinction as Utah's Gentile City, and in five years it had not exhibited the remotest promise of growing into something that would put Salt Lake City in the shade. It was time for the gentiles to have another try. The coming of the Pacific Railroad opened up exciting possibilities. A vigorous town athwart the railroad at some strategic location looked to be just what the situation demanded. Some shrewd gentile promoters who looked the possibilities over in the winter of 1868-1869 found a site that seemed to offer everything.

They reached an agreement with the Union Pacific by which the railroad should have every other town lot, and in February 1869 a railroad surveyor laid off the townsite at the point where the railroad right of way crossed the Bear. The town was named Corinne. There is much disagreement as to where the name came from— whether from a current popular novel, *Corinne of Italy,* from a reigning actress of the day, Corinne Lavaunt, or from the daughter of J. A. Williamson, subsequently mayor of the town; the last of these explanations seems most probable.

Corinne boomed from its first moment. The lots were auctioned off in March, and by the time the Union Pacific locomotive thrust across the Bear on April 7, Corinne was showing signs of growing straight over the horizon. Town lots sold for $100, for $500, for $1,000. In two weeks 500 tents and frame buildings went up and the population jumped to 1,500. A population of 10,000 within two years was seen as a practical certainty, even as the railhead moved on to Hell's Half Acre, Deadfall, Dead Man's Gulch, Commissary Camp and, finally, to Promontory.

During those hectic weeks, and during the month after the Golden Spike ceremony while the Union Pacific workmen hung around waiting to be paid off, Corinne resounded to the male uproar with which the Union Pacific had assaulted the continental silences all the way from Omaha. The combative young newspaper man, J. H. Beadle, who came to Corinne with the new *Utah Reporter* early in April, was impressed by the spectacle the town afforded.

"Nineteen saloons paid license for three months. Two dance-halls amused the elegant leisure of the evening hours, and the supply of 'sports' was fully equal to the requirements of a railroad town. At one time the town contained eighty *nymphs du pavé,* popularly known in Mountain English as 'soiled doves.'"

Beadle added, with no evident irony, that notwithstanding all the hullabaloo, Corinne basically was an orderly and quiet place: "Sunday was generally observed; most of the men went hunting or fishing, and the 'girls' had a dance or got drunk."

The founders of "the Burg on the Bear" rested their hopes in the belief that it must be found the logical junction city for the two railroads when the transfer point was removed from the temporary location at Promontory. Here the roundhouses and the machine shops must go up; here the hotels and restaurants must be built to serve the passengers changing cars.

It was a bitter disappointment when Ogden triumphed over its northern rival for the distinction of receiving the junction. But the founders of Corinne were fighters. The town was the best jumping-off place for freighters operating north to the gold camps of Idaho and Montana, and wagons rumbled in and out of town all day every day. Moreover, Corinne fronted opportunity on the south as well as on the north. In November 1869 one of Connor's schooners nosed up the Bear laden with silver ores, lumber, machinery and other cargo. Great Salt Lake made the Burg on the Bear neighbor to the booming mining camps down south, and the arrival of the schooner was hailed as the true inauguration of commercial traffic on the lake.

While Connor and other capitalists sank money in a smelter and new business enterprises of every kind in Corinne, while Utah's gentile merchants established branch houses and everybody with a grievance against the Mormons joined to organize the Liberal Party, Corinne acted to nail down its future. There must be an agricultural hinterland to sustain the gentile city, and Corinne's founders dispatched a memorial to Congress on the subject. They had a truly ambitious irrigation project in mind, envisioning nothing less than diverting the Bear from its channel where it emerged from the mountains and distributing its waters over the Bear River Valley. Here, almost alone, were there land and water unappropriated by the Saints. A grant of public land was asked to help finance the project. And why should the government exhibit this special generosity? The memorial was emphatic about that. Corinne's hinterland was "the only place where a truly American community can be brought into *permanent* and successful contact with the Mormon population, whose feet have trodden, and who hold in their relentless grasp, every other valley in Utah."

The memorial met with some favorable response in Congress, but in the end it died there and Corinne was left to its own resources. But the town displayed an endless ingenuity. If they couldn't take the Bear from its channel and grow crops with it, they would seriously sail ships up and down it. The river was, after all, 13 feet deep at the landing in Corinne and 300 feet wide. Though the *Kate Connor* came to an unlucky end sometime in 1871, when it sank in the river under a heavy load of ore, Corinne was already engaged with bigger and better things. One of the town's entrepreneurs, Fox Diefendorf, sank $45,000 into the most imposing boat that has ever sailed the Great Salt Lake.

Engines for this boat were built in Chicago by marine engine manufacturers serving the Great Lakes trade, and they were shipped around the Horn to California for transshipment to Corinne. From California came also the redwood lumber for the hull and beams. Christened *City of Corinne,* the steamboat was launched in the Bear on May 22, 1871. She made her trial trip on June 4 with 50 guests aboard, and a week later made the first experimental trip to the south shore, returning in 3 days with 1,150 sacks of ore—a 45-ton cargo. Before the month was out, she was sailing from her home port on a thrice-weekly schedule. The route ran down the Bear to its mouth, south down Bear River Bay to the channel between Frémont and Antelope and then west and south to Lake Point, on the south shore eight miles from Stockton.

The route up the Bear was doubtless unsuited for sailing vessels, for "Connor's Line of Boats" is shown by the maps of 1871 as plying between Lake Point and Monument Point at the head of Spring Bay.

The *City of Corinne* was a three-decker 150 feet long and of 250 tons burden, propelled by a large paddle wheel at her stern. Her first pilot was Captain S. Howe, but within the year he gave way to Captain Thomas Douris. Though the *City of Corinne* was not long destined to call the gentile city her home port, three times a week during the summer of 1871 Corinne swelled with pride as the steamboat nosed up the river to blow for a landing. The enterprising townsfolk had declared their city a "port of entry" and they were assured that not least among Western attractions for the tourist must now be "the voyage lengthwise of Salt Lake, the Dead Sea of America," an "interesting and agreeable diversion in the somewhat tiresome experience of the long rail ride across the continent."

Unfortunately, Corinne was not permitted for very long the enjoyment of her unique steamboat service. Tradition is that the *City of Corinne* was no longer able to ascend the river after the lake level fell and the Bear silted up. Tradition is not wholly reliable, for the lake continued at a very high level to 1875, whereas Corinne's history as a lake port came to its lugubrious end in the spring of 1872. Another tradition, that the steamboat could not negotiate the bar at the mouth of the river when heavily laden with ore, may be more authentic. Whatever the explanation, late in 1871 the boat was being reported a financial failure, and in April 1872 she was sold to the Lehigh and Utah Mining Company.

Her new owners promptly converted her into an excursion boat, and that was her congenial destiny for some 10 years. She was based, not at Corinne, but at Lake Side, on the east shore of the lake below Farmington. Legend would have it that during the course of a cruise on the lake on the occasion of James A. Garfield's visit to Utah in August 1872 his friends first broached to him the idea of running for the Presidency. Whether this be true or not, his second visit to Utah in June 1875 was made the occasion for renaming the *City of Corinne* in his honor. By her original name

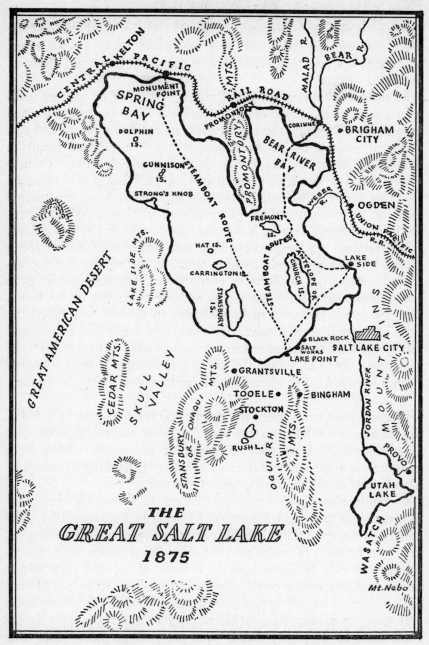

The Great Salt Lake at its commercial heyday and its highest recorded level.

the boat is almost forgotten in Utah, but as the *General Garfield,* she is still remembered, for she gave her name first to a beach resort and then to a smelting and refining center on the south shore of the lake.

So the fate that has pursued Corinne could not be content until it had wrested the name of the town from the steamboat launched in its honor! Nothing the town turned its hand to ever worked out. When it yielded up its steamboat, it began a railroad north to Idaho and Montana, the Portland, Dallas, & Salt Lake. Connor turned the first shovelful of earth in June 1872 and it was surveyed 50 miles north to Malad, Idaho, but the grades were constructed only for 10 miles before the railroad sank into ruin. When a railroad did go north, finally, it was the Mormon-built Utah Northern, which ignored the Burg on the Bear and robbed it of its freighting traffic. Oil and gas were found to underlie the region, but no successful commercial wells were ever driven. Mineral springs gave rise to hopes for a fashionable spa; nothing ever came of the hopes. Orchards were planted; alkali salts rose in the soil and killed the trees. Everywhere it turned, the town met with frustration, and finally infiltrating Mormon farmers took it over. Three-quarters of a century after its founding, the Burg on the Bear is indistinguishable from a hundred other Mormon country towns save only for its past.

During those years when the future was the brightest of bubbles, the islands of the lake, no less than the other mountainous areas of Utah, tantalized men with the prospect of wealth. Being in a measure more inaccessible than other parts of the territory, the lake islands seemed fraught with special promise.

Certainly they lured Reverend Ballard S. Dunn, the Episcopal minister who took up residence in Corinne in February 1871. His congregation was hardly sizeable enough to engross all his energies, and soon he went to mining on the side. From prospecting trips to the lake islands, he came back with loads of ore and rock which he crushed in a mortar with a pestle and washed out in a gold pan. Before long, as Alex Toponce tells the yarn, he had "all his members and vestrymen interested in his mining ventures and putting up grubstakes, for in reality that is what every congregation does with the minister, furnishes him with a grubstake."

Well, one Sunday morning only the vestryman, Nat Stein showed up for the services. Nat was interested in one of the parson's mines, so they sat and talked prospects and mines till long after the hour for the service. At last the pastor aroused himself. "Brother Stein," said he, "it looks as if no one else is coming. What shall we do, preach or pound quartz?" After the votes had been counted, they adjourned to the parsonage to spend the rest of the forenoon pounding up quartz in the mortar and testing it in the gold pan.

In the course of time an ungodly Californian jumped one of the parson's claims on Antelope Island, and as Alex Toponce heard the tale, when the Reverend Mr. Dunn visited the island and found the sinful interloper in possession, "he smote him hip and thigh and chased him off the island with a shotgun loaded with buckshot." Bishop Daniel S. Tuttle, in charge of the Episcopal missions in the Utah area, was known far and wide as a good fellow and a broadminded one, but this kind of thing he found hard to take, and the Episcopalian church and the Reverend Mr. Dunn came to the parting of the ways. That was all right with Mr. Dunn. Free to give all his time to the mining game, he became a mining promoter in the Idaho camps. Alex Toponce heard that he made quite a stake in the business.

That reminiscence of the wayward parson is almost the only echo of mining activity on Antelope Island, though the early maps indicate that a Church or Antelope Island Mining District was organized about 1871. Frémont Island, though it has barely rippled the surface of mining affairs in Utah, has left more discernible traces. A firm calling itself the Nebraska and Utah Mining Company turned up gold-bearing quartz ledges on the island in 1871, and on August 3 of that year organized the Island District. The Miller, Omaha, Queen Ann, Island, Davis and Shoebridge claims were vigorously worked that summer. Sad to report, nobody ever got rich, nor from that day to this has the Island District contributed anything to Utah's production statistics. The long, mountainous Promontory, largely neglected in the years of boom excitement, nearly half a century later produced modestly from a mine or two. But the lake islands and promontories, for all the recurring rumors that they possess hidden treasures of rare and precious minerals, have been no El Dorado.

Chapter 16

The Adventures of an Idea

IT WAS the misfortune of Dr. James Blake, Stansbury's surgeon, geologist, naturalist, meteorologist and scientific man of all work, that in the spring of 1850 he abandoned his scientific pursuits to go to law with his employer. Stansbury was left in no very amiable frame of mind after being dragged through a succession of lawsuits, and if anything was needed to give the captain a jaundiced view of his former associate, Blake's letters to Stansbury's chief, violently assaulting his character and integrity, did the job very thoroughly. So when the celebrated *Report* was finally published, Blake could riffle its pages in vain for any mention of his name. There was a noncommittal mention or two of "my doctor," but that was all, and Blake's scientific contributions disappeared into the records of the expedition without a word of appreciation.

Blake deserved better of history than that. For he it was who first realized the character of Great Salt Lake as the remnant of a vast inland sea. Though the mountain man Osborne Russell in 1840 had mentioned in his journal the fact that the lake level fluctuated so distinctly as to allow or prevent the passage of buffalo across the bar to Antelope Island, and though Frémont in his turn observed driftwood, proving that at times the lake level was higher than he found it, Blake was the first, so far as the record shows, to bend a thoughtful eye upon the hillsides adjacent to the salt lake and to decipher the singular story they waited to tell.

It was on October 24, 1849, as Stansbury's reconnaissance party was coming up the west side of Promontory, that Blake not only called to the captain's attention a remarkable succession of benches carved from the hillside but made the necessary inference; on reaching the head of Spring Bay next day, Stansbury recorded in his journal:

"This appears to be the northern extremity of the Great Lake, & has without doubt been at one time covered with its waters. The

Doctor counted in one spot 13 different lines or rings of elevation of the water on the shore yesterday. (Water lines)"

In his *Report* Stansbury amplified this mention, evidently by reference to Blake's own journal, which has now disappeared. Upon the slope of a ridge at the head of the lake, the *Report* observed:

"thirteen distinct successive benches, or water-marks, were counted, which had evidently, at one time, been washed by the lake, and must have been the result of its action continued for some time at each level. The highest of these is now about two hundred feet above the valley, which has itself been left by the lake, owing probably to gradual elevation occasioned by subterranean causes. If this supposition be correct—and all appearances conspire to support it—there must have been here at some former period a vast *inland* sea, extending for hundreds of miles; and the isolated mountains which now tower from the flats, forming its western and southwestern shores, were doubtless huge islands, similar to those which now rise from the diminished waters of the lake."

Blake had no part in the further explorations of the Stansbury expedition, and after his futile bouts with the captain in the Mormon courts, he took himself off to California. By a curious chance, however, in 1872 he had occasion to make a journey from Winnemucca, Nevada, to the Pueblo Mountains in Oregon. Here at the western end of the Great Basin he could see just such evidences of vanished lakes as he had pointed out to Stansbury, and in some observations communicated to the California Academy of Sciences he not only called attention to these but raised the interesting question whether at some time during the Quaternary period the waters of the Great Basin had found an outlet to the ocean.

Stansbury did not concern himself further with the problem of that ancestral lake from which Great Salt Lake had come, though he did jot down intermittent observations about the islandlike mountains in the Salt Desert, and the remarkable terraces cut on the islands of the lake. But Gunnison's curiosity was definitely aroused. During December 1849 he commented in his journal on the striking terraces seen in Salt Lake Valley, accounting for them as having been formed from "the crumbling down of precipitous cliffs into water which once made this region a vast inland sea," and subsequently, in his book, *The Mormons,* offering a tentative explanation. The waters of the ancient inland sea, he suggested, "had retired suddenly to certain distances, by regular upheavings of the land, or equal outbreaks, to a lower level. Three principal terraces, each retreating about fifty feet above the other, may be counted; and their exact planes and magnitude show the comparison of the works of nature with the feeble imitations of man, in beauty, sublimity, and permanence."

The signs were plain to see, once they had been pointed out, and for more than twenty years each new traveler of scientific bent pondered those clearly cut wave terraces along the shoulders of all the mountains bounding the valley of the Great Salt Lake. Lieutenant Beckwith, going west around the south shore of the lake in 1854, was especially struck with the old terraces, noting that one of them, on which his party traveled, was so remarkably distinct and peculiar in form and position as to attract the attention of the least informed teamsters of his party. Some of these terraces were at so slight an elevation above the level of the salt lake—from 5 to 20 feet—that Beckwith felt assured as to the geological recency of the subsidence of the lake, and doubted that the water which formed them could have escaped to the sea, either by underground convulsion or by the breaking of the shore line. On the adjacent mountains he could see terraces elevated from 200 to 800 feet above the present level of the lake; he was confident that these were ancient shore lines, and as they were so well marked, he felt that by tracing them it might be possible to determine the character of the sea which had formed them, "whether an internal one, subsequently drained off by the breaking or wearing away of the rim of the Basin . . . or an arm of the main sea, which, with the continent, has been elevated to its present position, and drained by the successive stages indicated by these shores."

The French traveler, Jules Remy, in 1855 decided that the Great Salt Lake was not the remains of an ocean which had receded after some vast geological commotion but was simply a small inland sea, receiving all the running waters of the vicinity and parting with them only by evaporation.

"This explanation ought to tranquillize the Mormons, who fear the lake will some day dry up. It cannot possibly disappear till all the watercourses of the great basin have previously become exhausted. . . . A change of climate, causing the diminution of the supply of water, has sufficed to reduce the salt-water to the present bed of the lake. A change of climate in an inverse sense would restore the lake to its pristine dimensions."

In 1859 Captain Simpson's geologist, Henry Engelmann, added his own observations to this problem presented by the salt lake; far to the south, at the rim of the Salt Desert, Engelmann found not only on-shore terraces but lacustrine silt and tufa and fresh-water shells. He pointed out that the saltiness of the Great Basin lakes was inconsistent with any idea of underground outlets. Variations in the lake level he ascribed to climatic reasons, pure and simple.

For his part, Sir Richard Burton in 1860 contributed the observation that the lake in geologic ages "occupied the space between the Sierra Madre [Wasatch Mountains?] on the east, and the ranges of Goose Creek and Humboldt River on the west." He computed the length at some 500 miles from north to south, and the breadth from 350 to 500, the area approximating 175,000 square miles. He added:

"The waters have declined into the lowest part of the basin by the gradual upheaval of the land, in places showing thirteen successive steps or benches. A freshet of a few yards would submerge many miles of flat shore, and a rise of 650 feet would in these days convert all but the highest peaks of the surrounding eminences into islands and islets, the kanyons into straits, creeks, and sea-arms, and the bluffs into slightly elevated shores."

The pursuit of the idea of an ancient lake had been spasmodic and disjointed, with a good deal of misinformation mixed in with the information. It was time that the ancestry of the salt lake be worked out with some degree of exactitude. And, now in fact, American geology brought forth an exciting idea of the past. Beginning in 1869, an extraordinarily brilliant company of geologists, in pursuit of one problem or another, made the valley of the Great Salt Lake the nation's geological crossroads. King, Hayden, Powell,

Thompson, Gilbert, Dutton, Holmes, Russell—these are great names, and their work has had a profound and lasting influence on American culture. Out of their labors has come the Geological Survey, the Bureau of Mines, the Bureau of American Ethnology, the Reclamation Service and a host of other handmaidens of science and technology.

Clarence King's Fortieth Parallel Survey reached the Great Salt Lake country in the summer of 1869. A Rhode Islander who graduated from Yale in 1862, King engaged for several years in geological surveys in California and returned east in the fall of 1866 with a plan for surveying a 100-mile strip of territory along the line of the Pacific Railroad, all the way from the foothills of the Rockies to the borders of California. Congress gave its sanction to the idea, and in 1867 King began seven years of field work.

The Fortieth Parallel Survey was a model of its kind, and sanction was promptly won for three other systematic surveys. Under F. V. Hayden, the Geological and Geographical Survey of the Territories took the field in 1867 to map much of Wyoming, Idaho, Montana, New Mexico and Colorado. The Hayden survey was primarily geological, but its work was fruitful of much other valuable information; the topographical maps it produced are beautiful still and have not been entirely superseded.

The third of the four surveys had its origin in the spectacular exploit of the tumultuously bearded John Wesley Powell in descending the Colorado River in 1869. Powell had studied for the Methodist ministry only to enlist in the Union forces on the outbreak of the Civil War. He became a captain of artillery and at Shiloh was so severely wounded that he lost his right arm at the elbow. Returning to service, by the close of the war he had risen to the rank of major. Although he had received his colonel's commission before he left the army, it was as "the Major," or "the Maj." that he became known the length and breadth of the Rocky Mountains. After his discharge from the army, the major served on the faculties of colleges in Illinois, and in 1867-1868 shepherded parties of students and amateur naturalists on scientific excursions to the Rockies. The gorges of the Green and Colorado seized upon his imagination, and in 1869, notwithstanding his missing arm, he organized a party to explore the legendary canyons of the Colorado. As a scientific sur-

vey the value of that exploration was nearly zero, despite its stature
as a breathless feat of adventure, but it immediately led to formal
explorations that were of great importance. The Powell Survey
mapped the Colorado and its tributaries in southern Utah and northern Arizona throughout the seventies, opening up a wide knowledge of areas which had been substantially a terra incognita since
Coronado's day. Like the Hayden Survey the Powell Survey was
under the direction of the Department of the Interior.

A fourth and no less momentous survey was the Geographical
Survey West of the One Hundredth Meridian, inaugurated in 1872
in charge of Lieutenant George M. Wheeler. Like the King Survey
it was under the jurisdiction of the War Department. Wheeler's
topographical engineers mapped wide areas of the West, including
large parts of Nevada, California, Arizona, New Mexico, southern
Colorado, southern Idaho and western Utah. For much of this
region, after three-quarters of a century, the Wheeler maps are still
the basis of our cartographical knowledge.

In their crisscrossing of the West all four of these surveys strangely
converged upon the valley of the Great Salt Lake. And all of them
almost simultaneously contributed significant information about
the lake and its geological ancestry.

Hayden himself in 1870 inspected the old shore lines in the vicinity of Great Salt Lake, and, as G. K. Gilbert says, "correctly correlated them with lacustrine deposits at various points, showed their
recency as compared to the later Tertiary beds of the vicinity, and
referred them to the Quaternary. He also found shells in the deposits, and from their character recognized the freshness of the old
lake." Two years later Frank H. Bradley, also of Hayden's party,
"recognized the broad terraces flanking Ogden River and other
streams of the vicinity as deltas built by the same streams in the
ancient lake, observed that the Ogden delta deposits extended into
the mountain canyon of the river, and drew the important conclusion that before the age of the high terraces Great Salt Lake was
not far, if at all, above its present level." A third observer, Henry S.
Poole, traced the shore lines of the ancient lake as far west as the
Deep Creek Mountains along the Nevada line.

Meantime, Clarence King, S. F. Emmons and Arnold Hague of
the King Survey had made extensive geological reconnaissances in

the valley of the Great Salt Lake. By the end of the field season of 1869 they were enabled to map with some precision the ancient lake that had filled the northeastern quarter of the Great Basin and extended long fingers farther south. They established that this prehistoric lake had reached a height at least 900 feet above the level of Great Salt Lake.

The salt lake itself took on fresh interest under the scrutiny of these geologists. Its bottom, they pointed out, was evidently even more level than the broad desert-valleys surrounding it, since at its deepest points its waters did not reach a depth of 50 feet, while a large proportion of its area, including the broad belts along its shore line and the partly enclosed bays, did not exceed 10 feet in depth.

It was fascinating to compare such a lake with the Dead Sea of Palestine. The level of Great Salt Lake was some 4,200 feet above sea level, while the Dead Sea was over 1,300 feet below the level of the Mediterranean. Great Salt Lake at its deepest point was hardly 50 feet deep; the Dead Sea plunged to depths of 1,800 feet. The mountain sea in this year near its high stage was about 80 miles long and 32 wide; the Dead Sea was 60 miles long by 15 wide. Both lakes were subject to fluctuations of their level, both drained a fresh-water lake by a Jordan River, both had extensive deposits of mineral salts on their borders, and both had heavy concentrations of brine. The Dead Sea, which was supposed to have been cut off at some time from the Mediterranean, had reached its heavy concentration of salts presumably by evaporation, and these salts much more nearly resembled the composition of ocean salt than those of the Great Salt Lake, the latter having in solution a smaller proportion of magnesia and lime. Of the two, in 1869, the Dead Sea was somewhat more dense, with a mineral content of 24.056 percent, as against a percentage of 14.994 for Great Salt Lake. (But the mountain lake in 1869 was very nearly at its highest stage, and other analyses over a period of years have shown mineral concentrations in Great Salt Lake up to 27.038 percent, virtually the saturation point.) The ocean was in no way comparable to either of these salt seas, having a mineral content of only 3.527 percent.

Clarence King and his associates moved on west in that 100-mile geological swath they were cutting across the country, and in the western half of the Great Basin they reported another such pre-historic lake as they had found in the eastern half. The Great Basin was no shallow depression rimmed about by mountains—there was a Utah Basin to the east, a Nevada Basin to the west and in between a mountainous upland which could be denominated the Nevada Plateau. Two immense lakes, it was now established, had filled the basins within the Basin. What should they be called?

Grove Karl Gilbert took the easternmost of these ancient lakes in hand before the King Survey could settle this problem. In 1872 he and Edwin E. Howell entered the Utah Basin with the topographical parties of the Wheeler Survey. Gilbert's duties required him to cross and recross the basin of that ancient lake until, rising in his mind, it began to drown out the rest of his geological interests. In April 1873 he told the Philosophical Society of Washington that this ancient lake in the Glacial Epoch had filled a portion of the Great Basin to its brim, a great, fresh-water lake which had flooded over to discharge into the Snake and Columbia. By the following year he thought the limits and history of the ancient lake so far established that he could venture to propose for it "the name 'Bonne-ville,' in honor of Captain B. L. E. Bonneville."

There was no ironic gleam in Gilbert's eye, but certainly there is an ironic aspect to the thought that Bonneville, who vainly endeavored to perpetuate his name by applying it to Great Salt Lake without ever having laid eyes on that lake, should find his immortality at last in a lake which no living man had ever seen.

Not to be outdone, the geologists of the King Survey came up with a brilliant name for the vanished lake in the western half of the Great Basin. Lahontan, they called it, in honor of the fabulous baron.

The several surveying organizations were showing signs of getting in each other's way, and in 1875 the Interior Department attempted to bring a little order into the operations of the two under its control. The Hayden and Powell Surveys were reorganized as the United States Geological and Geographical Survey of the Territories (re-named in 1877 the Survey of the Rocky Mountain Region), though Hayden and Powell remained in charge of the two divisions. Gilbert joined Powell's staff and with Almon Harris Thompson

The Great Basin, showing Quaternary Lakes (shaded) and residual lakes.

and C. E. Dutton spent the seasons of 1875-1876 working in the high plateau country of south-central Utah. In 1877 Powell's job took him into investigations of the irrigable lands of the Great Basin, investigations from which came his great *Report on the Lands of the Arid Region.* The field work for this report brought Gilbert back to his old love, Lake Bonneville, and to the bitter, blue lake which was its shrunken remnant.

There were all sorts of interesting questions it was suddenly necessary to start asking about Great Salt Lake. The lake was the best possible index to precipitation in the arid region. But how to establish the yearly fluctuations in its level?

On inquiry Gilbert learned that two years earlier Dr. John R. Park and others had erected a granite pillar at Black Rock, setting it in gravel beneath shallow water, with the zero of its scale near the surface. With the aid of this marker a record had been systematically kept between September 14, 1875, and October 9, 1876, but it had been discontinued. Gilbert himself, however, had made two observations in 1877. On the basis of this record it could be determined that the lake had risen 13 inches the first year and fallen 6½ the second.

Gilbert established another granite bench mark, higher up on the hill, to take care of the contingency that the lake waters might rise high enough to submerge the original pillar entirely, and he followed this up by establishing a new gage on the east shore of the lake below Farmington. Provision was thus made for the future. But what of the past? The exact records extended back only to 1875. How to get even approximate data for the preceding 20 years?

It was the trials and tribulations of those who had traveled across the Antelope bar from the island to the shore at various seasons of various years, which solved the question finally. Gilbert was able to learn that from 1847 to 1850 the Antelope bar had been dry during the low stage of each winter, and covered by not more than twenty inches of water in summer. Then had commenced the rise which had occasioned the building of Brigham Young's *Timely Gull.* The rise had continued until 1855 or 1856. With difficulty a horseman could ford in the winter, but there was no communication in summer except by boat. The lake level had then fallen again, so that in 1860 and 1861 the bar was dry in winter. The remarkable rise in the spring of 1862 had continued for several years, and by 1865 the bar was no longer passable. The lake level had continued to rise, and in 1868 it had reached a high point which it had roughly maintained since.

With Jacob Miller, the geologist voyaged to the bar in October 1877 to make careful soundings; he found the water standing nine feet deep on the sand bar that day.

So far, so good. But what of the period since 1865, for which the Antelope bar was of no service? Luckily, Stansbury Island came to the rescue. Stansbury was connected with the south shore by a bar seven feet higher than the Antelope bar. In 1866, the year after the Antelope bar had become unfordable, water had covered the Stansbury bar for the first time. Gilbert was able to learn that from 1866 on there had never been less than a foot of water on the Stansbury bar. Though the lake level had never risen so high as to prevent fording in winter, during the summer flood stages of 1872-1874, when the lake reached its highest levels, there was no access to the herds on the island except by boat.

Gilbert now had some interesting facts to chew on. For an indefinite period before 1865 the lake had not overstepped certain bounds, as could be determined by the shore-line growth of sage, which is inhibited by saline soils. Now, however, the lake had overstepped those bounds; the maps of the King Survey gave it a mean area of water surface almost a sixth larger than in Stansbury's time.

Three theories were offered to account for this rise in the lake level—volcanic, climatic and human agencies. The volcanic theory surmised that upheavals in the lake bed had displaced water which in consequence overflowed certain shores. This theory Gilbert dismissed at once, because obviously *all* shores had been encroached upon, and, moreover, the annual rises coincided with the seasonal increase from the inflowing streams. The second theory, that a relatively small increase in precipitation might have occasioned the rise, Gilbert thought tenable enough.

But much the most interesting was the third theory, advanced by Powell himself. It was the universal belief among the Mormons that wherever a settlement was made, within a few years an increase in the water supply followed. Powell was disposed to credit this theory on these grounds, that whatever man had done to clear the way for the flowing water had diminished local evaporation and helped to fill the lake; whatever he had done to increase local evaporation had tended to empty the lake.

Thus by plowing the earth he made it more porous, so that a smaller percentage of the passing shower ran off. Although he had taken water out of streams for irrigation purposes, he had also cleared out springs and drained bogs, making for less standing water to be lost as evaporation. Moreover, grazing livestock, by destroying the native grasses, decreased the efficiency of the earth as watersheds; there was more surface runoff than before. And the treading of many feet at boggy springs compacted the spongy earth and rendered it impervious, so that the water, unable to percolate, ran off in streams. The same thing happened in the beds of streams. And, finally, the cutting of trees for lumber and fence material and fuel increased the surface runoff.

Gilbert thought the question of where the water came from one best left for the future to determine, since there was no way of settling it with the available information. In the perspective of the decades since that time, it has become clear that a period of relatively wet years was primarily responsible for the rise in the lake level, though the human factor was a contributing agent—somewhat to the grief of those humans, who have had to reckon with the sad consequence of overgrazing and the destruction of native grasses, shrubs and trees on the watersheds.

At the moment all these questions interested Gilbert primarily for their bearing upon the subject of Powell's pending report on the use of the arid lands, for which he himself must write the chapter on water supply. But Lake Bonneville was much on his mind as he traveled here and there in the Salt Lake basin in the interests of the Powell report. . . . There was still the question of where the ancient lake had overflowed into the Snake. In the summer of 1876 Gilbert addressed himself to the problem. Patiently he pursued the old shore lines into Cache Valley, and there, at the northern extremity of the valley, Red Rock Pass, he found what was obviously the point of overflow. The old shore line was well marked to within half a mile of the pass, and as mute evidence of the long ago, there was a great channel cut perhaps 370 feet deep in the Rim of the Basin. Through that steep-sided, trenchlike, 1,000-foot wide passage had spilled a Niagara-like torrent in tumultuous escape from the mountain walls that had withheld it from the sea. The waters had roared down the valley of Marsh Creek to the Portneuf, and thence by the gorges of the Snake and the Columbia had found their way to the Pacific.

So much Gilbert had settled. But had there been other outlets? F. H. Bradley in 1872 had thought that there might have been a point of overflow at the divide between the Malad River and Marsh Creek; indeed, he was willing to conceive of no less than four points of overflow—Red Rock Pass, Soda Springs Pass and the head of the Malad, as well as the Malad-Marsh Creek divide. Though it was unlikely, there might have been small orographic movements to shift the outlet from point to point. Patiently, through the summer of 1877, Gilbert pursued this question. Finally he was satisfied that Red Rock Pass had been the only outlet. Its elevation was lower than the others, and here alone existed a channel and a break in the shore line.

All these findings Gilbert announced early in 1878 in the *American Journal of Science*. Though he and all his works were promptly attacked in the same journal by A. C. Peale, there could not for very long be any question of the correctness of his findings, and in 1880 a second communication he sent the *Journal* forever ended the argument.

Those researches of 1880 themselves represented a kind of fruition, not merely of the work that Gilbert had done in the old Bonneville basin, but of the work of all the geological and geographical expeditions. By 1879 it had become obvious that the King, Hayden, Powell and Wheeler surveys must be systematized and correlated, the more so because the Coast and Geodetic Survey had begun extending its work into the interior for the purpose of making geodetic connection by primary triangulation between the Atlantic and Pacific Coasts. Accordingly, early in 1879 Congress set up the Geological Survey, and gave to the Survey the responsibility of classifying the public lands and of examining the geological structure, mineral resources and products of the national domain.

Named director of the survey, Clarence King accepted the job to appoint the staff and institute operations and then resigned to enter private practice as a mining engineer. He was succeeded by "the Maj.," John Wesley Powell, who meantime had been engaged in setting up, under the direction of the Smithsonian Institution, the Bureau of American Ethnology—a scientific agency which has since carried on the anthropological, archeological and ethnological inquiries so brilliantly begun by the Powell Survey.

As first constituted, the Geological Survey limited its operations to the territory west of the 102nd meridian. The second of its four districts, the Division of the Great Basin, was set up at Salt Lake City with Gilbert as director. As the first large work of his division, Gilbert tackled the problem of the Pleistocene lakes—Lake Bonneville, which he himself studied intensively, and Lake Lahontan, which he named Israel C. Russell to investigate. More obscure lakes in the southwestern part of the Basin were reserved for later study.

Such plans were overturned when in 1881 the operations of the Geological Survey were extended over the entire country. Since there was no proportionate increase in appropriations, many activities had to be curtailed, including the study of the Pleistocene lakes. Work on Lake Bonneville and Lake Lahontan being far advanced, Gilbert and Russell were authorized to complete their classic monographs. Notwithstanding all the work that has since been done, very few discoveries have been made to modify materially their principal conclusions.

What was it, then, this Lake Bonneville to which a man could give the best years of his life, this lake which had overspread thousands of square miles, which had memorialized itself on the mountains that once walled it in and which had left so strange a heritage? The story pursued through all these years by all these explorers and scientists was a story fascinating and complex—and strange in this, that the history of that vanished sea was known at last more fully than that of most lakes still surviving.

The story goes back millions of years, to the time when the Great Basin itself was formed. This huge depression was created when the upward-thrusting earth crust broke along the line of two great faults, one at the west base of the Wasatch, and one at the east base of the Sierra Nevada. It is generally agreed by geologists that movement on the Wasatch Fault began no later than the closing stages of the Tertiary period, perhaps about the middle of the Miocene. Lake Bonneville was only the last of four lakes that have filled the great hollow at the base of the Wasatch Fault.

Those lakes were the product of the successive glacial periods. The time schedule of those periods has been roughly worked out like this:

Geological Epoch		Duration in Years
I	Glacial	25,000
	1st Inter-Glacial	75,000
II	Glacial	25,000
	2nd Inter-Glacial	200,000
III	Glacial	25,000
	3rd Inter-Glacial	100,000
IV	Glacial (Wisconsin Stage)	25,000
	Post-Glacial (Post-Bonneville)	25,000
	Total Duration	500,000

The successive lakes occupying the Bonneville Basin came and went, dependent on the vagaries of climate. Great Salt Lake as well as Lake Bonneville may have been thrice anticipated; well drillings in Salt Lake Valley show, by an alternation of subaqueous and subaerial deposits, that from time immemorial the waters of the Bonneville Basin have advanced upon the shores and withdrawn from them. The history of the three lost lakes of the older geological epochs cannot yet be reconstructed, but the record of Bonneville itself is amazingly clear.

Lake Bonneville was the creation of the fourth glacial age. Perhaps more rain and snow fell, but most important was the increased cold, which acted to reduce evaporation. Beginning as a brine pond much like the present Great Salt Lake, Bonneville slowly began to rise. Though the lake level many times advanced and retreated under the influence of dry and wet years, or warm and cold years, over the hundreds and thousands of years the movement of the lake level was upward.

Reed Biddulph   *Courtesy Provo Chamber of Commerce*

Gulls following behind the harrow in Utah Valley. Mount Timpanogos, 12,008 feet above sea level, in background.

Russell Lee, Farm Security Administration   *Courtesy, Library of Congress*

Picking berries in Cache Valley.

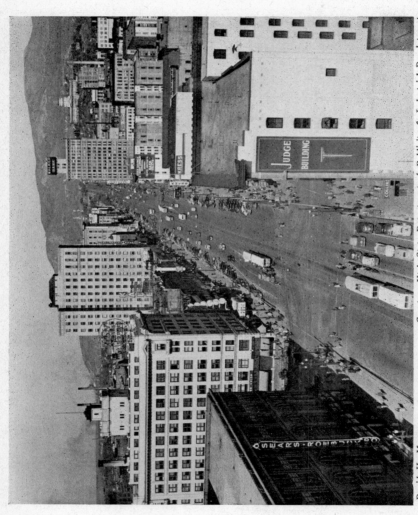

David H. Mann   *Courtesy Utah State Department of Publicity & Industrial Development*

Main Street, Salt Lake City, looking north toward Ensign Peak; in background, Mormon Temple and State Capitol.

Suppose that were to happen all over again; suppose a fifth glacial age should take the earth in its frigid grasp. Great Salt Lake begins to rise, and the markers at the lake shore record the first advance— 5 feet, 10. . . . At 25 feet the transcontinental railroads have been flooded out; the Lucin Cutoff is destroyed, and the Western Pacific's line across the Salt Desert is washed away, while also, the lake has crept east across the alkaline flats to inundate the Salt Lake airport. Still the water rises. At the 100-foot mark it invades Salt Lake City's business section, and 40 miles to the north, the water also invades the waiting room of Ogden's Union Depot.

No dikes can hold the water back. It keeps on climbing, to the 300-foot mark. All the farmlands of Salt Lake and Weber Valleys are submerged now, and the lake sends a thirsty arm up Bear River into Cache Valley. Fort Douglas, on the bench high above Salt Lake City, defends itself for a time, but at 600 feet it, too, sinks into the remorseless lake.

As the lake approaches the old Bonneville levels, Utah has all but disappeared from the map. Ninety percent of the state's population has been made homeless, and three-quarters of a million acres of the state's most fertile lands have been inundated, some to a depth in excess of 500 feet. Highways have almost been wiped from the map, together with 2,000 miles of railroad. Transcontinental railroad journeys are a thing of the past; travelers enroute to San Francisco by the Union Pacific must take a boat at Morgan, in Weber Canyon, and those going by way of the Denver & Rio Grande Western must take a boat at Thistle, in Spanish Fork Canyon, in either event sailing west 150 miles to the railheads at Lucin and Wendover. A still longer journey by water is required of those traveling to Los Angeles; from the railheads at Morgan or Thistle they must voyage 250 miles southwest to Modena, Nevada. The Mormon Temple in Salt Lake City is buried in 850 feet of water, as is the business section of Ogden. Provo is submerged in 650 feet of water, Logan in 500 feet. . . . Western Utah has been reduced to a vast water surface from which, as promontories or islands, the old mountain ranges lift their embattled heights.

But this image, while true in terms of prehistory, projects the reincarnated Lake Bonneville beyond the bounds of present possibility, for the old channel at Red Rock Pass, cut down to the 650-foot level, waits to drain off any surplus beyond that level. Unless some extraordinary earth movement takes place to uplift this spillway at the Rim of the Basin, no glacial lake of any future age will reach the topmost terraces of Lake Bonneville.

Starting as little more than a brine pond, Lake Bonneville grew into a lake 1,050 feet deep, 346 miles long and 145 miles wide. On the west it extended to the Pilot Range; on the south it rolled all the way to the Pine Valley Mountains, with long embayments extending over the Escalante Desert, Snake Valley, White Valley and Preuss Valley. Utah Valley, Rush Valley and Cache Valleys were other landlocked bays; the water spread up the canyon of the Weber as far as Morgan Valley, up Ogden Canyon to fill Ogdens Hole. The Promontory, Lakeside, Cedar, McDowell, Dugway and Beaver Mountains were converted into islands; Antelope and Stansbury Islands were largely submerged, and only the tip of Frémont Island showed above the surface. Essentially the waters of this lake were fresh; vegetation grew in green abundance on its shores; and long-vanished animals made trails through the tall grasses to drink from its verge. Mammoths, musk-ox, camels, horses, deer and mountain sheep all perished at times at the margin of the lake, their bodies sinking into the lacustrine silts which men in the far future would dig for gravel.

Had Bonneville gone up to its maximum level and then immediately shrunk back upon itself, no terraces would have been left to challenge thoughtful travelers. Wave-cut terraces are formed only when a lake maintains itself at the same level for a considerable period. Although other factors operate, the size of a terrace generally is proportionate to the time the lake maintained itself at that level.

The topmost terrace of Lake Bonneville, which Gilbert named the Bonneville terrace, was almost exactly a thousand feet above the present level of Great Salt Lake, and, as one of the most deeply etched of all, is evidence that the lake remained in equilibrium there for a very long time. Finally the water moved upward again, sufficient to reach the floor of Red Rock Pass. Quickly it ripped out a channel through the loose, unconsolidated sand and gravel, and cut downward and lakeward, so that when a hard limestone ridge was reached, 370 feet below the first point of overflow, the point of overflow itself had moved seven miles back into Cache Valley.

Gilbert estimated that Lake Bonneville had required perhaps 25 years to cut its way down to that limestone floor in Red Rock Pass, but there is no way of knowing whether climatic conditions produced a 25-year outflow in constant volume; there may have been fluctuations in the lake level to spread the work of erosion over a longer period. But in reaching that hard floor in the Red Rock channel, Bonneville reached a new point of equilibrium, and here the lake carved a second great terrace from the mountainsides, a terrace Gilbert called the Provo. Bonneville was now approximately 600 feet above the level of Great Salt Lake, and here it remained, longer than at any other level. Precipitation and stream inflow were in exact balance with evaporation and stream outflow. Eventually, however, as the climate again changed, the lake could no longer maintain itself. It sank below the Rim of the Basin, then ever lower as evaporation worked upon it. At times it halted to make new terraces, but nothing comparable to the Bonneville and Provo terraces was carved from its shores until the lake reached what Gilbert called the Stansbury terrace, nearly 300 feet lower than the Provo, and the same distance above the level of Great Salt Lake.

At the Stansbury stage Lake Bonneville had wholly withdrawn from the Sevier Desert and from Utah Valley but still reached into Cache Valley; most of Salt Lake Valley below the level of the State Capitol was covered, and it stretched far across the Salt Desert to the site of Wendover.

Now the final transformation from Lake Bonneville to Great Salt Lake could take place. Terraces show the entire course of the descent, without any single stage where the two lakes may be said to begin and end. The brackish Lake Bonneville of the Stansbury stage concentrated its salts as it shrank toward its identity as Great Salt Lake, strewing them prodigally over the Salt Desert, a poison to make that plain an irreclaimable desert, but retaining 5,000,000,000 tons of the salts in its waters to astonish the witnesses of its declining days.

That was the end of the 50,000-year adventure: that was what Lake Bonneville, finally, had to show for its geological labors—5,000,-000,000 tons of salt. It had started as a brine pond, and a brine pond was the identity to which it returned, with the carvings upon a thousand mountainsides the record of its extraordinary story. Is the lake near its extinction? No one can know. If man does not busily blow up the earth with his new bombs, the climate may grow increasingly more arid until all the affluent streams of Great Salt Lake disappear; evaporation will wrench from the resisting lake the water it still retains, and its salts will be precipitated as another and even more amazing Salt Desert. But if Great Salt Lake is a mere incident in the final extinction of Lake Bonneville, it seems assured, at least, of continued existence for centuries to come.

And of course there is no way of knowing whether we are done with ice ages, whether the recession of the last 25,000 years has not been merely an incident in the history of the ancient lake. Gilbert himself read a premature obituary for the lake. When its level began to fall in the eighties he foresaw a not too distant time when the lake would retreat for its last defiant stand into the depression west of Antelope Island. Diversion of water for irrigation seemed to him to assure the early finish of the salt lake. But a cycle of wet years in the early 1920's brought the lake level up again—not to the record height of the early seventies, but to heights surprising to all prophets. It was like a gesture of independence, a reminder by the lake that its destinies are in the hands of mightier forces than man has yet contrived to master.

Chapter 17

Three Lives

Brigham Young died on August 29, 1877, in the gabled Lion House in Salt Lake City. Black along Mormondom's horizons political storms were blowing up. Brigham's own last years had been ones of continual legal harassment, for U. S. Grant early showed a disposition to appoint officials who would roll up their sleeves and get to work on the Territory of Utah as upon an Augean stable.

These men with a mission made a beginning by attempting to enforce antipolygamy laws. Prosecutions against Brigham came to nothing, and the attempt to make a *cause célèbre* out of Ann Eliza Young and her suit for alimony petered out ingloriously. But in 1874 Congress passed the Poland Bill, which sharply curbed the jurisdiction of the Mormon courts. Later that year John D. Lee was seized in southern Utah, and after an abortive first trial, he was executed for participation in the Mountain Meadows Massacre.

Regarding the Lee affair as only a beginning, the crusading gentiles plunged into a violent political warfare. Polygamy was a made-to-order issue, for as early as 1856 the first national convention of the Republican Party had branded polygamy and slavery as the twin relics of barbarism. But the basic issue was not one of morals. Primarily the gentiles wanted to smash the political power of the Mormon Church. Laws against plural marriage had the merit of providing a ground of principle on which the Saints must take a stand and fight, and of dramatizing an issue in morals which could marshal national sentiment and bring about decisive intervention by the federal government on the side of the gentile minority.

These issues were fought out during the eighties. The Edmunds Act of 1882 disfranchised polygamists, redefined polygamy as a crime, and provided also for legal action against unlawful cohabitation ("u. c." in familiar Utah phrase ever after) where some difficulty might be met with in establishing the fact of marriage. A test case was brought against Rudger Clawson, and in November 1884 he was sentenced to four years in the territorial penitentiary. The appeal to the Supreme Court failed, and U.S. deputy marshals began "polyg hunts" the length and breadth of the territory. The polygamists were forced into hiding, some even going to Canada or Mexico in hope of finding a haven, but the raids kept a constant flow of polygamy and u. c. cases moving into the courts. The penitentiary filled with the resisting Saints.

The warfare intensified politically as well, the gentiles' Liberal Party fighting the Mormons' People's Party with occasional effective intervention by the sympathetic territorial officials. The Mormons had called constitutional conventions in 1856, 1862 and 1872 in vain efforts to obtain statehood, and the Edmunds Act goaded them to another unavailing effort in 1882. In 1887 the need was even more dire, for Congress passed the drastic Edmunds-Tucker Act designed to smash the Mormon Church completely. The church was dissolved as a corporation, and its property was confiscated by the federal government. A new constitutional convention in 1887 failed to obtain statehood, and the appeal to the Supreme Court against the constitutionality of the Edmunds-Tucker Act was lost. Moreover, the gentiles had broken through the Mormon political defenses to capture Salt Lake City and Ogden, the chief cities of the territory.

There was no alternative but surrender. John Taylor, who had succeeded Brigham Young as president of the Mormon Church, had died in hiding in 1887, resolute against yielding, but his successor, Wilford Woodruff, had to face up to the bitter necessity: the temporal salvation of the church was at stake. On September 25, 1890, he issued an Official Declaration, since famous as "The Woodruff Manifesto," announcing that inasmuch as laws had been enacted by Congress forbidding plural marriages, laws which had been pronounced constitutional by the court of last resort, he hereby declared his intention to submit to those laws and to use his influence with the members of the church to have them do likewise. "I now publicly declare that my advice to the Latter-day Saints is to refrain from contracting any marriage forbidden by the law of the land."

It was a momentous decision to take, and it could not solve the Mormon problem out of hand. Men who believed the injunction to take plural wives to be the command of God, could not at once reconcile themselves to this drastic change of front, and for years there was a diminishing flow of plural marriages; even a half century later a small, defiant knot of die-hards survives to preach and practice the doctrine. But at the same time there were Saints who had never approved of polygamy personally, even though they defended the doctrine itself, and these were made happy in being relieved of any obligation to contract plural marriages.

The position of the church was awkward and had to be left for time to work out. The Woodruff Manifesto was not issued as a revelation from God countermanding the revelation to Joseph Smith; it simply advised a suspension of the *practice* of polygamy. But after a half century the Manifesto for church members has come to have all the binding force of a revelation, and church theologians tend to argue that it always had that status. For most Mormons today plural marriage is simply a fossil relic of the past.

The Manifesto was regarded by the gentiles with the deepest suspicion, and they were hostile to the succeeding movement for statehood as being simply an expedient by which the Mormons schemed to get out from under the iron heel. But to show their good faith the Mormons dissolved their People's Party with instructions to the Saints to join one or another of the national political parties (the priesthood in some communities arbitrarily directed the members to join this party or that, an order which has produced generations of Republicans or Democrats innocent of how they happen to belong today to one party rather than the other). After some hesitation the gentiles followed suit. Statehood came rapidly after that, with a constitutional convention in 1895 and formal admission to the Union on January 4, 1896. The escheated properties of the church were returned by Act of Congress even before statehood was granted.

It is against this background of political strife and turbulent social change that one must set three lives lived on the islands of Great Salt Lake. Conflict makes news, and news makes history, yet men live rich and quiet lives outside the boiling currents of their times, and who shall say whether the thousand existences in quiet do not more nearly express the shape of human experience than the fiercely spotlighted existence that survives as history? The lives of George Frary, U. J. Wenner and Alfred Lambourne have only this in

common, that each found rich contentment on an island of Great
Salt Lake. None could be regarded as typical of his times. But no
man, himself, is ever typical. Uniquely he is himself, alone and
incomparable.

George Frary gave his life to Antelope Island, but not the Antelope Island that Brigham Young had known. After Briant Stringham died in 1871, the island horses ran wild for four years. During
that time they hardly saw a human being. In 1875, anxious to move
the horses off the island, the church contracted with Chambers,
White & Company to round them up and move them to Salt Lake
City, the contractors to receive half of all the horses they could get
off the long, hilly island.

The contractors embarked upon their job confidently, but the
horses displayed an almost diabolical ingenuity in eluding the
roundup artists and in getting out of the corrals. The large proportion of them were never caught, and their pursuers eventually
gave up in discouragement.

Freedom had its privations, however. Residents of Kaysville
stocked the island with 10,000 head of sheep, and feed became so
scarce that many of the horses died of starvation. This situation
improved in 1877 when Adam Patterson bought 10,000 acres of
railroad land on the island and moved the sheep off, but after the
Island Improvement Company bought out Patterson in 1884, the
horses still surviving were regarded as such a nuisance that John
White and several others took rifles to Antelope and exterminated
them. "Thus ended the horses of Antelope Island, once the pride
of such men as Brigham Young, Heber C. Kimball and hundreds
of others who knew the value of a good horse," Solomon Kimball
said with genuine sorrow.

As a boy, George Frary learned to sail on Lake Superior. It is
not strange that when he came to Utah he took a job herding cattle
on Antelope Island, for the job had in it almost as much of seafaring
as of ranching.

The sailboat which voyaged to and from the mainland is described as a "clumsy, scow-shaped cattleboat, sloop rigged with
mainsail and jib, and steered by an oddly placed wheel on the
forecastle deck." It was capable of carrying 40 head of cattle at

once, and in its time it was employed for interesting special duties, like moving to Antelope Island in 1892 the dozen buffaloes William Glasmann had bought in Nebraska and maintained at Garfield Beach. (The buffaloes flourished, growing at one time to a maximum of 400 head; it was on the island that the stampede scenes for *The Covered Wagon* were filmed in 1922.) In his clumsy sailboat George Frary sailed the lake in all directions. Eventually it was to the island that he brought his bride, and here their six children were born.

About 1895 Ninetta Eames was privileged to visit the island, and she wrote a charming account of the experience in *Outing* for March 1897. The boat owners, she said, communicated with the herdsman by signal fires. Two sage-brush fires lighted on the west face of Ensign Peak, above Salt Lake City, telegraphed the message, "Bring over a load of cattle." Within 24 hours, if the wind was favorable, the "patriarchal scow" made its way across the channel to the cattle chutes at Lake Side. The boat was brought alongside with poles, and then there was a downrush of canvas, a rattle of chains, and the rusty anchor went overboard with a splash. After a plank was withdrawn from the open stern, 40 excited Herefords were hustled off in the narrow, cradle-built chute and taken in charge by two mounted herders who would escort them toward the butchershops of the city.

Ninetta Eames insisted that the accommodations of the cattle boat were not to be despised.

"Barring the barnyard odor of the empty hold, a sail on the stanch old hulk has a charm of its own. A picture or a poem might be born to one while lounging a night out on the scrap of deck forward, a coil of rope for head-rest, a discarded sail for weather cloth, the ears hearkening to the roar of the wind in the rigging and the flesh stinging with the saltiest of salt spray, and the eyes strained to catch a glimpse of star or island in the pitchy darkness."

The crew was limited to the captain and a boy of 16, but she enjoyed the night sail. Frary never left the wheel, but he talked to her in the darkness, telling her the story of the Wenners on the island to the north, pointing out their own progress toward Antelope. Suddenly a feeble point of flame appeared on the dark, crouching mass off the bow, and the captain spoke up, "Wife saw us coming before dark, an' has hung out the lantern."

By that starlike gleam, Ninetta Eames writes, Frary—

"was enabled to steer straight for an invisible cattle-chute, where we landed before midnight. The Captain . . . was warmly welcomed by a demure little woman in clean calico, who had tucked in bed her two sleeping babies, and come down with the lantern to meet him. The family also numbered four hired men; so it turned out that this island-farm had something of the life and bustle that are common features of less romantically located ranches."

She was put to bed in a hammock swung under the beautiful honey locusts by the door of the old gray adobe house, the house that was the one dwelling on the island. It stood a few rods up from the surf, a small apple orchard and garden to the right of the rude porch giving a homelike air to the weather-cracked walls. It was, she thought, a gorgeous place to live; all up and down the shore the "long, salt-white fingers of the bay ran into the emerald of tasseled green—the hay crop for winter-feeding the cattle." And when one rode horseback to the island heights, "the immensity of sun-hot blue, sewn with islands," filled the mind unforgettably.

George Frary lived in this rich contentment only for another two years, for there was another and frightening side to this islanded isolation. One night in 1897 his wife was stricken with appendicitis. A nor'wester had been blowing all day, and the smashing salt waves made it impossible to take her to the mainland. The only alternative was to bring a doctor to her.

Leaving his wife and their six small children, Frary set out for the eastern shore in the clumsy old scow. It was pitch dark with a stiff gale and a heavy sea running, and it required all his skill to cross the 20-mile channel. He arrived long after daybreak, almost completely exhausted. Half the day was gone before he could find transportation to Salt Lake City, and three or four more hours before he could find a doctor willing to make the hazardous journey back to the island. He and the doctor got away from the landing, finally, at sundown. At dawn they reached the island—too late. His wife had died during the night.

There on the island he buried her. But with the six children he stayed on. In 1902, when the Lucin Cutoff was projected, he helped make the first soundings to enable the railroad to go to sea, and it was almost as by right that his daughter traveled as a passenger in 1903 on the first regularly scheduled train to cross the lake.

Finally George Frary abandoned the old house on Antelope Island with its sad and tender memories. But he could not bring himself to leave the lake. He made lonely sails to all its shores, and about 1911 became interested in a deposit of asphalt in the lakebed along the Promontory shore. In a weather-beaten shack he settled down to await a time when his discovery might find a market, happy with his books, happy with the sound of the salt surf and the smell of the salt air. The lake had been too much of his life for too long, and in the end he could not tear himself away from it.

Three lives, and kindred only in this, the love of the lake and the open sky and the thousand myriad faces of the days. U. J. Wenner had nothing in common with George Frary except that spacious appreciation of the world of the lake, and the rich, warm family world to which he gave himself.

He was a man of warm, romantic temperament, impulsive and kind. With his laughing young bride, Kate Greene, he came to Salt Lake City in 1880.

They built a home on South Temple—"Brigham Street" to everyone of that era—and he opened a law office. Their first son, George, was born in 1881, and two years later a daughter, Blanche, arrived. In 1885 they were caught up briefly in the territory's bitter political struggles when the governor named him probate judge of Salt Lake County. The Mormons fought the appointment in the territorial courts, but this was one among their many lost battles of that disastrous decade.

Judge Wenner's life, however, lay outside the militant current of the times. Consumption struck at him, and the doctors told him that his life depended on an existence in the open air and the sunshine.

It was Frémont Island that touched fire to his imagination. Late in 1885 with his friend, Shelton Baker, he visited the island to examine its possibilities. There was a spring of sorts, a seepage, really, near the north shore. Frémont had not found it nor had

Stansbury, but sheepmen who had pastured their flocks on the island had known of it. And it seemed likely that artesian wells could be driven. There was no place to live on the island, nothing but the tumble-down shack that dated from before the time of Jean Baptiste, but that held the promise of adventure, too.

Judge Wenner talked it over with his young wife, and they decided to sell their home in Salt Lake City and buy a part of the island from the Union Pacific, and homestead the rest. Kate Wenner loved the idea; it made her feel like a real frontier woman. Though relatives and friends were horrified, she and her husband would not be dissuaded. They intended to try it for at least one summer.

"We tried to think of everything we would need for camping and tent life," Kate Wenner wrote in her reminiscences, long years after. "We arranged for an old sail boat to carry us over. I thought of the Ark as we marched in two by two, the little boy and girl, age four and two years, two men, the hired girl and captain, as he called himself." What with calms, head winds, squalls and sea-sickness, the 20 miles to the island turned out to be a three-day voyage, and Kate Wenner made up her mind that she would not take her family back to the mainland very soon; perhaps she would even wait until the lake dried up.

They had come prepared for camping all summer, but when they unpacked, Kate discovered that she had left her small looking glasses behind. The judge was amused, she says, as he was to wear a beard for the protection of his throat, anyway. "He waited for my vanity to send for a looking glass and I did not have one for six months." When the old, salt-encrusted boat, after a month, came over with juniper posts, lumber and fresh provisions, the hired girl could not resist the opportunity to get back to the mainland—more, as Kate thought, to see herself than her friends.

The tents were pitched near the old shanty, not far from the beach. Spiders and creeping things alarmed the young wife, but only delighted the children. One "shalt not" alone existed for the youngsters—they were not to go into the lake unless their parents were with them.

Like a world lost in enchantment, the summer flew by. Judge Wenner seemed so much improved that they decided finally to live permanently on the island. Having no boat of their own, they made arrangements for the boat that had first brought them to come once a month, bringing mail and provisions. The captain knew their tastes and would arrive with a regular little store, from which they might select to satisfy their needs.

They owned a copy of Frémont's book, and often reread what he had had to say of their island. Climbing to the summit, they vainly hunted the lost object-end of his telescope. They found the cross his men had carved on the windswept rock at the summit, read vainly through Frémont for some account of how it had come there, and wondered whether it might betoken a visit by Spanish priests in some forgotten time. Indians had visited their island, for they found flint arrowheads.

The fall of 1886 was crisp and sunny. The Judge rented the boat for a month and brought from the mainland horses, sows, chickens, thoroughbred sheep from Iowa, a big wagon, and lumber for a house. With the judge's management and assistance the two men who were working for them built, Kate says, "a little house, which we thought should have a very small name; cabin sounded too pretentious so we named it the Hut. With a tent, a shanty and a Hut we were prospering." The old shanty, papered with gay magazine pictures, was her kitchen.

All hands combined in collecting rock, and by summer their rock house was finished, complete with upstairs and downstairs. Out of storage in Salt Lake City they brought their household things, lining the house with their books, and hanging on the rough, gray plastered walls the well-loved pictures Kate had brought back from Europe.

Trees and garden did not do well, but the sheep flourished, many lambs coming forth in the spring. This was what life could be, this peace, this contentment. Kate Wenner read with a kind of wonder the letters from relatives and friends insisting that they leave the desert island and come back to civilization.

"There was so much to do, so much to think about in this new life away from the world, the only family on the Island. I began to feel much of my life would have been wasted living in the outside world imitating fashions, wondering about neighbors' affairs, worrying about my children's companions. We learned to know ourselves, enjoy ourselves, children and books."

It was two years before she set foot off the island again; she went home to Illinois then because a new baby was coming. Her mainland finery she had packed away, forgetting it would be old-fashioned. So it was a funny procession that passed along the street in Ogden, the mother perfectly unconscious of her old-fashioned clothes, the little boy with a squeaking pet pelican close behind him, the little girl carrying a box of horned toads. The children would not leave their mother, nor would they leave their pets, so all went together. The lame pelican had been found by the children on the island shore, and had responded so well to domestication as to become something of a nuisance.

So, while Judge Wenner went back to the seasonal labors on the island, Kate and her two children went home to Illinois. "While East there was an epidemic of whooping cough and my father, concerned, said, 'Children, have you had it?' and little Blanche replied, 'Grandpa, I think we had all the diseases but Polygamy before we went to the island.' "

Three months later with the new baby, Lincoln, they all came back to the beloved island. Two Shetland ponies awaited the children, and a goat and harness and a little wagon, as well as a pedigreed shepherd dog.

It was, altogether, an idyll they lived. With their chickens, ducks, turkeys and sheep they lived well. They had bought an old boat, and they named her the *Argo,* made her seaworthy again, carved a ram's head on her bow and in her carried their fleeces and lambs to the mainland. Once a month they sent their herder for provisions and mail. "Oh the mail and how the newspapers were devoured—that part of life we never gave up. Crude as Island life was in many ways, there were certain amenities that we never neglected." The holidays all were celebrated, the Fourth of July not least among them; their Jersey cow once took refuge in the lake from the rockets bursting overhead; a Christmas tree was always brought from the mainland, and Santa Claus contrived to find his way there. Once, Kate remembers, the children decided they ought to be sick:

"they heard us reading letters about their little cousin being sick, and not to be outdone the two older ones began by letting 'the old cat die' in their swings, they caught hands and whirled as long as they could, then staggered over to a can of sheep dip and sniffed that until they knew they were sick or something. We found them laid out in the shearing shed and that was their only sickness on the Island and was brought on by their own determination."

On summer evenings the children would run down to the lake for a quick dip in the salt water, come back to the rock house and climb the stairs to their beds. Their father's voice would seek after them up the stairs.

> "Sleep, baby, sleep,
> Thy mother is shaking the dreamland tree.
> Down falls a golden dream for thee,
> Sleep, baby, sleep."

Through this joyous island existence sorrow stalked them. Judge Wenner's health did not improve. By the summer of 1889 he had become too weak to ride on horseback. His wife looked after the stock herself, attended to her house, taught her three children, nursed her husband and never for a moment admitted that death could seek them out.

On Wednesday, September 16, 1891, Judge Wenner had a severe hemorrhage of the lungs. It was stopped, and he said he felt more relieved than for months; though very weak, he was cheerful, and asked Charlie Rollins to sail the *Argo* over to Hooper and get the mail. On Friday morning the herdsman left. That was a good day for the judge, and he asked Kate to read from their favorite books and repeat whole poems that she knew by heart. Next morning, however, as she was cooking his breakfast, she heard his signal. She ran to him, to realize that now, indeed, he was dying. She took his head in her arms. "Do you love me?" she asked tenderly. He answered her, "Yes," and asked if she loved him in return. At her "Yes!" he smiled. In a few moments he was dead.

Kate had only the hired girl to help her, and the girl had such a horror of death that nothing could induce her to enter the room. Kate washed and dressed her husband's body, went outside and got a board, laid it on chairs beside the bed and contrived to move her husband's body to the plank. When all was composed, she went in search of the three children. As best she could she explained what death was, then took the children in and showed them their father's face. All kissed him and knelt and prayed beside him.

In the meantime a heavy storm had arisen, lashing the lake to fury and making it impossible for the herdsman to return. When darkness fell, Kate climbed the island slope and lighted two signal fires to tell the man of her extremity. All that night she alternately replenished the fires and watched beside the body of her husband. But throughout the night and all the next day the wind raged around the island, and smashing waves rolled in from the lake as though to tear it apart. It was nightfall, and the twin fires were blazing again, before the wind began to die down. "There came a faint light in the heavens," Kate says, "and gradually a broad stream of moonlight like a path of gold and I saw the *Argo* sailing 'wing and wing' toward me. I felt like an angel was treading softly across the water."

"What's happened?" Rollins called hoarsely. She explained, and said that he must make a casket of such boards as he could find on the island. He thought it impossible, but she encouraged him, and in the little barn they worked the night through. The box was ready at last; she lined it with a softly tinted shawl, and fixed a pillow for her husband's head.

In the first light of day the faithful Rollins dug the grave. There were no services but the prayers of Kate and the children, kneeling around the casket. As best they could they carried the box to the grave, and after the man drove stakes on one side of the grave and tied ropes to them, they lowered the rude casket into the grave. Kate went back to her children and Rollins filled the grave.

The storm had enveloped the lake again, so furious that it was almost a week before Kate could take her children and leave the well-loved island home. The editor of the Salt Lake *Tribune* talked to her when she arrived in the city, and paid her public tribute. "She did not shed a tear, she has not shed a tear since, she says very calmly that she never anticipated life without her husband, but that now her children need what strength she has got." These five island years and that final tragedy had been lived through, he desired to say, "by a little woman who never knew what work was, or what isolation meant; who knew nothing at all about the rougher side of life until she gave her heart up to her husband and thenceforth lived only for him."

Before leaving the island, Kate and the children took beautiful colored pebbles from the beach, and over the grave arranged them to spell the initials, "U.J.W.," with the word "LOVE." At a later date an iron fence was built around the burial plot, and letters of galvanized iron were made to contain the pebbles.

The widowed mother took her children to California. Later she married again and traveled to the far shores of the world. But she could never bring herself to sell the island; she herself ran it very efficiently for 10 years, and thereafter she leased it to men like Arnold and Orville Stoddard of Hooper, who continued to run sheep on it.

Fifty-one years later, the veteran yachtsman, John E. Jones of Salt Lake City, visited the island with Dr. Thomas C. Adams and two Sea Scouts. While the others explored the island summit, Mr. Jones walked about the lower slopes. To his surprise he came upon a small plot of ground enclosed in an iron fence set in cement posts. Within the fence were the disordered initials, "W.U.J.V.E.," partly buried in the sand.

His interest aroused, John E. Jones made inquiries in Salt Lake City. The island, he learned, belonged to Mrs. Kate W. Noble, living in Seattle. He wrote her early in November 1942 and she replied at once, the widow of U. J. Wenner, happy in reminiscences of the five years when Frémont Island had been her home—not then, she said, a neglected sheep ranch but a real home with a big library, pictures from abroad and Shetland ponies for her children. Her two boys were dead, but her daughter was with her in Seattle. She owned the island still, and her daughter Blanche, a high school teacher and war worker, hoped some day to make the improvements they once had. The galvanized letters Mr. Jones had found originally had been filled with bright pebbles, and V.E. were the last letters of the word LOVE, "a letter for each one of the family left behind."

Within two weeks Kate Wenner Noble, now a diminutive,

bright-eyed woman of 85, sent Mr. Jones the memoirs of her island life from which I have quoted. It was one of the last acts of her life, for she died before the month was out. In January her daughter Blanche wrote of her intention to place her mother's ashes beside her father's grave, and Mr. Jones replied, offering to obtain a boat for the voyage.

So, after so many years, the little girl who had been her father's "Cushla Machree" came back to her island home. Eight in all sailed from the Salt Lake Boat Harbor at 9:00 A.M. on Sunday morning, June 13, 1943. It was storming, but the crew was experienced and Blanche Wenner was unafraid. Though the heavy seas tossed the 10-ton boat around like a cockleshell, they reached the island after a 4½ hour voyage. They had to anchor 300 yards out and ferry in the party one by one, for the small rowboat was only large enough to carry two at a time—six trips in all. The owner of the boat had to stay aboard, as he dared not leave it alone in the storm.

Carrying picks, shovels, flowers and a box containing the bronze urn, together with a copper plaque Mr. Jones had caused to be made, the six men climbed the island to the burial place. Miss Wenner went off by herself while the men dug the grave for the urn. When all was ready, she placed the urn in the grave, said some prayers from the Episcopal Prayer Book and some verses that had been favorites of her mother and then retired while the grave was filled. She came back to arrange the flowers, and the men left her there for a time in the intermittent sunshine and storm.

They reunited at the beach and one by one were carried aboard again. As soon as all were on board Mr. Jones writes me, "the wind whooped it up again and blew fiercely all the way home. Only four of us ate anything on the way home—no, I wasn't sick—neither was she." The rain came down in sheets, with violent thunder and lightning, visibility so blotted out that landmarks could not be made out, and for a time they had to travel wholly by compass. The boat harbor was reached in the mingled gloom of the night and the storm at 10:00 P.M., and an hour and a half later Mr. Jones delivered Miss Wenner back to her hotel in Salt Lake City.

On the island the copper plaque remains to tell its cryptic story to all who may chance that way in time to come:

IN MEMORIAM

U. J. Wenner	Kate Wenner Noble
Born	Born
Bethlehem, Pennsylvania	Tallula, Illinois
July 31, 1849	April 1, 1857
Died	Died
September 19, 1891	December 29, 1942
Fremont Island, Utah	Seattle, Washington

LOVE

Three islands: three lives. In the book that he made of his adventure Alfred Lambourne wrote that on Frémont Judge Wenner had lived for health, and that Antelope early had an occupant. But he himself, he believed, "was the first to live for love on one of the islands of the Inland Sea."

This strange and rather charming person was born in England on February 2, 1850. In his childhood he journeyed to America with his parents and lived for many years in St. Louis before driving an ox team across the plains to Zion in the summer of 1866.

Though a boy of 16, art already had captured him, and he sketched the scenes by the way—drawings published years after in a book he called *The Pioneer Trail*. The first building he looked upon, as he entered Salt Lake Valley on a golden September afternoon, was one which shaped much of his life. He could see from the canyon mouth the city of the Saints, its streets and houses almost hidden by trees of many orchards, making as he remembered in after life, "an oasis of brighter green amid the sage-gray sadness of the open valley." In the midst of the green, above the trees, he could see as he came across the eastern benchlands, a great, white, oblong building—the Salt Lake Theatre.

In that theater, then in the fourth year of its famous existence, he found employment as assistant scenic artist. *A Play-House,* the most appealing of all his 14 books, is also the most warming account of the historic old theater, written from the vantage point of the Scene Painter's Gallery. For many years his life was bound up with the theater, first as an apprentice, later as chief scenic artist, and he there met the costumer, Wilhelmina Marie Williamson, whom on September 13, 1877, he made his wife.

He was a true artist, with an artist's independence of mind and mood and tastes. Though his parents were Mormons, and though he remained in good fellowship with the Saints, he had no religious affiliation until late in life, when he associated himself with the Unitarian movement in Salt Lake City. He had a taste for solitary rambles in the mountains; it was he who explored and named the Cottonwood lakes above Salt Lake City—Martha, for his mother, Minnie, for his wife, Lillian, for his youngest daughter. He was a close friend of the famous pioneer photographer, C. R. Savage, with whom he toured the West, one photographing, the other painting; he was one of the first to paint Yellowstone, Zion and Bryce.

Of shy and retiring disposition, modest, reticent and uncommunicative, he unbent only to his intimates—but to them as a man of singularly lovable character, with a keenly analytical mind and an astonishing fund of information. When he died, on June 6, 1926, it was said of him that pursuit of material wealth or the attainment of prominence through books or pictures seemed always farthest from his purpose; he lived in a world of his own making, a world of dreams and ideals—a true Bohemian.

The lake first enwrapped Alfred Lambourne in its spell early in the eighties, when Adam Patterson took him in his yacht, the *Maud,* to Antelope Island. On horseback Lambourne rode along the island's western highlands, and the infinitely varied mood of the lake, with the lonely magnificence of its far shores, filled him with a restless desire to sail the lake and sketch it, capture in water colors and oils the quality of its mingled desolation and beauty. In David L. Davis he found a man kindred in his love of the lake, though Davis was yachtsman, not artist. Innumerable happy cruises they made together in Davis' catamaran, the *Cambria.*

Skillfully as he wielded it, his brush alone was not adequate to his necessities, and Alfred Lambourne felt a need for the communication of words. The need for words grew upon him as the years went by, and by the end of his life he had all but abandoned the brush for the pen.

His first cruise in the *Cambria,* in June 1887, only spurred Alfred

Lambourne's passion to know the lake in all its moods. Gunnison Island, in the far northwestern part of the lake, began to fill his mind as an image, the unattainable that might somehow be sought out. It seemed as he dreamed of it, a realization of perfect solitude.

A second cruise, later in the summer of 1887, gave body to his dreams. The *Cambria* sailed north into a moment of true magnificence. In the waste of waters, as the golden-gray sunset gave way to the early stars, what an overpowering sense of solitude! And on the far horizon a purple speck no bigger than a boy's top—the first sight of his heart's desire.

Darkness closed down. It was an experience beyond describing to sail through those remarkable hours between the evening and morning twilight, while the water reeled in their wake like a mountain torrent. "How like a dream it was to be out there on the face of that mysterious sea! How like a dream to be moving in the deep midnight toward the shadows of its unknown shores! Every sight and sound had in it something of wonder or beauty."

The sky was blazing with morning when they reached the island. Lambourne leaped ashore, shouting, answered by a scream from the throats of myriad birds. "Not in our circumnavigation of the lake," he wrote, "had we looked upon another scene half as picturesque as that, nor one whose sombre features were enlivened with such a multitude of noisy life. Every hour of our stay at this island was filled with the echoes of a ceaseless din."

In some respects the island could be likened to an outlying fragment of "sea-beat Hebrides," but on a summer day,

"with the fervid heat pouring down on the lava rocks, with its lizards darting across the burning sands, the green and blue water lying glassy calm, and on the horizon gleams of snow-crested peaks, it more closely resembled some lonely rock of the Azores. Well could we ask, Where could we find another such lake, with another such island, where, in the noon of a summer day, we might fancy ourselves by the shore of some southern sea, and yet be standing on a spot that is howled across by the fiercest of winter storms?"

He enjoyed the clamorous gulls and the stolid pelicans, and he left the island with a sharp regret.

They ran into such heavy weather on the return voyage as taxed the strength of two men to manage the tiller of even the tiny *Cambria*. There was not a man of the six aboard, Lambourne was sure, who did not wish himself ashore—not in fear, but to have won through these dangers triumphant. Who but the born coward did not enjoy such an experience—"the thrill, the secret sense of exultation engendered by looking a danger full in the face; to fully realize its presence, yet not turn aside"? So he watched the spiteful, vicious waves, exulting to see the foam ripped fiercely from their crests, until the seas subsided, withstood—for this time.

Again and again, as the years went by, he made the cruise to the distant island. It filled his mind; it made him restless and unhappy, unfulfilled.

When Ninetta Eames was the guest of the *Cambria* on a two-day lake cruise in June 1895 Lambourne and the younger artist, H. L. A. Culmer, came along with their sketchbooks. She saw how Lambourne's eyes lighted when Davis mentioned the northern island. "Gunnison is the Ultima Thule of all this glorious island cruising," he said softly, "the realization to poet and artist of perfect solitude. I have always an insatiable longing to build me a lodge on some bleak shelf there, and hie me to it for brief periods to enjoy to the full my divine right to myself. The soul needs such seasons of unrelated environment."

But was not Gunnison a dead, a desert island? "I remember the fright of the gulls," he said, "and how the lizards skimmed the hot sands or peered like devils from holes in the rocks. Such a torrid sun, and the deafening clamor of those gulls! Never was anything more wildly picturesque—the gaunt white cliffs, the countless, furious gulls, pelicans on the shore-marge standing wing to wing as stiff and orderly as soldiers, and tall, blue herons posed at way-points with all the dignity of sentinels!" He brooded. "There certainly is life enough upon Gunnison of unfamiliar kinds, though the eyes of man rarely see it."

The dream of solitude! Yet he was a man 45 years of age, with a wife and four children (three others had died in infancy.) How was such a man justified in seeking out a solitude within his own soul? He thought long, and late in the year the answer came to him. He would homestead the island. The Homestead Law required a continuous residence, with the right of leaving for business or visiting, but not for labor or hiring out. He would live on the island continuously through 14 months, making of it a vineyard. "From my father," he reflected, "I have inherited these—a love for an island and a love for the vine. Two good reasons, it appears to me, why I may hope to succeed."

In November 1895 his friends carried him north to the bleak island that filled his heart. They helped him build a small, massive hut, its low, thick walls formed of untrimmed slabs of stone taken from the cliff by which the hut stood, its roof earth-covered, its chimney starting from the ground, almost as big as the hut itself. Though rough outside, the hut was bright and cozy within. It possessed a table, a rack formed from the skull of a mountain sheep, with curved and massive horns, a bin and the means for cooking, an easel and a piano encased in dark mahogany. There were shelves of books—the *Decameron,* Walt Whitman's *Leaves of Grass,* Herrick's *Hesperides, Don Quixote,* Caesar, Kepler, Gladstone, Webster, Paine, Montaigne, Rabelais, Swift. There was a statuette of Ariadne by Danneker and a Navaho blanket of bizarre design. On the wall was a plate after Titian, and an autographed portrait of a famous modern beauty, one among the innumerable great who had trodden the stage of the Salt Lake Theatre. Over the whole "a chain-dropp'd lamp" cast its mellow glow.

Nevertheless, as the sails of the departing yacht disappeared below the horizon, Alfred Lambourne felt a strange sinking of the heart. With winter coming on, this comfortless island could as well be some lonely spot in the Arctic.

How slowly the hours crept by! "Silent, implacable days," he called them, more trying than the furious times of storm. Yet what a wintry magnificence to the scene and the season! The distant mountain heights smoked in the dawn, he thought, like tired horses; the sun rose like a disk of copper through the spindrift brine.

With him he had brought two dogs, and one morning he found them worrying a raven, a great black thing with wing spread a full three inches beyond the four-feet-six supposed to limit the growth of his kind. Lambourne rescued the ebony-feathered bird, and named him Devil, for after that moment of first ascendancy, the dogs learned to fear him.

The long months of hermit existence ended in March. The rock once so desert, Lambourne made wondering entry in his diary, "has become a hive. The gloomy season is ended. I am lost in news of the world." There was a plenitude of shipping in the bay—the yacht of his friends with wet deck and tired crew, a 50-foot schooner, with another craft anchored close by, and a little sloop lying half-wrecked on the island sands alongside his own small boat, the *Hope*.

"Suddenly this island has become important. Short the time, since for the asking alone, the place had been mine. Now, as if it had become an actual beehive, a monster and animated emblem of the state, Science, Commerce, Agriculture, Education, *'Ars Militans,'* I might add, are contending for it—the corporation with millions of dollars, the private company, the individual, the state, each makes a claim. There have been Government surveys, railroad section surveys, local company and private surveys. There have been issued a Government Grant, the Desert Entry, the Homestead Entry, and the Mineral Claim. A coveted prize this island must certainly be."

He was saying that the state was claiming that part of the island which had fallen to it by the school grant; the Central Pacific was eager to establish whether any part had been given it by the railroad land grants; and private companies were seeking to patent a mineral claim. All this by reason of the new interest in the commercial possibilities of the guano.

Guano sifters would live with him on the island all the rest of the spring and the summer; already they were making themselves a home not a hundred yards from his own, a long and narrow structure built of rounded slabs. The homesteader peered within their cabin. The piled-up sacks of flour, the bags of beans, the boxes of candles, the flitches of bacon hanging from the beams, the pots, pans and kettles, as well as the numerous aids and implements of labor, were evidence that the men would make a protracted stay.

From the first hours he found it fascinating to watch the sifters at their labor. Three of them passed guano dust through sieves and put it into sacks while four others dug among the ancient bird deposits. Lambourne took up his notebook to fix the scene.

"Leaning against the wild March wind, their rustic clothing flapping in as wild disorder, and a cloud of the brown, snuff-like mineral hovering around them, or being carried by the fitful gusts far beyond the sieves, the men make extremely picturesque figures. One of the sifters will dwell here permanently. I expect to place him into many a future sketch. He is a Hercules in strength and of brawny stature. He moves from place to place all unconscious, and of course uncaring, of his pictorial value to me. Despite the season, his head and shoulders are bare to the sun and wind, his feet are encased in coarse brown sacking; and, as I write, he is, with that exception, naked. He is carrying a plank to a couple of his fellow laborers, and these are busy at work on the recently stranded boat. His yellow hair, his ruddy flesh tints focus a picture in which the broken sloop, the big black schooner, the white hull of the yacht, the turquoise blue waters of the Inland Sea, the warm gray of the island cliff, with the reeling clouds above them, are the splendid components. Only to realize to the full the effect of this momentary scene upon the mind, the describer must not omit the sounds. Two of my friends, with shouts and halloos, explore a corner of the transformed bay. There is a chattering of hammers made by the workmen overhauling the wreck: the dogs bark loud, and these united noises bring shrill, harsh cries from the island sea-birds, and these are answered in turn by a loud and indignant cackle from the sifters' score and two of newly-brought and astonished barnyard fowls."

On closer acquaintance Lambourne found the sifters an extremely varied lot. There was a Pole, a Russian, a Scot, and an Englishman who had visited the guano islands off the coast of Brazil, one who had doubled the Capes, one who had seen Mauna Loa, and the giant fellow he had first marked, and whom he denominated "the Drudge."

The pits and trenches, the numerous outworks, made the sifters' part of the island like a fortified camp. The posts and the trellis of his own vineyard followed the terrace lines of vanished Lake Bonneville. Stones enough and to spare existed for a retaining wall. Making the desolation to be fruitful was a great adventure. "This may be a question of will," he admonished himself. "Then let me endure. Perhaps this is a game of patience, and my part is but to watch and to wait. A work of redemption is a work that proves slow. . . . A Homesteader's vines, like a Homesteader's heart, must be filled with courage." Water must be had; he could hope for a well, and meantime carry water to his vines from his rain-filled tanks.

As the days lengthened, he longed to experience again the exuberance of spring. Here there was nothing of spring except qualities of the air. "A wind treacherous and soft," he described it. "As if made of burnished silver, shone the passing clouds. Lovely tints of pale, turquoise blue lay on the placid water, and the mountains, like vast crumpled foldings of cream-colored silk, stood shimmering along the horizon. . . . All of this, and yet once more the wild March blizzards come out of the north. The salt spray is hurled across my island."

And yet, when summer itself was come, "My days of trial are here. . . . My eyes ache. O, the insufferable brightness! O, the glare of light upon the waters of the Inland Sea! Like polished steel gleams the briny surface. . . . My brain seethes." The bird voices grew monotonous. The shy herons and pelicans had not returned this spring to share the island with him and the sifters, nesting instead on Hat Island, many miles to the south. But the brazen gulls came back fearlessly. "I am berated from morning to night. The gulls scream defiance . . . go where I will the untired birds await my presence with cries of resentment. Not content with this, they await not my coming, but come themselves to my very door. . . . It is painful to be so very unpopular." Yet there were compensating moments, nights when the gulls floated like a white, fallen cloud on the starlit water.

He was shocked to find a rattlesnake amid his vines. "This is a counter invasion," he reasoned. "There is no mistaking what this incident means. The desert retaliates, it puts into operation the natural law of self-defense. In this presence among the vines there is a lesson to learn." Perhaps this anger, this shock, was unreasonable; the island mice were making havoc of his bin, and his sketchbook had not escaped them. Even so, he did not like to think of a rencounter between the mice and the snake.

The Drudge's pick turned up a human skull and fragments of a skeleton—an Indian burial. The thought excited him. Even *here* the aborigines had dwelt. At what age of the earth; and how had they come here? Throughout the summer he speculated about these questions.

The autumnal equinox ended the sifters' labors; the season was over, and they awaited the schooner that would bear them to the mainland. Lambourne had found them picturesque in labor; he found them no less picturesque in idleness, and longed for an old Dutch master to paint them.

"The out door labor removed the men from vulgar commonplace, and now the night scenes of pastime are quite as good. Nature composes in the sifters' cabin a hundred pieces, each one better than those of the Little Masters. The sturdy or lank forms of the men, their eager faces, those who play the game, the onlookers, the drowsers, the candle flame—of such are pictures made. And in the background, the ruddy reflections on the smooth rim or bottom of pan or kettle, the shining of tin or copper against the brown blackness of bituminous shadow."

All at once the sifters were gone, and he was alone again. If spring had been tenuous, intangible, autumn was not. "A mighty drowsiness is on the land. . . . Haze-enwrapped are the distant Wasatch; through deepening shades of saddened violet, the Onaqui lapse into melancholia. The western headlands, the jutting promontories, appear as if cut from dim, orange crape, or maroon-colored velvet. Wistful and vague stand the peaked islands, and shell-like is the gleam of the far-stretched brine." Ah, this heavy lassitude, this voluptuous sadness, this wondrous effect of sensuous color! "Always there are the same great stretches of water around, always the same dreary and monotonous hills, ever the same strange walls of rock, and ever the same wild peaks. . . . But how the seasons and the great sun play with them!"

Winter was here again, the dark waters and the snow. The year turned, and on a day early in February there were white sails on the horizon and his friends had come for him. The 14-month vigil was ended. He could not feel that he had been imprisoned, now that his time was full; he would have disliked to part with the experience of having lived here, and he felt a need to state to himself the nature of this experience:

"Under certain conditions, a place becomes part of us; we own it. We absorb it into our lives. It cannot be taken from us. It is ours, and without title or deed. We are associated with a certain spot of earth; we have our lives shaped by it; or if that be not the case, we stamp the place with our individuality."

He had something to say to himself, something overflowing with meaning: "THIS PLACE IS MINE."

In the end that must be his satisfaction, the reward for 14 months of his life given to the inland sea and its island. Lambourne's friends loaded his things on their boat and carried him back to Salt Lake City. On February 9, 1897, he filed his application for Homestead Right No. 12592, covering 78.35 acres of the northern part of the island (the part that was grand with cliff and bay). Of the total island area of 155.06 acres, the rest was divided between a railroad grant and the State School Section.

Lambourne was two years too late; the guano had excited the avarice of his townsfolk, and as soon as his application was filed, suit was brought to void the homestead entry on grounds that the land was mineral rather than agricultural. For a few hopeless months he fought in the courts for his vines and his 14 months of island labor, but he had no money to sustain a long fight. On August 7, 1897, he formally relinquished his application, and the way was cleared for eventual patenting of the island by mineral claim.

He had only his memories, his notebooks, and his canvases, what he had given of himself to the lake and the island, and what they had given him in return. In 1902 he published a slender volume, *Pictures of an Inland Sea,* illustrated with some of his own paintings but essentially the story of his homestead venture. About 1908, five years after the Lucin Cutoff was completed, he visited the island again, and the year following expanded his book in a final form as *Our Inland Sea.* It was one of the Southern Pacific's launches, the *Augusta,* which carried him back to the island that last time. The

Cutoff with its long line of piles and rock filling had materially altered the conditions on the upper end of the inland sea. Stations existed at Promontory Point and near Strongs Knob. Naphtha launches or cutters had supplanted the sailboats, running in an hour or two across long reaches of water where the sailboats had lain becalmed or labored slowly against an adverse wind. "The machine has its practical superiority," he reflected, "the sail its poetry."

The view from the island was changed, the long line of the Cutoff to the south seen in silhouette against the shining water, the Lilliputian locomotives trailing plumes of smoke and long trains of cars. The island itself was very lonely and desolate, no living soul there. The door of his hut stood open, the sifters' cabin empty. His vines were dead—not a stem or shoot of his hope had lived.

Dry-eyed, he returned to the *Augusta*. As he stepped aboard, he saw near the boat's prow a drowning butterfly. Its extended, bright blue wings quivered convulsively as it drifted, helpless, on the brine.

Chapter 18

Place of Resort

THE IDEA that Great Salt Lake was above all else a place to have a good time took hold from the first, on the arrival of the Mormons in 1847. As one of the lesser wonders of the age, it was incumbent on all the Saints to go soak themselves in the salt water so that thereafter they might have a tale to tell.

Heber C. Kimball thought the salt breeze off the lake just like that off the ocean, if not more so, although most later visitors have disagreed with him, finding in the air, as one writer expressed it, not a salt freshness but rather "the warmth and electric dryness" characteristic of desert regions.

By chance Brigham Young's party in 1847, following the Hastings-Donner trail west to the lake, had been led to the only good beach, and all the excursions of nearly 25 years followed the beaten track to where Black Rock upthrust its somber bulk along the south shore. The first excursion in which the entire community participated came on July 4, 1851. This particular Glorious Fourth at Great Salt Lake City was ushered in at daybreak with three rounds from the artillery on the Temple Block. While an immediate far, faint echo sounded from Black Rock, the townsfolk set about lighting their fires, milking their cows, watering their horses, and attending to all the other chores from which even holidays could not exempt them. By 7:00 A.M., as the contemporary newspaper account quaintly puts it, "the city began to be in motion," with much rattling of carriages, rumbling of wagons, trampling of horses and loud preliminary *blarumphing* from Captain Pitts's Brass Band. After the throng was assembled, the cannon fired again, echoed faintly from Black Rock, and, at 8:00 A.M., the population of Great Salt Lake City arranged itself for the procession to the salt lake.

Out in front went the military escort, followed by the band carriage drawn by sixteen mules four abreast, with which rode six mounted guards. Brigham Young and Heber C. Kimball, with their expansive families, were third in the line of march, and after

348

them came three of the apostles with their families. The gentiles in town, invited to join with the community in this patriotic celebration, were fifth in line, and following them came the lesser dignitaries and the townsfolk themselves. Fifty mounted men were designated to remain in town as an armed guard, and additional watchmen were stationed here and there to safeguard the city.

It required four hours to reach the lake, where the Stars and Stripes in all its glory flew from a tall liberty pole that had been raised for the occasion. The carriages were corralled, horses unharnessed and given in charge of the herdsmen, and then the citizenry could give themselves up to the occasion.

After eating a picnic dinner embellished with snow brought down from the Oquirrh canyons, they assembled for the customary orations. The wind blew so hard, however, that the orators could not begin to compete, and the oratory was adjourned till evening. Everybody scattered to find their pleasures along the lake shore.

At 6:00 p.m. the orators were given another chance, and they did nobly through four hours. The cannon then summoned everyone for prayer, after which dancing continued till a late hour. Early next day the cannon summoned everybody for the homeward departure, and at 2:00 p.m. the procession was safe within the city limits again. There had been no drunkenness, no discord, nor even any accident, except the upsetting of the carriage of Ben Holladay, the future stagecoach king.

A visitor in town wrote home an account of the occasion which in one respect strikingly anticipated the future. The Mormon people, he said, "ever ready to take advantage of improvement by the public spirit, with which they seem to be inspired, intend building a Bathhouse and Hotel, together with their pleasure boats, which will make Great Salt Lake one of the greatest places of resort, not only to the citizens of the Mormon population, but a pleasurable excursion to the passing emigrants."

It is not clear why this idea had to wait 20 years for fruition. Perhaps the bathhouse erected at Warm Springs, just within the city limits, provided a sufficient place of resort for the immigrants, and perhaps the immigrants were disinclined to journey 35 miles out of their way even for the satisfaction of bathing in the unique mountain sea. There are, at all events, few accounts of gentile visits to the Black Rock beaches until the time of the Utah Expedition, and Brigham Young himself evinced a preference for Antelope Island when an excursion to the lake appealed to him.

As far as the Saints were concerned, the first novelty faded, and fewer and fewer of them hitched up their teams for the two-day excursion to the lake. However, a handful of visitors have left interesting accounts of their visits to the salt lake.

Among these was the French traveler, Jules Remy, in September 1855. He bathed in the lake several times, "rather from curiosity than taste." This scientific bent displayed by Remy and his companion was not at all shared by the gentiles who accompanied them on such excursions, for Remy remarks, "we were much amused at the astonishment which it always caused among the people of our suite, who took care not to imitate us, fancying that so salt a bath must be of necessity prejudicial to the body, especially to the eyes and ears."

Four years later the busy Horace Greeley found time during his hectic overland journey to report to the readers of his beloved *Tribune* his impression of this "deeply, darkly, beautifully blue" lake. You could no more sink in it than in a claybank, he reported, "but a very little of it in your lungs would suffice to strangle you." The bathing itself he thought delightful.

Captain Richard Burton, who next year made his own memorable visit to the city of the Saints, accompanied Governor Cumming to the lake in the last week of his stay. The empirical spirit was too much for Captain Burton, and he must find out for himself the effect of the brine. With opened eyes he ducked his head under the surface and smarted for his pains. "The sensation did not come on suddenly; at first there was a sneaking twinge, then a bold succession of twinges, and lastly a steady, honest burning." With no fresh water at hand, he was obliged to scramble upon a rock and sit there for half an hour, presenting, he said, the ludicrous spectacle of a grown man weeping flowing tears. He found fault with those who had averred that the buoyant water would support a bather as if he were sitting in an armchair, and float him like an unfresh egg; for himself, he experienced no difficulty in swimming, or even in sinking. He was struck, however, with his appearance on emerging

David H. Mann

Courtesy Utah State Department of
Publicity & Industrial Development

Andreas Feininger, Office of War Information

Courtesy Library of Congress

The Utah Copper Mine in Bingham Canyon, Utah's greatest treasure trove.

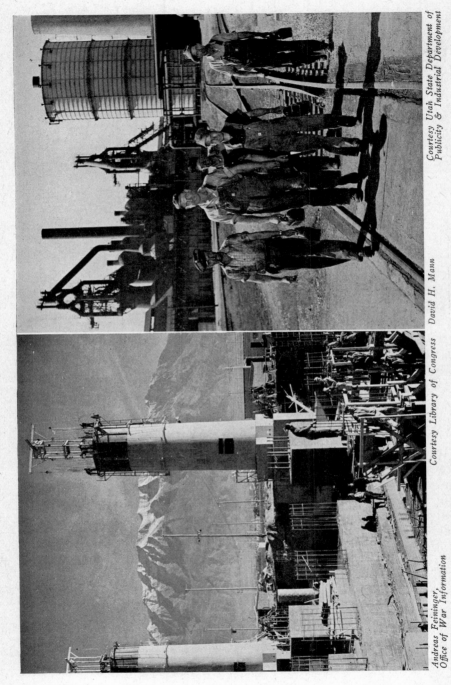

The Geneva Steel Plant: *at left*, under construction in 1942, Mount Timpanogos in background; *at right*, workmen leaving plant.

from the water; his hair was powdered, and there was a clammy stickiness exceedingly disagreeable. It was a novelty to be able to scrape salt from his skin, but he was happy to pour a jug of fresh water over himself.

In 1863 came the journalist Fitz Hugh Ludlow, among the earliest writers about Great Salt Lake with a feeling for its atmosphere. In his *The Heart of the Continent* he devotes an entire chapter to the lake. For him Black Rock rose "grim and ugly, like the foundation of some ruined round tower," and he was fully prepared for a grim and desolate landscape, a sullen waste of brine.

On the contrary, he found the view one of the most charming that could be imagined, the word "lovely" occurring to him instantly as its fittest description. The mountains around melted into "vapory streaks of pale turquoise on the far horizon, their northward terminations forming bold headlands, or long, low promontories, with dreamy bays setting back into the indentations of the coast between them." Though to the northeast the alkali plain was comparatively low and uninteresting, the lake itself seemed to him like a pavement of pure sapphire, flecked here and there with drifting whirls of marble dust, its heavy waves lifting more like lazy swells of quicksilver than of water. In the distance Antelope Island was reminiscent of Capri, as soft as a sunset cloud in tone of both feeling and color.

The water he found very exhilarating.

"It was as cold to the feel as the ocean at Long Branch in the bathing season, and from this cause, with its intense brininess in addition, gave me a tonic sensation like a brisk shower-bath. I felt none of the acidity and burning with which the lake affects some skins— only a pleasant pungent sense of being in pickle, such as a self-conscious gherkin might experience in Cross & Blackwell's aristocratic bath of condiments."

The adventure delighted him, and he could hardly bear to leave the water, even for dinner. Eventually, however, he stretched out on his back, head toward land, and allowed the breeze to blow him in on the long ground swells.

Salt drying in his long hair and full beard gave him the aspect of a shaggy Triton wreathed with seaweed and crystals, while the salt dried on his body in a crystalline film. He was happy to rinse himself off in fresh water, for as he got drier, the salt made his skin feel absolutely thirsty; a smarting, burning sensation lingered in his pores to some degree all day. So he was content to turn back to Townsend's Hotel in the city, rejoicing in the sunset effects upon the mountains—"such magical beauty as no pen or brush can hope to paint, no heart which it has filled with ecstasy can ever forget." He could well believe this mountainland part of heaven itself, "the very gates and foundations of the city of God."

Among these visitors who wrote of the lake in the years before the Pacific Railroad came must be mentioned William Elkanah Waters, whose little book, *Life Among the Mormons,* published anonymously in 1868, is distinguished by its temperate spirit and exact observation. On reaching Black Rock, Waters noted that peculiar smell all visitors to the lake forever remember, caused by the moisture in the air from the evaporating waters, "as well as the decay of myriads of little insects." He waded through the shallows to deep water, finally reaching a depth where he could wade no farther, "not because the water covered me, but because I couldn't reach the bottom with my feet—and there I was, bobbing about on the waves, head and neck above them, like an empty bottle." Turning upon his back, he found less difficulty in swimming, and by experimentation, remaining perfectly passive and holding up his hands before him, he concluded that he could have reclined there and read the morning paper with ease. There was a tendency to roll over, face downward, but no other inconvenience. To sink was impossible, as long as he lay passive on the water.

Waters was disposed to rebuke the unstable fancies of various writers. To those who said they found no difficulty in sinking, he made rejoinder:

"Neither would we find any difficulty in sinking a stick of soft wood for a moment in the Mississippi or North River if one should be dropped from a pier or a boat perpendicularly to the water. I have no idea that the body of a man, if he jumped on the water, would rebound like a rubber ball when struck against a marble slab; but I am very much inclined to think that if the gentleman named

[Burton] has five pounds of fat in his whole corpus some part of it would float above water."

But also he rebuked those tending to exaggerate the buoyancy of the water; being remarkable enough already, why spoil the idea by overreaching possibilities?

The idea that one could not drown in the Great Salt Lake, Waters gave short shrift. If a person should fall from a boat and lose the erect posture, he thought, his head, being the heavier part, would go under and the man would drown as his body floated on the surface. (In our own day it has been suggested, not altogether facetiously, that the best life preserver one could carry on the lake would be a ball and chain affixed to one's ankle, which would force the swimmer's body to a perpendicular position and bring the head well out of water.)

Altogether, Waters thought the bath one of the most pleasant he had ever had, with the temperature of the water delightful, and after remaining immersed half an hour, he left it feeling "invigorated and refreshed rather than debilitated."

After 1869 the experience of Great Salt Lake no longer had to be vicarious. Anyone who commanded the price could travel by rail to Salt Lake City and see the lake for himself. This significant change in the status of the lake dawned on the entrepreneurs of Salt Lake City very rapidly, and two resorts appeared on the shores of the lake.

The first of these was the idea of John W. Young, third of Brigham's 25 sons, and one of the most enterprising. Out of his subcontracting for the Central Pacific and the Union Pacific, "Prince John" had made some $50,000 and he had a hand in almost all railroad building in Utah during the next decade, not excluding the street railway system installed in Salt Lake City in 1872. The Utah Central, between Ogden and Salt Lake, ran close to the lake and though the eastern shore was inferior to the southern beaches, being shallow and muddy, its nearness to the line of the railroad made it an obvious location for a resort. Early in June 1870 Young opened his "pleasure grounds," Lake Side, near Farmington.

Within the year Jeter Clinton opened a rival establishment on the south shore. The occasion for his resort was the inception of steamboat service from Corinne. The "port of call" was variously called Lake Point, Steamboat Landing, Steamboat Point and Clinton's Landing before the first of these names won out. Clinton put up his "Lake House" early in 1871, and replaced it in the fall of 1874 with an impressive stone hotel.

For several years, however, Lake Side was the premier resort, and in June 1872 it became the home port for the *City of Corinne*. Excursions to "Prince John's" establishment frequently made news. One of these, of some importance for the history of the lake, occurred early in June 1872 when some Pennsylvania financiers who were interested in building the Salt Lake & Pioche Railroad were shown the sights. The party boarded the *City of Corinne* at Lake Side and sailed for Lake Point. At Clinton's Lake House they were served a dinner befitting the occasion, and after a day spent inspecting the mines in the near-by mountains, they returned to the steamboat and were carried north to Monument Point, to transfer to "the cars" for San Francisco. The financiers were sold on the new railroad which was to go west to Lake Point, thence to Tooele, Stockton and Tintic, and on to Pioche, Nevada, by way of Sevier Valley, and ground was broken on April 14, 1873. Depression times prevented its completion to Black Rock until January 10, 1875. By that time it had become reorganized as the Utah Western Railway, a name which in turn soon gave way to that of Utah & Nevada.

Until this railroad was completed, Lake Side largely monopolized the resort trade with a succession of Sunday school parties, reunions, ward parties and excursions in general. The *City of Corinne* was based at the resort, and excursions on it added much to holiday enjoyments. The Salt Lake *Herald* was of the opinion that there was probably no place in the territory where an excursion party could spend a day more pleasantly than by a steamboat sail on Salt Lake.

Gratified by this public approbation, the enterprising J. A. McKnight and H. Horsley in July 1873 came forward with the idea of a moonlight excursion from Lake Side to Lake Point and return on August 4. "The Party will be select," they advertised, "and will leave the Utah Central depot at 6:30 o'clock . . . returning thereto by 7:45 next morning."

But the *Deseret News* promptly put its foot down on such romantic nonsense. It was all very well to say that the party would be select, but if the general public was invited to join in it, how could it be? There was that class in the community (the *News* was squinting as much at the gentiles as at men of low character generally) which would seize such an opportunity to make acquaintances which under other circumstances they could not hope to obtain. "Certainly no parents, who have any sense of responsibility, would permit their daughters to go away from home for an entire night to mingle with a mixed company of people of whose antecedents and present lives they would be utterly ignorant."

Exit the Moonlight Excursion!

The south shore beaches resumed their old ascendancy in the spring of 1875, following the completion of the Utah Western to Black Rock. This excursion trade became the principal reason for being of the railroad, which, owing to failing activity in the mines around Stockton, was not extended beyond Black Rock for some years. The *City of Corinne,* newly renamed the *General Garfield,* abandoned her old base at Lake Side to sail from Clinton's landing, taking pleasure seekers 15 or 20 miles out into the lake in the course of two-hour cruises.

In 1876 Clinton's establishment was renamed Short Branch, obviously a pun upon New York City's watering place, Long Branch, and a pavilion was put up, with something like a hundred bathrooms. "The hotel is elegantly furnished and fitted up for parties," the *Deseret News* reported.

"The one great lack is a grove. An acre or two of trees, or an avenue a few hundred yards long, would add immensely to the attractiveness of the place. As it is, Short Branch may be termed wholly a marine pleasure resort, and as such, to many, it has no mean charms of its own. There are the extensive water and mountain views, the refreshing moist and cool breezes from the Lake, the steamer and row boat rides upon the waters, the bracing baths in the same, and the general calmness and quietude of the locality, all of which combine to render it an attractive and beautiful place to w[h]ile away a few hours, days, or weeks, as the case may be, in the pursuit of recreative pleasures and renewed health. There are those who claim that nowhere do they receive so much benefit to their health as at the lake, and to those who have shaky nerves or are slightly invalid from many other causes and in many other ways, an occasional visit to the Lake, or a stay there of a few days or weeks, might prove of signal benefit."

This was, of course, enchanting publicity. But there was a nettle in this reed; business at Short Branch proved altogether too brisk to remain long in Clinton's hands. By 1878 there was a small competing establishment at Black Rock, a little farther east, and in 1881 the skipper of the *General Garfield,* Captain Thomas Douris, took a running jump into the resort business himself. He beached his boat a short distance west of the Black Rock resort and added bathing and boating facilities. At first called Garfield Landing, Douris' resort soon became generally known as Garfield Beach. Douris had some backing from the railroad, it appears, but the Utah & Nevada showed a disposition to get neck-deep into this lucrative business and in 1883 took over the Black Rock property. By the mid-eighties, Clinton's old hotel had been squeezed out.

Her seafaring days ended, the *General Garfield's* job of catering to pleasure seekers was carried on by two saucy little steamers regarded as better adapted to the responsibility, and far less costly to operate—the *Susie Riter* and the *Whirlwind.* The *Susie Riter,* a brisk little side-wheel steamer, was a luckless craft; she remained in service only a year or two before going down by her anchor in a storm.

This lucrative business of acquainting tourists with the strange salt lake in 1886 brought a new resort to the eastern shore, a little north of Lake Side. Built and operated by the Denver & Rio Grande Western Railroad Company, Lake Park came into existence only three years after this railroad reached Ogden.

It had been the general opinion for some time that there was a crying need for better facilities on the lake. Edward W. Sloan, in his *Gazetteer* of 1884, had minced no words on the subject, saying that the several lake resorts were "anything rather than what the importance of the lake as a watering place or the patronage would justify. Garfield and Black Rock are within a mile of each other and belong to the railroad company which, for reasons best known to the owners, have made no effort to put the unequaled opportunities they have into execution in making a great inland watering resort on the shore of this remarkable dead sea."

The Utah & Nevada did not take this advice to heart, but the D & R G hearkened to it and when the season of 1886 closed, 53,347 visitors had paid their 50 cents to go to Lake Park as against the 48,279 who had chosen the resorts at the south shore.

Confronted by this challenge, the Utah & Nevada early in 1887 got to work. Douris' place was taken over and a new and more resplendent Garfield Beach resort was built. This new resort, the proprietors boasted, was distinguished by a magnificent pavilion, 165 by 65 feet, built over the water 400 feet from shore, and approached by a covered pier over 300 feet in length. The whole was surmounted by an observation tower overlooking the lake on all sides, and in this pavilion, every afternoon during the season, a grand concert was to be given by "a first-class orchestra of talented soloists." There were elegant dressing rooms, a handsome station building, a restaurant and lunchstand with a distinguished bill of fare, and a saloon where the choicest brands of liquors and cigars would be dispensed by polite attaches. It was also to be borne in mind that Garfield Beach was the only resort on the entire lake shore having a clean, sandy beach, free from mud, rocks and offensive vegetable matter.

In this last argument the proprietors of Garfield Beach had something, and they knew it. Lake Park had the advantage of being located along a main railroad line between Utah's two largest cities, but the east shore was flat, and the bottom too muddy for fine bathing. Some 60,000 visitors thronged to Lake Park in 1887, but the handwriting had to be read upon the wall.

When, in writing this book, I began to resurrect out of history lake resorts I had never even heard of and which, after the lapse of half a century, have been almost totally forgotten, for information about Lake Park I turned to Darrell J. Greenwell, editor of the Ogden *Standard-Examiner,* who unites a genial helpfulness and a vast knowledge of Utah with a salty brevity of phrase. He gave me an obituary for Lake Park which has been in no way bettered by the long researches into the subject I have since conducted:

"Lake Park was a resort which fully 50 years ago attracted throngs to the shore of Great Salt Lake west of Syracuse in Davis County. Boating, dancing, swimming and other amusements were provided. The beach, it seems, was sandy when the resort was opened, but the sand was merely a veneer, like civilization, and the sand vanished under the massage accomplished by thousands of well-shod visitors, a most sticky brand of blue mud replacing the sand. That was the end of Lake Park."

This sad end had been clearly forecast in a pamphlet discussing the resources of Utah published in 1889. After describing Lake Park, the author had gone on to discuss the still-feebly surviving Lake Side resort close by. "It is now proposed," he said, "to construct a gigantic swimming bath and pump the waters of the lake into it for bathing purposes. This, if it proves satisfactory as a bathing place, will probably be done at Lake Park, which suffers from the same drawbacks." But even such heroic measures seemed insufficient to re-establish Lake Park in the light of the destruction of its beach, and by 1890 Garfield Beach had the resort trade to itself again.

The year following, 1891, an effort was made in the Black Rock area to promote a real estate development envisaging privately owned beach cottages, but, notwithstanding the attraction of William Glasmann's herd of buffalo, Buffalo Park made no hit with the public. It was time, nevertheless, for a new and striking idea in the way of lake resorts, and this came in 1893 with the building of the great Moorish pavilion at Saltair. Work was commenced in February, and the grand opening was staged on June 8 of the same year.

Saltair caught everybody's imagination. The train was run on a pile-supported track 4,000 feet out into the lake to reach the pile-supported, crescent-shaped platform. The 2,500 10-inch pilings were driven into the lake bottom through salt dissolved by steam. Upon this platform was built a large two-story pavilion, with picnic tables and restaurant overlooking the lake on the ground floor, and an immense ballroom, locally thought to be the largest in the world, on the upper floor. The roof pattern of the dance floor was similar to that of the famous egg-shaped Tabernacle in Salt Lake City, and the proportions were about the same. On the pile-supported platform itself the pavilion was shouldered by concessions of all kinds and by long rows of bathrooms capable of serving thousands at a time.

There was no beach at Saltair as at Garfield, and bathers descended by steps directly into the water, but there was a novelty and even a convenience to this, and with $250,000 sunk in the new resort, its facilities were in all ways superior to those of Garfield.

Yet Garfield Beach was not put out of business until misfortune overtook it a decade later. In 1904 it caught fire, and both the resort and the old *General Garfield* were razed to the ground. This mischance extinguished the last of the old resorts at the south shore of the lake, and there was somehow an ironic flavor to the aftermath, as though progress were utterly relentless, for when the Western Pacific built around the lake and across the salt desert to San Francisco in 1906-1908, its roadbed ran ruthlessly across the charred remains of the *General Garfield*.

Saltair was left to reign over the lake in solitary splendor, but 20 years later it too felt the heavy hand of disaster. Early in 1925 fire swept the resort, destroying it completely except for the pilings. But with that much left to work with, a new resort replaced the old without delay.

Saltair had thus been tried by fire, but much more vexatious trials awaited it. After the great rise in the seventies the lake level had sunk, except for a brief upsurge in the mid-eighties, to its then lowest recorded level, in 1905. In the next five years the lake level climbed eight feet, and it remained relatively high until 1925, but then it began dropping swiftly, and by 1934 it had reached the "zero level" on the Saltair gage. Nor did it stop there: Saltair was subjected to the humilation of being left high and dry on its piling when the lake receded toward the horizon. All of a sudden, Saltair had become an orthodox beach resort, and by no means the best situated.

The time was ripe for a revival of the old beaches, a few miles south of Saltair. All the desirable beachland was owned by L. H. Gray, and in 1933 J. O. Griffith of Salt Lake City bought from him 3½ acres to open a new Black Rock Beach. The 3½-acre tract lying immediately east of this, comprising principally a rocky island called Fritch Island, was bought by Ira Dern, also of Salt Lake City, who opened Sunset Beach in July 1934.

Both of these beaches were built up to provide what Saltair could not, a comfortable beach sprawling along the lake shore for the convenience of beachgoers with automobiles. While bathhouses as well as luncheon boweries, cafés and bars were provided, it was not incumbent upon those resorting to the beaches to use the bathhouses, since their automobiles served very well for such purposes. Picnickers could sun themselves on the sand, wade or swim in the lake or roast weinies exactly as pleasure might dictate. Saltair reduced its prices and set up in competition its Crystal Beach, but the three resorts, right down to the end of the war, served, in general, two different clienteles. With its railroad facilities, its amusement-park concessions and its generally more elaborate setting, Saltair catered to the generality of tourists and the townsfolk of Utah without an automobile at their disposal, while the south shore beaches served those willing or able to make their own good time.

The war crippled both Saltair and the south shore resorts, the latter because of gas and tire rationing, the former because the rolling stock of the Salt Lake, Garfield & Western—the electrified railroad serving it—went off to war, to the Army's Hill Field. In 1946 both Saltair and the twin resorts on the south shore, Black Rock and Sunset beaches, hailed the return of the good old days, the rolling stock of the S L G & W returning to its own tracks, and John Q. Citizen's car returning from hibernation in the family garage.

Except for Lake Side and Lake Park no resorts have been established on Great Salt Lake except at the south shore. In 1905, after the completion of the Lucin Cutoff, enthusiasts in Ogden promoted a barbecue excursion to Promontory Point with an eye to building a resort at this picturesque location, but the facilities provided for this affair by the railroad were so inadequate that the idea died a-borning. Over the years it has been often pointed out that Antelope Island is a magnificent site for a resort, but the hard cash to finance one has never been forthcoming, and the sheep, cattle, horses and buffalo grazing on the island have been spared the ordeal of sharing their hilly homeland with unruly pleasure seekers.

The spectacular lowering of the lake level which brought Black Rock and Sunset Beaches into existence in the early 1930's brought to the south shore one of the developments most pregnant for the future of the lake—the Salt Lake Yacht Club Harbor. The beginning of an exciting new story, that boat harbor was also the end of a very old tale, the story of the boats and the boatmen who have sailed the mountain sea for the sheer joy of it during three-quarters of a century.

Brigham Young's converted horse boat, the *Timely Gull,* had been the first craft resembling a pleasure boat to sail the lake, though to the Walker brothers, a decade later, seems to belong the distinction of launching the first sailboat designed purely for pleasure purposes. The annals of Great Salt Lake yield up only the most reluctant information about the development of yachting on the lake, but by 1877 the Salt Lake Yacht Club was in active operation.

Among the early pleasure craft John W. Young's tiny steamboat, the *Lady of the Lake,* made much the biggest splash in her appearance on the scene, though she promptly disappeared in the prevailing fog of obscurity shrouding all the early boats.

The *Lady of the Lake* was built in Williamsburg and had her trial run on the Hudson June 29, 1871. The New York papers were much taken with her, describing her as the smallest steamer afloat and altogether "the most diminutive jaunty little thing that ever felt steam." She was 30 feet long and had a 10-foot beam, 7-foot cabin and weighed 7 tons. Inasmuch as she drew only 18 inches, her builder was optimistic that she would be able to steam up and down the Jordan River between Great Salt Lake and Salt Lake City at all seasons of the year.

Her trial run a success, the *Lady of the Lake* was pulled to pieces and shipped west; she was launched anew in the Jordan River on August 9. The Salt Lake papers agreed that she sat most jauntily on the river and foresaw a pleasant future for her, bearing "happy companies of pleasure seekers" up and down the river. Whether she paid the dividends in pleasure that had been expected of her, history has neglected to say, but any hopes that she could regularly navigate the Jordan must have disappeared by 1874, when the lake level began to fall so precipitately that even a rowboat would have experienced difficulty negotiating the bar at the Jordan's mouth.

The *Lady of the Lake* seems to have been the only instance during this first period of a powered craft used as a yacht. Sailboats were much more to the taste of the boating enthusiasts who in the seventies turned their attention to Great Salt Lake. The queen of them all was David L. Davis' *Cambria,* built in the mid-eighties.

The *Cambria* was a distinct departure from any boat yet launched in the waters of Great Salt Lake, and she proved much the fastest; she is said to have been the first boat of the English model of catamaran built in America. She was 20 feet long with a 10-foot beam, and with 5 feet of space between the two slim, pointed boats which formed her divided hull. With no cockpit or cabin, her deck from stem to stern was unbroken, except for the mast and tiller. She carried a mainsail and a forestaysail, and when not overloaded, drew less than 2 feet of water. Owing to the shallowness of the water, from the *Cambria's* time to the present, it has been generally recognized by yachtsmen that keel boats are unsuited to Great Salt Lake, and shallow-draft boats have come to dominate the lake.

Yachting activity was not confined to the great lake itself. During the late seventies Hot Springs Lake, below the hot and warm springs at the north end of Salt Lake Valley, was the scene of many a regatta. By the early eighties, however, the diminishing level of this lake as well as that of Great Salt Lake, together with the choking growth of cattails and other vegetation, drove the boats out into the larger lake and to the rickety pier at Lake Side. Though the south shore beaches remained the home ports for most of the sailing craft, they touched occasionally at Lake Side.

An offshoot of this interest in boating was the organization of rowing clubs at Lake Park, Garfield and Provo. The Garfield enthusiasts for a period after 1889 used the old *General Garfield* as their boathouse. After 1891 these rowing clubs declined. The high-water mark for rowing activity seems to have been 1888, when under the auspices of the Lake Park club the Mississippi Valley Rowing Association held a regatta on the lake; in the record time of 8:36 the Modocs, a four-oared crew, won the mile and a half race with turn. This time, being 34 seconds faster than the previous record, was hailed as showing the fastness of the water. Boats were declared to float nearly a third higher than in fresh water, and the local boosters were positive that Great Salt Lake must become the scene of countless record-breaking exploits.

Though the rowing clubs died, this argument about the fastness of the water of Great Salt Lake has continued down to our own time in its bearing on marathon swimming. Enthusiasts argued that as swimmers' bodies floated so much higher in the water, opportunities were unrivaled for setting speed records. The choking salt brine was unsuited to sprint events, for swimmers could not make free with it as they could with fresh water, but it seemed well suited for distance events.

In 1919 a professional swimmer, C. S. Leaf, negotiated the distance between Antelope Island and Saltair in 2 hours, 28 minutes and 27 seconds, and 7 years later a marathon swim was staged; the event was won by Chick Mitchell. The marathon was revived in 1930 and for 3 years was won by Orson Spencer; his record time, 2:20, was set in 1932. The receding lake level, which left Saltair high and dry, killed the event, but in 1937 it was again revived under the auspices of Black Rock Beach. The distance between Antelope and Saltair was never formally measured, the promoters and swimmers being content to estimate that the distance ranged between 6 and 7 miles. Continued agitation for national recognition of the event, however, led in 1927 to the survey of the new course, and the distance was officially established at 8.12 miles. Over this course Orson Spencer in 1937 and 1938 triumphed exactly as he had over the shorter one; his record time of 3:40:52 was set in the former year. In 1939, however, in rough seas E. C. Watson was not merely the winner but the only finisher, even Spencer being taken from the water a mile and a half from shore, nearly blinded by the salt, and far from the course.

The event was held for the last time in 1940, when Kenny Lyman finished ahead of Watson. Convalescent from an automobile accident, Spencer on this occasion was not a participant. The record for the Antelope-Black Rock course remains Spencer's time of 3 hours, 40 minutes and 52 seconds, set in 1937.

This pursuit of history down the bypaths of sport has taken us far from our primary interest, the development of yachting on the lake.

As with the rowing clubs, interest in boating faded after the turn of the century, though salt-water sailing was never without its die-hard enthusiasts. In the 1920's the old interest markedly reawakened as the lake level rose and in 1929 the Great Salt Lake Yacht Club was organized. In 1932 it was legally incorporated and opened a $200 clubhouse beneath the south pier at Saltair.

But that deadly lake level, which so often had disastrously intervened upon boating activities, either by rising to flood shore facilities or by so far withdrawing from them as to render them useless, once again began its assault upon the enthusiasm for yachting. The facilities at Saltair, between 1928 and 1935, became increasingly less satisfactory as the lake shrank upon itself. It was difficult to reach the boats, for the increasing shallowness of the water necessitated anchoring farther and farther out from the pavilion. And even when the water was deep enough to allow the boats to come to the pier, there was no protection from waves and storms.

The need clearly was for a harbor of some kind, and the yacht club began groping toward plans for building an encirclement of cribwork at Saltair. There was, however, no financial backing in sight, and all such plans were overturned by the swiftness with which the lake began sinking; the brine concentration became so great that precipitation of sodium chloride began. It collected on the boats moored near Saltair and substantially added to the difficulties of the club members.

It was noticed that the water in the vicinity of Garfield and Black Rock did not precipitate salt on the beach because of a small inflow of fresh water from springs along the lake shore. Though the inflow was not great, it was sufficient to prevent salt precipitation over a two-mile stretch of beach. Any idea of developing the Saltair area had also to be reconsidered because it would be necessary to go so far out from shore as to involve difficulties with the fresh-water supply, the access road and other utilities. Further, it was the part of wisdom to undertake to separate the boating center from bathing centers. A site accordingly was chosen about a mile east of Fritch Island (the Sunset Beach location).

The building of a boat harbor came about as a result of the co-operative endeavors of Salt Lake County, the state government and the various work relief administrations of the federal government. The yacht club fortunately had its plans well advanced when the federal relief program was inaugurated in 1933, and the backing of state and local government officials was obtained. It required almost two years to work out the details, but the boat harbor project was finally approved, and sponsorship settled down to Salt Lake County.

The first project, says Dr. Thomas C. Adams, commodore of the yacht club, was a modest one and set up in an impractical manner, but through sympathetic and intelligent consideration by the work relief officials, adjustments were made which permitted the project to proceed. Three or four extension projects were submitted and approved at later dates, and the work was carried on intermittently until the late thirties, when relief work was substantially curtailed.

Out of these co-operative efforts came the Salt Lake County Public Boat Harbor, located 17.8 miles west of Salt Lake City on U. S. 40. By this harbor the lake, so long all but inaccessible to boatmen, was made practical of access. Nevertheless, interest in boating far outpaced the facilities that could be provided. Plans for the harbor never were completely realized, and maintenance funds were scanty. There was insufficient space at the harbor for all who desired to operate boats on the lake, nor were the facilities adequate. At the time the war broke out, from 75 to 100 boats larger than rowboats were using the harbor, whereas the recreational potential could be estimated in the neighborhood of a thousand boats.

Alive to the magnitude of the recreational resource with which it was concerned, during the war years the yacht club prepared new plans looking to a co-ordinated development of the entire beach area from Black Rock to a point east of the present harbor. This plan, which has caught the imagination of city, county and state planning boards, envisions the building of a longer and larger breakwater on a reef of tufalike material found several hundred feet offshore, with another breakwater to be built near the harbor to enclose a substantial area of intermediate depth water and furnish protection for anchorage, small boat use, and other purposes.

It has further been proposed that a bathing resort be built at the west end of this development, in the vicinity of Fritch Island, and that a dike be constructed along the present water line, which is several hundred feet back from the existing breakwater. On top of this dike could be built a water-line highway four or five thousand feet long to connect Fritch Island with the boat-harbor access road, while the back of the shore-line dike could be made to retain a fresh-water lake about fifteen hundred feet wide and three or four thousand feet long, which would be connected to the harbor area with a marine railway and possibly a lock. Boats thus could go into the fresh-water lake and soak the salt from their planking before being hauled out for painting. This lake could also be used for small boating by youngsters and other learners, and for regattas would serve as an outboard motorboat racecourse. Provision would be made for private cabins along the lake shore and other attractive features. Since a development of such proportions was beyond the financial capacity of any local sponsoring body, in the summer of 1946 the state endeavored to enlist the services of the Army engineers, whereby the federal government, under the Rivers and Harbors Act, would build the enlarged boat harbor. Hearings were held by the Corps of Engineers in Salt Lake City in July 1946, and it was hoped that the outcome would be recognition by the federal government of the opportunity that offered for development of a national recreational resource of exciting potentialities.

Chapter 19

Birds and Beasts, No Flowers

I<small>T</small> <small>IS</small> a part of Utah's legend of the gulls that sea gulls were never known in the region of the Great Salt Lake until that June morning of 1848 when they winged in from the lake to war upon the revolting swarms of black crickets that were devastating the crops.

The guano deposits on the islands, however, are evidence that the gulls had colonized the islands of Great Salt Lake long before the entrance of the Mormons into Salt Lake Valley, and Frémont's half-starved party in September 1843 made a supper of sea gulls shot by Kit Carson near the lake shore. Not only California gulls but Treganza great blue herons, white pelicans, double-crested cormorants and Caspian terns have nested on the islands.

Stansbury encountered the colonial birds for the first time on April 9, 1850, when he erected a triangulation station on tiny Egg Island, a mile west of the northern tip of Antelope. The rocky islet was covered with wild birds—ducks, white brant, blue herons and gulls without number. Overhead he saw a pelican flying, with red gills and pink bill, and longingly he watched it disappear, covetous of a specimen for his collections. He had to be content with 76 heron eggs, as none of the other birds were nesting yet. The eggs, however, were obtained for gastronomic rather than for scientific purposes; they were roasted for supper that night.

Later in the month it fell to Albert Carrington's lot to chain Frémont Island, and on the third day of this four-day job he reached what he called Egg Point, at the south end of the island. As he had in 1848, he here collected a few good blue heron eggs, though most of the eggs, he says, had been set on too long, so that he left them for the herons to hatch. And "the same with the geese eggs which were not so plenty."

Stansbury got another distant look at a pelican on May 4, but his passion to examine one was not satisfied until May 8, when he visited Gunnison Island. As the yawl drew near, innumerable nests of gulls and pelicans were seen, strewing the ground in every direction.

The men splashed ashore and ran to seize a full-grown pelican just rising from the ground. The captive took no very philosophical attitude; he was, Stansbury says, "very indignant & fierce snapping with his long bill at every body that came near him & shewing determined courage."

When the party left the island next day, they took the captive pelican with them. He seemed now, John Hudson says, somewhat resigned to his novel position. But it was impossible to induce him to eat or drink. When Stansbury reached camp, rather than see him starve to death, he set the bird at liberty. "I had made some little progress in taming the fierceness of his nature," the captain says in his *Report*. "He would suffer me to assist him in pluming his feathers; but to all others he was sullen and intractable, snapping violently at every one who approached him."

But the sulky captive could not enjoy his liberty; in Hudson's words, he was not fated to return again to the bosom of his family. After sailing for some time in the wake of the boats, he was washed ashore, and accordingly, as Hudson tells the tale, was "recaptured & slain & boiled to a skeleton." It was in honor of this doughty old bird that Gunnison Island was given its first brief name, "Pelican Island."

Though the captured pelican monopolized attention, Stansbury's men found on the island 50 nests with young pelicans just hatched and still unfledged; they gathered a bushel and a half of gull and pelican eggs and came back well pleased with their adventure; Hudson was impressed to hear one of the men swear that he would not have missed seeing the island for five dollars—the equivalent of five days' work. The eggs were a happy plunder, the white pelican eggs about the size of a goose egg, the spotted brown gull eggs about the size of a hen's egg, and both delicious.

Two weeks later, while on one of his many voyages to supply his men, Stanbury revisited Egg Esland. The nesting season was well advanced now, and the whole islet was covered with eggs, chiefly of gulls, interspersed among "nests of hatched out herons or blue cranes & of a species of cormorant, which have a black shining plumage with a bill some like a mud hen, webb footed & very black & beautiful." He gathered half a barrel of eggs, but lamentably, most of these turned out to be bad.

On the last day of May Stansbury and his party returned to "Pelican Island." The gulls and pelicans, the captain observed, "had by no means decreased in number nor the latter in the continual clatter & noise, whilst we found that the latter had hatched out all the eggs we had left them, & numerous broods of youngsters were to be seen in various directions of all ages & sizes." This was Albert Carrington's first visit to the island, and he inspected it with interest, with its "myriads of gulls & Pelicans, quite tame on a/c of their eggs & young—the gulls screaming, the pelicans looking very grave." Hudson adds that on the approach of the boat the pelicans and gulls with loud screams "rose from the ground darkening the air & we had a canopy of fluttering wings. The pelicans grave & stately marched in battalions to the shore ready for flight should we approach nearer, than they deemed consistent with their safety."

It was at first a puzzle to determine what the birds could live on, but on seeing fish, the visitors decided that the pelicans made long flights to Bear and Weber Rivers, returning with full pouches to feed the helpless young. And the aged as well as the young were fed. Stansbury and Carrington came upon an old fellow "quite blind & hoary," though (Stansbury gives him his due) "ready for fight could he only find out the whereabouts of his enemy. From his good case he must have lived on the charity of his neighbours & like more civilized beggars he doubtless fared well."

Carrington took pains to give his journal some idea of the aspect of the island's population:

"gull screams every part of the time I have been awake, but pellican is too sedate, or in too high dudgeon to make a noise, they are about in squadrons & platoons, wherever their young are collected; the young are in squads of from 2 to a hundred together, & from very small to ½ grown, with no feathers yet, but covered with so thick a down that it looks like a young lamb's fleece, very fat & when you approach them the old ones fly & the young each with all his might tries to avoid being in the rear, hence they push & tumble over each other, makeing a very confused & amuseing heap of moveing matter —they live upon fish, and I saw one young one, (over tramped) disgorge a piece of quite a large trout."

Alas for sentimentalists, he noted that a hailstorm killed several young pelicans while the old ones consciencelessly took to the rocks for shelter, leaving the fledglings to make out as best they could by themselves.

Stansbury's third visit to Egg Island on June 16 was more interesting than either of the previous visits; for now gulls as well as pelicans had hatched out their eggs,

"& the island was full of little half fledged youngsters who ran off at our approach & hid themselves under the first rock they could find. We caught them however & amused ourselves by putting them into the water, where however young they instantly followed the instinct of their nature & paddled away with their little black feet most lustily. The young herons or cranes had grown since our last visit to nearly their full size although they were not sufficiently feathered to fly. They too fled as fast as they could at our approach, & 'cached' themselves in the most secret places they could find. When hard run however they would turn & fight most fiercely, striking furiously with their long sharp bills, & also with their claws, screaming the while with a discordant & angry note. They were very brave & evinced not the least disposition to succumb when attacked. The young cormorants were black & covered with a sort of fine wool. They also when pressed, struck with their beak & evinced considerable pugnacity. The greater part of these however took to the water, evidently for the first time in their short lives, where they too evinced the peculiarity of the habits belonging to their species by desperate attempts to dive & thus conceal themselves under the water. The Pelicans had commenced laying a second crop of Eggs. One little gull about 4 inches long, driven by the extremity of his fear took to the water, when he was swept out by the current to the distance of two or three hundred yards from the I. As soon as his situation was discovered by the older ones, who hovered around in the air by the thousands, watching us with great anxiety & noise, one the parent we judged by its great anxiety lighted down along side of it, & was soon joined by half a dozen more who began guiding it to the shore flying a little way before it & again alighting, the mother swimming along by its side. The little fellow seemed to understand perfectly what was meant, & when we sailed away he was proceeding rapidly & safely under conduct of his convoy, & was within a few yards of the shore, which he no doubt reached in safety."

In all this exact and conscientious reporting on the bird colonies of Egg and Gunnison Islands, there is one outstanding omission, and one would have to regard Stansbury and his men as scientific observers with a more than human detachment except for the saving clause provided by Stansbury's farewell to Egg Island: "The stench on the island was very offensive, from the amount of fish probably brought by the parent birds for the support of this very numerous colony."

The Stansbury expedition paid its last respects to the colonial birds on July 13, 1850, when in winding up the triangulation work a final visit was paid to Egg Island. The novelty had worn off for Stansbury, but Gunnison viewed the island with a lively interest. It was literally covered, he wrote in his journal:

"with gulls Herons, Pelicans, Cormorants—the Pelicans are breeding; there being several young ones just out of the shell & we found some eggs also. This appears to be a second brood. [Rather, a late nesting.] While taking the observation the young of these birds crowded the shores & the immense flocks of gulls hovered in the air— While the stately aged Pelicans navigated the water at a respectful distance & the old Herons eyed us closely from Rock Bluff point on Antelope island and the black cormorants played back & forth fearful either to leave their young to our inquisitive care or approach themselves to protect them."

These are the reports on the birds of Great Salt Lake carried back to Washington in the journals of the Stansbury expedition. It is not clear why Stansbury did not bring with him skins of the gulls, pelicans, herons and cormorants, for if he himself knew nothing of preserving them, Gunnison did. The lack was evidently felt, for in the summer of 1852 the Topographical Bureau wrote Carrington asking him to procure some skins. He was unable to oblige, writing back that it was impossible to supply any until next season, as the gulls had left for the winter. (He thereby gave evidence of knowledge that the California gulls which nested on the islands flew south in the late summer. The autumn and winter visitants, the Delaware gulls, have never, so far as known, nested in the vicinity of the salt lake.)

Apparently in 1850 the four principal species of colonial birds nested only on Egg and Gunnison Islands. At various times in the approximate hundred years since Stansbury's time, many other islands in the lake have served as nesting sites. Hat (or Bird) Island has been used by colonies of gulls, pelicans, blue herons and by Caspian terns. Dolphin Island, north of Gunnison, has been used by cormorants. Carrington Island has been used by gulls, and a sand bar between Carrington and Stansbury, locally called Badger Island, has been used by gulls and herons. Frémont was at one time used by herons, and two colonies of gulls have established themselves on Antelope. Stansbury Island, being relatively insecure from predatory animals, has not been found attractive as a nesting site by any of the colonial birds.

The birds have come and gone from all these islands. The usual colonists on Hat Island are gulls, pelicans and great blue herons, though of late years the herons seem to have deserted the island, and during the time of extreme low water in 1935 the pelicans abandoned it, too. Gunnison Island, which supports the largest of the colonies, has been host to the same three species as Hat Island, but the herons seem to have departed from here also. Gunnison is usually host not only to its seasonal tenants but to a pair or two of prairie falcons, and a few ravens and rock wrens.

Though the pelicans and herons have abandoned Egg Island since Stansbury's time, gulls are still found there, and it is the only present site on the lake where double-crested cormorants nest. Shore birds sometimes linger during their spring migration, and occasionally a few Caspian terns nest on this islet. In time past herons have nested on White Rock, off the west coast of Antelope, but gulls alone are found there at present. Frémont, Carrington, Dolphin and Badger Islands are not now known to be used by any of the colonial birds.

The nesting season varies for each of the species. They begin to straggle in from the south about the first of March. The herons start laying their eggs in mid-April, the cormorants in late April and May, the pelicans in early or middle May, and the gulls toward the end of May. The herons, pelicans and cormorants get along well with each other, but the gulls carry on an unceasing harassment of their neighbors when they can spare time from fighting one another; they are agrressive in destroying eggs and will pick young to death. The unsocial herons stand like sentinels at several yards' distance from each other, silent and watchful birds attending strictly to their own business, and the gulls are less disposed to quarrel with the herons than with the pelicans and cormorants.

In contrast to the herons, the Great Salt Lake pelicans, says Dr. William H. Behle, who has studied them more attentively than any other observer, "are very gregarious, meeting, resting and feeding in close proximity. They arrange themselves into small aggregations like family groups, and it is seldom that one sees a lone pelican. The cormorants are similar in these respects, as one would expect from the circumstances that they are closely related. The pelicans and cormorants show little animosity toward their own kind or to other species."

Since the nesting habits of the pelicans and the gulls bring them into closest proximity, it is the pelicans that suffer most from the gulls' bad-neighbor policy. On occasion pelicans will strike at brazen gulls which attempt to walk between their nests, and Dr. Behle has seen them snap at low-flying gulls.

Visitations by men during the nesting season tend to weight the balances of survival in favor of the gulls, for they are least afraid of men. Herons are most timid, but pelicans and cormorants are also shy. When disturbed, these birds leave their nests unprotected much longer than do the gulls—and unprotected from the gulls as well as from the elements, for the gulls have been seen going about shattering the eggs of the other birds without stopping to eat or drink the contents—out of no nobler impulse, it would seem, than a natural-born itch to raise hell.

Gulls have thus had all the advantages in reproducing their kind. The great blue herons have already abandoned all their nesting sites on the lake proper, though some have established themselves at the near-by Bear River Migratory Bird Refuge. Cormorants, now found only on Egg Island, are barely holding their own. In the face of a multitude of difficulties, especially including the lowering lake level, the white pelicans for a time seemed doomed, but, even if precariously, they are showing signs of recovery.

On any long-time outlook the gulls are by far the best bet to survive. Sassy, clamorous and obstreperous as they are, and often thievish in their inclinations, they are yet protected by Utah's social taboo—protected more effectively than by the formally written law. The fish-eating herons, cormorants and pelicans, on the other hand, not only are warred on by the gulls but are regarded by sportsmen with a deep dislike which in the past has had such expression as the shooting and clubbing to death of several thousand pelicans at a time, an atrocity perpetrated on Gunnison Island in 1918 under the auspices of the State Fish and Game Department. All three birds, because of the danger of extinction, are today protected by state law, but killing may be authorized by the Fish and Game Department.

A better public attitude toward the fish-eating birds of Great Salt Lake is likely to result from the studies of scholars like Dr. Behle, who has learned from stomach contents that the Salt Lake cormorants and pelicans today feed almost entirely on trash fish like carp, chubs and suckers, not upon trout and other game fish. As the sportsmen themselves inveigh against the trash fish, they may come to forget their long hostility and accept the fisherbirds as allies.

For the fish on which they subsist, the birds must fly round trips of from fifty to one hundred miles from the Hat and Gunnison Island nesting sites. Utah Lake is a favorite foraging ground, as are the mouths of the Bear and Weber Rivers. The necessity of flying so far for food may be a serious disadvantage at a time of drought like 1935, when Utah Lake all but dried up and blew away. In that year the pelicans seriously suffered from starvation. The older birds on occasion were too weak to fly to the foraging grounds, and the young could not forage for themselves in the salt water surrounding the nesting sites. Hundreds of dead young pelicans were found along the line of the Lucin Cutoff, washed down from Gunnison Island. "Adults were seen to drop out of flight lines too exhausted to continue," Dr. Behle writes.

"Many helpless birds were seen floating on the briny waters, too weak to fly. Great Salt Lake itself reached one of its lowest points in history which so concentrated the salt solution that a supersaturated condition existed. Salt crystallized very readily on objects on the lake. As a result the pelicans, dead and near dead, became covered with an immense weight of salt. This circumstance gave rise to the supposition that the salt crystallization was responsible for the death of the pelicans, whereas the basic cause was starvation."

What do the lake islands have to offer colonial birds, outweighing such disadvantages? Above all, security. Security from predatory animals and security from predatory or idly curious human visitors, though the development of boating in recent years has made the intrusive human race a fresh problem for the birds. Gunnison Island offers a maximum of security. It is somewhat walled off from the rest of the lake by the Lucin Cutoff; it has always retained its status as an island even when the lake is at a low level (unlike Hat Island, which is then connected with the western shore, and Egg Island, which is joined to Antelope); and it is high enough to be secure even against such a rise in the lake level as occurred in the early seventies, when other nesting sites were largely inundated.

The nesting season roughly lasts until July 15. Visits to the bird colonies during the preceding three months always involve the hazard of destroying the season's brood. When a party of boatmen was marooned on Gunnison Island in 1936, and the frightened pelicans abandoned their nests, the entire year's hatch was lost. Beginning in mid-July, some of the young are sufficiently matured to fly, and soon they begin to leave the island. The population of all the colonies grows progressively less, and by late August is reduced usually to a few crippled birds and a few loitering adults. By September the islands are almost completely abandoned, and they so remain until the birds fly north from Mexico in the spring.

Guano gatherers came to the islands in the mid-nineties; the first carload of Utah guano was placed on the market April 9, 1895. Alfred Lambourne saw the guano sifters come to his homestead on Gunnison Island, and they worked also on Hat Island, building a lonely cabin which stood on the island for many years until it was removed to Carrington by a homesteader. Both Gunnison and Hat Islands are held on mineral patents by Salt Lake City business interests, and though guano gathering has never been a commercial success, in part because of the difficulty of procuring it, and in part because the seasonal rains wash it into the lake as it accumulates, these patents have balked efforts to have the islands set aside as federal refuges.

The colonial birds are much the most interesting habitants of Great Salt Lake. But they are by no means the only ones. The often-heard remark that Great Salt Lake is so salty nothing can live in it is unjust to Nature's infinite resourcefulness. A limited variety of organisms has adjusted to even so hostile an environment as Great Salt Lake.

The problem of meeting the peculiarities of the Great Salt Lake environment, Dr. A. M. Woodbury has written, is largely physiological—that of extracting moisture from a salt solution. The principal food makers in the lake are blue-green algae and two flagellates, with others of lesser importance. These in turn are the food base for an extremely limited fauna of protozoans and invertebrates able to withstand immersion in the lake brines. The visible life forms of chief importance are the brine shrimp (*Artemia gracilis* Verrill), and two brine flies (*Ephydra gracilis* Packard and *Ephydra hians* Say).

The gulls have fed upon all of these, and at one time the Indians did also. Tastes that their possessors regard as more discriminating would reject all three as food, but the brine shrimp, at least, has had the gastronomic sanction of respectable authority. Dr. James Talmage in September 1892 after rinsing the brine shrimp in fresh water and cooking it with a little butter and pepper, pronounced it "actually delicious," and in this he was only echoing the verdict of David L. Davis, master of the *Cambria*. As the crustacean is only about one-fourth of an inch long, however, it would require great numbers to satisfy the average appetite.

The other notable life forms in the lake, the two varieties of brine fly, the average visitor to Great Salt Lake would gladly see pickled into extinction, for at all stages of their life cycle they are worse than pestiferous.

Although he did not associate cause with effect, Stansbury was first to run up against the life cycle of the brine fly. On April 11, 1850, near the mouth of the Weber he found the shore covered with a substance—

"precisely resembling in color & appearance the excrement of cattle dried in the sun. Underneath the upper surface which is dry, is a sort of black & sometimes greenish mud, which when the cake is moved by the foot yields allowing the top dry surface to be slid or pushed off; it emits a most foetid & offensive sulphureous smell & the whole air is poisoned with it.... In dragging the boat to the shore the men waded thro deep mud, which consisted almost entirely of the larvae of some insect which was nauseous both to the sight & smell. A belt of soft black mud lay between the water & this hard rocky beach, of the consistence of morter & very black slimy & offensive."

The larvae were the larvae of the brine flies, and the disgusting smell was occasioned by their decomposition. Three weeks later along the western shore of Promontory Stansbury collected masses of insect larvae which had been driven in by the lake to dry between the rocks in the semblance of horse dung. Under the magnifying glass this was found to consist almost entirely of the larvae or dried skins of insects. The captain was puzzled. Where had these insects lived? Nothing living had yet been observed in the lake.

"That they have existed in prodigious numbers is evident, as the shores, & the bottom for some distance out is covered with them, especially in the N. E. part of the lake, when they lay on the bottom a foot thick, & mingled with the cozy mud of which they form a very considerable percentage. Yesterday I observed far out in the lake several dark patches of apparently a dull reddish looking water, looking very much like shoal. Upon rowing over there the water being very shallow, I found that this colour was given by the bottom being covered with these larvae which the oars raised at every stroke rending the water turbid & offensive. Some of these deposits were very large & must have covered many hundred acres."

On June 14, as Stansbury was shepherding his party south along the west shore of the lake, the answer to this riddle was presented to him, without his quite grasping it. On the shore he noticed

"a large quantity of white translucent, pink & blood coloured gelatinous & mucilaginous matter spread about over the land, washed up from the lake by yesterdays North wind The quantity was very considerable, & if the whole extent of the sand flat was similarly covered must have been very great. An immense number of small black flies also covered the flat, apparently driven from their refuge in the sand by the overflow of the beach by the water of the lake driven up by the wind."

The flies, of course, came from the larvae. They emerged from the pupal state in incredible numbers during the next two weeks, driving the men almost mad with their swarming, and hardly pleasing them with the noisome stench that arose —— flies, larvae and scum rotting together in the salt water.

The brine flies were ultimately named by the scientists associated with the King Survey, but the priority of discovery seems to belong to the journalist Fitz Hugh Ludlow, who visited the lake shore in July 1863. When he returned to his hotel room in the city, he took with him a quart bottle of the salt water. He happened to place it in a west window of his room, where it had five hours of sun in the afternoon. To his surprise, about the third day he observed "small vermicular animals" in it. He forgot about it, but three or four days later, as he began packing his things, he discovered a number of minute *Diptera* floating dead in the bottle. "They resembled, in all but size, our common house-fly, or the Platte River buffalo-gnat, rather than a mosquito," he decided. He was positive the flies had not been in the bottle when he sealed it, and it was impossible that they could have got into the bottle afterwards. He thought, and quite rightly, that he had stumbled on the answer to the mystery that had baffled Stansbury.

Later travelers reported that the Indians and ducks fed on the flies and waxed fat, but the ducks at least were said to have a disagreeable taste at the table. It does not appear that anyone sampled the Indians. Stansbury himself observed the gulls feeding on the flies, and they still do, as on the brine shrimp, though these form an inconsiderable portion of their diet.

In our own time the "buffalo gnats," as they are locally called, exert some influence upon the pursuit of boating on Great Salt Lake; it is an enthusiast indeed who sails the lake in July when the brine flies are hatching. The larvae, or pupae, still bespeckle the waves of the lake at many seasons, though rarely in such masses as assaulted the sensibilities of the early observers.

Any discussion of the natural history of Great Salt Lake would be incomplete without a disquisition upon the Salt Lake Monster. Scholarship here, however, is not something that can be pursued into the laboratories or the back shelves of the libraries. This scholarship, in fact, runs up some strange back alleys.

The humiliating fact about the Salt Lake Monster is that except for J. H. McNeill, who in 1877 was numbered among the citizens of the flourishing metropolis of Kelton, on the north shore of the lake, science might have remained ignorant of its very existence, for it was only after Mr. McNeill supplied the clue that a rather wonderful collection of facts fell into a pattern.

Since history is an exact and just process of record, commendation must be given one Brother Bainbridge of the Mormon community, who at some time in 1847-1848 first laid eyes on the monster. Brother Bainbridge's eyesight was not of the best, however, for he considered that it was a dolphin he saw; in point of fact, had it not been for the observations of Mr. McNeill, history could even have wondered whether it was not merely a salt crystal that had got into Brother Bainbridge's eye.

But to return to Mr. McNeill: In an affidavit transmitted for publication in the Corinne *Record* of July 11, 1877, he swore to a somewhat unnerving experience undergone a day or so before at the northern lake shore near Monument Point. Several honest citizens employed at Barnes & Company's saltworks, so he made affidavit, had been startled to hear an altogether frightful bellow. Glancing up, they saw out in the lake a huge and fearsome creature having a body resembling that of a crocodile and a head resembling that of a horse. Even as they stared in horrified fascination, it came charging in upon them.

The men employed at the saltworks were men of superior mind, and knew exactly what to do in such circumstances. They stampeded up the side of the mountain and hid themselves securely amid the sage and scrub oak, remaining there throughout the night. By the time the sun rose next morning, it seemed evident that the monster had gone about its business, and since such occurrences were all in the day's work, the men returned to their usual labor of extracting salt from the lake brines.

A day or so later, chancing to be in Corinne, Mr. McNeill bethought him that the occurrence was a little out of the ordinary, and he strolled around to the newspaper office to give the monster such immortality as the public press affords. It made a nice story for the Corinne *Record* and was picked up by the newspapers in Salt Lake City.

Science must always make its way, however, against the absurd inelasticity of congealed attitudes and popular prejudices; a rather shocking levity was displayed toward the report of the monster. The *Deseret News* went so far as to suggest that a monster should find the lake plenty salt enough without applying for more at anybody's saltworks; and a little later, when the news got out that the *Record* was having to change from daily to semiweekly publication, added that the monster must have swallowed most of the *Record's* subscribers and advertisers.

Such hidebound attitudes were unfortunate because, as one looks dispassionately at the facts now, it should have occurred immediately to the press to put two and two together. The more so, because almost simultaneously a report came up from Lehi that something huge and reptilian had been seen in Utah Lake. The most elementary thinking should have sufficed to realize that here was nothing less than a biological triangulation. In a word, important new facts had come to light relating to the habits and habitat, not to speak of the range of migration, of the famous Bear Lake Monster.

The Bear Lake Monster, that singular beast, was introduced to the world of science by Joseph C. Rich. When a specimen is finally caught and classified, it would be no more than is due to tack "Rich" on the involved Latin name that is applied to it, for the whole natural history of the monster may be traced back to Rich's dispatch published in the *Deseret News* of August 3, 1868.

The credibility of witnesses is always a matter of moment in affairs of this kind, so let it be said without delay that Joseph was the son of the apostle, Charles C. Rich, and it is a fair presumption that he was brought up in ways of rectitude and sobriety. Moreover, he served as correspondent for the organ of the Mormon Church, which has been known to exhibit a certain narrowness of attitude toward any but the pure in heart.

In his historic dispatch Joseph Rich wrote that at various times since the settlement of Bear Lake Valley began in 1864, several persons had reported seeing in the lake a huge animal of some kind which they were wholly unable to describe. As these individuals had generally been unaccompanied, little credence had been given their stories, even though it was said that there were traditions among the Indians of some nameless animal which, in the days before the buffaloes disappeared, had carried off red men venturesome enough to swim in the blue mountain lake. This monstrous beast was represented by the Indians as being "of the serpent kind, but having legs about eighteen inches long," on which it sometimes crawled out of the water a short distance. This beast (these little details are always significant to science) was said to have the ability, when it chose, to spurt water upward out of its mouth.

All this was very insubstantial as natural history, but early in July 1868 S. M. Johnson of South Eden saw in the water what he took to be a drowned person. As the waves were running rather high, he thought the body would soon wash in to shore. But in a few moments—it must have given him a rather nasty shock—

"two or three feet of some kind of an animal that he had never seen before were raised out of the water. He did not see the body, only the head and what he supposed to be a part of the neck. It had ears or bunches on the side of its head nearly as large as a pint cup. The waves at times would dash over its head, when it would throw water from its mouth or nose. It did not drift landward, but appeared stationary, with the exception of turning its head. Mr. Johnson thought a portion of the body must lie on the bottom of the lake or it would have drifted with the action of the water."

This was close and exact observation, and we have Joseph Rich's word that it was faithfully reported: "This is Mr. Johnson's version as he told me."

Quickly there was corroboration. Next day a man and three women saw a monstrous animal of some kind near the same place. "They represented it as being very large, and say it swam much faster than a horse could run on land." In the light of such reports, the old stories about the monster were revived, and, Rich advised, many people began to think the story not quite the moonshine they had hastily suspected it of being. And at this juncture came a development to pale everything that had gone before:

"On Sunday last as N. C. Davis and Allen Davis, of St. Charles and Thomas Slight and J. Collings of Paris, with six women, were returning from Fish Haven, when about midway between the latter named place to St. Charles their attention was suddenly attracted to a peculiar motion or wave in the water, about three miles distance. The lake was not rough, only a little disturbed by a light wind. Mr. Slight says he distinctly saw the sides of a very large animal that he would suppose to be not less than 40 feet in length, judging by the wave it rolled upon both sides of it as it swam, and the wake it left in the rear. It was going South, and all agreed that it swam with a speed almost incredible to their senses. Mr. Davis says he never saw a locomotive travel faster, and thinks it made a mile a minute, easy. In a few minutes after the discovery of the first, a second one followed in its wake; but it seemed to be much smaller, appearing to Mr. Slight about the size, of a horse. A larger one, in all, and six small ones had [gone] southward out of sight.

"One of the large ones before disappearing made a sudden turn to the west, a short distance; then back to its former track. At this turn Mr. Slight says he could distinctly see it was of a brownish color. They could judge somewhat of their speed by observing known distances on the other side of the lake, and all agree that the velocity with which they propelled themselves through the water was astonishing. They represent the waves that rolled up in front and on each side of them as being three feet high from where they stood. . . . Messrs. Davis and Slight are prominent men, well known in this country, and all of them are reliable persons whose veracity is undoubted. I have no doubt they would be willing to make affidavits to their statements."

There is a fine, honest ring to these reports, and Joseph Rich showed himself possessed of the true spirit of scientific inquiry. "Is it fish, flesh, or serpent, amphibious and fabulous or a great big fish, or what is it?" he demanded to know.

Encouraged by the devotion to scientific truth Rich had displayed, other witnesses were found willing to make public certain sights and experiences about which they had felt a degree of reticence; hardly three weeks later reports were published of monsters in Utah Lake. Thus, even so early as 1868, a record was forming which could be interpreted to mean that the Bear Lake Monster had a tendency to roam around. Unfortunately, the data are insufficient to establish whether this migratory tendency was seasonal, sexual or otherwise to be accounted for; there was always the possibility that any one monster might have become bored with the narrow waters of Bear Lake and headed down Bear River toward more spacious seas. The strong probability is that the creature spawned (or bred) in the vicinity of Bear Lake; most reports came from this quarter, and it is often a characteristic of aquatic denizens to seek out higher waters to reproduce their kind.

There was, of course, an obstinate delaying action fought against public acceptance of so strange an animal as the Bear Lake Monster. The combative J. H. Beadle in one of his books summarily dismissed the monster as:

"a nondescript with a body half seal, half serpent, and a head somewhat like a sea lion, which has often been seen and described by Indians and Mormons, but never by white Christians, that I have heard of. It has never been properly classified or named, as it is invisible when scientific observers are at hand, but from the descriptions current among the latter-day Philosophers, I judge it to be a relic of that extinct species generally denominated the 'Ginasticutis.' "

Beadle did science no service in muddying the waters with this frivolous reference to the gyascutus, a curious beast indigenous to western America but known to be wholly fabulous. It is evident that Joseph C. Rich had to contend with many such skeptics, for in a letter published in the *News* of September 25, 1868, he expressed the pain he felt that people should doubt his story and explained that plans were on foot to capture a specimen.

Conference crowds in October were attracted in great numbers to Savage & Ottinger's window in Salt Lake City, but the specimen of the monster there exhibited was no doubt manufactured in the photographer's back room, for there is no evidence in the news out of Bear Lake Valley that fall that a specimen of the monster had been captured. A letter from the upper lake country published in the *News* of October 30, as a matter of fact, had more to say about some very peculiar birds lately seen flying over Bear Lake than about the monster; and a November visitor, by announcing his intention of branding the monster if he could find it, gave evidence by indirection that no capture had yet been made.

It might be thought that the Bear Lake Monster was a nine days' wonder. On the contrary, reports of it were published at frequent intervals throughout the seventies. And the stories did not issue from the Mormon press alone; the traveler, John Codman, who visited Bear Lake Valley in 1874, made a substantial contribution to the body of our knowledge.

Codman had first to tell an Indian legend about two lovers, pursued by their tribesmen, who had plunged into the lake to be changed by the Great Spirit into two enormous serpents. But aside from all such superstition, he said:

"there really is good reason to believe that the lake is inhabited by some abnormal water animals. We conversed with seven persons, among them our friend, the bishop, who at different times had seen them, and they told us that many other individuals could verify their report. The length of these monsters varies from thirty to eighty feet, and their bodies are covered with fur like that of a seal. The head is described like that of an alligator. In one instance the animal came close to the shore, and was entangled in the rushes, where he squirmed and splashed, and made a horrible noise like the roaring of a bull."

Though Codman was disposed to think the Mormons a somewhat credulous people, with their belief in all sorts of revelations and appearances, angelic and diabolical, still he could not think it possible for so many people to be utterly mistaken. Unquestionably, he said, there were in Bear Lake some fish larger than the ordinary salmon trout. But, whatever they might be, "they did not exhibit themselves for our benefit."

The question of the migratory habits of the monster takes on some importance in view of the persistent reports of its appearance in Utah Lake. The English traveler, Phil Robinson, who journeyed up and down Utah in the summer of 1882, wrote of the monster in Utah Lake without any apparent knowledge of its occurrence in Bear Lake. The southern lake, he said, in late years had come to have an uncomfortable reputation as "the domain of strange water-apparitions," somewhat after the likeness of sea serpents. He agreed that science was indisposed to credit the existence of sea serpents, but in view of the wondrous fossils lately found in Arizona, he thought it not beyond American resources to produce even the kraken. In the meantime, as a very tolerable substitute, he commended to the attention of science "the great snake of the Utah Lake. It has frightened men—and, far better evidence than that, it has been seen by children when playing on the shore. I say 'better,' because children are not likely to invent a plausible horror in order to explain their sudden rushing away from a given spot with terrified countenances and a consistent narrative." Robinson demanded, "Does the Smithsonian know of this terror of the lake—this fresh-water kraken—this new Mormon iniquity?"

On the basis of the evidence which I have painstakingly assembled, it is clear that the monster was a most interesting beast, and it is much to be regretted that no specimen has yet been taken for purposes of classification. Since it is my earnest desire that this book be a contribution to the natural sciences, as well as a work of history, I will undertake to summarize what is known of the monster. Its head resembles that of a horse or an alligator or a great serpent or a sea lion; at all events, it has ears or bunches on the side of its head as large as a pint cup. Its body resembles that of a seal or a serpent or a dolphin or a crocodile; at all events, it is covered with brownish fur, has legs 18 inches long and ranges up to 80 feet in length. The beast can roar very loudly; it makes much noise when it thrashes about near shore; it has the ability to spout water from its mouth; it can travel through the water at the rate of a mile a minute; and, the inference seems justified, it has a distinct migratory tendency.

Assuming that the Salt Lake Monster, the Utah Lake Monster and the Bear Lake Monster were of the same species, if not even the same animal, one may make certain postulates. The beast was possessed of considerable agility, for it was able to make its way up and down the canyons by which Bear River flows to Great Salt Lake, and up and down, similarly, the Jordan Narrows—no mean feat for so large a creature. That it was able to pass through, if not flourish in, the waters of Great Salt Lake seems a fact of high importance, for it has already been pointed out that Great Salt Lake presents a hostile environment to most living organisms. It should be remembered, as Dr. A. M. Woodbury puts it, that "those who would survive the rigors of this aquatic desert must either be equipped to meet the exactions imposed or to avoid them," and the monster evidently did not have to avoid them.

In general, the monster does not seem to have exhibited a carnivorous appetite. Apart from the problematical Indian traditions, J. H. McNeill's affidavit is the only evidence tending to a contrary conclusion, and special circumstances were operative in that instance. The lake is devoid of fish, and a monster would have to eat extraordinary quantities of brine shrimp and brine flies to fare very well. Doubtless the men working on shore attracted the attention of the monster in an especially ravenous moment, so that it blindly charged on the saltworks in an effort to satisfy its terrific hunger.

Of late years, the monster has not been seen, but it is premature to suppose that it has become extinct. The attention of aspiring zoologists is called to a real opportunity. Someone might very profitably devote a summer in Utah to an investigation. The new radar devices need not be restricted to the pursuit of mackerel and sardines in the ocean seas; there is no such difficulty about locating a specimen as existed 75 years ago; and the rewards, in the event of success, should be substantial. The scientist who captured a specimen could feel assured of a full-page picture in *Life;* he would be implored to accept a chair at Harvard; and assuredly he could look for an invitation to lecture in Australia.

Chapter 20

Door Upon the Future

"History!" the young man insisted. "Utah doesn't have history any more, only business!" He meant that Mormons and gentiles have learned to get along with each other, that Utah's early social conflicts have largely been resolved without being succeeded by new ones, and that the political and social institutions of the state have evolved to a point where they can be largely taken for granted. But business, the terms on which men contrive to live from day to day, is not to be dismissed from the province of history, though the Great Salt Lake itself has only dabbled in such matters.

The Mormons no sooner established themselves on its shores than they sought out the salt lake in full appreciation of God's abundance in providing for his Saints; in the East salt had been a commodity no less scarce and expensive than necessary. Some of the brethren who traveled to the lake for salt in the summer of 1847 made a happy discovery of a whole bed of it, beautifully white and ready to shovel into wagons, but it turned out to be better to boil down the salt from lake water, to avoid mud and other impurities, than to dig it from dry beds at the shore.

From that first summer on, there was rarely a time when fires were not burning under the great iron kettles at the south shore of the lake. The better to carry on the business, Charley White and his wife built a hut at the lake shore. At the time of the Stansbury survey, Gunnison made interested inquiry, and was told that in his 6 kettles, holding perhaps 60 gallons, White could boil 300 pounds of salt a day. White judged that in summer he obtained a pail of salt from 4 of water, and that in winter he obtained one of salt from 3 of water. This could not, however, have been very precise observation, for at 25 percent a salt solution is very close to the saturation point, where precipitation begins.

The unrefined salt was not perfect for all uses. The chemical analyst to whom Stansbury referred his samples discovered that in addition to the 20 percent of common salt the lake contained about

2 percent of foreign salts, the most objectionable being chloride of lime and chloride of magnesia. These had a tendency to absorb moisture from the air, moistening and partially dissolving the common salt so that when it was exposed to dry air or heat, it caked with a hard crust. A suggested remedy was to heap up the dry salt and sprinkle it with a concentrated brine from the lake at intervals of a few hours during a single day. Though the chloride of sodium would not be dissolved, the chloride of calcium and magnesium would be drained off. By allowing the heaped-up salt to drain and dry at night, then spreading it to the sun for an hour or two next morning, the salt boilers could obtain a relatively pure and free-running salt.

Alas for technology, the salt boilers would not put themselves to any such trouble. The unrefined salt was good enough for them, and those who wanted a superior grade could import it from Liverpool. The result was, however, that the lake salt often sold as low as 50 cents per hundred pounds.

Fresh interest in the commercial potentialities of the lake was aroused by the coming of the transcontinental railroad. Early in 1869 the firm of Smith, Housel & Hopkins began some serious investigations, so that the Salt Lake *Herald* on February 1, 1871, was pleased to boast that the Salt Lake salt was, for all the local prejudice about its being impure and unfit for commercial uses, the peer of the world's finest, the Turk's Island and Onondaga varieties. "This thing should rise above the magnitude of an ordinary business," the *Herald* lectured the people of the Territory, "Salt Lake City lying within a few miles of the Great Salt Lake, should have enterprise enough to furnish all the salt required for culinary purposes in the same region; and should send car-loads daily east and west by the P. R. R. to meet the wants of the millions of American citizens." In true booster fashion the *Herald* trumpeted, "There is a vast trade here to be opened up. Where are all the salt boilers?"

The journalist of the itching feet, J. H. Beadle, got back to his old stamping grounds at the north shore of the lake long enough in 1873 to supply history with a tantalizing footnote. At Kelton, so he wrote in *The Undeveloped West,* an enterprising firm was proposing "to dam the mouth of a long bayou near, and place a windmill on the lake shore, with force sufficient to keep the pond thus created full all summer; the evaporation would be continuous and rapid, making, in one season, half a million tons of salt."

Did anything ever come of this idea? History would be interested to know. But unless this was the establishment of Barnes & Company (to whose operations we are indebted for the details concerning the Salt Lake Monster), that windmill-powered evaporation works has sunk from sight.

All really important developments in salt refining have occurred along the east shore. Three companies assumed prominence, the Jeremy Salt Company, the Intermountain Salt Company and the Inland Crystal Salt Company, the last being founded in 1889. The Jeremy firm eventually failed but the other two merged and under the successive names of Inland Crystal Salt Company and Royal Crystal Salt Company have manufactured salt into our own time.

The Royal Crystal plant lies on the low plain east of the lake, below Salt Lake City. The brine is pumped from Great Salt Lake into large concentration ponds to be evaporated by the sun. The flow is so regulated that only sodium chloride, common table salt, crystallizes from the saturated solution. In the fall of each year the dried salt in the concentration ponds is loosened by tractor-drawn plows, and, after being cured in long mounds, is hauled to the mill for refining and packing. The salt comes from the ponds in crystals ranging in size up to the proportions of a large pea. At the plant, after being dried and heated to a temperature of 300° F., it is crushed and screened to produce the grades and sizes in commercial demand. Annual production approximates 80,000 tons, about one percent of America's total production.

A kindred undertaking is the Salt Lake Sodium Products plant, three miles closer to the lake. This company manufactures sodium sulphate from Glauber salt; the refined product is principally used for processing wood pulp in the manufacture of kraft paper. One of the few plants in the United States manufacturing sodium sulphate as its principal product, it has a daily capacity of 100 tons.

In times of extreme low water, when the lake waters are a heavily saturated brine solution, Great Salt Lake goes on manufacturing enterprises of its own. The lake precipitates sodium chloride on its shores, on structures in the water, and on bottoms of boats, in beautiful, white, hard, cubic crystals. It is a phenomenon boatmen do not regard with extreme pleasure, for it makes anchoring difficult, slows boats as barnacles would and seals in centerboards. Objects placed in the lake at such times clothe themselves in a coat of crystalline salt, and boatmen, whose whim it has been to make anchors of compressed salt, have seen the anchors, so far from dissolving, even grow a little.

The lake has its chemical caprices with respect to its sodium sulphate content, also. When the weather is cold and the stage of the water low, sodium sulphate is precipitated, as Dr. Thomas C. Adams describes it, in the form of "a light, soft, snowlike mass of crystals which cover the bottom of the lake and are washed by the waves into bars of surprising size along the shore."

Imaginative souls have not been wanting to find other uses for a salt lake. The idea of oyster culture was advanced as early as 1853. Though admittedly the lake was too salty for oysters, an ingenious mind, writing in the *Deseret News,* suggested that a dry bay lying near the outlet of some large creek or river be excavated behind an embankment and filled with a solution of the proper salinity. Then "put in your oysters, taking care to change the salt and fresh water currents, as occasion may require to preserve the proper temperature of salt, and when your oysters are old and fat, dig and eat them." This was the most modest of beginnings. Not only oysters but clams, crabs, lobsters and any other shellfish might be so deposited; "give them a chance to be neighborly, as in the ocean, and maybe they will thrive the better, by keeping up each others spirits." Moreover, "these clam pools will be just as good for salmon, shad and other fresh-salt-water-fish, as they are for oysters, and the shell tribes; and when the season of country immigration and multiplication arrives, give them a free passage to all our big streams, and they will fill them with their scaly dainties in miniature and return to [the] lobster pond for winter quarters."

It sounds wonderful. It sounds, as the phrase has it, as if there might be millions in it. And if J. H. Beadle can be granted authority, someone was sufficiently taken with the idea to try something approaching it, 20 years later. Oysters and eels, Beadle says, were actually planted in the rivers at their mouths. Regrettable to report, they were promptly pickled by the marauding brine.

Nothwithstanding a certain charm of the unconventional that is found in the business thinking that has wrestled with Great Salt Lake, the lake itself has had only the most negligible of influences in the economy of its hinterland. One must look farther from its shores for an insight into the economic vitality of Salt Lake City, a vigorous young metropolis large and influential enough to constitute a regional capital, dominating the area east to the Colorado line, north to the Snake, south to the Grand Canyon and west to the Humboldt Valley of Nevada. Thirty percent of the population of that whole vast region lives in Salt Lake City.

The rich farmlands of the Wasatch Oasis, Brigham Young's heritage, have played their full part in the growth of such a metropolis. Grains, sugar beets, fruits, truck garden crops and forage for dairy cattle have been produced in abundance, and many secondary industries—mills, canneries, meat-packing plants and creameries—are directly dependent upon these green fields and their silver network of irrigation canals. But the economic dynamism of the Great Salt Lake region owes to the sharp juxtaposition of these farmlands with mining districts no less rich.

The mines underwrote Utah's first social revolution, beginning in Connor's time, but they were also the instrument that created most of the railroads. The rails that went here and there across the face of Utah, penetrating far down the central valleys of the territory, primarily sought out the ores that were being dug from the mountains. Some of these railroads died, but others, which were incorporated into the Union Pacific and Denver & Rio Grande systems and survive as integral parts of transcontinental routes to Los Angeles and San Francisco, serve the mines still.

The mines, moreover, provided a great part of the market for the produce of the agricultural oasis. The farmlands, the mines and the transportation facilities that bind them together have made Salt Lake City, the economic heart of all this activity, an ever-expanding force in the economic life of the West.

No single resource of the Great Salt Lake country is comparable with the open-cut copper mine in Bingham Canyon, a narrow slash in the Oquirrh Mountains a few miles beyond the southeastern extremity of the lake. Bingham was the locale of one of the earliest strikes in Utah, when Connor turned his men loose to prospect the country, but originally the low-grade copper deposits were held in contempt. Placers and then lode mines gave Bingham Canyon its rousing early vitality. Those were the great years of the Cottonwood mines in the mountains southeast of Salt Lake City, including the famous Emma, and like those mines the Bingham mines eventually played out. At the turn of the century, Bingham's finish seemed near, just another ghost camp from which the silver and gold had been dug.

Yet there remained those known, known-to-be-useless, low-grade copper ores. Colonel Enos A. Wall would not give up his conviction that a means could be found for recovering low-grade copper at a profit. He interested an old friend, Joseph De Lemar, who hired two young engineers, Daniel C. Jackling and Robert C. Gemmell to work on the problem. Their report, published in 1899, revolutionized copper mining. Though Jackling met with much ridicule, he was convinced that his improved metallurgy, united with mass-production methods, could produce large profits from low-grade copper. He obtained backing from Charles MacNeil and Spencer Penrose of the United States Reduction and Refining Company and bought out Wall and Lamar. The Utah Copper Company, organized in 1903, erected a pilot plant and began operations. Old-fashioned underground mining methods were used at first, but Jackling was convinced that in dealing with an entire mountain of copper ore surface operations would pay off best. Open-cut mining began in 1907, and met with such success that in 1910 the firm merged with Boston Consolidated and Nevada Consolidated as a $100,000,000 copper company.

The mountain that has gradually been cut down by the voracious steam shovels has produced, since 1907, more than 6,000,000,000 pounds of copper, with gold, silver and molybdenum as by-products. Its total production is valued in excess of $1,214,449,000, and its copper totals approximately a fourth of that annually produced in the United States.

Though the Utah Copper Company is rivaled by no other mining property in Utah, other mines around the Great Salt Lake periphery throw their wealth into the economic balance. The mines in Big and Little Cottonwood Canyons have gone the way of the Emma, and winter sports enthusiasts and summer vacationists have ousted even the ghosts of the past. But Park City, in the Wasatch Mountains 20 miles east of Salt Lake City, with its 12 large mines and 500 miles of underground workings, is still the heavy producer of silver, silver-lead and zinc-lead ores that it has been since 1870, its output in that time approximating a third of a billion dollars. The Tintic mines in Juab and Utah counties, 75 miles south of Salt Lake City, have produced silver, lead, gold, zinc and copper to fully rival the Park City mines, and depletion is not yet in sight.

Certainly not less significant are the coal deposits, found notably in Carbon County, in central Utah, and the iron ores found in the Iron Mountains at the South Rim of the Great Basin. A Mormon exploring party found the hematite deposits in the winter of 1849-1850, and the settlement of Little Salt Lake Valley a year later had as its direct objective the exploitation of these ores. However, an ironworks built near Cedar City, notwithstanding a struggle continued over many heartbreaking years, proved incapable of dealing with the ores. It was not till 1924 that small-scale utilization really commenced. At that time the Columbia Steel Company built a reduction works at Ironton, just south of Provo, to which the ores were shipped. The Ironton blast furnace reduced about 500 tons of pig iron a day, most of which was shipped to the Pacific Coast, but until the shadows of the Second World War lengthened over America, there seemed no prospect of any really extensive exploitation of the southern Utah iron deposits.

Right up to the outbreak of the Second World War, Utah had struggled to get a hold on its economic bootstraps sufficient to lift itself into an age of abundance befitting its resources. Not exactly by chance, the coming of war to America found the state government better equipped to wrestle with its destinies than it had been at any time since statehood was attained in 1896. The progressive Herbert B. Maw won the governorship on the Democratic ticket in the elections of 1940 and immediately on taking office set about reorganizing the state government. As a part of this reorganization he established a Department of Publicity and Industrial Development, which was given the duty of providing employment for the citizens of the state and raising their earning level. The department was set up on July 1, 1941, in the midst of the national defense emergency, and throughout the war period it worked hand-in-glove with the federal government and private business interests to develop Utah's resources concurrently with the national industrial machinery.

In the immediate prewar years, Utah's economy was based primarily upon metal mining, agriculture and livestock production, manufacturing and food processing. Primarily, the state was a producer of raw materials which were processed elsewhere with a consequent economic loss to the state, nor did the people of Utah have any voice in or control over the economic and market conditions which fixed the prices paid Utah for its products. A serious effect of this economic maladjustment was that a rising proportion of the young people of the state was migrating to other areas in search of the opportunities that were lacking at home. Since Utah has one of the highest literacy rates in the country and extremely high standards of education, a direct monetary loss was involved here; the state was footing the educational bill for the more wealthy states to which its sons and daughters were migrating; this was erosion of a human asset of the highest importance.

It was clearly the part of high government policy to reinvigorate the Utah economy on the widest possible base. Eight categories were seen as offering hope for a freshly varied economy—iron and steel industry, nonferrous metal mining, agriculture and livestock, manufacturing and food processing, coal mining and processing, mining of nonmetallic minerals, tourist trade and motion-picture making.

The war had an immediate bursting effect upon the entire economy of the state. Important beyond any other single development was the building by the federal government of the $200,000,000 steel plant at Geneva, on the northeastern shore of Utah Lake. Its location was approximately equidistant from Los Angeles, San Francisco, Portland and Seattle, and it was close enough to reduce the transportation problem yet sufficiently removed from the West Coast to be secure from Japanese attack. Since a good grade of surface-mined iron ore, coking coal and limestone all were close at hand, and since the Geneva area had a good water supply, an adequate outside power supply, and a good plant site in an area that was not congested, the War Production Board ordered the building of the plant early in 1942.

Geneva was designed to meet the war demand for plates, ship shapes and shell steel, but its postwar potentialities were kept in mind, particularly in view of the heavy government investment involved. Room was therefore left for the building of a postwar plate mill for rolling sheet and strip steel, together with other important facilities. At the close of the war, the fate of the Geneva plant being of prime importance to the industrial future of Utah, the state government took an active part in the negotiations by which the $41,000,000 bid of the United States Steel Company was approved by the federal government; the need for a Western steel industry, to pave the way for full economic development of the West after the war, had made the disposition of the Geneva plant a public issue for the entire West.

U. S. Steel announced that it would increase facilities to whatever extent the demand would justify, and it embarked upon a reconversion of the Geneva plant which it hoped to finish by the end of 1947. Natural resources for a steel industry seem virtually unlimited, and the Utah iron ores, which are of as high grade as the famous Mesabi iron ores in Minnesota, are of particular importance now that the highest-grade Mesabi ores face early depletion. In 1945 Utah shipped 1,987,000 tons of iron ore, almost a million tons more than all the other Western states combined, hardly comparable with the 75,071,000 tons shipped from the Lake Superior region, but significant because it was the only iron-shipping area in the United States to expand its production in 1945 over that of 1944.

The first dividend on Geneva came to the state in the fall of 1946, when the Besser Manufacturing Company of Alpena, Michigan, announced plans to establish a concrete-block machine manufacturing plant in Salt Lake City. The state had been confident that steel fabrication plants would throng to Utah once steel was assured, and this manufacturing company was regarded as the first of many which would cross the threshold of the door that had been opened.

The inception and development of fabricating industries, however, to some degree is dependent on power as well as basic steel supply. Since Utah's present power supply is inadequate for proper economic development of the state, Governor Maw has thrown his weight behind the so-called Central Utah Reclamation Project, which envisages damming the Green River at its junction with the Yampa, in Dinosaur National Monument, and impounding some 600,000 acre-feet of water which on the one hand will produce vast new quantities of industrial power, and on the other hand will reclaim some 200,000 acres of land where the desert now reigns.

Nonferrous metal mining is already well developed in the state; virtually all the useful metals, save only tin, are now mined. Utah is the only state among the half-dozen top producers of all five of the chief metals; in 1945 it was first in copper, second in lead, fifth in zinc, third in silver and first in gold. Total production was valued at $89,575,200, second only to Arizona's total of $95,034,700. It is instructive to note that Bingham produced 89 percent of this wealth, Park City 5 percent, and Tintic 3 percent.

In 1947 as it had been in 1847, irrigation was still the crucial problem for agriculture in Utah. Notwithstanding the labors of a century, notwithstanding all the labors of Mormon desert-breakers and the large-scale projects of the U. S. Reclamation Service, only 2½ percent of the total state area was under irrigation—a little less than 1,200,000 acres. Plans for further development contemplated bringing an additional 900,000 acres of land under irrigation, at least half of it in the Colorado River drainage basin previously beyond the possibility of reclamation. The Central Utah Irrigation project, to divert the waters of the Green and Yampa, was being especially pushed as Utah's second century of settlement opened, and a priority rating by the Reclamation Service encouraged hopes that it might become an early reality.

On its 1,194,578 acres of irrigated land, its 560,000 acres of dry farms and its 5,547,429 acres of range and grazing lands, agriculture in Utah flourished during the war years. Looking beyond the war, the state's program of internal development emphasized new possibilities in crop diversification, better grading and packing methods, more efficient marketing procedures and co-operative group action to improve the situation of Utah's farmers. The three largest crops, as the state emerged from the war, were turkeys and poultry products, dairy products and lambs and wool, though fruits and vegetables and sugar beets were important cash crops.

The importance of manufacturing, and the reason for the particular emphasis laid upon it in such issues as the Geneva steel plant, is that it adds, through processing, such added value to raw materials. Governor Maw and his aides considered that even though, prior to the war, manufacturing in Utah had reached an importance rivaling agriculture and mining in the Utah economy, the loss to the state in the export of its raw materials was so disproportionate as to demand an energetic effort toward the establishment of new fabricating and processing industries. It was felt that since Utah had an increased population, a good and stable labor force, abundance of raw materials, excellent transportation facilities, adequate fuel and power, good living conditions, a climate remarkable in its low humidity and abundant sunshine and a favorable public sentiment, it had something to sell.

The resources on which enterprises can draw are extraordinarily varied. The coal deposits in Utah are, by reckoning of the U. S. Geological Survey, as extensive as those in any state, including Pennsylvania and West Virginia; more than a seventh of the total area of the state contains workable coal deposits, usable not only for fuel, the chief use of the past, but for the production of plastics, resins and oils. Hydrocarbons like asphalt and gilsonite are found in large deposits in eastern and central Utah. Oil production has never become commercially important, though a refining plant in Salt Lake City processes crude oil piped from the Baxter Basin field in Wyoming; oil shales, however, underlie wide areas of eastern Utah and may yet produce petroleum on a substantial commercial basis. Phosphate the state has in abundance rivaling its salt supplies; there is more of both in sight than any conceivable market can fully use.

With all this economic potential the fact remains that much of it, as it was before the war, is a potential only. Geneva is the one big toe hold the state has on its future. What of the intervening time while slow and patient work transforms the state industrially? The tourist trade is looked to, primarily, to see the state over the difficult period before the new era can materialize. Unless the matchless scenic resources of the state are exploited to such end, there is bound to be an economic shock following the cessation of federal spending.

The extent of this shock is better understood if the direct military impact of the war upon Utah is held in view. The First World War was for Utah a thing of subtraction only—its thousands of boys who went off to war, its millions of dollars spent for Liberty and Victory bonds. But in the Second World War the American people fronted an enemy in the Pacific. Thus the valley of the Great Salt Lake had a new strategic significance.

The Army established its $25,000,000 Hill Field on the lake plain between Ogden and Salt Lake City, and at near-by Clearfield the Navy located its $32,000,000 Naval Supply Depot. A $55,000,000 Army Service Forces Depot was established at Ogden, a $30,000,000 Ordnance Depot at Tooele and a $40,000,000 Army Ordnance plant at Salt Lake City. Additions to the Ogden Arsenal cost $9,000,000, and this was the cost also of Bushnell Hospital at Brigham City.

At the same time the $50,000,000 training camp, Kearns, went up on the alkaline plain at the heart of Salt Lake Valley, an installation which, three months from the time the first dust was stirred up, grew into the proportions of Utah's fourth largest city. The Army Air Forces took over the Salt Lake Airport and built another air base at Wendover, on the western rim of the Salt Desert, while it converted a considerable area of the desert itself into a bombing range.

There were numerous other installations. Altogether, it was estimated, the war poured more than a billion dollars into Utah for the construction of facilities alone. Pay rolls added fantastically to the sums that were spent in the state. Pay-roll totals in Utah had averaged $90,000,000 annually during the 25 years before the war. They jumped under the onset of defense activity to $102,000,000 in 1940 and $126,000,000 in 1941. This was only a beginning. Under the impact of the war itself the totals soared to $208,000,000 in 1942 and to $225,000,000 in 1943 before finally turning downward again. The annual average for the final months of the war approximated $203,-000,000.

Obviously, the state cannot go back to the subsistence level of $90,000,000 a year. And since it has everything to offer the almost inconceivably rich tourist industry (tourists spent perhaps $6,000,-000,000 in 1940, making the industry the largest immediate source of cash income in the United States) it has embarked upon a program to lure visitors to Utah and make them want to come again.

The scenic splendor of the state has led to its increasing use for location purposes by motion-picture companies, particularly for technicolor productions. Since the companies get into areas commonly lacking in other economic resources, the state finds it to its benefit to build access roads for the use of the film companies and otherwise to co-operate with them, both for the sake of the cash income to residents and for the sake of the facilities that remain when the companies, which rarely make more than two pictures with the same scenic background, move on to fresh locales. The motion-picture industry consequently is tied in at many points with tourist trade as a part of the general economic development of Utah.

So these are the economics of survival: Here is the history of the half century since statehood while business has been the constant force to work the shape and pattern of life in the Great Salt Lake country. Yet a question remains: What of the people who have created and lived this life, and what of their cultural inheritance?

... Turn back through the pages of Mormon history. You come upon a certain striking disproportion; time has got strangely askew. Summon up the Manifesto of 1890 and you seem to touch the events of yesterday. Seek after Joseph Smith and the Mormon beginnings and you seem to stir in the dust of a timeless antiquity; whole millennia appear to intervene. Yet the Manifesto is almost as far removed from our own time as it is itself removed from the inception of Mormonism.

The difference is not one of perspective only. The disproportion follows directly from the detail of history. Mormonism's early years were volcanic with energies loosed against the walls of American society, American life, American mores. The clashes of emotions, ideas and social and economic systems showered events as a blowtorch showers sparks. To the time of the Woodruff Manifesto Mormon history is a continual blaze of event. That history since 1890 seems by contrast almost barren of happenings.

The old conflict ended rapidly after the Saints made the fundamental surrender. The Mormons and the federal government resolved their difficulties with only such minor irruptions as the exclusion in 1898 of the polygamist, Brigham H. Roberts, from the

House and the four-year fight (1904-1907) that the Apostle, Reed Smoot, had to make for his seat in the Senate. Anti-Mormonism as a political issue in Utah died after a final flare-up of an anti-Mormon "American Party" in Salt Lake City and Ogden between 1905 and 1911, and the long decades of journalistic preachment on the Mormon Problem came to an end with the muckraking "magazine crusade" of 1910-1911.

Almost indistinguishably during all this time the presidents of the church have succeeded one another, Lorenzo Snow taking office in 1898, Joseph F. Smith in 1901, Heber J. Grant in 1918, George Albert Smith in 1945. No longer is the question of succession attended by a loosing of energies disruptive with schism and apostasy. Although church law does not specifically so provide, the senior member of the Quorum of the Twelve Apostles will always be advanced to the presidency on the death of the incumbent; the precedent has become binding and powerful, and safely removes the succession from the realm of conflict and schismatic intrigue.

The Manifesto, it must be pointed out, was the admission, more than the instrument, of a fundamental surrender. It placed on a documentary basis what was already a condition of fact. The Mormon position had begun to disintegrate in the late eighties as the membership, which in overwhelming proportion had never entered into polygamy, began to reveal a sense of a cleavage between themselves and the stubborn adherents to the principle of plural marriage. And the political battles lost in 1889 and 1890 had led directly to another defeat, in the domain of education; in 1890 the territorial legislature had established public schools throughout the territory, placing them for the first time on a nonsectarian basis.

Possibly the gentile victory on the battlefield of education was the most pregnant of all. Though the Mormons established seminaries to complement the teachings of the public schools, the emphasis was changed, subtly and effectively. The seminaries were peripheral only, and the large assumption was inescapable: the central truths of education did not necessarily coincide with the central truths of Mormonism. Here was a fundamental shift in values, intangible but drastic in its long-range effect. Moreover, Saints and gentiles intermixed at the age level where significant social attitudes are formed. Here in the schools began the subtle disintegration of the rigid attitudes which had socially differentiated Saints and gentiles for a generation.

Over a span of half a century the crumbling of old attitudes within and about the Mormon Church has had its effect. Both persecution and the idea of persecution were cohesive forces which operated powerfully to shape Mormonism and the Mormon people in the first 60 years of their existence. No one may say what kind of Utah might have resulted had statehood been granted in 1850; for a time the Mormon State of Deseret might more nearly have resembled a theocratic kingdom, the Kingdom of God, than a sovereign state of the Union. But inevitably a social erosion would have begun from within, and without the binding power of real or fancied persecution to hold the Mormon people in close ranks, the normal human waywardness and obstinacy and reluctance to submit for very long to any very rigorous social discipline would have got in their deadly work. Social changes which have operated since 1890 would have commenced earlier, though the evolution would have been slower, in the context of the frontier.

These might-have-beens are problematical. But there is no difficulty in establishing the broad outlines of what has happened to the Mormon people and their church since 1890. An entire evolution can be summed up in a new word that has come into the Mormon vocabulary, "Jack Mormon." Actually not a new word, it is one that has undergone an extraordinary change in definition. During the turbulent months in 1846 before the Saints finally evacuated Illinois, "Jack Mormon" was a term opprobriously applied by the anti-Mormons to a gentile exhibiting Mormon sympathies. But in the new vocabulary it describes a nonpracticing member of the church. The Jack Mormon constitutes a blurred human middle ground between Saint and gentile. He goes to church in the Mormon chapels when he goes at all, and is bound by varied emotional loyalties, but he has as cheerful an irreverence toward constituted Mormon authority as any gentile.

The Jack Mormon is the product of an internal disintegration of Mormon society, and perhaps it is no exaggeration to describe him as the chief annoyance and the chief problem of the church today. He cannot be depended upon to pay his tithing; he looks with complacence on the marriage of his children outside the church; he is in no way deterred by the Word of Wisdom from enjoyment of his morning cup of coffee, a glass of iced tea or even a frosted glass of something stronger, and he thinks nothing of offering you a cigarette. If he were a type, to be isolated as such, he would be no cause for worry, but there is a strong element of the Jack Mormon in all the body of the Saints, and the iniquity he represents is not to be abated simply by the passing of time; time, indeed, is his ally. Though upbraided from the pulpit, he is unruffled. He bears no grudge toward the Authorities who preach against the sins that he embodies, for after all, he is willing to concede, they are doing their duty as they see it. But there are things a man must adjust within his own conscience, and the Mormon conscience is not only more elastic than it was, but less amenable to management by the priesthood.

The church itself exhibits a certain incomprehension as to what has befallen it. By the operation of seniority among the hierarchy, which makes for government by an aging group of men, old ideas and old traditions longest survive at the highest levels of the church. Voices are not wanting to speak out to the membership in the old accents. But dubious results issue from attempts to exercise an authority which history has made obsolete. The intervention of the church in three presidential elections, with public pronunciamentos against Franklin D. Roosevelt, was worse than futile; it possibly militated to the disadvantage of the Republican Party, and it remarkably demonstrated the political impotence of the present-day church.

It is not alone the rise and spread of the Jack Mormon that has altered the relations of the church with its membership. The world has undergone drastic change during the lifetime of Mormonism. The missionaries of the church no longer find the receptive religious environment, the emotional and intellectual ferment, that existed a century ago. The anxious preoccupation with the Bible which characterized wide areas of nineteenth century America has given way to a preoccupation with the bridge club, the movies and next Saturday's football game. The missionaries find themselves no longer classic figures going to the world without purse or scrip; suddenly they are the agents of a public relations program, complete with men's choruses and basketball teams. The young missionary writes home to his parents: "I know that my message is true, *if I could just get somebody to listen to it.*"

It is not only the social environment that has changed. The Mormon Church was an instrument admirably fashioned for the taming of a desert land. But what is to be done with an instrument that has lost its function? The Mormon desert settlements overspread all the fertile areas in the intermountain empire, spread beyond them to the submarginal lands where even the Mormon techniques of settlement and the Mormon social discipline were insufficient and must recoil. The Mormons were able to dedicate themselves to faith and hard works in a peculiarly intimate relation with the land. But when the land is gone, when it can no longer support the whole posterity that issues from it, where then shall the church turn?

To a notable degree the church has turned in upon itself, conducting crusades among the membership on such small moral issues as use of tea, coffee and tobacco. Perhaps this is merely a passing phase as it seeks out a new and vital social function. The church, of course, regards its religious function as eternal and unchanging, to bring mankind to salvation in the New and Everlasting Covenant.

The structure of the church, which articulates, and is always regarded as energized by, a downward impulsion from a single authority who alone receives revelations for the church, always has been and still is essentially antidemocratic in nature; its only democratic characteristic inheres in the right of the membership to accept or reject law or doctrine transmitted from on high. There is no provision in the church for nomination by the membership of the governing authorities, and church elections have the doubtful status of oral plebiscites. This organizational structure has come down intact to our own time from the early years of the church; it is perhaps a necessary condition for survival, since human experience has gone to show that a truly democratic church characteristically is schismatic and self-destructive.

It is inconceivable that the generality of the membership will ever rise in rebellion against the self-perpetuating hierarchy. In a certain negative fashion, however, the Saints do now and will hereafter exert every necessary influence upon the constituted authorities. The lives of an older generation of Saints centered around the church; it *was* their life. That is no longer true. The church has become only marginal to the lives of its members. It is a reluctant admission for the church to make, but the Saints have become members of a larger community than the community of religion. War and depression alike are beyond the power of the church to forestall or withstand; both membership and church are shaped by forces beyond their control. So now a curious democratic force begins to operate in the theocratic structure of the church: It must accommodate itself to its membership because, save within a very narrow tolerance, there is no longer any question of the membership accommodating itself to the church. There is nothing to bind the membership except a community of interest and feeling, for the church can no longer serve any dynamic purpose as a social and economic instrument of the membership. The Jack Mormon's undependability, his lack of interest, his easy tolerance, paradoxically exert a greater leverage upon the officialdom of the church than the earnest pieties of the conscientious Saint. For the Jack Mormon is disintegration embodied. To the extent that his number grows, the church or its authorities have failed to adapt to the needs of the membership.

It is a strange place to come out at. The redefinition of loyalties, the shift in attitudes, has been intangible. At no time have there been public crises to dramatize fundamental alterations in social relationships; it is not possible to say that at this time or that some significant change occurred; but over a period of 25 or 40 years the fact of change is beyond all question.

Yet it oversimplifies the character of social change in Utah to interpret it solely in terms of the church's problems of internal adjustment. Even the Jack Mormons are bound up within ancestral loyalties and stand foursquare with their brethren at the essential points. They may become politically indignant with the president of the church, burlesque the business interests of the General Authorities, or write off certain of the officials as meddlesome busybodies. But let the church or the Mormon people be brought under attack from outside, and Jack Mormon is suddenly indistinguishable from his orthodox brother. Both are well persuaded that Utah is the fairest place on earth, the truly chosen land; and both are persuaded that the Saints, any way you look at them, are just about what

Brigham Young always said they were, "the best people on earth."

No less than the Saints, the gentiles have been changed by time. ("Gentile" in Utah now is almost a disused word.) A few gentiles of the old, militant strain yet survive, but for the most part the gentile is indistinguishable from the Jack Mormon.

Even so, there remains an undercurrent of social antagonism. In some part it is the fossil remnant of old attitudes, and in some part it is the reaction of minority to majority in any place or time. It delights the gentile to set up the Saints as a straw figure, a creature all ears and mouth, pompous, complacent, credulous and sancti-monious. And he is immediately busy with his wit when any crack appears in the holy edifice the Saints have builded about themselves.

All this is a kind of social corrosion surviving from the savage hostilities of the older time, but there is no absolute ill feeling about it, and in time it will pass away. That is the shape, if not necessarily the promise, of the future. Through two generations the schools have done their work; in the last generation the old clannishness in the area of marriage has begun to break down; and politics and business no longer take account of religious differences. Mormon and Methodist in the valley of the Great Salt Lake are not much further removed than Methodist and Baptist, or Lutheran and Presbyterian, in the valley of the Ohio.

Mormons and gentiles, simply as citizens of Utah, have shared the events of the half century since statehood. Elected officials have been indiscriminately Mormon or gentile, Democrat or Republican. When the Saints broke apart their People's Party in 1891, they set up an approximate balance between the two national political parties, and this was not upset when the gentiles in turn dissolved their Liberal Party in 1893. A sufficient edge of superiority fell to the Republican Party to enable it to dominate the first state elections, and, after some seesaw years, to take a firm grasp on the governor-ship, the senatorial representation and the state legislature. However, in 1917 William King achieved the Senate under Democratic auspices, and in 1924 George H. Dern made the governorship a Democratic prize. Reed Smoot, representing the Republican Party, retained the senior senatorship, however, and in local elections the Republicans held their own until the depression of 1929.

The Democratic landslide of 1932 extended to Utah, and so forcibly that the Democratic Party was politically dominant in Utah until 1946. Not least among the sensations of the 1932 Republican debacle was the ousting of Reed Smoot by Elbert D. Thomas, then professor of political science at the University of Utah. As dean of the Senate and one of the General Authorities of the church, Smoot had seemed so firmly entrenched in his job that up to 1929 few could have been found willing to wager that he would not die in office.

Politics and business have been meeting grounds, an area to obliterate the old distinction of Saint and gentile. But war, above all, has welded a people who belong one to another.

The Mormons "sat out" the Civil War while the gentiles railed at them. But Mormons and gentiles rushed to enlist in the war against Spain. The new state supplied three batteries of light artillery and two troops of cavalry, the men seeing action in the Philippines and Cuba. Eight men were killed in action and five others died overseas.

It was a different, grimmer war that was fought a half generation later. To the First World War Utah sent 21,000 men, and its sons principally composed the 362nd Infantry of the "Wild West Division," which engaged in the St. Mihiel and Meuse-Argonne offensives and other actions. With 760 war dead few towns in the state did not have a Gold Star mother.

But even that world convulsion did not compare with the war that yet aches in memory. Utah's fighting generation was already being drafted when the incredible news from Pearl Harbor came on that sunny December Sunday of 1941, and before the climactic surrender of Japan 3½ years later, 69,000 men and women from Utah had donned their country's uniform. Casualties reached a total of 1,826 dead and missing.

Mormon, gentile or Jew, enemy gunfire had been impartial. The boys had fought together, and together their folk, Mormon, gentile, or Jew, had suffered in their absence and mourned the word that they would never come back. The memory of the war will dim, as time dims the memory of all wars, but those who fought it together, in their several ways, cannot be the same again, and the sense of the irrevocable fellowship will remain.

ACKNOWLEDGMENTS,
BIBLIOGRAPHICAL NOTE AND INDEX

ACKNOWLEDGMENTS

THE pleasantest thing about the writing of a book is that at the end of it one is enabled to make some small return for freely given help. No acknowledgment can ever discharge the debt, but it is gratifying to make record of it. So to all those who did for me what I could not do for myself, who in all parts of the country provided information or who undertook those heroic investigations that can yield only the barren satisfaction of having established that information does not exist—to all who helped in these and a hundred other ways, I express my thanks and appreciation.

It is a source of high regret to me that Maurice L. Howe did not live to learn that this book was to be dedicated to him and to his gallant wife as an expression of my appreciation of them both. This book reflects a thousand interests we shared in common and sheds fresh light on many matters that at various times we wondered about together. Maurice would have brought a special discernment and enjoyment to much that is written here, and in this among other things I feel bereft by his death, on June 6, 1945.

Darel McConkey has once again placed me in his debt for his characteristically constructive reading of the manuscript, for his patience and high good humor, for his engaging point of view and critical detachment and for his stimulating interest in the book at all stages of its writing.

I am happy, too, to render my thanks to Winnifred Henry, Mary R. Gaither and Agnes Shelor, who brought to the typing of the manuscript not only a high technical proficiency but an unflinching willingness to work at it, at a cost of what must often have been great personal inconvenience.

Except for John D. Thornley's willingness to sacrifice his own interests for mine, I should hardly have been able to write this book, and I am happy to express appreciation of his friendship and his generosity. I am still further indebted to him for reading a considerable portion of the manuscript and for providing me with rare photographs. Louise C. North also read much of the manuscript and gave me valued technical advice. Significant contributions were made to my text by John E. Jones, Blanche H. Wenner, Antoinette Lambourne Fowler, Darrell J. Greenwell, J. Roderic Korns, Charles Kelly, Ira Dern and Brenda R. Gieseker.

My discussion of the colonial birds rests squarely upon information generously made available to me by Dr. William H. Behle of the University of Utah, including a preliminary draft of a most interesting and exhaustive work on these birds which, it is to be hoped, will soon see print. I feel a major obligation to him as to Dr. Thomas C. Adams, who as an engineer long concerned with the lake and as commodore of the Great Salt Lake Yacht Club has an unequaled fund of information about the lake which he has been at pains to place at my disposal. I am again indebted to a major degree for the extraordinary kindness of Arthur L. Crawford of the Utah State Department of Publicity and Industrial Development, who procured at the cost of much time and labor information of great importance to me. I am still further indebted to Mr. Crawford, as to David H. Mann of the department, for excellent photographs made especially for this work.

In having delayed mention even so long, I have failed in expressing the extent of my personal obligation to D. L. Chambers, president of Bobbs-Merrill. It was at Mr. Chambers' earnest solicitation that I embarked upon the book, and throughout the trying period of its writing, he exhibited a personal kindness, patience, interest and enthusiasm for which it is difficult to find adequate words of appreciation. Dr. M. M. Quaife has also contributed much to the book, and I am only less indebted to John L. B. Williams, Guernsey Van Riper, Jr., Elizabeth Bridwell and Harrison Platt of the Bobbs-Merrill staff.

Much information of importance was obtained for me by T. Gerald Bleak, who searched dusty newspaper files otherwise beyond my reach and enabled me to fill in what must have been many blank spaces in the narrative. My grandfather, James S. Morgan, also went to much trouble to provide information; and it would not be possible to itemize in detail all the small and large services done me by my mother, Emily H. Morgan, during the time the book was in preparation.

Others, both my friends and those who are strangers to me outside the fellowship of letters, have contributed important miscellaneous information or done me significant services; I express thanks freely to Charles D. Wood, Madeline Reeder, Anna McConkey, Juanita Brooks, Gail Martin, W. W. Hardy, Douglas Hardy, Charles L. Camp, Marguerite L. Sinclair, Clayton Jenkins, Leroy R. Hafen, Harold H. Jenson, Wallace Stegner, Nels Anderson, A. William Lund, Alvin F. Smith, Lee Greene Richards, Stanley Ivins, Alice B. Maloney, Walter C. McCausland, M. T. Wilson, Ralph V. Chamberlin, Elmer R. Smith and C. K. Greening.

No work of history is written in these times without recourse to the collections of the country's great libraries, and for much help it is a pleasure to thank the Library of Congress, the Library of the Geological Survey, The National Archives, the Bancroft Library, the California State

Library, the Henry E. Huntington Library and Art Gallery, the **L. D. S.** Church Historian's Office, the Salt Lake City Free Public Library, the Utah State Historical Society, the Missouri Historical Society, the Kansas State Historical Society, the Chicago Historical Society, the Oregon Historical Society, the Connecticut State Library, the New York Public Library, the Free Library of Philadelphia, the University of Chicago Library and the Library of the Salt Lake *Tribune*. I am also indebted for special help to the Salt Lake City offices of the U. S. Weather Bureau, the Geological Survey and the Bureau of Land Management.

For much information of value about the experiences of Judge **Wenner** and his family on Frémont Island I am indebted to Blanche H. Wenner and John E. Jones. Miss Wenner generously made available to me the interesting memoirs of her mother, and quotation from these memoirs is with her permission.

The numerous quotations in my text from the original journals of the Stansbury Survey are from a transcript which I am now editing for publication; the manuscript journals themselves are in the possession of The National Archives.

Photographs have been provided without stint by the Utah State Department of Publicity and Industrial Development, many of them taken especially by David H. Mann of the Department, and by L. Clyde Anderson, Clayton Jenkins of the Provo Chamber of Commerce, Charles Kelly, John E. Jones, John D. Thornley, D. Eldon Beck, the Geological Survey and the Library of Congress.

The maps have been drawn by Clarance Smith from base maps of my own devising.

BIBLIOGRAPHICAL NOTE

Works immediately relating to Great Salt Lake make up a small and fragmentary literature, and the story of the lake and the people who have dwelt at various times near and upon its shores must be pursued to widely scattered and diverse sources.

The only general work that has concerned itself with the lake is James E. Talmage's *The Great Salt Lake Present and Past* (Salt Lake City, 1900). Primarily this is a collection of monographs on scientific aspects of the lake published by Dr. Talmage at various times. Useful for a more extended inquiry into the many fields of scientific interest on which the lake impinges is Ralf R. Woolley and Ray E. Marsell's "Great Salt Lake:

A Selected Bibliography With Annotations," in the American Geophysical Union's *Transactions,* February 1946.

The geological history of Great Salt Lake has been the province primarily of G. K. Gilbert's notable *Lake Bonneville* (Washington, 1890). A companion work is Israel C. Russell's *Geological History of Lake Lahontan* (Washington, 1885). Gilbert's great work is the classic source on Lake Bonneville, but Ernest Antevs has written "On the Pleistocene History of the Great Basin," in Carnegie Institute of Washington, *Publication No. 352* (Washington, 1925), and Frederick J. Pack has published *Lake Bonneville* (Salt Lake City, Bulletin of the University of Utah, 1939), a highly interesting popular account of the vanished lake based on Gilbert's book but incorporating recent geological findings.

Archeology and ethnology in the Great Salt Lake region are best pursued in a series of publications by Julian H. Steward of the Bureau of American Ethnology, notably including "Native Cultures of the Intermontane (Great Basin) Area," in *Essays in Historical Anthropology of North America* (Smithsonian Miscellaneous Collections No. 100, Washington, 1940); *Ancient Caves of the Great Salt Lake Region* (Bureau of American Ethnology Bulletin 116, Washington, 1937); *Basin-Plateau Aboriginal Sociopolitical Groups* (Bureau of American Ethnology Bulletin 120, Washington, 1938); and "Changes in Shoshonean Indian Culture," in *Scientific Monthly,* December 1939. Archeological labors earlier than Steward's are described in Neil M. Judd's *Archeological Observations North of the Rio Colorado* (Bureau of American Ethnology Bulletin 82, Washington, 1926), while the latest work in the field has been described in part by Elmer R. Smith in *The Archaeology of Dead Man's Cave* (Salt Lake City, Bulletin of the University of Utah, 1942). Frank C. Hibben's *The Lost Americans* (New York, 1946) is a highly readable account of the hunt for early man in the Americas. Two instructive monographs by Ralph V. Chamberlin are "The Ethno-botany of the Gosiute Indians" in the Academy of Natural Sciences of Philadelphia *Proceedings,* 1911, and "Place and Personal Names of the Gosiute Indians of Utah," in American Philosophical Society *Proceedings,* January-April 1913. William R. Palmer has published many articles on the Paiute in the *Utah Historical Quarterly* and the *Improvement Era.* Elijah Nicholas Wilson's *Among the Shoshones* (Salt Lake City, 1910), more frequently seen in a revised version, *The White Indian Boy,* is the story of a Mormon boy who in 1856 ran away to live with the Shoshoni for two years. A somewhat disconnected account of Indian conflicts in Utah is the compilation by Peter Gottfredson, *History of Indian Depredations in Utah* (Salt Lake City, 1919). No adequate history of the Indians of the Utah area has been written, nor, so far as the Ute are concerned, has any adequate ethnological study been made.

The mythological period in the history of the lake is best illustrated in the comprehensive collections of the Map Division of the Library of Congress, but a sufficient number of early maps has been published so that development of the mythological conceptions of Great Salt Lake may be readily traced. Manuscript maps resulting from the expedition of Escalante and Dominguez are reproduced with allied material in the *Utah Historical Quarterly*, 1941-1943. Early printed maps, constituting a fairly good sampling, are reproduced in H. H. Bancroft's *History of Utah* (San Francisco, 1889) and *History of the Northwest Coast* (vol. 1, San Francisco, 1884); in the *Reports of Explorations for a Pacific Railroad* (vol. 11, Washington, 1859); and in F. S. Dellenbaugh's *Frémont and '49* (New York, 1914). Other individually important maps of later date are published in books relating to fur trade and exploration mentioned below.

The slow accretion of concrete knowledge about the Great Salt Lake country prior to actual exploration may be traced through George P. Hammond and Agapito Rey's *Narratives of the Coronado Expedition, 1540-1542* (Albuquerque, 1940), Alfred B. Thomas' *After Coronado* (Norman, Oklahoma, 1935), Baron de Lahontan's *New Voyages to North America* (London, 1703; reprinted New York, 1905), and Joseph J. Hill's article, "Spanish and Mexican Exploration and Trade Northwest from New Mexico into the Great Basin," *Utah Historical Quarterly,* January 1930 (a revised version of his "The Old Spanish Trail," *Hispanic-American Historical Review,* August, 1921).

Herbert S. Auerbach's edition of Escalante's journal, printed with much collateral material in the *Utah Historical Quarterly,* 1943, is the only one generally available in English, though an earlier translation was published in W. R. Harris' *The Catholic Church in Utah* (Salt Lake City, 1909). The fragmentary Spanish documents covering the period after Escalante have been treated only by Joseph J. Hill, in the article listed above. The original journals of the Lewis and Clark expedition, with their remote perspective on the Great Salt Lake country, are available in the monumental edition edited by Reuben G. Thwaites in 1904-1905, supplemented by Ordway's journal, edited by M. M. Quaife and published in 1916 as volume XXII of the *Publications* of the State Historical Society of Wisconsin.

Within the last generation a great deal of important research has been done on the era of fur trade and exploration. There are many gaps in the record still; indeed, it is amazing that so much of the record can be recovered, since it is one essentially ephemeral in character; but the source literature has outpaced the historians who specialize in the synthesis of it. There is a serious need for a vigorous rewriting of the entire history of the fur era on the basis of the record now available. Such a work, however, will be liable to revision when important journals known to be extant are published. The long-lost Peter Skene Ogden journal of 1824-1825, together with that of his subordinate, William Kittson, covering the expedition into the Great Salt Lake country, has turned up in the Hudson's Bay Company archives in London, and I am informed that preliminary editing is being done looking toward publication, though this may not come to fruition for 10 years. A fragmentary journal of 1825 kept by William Sublette will ultimately be published by the Missouri Historical Society, and these three journals are certain to throw a great deal of new light upon the early exploration of the Far West in general and the Great Salt Lake country in particular.

In the meantime, W. J. Ghent's *The Early Far West* (New York, 1931) provides an over-all view of Western history down to 1850. The classic account of the fur trade is Hiram M. Chittenden's *The American Fur Trade of the Far West* (New York, 1902; reprinted with additional matter, New York, 1936). Although largely outmoded on individual traders and enterprises, its general treatment of the subject, even with its neglect of the Southwest, is so sound that it will doubtless stand indefinitely.

Harrison C. Dale's *The Ashley-Smith Explorations and the Discovery of a Central Route to the Pacific, 1822-29* (Cleveland, 1918; revised edition, Glendale, 1941) has acquired a classic stature. This monograph, brilliant both for its energetic method and for its critical acumen, has made its impress on everything that has been written on the fur trade since 1918. Unfortunately, the 1941 revision was not thoroughgoing.

Individual mountain men have preoccupied historians of the fur trade during the last generation. Edwin L. Sabin's *Kit Carson Days* (Chicago, 1914; but primarily important in revised edition, New York, 1935) is in a class by itself, exhaustive in its treatment of Carson and hardly less than a social history of mountain life. J. Cecil Alter has recreated Jim Bridger (Salt Lake City, 1925), Leroy R. Hafen and W. J. Ghent have written up Thomas Fitzpatrick (Denver, 1931), Maurice S. Sullivan has done Jedediah Smith (New York, 1936,) and Alpheus Favour has depicted Old Bill Williams (Chapel Hill, 1936); these are among the more important. "Popular" treatment of Kit Carson (Boston, 1928) and Jim Bridger (New York, 1946) by Stanley Vestal are of little value.

For the general reader as for the student, the source works on the fur trade are really more fascinating than most of the formal histories and biographies. Philip A. Rollins has revised and extended Washington

Irving's classic account of the Astorian enterprise with his *The Discovery of the Oregon Trail* (New York, 1935), which not only prints the journal of Robert Stuart, leader of the returning Astorians, but with it a contemporary French redaction of the now-lost journal of Wilson Price Hunt, covering the outward journey. Although books and articles about the Astorians make up a considerable literature, only the works of Irving and Rollins bear intimately on the history of the Great Salt Lake country.

Information about the southward penetration of the Hudson's Bay Company is to be had principally from the journals of Alexander Ross, Peter Skene Ogden and John Work, published in the *Oregon Historical Quarterly* at various dates between 1909 and 1913. The only biography of Ogden is a monograph by T. C. Elliott in the *Oregon Historical Quarterly,* September 1910. Alexander Ross's *Fur Hunters of the Far West* (London, 1855) is almost the sole record of the North West Company in the Snake country and as far south as the vicinity of Bear River, after the time of the Astorians and prior to the merger with the Hudson's Bay Company in 1821. The first of the two volumes comprising this rare work has been reprinted by the Lakeside Press (Chicago, 1924), edited by M. M. Quaife. Unfortunately the second volume, covering Ross's expedition of 1823-1824, when he encountered Jedediah Smith, has not been reprinted and is generally unavailable. Frederick Merk's *Fur Trade and Empire,* (Cambridge, 1931), printing George Simpson's journal of 1824-1825 and important Hudson's Bay Company letters for the period 1822-1837, has most interesting information about Ogden's expeditions as well as about the character of the international rivalry in the fur trade. Hardly less important are letters written by Ogden in the summer of 1825, containing practically all that can be known of his expedition of 1824-1825 until his journal itself is published; these letters Dr. Merk printed simultaneously in the *Mississippi Valley Historical Review* and the *Oregon Historical Quarterly,* June 1934.

Etienne Provost remains one of the least-known of the master mountain men, and only the slim sketch of his life published in the WPA Utah Writers' Project's *Provo: Pioneer Mormon City* (Portland, 1942) correctly differentiates him as having been an independent trader rather than an Ashley man, and as having come into the mountains northwest from Taos rather than across South Pass. Harrison C. Dale in 1918 published virtually all that was then known of William H. Ashley and Jedediah Smith. The Ashley record has since been amplified somewhat by Donald McKay Frost in his *Notes on General Ashley, the Overland Trail, and South Pass* (Worcester, 1945), while our knowledge about Jedediah Smith has been greatly extended by Charles L. Camp, in his publication of the reminiscences and journals of James Clyman (San Francisco, 1928), by Merk in the works listed above, and by Maurice Sullivan, who preceded his biography of Smith with a more valuable documentary volume, *The Travels of Jedediah Smith* (Santa Ana, 1934). A few of Smith's letters have been published in the Historical Society of Southern California's *Annual Publications,* 1926.

The grandiloquent James P. Beckwourth's *Life and Adventures* (New York, 1856; reprinted with interesting introduction and notes by Bernard DeVoto, New York, 1931), is at once the despair and delight of historians and the general reader, for much in his highly colored pages with respect to the Ashley expeditions is found nowhere else.

Joe Meek's gaudy reminiscences, as set down by Frances Fuller Victor in *River of the West* (Hartford, 1870), take up where Beckwourth leaves off, in the summer of 1829, and are hardly less a delight for the general reader or a problem for the historian, though H. E. Tobie in the *Oregon Historical Quarterly,* 1938-1939, has tried to sort out the probabilities. An important unpublished record is that of Robert ("Doc") Newell, who came to the mountains with Meek in 1829 and left with him in 1840; a copy of his "memoranda" is in the library of the Oregon Historical Society.

Warren Ferris' *Life in the Rocky Mountains* (Denver, 1940) depicts mountain life from 1830 to 1835 from the point of view of the American Fur Company. The Wyeth expeditions of 1832 and 1834 are reflected in numerous records by fur traders, travelers and missionaries. Most important for their bearing on the Great Salt Lake country are Wyeth's own "Correspondence and Journals," printed as *Sources of the History of Oregon* (Eugene, 1899), Osborne Russell's *Journal of a Trapper* (Boise, 1914; reprinted 1921), and Isaac P. Rose's narrative, set down by James B. Marsh as *Four Years in the Rockies* (New Castle, Pa., 1884).

Washington Irving's classic account of the adventures of Captain Bonneville, *The Rocky Mountains* (Philadelphia, 1837), is necessarily supplemented by the Wyeth journals, to which, indeed, Irving had access, and by *Zenas Leonard's Narrative* (Clearfield, Pa., 1839; reprinted 1904 and 1934), the latter being the key source on Joe Walker's expedition to California. George Nidever's *Life and Adventures* (Berkeley, 1937) also bears interestingly on this expedition.

The closing years of the fur trade are depicted by the Oregon missionaries in particular. The extraordinarily helpful bibliography of trans-plains travel compiled by Henry R. Wagner and Charles L. Camp, *The Plains and the Rockies* (San Francisco, 1937) lists many of these missionary records. Others have been published in the *Transactions* of the Oregon Pioneer Association, the *Oregon Historical Quarterly,* the *Pacific North-*

west Quarterly and the *Whitman College Quarterly*. The missionary records are interestingly supplemented by F. A. Wislizenus' *A Journey to the Rocky Mountains in the Year 1839,* originally published in German (St. Louis, 1840) but reprinted in translation (St. Louis, 1912) and by E. Willard Smith's journal of 1839-1840, in the *Oregon Historical Quarterly,* September 1913.

No satisfactory account exists of the operations of the Robidou brothers in eastern Utah, western Colorado and northern New Mexico. Oral Messmore Robidoux' *Memorial to the Robidoux Brothers* (Kansas City, 1924), is undependable, and Joseph J. Hill's slight sketch of Antoine Robidou in *Colorado Magazine,* January 1930, is not very largely helpful.

A comprehensive treatment of the Spanish Trail is a serious want, and it is to be hoped that works in progress by Charles Kelly and Leroy R. Hafen will clear up many matters that are now obscure. My own text summarizes much of what is known about the subject and makes an original contribution in its interpretation of the baffling Armijo "Itinerary," the scant record of which is translated by Archer B. Hulbert in his *Southwest on the Turquoise Trail* (Denver, 1933). Eleanor Lawrence, in the *California Historical Quarterly,* December 1931, has pieced together the scanty records relating to the caravan trade, and there are fragments of information in Charles L. Camp's "Chronicles of George C. Yount," *California Historical Quarterly,* April 1923, and in Joseph J. Hill's "Ewing Young in the Fur Trade of the Far Southwest 1822-34," *Oregon Historical Quarterly,* December 1922. Frémont is the main authority for the location of the trail in its later phase, but he traveled over only its western reaches.

Frémont's report (Washington, 1845), of course, is the basic account of his own explorations. I have consulted in The National Archives the manuscript original of his report of his 1842 expedition and have drawn upon it for some small details. Theodore Talbot's engaging journal (Portland, 1931) adds much of interest, and there are some absorbing items in the letters of Marcus Whitman in Archer B. Hulbert's *Marcus Whitman, Crusader* (Part 2, Denver, 1938). For the trip to and from Great Salt Lake, *Kit Carson's Autobiography* (Chicago, 1935) supplies important details, as for the expedition of 1845. By the time Frémont came to write his *Memoirs* (Chicago, 1887) he had lost his journals and forgotten most details of the 1845 expedition, so his account of it is eked out from his *Geographical Memoir Upon Upper California* (Washington, 1848) and from DeWitt Peters' biography of Carson (New York, 1858), with a few additional details dredged up from memory. Alpheus Favour has determined the date Old Bill Williams left Frémont on this expedition, and an interpretation of my text hinges upon that date.

Allan Nevins' *Frémont: Pathmarker of the West* (New York, 1939) is much the best of the Frémont biographies, but in interpretation of the explorations Nevins leans almost entirely on Dellenbaugh's *Frémont and '49*, which indeed is an education in miniature. I have stated some of the Frémont routes in the Great Salt Lake country more closely than has hitherto been attempted.

For overland immigration generally W. J. Ghent's *The Road to Oregon* (New York, 1929) is a superior treatment, but Bernard DeVoto's magnificent *The Year of Decision: 1846* (Boston, 1943), however limited in time, is almost *sui generis*. The Bartleson party of 1841 has left a rather extensive literature, especially including John Bidwell's journal (Weston[?] 1842[?]; reprinted San Francisco, 1937) and his reminiscences, published in *Century Magazine,* 1891, and several times reprinted as *Echoes of the Past*. The *Narrative of Nicholas "Cheyenne" Dawson* (San Francisco, 1933) is informative, and additional details are provided by Joseph Williams' *Narrative of a Tour from the State of Indiana to the Oregon Territory in the Year 1841-2* (Cincinnati, 1843; reprinted New York, 1921) and by P. J. De Smet's *Letters and Sketches* (Philadelphia, 1843), though Williams and De Smet parted from the California-bound immigrants at Soda Springs. All these documents, in conjunction, show that, contrary to popular belief in Utah, Father De Smet was never nearer the Great Salt Lake Valley than Soda Springs.

Charles Kelly's fascinating *Salt Desert Trails* (Salt Lake City, 1930) works out the routes of these immigrants and those of 1846 around and across the Salt Desert. I have myself ventured to state routes with some precision, occasionally at variance with Mr. Kelly. In bringing the 1841 immigrants to the Humboldt Valley by way of Secret Pass, I come to agreement with F. N. Fletcher in his *Early Nevada* (Reno, 1929) and differ with most other authorities.

Miles Goodyear (Salt Lake City, 1937) by Charles Kelly and Maurice L. Howe is the basic account of Utah's first white settler. However, I have extended the record of Goodyear's life in a number of respects, drawing information from the manuscript diaries of Matthew F. Field in the Missouri Historical Society, generously placed at my disposal by Mrs. Brenda R. Gieseker, librarian; from Field's correspondence in the New Orleans *Picayune,* 1843-1844; from the Joseph Williams *Narrative;* from a hitherto unguessed story in the *Platte Argus,* September 26, 1845, and from a letter by James Frazier Reed in the *Sangamo Journal,* November 5, 1846. I have interpreted John Minto's reminiscences in the *Oregon Historical Quarterly,* June 1901, to refer certainly to Goodyear at Fort Bridger in the late summer of 1844, though in after years Minto was disposed to think (an untenable idea) that it must have been Kit Carson he saw there.

The experiences of the immigrants of 1846 have produced a considerable literature. Clyman's journal is almost the sole source on the eastbound parties, but the experiences of the parties guided by Hastings and the Donner-Reed party have resulted in a literature of considerable proportions, most of it cited in the edition of C. F. McGlashan's *History of the Donner Party* edited by George H. and Bliss McGlashan Hinkle (Stanford University, 1940). The best single book on the Donner Party is George R. Stewart's *Ordeal by Hunger* (New York, 1936), but the tragedy is described in special perspective by Bernard DeVoto in *The Year of Decision: 1846*. A different interpretation of the interrelationships of the several immigrant parties which broke trails across Utah that summer and fall is required after thoughtful study of T. H. Jefferson's *Map of the Emigrant Road from Independence Mo. to St. Francisco California* (New York, 1849; reprinted San Francisco, 1945). My text is the first to wrestle with some of the new problems presented. John R. McBride's "Pioneer Days in the Mountains," *Tullidge's Quarterly Magazine,* July 1884, is of interest as decribing a visit to Salt Lake Valley by a party of Oregon immigrants earlier in the summer of 1846.

Fawn M. Brodie's brilliant biography of Joseph Smith, *No Man Knows My History* (New York, 1945), is the only thing like an adequate history of the early Mormon Church, though, as it came to adverse conclusions about the Mormon prophet, it was not well received in Utah. Within the Mormon Church itself the outstanding scholar has been Brigham H. Roberts, with his 6-volume *Comprehensive History of the Church of Jesus Christ of Latter-day Saints* (Salt Lake City, 1930) and the 7-volume *Documentary History of the Church* (Salt Lake City, 1902-32) which he edited. The latter relates almost entirely to the period prior to the Mormon migration to Utah.

A number of unsatisfactory state histories exist, including those of H. H. Bancroft (San Francisco, 1889), Orson F. Whitney (Salt Lake City, 4 vols., 1893-1897) and Andrew Love Neff (Salt Lake City, 1940). Two works of distinction are Robert J. Dwyer's *The Gentile Comes to Utah* (Washington, 1941) an objective study of religious and social conflict from 1862-1890, and Nels Anderson's *Desert Saints* (Chicago, 1942), an essentially sociological history of Utah's frontier phase. A proper biography of Brigham Young does not exist yet, M. R. Werner's rather casual study (New York, 1925) being the best available. Fred B. Rogers' *Soldiers of the Overland* (San Francisco, 1938) is the principal authority for Connor's life, but much about him and the times in which he figured is recoverable from the several works of Edward W. Tullidge, including his *History of Salt Lake City* (Salt Lake City, 1886), *Tullidges Histories* [of Northern Utah and Southern Idaho] (Salt Lake City, 1889), *Tullidge's Quarterly Magazine* (3 vols., 1880-84) and *Western Galaxy* (monthly, March-June 1888).

Descriptive works on the state and its people include the comprehensive *Utah: A Guide to the State* (New York, 1941) by the WPA Utah Writers' Project, Wallace Stegner's superb *Mormon Country* (New York, 1942), Maurine Whipple's *This Is the Place: Utah* (New York, 1945) and George Wharton James's *Utah, the Land of Blossoming Valleys* (Boston, 1922). A well-rounded classified bibliography in *Utah: A Guide to the State* enables me to restrict these annotations to works more intimately connected with the history of Great Salt Lake itself. However, two works of high interest and value should be noted, Chauncy Dennison Harris' *Salt Lake City: A Regional Capital* (Chicago, 1940) and Frank Herman Jonas' "Utah: Sagebrush Democracy," in Thomas C. Donnelly's *Rocky Mountain Politics* (Albuquerque, 1940).

Howard Stansbury's *Exploration and Survey of the Valley of the Great Salt Lake of Utah* (Washington, 1852) is the famous Report from which most of our knowledge of the Stansbury Survey has come, supplemented slightly by J. W. Gunnison's *The Mormons* (Philadelphia, 1852), but I have more frequently preferred to quote from the original journals I am preparing for publication.

The early history of Antelope Island is principally recoverable from the reminiscences of Solomon F. Kimball, published first in *Improvement Era*, 1907, and reprinted in his *Thrilling Experiences* (Salt Lake City, 1909).

The only previous account of the Wenners on Frémont Island has been that by Charles Kelly, "They Built an Island Home in the Desert," *Desert Magazine*, February 1944. Like my own, this is based primarily on the memoirs of Mrs. Wenner. I have extended this account somewhat from sources indicated in my text. Kelly has also published an article in *Desert Magazine*, February 1942, on the "Carson cross" on Frémont Island, and I am indebted to him for photographs of it.

Alfred Lambourne wrote a number of articles and books about the lake. As early as 1888 he projected the idea of an article to be called "Shores of an Inland Sea." He published some prose pictures, in association with reproductions of some of his sketches and paintings, in *Western Galaxy*, March 1888. Recast and amplified, this material was published by the Union Pacific Railroad in 1890 as *A Glimpse of Great Salt Lake*. This pamphlet went through a number of editions, and the text was apparently printed also in a few copies as a Christmas gift book in 1895. In 1902, after his experience on the island, he published *Pictures of an Inland Sea,* which united some of the old material with the fresh experiences, and in 1909 his ideas about Great Salt Lake crystallized in a final form as *Our Inland Sea.* Although he wrote with the eye of a poet, he had a realistic point of view, and was displeased by indiscriminate praise of the lake that ignored its desolateness, even its ugliness, to him an essential part of its character.

Ninetta Eames's (Payne's) article, "Cruising Among the Salt Lake Islands," *Outing,* March 1897, belongs to the small literature of appreciation. Other accounts of cruises on the lake include Leo A. Borah's "Utah, Carved by Wind and Waters,"*National Geographic Magazine,* May 1936; Donald Edward Jenkins, "On the Great Salt Lake," *Improvement Era,* January 1932; and Thomas J. Holland's "Cruising on Great Salt Lake," *Improvement Era,* August 1946. Dr. Thomas C. Adams, commodore of the Great Salt Lake Yacht Club, has prepared information for the benefit of actual or intending boatmen on Great Salt Lake, and this experienced technical advice is obtainable in mimeographed form from his offices in the Utah Oil Building, Salt Lake City.

Automobile racing on the Bonneville Salt Flats has been described by George E. T. Eyston and W. F. Bradley in *Speed on Salt* (New York, 1936) and by Ab Jenkins and Wendell J. Ashton in *The Salt of the Earth* (Salt Lake City, 1939). Charles Kelly's *Salt Desert Trails* describes troubles of railroad and highway builders on the salt desert in the years before the salt flats were formally "discovered."

Resorts on the lake, particularly those dead and gone, must be tracked down through an extraordinary succession of booster pamphlets relating to Salt Lake City and vicinity. The more significant among these, and the sources of information for most of the others, are Ovando James Hollister's *The Resources and Attractions of the Territory of Utah* (Omaha, 1879), which describes the early facilities at the south shore of the lake, and Marcus E. Jones's *Resources and Attractions of Salt Lake City* (Salt Lake City, 1889), which describes in careful detail both Lake Park and Garfield Beach. The early resorts also are described in detail in *A Complete and Comprehensive Description of the Agricultural, Stock Raising and Mineral Resources of Utah* (St. Louis, 1893), written by S. A. Kenner and published by the Union Pacific Railroad. Dr. Talmage's book also has material on this subject.

My account of the colonial birds on Great Salt Lake is based primarily on an exhaustive history William H. Behle has in preparation; until that is published, his shorter "A History of the Bird Colonies of Great

Salt Lake," in *The Condor,* January-February 1935, will be the best available authority. A bibliography appears in that work, but does not include an interesting article by Charles G. Plummer, "Pelican Days and Pelican Ways" in *Country Life,* April 1920, describing his 26-day stay on Hat Island in 1917. Kimball Young's "Story of the Rise of a Social Taboo" *Scientific Monthly,* May 1928, is a sociologist's point of view on the famous sea gull episode. Those with a narrower biological interest in the lake should consult the bibliography by Woolley and Marsell cited earlier; however, I should like to remark on A. M. Woodbury's "Animal Relationships of Great Salt Lake," *Ecology,* January 1936, as of special interest.

Saltmaking from the lake brines has been described by Dr. Talmage, and more recently by T. R. Brighton in the *Journal of Chemical Education,* March 1932.

Few works of fiction have used the lake as a locale. Orvilla S. Belisle's *The Prophets, or, Mormanism Unveiled* (Philadelphia, 1855) an ancestral form of the Mormon novel, has an incredible scene on an incredible island of an incredible lake. Villainy is foiled and fair beauty escapes; the lake, too, fortunately, has escaped a second such experience. At the other extreme is Wallace Stegner's *The Big Rock Candy Mountain* (New York, 1943), as fine a novel as has been written about the West, which has an effective scene at the Saltair of the early 1920's.

On the shelf with these two novels must be put two juvenile novels of adventure, *Trust a Boy!* (New York, 1923) and *The Measure of a Boy* (New York, 1925) by Walter H. Nichols. Though undistinguished as literature, these stories of adventure on Great Salt Lake and in and around the Salt Lake City of the eighties have an undeniable charm, and exhibit a most interesting familiarity with the lake.

INDEX

423

PREHISTORIC RELIGION

By the same Author

PREHISTORIC RELIGION

A Study in Prehistoric Archaeology

by

E. O. JAMES

D.Litt., Ph.D., F.S.A.

*Professor Emeritus of the History of Religion in the
University of London. Fellow of University College
and Fellow of King's College*

BARNES & NOBLE, INC.   ·   New York

Publishers   ·   *Booksellers*   ·   *Since 1873*

*Published in the United States
in 1962
by Barnes & Noble, Inc.
105 Fifth Avenue, New York 3*

Second Printing, 1963

Printed in the United States of America

CONTENTS

5

ILLUSTRATIONS

SOURCES FOR ILLUSTRATIONS

G. H. Luquet: *The Art and Religion of Fossil Man*, 1930 (1, 8, 9, 12); T. E. Peer: *Harmsworth's Universal History*, vol. v (2); Daryll Forde: *American Anthropologist*, N. S. vol. 32, No. 1, 1930 (3, 4, 5); W. J. Hemp: *Archaeologia*, vol. xxx, 1930 (6); T. G. E. Powell: *Proceedings of the Prehistoric Society*, N. S. vol. IV, Pt. 2 (7); G. R. Levy: *The Gate of Horn*, 1948 (10); V. Gordon Childe: *The Dawn of European Civilization*, 5th ed., 1950 (11); Max Raphael: *Prehistoric Cave Paintings*, 1945 (13); Ashmolean Museum, Oxford (14).

PREFACE

In the considerable literature on prehistoric archaeology that has accumulated in recent years, covering almost every aspect of the subject, so far as I am aware there has been no attempt in this country to bring together and interpret in a single volume the available material relating specifically to religious phenomena. There have been and are, of course, many excellent and quite invaluable regional studies which describe and discuss much of the data in particular areas and cultures—indeed but for them the present volume could not have been produced. There are also a number of works on various aspects of prehistory in general, directly or indirectly bearing on evidence analysed and reviewed in this book to which reference frequently has been made in its compilation, as will be seen from the footnotes and bibliographies. Nevertheless, for some time, and especially when the subject was discussed at a conference of the Prehistoric Society at the London University Institute of Archaeology in 1953, and at the meeting of the British Association at Bristol in 1955, it has seemed that an investigation of the field as an organized whole should be undertaken in the light of the evidence now at hand.

In opening such an inquiry an initial problem was to decide how the term "prehistoric" should be interpreted, and what should be the *terminus ad quem*. To have drawn the line at the invention of the art of writing would have excluded all consideration of the texts, documents, and inscriptions written or carved on prehistoric or protohistoric tombs, temples, stelae or tablets which, particularly for this investigation, constitute an all-important source of information, not only for contemporary belief and practice but also for their more remote background. The main purpose, however, of a study of Prehistoric Religion must be an examination of the discipline in its earliest manifestations prior to the recording of events in written documents in sufficient quantity to make possible a precise determination of their occurrence, chronology and significance through the

13

ordinary channels of historical research. Therefore, it has been upon the Palaeolithic and Neolithic periods that attention has been primarily concentrated, where no written records obtain.

The term "Neolithic" however, is now exceedingly diffi-cult to define and determine as the transition from food-gathering to food-production certainly was not a uniform and orderly sequence of events, as was formerly supposed, even though it may not have been quite so revolutionary as is now sometimes asserted. Thus, as the use of metals was firmly established in the Near East at least 2,000 years before it was introduced into Britain and other outlying regions far removed from the centre of prehistoric civilization, it is impos-sible to draw a hard and fast line in any chronological sense between the Neolithic and the Bronze Age in the study of a specific aspect of prehistory which covers the whole field. Therefore, I have not hesitated to include the developments in the second millennium B.C. in the background of the higher religious systems of the Fertile Crescent and Western Asia, of India and of pre-Homeric Greece, calculated to throw light on their prehistoric antecedents, though in some instances the faiths may have passed into the realms of recorded history.

At the other end of the scale a quantity of material exists concerning the observable beliefs and practices still, or until very recently, current in primitive societies on the fringes of civilization, or in its background, all over the world, many of which appear to have persisted little changed throughout the ages. Some of them, in fact, go back apparently to a very remote period in the prehistory of mankind. In employing these sources of information to throw light on ancient institu-tions, customs and traditions extreme caution is needed, fore-warned by the uncritical theoretical reconstructions of "origins" and "developments" of an earlier generation of social anthropo-logists. Then general conclusions were drawn from disparate phenomena, often haphazardly assembled and brought together on the principle of superficial resemblance, regardless of their diversities, comparability and provenance.

But notwithstanding these fruitless attempts to produce an

orderly stratified sequence of cultural and "spiritual" ascent from savagery to civilization, successive in time and progressive in development, reasonably reliable first-hand accounts, and especially intensive studies of existing primitive societies by properly trained observers for the purpose of ascertaining the part played by beliefs and institutions in a given social structure (which happily now are becoming increasingly available), constitute valuable data for the interpretation of the archaeo-logical data. Such studies are able to throw light on analogous activities and organizations, beliefs and practices, and their significance within living religious systems under conditions not very different from those which prevailed in prehistoric times. This is most apparent in the case of the anthropological evidence derived from existing peoples, like, for example, the Nilotic tribes in East Africa representing the remnants of the substratum out of which the higher civilization of the Nile valley arose, and who have retained in their material and spiritual culture and linguistic affinities definite links with the prehistoric Egyptians.

It cannot be denied, then, that the past is contained in the present, even though the earlier theory of "survivals" has had to be abandoned in the form in which it was formerly held. Moreover, while it may be impossible to determine what lies behind the existing culture in some primitive societies devoid of any ascertainable history, this certainly does not apply in the case of the ancient civilizations out of which the higher religions emerged with their roots deeply laid in a prehistoric past now in process of recovery by the spade of the archaeologist. Herein lies the justification for a study along the lines adopted in this volume, prehistoric religion having been one of my principal preoccupations since, after completing my anthropological training at Oxford, I first became acquainted with ancient Near Eastern religions forty years ago as a post-graduate student working under the supervision of Sir Flinders Petrie. In the intervening period much of the data here reviewed and discussed have been collected or examined at first hand in decorated caves and rock-shelters, tumuli and other prehistoric sites and excavations (as well as in many museums), especially in the Dordogne, Ariège and the Pyrenees; in Brittany, Ireland, Wessex and the adjacent region; in Spain, the Aegean and the Eastern Mediterranean. As the book has been written mainly in the excellent library of the Ashmolean Museum, it has been possible to consult the original sources with comparative ease, aided by its efficient staff, who have been always so willing and anxious to be helpful. While in preparing the text a general knowledge of prehistoric archaeology has been assumed, I have endeavoured to make the inquiry intelligible to as wide a range of readers as possible, without, I hope, diminishing whatever value it may have for professional archaeologists.

Oxford   E. O. JAMES

CHAPTER I

Palaeolithic Burial Ritual

SINCE of all the mysterious, disintegrating and critical situations with which man has been confronted throughout the ages death appears to have been the most disturbing and devastating, it is hardly surprising that the earliest traces of religious belief and practice should centre in the cult of the dead. Therefore, an examination of mortuary ritual constitutes a convenient and appropriate starting-point for an investigation of the archaeological evidence relating to prehistoric religion, and takes us back at once to a remote period long before the arrival of *Homo sapiens* on the human scene, or even of his predecessor, *Homo neanderthalensis*.

THE CULT OF SKULLS

Choukoutien

In the caves at Dragon-bone Hill near the village of Choukoutien in China, about 37 miles south-west of Peking, fossil hominid teeth were found in Middle or Lower Pleistocene strata in 1922, but it was not until 1927, on the strength of a very youthful molar unearthed by a Swedish excavator, Dr Bohlin, that Professor Davidson Black announced the discovery of a new genus of very Early Man, *Sinanthropus pekinensis*. This event, in addition to the light it has thrown on human origins, for the time being at any rate may be regarded as affording the earliest evidence of the ritual treatment of the dead, since the remains of Peking Man in the Choukoutien deposits are believed to be the debris of cannibal feasts. Unfortunately, the exact age of the strata is as difficult to determine as is the precise correlation of the phases of the Pleistocene in China with the European glaciations and interglacials. The layers being 50 feet in depth, they extend over a very long period, but the fauna was the same throughout, and as the bison, mammoth and woolly rhinoceros have not been detected it would seem to be older than the Upper Pleistocene (Loess) and younger than the Late Pliocene.[1] On Zeuner's calculation *Sinanthropus* is dated "in the neighbourhood of 500,000 years". The crude pebble and flake implements that were scattered through the caves had affinities with their Clactonian counterparts in Europe and the Soan artifacts of North-west India. If the industry that takes its name from the East-Anglian type station was an offshoot of the Choukoutien-Soan prototype, as has been suggested, it may have flourished in its original form in China in the Middle Pleistocene contemporary with the Javanese deposits.

So far as the skeletal remains are concerned, with which we are here primarily concerned, since the discovery of the molar in 1927, fragments of human skulls of at least fourteen individuals of varying ages have come to light with teeth and pieces of jaws belonging to more than forty persons, together with a few long bones. These in their general features conform to those of the pithecanthropoid type of hominid, familiar in the notorious *Pithecanthropus erectus*, the so-called ape-man of Java, and the subsequent Javanese examples of the species.[3] They are, therefore, proto-Neanderthaloid just as the implements foreshadow the Mousterian flint tradition. The bodies had been decapitated after death, buried until they had decomposed, and the heads were then carefully preserved for ritual purposes, doubtless, as in Borneo today, because in them it was supposed that soul-substance resided having the properties of a vitalizing agent.[4] As the skulls show signs of injuries they may have been those of victims who had been killed and their crania broken open in order to extract the brain for sacramental consumption. If this were so, probably they represent the remains of cannibal feasts, organized cannibalism in that case having been an established feature of the cult of the dead in the Mid-Pleistocene in North China in which the cutting off and preservation of the head, skull or scalp was a prominent feature during or after the sacred meal, either to extract its soul-substance or as a trophy.

Monte Circeo

That this practice was widely and persistently adopted in prehistoric times, doubtless for a variety of reasons, is clear from the numerous skulls and headless bodies that have been found in Palaeolithic, Mesolithic and Neolithic sites.[5] An interesting and significant example is that of a Neanderthal skull discovered in 1939 in the grotto at Monte Circeo on the Tyrrhenian coast of the Pomptine Fields within a circle of stones in a small inner chamber. Bones of deer, horse, hyena, elephant and lion were on the floor and heaped up round the walls in piles, and on the floor beneath the cranium were two fractured metacarpals of an ox and of a deer. The skull showed signs of having received a fatal blow on the right side of the temple, and at its base the foramen magnum connecting the brain with the spinal cord had been cut away after death, probably to extract the brain.

It would seem, therefore, that here we have the trophy of a Neanderthal man who in the last glaciation, after having been murdered or killed by a serious accident perhaps 70,000 to 100,000 years ago, was deposited ceremonially in a cave used for ritual purposes as a sacred ossuary. It would appear further that the brain had been extracted and eaten to imbibe its magico-religious qualities very much as in the Ngandoeng terraces of the Solo river in Eastern Java (which may correspond in time to the Riss-Würm Interglacial in Europe) skulls appear to have been hacked open, possibly at a cannibal feast, and subsequently used as bowls.[6] Thus, in an Upper Palaeolithic cave at Placard, Charente, drinking cups made from the upper part of the vault of human skulls occurred in the Magdalenian and Solutrean layers.[7] At Krapina near Zagreb in Croatia in a Mousterian deposit on a terrace which also belongs to the Riss-Würm Interglacial, a quantity of human and animal bones occurred in a fragmentary condition, some having been split open to obtain their marrow and charred, suggesting the remains of a cannibal feast. One of the skulls contained artificial cuts, the result doubtless of a deed of violence.[8]

Ofnet

The most convincing evidence, however, comes from two deposits near Nördlingen in Bavaria, where in a spur of the Jura known as Ofnet, and assigned to the Mesolithic period after the last glaciation, a nest of twenty-seven human skulls was found in a group embedded in red ochre, the skulls looking westwards. A few yards away was a second identical group of six skulls. In some of them the cervical vertebrae were still attached, and from their condition the heads must have been severed from the body after death with flint knives, and ceremonially preserved when they had been dried. As those in the centre were more tightly packed together and crushed, it seems that they had been added one by one from time to time. Since some of them were brachycephalic and others dolicho-cephalic they must have belonged to two distinct races, the one broad-headed and the other long-headed, probably survivors of the so-called "Brünn race" from the Upper Palaeolithic. Twenty were those of children ornamented with snail shells, nine were of women with necklaces of deer teeth, and four only were of adult males.[9] To explain this high proportion of women and children it has been suggested that they were the victims of an attack in which most of the men escaped, leaving the women behind to be decapitated. This hardly accounts for the ornamentation of the skulls with shells, the burial in red ochre, and the provision of all but one of the men with their implements, and signs that fires had been lighted near them. From the equipment it would seem more likely that some particular significance was attached to the skulls, whether the victims had been killed *en bloc* or singly, and so they were treated as trophies comparable to those collected in head-hunting expeditions in Borneo and elsewhere in modern times.

In the grotte de Trou-Violet at Montardit a fragment of a skull from which the flesh had been peeled off, together with a few small bones and a number of pebbles arranged in the form of a human body, may have been in the nature of a cenotaph commemorating some notable person, the head being the object of veneration.[10] In the pre-pottery levels at Jericho seven skulls in varying states of preservation have been recently discovered with features moulded in plaster and shells, including in one case cowries and in the others flat shells in two leaves, separated by vertical slits to represent the pupils of the eyes.[11] Here, again, some form of trophy, or object of worship possessed of great potency, is suggested. For the same reason animal heads were interred, it would seem, as, for example, those of bears in two Mousterian caves at Drachenloch in Switzerland, collected into groups and orientated in stone cists covered with a rock slab. At Petershöhle near Nuremberg bear skulls were erected in niches along the walls of a cave of the same period, and on a stone platform, while in Austria at Drachenhöhle in Styria fifty-four bear femurs were orientated in another Mousterian site.[12] Doubtless it was the great strength of the bear that caused it to become a cult object at a very early period, and as this was likely to be concentrated in the head it would be the skull that would be preserved and venerated.

CEREMONIAL INTERMENT IN THE MIDDLE PALAEO-LITHIC

Le Moustier

It was not, however, only the cranium that was ceremonially treated after death in Palaeolithic times. Thus, at Le Moustier, the site that has given its name to the characteristic industry of the last group of flake tool-makers in the middle of the Palaeolithic, situated near Peyzac on the right bank of the Vézère in the Dordogne, the skeleton of a Neanderthal youth was discovered in 1908 under fragments of animal bones. It had been placed with the back upwards, the forearm under the head, which rested on a pillow of flint flakes. Near the left arm were a fine Acheulean hand-axe and a scraper. In the grave were the bones of the wild ox, charred and split, suggesting the remains of a funeral feast.[13]

La Chapelle-aux-Saints

The similar interment in a small low-roofed cave near the village of La Chapelle-aux-Saints in the department of

Corrèze lay in a pit dug in the floor surrounded with flints which included excellent scrapers and quartzite and crystal flakes of various colours. Near the hand was the foot of an ox, and behind it part of the vertebral column of a reindeer. Above the body, which had been buried in the contracted position, the earth contained broken bones of the woolly rhinoceros, bison, horse and ibex, together with Mousterian implements. Near the skeleton was the leg of a bison buried apparently while the flesh was still on it.[14] Some of the flints were broken near the point, probably in the process of splitting the long bones of the animals to extract the marrow[15] consumed at the funerary feasts held in the cave. Judging from the quantity and variety of the bones, these must have been considerable and could hardly have been confined to the time of the interment.

La Ferrassie

In a cave at La Ferrassie near Les Eyzies in the Dordogne the remains of a man and a woman occurred, the head and shoulders, the right leg and the left forearm of the man having been protected with slabs of stone and covered with bone flakes. In the trenches near by lay the remains of two children, while those of a baby were found under a tiny mound. A fourth child was buried in a grave in the floor and covered by a stone with artificial cup-markings on it. All the skeletons, which may represent members of one family, were orientated east to west, and associated with Mousterian implements. In front of the graves of the children a ditch containing bones and ashes (perhaps those of an ox) may have been a funerary deposit.[16]

The care bestowed on the disposal of these bodies leaves little room for doubt that a cult of the dead was definitely established in the Middle Palaeolithic, though, of course, it was only in districts like the Dordogne where caves and rock-shelters were readily available that intentional interments have survived the ravages of time, weather and wild beasts. At this stage it may not have gone further than a belief in human survival under conditions in which food and implements would be required

eyond the grave in a life like that lived before death, for none
ther could be conceived. The attitude towards the dead which
ound expression in the funerary ritual may have been a com-
ination of respect, fear, veneration and concern for their
vell-being. All of these, however, presuppose a prolongation
f existence after the dissolution of the body.

HE UPPER PALAEOLITHIC

This becomes clearer in the Upper Palaeolithic with the
rrival in Western Europe of a variety of forms of *Homo sapiens*
f which the Crô-Magnon type, named after the rock-shelter
ear Les Eyzies in the Dordogne where it was first detected in
868, is the most characteristic in the later stages of the last
laciation. Nevertheless, as the burials reveal, in addition to
ne tall, dolichocephalic, muscular, well-proportioned Crô-
Magnons there was a shorter rather less advanced type with a
omewhat higher head and broader nose, exemplified in a
keleton at Combe Capelle, Dordogne, and in Moravia at
rno (Brünn) and Předmost, where in a collective burial in
common grave containing fourteen complete skeletons and
ix fragments, a third variant occurred with heavy brow-ridges,
igh-vaulted skull and more prognathous jaws. Finally, in the
owest level of the first of the series of caves at Grimaldi on the
talian side of the frontier between Mentone and Ventimiglia
–that known as the *Grottes des Enfants*—an old woman and
youth were found in 1901 who differed considerably in their
hysical features from the rest of Upper Palaeolithic Man.

he Grimaldi Burials

The boy was about sixteen years of age and lay on his right side
vith the legs doubled back under the thighs so that the heels
lmost touched the pelvis. The woman was tightly flexed with
er knees as high as her shoulders, and her feet touching her
elvis. She was laid to the left of the youth. Round his head
vere four rows of pierced shells, and his skeleton was stained
ed with peroxide of iron. On the arms of the woman
vere shell bracelets. Between the heads lay two pebbles of

serpentine, another pebble against the jaw of the woman
The trench had been dug in a Mousterian stratum immediately below the first Upper Palaeolithic level to which the
grave belonged. The heads were protected by a flat stone
supported by two others, and the space between them was
filled with peroxide of iron.[17] The skulls are high and very
dolichocephalic; the nose is flatter and broader than in the
Crô-Magnons, the jaws are prognathous, and the proportions
of the limb bones and the dentition have suggested negroic
affinities. About this, however, expert opinion is divided, and
the Grimaldi remains may be merely a variant of the Combe
Capelle and Předmost types, or possibly of the Crô-Magnon
variety of Upper Palaeolithic Man. Thus, a somewhat similar
skeleton was found in 1927 at La Genière in Ain, and Keith
maintained that the relatively greater length of the forearm and
shin as compared with the upper arm and thigh respectively
was a recurrent feature in Crô-Magnon skeletons.[18]

In the stratum above this burial were the remains of a very
tall man of normal Crô-Magnon type in the extended position
with his forearms drawn up, bringing the hands to the level of
the neck. The head had a similar crown of shells to that on the
youth below, and about its thorax was a quantity of shells
which apparently had been fixed to a sort of apron made
perhaps of hides. Over the body stones had been placed and
the head rested on a block of sandstone reddened with ochre.
On the hearth on which it was laid were rough limestone and
quartzite tools. Above this came the two young children clad
in a shroud composed of nearly a thousand Nassa perforated
shells. From this interment the cave has been named. Nearer
to the surface were the mutilated remains of a woman which
appear to have been re-buried and surrounded with trochus
shells.[19]

The adjoining Grotte du Cavillon, the fourth in the series,
contained 7,868 marine shells (*Nassa neritea*) of which 875
were pierced. Of these over 200 were about the head of a
Crô-Magnon man in the contracted position. The skeleton
was covered with powdered haematite so that it was coloured

Fig. 1. Collar on a skeleton from Barma Grande, Mentone

carlet. On the cranium was a fillet of seashells, and twenty-two perforated canine teeth of deer were near the frontal bones. A bone point made from the radius of a deer lay across the forehead, and two flink flakes against the occiput.[20]

At Barma Grande, the fifth cave, the bodies of a tall man, a young woman and a boy occurred in a grave lined with red ochre. The male skeleton, which lay on its back with the head resting on the thighs, was adorned with Nassa shells, the canine teeth of deer and a fish's vertebrae, all perforated, together with ivory pendants, a necklace and two large perforated cowries (*Cypraea millepunctata*), originally apparently a garter.[21] The female was similarly ornamented and in her left hand she held a flint knife, 26 centimetres in length. Beside her, also lying on his left side, was the boy, whose head was covered with fish vertebrae and Nassas divided into groups by deer teeth (Fig. 1). Above these remains, towards the back of the cave, were two skeletons in the same extended position with an array of Nassa shells, deer teeth and pendants of ivory disposed about the bodies in similar fashion. All these lay in a trench filled with red ochre and were covered with it. Finally, in the sixth cave, Baousso da Torre, a shell collar, a fillet and a girdle with shell pendants recurred in a disturbed burial. Two other skeletons were found in this cave, one of which had been sprinkled with ochre.

Paviland and other Upper Palaeolithic Sepultures

The custom of burying the dead in a deposit of ochreous earths was widespread in the Upper Palaeolithic. Thus, as far from the Italian riviera as the Gower coast of South Wales a skeleton of this period, long known as the "Red Lady of Paviland" was discovered by Dean Buckland in 1822 buried in red iro ore which had coloured the associated objects. These include a number of Pleistocene animals such as mammoth, wooll rhinoceros, reindeer, bison, hyena, horse and cave bear, togethe with a quantity of Aurignacian implements and other object in bone and ivory, and pendants in the form of beans. By th side of the body were small shells (*Neritea littoralis*) and th head and tusks of a mammoth. Only the limb bones of the le side of the skeleton have survived and these, now preserved i the University Museum, Oxford, are thought to be those of tall Crô-Magnon male.[22]

Between Mentone and Paviland a number of similar burial have been found in Upper Palaeolithic deposits. Thus, a Crô-Magnon among the bones of the skeleton which had bee stained red by pieces of haematite were nearly 300 shells, mainl of *Littorina littorea*, and perforated pendants. At Brno (Brünn immediately above the skeleton were a mammoth tusk and shoulder-blade, and around it were more than 600 conical tubes of a fossil shell (*Dentalium badense*), used apparently as breastplate, an ivory male figurine without legs, perforated disks in bone, quartzite and stone, and three cut from a mammoth tooth.[23] The skeleton was coated with an iron oxide ochreous powder, and the traces of this red colouring matter occurred on the statuette.

The remains of the tightly flexed body at Raymonden, Chancelade, near Périgueux in the Dordogne, was covered with a layer of peroxide of iron and associated with Magda-lenian implements. Although attempts have been made to interpret the anatomical features of the skull as Eskimoid, the skeleton is probably that of a dwarf variety of Crô-Magnon Man considerably later than the Grimaldi type.[24] Thus, three skeletons excavated in the valley of the Roc in Charente in 1923 bear some resemblance to the Chancelade remains. It is clear from other Magdalenian interments, such as those at Obercassel near Bonn and at Laugerie-Basse near Les Eyzies, at Grotte des Hoteaux near Rousillan, Ain, and at Sordes in e Landes, that the Magdalenians were not homogeneous. As a ethnological group they emerged as the consummation of e Upper Palaeolithic with no less than six phases in their dustry, establishing themselves mainly in France (with the ve of La Madeleine, Dordogne, as the type station), Spain, aly, Moravia and Poland, with local variations in England tected at Cresswell Crags in Derbyshire, Cheddar in the lendips and Kent's Cavern in Devon; while in the Rhine illey in Holland, the vicinity of Hamburg in Germany, and . Eastern Europe, independent groups persisted. That they intinued the Gravettian (i.e. the former Upper Aurignacian) adition in sepulture as well as in art and blade culture is shown y the recurrence of ochreous burial often in association with 1 elaborate shell, bone and ivory equipment, as at Grimaldi, aviland, Brno, Hoteaux, Obercassel and Chancelade.

If the Gravettian culture took the firmest root in the Upper alaeolithic in Europe, in the second phase of the Würm laciation the Solutreans from their cradleland, either in the iountainous country of Northern Hungary or in North-west ifrica, established themselves sporadically over Western and central Europe. While their composite culture flourished with s fine pressure-flaking of leaf-shaped points and bas-reliefs in hallow rock-shelters, before it was succeeded by the Magda nian, the mortuary tradition continued little changed. At the rpe station of Solutré near Mâcon in Saône-et-Loire were earth-burials varying in size and associated with perforated hells, pierced phalanges of reindeer, engraved figures of animals 1 limestone and bone, and the remains of funerary feasts.[25] Unfortunately we know practically nothing about the circum tances and conditions in which a skeleton was found in the mportant Solutrean site at Laugerie-Haute near Les Eyzies, iut at Předmost near Brno there was an intentional burial in . common grave of fourteen bodies with mammoth bones, vory and reindeer-horn artifacts and a flint industry in a ransitional stage from Gravettian to Solutrean. The physical ype has affinities with that revealed at Brno and Combe Capelle, and though it may not have been responsible for the

Gravettian industry, or the introduction of the Solutrean i
Central Europe, it would seem to have been one of the contri
butory elements in a composite culture. But from whateve
sources the Solutreans and their techniques came, from the fev
traces left of their graves they appear to have buried their dea
in the established manner, which included, as we have seer
a cult of skulls with drinking-cups at the Grotte du Placarc
Charente.

The Palaeolithic Cult of the Dead

Thus, from the available evidence concerning the disposal o
the body under Palaeolithic conditions it seems that from th
beginning of the Pleistocene period a cult of the dead wa
practised which found expression in the preservation of th
skull and the extraction of the brain, ceremonial interment i
either the extended or contracted positions with flint imple
ments, and sometimes animal bones suggestive of a funera
feast. In the Upper Palaeolithic the body often was deposited
in a grave containing ochreous powder with an abundance o
shells and other ornaments in bone and ivory, sometime:
apparently after the flesh had been removed from the bones
thereby colouring them red. This widespread custom of coating
the corpse with red ochre clearly had a ritual significance. Rec
is the colour of living health. Therefore, as Professor Macaliste
has pointed out, if the dead man was to live again in his own
body, of which the bones were the framework, to paint them
with the ruddy colouring of life was "the nearest thing to
mummification that the Palaeolithic people knew; it was an
attempt to make the body again serviceable for its owner's
use".[26]

Moreover, as blood has been a vitalizing agent from time
immemorial, so certain shells, such as the cowrie shaped in the
form of the portal through which a child enters the world,
seem to have been connected with the female principle and to
have been widely employed as fertility charms.[27] It is no
improbable, therefore, that this recurrent feature in Upper
Palaeolithic interments was in the nature of a life-giving rite

hich later found expression in female figurines and other
pects and symbols of the Great Mother with which the cult
the dead became associated. Thus, at Laugerie-Basse,
Dordogne, cowries were arranged in pairs upon the body: two
airs on the forehead, one near the humerus, four in the region
f the knees and thighs, and two upon each foot.[28] Such a
istribution can hardly have been other than for the purpose of
iving life to the deceased rather than for ornamentation.

On the other hand, the suggestion repeatedly made that the
exing of the body symbolized the foetal position of the
mbryo and was inspired by the idea of rebirth beyond the
rave is most unlikely, at any rate in Palaeolithic times. That
ie prenatal attitude was then understood or that Early Man
vould have reasoned along those sort of lines, even supposing
nat he had any such embryological knowledge, is highly
nprobable. In some cases the binding was done undoubtedly
efore rigor mortis had set in, and where this practice has been
dopted by modern primitive people normally its purpose has
een to prevent the return of the deceased to molest the living.
This motive hardly can be eliminated from the Palaeolithic
nortuary cult and may very likely explain rigid flexing and
urying beneath heavy stones, especially when economy of
pace is not involved.

Nevertheless, the care taken in the disposal, ornamentation
nd protection of the body, and sometimes its re-burial,
ogether with its equipment with amulets, fires and the means
f sustenance, seem to indicate a respect and regard for the
eparted that goes beyond fear. The grave was not so much a
rison in which the dead were incarcerated within stone walls
nd made secure from escape by being tightly bound, as a portal
o an after-life on the other side of the grave. Even Neanderthal
Man, degenerate though he may have become and doomed to
xtinction as a type in the maximum glaciation, had begun to
ook forward to survival after death; to a life like that which he
ad lived on earth, where he would still need food, tools and
varmth, as he had always required. The Crô-Magnons appear
o have gone a stage further in the development of a cult of

the dead by resorting to magico-religious devices, such a
surrogates for blood and life-bestowing amulets, in order t
re-animate the mortal remains.

Side by side with these attempts to secure a renewal of li
in the hereafter there may have been a very real, and perhap
increasing, fear of the return of the dead to exercise vengean
and pay off old scores, or avenge any neglect in the di
performance of the mortuary ritual. It is possible that fir
trussing of the corpse immediately after the dissolution ma
have been employed as a precaution against "walking", thoug
the widespread adoption of the contracted position (as distin
from complete and tight flexion in an unnatural posture) ma
have been merely an imitation of that of sleep and rest c
sometimes an economy of space. Among the examples th
have been described, however, those of the "negroid" woma
at *Les Grottes des Enfants* and the flexed body at Chancelac
are very difficult if not impossible to explain on any suppositio
other than that of fear as the underlying motive of this mode c
disposal. On the other hand, the preservation of trophies, as i
the cult of skulls, seems to have been inspired by a desire t
retain a potent relic of the dead, while brain-extraction was
means of communion with them, or of imbibing their virtu
and strength.

THE MESOLITHIC TRANSITION

Azilian-Tardenoisian Interments

That this practice continued into Mesolithic times is estab
lished by the nests of skulls at Ofnet, to which reference ha
been made (cf. pp. 20 f). This remarkable ceremonial inte
ment with its thirty-three heads embedded in ochre an
ornamented with shells, successively buried in a grotto revealir
a sequence of cultures from the Aurignacian and Earlier Sol
trean to the Late Magdalenian and Azilian-Tardenoisian, shov
that the Palaeolithic funerary cult survived unchanged from th
beginning of the Upper Palaeolithic well into the Transition
period at the end of the Pleistocene. Moreover, in addition to th
great ossuary, ten burials, including the remains of twenty-thre

ndividuals, were discovered in 1928 in another Mesolithic ettlement, that at Téviec off the Quiberon peninsula in Brittany. The bodies were crouched in shallow trench graves near the hearths, accompanied by Late Tardenoisian imple‐ ments, perforated shell necklaces and bracelets, and covered with red ochre and stone slabs, over which small cairns were rected. From the cloak‐fasteners it would appear that the bodies were clothed when they were interred, or re‐buried, and n one case red deer antlers had been stacked over a skull. On he neighbouring island of Hoëdic male skeletons were similarly rowned with deer antlers.[29] An infant was buried beneath hearth at Téviec, and at Mugem in Portugal a number of burials have been found under the great middens on the Tagus stuary. In an oval tumulus called Cabeço d'Arruda on these marshes were human skeletons in association with marine hells, a perforated pebble, Tardenoisian flakes and a trapeze.[30]

In Spain near Tres Puntes, Alava, in the neighbourhood of Vittoria, under a tumulus at a mill called Axpea, a number of human bones, including the mandibles of five children, were discovered in 1918, together with pierced shell beads, ochre nd Late Tardenoisian geometric flints.[31] At Furfooz on the iver Lesse in Belgium, one of the seven caves was an ossuary n which the bones of about fourteen skeletons had been deposited after the flesh had decayed,[32] just as at Mas d'Azil n Ariège portions of two skeletons had been treated in the same way, and painted red after interment.[33]

Maglemosean

Therefore, ritual burial was well established in the Azilian‐ Tardenoisian culture soon after 12000 B.C., but no clear evi‐ dence has so far been produced of intentional disposal of the dead, either in the Maglemosean culture, which flourished in Denmark and along the Baltic coasts about 7000 B.C., or in that of the somewhat later Kitchen middens near the coasts of South Scandinavia and the southern shores of the Baltic about 000 B.C. Thus, no definite burials have been discovered under he great bog of Mullerup on the west of the island of Zealand,

or in any of the other Maglemosean sites, such as Svaerdbor
or Holmegaard in the same vicinity, though a few huma
bones have been found in the peat at Maglemose.

Ertebølle

When salt water poured into the Baltic depression to form th
Litorina Sea, near its oyster-beds the people called Ertebølle
after the name of one of their middens, settled down to
sedentary life with shell-fish as their staple diet. In the debris o
their refuse they buried their dead in the extended position, an
sometimes surrounded them with a few large stones.[34] Bu
there is no indication of their having practised any mortuar
ritual, or of their having provided their dead with grave goods
Their outstanding achievement was the production of coars
and roughly made pots for the storage of food, but althougl
some of the later vessels at Havnelev near Strandegaard i
South Zealand bore impressions of grain (wheat and barley
no such imprints, or any querns, occurred in the rectangula
log-houses inhabited by late Ertebølle folk at Strandegaard.[3]

The earliest signs of agriculture in Denmark came from th
Solager midden in North Zealand, and from Brabrand i
Jutland in the form of impressions of wheat on potsherds, whil
simultaneously the bones of the domestic ox, pig, sheep an
goat appear in the Ertebølle middens. When the middens wer
abandoned is uncertain, but it seems that the Mesolithic inhabi
tants of the region must have been in contact with Neolithi
settlers for some time before the arrival of the megalithic migra
tion (*c.* 2300 B.C.), or encamped on sites which had bee
occupied previously by food-producers who may have com
along the Danube and spread between the Oder and th
Vistula beyond the loess lands until they reached the Balti
coasts.[36] In Denmark they continued their tradition o
extended burial in earth graves defined by a ring of smal
stones round the body and covered with a large earth mound
The only stones available being boulders which could not b
split into slabs, the Neolithic farmers were the first group i
this region to erect small rectangular chambers with singl

capstones, known as "dolmens" or *dyssers*, like those in the cemetery of Jordansmühl in Silesia in which Danubian and northern grave goods were combined.

Danish Dyssers

The origin of these Danish *dyssers*, however, is far from clear. That they represent the starting-point of the long and complicated process of megalithic burial in slab-built tombs and the associated cult can be dismissed at once. The notion of a unilineal development from the small rectangular chambers consisting of about four large stones set on edge with one larger slab forming the roof, commonly called "dolmens", through passage-graves with round or polygonal chambers leading out of a passage of large slabs and roofed with huge capstones, and the long galleries with forecourts and side-chambers, to the great corbelled vaults of Spain and the Aegean, along the lines suggested by Montelius, has now been abandoned in favour of a series of movements from the Mediterranean and Atlantic littoral during the third millennium B.C. making their way northwards to the British Isles and Denmark, as will be considered in greater detail later (Chap. III). Thus, the "simple dolmen" often has turned out to be nothing more than a late fragment or degeneration of an earlier complex tumulus, and, as Professor Daryll Forde concluded, the traditional classical typology had begun at the wrong end.[37]

In the light of the existing evidence it seems certain that by whatever route the megalithic culture was introduced into Denmark and Sweden, the dolmen tomb-form was the first to arrive. Although it is true that in the Baltic the cult developed along its own lines, with its own Mesolithic tradition in the background, nevertheless its significance can be understood only when it is viewed in relation to all that lies behind the megalithic movement as an integral element in the rise and diffusion of Neolithic civilization in Europe. To this inquiry, therefore, we must now turn, beginning in the Ancient Middle East.

CHAPTER II

Neolithic Burials in the Ancient East

ALTHOUGH the transition from food-gathering to food-production was a very gradual process localized in certain regions, notably in the Fertile Crescent in the Ancient Middle East, where it became an accomplished fact it had a marked effect upon the disposal of the dead in more elaborate tombs and with a more complex mortuary ritual. Graves, however, were still dug in the ground, sometimes covered with a mound of earth or a stone erection, and caves were also used for burial purposes. With the rise of the megalithic tradition massive sepulchral structures developed, while in Egypt a funerary cultus assumed such gigantic proportions that it became the characteristic feature and focal-point of the remarkable civilization of the Nile valley. Indeed the monuments it created have remained throughout the ages the chief sources of information about the culture of which they constitute a permanent record. Upon the decoration and furnishing of their royal tombs the Egyptians lavished their art in mural paintings, sculpture and architecture, and gave expression to their beliefs, hopes and achievements, here and hereafter.

EGYPTIAN NEOLITHIC CEMETERIES

Since Sir Flinders Petrie first discovered the Predynastic cemeteries at Naqada in 1895 hundreds of prehistoric graves have now been excavated which take back the cult of the dead in the Nile valley to well before 4000 B.C. While in Lower Egypt a very early settlement with Mesolithic affinities has been found at Merimde Benisalame near the western edge of the Delta, the three main Neolithic cultures, termed respectively Badarian, Amratian (Naqadaean) and Gerzean

34

(Semainian), are differentiated in Middle and Upper Egypt. Behind the earliest of these Dr Brunton claims to have detected at the village of Deir Tasa a less developed semi-nomadic cultural phase which he has named Tasian, contemporary with the Merimdian, and which he thinks preceded in the fifth millennium B.C. the more settled agricultural Badarian community.[1] About this, however, there is now some doubt since the graves at Deir Tasa were found in the same cemeteries as the Badarian tombs, and some of them cut into each other.[2] But in any case ritual burial was firmly established in Neolithic Egypt.

Badarian

Thus, at Badari graves occurred in small and scattered groups dug in soft, sandy gravel or limestone detritus on the spur of the desert near to but independent of the dwellings. The bodies were clothed and adorned with their ornaments. One man had a girdle of over five thousand blue glazed steatite beads, and in the hair of a baby were ostrich-tips, while near another infant were a bowl and an ivory spoon. Among the graves were cooking-pots and food bowls, either empty or containing grain and meat, suggesting that funeral meals probably were a feature of the mortuary ritual. Near the hands were slate palettes and pebbles for grinding malachite as eye-paint. The corpse was laid on a reed mat, often on its left side with the head facing west or south, and surrounded with beads, perforated shells, ostrich-shell disks, ivory hair-combs and female figurines, as well as with pottery. Over it was a roofing of matting and sticks, and occasionally hides. The contracted position was adopted with the thighs forming an angle of about 60° with the spine, or at right angles, but tight flexing was rare. The head rested sometimes on a pillow in an attitude which Dr Brunton describes as that for "comfortable sleep".[3] No traces have been discovered of coffins of wood or clay, or any indications of attempts at the preservation of the body, though the skin sometimes was visible as a result of natural desiccation. In some cases the head was wrapped in cloth, but skins were the normal clothing of the dead below the neck. No traces occurred of multiple burial, and females were buried alongside of males in separate graves, though sometimes men were grouped together in a particular part of the cemetery.[4]

Amratian

In the First Predynastic or Amratian culture of Upper Egypt, soon after 4000 B.C., the same general procedure was maintained in spite of infusion of Getulan or Libyan strains from the margins of the desert. The graves continued to be oval with a tendency to become straight-sided with rounded corners, and finally rectangular. Occasionally they were plastered with mud or lined with brick. The bodies were wrapped in matting, though this custom tended to be abandoned in due course, since in the later graves it did not appear. A few traces of wooden coffins were discovered. The contracted position and orientation towards the west, the Land of the Dead, continued, but burials became more communal. Sometimes the body appears to have been dismembered, and in certain instances the head was removed and preserved, and for it either a pot or an ostrich egg was substituted. Pots and animal bones occurred on the grave floors together with fragments of ivory, slate palettes, mace-heads, beads, shells, flint flakes and malachite.

In an undisturbed grave of a female the beads were placed at the neck, mostly carnelian with four turquoise, three calcite and several lapis lazuli. On the right wrist was an ivory bracelet, and on the left two cowries. A slate palette, an ivory pin and resin were at the hands, and close to the head and hands were two pots. On each wrist was a bone bangle, and the leg of a very small animal in front of the face. In another undisturbed female interment, behind the head of the woman was the body of an infant, and both lay on their right sides. At her elbows was a string of carnelians with four blue glazed steatite beads, a white pebble pendant and a short string of columbella shells. A slate palette, a brown jasper pebble, a basket containing malachite, two flint flakes and three limestone "stoppers" were in front of the arms.[5]

Merimdian

On the western marshes of the Delta at Merimde, west of the Rosetta branch of the Nile, where the black soil brought down the river from Abyssinia, a prosperous agricultural community more or less contemporary with the Badarian settlements in Middle Egypt flourished on the fertile soil among the network of small streams until the encroachment of the desert caused it to be abandoned. Like the Badarians and Amratians, in life they wore linen clothes and decked themselves with necklaces of shells, bone rings and ivory bangles. Women had slate palettes on which they ground malachite for painting their eyes to counteract the glare of the sun. As the communities were small no extensive cemeteries have been found, the dead having been buried in trench or pit graves in the flexed position among or within the huts of the settlement near the fire-place, but without any furniture. There is the same lack of evidence in the Fayum lake-side settlements which may be rather later, though closely related to the Merimdians, if rather less advanced.[6]

Gerzean

As Asiatic influences began to make their way in Lower Egypt in the fourth millennium B.C. (*c.* 3500) they gave rise to a more advanced culture in which copper, painted pottery and cult objects were features, together with marked changes in dress, weapons and religion. In the mortuary tradition no very significant break occurred. Burial in the contracted position in oblong trench graves, dug rather deeper than formerly, was continued. But either a ledge was added for the rapidly increasing offerings, or, if they were placed in the grave, the corpse was laid on a bier of twigs, or in a niche cut in the rock, unless it was enclosed in a coffin. In the Gerzean cemetery at Hierakonpolis, the predynastic centre of the Horus cult of Upper Egypt, a late prehistoric brick-lined tomb decorated with coloured drawings consisted of a chamber 15 by 6½ by 5 feet, divided into two equal parts by a low transverse wall of small crude bricks, like those with which the floor was paved. The whole was plastered over with mud mortar which on the

walls was then covered with a coating of yellow ochre. On i
hunting scenes, combats and ships had been painted in red,
black and white, the designs resembling those on the pottery
of the period found in the tomb, together with a flint lance and
a small limestone or chert vase. But there was no trace of the
body, which can hardly have been other than that of a chief
in view of the proportions and decorations of the sepulchre
Near by were two more brick-lined decorated tombs with
divided compartments, but as they had been plundered no
furniture remained except a few jars. The rest of the graves were
rectangular trenches often roofed with wood, mostly disturbed
and containing little except coarse pottery and spheroidal
spindle-whorls.[7]

Thus, throughout the Neolithic period in Egypt the disposal
of the dead followed the same general pattern. Interment invariably was in the contracted position in graves dug in the ground
in cemeteries near but, except at Merimde, not within the
settlements. The bodies frequently were clothed in skins and
provided with ornaments, amulets and the means of sustenance
and at Merimde they were buried near the fire within the family
circle. At Badari the burial grounds were near the village and
so in close touch with the relatives of the deceased. But later
they were placed at a distance from the habitation, suggesting
that the next life was becoming less closely connected with that
in this world.

Orientation towards the west may indicate that already an
occidental land of the dead, which became so prominent later,
was in process of development. This ancient doctrine of the
"West" as the permanent realm of the dead was submerged
however, in the Dynastic Pyramid Texts in favour of the East
as the region in which the dead pharaoh had his abode.[8]
Moreover, at the end of the prehistoric period at El Amrah,
Gerzeh and Turah the head faced eastwards, while at Merimde
the graves were so arranged that the body looked towards the
north or the north-east. There was, therefore, no hard and fast
rule about orientation, or the side on which the body lay. The
normal position for the corpse in the grave was on the left side

om the Badarian period to the Middle Kingdom in the
econd millennium B.C. Where this was not adopted it is
ossible that if the land of the dead was thought to be where
ne sun sets, the renewal of life after death was more appro-
riately associated with the east, since it was there that the sun
ose in the morning.

Another home of the dead in some of the Pyramid Texts was
mong the circumpolar stars in the Elysian Fields in the northern
ky. But to what extent, if at all, these beliefs about the realms
f the dead in the historical period have their antecedents in
ne Neolithic mortuary ritual can be only conjectures in the
bsence of precise information other than the evidence concern-
ng modes of disposal of the body and the position of the tombs
nd their contents. All that can safely be affirmed is that a life
fter death was an established belief, and from all appearances
 was not very different from that which had obtained else-
vhere from Palaeolithic times, since it found expression in
lmost identical funerary practices.

HE EARLIEST DYNASTIC TOMBS

Vhen the unification of Upper Egypt was effected, it would
eem by a king of Hierakonpolis soon after 3000 B.C., with the
stablishment of the First Dynasty of the pharaohs, significant
hanges in tomb construction became apparent. The simple
redynastic pit graves continued to be the normal method of
epulture for the mass of the people but the elevation of a local
hieftain to the exalted position of the single ruler of the "Two
Lands" of Upper and Lower Egypt, with all the divine
rerogatives the office acquired, found expression in a rapid
laboration of the royal tombs and their contents and cultus.
Already, as we have seen, the sides of predynastic graves had
een lined with bricks made of Nile mud dried in the sun, and
quipped with a plentiful supply of offerings. They were also
overed with sand or stones over a wood roof, the brick lining
ften being carried up to contain this covering and make it
ecure from hyenas and jackals. The pit was undercut on one
de to allow more space at the bottom for the grave-furniture.

As the digging proceeded deeper and deeper into the sand, rock steps were required to gain access to the chamber below, which was also expanded by the addition of smaller rooms to contain offerings. The royal tombs at Abydos illustrate several varieties of this phase in the development in attempts to construct subterranean reproductions of the houses (or palaces) of the living.

The Mastaba Tomb and the Pyramid

Thus, in the centre was a large chamber under the superstructure with the smaller tombs grouped around it containing the bodies of courtiers and servants who in all probability had been sacrificed during the royal obsequies. The floor of the tomb of King Den at the end of the First Dynasty was composed of slabs of granite, while in that of Khasekhemui of the Third Dynasty a room was lined with limestone. In the Second Dynasty the wooden roof was replaced by a corbelled vault of mud brick with a small rectangular brick structure resembling the shape of a house (or palace), with a slight slope to its side and a niche in one face in front of which offerings were laid. The outside walls became ornamented with a series of vertical recesses and projections. In this way the mastaba tomb as a vast rectangular brick creation arose over a series of chambers and a shaft leading to the grave (Fig. 2). The niche or chapel of offerings was sometimes represented by a "false door" on one side, but in royal tombs its place was taken by a temple. In the Third Dynasty stone was substituted for brick to make the tomb an "everlasting habitation" for the occupant. Thus, Zoser had a vast stone oblong constructed of five other mastabas superimposed on each other in steps of decreasing height and size in the form of a pyramid. In the next dynasty the steps were filled in with stones, the ground plan was made square, the sides were straightened and brought to a point at the top. Surrounding these vast royal pyramids, which about 2900 B.C. reached their climax in those erected at Gizeh for the kings Khufu (Cheops), Khafra and Menkaura, are smaller stepped pyramids constituting the mastabas of royal relatives, courtiers and officials, arranged in rows at a respectful distance.[10]

Fig. 2. The development of the mastaba tomb

The burial in the pyramid was in a rock-cut chamber below the surface, and, as in the mastaba, the gigantic superstructure formed the memorial pile above the tomb. Whereas access to the burial chamber under the mastaba was through the vertical shaft which was filled in after the burial, in the pyramid the entrance was in its northern side, near ground-level, along a passage leading to the chamber in the pyramid or in the rock under it. The temple of offerings was in the front of the pyramid on its east side and consisted of several rooms devoted to the royal cultus, corresponding to the chapel and storeroom on the east side of the mastaba, containing provisions for the deceased in the west wall of the chapel and a portrait statue of him sitting at a meal before a table of offerings.

At first the offerings were made at the tomb, and this continued to be the normal practice for all ordinary Egyptians.

Thus, in the mastabas when a niche replaced the tablet of the table of offerings and a "false door" was added, it was through it the *ka*, or guardian *alter ego* guiding the fortunes of the individual in the hereafter, was thought to emerge to partake of the offerings and behold the rites performed in the chapel. But at the end of the Third Dynasty, when the place of offerings in the royal tombs was in a separate court attached to the side of the tomb, it developed into a stately and elaborate independent temple which by the Twelfth Dynasty had become entirely separated from the tomb in the desert.

Originally, however, as the pyramids and their temples stood on the desert plateau 100 feet above the plain, they were approached by a sloping covered passage or corridor of stone at the lower end of which stood a small introductory chapel. Khafra appears to have introduced the custom of placing statues of himself in front of, or between, the pillars of his temple, and the so-called Sphinx temple at Gizeh is the entrance to the corridor of the second pyramid, surmounted by the portrait statue of the pharaoh (Khafra) himself attached to the body of a lion, guarding the great cemetery of Gizeh, the most imposing city of the dead ever conceived. Thus, in the course of a few centuries, between about 3200 and 2900 B.C., the simple grave with its sand heap surrounded by a circle of stones assumed the gigantic proportions of these mighty pyramids, the greatest of which covers thirteen acres and contains over two million blocks of limestone, each weighing on an average two and a half tons, and stands nearly 500 feet high. It may well have been, as an ancient tradition recorded by Herodotus maintained, that 100,000 men were involved in its construction.

Thus, the prehistoric belief that the dead lived in or at the tomb, which must be adequately equipped, therefore, as an "everlasting habitation", persisted until at length it acquired the vast dimensions of these monumental structures which have remained throughout the ages as the most impressive expression of this conception of the hereafter in the ancient world. Even after the Fifteenth Dynasty, when the mortuary ritual and the cult of the dead became crystallized in their final form, the sojourn in the tomb subsisted side by side with the belief in remote realms of the dead in distant regions. When the pharaoh of the Old Kingdom became a god in the celestial realms, the nobility in the Pyramid Age began to seek their own eternity, and so they moved away their tombs from the royal cemeteries to their own domains in sure and certain hope of being able "to join their *kas*" in a future life in their own right. So eventually ordinary mortals, including commoners, returned to the Neolithic and earlier conviction of continued existence beyond the grave as an "effective personality" (*akh*); for every Egyptian at death now was destined to become an Osiris, and so to attain eternal blessedness.

NEOLITHIC TOMBS IN MESOPOTAMIA

In Mesopotamia, on the other hand, the sustained Egyptian preoccupation with the hereafter was conspicuously absent. The contrast between the regularity of the rise and fall of the Nile and the unpredictability of the Tigris and Euphrates, always liable to cause disastrous floods, seems to have been reflected in the cult of the dead. Thus, in Babylonia the hereafter was regarded as a sombre place of darkness and dust beneath the earth, to which all men, both good and bad alike, descended. Therefore, great cemeteries, enduring pyramids and elaborate tomb equipment, which reveal so much about the civilization of Ancient Egypt, are not to be found in Mesopotamia to anything like the same extent. In Sumer, apart from the royal tombs at Ur, the normal procedure was for the body to be clad in its ordinary clothes and wrapped in a mat, or in a linen winding-sheet, in the flexed position with the head resting on a fringed and tasselled cushion. It was then enclosed with a bowl of water and a few personal belongings (a dagger or razor, or a necklace and bracelets) in a wicker or pottery coffin (*larnake*), or in two large pottery jars with their open ends together (*pithoi*), and placed in a simple earth grave, or in a small brick-built vault. In towns the grave often was dug beneath the house in which the deceased had lived, under the pavement of one of the rooms. When the funeral rites had been performed the flooring was relaid and the occupation of the house continued in the customary manner. In the case of family vaults, after each interment the door was bricked up and the food vessels were placed outside before the earth was filled in.[11] Relatively few cemeteries have been discovered as yet in Mesopotamia, but at Ur among the royal tombs in some of the early graves of the commoners (*c.* 3500 B.C.) there were signs of burning in the upper part of the body. Cremation, however, was not practised in the historic period, and this incineration may have been accidental. Near or over the grave sometimes a model boat of bitumen with a cargo of clay vessels containing food was placed.[12]

Hassuna

West of the Tigris at Hassuna near Mosul in Assyria burials were found at almost all levels in the mound situated in the earliest known Neolithic settlement in Mesopotamia. In the lowest stratum (Level IA) an adult skeleton occurred in a loosely contracted position between two hearths in association with a Neolithic storage jar and a stone hoe, though it is not certain that this was a deliberate interment. From Level IB upwards infant burials in coarse incised and painted and incised jars occurred and beneath the floor of a room in Level IC was an undisturbed burial in the fully flexed position with the head to the north. Three sides of the grave were formed by the foundations of the walls of the room, and the fourth side consisted of a row of large stones. No traces of funerary furniture were seen. There seems to have been no uniformity of burial practice in this period, and two skeletons had been flung apparently unceremoniously into a grain bin of Level III, while in a rubbish pit in Level IV there was a skull. In the corner of a room in this level a collection of human bones were found.[13]

Tell Halaf

At Samarra, north of Baghdad on the Tigris, beneath the pavements of Islamic houses are a number of badly preserved graves in a cemetery in a layer showing no stratification. While most of them were simple inhumations, a few were surrounded by a row of mud bricks. The bodies were flexed but gave no indication of having been orientated. There was the body of a new-born infant inside a pot of Samarran ware.[14] Both these sites, Hassuna and Samarra, were earlier than that of Tell Halaf on the Upper Khabur on the Anatolian border, which has given its name to the painted pottery it has yielded, and marks a definite advance in culture. Not only did the new technique in well-fired pottery replace the earlier styles, but it was accompanied by beads of metallic copper, emmer wheat and barley, and the remains of domesticated cattle.

At Tepe Gawra near Nineveh peculiar circular stone structures (*tholoi*) with a domed roof and in some cases a rectangular chamber attached to them, as in the Mycenaean beehive tombs, were used for ritual purposes, and many of the graves were associated with them. Moreover, that they were dedicated to chthonic deities is supported by the concentration of graves within and around them.[15] Throughout the greater portion of its long history the mound of Gawra was used as a burial ground though doubtless other cemeteries await discovery, since less than 500 tombs and graves have come to light during the excavations. This must represent a small proportion of the population during the many centuries of occupation from perhaps 5000 B.C. to the Bronze Age.[16] A pit was found below layer f. sunk into virgin soil, filled with earth and containing skeletons and artifacts at four levels. In the lowest was an adult in a contorted position; above this were the bones of nine skeletons all intermingled as though thrown into the pit. Higher up were the scattered remains of twelve more bodies, together with a pot, two stone pendants and a basalt pestle. Just below the mouth of the well were two more adults, one of which seems to have been a case of burial in the flexed position; the other was thrown on top of it. It may be, as Dr Perkins suggests, that originally it was used as a cistern or well, and later, after it had been filled with soil, it became a place for burial, as twenty-four skeletons were found at different levels.[17]

Al 'Ubaid

At Gawra flexing was the normal mode of inhumation, and only a few skeletons were laid in the extended position, whereas in the Tell Al 'Ubaid deposits, which represent the earliest phase in Sumer, named after a mound near Ur excavated in 1922, the bodies invariably lay on their backs, rigidly extended with the hands crossed below the chest. This, as we have seen, was an unusual practice which seems to indicate a break in the mortuary ritual in Mesopotamia to be explained in all probability by foreign intrusion.[18]

At Tell Arpachiyah near Nineveh, out of the fifty Ubaid graves discovered forty-five were found in the cemetery from which most of the painted ware of this period came. With many of the burials were votive-painted vessels, and the bodies generally were orientated east by west, though the heads lay sometimes at the east and sometimes at the west end of the grave in spite of the orientation of the body. The grave goods were placed at the head or the feet of the deceased. Fractional burial was widely practised, but even so what remained of the body was laid in an east-west direction. This mode of interment has never been recorded in the Halaf period as the pottery suggests, and it may have been introduced from Iranian sources.[19]

Halaf pottery was associated with two or possibly three of the five graves in the Middle phase, but the catalogue of the tombs in the report is not very explicit about the contents of the interments, and Sumerian tradition placed the foundation of their civilization in Dilmun, perhaps the modern Bahrein, on the Persian Gulf. Therefore, Professor Childe thinks that the starting-point may have been farther south, the distinctive features of the Ubaid culture representing merely adaptations of an imported "Eridu culture" to the peculiar conditions of the Delta.[20]

Be this as it may, while the peasant culture of North Iraq gradually changed character the first Al 'Ubaid settlements appeared in the drying Delta in the south. Further immigrations from Anatolia or Trans-Caucasia are associated with the

Uruk (Warka) civilization, and those from Iran with that of Jemdet Nasr, both of which lay behind the First Dynasty of Ur. In these proto-Sumerian cultures sepulture followed a fairly consistent tradition. In the Ubaid period the extended position was maintained, except, as we have seen, at Gawra, where flexing as the normal mode of Neolithic interment was commonly adopted.

In the Ubaid cemetery outside the retaining wall of the acropolis at Eridu extended collective burial occurred orientated to the north-west, consisting apparently of family graves with a flat shallow dish and an inverted bell-shaped cup, and one or more jars or stone vessels placed near the head.[21] Adults generally were interred in cemeteries outside the settlements of the living while infants frequently were laid among the dwellings. In the cemetery at Ur, which goes back to the Jemdet Nasr and Uruk periods, the bodies were definitely contracted and with them were stone vessels, lead cups and painted pots with sharp angular outlines, lug handles and spouts, and an inverted lead tumbler over the mouth of one of the pots.[22]

In the next stage the stone vessels were more numerous and varied with slip decorated ware. In the uppermost level pottery was scarce and its place was taken by cups, bowls and vases in limestone, diorite, steatite and alabaster. The abrupt ending of the Jemdet Nasr period suggests that the infiltration of an alien people with their own funerary tradition was summarily brought to a close when the old inhabitants reasserted their rule and established a new régime marking the beginning of the Dynastic period of Ur.

The Royal Tombs of Ur

In the great cemetery outside the walls of the old town two types of burials have been discovered, the one being the graves of commoners, the other, at a deeper and apparently an earlier level, those of the kings. These royal tombs are dated by Sir Leonard Woolley soon after 3000 B.C. (i.e. between 2900 and 2700),[23] and differ from the graves of their subjects by being stone and brick-vaulted, chambered structures rather than simple rectangular pits. They do not, however, follow any uniform plan. Usually they consist of one or more long outer chambers which are vaulted, and one or two smaller chambers roofed with domes in stone or brick, together with a pit for offerings and additional burials.[24]

The outstanding features are the amazing wealth of funerary furniture and a ritual involving human sacrifice on a grand scale. The grave goods included a fine head of a bull in gold with eyes of lapis lazuli, exquisitely fashioned stags, gazelles, bulls and goats also in gold with clusters of pomegranates and branches of trees with stems and fruits of gold and carnelian, silver and gold bowls and stone vessels, clay jars, silver tables for offerings, harps or lyres, an inlaid gaming-board, the statue of a ram on its hind legs with its front legs bound to the branches of a tree with silver chains, a wooden chariot decorated with mosaic and golden heads of cows and bulls, and cockle-shells containing green paint. With such a galaxy of priceless objects it is not surprising that many of the tombs had been rifled so that it is impossible to estimate the total wealth of the contents of the cemeteries. But it must have been immense.

Moreover, the bodies on their biers were richly clad and ornamented, and accompanied by a retinue of courtiers, attendants and guards also dressed in their finery. The soldiers were in two ranks with copper spears by their sides and were distributed elsewhere in the chamber carrying daggers and spears with heads of silver or gold. The women wore a gala head-dress of lapis and carnelian beads with golden pendants of beech leaves, ear-rings, necklaces of gold and lapis lazuli, and on top of their bodies were two wooden harps with the head of a bull in gold and copper respectively. These remains were those of victims who were sacrificed during the obsequies of a ruler who, according to an inscription on a cylinder seal found in the tomb, was named A-bar-gi, and his supposed queen was called Shub-ad. The stone chamber of the king had been plundered, but traces of a retinue survived, together with two model boats. Behind it a second vaulted chamber with a ylinder seal of lapis lazuli above the roof bearing the name of he occupant, Shub-ad, was undisturbed.

Here by her body on a wooden bier was a golden cup near er hand and a large quantity of beads from the cloak in which he must have been clad. Three fish amulets and three gold pins vere against her arm. Over the skull was a head-dress of greater elaboration than those of the court-ladies, fortified with mulets in lapis shaped as a bull and a calf. Near it was a econd head-dress composed of thousands of lapis beads and ome gold animal figures, with the bodies of two female ttendants, one at the head and the other at the foot of the bier. nside the entrance stood the wooden chariot used as a hearse. The chamber was strewn with offerings and around the inter-ment were the remains of fires and of a funeral feast.

In another similar grave lay the bodies of six men and ixty-eight attendants arranged in an orderly manner in the ectangular pit in the slightly flexed position, suggesting the bsence of a struggle of any kind or a violent death. The women vore head-dresses and were arranged with all their ornaments ver crimson garments, adorned in their full glory to accompany heir sovereign to the next life. The supposition is that they valked to their appointed places in the chamber and then took a drug such as hashish or opium, and after their sleep of death he gaily dressed voluntary victims were put into position before he grave was filled in.[25] Therefore, it is suggested that the kings f Ur were regarded as divine rulers who "did not die as men lie, but were translated". Under these circumstances it would be a privilege for his courtiers to continue their service beyond he grave.[26]

Nevertheless, though kingship in Sumer is said to have "descended from heaven" after the flood in the third millen-ium B.C., presumably as a gift of the gods, it never occupied he position attained by the pharaohs in Egypt; Mesopotamia being divided up into a series of city-states loosely bound ogether rather than a single nation with the throne as its lynamic centre, as in the Nile valley. No Sumerian king, herefore, was a cohesive force in the entire realm. This,

however, apparently did not prevent the prehistoric rulers of Ur
from acquiring a divine status by virtue of their office and its
insignia in which divinity was inherent,[27] and so of gathering
around them at death a select company of the devoted members
of their court and of their bodyguard to accompany them to
their final abode, there to carry on their customary service. If
this interpretation of the mortuary ritual is correct it follows
that the conception of "the Land of No-Return" where rulers
and commoners alike dwelt in darkness and dust was a later
development as in Israel, where the notion of Sheol arose
largely under prophetic and Babylonian influence in the eighth
century B.C. In the royal tomb ritual in the Early Dynastic
period in Mesopotamia there was some approximation to the
Egyptian cult of the dead, and in prehistoric times the two
contemporary civilizations seem to have developed along more
or less parallel lines in respect of funerary practice and belief,
until in the third millennium B.C. they diverged as the structure
and functions of the State in the valleys of the Nile and the
Euphrates underwent a fundamental change.

BURIALS IN ELAM AND BALUCHISTAN

Susa

In Elam, where at Susa in the lowest level of the site (Susa A)
a culture flourished contemporary with that in Sumer, the
grave goods in the cemetery were in advance of those in the
Ubaid burials.[28] In the succeeding higher levels, corresponding to Uruk (B), Jemdet Nasr (C) and Early Dynastic (D),[29]
the cultural development was maintained. Interment was in the
extended position coupled with some flexed bodies which
de Mecquenem thinks had been inserted in the graves after
decomposition.[30] The funerary pottery was of a very high
quality in form and design, based mainly on basketry models
and ornamented with magico-religious patterns and symbols.
Stamp seals were engraved with animal figures and female
figurines moulded in clay. Children's graves contained toys,
as in Warka IV in the Uruk culture in Southern Mesopotamia,
but inscribed tablets do not occur in these earlier levels (A, B).

It is not until c level is reached at Susa that proto-Elamite tablets appear together with food vessels and seals of the Jemdet Nasr period.[31] The tombs become richer but similar to those below, though they contain little pottery. At the D level the designs reveal affinities with the Early Dynastic scarlet ware in Mesopotamia[32] and the seals, pins and metal vases resemble those found in the Ur royal cemeteries and the "A" cemetery at Kish.[33] The polychrome vases, however, suggest relations with Baluchistan rather than with the Euphrates valley.

From Early Dynastic times in Sumer a fairly uniform culture seems to have existed in the Zagros mountains from Susa to Tepe Giyan, near Nihavend in Va, the divergences being most marked in the north and south. That Dynastic influences predominated in the cult of the dead can scarcely be doubted in the light of the evidence from the cemeteries concerning mortuary procedure. In the Musyan area on the Mesopotamian border the tombs and their contents conform to Sumerian types in relation to the royal cultus, and in both regions the sacred kingship seems to have been an established institution. But in which of the two areas the "dynasty" arose is a matter of conjecture.

The Iranian highlands geographically represent the natural position for a common cradleland of the whole range of cultural achievements in the Ancient East in the fourth millennium B.C. If it was the source of the first civilization of Elam, it may well have been the centre from which similar movements and influences radiated across the Zagros mountains into Mesopotamia through Baluchistan and the Himalayas to India. In Western Turkestan at Anau near Askabad the settlements unearthed by Pumpelly in 1904 have revealed further evidence of another outpost of the same civilization on the alluvial land of Transcaspia, while in Baluchistan Indian pottery has been found in association with wares having Persian affinities (Hissar I).[34]

Baluchistan

Although the course of events in Baluchistan before 3000 B.C. is still obscure, it would seem to have been in the small settled farming communities there that the sources of Indian civilization are to be found. These villages had behind them the earlier Iranian settlements such as Sialk and Giyan, but in addition to these centres on the edge of the Persian desert, the ancient cities of the Tigris-Euphrates valley made their contribution to the urban culture of Mohenjo-daro and Chanhu-daro on the Indus, and Harappa on the Ravi, which flourished in the third millennium B.C. Thus, Baluchistan appears to have been the connecting link between the Indus valley civilization and that of the Fertile Crescent and Western Iran, though neither in Baluchistan nor in Sind was there apparently a genuinely Neolithic stage, such as occurred in some parts of Europe, in which cultivation, herding and pottery-making were practised without any knowledge of metal. This indeed applies throughout the greater part of the Ancient East.

In the secluded mountain valleys of Baluchistan the self-contained peasant communities at Quetta, Nal, Kolwa and Zhob developed a prehistoric culture with a considerable measure of uniformity but with certain local distinguishing features. Thus, in the pottery techniques, while, as in Persia, buff ware was characteristic of the south and red ware of the north, black on red predominated in the Zhob valley in the north and black on buff in the south at Nal, Quetta and Kulli, and at Amri in Sind, where typologically the earliest pottery occurred.[35] The latest came from a mound near Nal in Southern Baluchistan, first described by Sir John Marshall in 1904.[36] This proved to be a necropolis which had been excavated in a very unscientific manner at the beginning of the century by an antiquarian in search of pottery before Mr Hargreaves of the Archaeological Survey began operations there in 1925. These "pioneers" had dug down on the western slope of the mound and further excavation revealed stone structures which may have been used for funerary purposes, as they were part of the necropolis in which some forty groups of burials were discovered associated with 270 mortuary potsherds.

he Nal Cemetery

veral methods of inhumation appear to have been practised
the same time, but fractional burial predominated. Only one
mplete adult skeleton and those of three infants were dis-
vered intact, the rest consisting of a few bones scattered among
: pots. Some of the vessels contained bones or fragments
xed with earth. Two phalanges were in one vessel, parts of
o small ribs in a second, and three metatarsals in a third, and
on, whether they were placed there deliberately or had
rely drifted in by accident. Bones of animals were also
overed from the groups. In one grave a broken bowl con-
ned earth and five other smaller vases, with pieces of a rib,
t of a pelvic bone and many small bones in the earth and
ween the vases. These would seem to have been placed
re, and may have belonged to a single individual, probably
voman. Besides these fractional burials, the three complete
umations—the adult and two infants—were enclosed in
tangular sun-dried brick graves. With the infants were six-
n beads and a pear-shaped crystal pendant. The adult lay on
left side with the head to the east, face to the south, and the
and right arms bent in a slightly contracted position of
ut 50°, suggestive of sleep. In this grave there was no
niture. Near the grave of the infant a skull and some bones
re found, and around the neck the remains of a necklace of
hty-nine white disk beads.[37]

Making due allowance for disturbance by the earlier excava-
s, there can be little doubt that at least some of the bones of
fractional burials had been interred as fragments and not as
nplete bodies. As in the Damb Buthi cemetery in Makran
Sind,[38] they had been collected after the body had been
osed for some time and then either put in a pot or laid on
floor of the necropolis without any protection. The grave
ds were chiefly pottery vessels, apart from the bead necklaces
l pendant and the discoid beads found with the second
int's skull. There were also a grinding stone, a stone weight,
tone chisel, copper tools, and a marble ringstone. The
sence of a piece of red ochre in one of the funerary vessels,

and of a carefully moulded cake of red ferruginous earth in
broken vessel with a colour grinder, hardly can have bee
fortuitous, especially as red pigment recurs at Damb Buth
and, as we have seen, it has a long history in ceremoni
interment going back to Palaeolithic times.

THE INDUS VALLEY

Mohenjo-daro

In Sind and the Punjab the remarkable homogeneous urba
civilization which flourished from 2500 to 1500 B.C., reveale
by the excavations in and around the Indus valley at Mohenjc
daro, Chanhu-daro and Harappa since 1922, has produce
singularly little evidence of the disposal of the dead and c
funeral ritual. At Mohenjo-daro no trace of a cemetery has bee
discovered, and the few bones in the vicinity of the houses an
in pits seem to have been those of people killed when the cit
was raided in its last period and their bodies summarily throw
away.[39] As some of the bones show signs of charring it ha
been suggested that cremation was practised, generally on th
banks of a river, and the incinerated remains collected for th
performance of funerary rites before they were deposited in th
"ossuary". But the skeletons in the pit on the southern side c
the city in what is called North Lane give every indication c
having been disposed of in haste and disorder, and at least or
had been decapitated. If cremation was in vogue some attem;
at incineration may have been made by the relatives when th
raid was over, but the general conditions, as Mackay ha
suggested, point to a massacre by raiders among a group tryin
to escape, whose bodies were hurled into a pit near an exit c
the city.[40]

Much the same explanation applies probably to the oth
fractional burials which have been noted. Thus, the twenty-or
skeletons recorded by Sir John Marshall do not represer
intentional burial and their attitudes point to simultaneot
death. None was deposited in an orderly manner or provide
with grave goods.[41] Moreover, they belong to a late perioc
In one case a tragedy seems to have occurred in the last pha

the city, in an attempt to escape from a well-room, during
hich four persons were killed. Two lay on or below the stairs
here they died, trying to climb to the street; one of these
·ms to have fallen backwards. The other two came to an un-
nely end in the lane outside or near by, where some of their
·nes were found.[42] At Chanhu-daro near Sakrand in the
uwabkah district of Sind, the only graves came from the
uhammadan cemetery.[43]

ırappa

n the south-eastern outskirts of the ancient city of Harappa
the Montgomery district of the Punjab, a lightly packed
ass of twenty complete skulls and other fragments inter-
ingled with long bones, animal remains and pottery were
ınd in what seems to have been an ossuary.[44] In the
serted corner of a house fragments of two skulls were
:overed and said to have been a fractional burial,[45] but it
·ms more likely that it was a modern interment. Some of the
nes had been buried with the ligaments upon them, and
r Mortimer Wheeler suggests that they may have been
:erred ceremonially after a plague or battle when vultures and
:kals had done their grim work on the bodies.[46]

Cemetery R 37. To the south of the citadel mound in what is
own as cemetery R 37, fifty-seven graves have been identified
belonging to the main Harappan period. The bodies in them
·re extended from north to south with the head towards the
·rth. Large quantities of pottery were placed at the head, some
the feet and along the sides, and occasionally below the
dy, ranging from as many as forty pots to from fifteen to
enty as a fair average. Personal ornaments and toilet objects
·re sometimes worn. These included a copper ring found on
·e skeleton, and on others a necklace of steatite beads, two
·klets of paste beads, a copper ear-ring and shell bangles,
;ether with a copper mirror, a stock of antimony, a large
·ll spoon, and mother-of-pearl. In one grave was a small
·ttery lamp and bones of a fowl on the floor near the feet of
· deceased. One of the graves was lined with mud-brick as

at Nal in Southern Baluchistan,[47] and in another the bod‑
probably that of a girl, had been buried in the extended positio
in a wooden coffin and wrapped in a shroud of reeds, of whic
traces remained. With it were thirty‑seven pots, the majori‑
near but outside the head of the coffin. On the right midd
finger was a copper ring, to the left of the skull a shell rin
(perhaps an ear‑ring) and two others above the left shoulder.[4]

Cemetery H. Between this cemetery and the citadel on th
south side a second cemetery in Area H was excavated by Va‑
in 1929 and the succeeding seasons, in the lower and old‑
stratum of which were extended burials, sometimes with th
knees slightly bent, orientated towards the east or north‑eas‑
Some of them may have been fractional, unless they we‑
normal interments disturbed by later burials or other cause
The red ware was not Harappan, and among the food offerin‑
was a dismembered goat. Apart from a gold bangle on th
wrist of a woman and three teeth on a gold wire on the sku
of another, no ornamentation occurred. On the stratum abov
this lower level about 140 true fractional burials were foun‑
together with babies enclosed in urns in the contracted positio‑
The jars, again, are not Harappan, and on them are depicte
scenes which it has been suggested have Vedic affinities.[4]
Although the friezes on the urns display the same decorativ‑
characters in both the upper and lower strata, the symbolisn
with its bulls, goats, waisted animals, crested peacocks betwee‑
groups of stellar or solar motifs with the figure of a centaur wi‑
horns, has no really convincing parallel in any of the cultur‑
of the Ancient East. But as cemetery H is subsequent to th
true Harappa civilization, its contents do not come within ou
present inquiry.

What is significant is that in the earlier Harappa cemete‑
R 37 inhumation in the extended position was the norm‑
mode of disposal, and that it conformed to the usual mortua‑
procedure in respect of food offerings, grave goods and person‑
ornaments, though fractional burial also may have be‑
adopted. If cremation, which subsequently became predom‑
nant in Vedic India, was practised it has left no very convincin‑

traces of its occurrence prior to the destruction of the cities in the middle of the second millennium B.C.

Throughout the Ancient East, from the Fertile Crescent to the Indus valley, the funeral ritual underwent singularly little change from the beginning of the Neolithic to the break-up of the urban cultures. This uniformity is an indication of the solidarity of the area as a cultural unit in which, despite marked differences in climatic and economic conditions and in respect of the social and religious structures, there was a uniformity of procedure in the burial of the dead, and in the funeral ritual and equipment. In the Indus valley the evidence is surprisingly meagre, and although it appears to have had a theocratic state with a sacred kingship,[50] no royal tombs, comparable to those in Egypt or at Ur, have come to light. Whether or not the practice of cremation played any part in the absence of extensive cemeteries has yet to be determined by further excavation.

Megalithic Burial in Europe

WHEN the Neolithic culture passed from the Ancient East westwards into Europe in the second half of the fourth millennium B.C. (i.e. from about 3500 to 3000 B.C.), following either an overland route from the south-east to and along the Danube or by way of the Mediterranean littoral to Spain and France and the north-west, with in addition a continental route from South Russia, Poland, Central Europe and Germany, the cult of the dead underwent considerable development. If in the Middle East the use of copper and later of bronze played an important part in the beginnings of the more highly organized urban communities, in Europe the knowledge of metal spread relatively slowly in a northerly direction and was still unknown long after it was well established in the Fertile Crescent, Iraq, Persia, Turkestan and Anatolia. But this did not prevent a general advance in culture over the greater part of Europe in the third millennium.

EASTERN MEDITERRANEAN

Tholoi in Cyprus

So far as the disposal of the dead is concerned, in Cyprus with its close links with the neighbouring Chalcolithic cities of southern Anatolia, at Khirokitia, between 4000 and 3500 B.C., the remains of tholoi have been found similar to those of the Tell Halaf period at Arpachiyah in Iraq near Nineveh.[1] These lie on either side of a long wall resting on the older structure of the small tholoi, 4 to 6 metres in diameter, made of *pisé*, or sun-dried bricks, forming a kind of corbelled roof, or with mud-plastered reeds or brushwood. The larger ones, 10 metres wide with walls 2 metres thick, are fewer in number and were built on either the left or the right of the wall. In many cases they are surrounded by open spaces enclosed by walls. In the area were round tables built of stone slabs and burnt bones. The foundations are deeper and more substantial than are those of the smaller tholoi, and on them the earliest attempt at corbelling in the whole of the Mediterranean was constructed in the form of a vault built of river stones and resting on the walls.

The floors were usually made of beaten earth or mud, sometimes plastered with a layer of fine mud, and in them the graves were dug. Whether large or small, nearly every tholos contained one or more skeletons, mostly in the contracted position. Over the head or chest a large stone quern was placed, necklaces of beads and shells sometimes were worn, and bowls, intentionally broken, surrounded the body. In one of the larger tholoi a woman had been buried under a square platform in the foreground, with the hands, it seems, bound behind the back, as in the Neolithic strata at Jericho. Near the summit of the hill two skeletons were found below a rectangular platform of mud plastered over with clay on the floor of a fine tholos. One had a necklace of carnelian beads and dentalia, and was surrounded by broken vases. The other, that of a young person, had the hands behind the back and a bowl under the middle part of the body.

One of the most important of the upper group of tholoi contained twenty-five infants in successive floors, in some cases buried on top of adults, elsewhere in small holes surrounded with stones or covered with slabs. On the lower floor were a "throne", or seat, made of river-stones, and three small round hearths, on one of which lay the skeleton of an adult. Higher up was a clay head of a figure, probably representing a male god, ornamented at the back with what appears to be a snake design. This may suggest a connexion with the cult of the Great Mother whose emblem in Crete was the snake. Or the head may represent a chthonian deity with the snake as his attribute; a belief that recurred in the Bronze Age in Cyprus.[2] The infants may have been sacrificed as part of the funeral ritual, and the whole tholos and its equipment indicate that it was a place of peculiar sanctity. In fact, all the larger structures and many of the smaller ones seem to have been connected with the cult of the dead as their contents show that they were reserved for burials and the prescribed mortuary ritual, which may have included sacrifices in honour of the chthonian deities. Some of the smaller tholoi, on the other hand, appear to have been habitations, or used for grinding grain, without any connexion with burials.[3]

In the succeeding culture localized at Erimi (3500–3000), which marks the transition from the Chalcolithic to the Bronze Age in Cyprus, the tholoi have a stone substructure with a central support. On or along the inner face of the foundation post-holes occur, suggesting that there had been a superstructure of brushwood or reeds supported by posts and covered with mud. On the floor of rammed earth there were traces of occupation, but burials have been found along the outer ridge of the stone foundation or under the floor. Towards the end of the period, in addition to the mortuary ritual practised at Khirokitia, the presence of female figurines in graves suggests that the cult of the Mother-goddess had been introduced, probably as a result of foreign influence.[4]

In a later necropolis at Vounous Bellapais (*c.* 2800–2000 B.C.) a vase from Palestine shows that contacts with the Fertile Crescent continued into the Bronze Age (i.e. 2800–2600 B.C.). The cult of the dead became more developed and tombs cut in the rock were either short with roughly parallel sides and rounded back, or long and narrowing towards the end, which was either straight or rounded. The long sides sometimes sloped inwards. Each *dromos* gave access to a main chamber through a rectangular or rounded doorway. On either side of the tomb were from one to three smaller side-chambers blocked by rectangular, rounded or irregular slabs of rough blocks of limestone. In some the bodies were placed in niches with grave goods on the floor. In the earliest period the burials generally were in the right and left parts of the chamber with large vessels on top of them, though in one case they covered the greater part of the floor. The bodies were clad in their usual clothes with bronze daggers, pins, necklaces and small bottles or near them. Large bowls containing animals' bones and smaller vessels were used in the sacrificial ritual in honour of the dead, the animal victims having been deposited on the floor of the chamber with vases placed over their remains. As new burials were introduced in the family or clan tomb the previous ones and their furniture were grouped along the back wall of the chamber.[5]

Vaulted Tombs in Crete

In Crete a succession of vaulted beehive tombs have been investigated along the borders of the plain of Mesara since 1904, containing hundreds of interments. Those grouped round Koumasa, south-east of Gortyna on the upper slopes of the Kophina mountains, consisted of four tholoi, three circular and one square, varying in internal diameter from 4·10 to 13 metres. They were enclosed within dry-stone walling composed of undressed stones bonded by a quantity of clay and projections inwards. The whole had been roofed with a corbelled vault, or with wood and thatch. It was entered through a doorway to the east, formed by two large stone uprights supporting a massive lintel. In one case (tholos B) the doorway was divided into two by a large upright stone deeply fixed into the ground. The natural rock was left as a floor, as was also the case at Hagia Triada and Platanos. On the outside of the northern wall five slabs in a row projected from 0·15 to ·20 metre at a height of about 1 metre from the ground, possibly to serve as scaffolding during the building of the upper part of the tomb, or if it was covered with earth it may have been a key binding it with the earth to make it more compact. A square pit lined with stones often stood before the doorway, and a court paved with slabs recurred in front of several tholoi.

Inside was a hearth at which numerous fires must have been lighted in the middle of the circle immediately under a smoke-hole. But it would seem to have been for ritual purposes other than cremation, as no genuine evidence exists for this mode of disposal having been practised in these tombs. The thickness

of the burial stratum and the mass of bones indicate hundre
of interments, which at Hagia Triada were estimated k
Professor Halbherr at 250, and at tholos B at Koumasa tl
number was far larger.[6] The bones, however, were so dislocate
and often heaped together in various parts of the chamber t
afford space for subsequent burials, that the manner of dispos
could not be ascertained. Throughout the Mediterranean con
munal sepulture was the common custom, a communi
burying in the same ossuary for hundreds of years, generatio
after generation in this way being "gathered to their fathers'
Thus a chronological sequence of objects occurred in tl
tombs though the more valuable articles, especially those d
metal, frequently were extracted from the preceding interme
when a tholos was reopened. To judge by such things a
remained, the equipment included stone vases and palettes n
unlike those in the royal tombs in Egypt at the beginning d
the Dynastic period,[7] cylinder seals and clay figurines, amulet
scorpions on ivory seals, and pins, awls and daggers in coppe
suggesting intercourse with Egypt and the Aegean, whi
geometric vases, the spiral motif on seals and vases, an
obsidian, show Cycladic influences. Fires were burnt on tl
floors of the tombs but no traces of cremation occurred, an
although no evidence was obtainable from the Mesara thol
concerning posture, elsewhere in Crete contracted burial i
coffins or clay pithoi was the usual procedure.[8]

In Eastern Crete single graves or cists were grouped in sma
cemeteries, and at Mochlos large ossuaries or chamber tomb
were entered through doorways closed by huge upright slat
of stone, or cists were constructed with walls of similar slab
Sometimes the walls were built of small stones like those use
in house construction, or with a combination of large an
small stones. Occasionally bodies were interred in holes in tl
rocks with no attempt at a fashioned grave and very little i
the way of mortuary objects. These all belonged to the Earl
Minoan period, but in the Middle Minoan large terra cotta jar
or pithoi, came into use. These were found standing upsid
down over the earlier tombs or in cemeteries, as at Pachyamm

d Sphoungaras, in a state of confusion as a result of subse-
ient interments. The body had been placed in the jar with
e head downwards, and the jar had been then put in the
ound bottom up, the corpse occupying a sitting or crouched
osition; the knees often trussed up under the chin and the
ms doubled back against the body.[9]

The Cycladic Tombs

Notwithstanding the influence of Egypt on the Mesara tholoi,
which may indeed have been erected by Libyan settlers soon
fter 3000 B.C., in Early Minoan II and III in Crete and the
Aegean, collective burial in stone-built or rock-cut tombs, or
n natural caves, prevailed in successive interments numbering
many hundreds, as against the separate sepulture in Egypt and
Mesopotamia. In the Cyclades, connecting Crete with the
mainland, the early graves included cave-burial, rock-cut
ombs and small slab-cists. In these barren islands, however,
olonized from Anatolia about 3000 B.C., as in Eastern Crete
ndividual burial in the contracted position was prevalent in
he later tombs (i.e. Early Cycladic III, about 2400 B.C.)
containing human figures called "idols", marble vases and
weapons. In the oldest prehistoric cemeteries at Pelos in Melos
he graves were cists constructed of four erect slabs from the
neighbouring hill-side with the bottom paved with thin plates
of schist and covered with a huge capstone, roughly flattened
on the underside. Burial apparently had been in the contracted
position, and several of the graves had held at least half a dozen
bodies, as at the cemetery of Antiparos, where most of the tombs
contained more than one skeleton. The head in most cases was
laid against the west wall, but no attempt was made at orientation. The vases were at one end but not more than two were
found in a single grave.[10]

In the majority of the island tombs the contents were much
the same and included earthen or stone pots, varying in shape
and colour from light red to black, marble idols, sometimes
shaped like a "fiddle", obsidian blades, copper daggers
and axes and silver ornaments, but in later cemeteries (e.g.

Antiparos II, Amorgos, Siphnos, Syros) the metal ornaments were prevalent, the idols better shaped and the grave more elaborate. For example, at Antiparos I on the western side, bones were heaped together in confusion, and most graves contained the remains of several bodies which would seem to have been cut up and tightly wedged together between the side slabs. In the later sites on the south-east of the island the tombs were longer and better built, and contained only one body in each, the head resting on a slab or pillow. In both, the nature of the goods was the same, but the large marble bowls and plates, obsidian implements, pottery designs and representations of the human form in marble, showed an advance in technical skill.[11]

In the southern group of tombs at Phylakopi in Melos irregular pits, sometimes semicircular, were sunk beneath a shelf of rock, or subterranean rectangular chambers were cut out of the soft rock, entered through a rectangular doorway and approached by a short uncovered dromos about 1 metre in length and 1·60 metres in width. Unfortunately these chamber-tombs were not reopened or thoroughly examined when they were found. They and the shaft-graves of uncertain date are by no means rare in the Phylakopi district, trapezoid cists being the earlier mode of burial. On the west side of the Bathing Creek, the graves are quite small, sometimes round with a dromos and a low beehive roof. On the east side is a two-chambered tomb with a gable roof, well-squared walls, and a ledge for the head of the corpse to rest on. The pottery was mainly of local geometric ware, with obsidian chips lying about. Fragments from the chambers included Mycenaean imports, showing that later influences were felt in the Early Cycladic settlements.[12] In Guboea, only single interments occurred in the pit-grave excavated in the ground, and the same applies in the rectangular or oval corbelled tombs in the hill-side of Syros. On the island of Pantelleria between Sicily and Africa are a series of elliptical structures, locally called "sesi", containing one or more burial chambers approached by a passage to which a low door gives access and having a corbelled roof. They are solid masonry with an outer casing of large blocks of stone, and are believed to be Neolithic in origin.[13]

The Siculan Rock-cut Tombs

Farther to the west, Sicily became a cultural centre in the third millennium B.C. As early as 2500 agricultural settlements of Eastern-Mediterranean type situated on hill-tops began to replace Neolithic villages. The cemeteries were composed of rock-cut tombs, usually entered through a *domos* leading to oval or circular chambers which contained a number of burials. The narrow portal or window cut out of the slabs at the top, probably a survival of the doorway of the chamber-tomb, was sealed with a slab which in one case at Castelluccio near Syracuse was decorated with spirals in relief. In the same cemetery another tomb was closed with two carved slabs which together represented a breasted female figure.[14] At Monteracello the vault was later reproduced above ground as a rectangular cist built of squared slabs of limestone set on edge with a window-entry at one end to represent the door. The chambers, however, were generally more or less circular in plan, though natural cave-tombs and old flint mines were in use as family graves, and followed the Aegean funerary technique and ritual in its main characteristics.[15]

WESTERN MEDITERRANEAN

Sardinian Gallery-tombs

The elaborately constructed Siculan port-hole slabs ornamented with raised bosses and engraved spirals recur in the Sardinian gallery-tombs, in the Maltese tholoi, and in the Spanish passage-graves, while a similar entrance is found in British barrows and in cists in Brittany, in the valley of the Seine and in Sweden. In Sardinia, where collective burial in caves and rock-cut tombs was common, gallery-graves, known locally as *tombe di giganti*, or giants' tombs, were constructed of rude blocks roofed with flat capstones or corbelling and covered by a cairn enclosed by masonry walls rounded at the closed end. At the front the entrance was effected through a huge slab carved and bordered in relief with a small hole at the base and gabled above.[16] The narrow corridor of dressed slabs opened into a rectangular chamber enclosed by large slabs of stone set on edge and roofed with similar slabs, the intervening space being filled with earth. The chamber was a family tomb, and from the entrance two wings branched off, prolonging the double walls of the corridor, which were sometimes covered with clay mortar, not unlike in plan the horned cairns of Northern Ireland except that the stones were dressed with metal tools. Some of the Giants' Tombs were contemporary with the rock-cut graves known as *domus di giganti*, or "Witches' Houses", with an upright slab forming the entrance to both of them from a semicircular space flanked by masonry.

The rock-cut tombs consist of a circular or elliptical chamber with a beehive ceiling and approached by a short corridor rectangular in form, though sometimes the chamber is rectangular with a flat roof. It is not easy to date these graves in the absence of very much in the way of well-attested furnishings. Mackenzie attempted to establish a typological sequence from the "dolmen" to the Giants' Tomb,[17] following that of Montelius for the evolution of megalithic monuments in general. But the process can as easily be reversed unless it is supported by datable contents. The connexion would seem to be rather with the Mediterranean tholos type of tomb, though there may be some relation between them and the truncated conical dry-stone towers of clay mortar and blocks of stone called *nuraghi*, which in their more complicated forms continued in their final development until the Late Bronze Age in the first millennium B.C. as fortified refuges, sometimes containing traces of a third upper chamber approached by a stairway, and revealing signs of habitation.[18]

Rock-cut Tombs and Navetas in the Balearic Isles

In the Balearic Isles a similar mystery surrounds the *talayots*, commonly found in Menorca, which while sometimes used for burial purposes generally had neither entrance nor interior hambers. In construction they resembled the *navetas*, or stone-built tombs shaped like a ship, built of cyclopean masonry in which a slab-roofed passage leading to a rectangular burial chamber had a very small door.[19] Closely associated with them in Mallorca were a number of rock-cut tombs, dating from the Bronze Age, consisting of a long narrow gallery with one or more smaller side-chambers opening out of it. Those on the level ground are approached by a descending stair contained in a chamber cut in the rock and open to the sky. Others are entered through a low opening cut in the rock and giving access to an uncovered courtyard in the hill-side. Both types may have courtyards and a single or double vestibule which may or may not contain a stair. In one instance a mound was erected over a cave covering the entrance. The main chamber was filled with earth in which the bodies were buried in the extended position with pottery, copper or bronze daggers and awls, perforated shells, and buttons. In the side-chambers they were laid in the contracted posture, and in some of the vessels human bones and ornaments were found.[20]

In the *navetas* of Menorca the structure of the rock-cut tombs is reproduced above the surface of the ground in the form of megalithic chambers along boat-like lines. That known as Es Tudons ("the wood-pigeons") stands on slightly rising ground in a sloping valley, measuring in length about 45 feet with a height of rather under 15 feet. The entrance at its western end is nearly square with three courses of upright masonry inclining towards an angle of 67°. The eastern end is rounded and gathered in at an angle of about 55°, the sides perhaps meeting originally in a ridge before the upper part collapsed. The appearance was that of an overturned ship (*naveta*) with a square stern and rounded prow. The monument stands on a platform above the level of the rock, and forms the forecourt bounded by rough stones. In front of the entrance are two slabs which formed a second semicircular area concentric with the forecourt. The door of the entrance may have been a slab of stone, suggested by a groove shown in the floor, and through this opening a passage led to an antechamber some 10 feet high.

A second narrow passage led into the main chamber con-structed like that in the rock-cut tombs, except that the roof made of great slabs is flat instead of being rounded. At the far end is a terminal ledge, 2 feet above the floor-level, as in the caves, but no side-chambers have been discovered. Since in all probability the *navetas* were used as tombs for chieftains in the manner of the Giants' Graves in Sardinia, while commoners were buried in the rock-cut tombs, they doubtless were carefully sealed after interment. This is indicated by the rebate for a door-slab at the two Rafal Rubi *navetas*. At Es Tudons frag-ments of prehistoric pottery and two pieces of a bronze armlet in the soil by the entrance suggest that it was a tomb which remained unopened until fairly recently.[21] But until more is known of their contents the Balearic graves will remain obscure notwithstanding their structural importance in the megalithic tradition of the long cairn type of grave.

Maltese Megaliths

Of all the islands in the Western Mediterranean, however, the one of greatest sacred significance from the third millennium B.C. was Malta. Although it was uninhabited apparently until the megalithic civilization reached its barren shores about 3000 B.C., it was there that the elaborate labyrinthine burial vaults or apsidal "temples" of Mnaidra, Hagia Kim and Hal Tarxien were created, with the Gigantea on the neighbouring island of Gozo and the Hal Saftieni Hypogeum to the north-west of the village of Tarxien, prior to the arrival of the Bronze Age immigration about the middle of the second millennium when cremation was introduced at Tarxien. It is true that Ugolini has endeavoured to make the island the centre from which Mediterranean civilization originated,[22] but this claim can hardly be seriously maintained. Nevertheless, it certainly does seem to have been the meeting-place of a number of streams of culture over a considerable period from western Asia and the Eastern Mediterranean, including Thessaly and the Balkans, as well as from Egypt, and nearer at hand from Italy, beginning perhaps, as Zammit contended, about 3000 B.C.[23]

It may, however, have been rather later that the tholos-architecture of Near-Eastern (Sumerian) origin, in its western diffusion, reached the island.[24]

The three successive Neolithic temples at Hal Tarxien reveal a chronological series extending from the Neolithic in the third millennium B.C. to the Bronze Age in the middle of the second millennium. Within these broader periods, which in Malta in the Phoenician colonization continued into the first millennium B.C., contemporary with the final phases of the nuraghic culture in Sardinia, there were subdivisions each displaying its own insular characteristics as well as its contacts with the out-side world, ranging from the Near East and Anatolia to the Cyclades, Italy and Sicily. It was, in fact, not until the Bronze Age that this seclusion was interrupted by the arrival of a cremating immigration at Hal Tarxien from the Eastern Medi-terranean, and only there has a cremation cemetery been found containing copper and bronze implements and a type of pottery with its duck-shaped vessels, quite distinct from the preceding Neolithic ware.[25] It may be that it was only one of several similar groups which happened to have been isolated before it was influenced by the native Neolithic culture, but in any case it shows how vigorous was the indigenous prehistoric civilization known to us very largely from its megalithic monuments.

Notwithstanding the complexity of their structure, the general plan is that of the megaliths of the Siculan and Sardinian type with corbelled vaulting, a curved forecourt and a passage leading to several chambers. Thus, at Mnaidra two elliptical chambers are placed one behind the other, the southern half consisting of a paved passage of upright stones leading to an enclosure composed of a wall of vertical and horizontal masonry. To the left of the entrance stands a trilithon table with a horizontal block above it. A window 16 by 12 inches has been cut in the vertical slab of the wall of the enclosure beyond the aperture, and similar port-holes occur in the south-west wall communicating with two other rectangular spaces, while the whole of the southern half of the structure is surrounded by a series of rough stones set alternately with the broad faces and their narrow edges outwards. The roofing of the apses was by corbelling, of which a few traces are still visible.[26] The northern half of the temple was added later, and at Hagia Kim and Hal Tarxien a complicated sanctuary was produced, apsidal elliptical chambers with cup-marks and spiral cuts on many of the slabs being suggestive of Minoan influences.

The Hal Tarxien group of temples, to which a fourth has now been added, are all prior to the Bronze Age influx with a common approach from a large semicircular forecourt leading to a corridor terminating in an apse. The succession of developments was spread over centuries within the Neolithic period, with a fourth smaller temple to the east dating from the Bronze Age more or less contemporary with the cemetery overlying the other temples. The whole structure may have been surrounded by a mound of earth up to the level of the capstones, while the apses were domed with corbelled cupolas and the corridors sheltered by long horizontal slabs, with the spaces between the apses only open to the sky. The walls were decorated with geometric designs, spirals and friezes of animals.[27]

The temple called Gigantea in Gozo, which originally consisted of a single shrine, contained stones with spirals and animal designs in relief, and ornamental pittings. Like Mnaidra, when a second temple was added it became two separate buildings, each having two sets of parallel elliptical areas with the remains of niches and altars in the second elliptical enclosure.[28] The great rock-cut Hypogeum at Hal Saflioni with its domed vaults decorated with spirals is an underground series of caves, passages and chambers with trilithons built in front of them, reproducing below ground in three storeys the main features of the temples. The middle room is the largest and has a number of small chambers and two decorated rooms, with the lowest storey reached by a flight of steps partly cut in the rock. Before it became a vast ossuary extensively used for burial purposes, containing, it is estimated, 7,000 interments with shell necklaces, polished stone amulets and funerary pottery, it may have been used as a sanctuary for oracular and initiatory rites, as Zammit has suggested,[29] in which, as will be considered later,[30] the Asiatic Mother-goddess probably played an important part. But whatever may have been the precise nature of the cultus performed in these sacred edifices, Malta unquestionably was an important religious centre in the third millennium B.C., and while its megalithic cult may not have been essentially a mortuary ritual, despite the absence of burials except at Hal Saflieni, the plan of construction adopted with the semicircular court with apses, port-holes and slabs used as doorways and approached through a passage, conforms to that of the collective tombs of the Eastern Mediterranean. The oldest examples were elliptical apsidal shrines with a door on one long wall and a niche facing it on the other, branching into lateral and terminal apses. This is merely an extension of the rock-cut tomb, familiar as we have seen elsewhere in the Western Mediterranean in the tholos tradition, with the addition of a semicircular paved forecourt.

The numerous graves cut in the rock at Malta are assigned to the Phoenician occupation in the first millennium, prior to the Roman domination in 218 B.C. The earliest of these are circular tombs with a domed ceiling and shallow circular shaft and a square entrance sealed on the outside by a rectangular stone slab. Cinerary urns of an amphora type, globular in form and covered with a circular plate, occur in them, with ashes in one or more urns. These oldest graves were followed by an almost identical structure except that the shaft became deeper and rectangular, until in the third stage the funeral chamber was rectangular with a flat ceiling and the floor ran at right angles to the entrance dividing the tomb into two parts with a flat ledge on each side of the trench on which two bodies were laid. Occasionally, rectangular chambers were added to the single shaft. The furniture became progressively more and more abundant and varied in the later graves, inhumation being the rule in the second stage, though cinerary urns in the shape of a simple Maltese olla persisted throughout the sepulture. Copper jewellery occurred in the third type of rectangular tomb as well as glass, beads, stone and ivory objects, and a bilychnis lamp with Carthaginian affinities. Roman influences were very evident in the later graves, but although they were used by the Phoenicians and their successors down to the Christian era, some of the rock-cut tombs may have been built in the pre-Phoenician period. Indeed Zammit maintained that some of those of the first stage cannot be much later than about 3000 B.C.[31] If this can be substantiated by further discoveries and examination of the furniture, the sepulchral origin of the temple architecture will become more apparent.

Isolated from commercial relations with the Aegean the culture contacts of Malta in Neolithic times seem to have been mainly with Anatolia and Western Asia, notwithstanding the presence of querns of lava from Sicily, and Siculan bossed bone-plaques, and the spiral designs and other Minoan influences which reached it by the second phase of Hal Tarxien. The pottery shows resemblances to that of Southern Italy and Sicily, while the rotund female figurines and ancient figures in bas-relief are Thessalian and Asiatic in appearance, and the polished grey ware is reminiscent of Syria and Palestine. Besides Danubian, Macedonian and other Eastern European connexions, the closest affinities appear to have been with Sardinia. Notwithstanding the traces of Minoan contacts the sacred isle stood apart from the rest of the Aegean world, and having practically nothing to export it remained relatively in isolation from the commercial activities of the region. This doubtless explains the survival of the Neolithic culture long after the use of copper and bronze had become established elsewhere. But as the centre of the megalithic cult it occupied a unique position in the Western Mediterranean in the third millennium and exercised a far-reaching and powerful influence in the diffusion of this essentially religious prehistoric civilization.

IBERIAN PENINSULA

The Almerian Megaliths

It was, however, on the southern and eastern shores of the Iberian peninsula that the commercial and cultural enterprises were most apparent from about 2600 B.C. onwards, and nowhere is the megalithic tradition more strongly represented than in Almeria and the surrounding district. Communal graves, ossuaries, cists, simple and chambered or galleried "dolmens", corridor-tombs, corbelled vaults with or without entrance passages; in short, practically every known type of great stone monument is to be found on the land bridge in the sea route from the Ancient Middle East to the Atlantic littoral and the North-west. Its wealth in metals made it a centre of commercial enterprise for traders and voyagers, and the Chalcolithic invasion of Spain, which introduced the megalithic cult, may have been preceded by metal-using navigators who settled at Valez Blanco, Palaces, Campo and Puerto Blanco, where they buried their dead in stone-walled trenches containing from eight to ten bodies, or in stone cists, each under a round cairn, rather like the North African pit-graves or the Early Minoan rock-cut cists. But collective burial in natural caves and circular cists was also coming into vogue with collective necklaces, stone beads, bracelets, *Pectunculus* shells, stone figurines, and copper pins, among their funerary furniture.[32]

The Neolithic folk settled on hill-tops like El Garcel near the Mediterranean coast in South-east Spain, and brought with them a culture having affinities with that of the Badarians and Merimdian peoples of prehistoric Egypt and the Fayum. But they also had adopted collective burial and the use of calläis beads which might connect them with Brittany rather than the Fertile Crescent. It was apparently upon this first genuine Neolithic civilization in Western Europe that the megalithic voyagers made their impact when they established themselves in Almeria among the hills at Los Millares. There within very easy reach of the coast in a region rich in copper, gold, silver and lead, they erected a settlement on the spur of a plateau overlooking the fertile valley of the Anderax river with a cemetery of collective tombs behind the town containing copper daggers and axes, flint arrow-heads, ornaments of ivory and calläis, amulets, bone figurines, stone jars, beakers, bowls and vessels decorated with conventionalized animals.

Rectangular houses were built with dry-stone walling and supplied with water by an aqueduct from a spring in the hill-side. Whether or not it was contemporary with or subsequent to the Garcel Neolithic culture is a matter of debate, but in any case it represents an influx of a group of megalithic builders in Almeria who became sufficiently powerful and established to fashion and erect imposing stone tombs with corbelled roofs.

Over a hundred of them were constructed in small groups, either with entrance passages, circular corbelled chambers and dry-stone walling, like those at Khirokitia in Cyprus or at Mesara in Crete, or as quadrangular megalithic gallery tombs. The chambers in the tholoi generally are from 3 to 6 metres in diameter, and the walls are lined with stone slabs plastered and painted, while pillars of stone or wood support the roof. A single or double ring of upright stones constitutes the retaining wall of the earth mound, and on the side where it descends, generally on that facing the sea (i.e. the east), the

Fig. 3. Entrance to passage-grave at Los Millares, Spain

Fig. 4. Reconstruction of entrance to passage-grave
at Los Millares

wall of the chamber and the slab at the entrance are pierced by
a doorway or port-hole, frequently divided into a series of
antechambers by other doors. This passage is constructed with
upright slabs or dry-stone, the roof is of flat slabs or corbelled,
and the portals are formed of several slabs or of a single holed-
stone (Figs. 3, 4). Access to the circular mound is gained by two
or three steps leading down to the passage. The semicircular
forecourt where the rites were performed, often is outlined by
stone slabs.[33]

In one tomb up to a hundred burials were found, and everywhere there are indications of collective interment on a considerable scale over long periods, the earlier bones having been
put on one side to make room for later additions to the necropolis. The skeletons often overflow into the passage, and it has
been suggested that a family likeness occurs in some of the
skulls. Be this as it may, there is little room for doubt that these
great tombs belonged to a family or clan, as elsewhere in the
megalithic region. In this neighbourhood in South-eastern
Spain similar cemeteries existed at Almizaraque and Las
Canteras, and farther to the west at Belmonte, Purcherra,
Tabernas and Velez Blancho.[34] There were also in the area
slab-built graves, some rectangular or in the form of trapezoid
cists with short entrance passages.

Although there were traces of partially burnt bones, inhumation was the normal method of sepulture, the fires probably
having been for ritual purposes as purifying agents. The furniture everywhere was rich, and while this included an abundance
of copper daggers, awls and pins, there were also superbly
flaked flint arrow-heads, halbert blades and knives together
with ivory, turquoise, calläis, *pectunculus* shell, amber and jet
objects. The pottery was mainly Almerian with decorated
incised geometric and ritualistic designs, but a few beakers
occurred in some of the tombs as an intrusive element. Highly
stylized female figurines made by painting or incising knuckle-
bones were among the cult objects in the graves, which
included flat-stone croziers, a few undecorated schist plaques,
and stone or bone models of sandals used apparently as
amulets as were the stone-axes.

South-west Iberian Tombs

Granada on the plateau also contains several large cemeteries
of collective burials in the neighbourhood of Guardix, Gor
and Gorafe. A few were corbelled tholoi, but most of them
were smaller cists, often entered through port-holed slabs, and
containing Almerian funerary furniture, but of a rather inferior
and less varied character. In fertile Andalusia, rich in minerals,
vast tombs were erected, as, for example, at Antiquera at the
base of the Sierra de los Toreales, between Malaga and
Granada. There the Cueva de Menga consists of a short lofty
passage leading to a rectangular chamber, 25 metres in length
and 6 metres in width, rising to 3 metres in height at its inner
end, which is cut out of a ridge of a cliff and covered with
four large slabs and a low mound of earth supported by three
large central pillars. The chamber is walled with carefully
dressed upright stones inclined inwards, and the gallery is
covered with a single slab. The entrance is composed of four
stones rather lower in height than the rest of the uprights but
showing no indication of an inward incline. On the last of
the vertical blocks on the left wall of the passage elongated
cruciform figures are incised comparable to the designs of

Neolithic shelters in the provinces of Malaga and Granada, and similar in patina to that of the surrounding rocks. These may have been a later addition, but they reveal the antiquity of the monument.[35]

On the same hill overlooking the plain, about 80 yards from the Cueva de Menga, there is a second chambered tomb, the Cueva de Viera, following the same method of construction but on a smaller scale and entered through a long gallery divided from the chamber by a stone doorway at one end and by a similar portal from an outer passage of rough stones at the other end. The cover-stones of the inner gallery and chamber are less regular than those of the Cueva de Menga, and on the stones of the outer passage are cup-markings. Two kilometres away a double-chambered tomb of cupola-type, the Cueva de Romeral, stands on an isolated hill, while a simpler form of the same construction recurs at Gor in Granada, and Matarrubilla in Sevilla.[36] In fact, from Almeria to the Portuguese province of Algarve on the South-west Atlantic coast, a long line of megalithic collective tombs mark the sites of ancient settlements in this metalliferous region. Thus, in the cemetery of Alcala in Algarve there are seven corbelled tombs of the Los Millares type with galleries, portals leading to a circular chamber, paved and divided into rectangular compartments, though in some dry-stone walling takes the place of vertical slabs.[37]

At Palmella in Estremadura on the Tagus estuary near Lisbon circular rock-cut tombs approached by passages with antechambers reappear and extend along the Atlantic coast to Alapraia (Cascaes), and Folha de Barradas (Cintra), and inland to Badajoz and Salamanca in Spain. In them the funerary furniture was less elaborate and metal objects were rare. Nevertheless, the essential features of the Almerian characteristics were retained in the cylinder-head pins, clay plaques, marble figures, often with incised eyes and bands, and excellently fashioned and polished halberd blades in flint and arrow-heads. From elsewhere came callais beads, schist plaques, gold, amber, ivory and croziers decorated with rectilinear designs and a squat type of beaker ware, globular pots and carinated bowls. Copper was only used for small objects in most of the graves, its place being taken by stone and flint axes.[38]

Pyrenaean Megaliths

While Almerian influences were extending westwards to Portugal, along the east coast and the Ebro valley, they were also penetrating northwards until they reached Catalonia and the Pyrenees. The indigenous population continued to bury their dead in caves and trench graves but in North-eastern Catalonia, Navarra and the Basque province megalithic passage-graves under round cairns, gallery and bottle-shaped tombs, dolmens with polygonal chambers and short passages began to make their way from the south, together with an abundance of copper objects, calläis beads, cylinder-pins, *Pectunculus* bracelets, zoned beakers, bone buttons, and knuckle-bone figures. The segmented galleries divided into two compartments by slabs like a series of cists, prevalent in the Pyrenees, may have arisen as a result of a fusion between the Almerian and El Garcel immigrations in this area.[39] Caves were still used, however, for burial, but it was the gallery-graves and their culture that became the dominant influence in the Pyrenaean region, spreading from Catalonia across to the west coast of France, representing a combination of the passage-tomb and the slab-cist of the original Almerian colonists.

On the Atlantic littoral and in the hinterland a similar movement occurred, with the megalithic architecture becoming less complex, with small passage-dolmens of inferior workmanship taking the place of the great tombs of the south, until in Galicia, the Basque provinces and the Spanish Pyrenees free-standing rectangular closed dolmens or cists became prevalent, polygonal in the north-west and square in the north-east. These are mere shadows of the great megalithic tombs of the south with their long ancestry in the Middle and Eastern Mediterranean.[40] The rarity of metal in these more remote megaliths is, however, no indication of their age, since the Neolithic culture persisted in North-west Iberia and Northern Europe long after copper and bronze were in general use in the Middle East and the Mediterranean littoral. Nevertheless, it suggests that the quest of ore was not the principal motive of the diffusion in his region, however much it may have been one of the articles sought in the south. Indeed there is no single object, or group of objects, which characterizes these graves, notwithstanding the fact that beaker pottery has revealed the spread of a new cultural influence not only in the Iberian peninsula but through out western and Central Europe from Brittany and the Rhine to Bohemia and Moravia, and sporadically in Sardinia, Sicily and Northern Italy.[41] But this diffusion could not have given rise to the megalithic civilization, in either the Eastern Mediter ranean or Atlantic Europe because, as will be considered later, while the Beaker folk buried their dead in megalithic tombs, they merely adopted the practice when they settled in areas in which the cult was already established.

ATLANTIC EUROPE
Megalithic Tombs in Brittany

Undaunted by the hazards of the Bay of Biscay, the megalithic mariners after colonizing Iberia made their way in a north westerly direction from Portugal and Galicia to the Breton peninsula. Thus, in the Gulf of Morbihan and the neighbour ing isles, which with Jersey may have been joined to the mainland, five types of tombs are distinguishable based on the Iberian tradition but adapted to local conditions and materials. While the corbelled passage graves on the coasts and islands reproduce their Portuguese and Spanish prototypes, they are clearly imitations displaying local variations. In Southern Morbihan the Iberian plan reappears, although corbelling is less frequent than in the south of Spain and is distinct from the small corbelled graves of the Breton Bronze Age. To the north east of Carnac the great passage family dolmen of Kercado in the form of a circular tumulus, 20 metres in diameter and 3·5 metres in height, is surmounted by a menhir over the burial chamber and surrounded by a stone circle (Fig. 5). Originally it had an ashlar retaining wall which splayed out towards the entrance to form a forecourt with a stone-built portal in the centre and a huge slab on each side of it. Encircling the mound was a causeway at the base of the wall constructed of closely packed stones from 3 to 6 metres wide flanked by the stone circle which seems to have been a development of the ritual enclosure at the entrance to some of the tombs at Los Millares and of forecourts in the Aegean tholoi and rock-cut tombs, but extended to embrace the entire structure.[42] Of the rites which were performed in it the only indications are two hearths and a slab on which offerings may have been cooked before presentation to the dead or to their tutelary spirits.

In some of the Breton passage-graves several chambers occur, as, for example, in the tomb of Mané Rutual, Locmariaquer, where behind a smaller rectangular chamber lies a larger polygonal chamber covered by a huge slab, as in the Spanish megaliths. But in Brittany sometimes transepts were added on either side of the gallery at or near the inner end (e.g. Mané-Bras (Goderon) and Clud-er-Yer). Whether or not these transepted galleries evolved in France out of normal Iberian tholoi with lateral cells as at Los Millares,[43] or, as Dr Daniel now maintains, they represent an independent line of diffusion from the gallery-graves set in wedge-shaped barrows related to the Balearic *navetas* and the Scandinavian *giganti*,[44] the elongated straight covered chamber indistinguishable from the passage-grave became a prominent feature in megalithic construction in Brittany (other than in Southern Morbihan) and in the basins of the Loire and the Seine. It is common also in the south of France and in many islands of the western Mediterranean, often covered with a long barrow in contrast to the Breton passage-graves in round barrows. In Morbihan, however, the unchambered long barrows of the Manio type near Carnac, which are not strictly megalithic in structure, may not have been inspired by the great Iberian megalithic tombs,[45] and, unless Dr Daniel is correct in deriving the *allée couverte* from the gallery series in the islands of the Western Mediterranean,[46] which is by no means improbable, the transepted galleries may have been borrowed from the long cairns.

KERCADO
(CARNAC)

Fig. 5. Passage-grave at Kercado, near Carnac, Brittany

Another type of gallery occurs in Brittany consisting of two sections at right angles, the one leading into the other, with carvings of an exclusive design on the vertical slabs. Since this form is unknown south of the Pyrenees, probably it represents a Breton peculiarity. In Southern Morbihan shortened galleries without entrances, such as the closed chamber in the tumulus of Tumiac, Arzon, are built largely of dry-stone walling under huge barrows. That at Mané-er-Hroeck was 100 metres long and covered a square chamber of very large slabs placed horizontally to form a chamber roofed with capstones. On one side of the chamber an upright was decorated with schematic sacred carvings like those on the Iberian chamber tombs, idols and plaques. Spiral designs recur on the pillars at Gavr'inis and Mané-Lud, similar to those in the Middle Mediterranean megaliths.[47] At Mont S. Michel the central chamber was surrounded by a number of small cists, and although they have been assigned to the Bronze Age,[48] green-stone ceremonial axes and calläis beads, which abound in them, suggest that they belong to the established tradition in Brittany, where practically every example of megalithic monument is to be found from corbelled tholoi to small cists.

Corbelling, in fact, is not a prominent feature in this area, having been introduced in all probability by the mariners from the south. A few rock-cut tombs were dug in the softer rocks, but the common practice was to bury commoners in stone cists, or dolmens, consisting of three or more upright slabs roofed with one or two capstones, either under small tumuli or sunk in the ground, containing jadite axes and bracelets, calläis, amber and rock crystal beads, together with some copper and gold objects, stone double axes, mace-heads and ritual carvings. This assortment of grave goods shows that Brittany became the centre of the megalithic cult in north-western Europe, and so attracted devotees from a very wide area. In addition to those who brought the chambered-tombs with their forecourt and walling and Mediterranean antecedents from Southern Spain and Portugal, there were unmistakable connexions with the valley of the Loire and Southern France; while from the Paris basin came the galleries with port-hole slabs, figurines of the Mother-goddess and "collared flasks" characteristic of the Seine-Oise-Marne (S.O.M.) culture. The occurrence of beakers in most types of graves, except the corbelled tombs of Morbihan and Jersey, indicate that the Beaker folk were also a dominant element in the population, since they adopted the local cult and buried their dead in megaliths with their own drinking-cup.

The S.O.M. Culture

The distribution of the monuments suggests in the first instance a maritime diffusion with concentrations at certain focal⁄points, such as the Gulf of Morbihan, Southern Finistère and, in a lesser degree, the Lower Loire and Vendée with extensions to the Côte du Nord and Jersey. But they are densest in the Breton coastal districts and the lower reaches of the estuaries, diminishing on the western coasts and dwindling to a few isolated spots in the north⁄east. From the Paris basin a late form of megalithic cult, characteristic of the S.O.M. cultus, made its way to Brittany with its collective burial in rectangular chambers and its appropriate furniture as indicated above, while commoners were interred in family ossuaries. This tradi⁄ tion had been inherited from the Pyrenaean region in the south of France, Sardinia and the Balearic Isles, as appears in the gallery of Grotte des Fées, 82 feet long, derived from the rock⁄ cut tomb of St Vincent in Mallorca. Passing up the Rhône valley to the Paris basin, it then spread westwards to Brittany and Jersey but not to Guernsey. To the north⁄east the S.O.M. galleries occurred in Belgium and Westphalia, and finally reached the south of Sweden. In the Marne, chalk cemeteries have been found containing rock⁄cut graves entered by a descending ramp or dromos, as in the Mycenaean tombs, and in the more elaborate structures equipped with richer furniture but fewer bodies than the smaller collective burials of forty or more corpses. In the valley of the Seine and Oise slabs generally have been used to produce a trench with a chamber at one end divided from the rest by a port⁄hole at the entrance, often with a conventionalized figure of the Mother⁄goddess inscribed on the wall.[49] In the Paris basin trepanning holes in the skull was practised as a magical device.

THE BRITISH ISLES

From Brittany the megalithic mariners proceeded northwards across the English Channel soon after 2500 B.C., settling on the chalk downs and uplands in the south of England from Sussex to Eastern Devon in an environment not unlike that to

which they had been accustomed in their continental homelands. They organized themselves in small agricultural communities on patches of arable land and pasture with causewayed
enclosures on high ground, perhaps for impounding cattle at
the end of the summer, in such places as Windmill Hill near
Avebury in Wiltshire (the site which has given its name to the
earliest or "A" Neolithic culture in Britain), Knap Hill between
Marlborough and Devizes, Whitehawk Camp near Brighton
race-course, Goodwood near Chichester, Coombe Hill near
Eastbourne, Maiden Castle in Dorset, Hembury near Honiton
in Devon, and Carn Brea in Cornwall. Near the Thames at
Abingdon a Neolithic promontory has been identified on
low-lying ground.[50]

The absence of metal in these sites and in the graves indicates
that the first Neolithic colonists arrived before they had become
acquainted with the processes of metallurgy, and their pottery
was also of the pre-Beaker type, consisting of well-proportioned
round-bottomed, baggy or carinated bowls, sometimes copied
from leather models, with moulded rims and upright lips. They
were well baked and often burnished, either plain or ornamented by drawing the finger or a comb over the wet clay and
making imprints with the finger-nail, and pricks by bone-pins
under the rims. They engaged in large-scale flint-mining on the
open chalk of the downs at Cissbury, Harrow Hill, Blackpatch
and Easton Down in Sussex and Wessex, at Peppard on the
Chilterns, and Grimes' Graves in Norfolk, where phallic
figures carved in chalk or bone have been found.

British Long Barrows

Skeletons having been discovered in the shaft of a flint-mine
and in the ditch at Whitehawk Camp, it might appear that
commoners were not interred in prepared tombs. Collective
burial in communal graves, often in a confused condition, was,
however, a feature of the Windmill Hill culture, together with
secondary interment in stone vaults or chambered tombs
covered with an earth mound. These long barrows are of very
frequent occurrence on the downs from Sussex to Dorset, and

on the Yorkshire and Lincolnshire Wolds; the primary interments in the chambers beneath a small cairn or sods at the end
of the mound usually are associated with Windmill Hill
pottery. In districts where stone was not available—e.g. in
South Wiltshire, Hampshire, Dorset, Sussex and Berkshire—
these elongated mounds were composed of earth, chalk and
timber heaped over with subsoil excavated from ditches, as in
the very long unchambered Holdenhurst barrow near Bourne-
mouth. In Brittany, as we have seen, long mounds as an
alternative to burial in round cairns were in vogue before this
mode of sepulture reached Britain, soon after 2400 B.C., and
became a characteristic feature of the Neolithic "A" culture. It
was also under Breton influences, it would seem, that chambered barrows began to make their appearance rather later on
the Cotswolds and in the neighbourhood of the Severn in the
form of genuine megalithic gallery-graves, where suitable stone
was readily obtainable, as it was in Ireland, Scotland and the
Orkneys.[51]

The origin and relation of these two types of barrows, however, is still a matter of debate. The earth mounds on the Sussex
Downs are situated near the causewayed camps rather than in
association with the flint-mines, but their focus would appear
to have been Salisbury Plain, where stone was accessible and
megalithic monuments abounded. Indeed the great long
barrow at West Kennet, which was virtually an appendage of
Avebury, contains stone chambers. But stone was not difficult
to obtain on the Yorkshire Wolds where earthen barrows were
erected. The distinction between the two techniques, therefore,
has the appearance of being an established tradition rather than
a matter of the material, though doubtless accessibility of stone
facilitated its use in tomb construction. It may be, as Hawkes
and Piggott suggest, that earth barrows were introduced by the
Neolithic "A" immigration from Brittany before the megalithic
builders arrived.[52] But the two groups of tombs seem to have
been more or less contemporary in the Windmill Hill and
Cotswold-Severn regions, and they may have reached their
respective destinations along parallel but distinctive routes, the

one landing on the south coast of England, the other making its way along the Bristol Channel and settling on the Gower coast of South Wales, and on the opposite side in the Mendips, spreading thence to the Cotswolds where it continued the megalithic tradition.

The Severn-Cotswold Barrows

Thus, the great mound known as Belas Knap near Charlton in Gloucestershire, 200 feet long and 75 feet wide, has at the end a false portal with uprights, lintel, blocking-stone and dry-stone walling curving inwards, together with the remains of a forecourt in which the funerary rites were held. On the west and east sides are openings leading to a small chamber composed of five great slabs of stone with a second long narrow chamber on the east side, and a passage running north and south at the southern end. It is said to have been surrounded by a circle of stones, but no trace of it has been found. Numerous dolichocephalic skulls occurred in all the chambers, and below the portal were those of five children. The remains of a brachy-cephalic young man, it has been suggested, may have belonged to a prisoner of war sacrificed during the funeral ceremonies.[53]

At the east end of a very long barrow at Maiden Castle a body apparently had been hacked to pieces and the brain extracted from the skull in the same manner and doubtless for the same reasons as those we have already considered.[54] Near by were pits which could have contained offerings for the dead, and judging from the length of the barrow (1,790 feet) the person interred in it must have been of some significance unless the site was a place of peculiar sanctity. In the communal tumuli the dead apparently had been deposited in the family vault to be gathered to their fathers without very much circum-stance or elaboration of furniture.[55] Only at Nympsfield in the Cotswolds have infant bones been recorded in barrows in southern England.[56]

On the other side of the Bristol Channel long cairns of the Cotswold type recur in Wales along the Glamorgan and Gower coast, in the Black Mountains in Brecknockshire, and

Fig. 6. The Bryn Celli Ddu chambered cairn, Anglesey

n the Conway valley in the north. In the western peninsulas
hey are more prevalent in the north of the Principality than in
he south, and reveal connexions with North Ireland and
South-western Scotland. Thus, Bryn Celli Ddu in Anglesey
s a chambered cairn consisting of a single polygonal chamber
bout 8 feet wide covered by two capstones, and approached
by a passage 6 feet in length with a roofed portal and an inner
passage 20 feet long, and originally placed in a round barrow
o feet in diameter with a ritual pit behind the chamber and a
nenhir in the centre of the tomb. Inside the portal are two
ecesses which may have been an antechamber, and outside the
ircular wall were the remains of a forecourt, suggesting
possible parallels with the Mallorca tombs[57] (Fig. 6). Ten

miles to the west at Trecastle Bay is a similar round barrow
80 feet in diameter with a passage leading to a small central
chamber with three side-chambers opening out of it, and at
Plas Newydd near by a small chamber opens out of a larger
one, either as a single chamber with an antechamber at the
south,[58] or, as Dr Daniel maintains, a side-chamber with a
passage running to the east.[59] In any case both Bryn Celli Ddu
and Plas Newydd are passage-graves displaying the customary
features.

The Boyne Passage-graves

The centres of this widely dispersed group of tombs with an
elongated gallery divided into segments by upright slabs and
often opening on to a forecourt with stone-walling recessed at
one end to form horns, seems to have been the estuary of the
Clyde and Carlingford Lough in Northern Ireland. From
these two ports of entry the colonizers spread through the
Hebrides, Arran, Bute, Kintyre and Galloway in Scotland,
to the Isle of Man, Anglesey and Ulster, with westward extensions as far as Sligo and County Mayo, bringing with them
the gallery-grave tradition of Sardinia, Southern France and the
Pyrenees. Meanwhile, around Dublin a passage-grave cult had
been established with tholoi tombs in the Boyne valley beneath
circular cairns on high ground arranged in cemeteries. The
best known of these, New Grange, is a circular chambered
barrow 280 feet in diameter and 44 feet high (Fig. 7) surrounded by a stone circle originally numbering probably not
less than thirty-five free-standing menhirs now reduced to
twelve. Around the mound runs a kerb of large flat stones on
end, each about 10 feet long, some of which are decorated with
sculpture and geometrical patterns in low relief typical of
Breton and Iberian tombs. The octagonal chamber with a
corbelled vault 20 feet high is approached by a passage 62 feet
long roofed with capstones and having three cells opening out
of it independently roofed. On the floor of each cell and in the
centre of the main chamber are large shallow stone basins.[60]
When the mound was first opened in 1699 it is said that a

Fig. 7. New Grange chambered tomb, Co. Meath, Ireland

menhir lay on the ground in the burial chamber, and another stood on the summit of the hill.[61] In the neighbouring tumulus of Dowth two sets of chambers occur, one of which is cruciform in plan but with a subsidiary passage opening out of one of the side recesses. The other is circular with an antechamber leading out of it. The stones in both these tombs have sculptured symbols and elaborate incised conventionalized designs on the walls and roofs, including those of the Goddess,[62] suggesting their Breton and Iberian prototypes.

The passage is not divided into segments as in the Clyde-Carlingford graves, and although entrances in the Boyne group often splay to form a forecourt, this feature is not prominent. At Carrowkeel in Sligo a vast corbelled tomb has sills in the passage and at the entrance to the three polygonal chambers, reminiscent of that at Antiquera in Spain;[63] a feature that recurs at the magnificent tomb of Maes Howe in the Orkneys, where it was doubtless reproduced from the Boyne model

rather than from the Iberian original structure. Closed roun
cairns at Carrowkeel resemble those of Mané and Tumaic i
Brittany, but by the time the cult had reached Sligo it ha
passed its zenith apparently, as burial in simple round ston
dolmens in walled cairns was the more general procedure.

From Dublin, Boyne, Armagh and North Antrim th
passage-grave tradition developed along familiar lines wit
inland and southern outliers.[64] The chambers with one or tw
cells are reminiscent of the plan of Los Millares and Alm
zaraque in Almeria, and at Alcala in Algarve. These featur
were further developed at New Grange and Dowth into thre
cells as apse and transepts. In the Dublin group at Tibradde
Mount the tholos scheme of a circular chamber with corbelle
roof (now mainly destroyed) and dromos built of dry masonr
together with chambers having cells opening out of them,
reproduced.[65] Furthermore, the Iberian tradition of erectin
the tombs on mountains or hills in groups was followed, whi
the symbolic and geometrical stylized designs recall simila
patterns on Iberian passage-graves.[66] Another common featur
are the large shallow stone bowls. Therefore it is in Spain tha
the origins of the Boyne Hill megalithic tradition would appea
to lie, with Brittany as its area of characterization.

The Clyde-Carlingford Gallery-graves

The Clyde-Carlingford galleries, on the other hand
belonged, it would seem, to the Severn-Cotswold group
derived ultimately from the Pyrenees and Southern France
Sardinia and Sicily, introduced into Ulster and Sligo eithe
direct from its continental cradleland, or as a secondary coloni
zation from Scotland. The resemblance to the Sardinia
Giants' Graves is so close that it could be explained as th
result of an immigration from the Western Mediterranean, an
the decorated pottery conforms to the Pyrenaean technique
But in the absence of a chronological sequence in the Sardinia
megaliths all that can be affirmed is that the Clyde-Carlingford
"horned cairns" have remarkable affinities with their prototype
in Southern Europe by whatever route they may have reached

ie North Channel and settled in small agricultural communi-
ies in Ayrshire, Galloway and the Hebrides, and on the Irish
ide in Ulster and Sligo. There they may have found the
·assage-grave people in possession of the uplands near the coast
f Dublin and the Boyne valley, and on the limestone hills in
iligo and the formidable headland of Antrim. Therefore, they
oncentrated on the light soils above the 400-foot level to the
iorth of the region occupied by the Boyne group. Nevertheless,
·assage-graves and galleries exist side by side, both at Carling-
ord Lough and in the Hebrides and Skye, suggesting that the
wo intruders probably overlapped, and perhaps intermingled
n certain districts to some extent while retaining their respective
haracteristic modes of sepulture, both of them being essentially
olonizers and devotees of a megalithic cult rather than
.ggressive conquerors of territory.

If they were primarily a religious movement led by sacred
hiefs, as Childe suggests, whose magic power ensured the
ertility of the crops and herds, of game and fish, the two
;roups may have been sectarian branches of the same cult, not
idverse to intermarriage—a union that found expression perhaps
n "hybrid" tombs in which a passage-grave might be enclosed
n a gallery.[67] Be this as it may, whatever may have been the
object of their quest, they wandered freely and fearlessly by
oerilous maritime routes in the northern seas, and settled often
n the bleakest and wildest places—the Hebrides, Caithness
ind the Orkneys—as well as in more congenial and fertile
ocalities in Ulster, Galloway, the Isle of Man and Anglesey.
Thus, an Iberian type of passage-grave, known as Rudh'an
Dunain, similar to New Grange or Bryn Celli Ddu, stands
n a remote hollow on the western coast of Skye. At Callernish
on the stormy coast of Lewis a small circular cairn 21 feet in
diameter encloses a rectangular chamber $4\frac{1}{2}$ feet deep and
$5\frac{2}{3}$ feet wide, entered by a passage from the east, with a portal
formed by two slabs on end. Surrounding the cairn is a circle
of thirteen stones having a diameter of $37\frac{1}{2}$ feet with four
avenues of menhirs leading to it from the four points of the
compass.[68] On the top of it is a single tall menhir nearly at

the centre of the circle, doubtless for the same purpose as the
cylindrical pillar in the chamber at Bryn Celli Ddu in
Anglesey.[69]

Other Hebridaean cairns stand within circles, suggesting
that collective burial persisted on these islands, while in
Caithness the cairns often occur in cemeteries, as at Camster
on Warehouse Hill, comprising in addition to chambered
cairns, others covering merely a short cist designed for individual interment. These may have been used by the Beaker folk
who settled in Caithness while collective burial was still in
vogue. In fact, Childe regards them as the last degeneration of
the long cairn under the influence of the individualist tradition,
the round-chambered cairns being intermediate forms.[70]

The Medway Megaliths

At the other end of the British Isles a small group of megaliths
occur in Kent on the uplands of the Medway valley. These
small closed chambers in long mounds enclosed by rectangular
palings of large blocks were erected apparently by immigrants
from Holland and North Germany. If Stukeley's sketches of it
are accurate, Kits Coty House at Aylesford, with what
Crawford believes to be a dummy portal like Belas Knap in
the Cotswolds, and the rectangular barrows at Addington and
Coldrum, have distinctive features of their own,[71] suggesting
a separate colonization. But they seem to have been derived
originally from the Dutch or Baltic chambered tomb[72] rather
than, as Crawford contends, from the Severn-Cotswold group.
The skeletons buried in them were on the whole shorter than
those found in other British megaliths,[73] and all the circumstances indicate a settlement in the Medway valley from the
Low Countries practising collective burial in chambered
barrows.

Thus, the British Isles became the meeting-place of a number
of streams of megalithic peoples after the foundations of the
Neolithic "A" (Windmill Hill) peasant culture had been laid
about 2500 B.C. on the uplands. In the river valleys and
marshes of East Anglia and the Thames basin, and along the

ast coast, in Yorkshire, and subsequently in Anglesey, Ulster nd Galloway, the Neolithic "B" Peterborough immigrants om the Baltic had established themselves relatively undis-irbed by the Neolithic "A" settlements on and beyond the halk massif of Wessex and Sussex, the wolds of Yorkshire nd Lincolnshire and on Lyle's Hill near Belfast in Ulster. Neolithic communities accustomed to burying their dead ollectively in long cairns reached the Cotswolds and South Wales via the Bristol Channel from Brittany and the mouth f the Loire. Thence they penetrated to Berkshire, and probably o North Wiltshire, and to the Black Mountains of Brecknock-hire up the valley of the Usk. From the south of France and he Western Mediterranean the Clyde-Carlingford gallery-raves were introduced into Northern Ireland, South-west cotland and the adjacent islands, while from Spain and Brittany came the Boyne group of passage-graves to the south f the Irish gallery territory, with closely related chambered ombs in Tramore near Waterford in the Scilly Isles and in the vest of Cornwall. These represent local colonizations from the ame sources on both sides of the Irish Sea in the south,[74] orresponding to those in the Hebridaean group at the other xtremity.

In Eastern Britain the contacts were with the Low Countries, he Rhineland and Scandinavia. Some of these were of con-iderable antiquity, going back to Boreal times in the Meso-ithic, when land communications with the Continent still xisted. It was from this direction apparently that the Medway negaliths came into being as an isolated group, introduced by nariners who reached the Netherlands, North Germany and Scandinavia, either by proceeding straight up the English Channel or by a circuitous route through the Pentland Firth o the Scandinavian littoral. Thence eventually they made heir way through Holland to Kent, having in the course f this diffusion developed their own characteristic features, ome of which may have been borrowed from other sec-ions of the megalithic culture with which they had come in ontact.

THE NORTHERN MEGALITHIC TOMBS

The Danish Passage-graves

As has been considered in an earlier chapter,[75] the cult wa
firmly established in Denmark on the islands of the Cattega
and the East Danish coast not later than 2200 B.C., bu
whether or not it came via the British Isles or direct from th
south of France is by no means clear. The first Danish farmer
appear to have buried their dead in single earth-graves in th
extended position within a ring of stones, protected probabl
by wooden planks and covered by a low elongated mound
from which the *dyssers* may have emerged.[76] Collective inter
ment in passage-graves with round or polygonal chamber
approached by short passages covered by capstones, reminiscen
of Iberian and Irish forms, except that corbelling was no
adopted and dry-stone walling was rare, gives every appearanc
of having been introduced from the original home of this typ
of sepulture. In Jutland a smaller side-chamber from 4 to :
metres in length often was added, with larger dimensions ii
Sweden,[77] while in Eastern Denmark double passage-grave
occur in which one mound encloses two chambers, each witl
its own entrance. In the latest form the passage opens into
short side flush with the floor of the chamber, and at Alsbjerg
a triple-chambered tomb occurs bearing some resemblance t
the Caithness graves.[78] Since as many as a hundred skeleton
have been found in some of the passage-graves,[79] they mus
have been used for collective burial for a very considerabl
time, and this is confirmed by the sequence of indigenou
pottery in them.

The angular decorated bowls, however, resemble the Rösser
ware of Central Germany and the Rhine valley, a coppe
dagger could have come from Los Millares, beads from
Brittany, and hammer-headed pins from the Kuban tombs
But metal ornaments usually were copied in amber, bone o
stone, amber being the chief export and the most widely usec
material for necklaces and pendants. Denmark, therefore, mus
have been a cosmopolitan centre to which the megalithic influx

brought cultural traditions culled from a variety of sources deeply laid in their ancestry in Iberia, Brittany, and subsequently in Ireland.

Battle-axes and Single Graves

Meanwhile there were also substantial infiltrations from North-west and Central Germany, together with Danubian merchants exchanging metal weapons and tools for amber ornaments and amulets. The most disturbing influence, however, came from the virile Nordic warriors with their battle-axes, who from about 2300 B.C. pursued their aggressive course from the Black Sea and the Urals through Central Europe to the Baltic, passing down the Elbe to Holstein and Jutland. Unlike the megalithic people in the centre and on the east coast of the peninsula, the Battle-axe conquerors buried their dead in the contracted position in single graves dug in the earth and generally covered them with a round mound. In the earliest of the separate graves in Jutland ovoid beakers with an S-profile decorated with horizontal cord-impressions occur, together with polished stone battle-axes, thick-butted flint axes, spherical maces and amber rings and buttons.[80] When subsequently interments were made in the existing barrows the axes had deteriorated and herring-bone designs had taken the place of cord-ornamentation on the beakers, until at the end of the passage-grave period in the adjacent islands (*c.* 1750 B.C.), and in Zealand, where the megalithic tradition survived much longer than in Jutland, the Battle-axe warriors had consolidated the civilization under their rule, and established themselves as the dominant power in Sweden and Finland.

In North-west Germany and Holland they expanded in a southerly direction, swarming over the plains of Schleswig-Holstein, probably driving the peasants in the Elbe-Weser region to seek refuge in Mecklenburg and in the Drenthe-Ems provinces in Holland. There the Elbe-Weser folk continued the megalithic technique, erecting stone cists often with very long galleries entered by a short passage in the middle on the

long side, covered by an elongated mound, known as Hun
Beds. In Jutland, passage-graves persist only near the coast
and there they are exclusively of the earlier variety, while i
Zealand later types occur. Only on the islands did the traditio
continue without a break. Elsewhere in Denmark the sing
graves extended northwards until they reached the extren
northerly end of Jutland, and in many of the passage-tomb
the megalithic contents in the deepest layers are overlaid b
single-grave relics.

On the islands it is estimated that there were nearly 3,50
megalithic graves, and 4,000 in Northern Sweden, mostly i
Västergötaland and on the south-west coast, in all probabili
built by refugees from Jutland. Like the Beaker folk, th
Battle-axe warriors sometimes buried their dead in the existin
megalithic tombs, but their normal mode of sepulture was the
own individual burial with the knees bent in earth grav
paved with small stones. The sides were walled with ston
and then lined with wood, closed by wooden planks an
covered by a low mound. The furniture, though variabl
generally, in the case of a man, included a battle-axe or
butted-axe of ground flint, a beaker, a stone mace and tw
large disks of amber; in that of a woman, a necklace of amb
beads. But whereas in the megalithic tombs the contacts wei
mainly with the Western Pyrenaean and Mediterranean regior
in the single graves they were essentially with Central Europ
and the Danube, with local characteristics and variations.

Whether the megalithic tradition came to the Baltic by wa
of the Atlantic route via the British Isles, or directly from Spai
through the English Channel, it was an intrusion from th
south which became centred in the Danish Isles, especially i
Zealand, with concentrations in northern and eastern Jutlan
and south-western Sweden, and south of Lake Väner, wit
extensions in the central region and in Norway. Once estab
lished in Denmark and Scandinavia, it developed its ow
peculiar features until in the long cist period it was brought t
an end, probably about 1700 B.C., when the warrior cultu
from Central Europe predominated in the Baltic.

CHAPTER IV

Cremation, Inhumation and Mummification

CREMATION IN EUROPE IN THE BRONZE AGE

In the opening centuries of the second millennium B.C. when the Neolithic civilization in the greater part of Europe had run its course and new cultural influences and traditions everywhere were rampant, the cult of the dead underwent a fundamental change. Before the Bronze Age was firmly established, however, metal had been in general use over a wide area and new modes of sepulture were beginning to appear, so that no sudden or revolutionary transition occurred from one epoch to another, as was formerly imagined. Thus, the elusive but influential people distinguished by the bell-beaker as their characteristic product roved about early in the Chalcolithic period as merchants and traders, opening up new lines of communications diffusing a uniform culture. This included the practice of metallurgy, which had been adopted in their Almerian area of characterization in Southern Spain, but unlike the megalithic mariners they had no hard and fast rule about the disposal of the dead.

As we have seen, they frequently resorted to burial in megaliths, so that beakers have been found in the rock-cut tombs and natural caves in Sardinia, Sicily and Portugal, in the great tholoi of Almeria, in the French galleries, the Catalonian cists, the British round barrows and the Danish passage-graves. But they readily reverted to their original custom of inhumation in single graves in the cemeteries of Moravia, Saxo-Thuringia and the Rhineland, where they mingled with the Battle-axe people, and eventually made their way to the lowlands in South-east Britain, East Anglia, Yorkshire and Scotland, continuing earth burial in isolated graves or grouped together in small cemeteries. Occasionally the dead were placed in stone cists, round barrows or cairns with circular ditches, and sometimes there were indications of cremation.

Partial Cremation under Long Barrows

In Yorkshire, bodies were actually burnt in a trench or flue at the end of some of the long barrows after having been dis, membered and placed under chalk-rubble and wood, among which charcoal and other charred matter were found.[1] But on the wolds inhumation was by far the most frequent practice, and out of 379 burials opened by Greenwell only 78 contained cremations.[2] Moreover, in many cases it would seem that bodies were burnt accidentally as a result of purificatory fires having been lighted in graves, or for the purpose of desiccating the corpse. In many of the British barrows burnt and unburnt bones occurred, and only in relatively few was cremation the rule. When a trench was especially constructed with a flue to aid combustion, as in some Yorkshire barrows, there can be little doubt that genuine cremation was intended. The same applies in the case of those in which the bodies were burnt on a platform of gravelly material and sand reddened by fire as at Tilshead and Winterbourne Stoke in Wiltshire, and at West Rudham in Norfolk.[3]

In the Leighterton barrow in Gloucestershire three vaults arched over like ovens are said to have been found with an urn at the entrance to each containing ashes and human bones imperfectly burnt and broken.[4] Similarly, in the Huggard Wold group of barrows in the East Riding the calcined remains appeared to have been placed in a wooden receptacle, traces of which had survived, but they had seldom been reduced to ashes. Generally they consisted of pieces of charred bones mixed with burnt chalk and soil reddened by fire, the pyre extending outside the area containing the actual crema, tion. The charcoal from the trenches sometimes was several feet long in a horizontal position, the floor of the trench being a continuous stratum of incinerated adult and juvenile bones, broken and splintered by the action of fire.[5]

It seems, therefore, that while in some cases genuine cremation probably was attempted as a means of disposal of the dead in the Neolithic and Early Bronze Age, partially burnt remains may be merely the result of an accidental conflagration arising from a variety of causes. Sometimes, as Childe suggests, the wooden chambers in the crematorium trenches may have caught fire,[6] if and when it was the custom to burn fires in the graves for purificatory purposes, or to dry the corpse to preserve it from decay; a practice, as will be considered later,[7] which has been widely adopted in primitive societies in modern times. In any case, the use of fires in mortuary ritual preceded the adoption of cremation as an established mode of disposal of the dead towards the end of the Bronze Age. Prior to this it had occurred only sporadically, perhaps in Syria at Byblos, in Palestine at Gezer, in the Peloponnese at Argive Heraeum, and without doubt in Bohemia, Moravia, Hungary and Central Germany, and in megalithic tombs in Brittany, Wessex and Ulster, where in the Clyde-Carlingford galleries it predominated.

Round Barrows

Inhumation, however, was the normal form of sepulture in unchambered and in chambered graves in Neolithic Britain, although burnt bones are of fairly frequent occurrence in passage-graves like Bryn Celli Ddu in Anglesey, Nympfield in the Cotswolds, and in two circular cairns in the Scilly Isles. It would seem, therefore, that the two practices existed side by side, though cremation usually was of the partial variety, either outside the tomb before the incinerated remains were deposited in the grave, or in a specially constructed wooden hut or in a flue-like trench, while a few barrows covered cremations on platforms. At Dorchester-on-Thames the bodies were burnt on pyres within the circular sanctuary and the incinerated bones were then interred in bags in cremation cemeteries. In Dorset four out of five of the round barrows contained cremations, while in Cornwall the practice was almost universal.

The "Disk Barrows" around Stonehenge, composed of one or more small mounds on a circular platform with a small ditch inside it but no entrance passage, had cremations with blue faience beads from Egypt (*c.* 1400 B.C.), together with amber beads from the Baltic and Central Europe, and jet beads from the north-east coast of Yorkshire. Beneath the chalk patches outside the sarsen circle at Stonehenge (i.e. the Aubrey Holes) a number of cremations have been recorded, and also in the bank and in the silt at the bottom of the ditch in the south-east quadrant. One hole was nearly full of wood ash, but the smallest contained only the remains of a partial incineration in the lowest levels. Although most of the holes bore traces of cremations, the furniture accompanying them was confined to a few bone pins, flint implements, and in Hole 29 a lugged "pygmy" cup bearing some resemblance to a Neolithic "B" Groved Ware vessel of Rinyo type from the Woodhenge area,[8] a few miles to the north-east of Stonehenge, where (i.e. at Woodhenge) only one cremation has been found.[9]

While the ditch, bank and Aubrey Holes may belong to the Late Neolithic period (*c.* 1900–1800 B.C.), the main structure of the sarsen circle and its "bluestones" probably are contemporary with the round barrows, and may be some 400 years later than the earliest features of the site (i.e. 1500–1400 B.C.).[10] It was then, in the Early Bronze Age, soon after the arrival of the Beaker "A" people from the Lower Rhineland, that a small influx of warrior chiefs from Brittany practising cremation established themselves temporarily in Wessex, equipped with a new type of flat dagger having a tough midrib and mounted on wood or amber, spherical stone battle-axes, sceptres, and blue glazed beads from the Eastern Mediterranean.[11] It may have been this invasion which facilitated the transition from the Early Bronze Age to the Middle Bronze Age in Britain, characterized by the change from inhumation to cremation as the established mode of disposal of the dead, associated with round barrows.[12] Many of their graves occur at the two principal cult centres of this period, Avebury and Stonehenge, nd very probably it was these warrior chiefs who were esponsible for the remodelling of Stonehenge. Outside Wessex hey expanded to Exmoor, the Mendips and along the Icknield Way from South Wales to East Anglia, and established colonies round sacred sites marked by clusters of their bell-barrows ontaining mainly primary cremations.

Urn Burial

Parallel with the Wessex culture a more permanent Middle Bronze Age culture flourished in Britain marked by cremations with the remains buried in cinerary urns, frequently under parrows or in cairns, except in the north, where they were grouped in cemeteries. These urns were made of coarse clay nd were similar in design to the food-vessels with flat bottoms which accompanied interments in the contracted position n stone cists and under barrows in the British Isles about .700 B.C., immediately after the Beaker invasion. With them occurred also stone axes, metal ear-rings, buttons with V-shaped perforations, bracelets and crescentic jet necklaces with gold *lunulae* of Ireland. Therefore, if the antecedents of he Urn culture are to be sought in that of the Food-vessel olk, a fundamental change in the disposal of the dead must ave occurred by the Middle Bronze Age, inhumation having iven place to cremation in the meantime.

On the Continent, cremation cemeteries in the form of urn-elds became general at this time (i.e. from the Middle Bronze Age to the Early Iron Age, from about 1500 to 800 B.C.), first n Hungary and Northern Italy, and then extending from Western Asia Minor throughout Western, Central and Northern Europe to Ireland. Genuine cremation with the ashes deposited n urns which were buried in large cemeteries now was so widely adopted that it marks a definite transition in the cult of he dead, notwithstanding the fact that partial incineration, as ve have seen, was prevalent in the Early Bronze Age and the Late Neolithic from the Early Helladic graves in Greece to he British barrows. Even in Food-vessel graves cremated shes are not unknown, and as cremation increased, the food-vessels seem to have become cinerary urns, though as a general practice this transition was not effected until the Middle Bronze Age.

The Terramara Cemeteries

Thus, in Northern Italy south of the Po and Lake Garda, westwards towards Brescia and Cremona, outside the settlements of pile-dwellings known as Terramara, were cemeteries on small piles and protected by moats containing ashes in urns closely packed together and covered with basins. It is possible that these prosperous agriculturists (*terra-maricoli*) may have arisen as an Urnfield group with Danubian, Asiatic and Iberian affinities, crossed with those of the Corded-ware warrior Nordic and Slavonic intruders in the Middle Danube basin,[13] before they were driven into the Middle and Lower Po valley and Taranto by a general westward movement, and there established themselves as a dominant but localized group. In any case they had come into contact with the practice of cremation and urn burial before they reached Italy about 1500 B.C. in the Middle Bronze Age, probably in Hungary where in the Pannonian cemeteries, extending from the Austrian border to Central Hungary, and in those of the Banat and North-east Serbia, urn burial was the only mode of disposal of the dead. Elsewhere inhumation was generally adopted.

It was this expansion from Hungary which took cremation in urnfields through North-western Serbia and Slavonia and the intermediate regions along the Save and the Danube to Transylvania, and along the Theiss to Perjamos and Tószeg where after 1400 B.C. it gradually ousted inhumation.[14] In Saxony and Western Silesia and Brandenburg the Lausitz culture became a powerful influence from about the middle of the second millennium B.C., which eventually was destined to play an important part in the establishment of cremation. When iron was just beginning to come into use in Italy for small objects, the vigorous community of peasant farmers called Villanovans, after the suburb of Bologna where their culture was first identified, had become established in what are now Umbria and Tuscany. Randall-MacIver regards them as an immigration from Hungary,[15] but they may have been merely descendants of the Terramaricoli[16] who continued the cremation and urnfield tradition.

The Villanovan Cemeteries

Around their villages, composed of small huts which were reproduced in the hut-urns that became common in Latium in the south,[17] graves were dug in the adjacent cemeteries, sometimes lined with stone slabs in which the cinerary urn was placed. The ossuary and grave furniture were often enclosed in an immense jar, or *dolio*, marked in several instances by sandstone stelae roughly carved with rosettes, human figures or animals. The *dolio* generally is a two-storeyed structure resembling a bowl with an inverted rim and a horizontal handle surmounted by a conical neck with splayed rim. It might be covered with a slab of stone and within the jar was the pottery ossuary, with its cover and several other pottery vases ornamented with meander patterns in high relief. In the graves were bronze pendants, palette-knives with handles, armlets, fibulae inlaid with amber, and bronze pins headed with disks of bone and spheres of glass, gold and glaze pendants, gold head-bands with four masks of human heads, and a gold fibula covered with figures of lions.[18] While they employed iron, the Villanovans were expert workers in bronze and exported their products as far north as the Balkans and east as Transylvania. They also had contacts with Phoenicia and Assyria, whence from the south the knowledge of iron may have spread through Italy.

Only a very small number of inhumations occur in their cemeteries. Thus, at Villanova only 14 skeletons were found as against 193 cremations, and these are said to have lain "pell-mell among the tombs containing burned bodies, almost at the same level", and with the same grave furniture.[19] These inhumations may have been the interments of members of adjoining communities who died among the Villanovans but continued their normal mode of disposal of the body in the local cemeteries. This would explain the absence of any such intrusions in those of Selciatello at Corneto in Etruria, and in the Etruscan Vetulonia near the village of Colonna.

The Lausitz Urnfields

While Italy and Southern Europe were experimenting with iron at the beginning of the first millennium B.C., the central region north of the Alps was still in the Bronze Age, and in the thirteenth century was in a state of ferment. The Barrow and Tumulus culture of the Middle Bronze Age, which survived in the highlands, was invaded by the Urnfield folk who occupied the valleys and the plains of the Upper Danube basin and practised cremation and the deposition of the ashes in large urns after the manner of the Terramara people, but sometimes under barrows. A smaller vessel for votive offerings, familiar in the Villanovan graves, was associated with these urns, revealing affinities with northern Italy, suggesting that they may have come from south of the Alps. It was, however, in that part of eastern Saxony and western Silesia known as Lausitz that it developed its characteristic features, among which were its ossuaries constructed by placing two truncated cones base to base and covering them with an inverted dish. In the earlier burials a hole was bored in the sides, presumably to enable the soul to leave it at will, and with the ossuaries were buff-coloured pots ornamented with large conical warts (*Buckeln*). In the later graves the warts became flutings or corrugations and the ware was dark-faced. Vases with side spouts called "feeding bowls", and vessels shaped as animals and clay rattles appeared. Since moulds have been found in the graves, the Lausitz folk must have been metallurgists, and they may have invented the socketed celt, developing it out of a flanged celt with a bronze sleeve.[20]

Wherever they may have originated, having established themselves in Eastern and Central Europe they carried on the Early Bronze Age cultural tradition called Aunjetitz, after the cemetery at Unĕtice near Prague, and extended their sphere of influence across Southern Germany and Upper Italy to the Rhône, although in the Lausitz culture inhumation in stone graves was abandoned in favour of cremation. Like their predecessors, the Lausitz people controlled the trade-routes and valleys on the loess between the Elbe and the Oder. Thence their culture spread to the Vistula, the Austrian Danube and the mountains of Slovakia, its influence being felt farther afield in Spain, the British Isles and Scandinavia, so that it became a predominant unifying force in the Late Bronze Age, and continued to flourish when iron was beginning to make its way northwards from Italy into Bohemia, Moravia and East Prussia. Throughout its diffusion urnfield burial in extensive cemeteries was retained, and the biconical ossuary was of frequent occurrence in the graves.

The Alpine Urnfields

In the North Alpine region a less coherent urnfield culture developed on the Upper Danube and its tributaries, and spread down the Rhine and across Switzerland, establishing itself in the fertile valleys and along the trade-routes as in the case of the Lausitz. Its main centres, however, were the copper mines of the Tyrol and the salt deposits at Hallstatt and Hallein in the Salzkammergut, Reichenhall in Upper Bavaria and Mergentheim in Württemberg, where it absorbed elements from trading contacts with the Tumulus culture, and especially with the Lausitz folk who may have settled within its borders.[21] But while cremation was universally practised, the urnfields were less uniform than those of the Elbe and the Middle Danube. Some of the urns were under barrows in Bavaria, the Rhineland and Eastern Bohemia, while inhumations in cists were not unknown.

In the graves stone axes and winged celts were common, together with socketed chisels, bronze swords with engraved hilts, rapiers, knives, razors, fish-hooks, sickles, bronze-tipped arrows and a great variety of ornaments. The urns were globular or piriform, sometimes fluted or roughened, with a cylindrical neck and wide brim which in the Tyrol was supported by pillar-like handles. Biconical ossuaries of Lausitz type occurred sporadically in the earlier urnfields throughout the region. Even the Tumulus-builders, who survived in the highlands above these valleys inhabited by the Urnfield folk, practised crema-tion, though, except in Bohemia, they seldom deposited the ashes in urns. Beyond the Main and Saône the culture declined, judging from the impoverished conditions of the cemeteries in this area. This may have been a result of its having become isolated from its Alpine centre as it spread into Central France and the Low Countries, where it mingled with the surviving elements of the earlier Tumulus culture and was overlaid by influences from north-western Bohemia.

It was not until towards the end of the Bronze Age that urn burial and Lausitz ossuaries reached Northern Germany and Scandinavia, notwithstanding the contacts between the Baltic and Central Europe at the beginning of the period. From the Eastern Mediterranean, probably inspired ultimately by Egypt and travelling along the amber route, came the custom of representing the grave in the form of a ship in which the deceased made his voyage to the next life. This practice was common in the Iron Age and reached its climax in Viking times. Boat-burial also appeared in Britain in the middle of the second millennium with other Scandinavian affinities like the amber cup found at Hove. It was not until much later (*c.* 700 B.C.) that groups of Late Bronze Age Alpine urnfield invaders reached the southern shores of England and settled in the Thames valley at Brentford and elsewhere in the lowlands, bringing with them bronze swords with a point shaped like a carp's tongue, together with "winged axes", horse trappings and knives resembling a hog's back. As would be expected, they buried their dead normally in urnfield cemeteries, accord-ing to their established custom, or sometimes at the south or south-east end of barrows of the Early or Middle Bronze Age, as, for example, at Deverel and Rimbury in Dorset. In the Deverel barrow the burials were placed at the foot of slabs arranged in the shape of a horseshoe, while in some of the cemeteries they were circular in plan.

The Hallstatt Cemetery

These immigrations from the Continent between 850 and 700 B.C. were the result of widespread movements of peoples at the end of the Bronze Age, characterized by the urnfield cultures based on Central Europe. It was at this time that the classic site in the Austrian Alps above Lake Hallstatt came into great prominence with an increased demand for the salt that was mined there. This is shown by the dimensions of the cemetery excavated in 1846, which dates from about 1000 to 450 B.C. The first phases appear to fall within the Bronze Age because the earlier fusions of peoples in the Alpine region lingered on, and towards the end of the period they sought shelter in the mountain valleys from the warlike invaders on the highlands. Thus, the harp fibula of Late Bronze Age type was a characteristic object at Hallstatt, together with the leaf-shaped bronze sword in which the flanges round the hilt disappeared and the tang terminated in a semi-hexagonal finial; the blade being narrower than in most preceding types and the rivets smaller.[22]

Of the 2,000 or more graves that originally were contained within the cemetery, 455 cremations and 525 inhumations have been identified. The bronze objects, numbering 179, were associated with the cremations and only three with the burials. In the case of the cremations, which are the older of the two modes of disposal in this cemetery, urns were rare and iron was confined to a few small knives. The bronze fibulae suggest contacts with East Central Europe, and it is not improbable that at the end of the Bronze Age pressure from the eastern side of the Lausitz province was responsible for a modification of the culture both at Hallstatt and in the West Alpine region, causing further extensions westwards and possibly to Catalonia in North-east Spain. The similarity between the Hallstatt and Alpine cultures may be explained largely as a result of the intrusion of the Lausitz urnfield folk, and it was under Hallstatt influence that the Lusatian urnfield people of Poland adopted the use of iron. The Tumulus-builders of the Middle Bronze Age (*c.* 1450 B.C.), on the other hand, continued to practise inhumation in the First Iron Age when elsewhere cremation predominated, and even in the Late Hallstatt period (C.D., 800–400 B.C.) intrusive inhumation graves occurred containing objects derived from the south-eastern sides of the Alps.

Urnfield cremation-burial, however, would seem to have come into Central Europe from the south-east out of Anatolia by way of Thrace.[23] By the thirteenth century, urnfields were established in Northern Syria at Carchemish and Ras Shamra, when cremation replaced inhumation,[24] while at the Sixth City of Troy an urn cemetery goes back to the fourteenth century, and can hardly have been derived from Central Europe or the North Alpine region.[25] From Western Asia it reached Hungary and Austria in the Middle Bronze Age (e.g. Tószeg C), following the tracks of the Neolithic colonists 2,000 years before, and interpenetrated the Tumulus culture as it moved towards the Rhine about 1100 B.C., eventually reaching Britain about 750 B.C.

CREMATION AND INHUMATION

While cremation and burial in urnfields were widely adopted in the Bronze Age and in the Middle and Late phases of the period, becoming the predominant mode of disposal of the dead, especially in Central and Northern Europe from the Alpine region to the British Isles, the practice appears to have been an intrusion from the Near East. Inhumation, however, in its various forms persisted everywhere as the basic rite, and not infrequently the incinerated ashes were buried with interments under barrows or cairns, suggesting that cremation was a new element superseding the earlier sepulture without completely eliminating it, except in a few localities towards the end of the Bronze Age. Moreover, as we have seen, partially burnt bones were of fairly common occurrence in graves from Neolithic times onwards. These were really inhumations which had been subjected to incineration to a limited extent, sometimes apparently for the purpose of desiccation, or as a result of accidental firing during a purificatory rite. Or, again, when secondary burial was practised, the body might be reduced to ashes, wholly or partially, after it had been interred for a period for a variety of reasons, as in primitive states of culture today.[26]

MUMMIFICATION IN ANCIENT EGYPT
Natural Desiccation

Although cremation has been a recurrent feature in the cult of the dead since the Bronze Age, the predominant and persistent tendency has been to give some measure of permanence to the mortal remains either in an "everlasting tomb" or through a process of natural or artificial preservation of the body. This was most conspicuous in prehistoric Egypt, where frequently the dead were buried in the hot dry desert sand, which was often impregnated with natronous compounds, so that decom position was arrested for an indefinite period, as in the case of the natural mummies in the more recent saltpetre caves in New Mexico.[27] The continual discovery of corpses in this condition probably concentrated attention upon the physical survival of the body after death, which soon found expression in a more ample provision of grave furniture and eventually, as we have seen, in elaboration of tomb construction. But burial in more spacious brick-lined graves removed the corpse from the desiccating sand and, therefore, defeated the effects and the purpose of the interments and their equipment. It may have been, as Elliot Smith suggested, that it was as a result of this that attempts were made at the beginning of the Dynastic period to discover ways and means of artificially preserving the bodies of the dead.[28]

Preservation and Embalmment

Thus, the flexed body of a woman has been found from the Second Dynasty which was wrapped in numerous layers of bandages, each leg having been separately treated. Between the bandages and the bones there was a mass of linen corroded probably by crude natron which had been applied to the body to preserve it.[29] Similar contracted burials have been discovered in the tombs of the Third and Fourth Dynasties near Nuerat, Beni Hasan, with the limbs separately wrapped in linen and the whole body covered with cloth.[30] No traces were found of attempts to embalm the tissues, whereas the body in a mastaba of the Pyramid Age (*c.* Fifth Dynasty) at Medum was shrunk, wrapped in a linen cloth, then modelled all over with resin into the natural form and plumpness of the living figure, completely restoring all the fullness of the form. The eyes and eyebrows were painted on the outer wrapping with green, and the generative organs were modelled with precision showing signs of circumcision. The viscera had been removed and embalmed in a recess in the south end of the chamber in the form of lumps of resined matter wrapped round in linen, while the body cavity of the mummy had been packed with linen soaked in resin. The head had been broken off by violators of the tomb but carefully replaced with a stone under it to keep it in position.[31]

At Deshasheh on the western edge of the plain about sixty miles south of Cairo, in a long trench grave of the Fifth Dynasty on the top of the hill lay the body of a young man on its back with the head towards the north in a coffin carefully placed in a recess. Upon the breast a stout head-rest was set on end, and the generative organs were modelled in cloth in their correct positions. The body was fully wrapped in linen, and the skin and ligaments were firm and strong. There were no signs, however, of embalming or mummification, but, nevertheless, the body had been preserved intact by desiccation. In the well at the foot of the coffin the head of a calf lay face downwards, and on the floor of the well at the other end was the calf's haunch. On the left side, looking out to the well, were two eyes painted opposite the head, and on the inside in addition to a list of offerings was a list of seven sacred oils which might indicate an acquaintance with embalmment.[32]

"Substitute Heads"

In two graves of the Sixth Dynasty, Professor Junker found the corpse covered first with a fine linen cloth to protect the mouth, ear and nose from a layer of stucco-plaster which was then applied and modelled according to the form of the body. The head was so accurately followed that in one case the fallen-in nose and twisted mouth could be clearly seen. In two other instances only the head was covered with the plaster, and on the linen enveloping the head of Idew II the face was painted.[33] These plaster-covered heads he connects with the "substitute heads" carefully portraying the facial features in limestone found among the grave furniture at the beginning of the Old Kingdom (c. 2900 B.C.). Their function, he suggests, was, therefore, that of a portrait statue of the deceased to take the place of the mummy if and when it should fall to pieces. For this reason they were made of the natural size, and they occur only in tombs in which statues or statue-chambers are absent.

Portrait Statues

That effigies of the dead were regarded as permanent substitutes for the corpse is shown by their being accorded the same ritual treatment by the mortuary priests as the actual mummy. Thus, in the periodical funeral services performed in the tomb-chapel it was important that the smoke of the incense should envelop the statue, and to it the food offerings were made in the prescribed manner.[34] Indeed, it would seem that in early times the reanimation of the dead man took place before the statue and not before the mummy. Thus, the rubric states that the ceremony called the "Opening of the Mouth" be performed on behalf of the statue in the "House of Gold"; that is to say, in the actual workshop where the statue was made. Even as late as the New Kingdom (c. 1546 B.C.) it was still depicted in the wall-paintings sometimes as the recipient of these rites.[35]

It is hardly surprising, therefore, that the sculptor was called "he who makes to live" (s'nh), and the making and reanimation of a portrait statue was described as a creative act; a rebirth or renewal of life. Similarly, the mortuary priest whose duty it was to supply the needs of the deceased in the hereafter, was for this reason called "servant of the ka", and whatever he provided for the ka was shared by him with his protégé.[36]

The corpse lying at the bottom of the tomb-shaft in the mastaba[37] was too inaccessible for ritual purposes to be the actual recipient of the funerary rites performed in the chapel above ground, or in the case of the pharaoh, in the pyramid temple. Therefore, it was to the statue as the substitute for the body that the libations were offered and the food and drink presented, just as in the temples the cultus was held before the statue of the god. But before the portrait statue could be employed as the *simulacrum* of the deceased it had to be fashioned with as close a resemblance to the actual person as possible, and then as it were "brought to life" by an elaborate ritual process of restoring the bodily functions and attributes one by one. This act of "Opening of the Mouth" (*Upt-ro*) is mentioned in the ancient texts in close connexion with the fashioning of the statue by the sculptor.[38] In all probability the rite was held where the statue was actually made; in the first instance perhaps in a chamber in the pyramids, since the Egyptian mortuary ritual was derived ultimately from that performed on behalf of the pharaoh in death and in life (e.g. the Toilet ceremonial). Thus, the lustrations in the "House of the Morning" which the king underwent daily, and especially before officiating as the high priest, were repeated at death in the process of the mummification of the corpse and the creation of the portrait statue, the royal ritual being extended to all and sundry when the hope of becoming Osiris after death became a universal aspiration.

The "Opening of the Mouth" Ceremony

Although "The Book of the Opening of the Mouth" was not compiled until the Nineteenth Dynasty, it and the subsequent copies in the Twentieth and Twenty-sixth Dynasties describe rites which originated among the early inhabitants of the Nile valley, and reproduce ancient formulae recited during their performance to reconstitute the body of the deceased and restore to it its *ba* and *ka*.[39] The earliest mention of the observance is in the sculptured tomb of Methen belonging to the Fourth Dynasty[40] when the cult of Osiris came into increasing prominence, but some of the rites may have been in use in predynastic times.[41] In any case, it seems to have been performed on a statue in the first instance and to have consisted in its purification with holy water sprinkled from different vessels, censings and the presentation of balls of natron. An ox was then slain and its foreleg cut off and given to the statue. The eyes, nose and ears were touched with a copper chisel and various magical instruments, one of which was a rod ending with the head of a ram and called "Great Magician". With this the priest pronounced the formula, "I open thy mouth with the Great Magician wherewith the mouth of every god is opened". Then finally, after a goat and a goose had been beheaded, the statue was invested with a head-dress, clothes and jewels and royal insignia. So arrayed it was anointed and again censed, the rite terminating with a sacred meal served on an altar. It was the duty of the king to perform the reanimation ceremony of the portrait statue of his father.

With the development of the worship of Osiris the rite became practically a repetition of that which was said and done by the sons of Horus for his father (Osiris). As Osiris had become a living soul by receiving from his son Horus the latter's eye, which had been lost in the conflict with Seth, so the body of a dead man must be similarly reanimated by the restoration of the faculties of the living person. It was this that was accomplished in the Opening of the Mouth ceremony, first on the portrait statue, and finally, as it was stereotyped in the Eighteenth Dynasty, on the actual mummy, so that the deceased might be able to take part in the funerary ritual in the chapel at his tomb.[42] The procedure was, however, practically identical with that adopted in the Opening of the Mouth of the statue. The body was purified with holy water, embalmed and censed; the mouth of the mummy was touched with the foreleg of the ox and other sacred objects; the faculties were restored one by one; the toilet ceremonies were re-enacted; a sacred meal was eaten by the mourners, and the coffin was duly installed in the grave.[43]

Making a Mummy

The process of mummification which found its climax in the Opening of the Mouth was essentially a religious act whereby the dead man was made into a living soul (*ba*) after the technical skill of the embalmers had rendered the body imperishable and the ritual acts of the priests had reconstituted the mental faculties. First, after washing the corpse in Nile water, the brain was extracted through the nostrils by a metal hook and the internal organs were removed, leaving only the heart (and possibly the kidneys) in position. The heart being the seat of life, it had to remain to resume its functions when the operations were complete. The corpse was next soaked in a salt-bath for a considerable time and the epidermis peeled off, while the viscera was embalmed separately, and until the Twenty-first Dynasty placed in canopic jars with stoppers representing the heads of the four sons of Horus familiar in tombs from the Fourth Dynasty onwards. When the body was taken out of the salt-bath it was washed in a conventionalized manner before it was carefully desiccated to free it from all moisture by either placing it in the sun or over a slow fire. When this had been accomplished—and the permanence of the preservation depended largely upon efficient drying of the corpse—embalmment began.

Resin mixed with natron and animal fat were applied to the surface, or poured over the body in a molten condition, and caused to penetrate into every cavity and crevice, and into the structure of the bones. Linen wads dipped in the mixture were packed into the body-cavity, the cranium and the nostrils, the orifices being sealed sometimes with a lump of resin or wax. The body and limbs were then treated with resinous paste and separately wrapped, appropriate spells from the prescribed liturgy being recited during the anointing and bandaging. In and after the Twenty-first Dynasty the viscera was separately embalmed and wrapped in linen parcels and restored to the body-cavity before it was finally packed with preservative material.

The substances used for embalming, which included in addition to natron and resin, incense, cedar oil, honey, olive oil and wax, were regarded as possessed of life-giving qualities which it was maintained had exuded from the body of Osiris, or some other god, or to have been the tears of the gods when they wept for the murdered divine hero (Osiris). Amulets of great potency were inserted in the bandages, on the body, and round the neck, long utterances being recited by a priest during their placing in position. They included a model of the Eye of Horus and the heart-scarab in hard greenstone, or the *crux ansata*, bestowed for the purpose of restoring life to the heart and preventing it witnessing against the owner at the time of judgment. Upon it was inscribed a legend in which it was addressed as the *ka* of the body, "the Khnum (ram-headed Creator-god) who makes my limbs to prosper".[44]

The Burial Rites

The mummification ritual having been completed in strict accord with that which was done by Anubia, the divine funerary physician, to the dismembered body of Osiris to restore it to life and to render it immortal, the mummy was placed in an elaborately decorated coffin, and together with the canopic jars containing the viscera, returned to the family for the burial rites. From its home it was taken to the place of burial in solemn procession on a sledge drawn by a pair of oxen, or in earlier times it was transported in a boat by canal and along the Nile, accompanied by professional mourners, priests and relatives. At the necropolis, ornamented with pictures and hieroglyphic inscriptions illustrating the cult of the dead, the procession was met by musicians and dancers, and the mourners partook of a meal before the ceremonial entrance into the tomb was made and the Opening of the Mouth ceremony performed, when the rites had been transferred from the statue to the mummy. Finally, to enable the dead man to leave the tomb and enjoy the delights of the next life depicted on the walls of the necropolis, he was equipped with the Book of the Dead.[45]

When the worship of Osiris was first established at Abydos it was believed that those who were buried there would come under his protection in the next life, rising from death to immortality, and share in his offerings on festivals. Therefore, in the first instance the bodies of the kings, and then those who could afford the very heavy costs of elaborate mummification, the purchase of a tomb at Abydos and the transport of the mummy to it, were taken to the cult-centre of Osiris (Abydos), often by way of Busiris in the Delta where the "House of Osiris" was situated, there to appear before the dead god. If it was not possible to buy a tomb at the sacred site the mummy was transported to Abydos to rest there for a time in order to imbibe its life-giving qualities and its holy influences and associations before being buried in its local cemetery. Even commoners depicted on the walls of their tombs representations of the royal obsequies, though the transportations of the deceased was in their case purely a ritual procedure. For the most part they had to rely on natural desiccation or simple methods of embalmment, and on portrait statues, for their survival in and beyond the grave.

That attempts at mummification go back to Neolithic times is suggested by the retention of the hieratic use of a flint knife to make the incision for the extraction of the viscera throughout the history of the ritual. This is supported by the occurrence of canopic jars, and the bandaging of bodies, sometimes with traces of embalmment, at the beginning of the Dynastic period. It was not, however, until the Fifth Dynasty that the more elaborate methods were crystallized in the form in which they became the characteristic feature of the cult of the dead in Ancient Egypt.

CHAPTER V

The Cult of the Dead

HAVING examined in some detail the available material connected with sepulture and mortuary ritual that has survived from prehistoric times, it now remains to attempt an interpretation of the data in the light of an anthropological study of the cult of the dead among living primitive peoples. Although this evidence cannot be expected to yield precise information about the significance of the beliefs and customs of Early Man, nevertheless it affords a glimpse of the meaning and purpose of identical practices in vogue under conditions not very different from those that prevailed at the dawn of human history. As man always has been phenomenally conservative in his attitude towards death and the dead, there can be little doubt that in these respects the cultus in remoter regions on the fringes of civilization has not undergone very fundamental changes throughout the ages.

THE DISPOSAL OF THE BODY

Thus, the treatment of the body before civilization had truly begun was almost identical with that adopted in areas where it was scarcely yet penetrated, at any rate until very recent times. From the Mousterian onwards, in both cases, the dead have been placed in graves dug in the ground, often but not always in the contracted position, and supplied with food and drink and other offerings, such as red ochre, shells, amulets and ornaments, believed to be necessary for sustenance on the journey to the next world and efficacious for the renewal of the life of the body, or its spiritual counterpart, beyond the grave, and for its status in the hereafter. The simplest procedure has been interment either in the contracted or extended position in a trench or in a cist of stone slabs, sometimes impregnated with red ochre as a vitalizing agent, and generally equipped with grave-goods. As in the Dordogne in the Palaeolithic, buria[l] of this nature often have been in caves, which may or may n[ot] have been used for habitation.

Cave-burial

Disposal in caves, adopted in the first instance for practic[al] reasons of security and secrecy, may have suggested the wid[e-] spread belief in a subterranean land of the dead, since caver[ns] appear to lead into the depths of the earth. Kruijt, in fac[t] maintains that in Indonesia the mortal remains are placed i[n] a cave or hole in the ground because these are regarded as t[he] entrances to the underworld. So fundamental was this belie[f,] he contends, that at one time it was universally held in th[e] region, as is shown, he thinks, by the existence of bone-cav[es] among peoples who now place their hereafter in a mountai[n] or a valley.[1] But although it is prevalent, cave-burial is an[d] has been more widely adopted than the conception of a subter[-] ranean hereafter, and the correlation is by no means establishe[d.] Not infrequently the souls of the dead are thought either t[o] remain on earth or to return to the island which was the original home.[2] Therefore, it would seem more likely that i[n] Indonesia the association of the underworld with cave-buri[al] arose as a later interpretation of the earlier form of disposal.

Elsewhere in the Pacific where the dead are interred in cave[s,] particularly in the case of chiefs, the practice often has bee[n] adopted to prevent the bodies being molested. In Easter Islan[d,] for instance, the corpses of an uncle and two nephews, aft[er] being exposed, were lowered with a rope down the crevass[e] of the cliff in order to evade the enemy.[3] In Aneityum, Ne[w] Hebrides, where the underworld belief does not occur, it w[as] the custom to bury a chief with his head above ground. Fema[le] mourners watched the grave until the skin on the skull w[as] decomposed, after which it was deposited in a cave.[4] In t[he] Banks Islands the normal method is inhumation, but burial i[n] caves also occurs,[5] though it does not appear to have a[ny] particular significance with regards to the hereafter. The sam[e] applies elsewhere in southern Melanesia, where, in spite of t[he]

redominance of the belief in an underworld, a variety of very
diverse ways of disposing of the dead have been adopted. Of
these the commonest has been interment coupled with the
preservation of the skull and certain other bones of the skeleton
fter exhumation, which sometimes may be kept in caves or in
houses for safety.[6]

The Skull-cult

The special attention paid to the skull is reminiscent of the cult
f skulls which, as we have seen, has been a recurrent feature
f the mortuary ritual of Early Man since it was first encountered
n the caves on Dragon-bone Hill near Choukoutien in China
t the beginning of the Pleistocene period.[7] While commoners
re interred in the usual place of burial where the bones are
collected after the flesh has decayed, and heaped on one side,
s in the collective Almerian tombs,[8] the corpse of an impor-
ant person is hung up in his son's house, either in a canoe or
nclosed in the figure of a sword-fish. After the lapse of perhaps
year, the bones are buried in the family ossuary but the skull
nd jaw-bone are enclosed in the figure of a bonito-fish, and
et up in the house or in the public charnel-house (*oba*), where
hey remain. A man may treat the body of his wife in this way
nd keep her jaw in a basket in the house as a memorial,
ffering food to the relics from time to time.[9] In the Malay
Archipelago after the funeral feast the skulls are washed and
aken to the house in baskets where offerings are placed before
hem. In due course they are deposited in a cave in the
mountains.[10]

Secondary Burial

Among the Trobriand islanders, two months after burial the
ody is exhumed and the bones collected, taken to the sea-
hore or into the bush, where they are smoked over a slow fire.
When this process of desiccation is complete they are put in
basket and given in charge of the widow, who keeps it by
er side. Three months later a feast is held, and she is then
lowed to go to the gardens, but before doing so she must

make sure that the basket is guarded by one of her children
until she returns to the house. At the end of two months it i
placed in a cleft of the cliff, the widow having first painted
horizontal black mark across the forehead of the skull.[11] I
Australia the bones are collected from the tree or platform o
which the body has been exposed after death, packed in sheet
of paper-bark and hidden in a cave, buried in an anthill, o
put in the fork of a dead tree. The Warramunga smash int
fragments the cranium and all the bones except the radius, an
bury them in an anthill. The radius is carefully wrapped up i
paper-bark and fastened with fur-string in the shape of
torpedo about 18 inches long and 3 or 4 inches in diamete
One end is decorated with owl or emu feathers, and secrete
in the hollow of a gum-tree. The next day it is taken back t
the camp just before sunset, where it is wailed over by th
women, who cut their thighs and scalps with yam-sticks. Fc
seventeen days the bone is hidden away in the wurley, or boug
shelter, of an old woman in whose charge it is placed until a
the final ceremonies it is broken with a tomahawk and interre
in a little pit on the ceremonial ground near a drawing of th
totem of the deceased and certain sacred trees. The grave i
filled in with earth and the opening closed with a large fl
stone.[12] Thus, the deceased is gathered to his or her totem.

In the Narrinyeri and some of the tribes on the Adelaid
plain the skull has been used as a drinking-vessel. A piece c
fur-string was fixed to the occiput through the foramen mag
num on one side, and to the frontal portion on the othe
through the orbital cavities.[13] Parts of the body must be eate
by the mourners in Queensland and the Northern Kimberle
and elsewhere, either before it is exposed in a tree or durin
the process of drying over a fire or in the sun after the interna
organs have been removed and the bones and dried skin mad
into a bundle to be carried by the mourners from camp t
camp. This cannibalistic feast is said to be a symbol of respec
and regret for the dead,[14] but over and above this it was doub
less for the purpose of imbibing their qualities. In the Queen
land region it is associated with attempts to preserve the bod

for the period of mourning by evisceration, until at the end of the rites it is cremated, interred or placed in a cave or in the hollow of a tree. On the south-west of the Gulf of Carpentaria usually it is a preliminary to exposure on platforms, and in the south-east it forms parts of the interment ritual. In the north the bodies of the mourners are smeared with the exudations from the corpse.[15] These more elaborate modes of disposal are reserved, however, for chiefs and members of their family, warriors and other fully initiated men who are in the prime of life and full of vitality. But since the bundle is to be preserved only for the duration of the period of the mourning ceremonies, which coincide with that of revenge to compensate for the death, it is in a very different category from that of the mummy in Ancient Egypt.

Concerning the ultimate fate of the departed in primitive society generally there is little or no interest. As one member of the community after another is dispatched to the unseen world with the prescribed mortuary rites, gradually each in his turn is forgotten by his kinsfolk and descendants, his name is never mentioned, and his mortal remains are concealed in some secret and inaccessible spot, such as a cave or crevice, lest molestation of the body should bring vengeance on the survivors. As a precaution against the return of the dead to their former haunts and relatives, tight flexing, blindfolding or mutilation is not infrequently adopted; or the corpse may be taken by a circuitous route to the grave, the mourners making loud noises, unpleasant odours, and brandishing weapons to scare away the ghost. In Melanesia it is driven forth with bull-roarers and conch-shells in the Banks Islands,[16] and everywhere the final funerary feast is the occasion for speeding the departing guest to a land of no-return through a process of initiation into the next life and the ceremonial disposal of the body. Revenge is liable to occur in the case of those who have died violent deaths, or who may be thought to have a grudge against the living or against life for any reason (e.g. childlessness and the unmarried). Since so much depends on the valid and punctilious performance of the obsequies in keeping the dead at bay and happily installed in their proper realm and status, no pain, must be spared in conforming to the prescribed procedures which very often includes the taking back of the body, or of some vital part of it like the skull, to its home when death has occurred at a distance.

Nevertheless, while fear is and has been a very prominent feature of the cult of the dead, the main purpose of the mortuary ritual is by no means confined to rendering the deceased harm-less to the survivors. When this is the motive it is accomplished by making him at peace with himself and in harmony with his new surroundings in the spirit-world; and also by removing from those who have come into intimate contact with the corpse and the mystery of death the dangerous sacred contagions they have contracted. The general attitude displayed in the cult of the dead, therefore, is that usually adopted by primitive people in the presence of any ambivalent sacred object, namely a combination of the fear, respect and reverence shown to a being who is half-god and half-devil, or perhaps god and devil by turns.

Preservation and Cremation

Thus, on the one hand a determined effort is made to dispose of the dead as summarily and surely as possible, and, on the other hand, to keep the physical body, or its surrogate, intact either permanently or for a specified period. How closely these two desires are connected is shown by the intimate relation which exists between what might appear to be diametrically opposed modes of disposal, i.e. preservation and cremation. In Australia, as we have seen, after the flesh had been consumed at a cannibalistic feast the bones and desiccated skin sometimes have been made into a mummy bundle by the legs being flexed tightly against the body and the knees trussed up, and in this form preserved for ritual purposes until it was disposed of, often by cremation. Peruvian mummies are similarly compressed, and in Nicaragua a chief after death was wrapped in clothes and suspended by ropes before a fire till the corpse was baked to dryness. When it had been preserved for a year, it was taken to the market-place and burned, the belief being that the smoke went "to the place where the dead man's soul was".[17] In Florida, where the dead are said to have been clothed in rich coverings, dried before a fire, and placed in a niche in a cave, fragments of half-incinerated human bones were found in a mound at Cade's Point near Santa Fé Lake in association with other skulls showing no signs of the action of fire.[18]

Similarly blackened human bones embedded in charcoal have been discovered in native cemeteries in British Honduras[19] and east of the Mississippi.[20] In a Cherokee mound at Chote, in the valley of the Little Tennessee, skulls and other bones have been found resting on coals and ashes, and in one burnt-clay sepulchre in this district a corpse had been placed face upwards and covered with mortar. On this was built a fire so that the body was encased in an entire shield of pottery.[21] Among the Aztecs in Mexico the corpse was washed in aromatic water before it was placed on the pyre. This may have been a survival of mummification, since in the series of pictures depicting the Michoacan funeral rite in the sixteenth-century Spanish MS. *Relacion de los ceremonios y rites de Michoacan* the actual body is shown swathed in rolls of cotton and carried on the heads of bearers to be consumed on a blazing fire. Or, again, in a painting at Chichen Itza in Yucatan the preparation of a corpse for cremation is represented with the body opened to extract the heart and viscera, which, after being charred, are to be preserved in a stone urn with cinnabar.[22]

Desiccation and Mummification

In the Basket-maker caves in Northern Arizona bodies were sometimes wrapped in blankets and woven clothes and strung together in the flexed position in the form of mummy-bundles resembling those depicted in the Mexican MSS.[23] At Kimboko in the Kayenta district they were encased in masses of hardened adobe, indicating that they had been packed into cists at the time of interment.[24] In the Lower Mimbres valley in Southern New Mexico the skeletons were tightly packed in red clay, each one resting separate and alone, with large perforated dishes placed over their faces,[25] as in the Lausitz ossuaries.[26] The saltpetre caves in this region have been used extensively for burial, the bodies found in them having been desiccated intact with the skin on most of them almost unbroken, and adorned with anklets, shell ornaments and bracelets of beautifully plaited straw. Next to the skin was a coarse cotton cloth, between the legs a large wad of cotton (sometimes dyed red or indigo) with the feathers of the turkey, the large woodpecker, and the blue jay. Near the head stood a large earthenware jar and in some cases drinking gourds.[27]

In the Eastern States similar burials occurred in the saltpetre caves in Kentucky. In one instance the mummy was placed in a sitting position between broad stones arranged edgewise with a flat stone covering the whole structure. The corpse was enveloped in coarse clothes and wrapped in deer skins, the hair of which was shaved off. Utensils, beads, feathers and other ornaments were enclosed with it in the stone coffin. In the mammoth cave, Kentucky, the body of a woman was in such a remarkable state of preservation that many of the features were discernible. But in none of these natural mummies was there any sign of a suture or incision in the abdomen indicative of the removal of the viscera.[28] This suggests that the process of mummification had been purely natural by desiccation. Nevertheless, the fact that they were clad and adorned with ornaments, or mudded into cists, shows that the bodies had been deliberately placed in the caves because of the preservative properties they contained.

Along the Alaskan coast, on the other hand, evisceration was practised, evidently through the pelvis. After cleansing the cavity from fatty matter, it was then dried in the sun, wrapped up in the form of a mummy-bundle, unless it was placed in a life-like posture, dressed and armed.[29] The Aleutian islanders embalmed the bodies of the men with dried moss and grass, buried them in their best attire in a sitting position in a strong box with their darts and instruments, and decorated the tomb with varied-coloured mats, embroidery and paintings.[30] In a cave in the island of Kagamale, the body of a chief was covered with the fine skins of the sea-otter, as a mark of great distinction, and enclosed in a basket-like structure over which a fish-net was thrown made of the sinews of the sea-lion, and a bird-net. Among the grave furniture were wooden vessels, green stones used for tanning skins, and locks of hair.[31] It is not improbable that these more elaborate methods of preservation were introduced from Asia where among the Ainu anal evisceration was practised and the body dried in the sun. In Virginia the skin was flayed off the bodies of kings, the flesh was removed from the bones which were dried in the sun before they were put back into the skin and the empty spaces filled with white sand. To prevent the skin from corrupting or shrinking, it was oiled.[32]

In the Pacific, evisceration and artificial embalming, though by no means unknown in the obsequies of chiefs and their families, is of comparatively rare occurrence. In Samoa the operation was performed by women in houses built for the purpose. The viscera was removed and buried, and then the body was anointed daily with a mixture of oil and aromatic juices. To enable the juices of the body to escape it was punctured all over with fine needles, and after a lapse of about two months the process of desiccation was completed. The hair, which had been cut off, was then glued on the scalp by resin, the abdomen was filled with folds of cloth with which also the body was bandaged and laid on a mat with the face and head exposed. From time to time the face was oiled with a mixture of oil and turmeric, and so successful was the mummification that bodies embalmed and exposed for over thirty years were found in a remarkable state of preservation. The practice, however, has now been discontinued because the family of chiefs responsible for it has died out.[33]

Similarly, in addition to their established custom of preserving human heads, the Maoris in the South Island of New Zealand sometimes have preserved for considerable periods the bodies of their chiefs and revered dead by draining the contents of the stomach through the anus and removing the brain, in small enclosure erected for the purpose and decorated with bird feathers and sacred carvings. The body is then very carefully dried in an oven beneath it containing special preservative woods and leaves so that the likeness of the individual is retained. It is placed in a sitting posture inside its own hut, and in the case of a chief the door is opened on occasions to enable people to gaze upon him and make addresses to him.[34]

In Mangaia Island, one of the Cook group in the South Pacific, the bodies of the dead were anointed with scented oil, carefully wrapped up in a number of pieces of cloth, and either buried in the earth within the precincts of the sacred enclosure (*marae*), or hidden away in caves which constituted the royal mausoleums of the ruling families, in which hundreds of mummies are well preserved on ledges of stalactite or wooden platforms. When the bodies were buried in the ground they were laid face downwards and tightly flexed with sennit cord, the chin and the knees meeting. The body was covered with earth and large stones were placed over the grave, which was visited periodically by relatives. Occasionally the corpse was exposed to the sun, reanointed with oil and wrapped in fresh cloth, but it was not eviscerated.[35]

In Tahiti desiccation was effected by pressing the different parts of the body, drying it in the sun by day in the sitting position, and anointing it with fragrant oils. At night it was turned over so that it might not remain long on the same side. Sometimes the intestines and the brain were removed and the cavity was filled with cloth saturated with perfumed oils, which were also injected into other parts of the body, and rubbed over the skin every day. When the muscles were completely dried up the mummy was clothed and placed in the sitting posture before a small altar at which fruit, food and flowers were offered daily by the relatives or the "chantry" priest. In this condition it was kept until it began to decay after several months. The skull was then carefully preserved by the family and the bones and desiccated remains were buried within the precincts of the family *marae*.

When the embalmment began a special priest, known as "the corpse praying priest", interceded with the god, by whom

was thought the soul of the deceased had been required, that
ll the guilt he had incurred might remain with him. A hole
as dug and a post was set up in it as a personification of the
ead man, to remain after the mummy had decayed. Earth was
hrown over it and the hole filled in to conceal and contain the
vil. Taking a number of slips of the plantain leaf-stalk, the
riest placed two or three under each arm of the corpse and on
he breast, saying "there are your family, your child, your wife,
our father and your mother. Be satisfied in the land of spirits,
nd look not towards those who are left in this world." Until
his ceremony had been performed all who were employed in
he embalmment were carefully avoided since they were in a
aboo condition both as a result of their contact with the corpse
nd with the guilt of the sin for which he had died. At its
onclusion they fled to the sea to cleanse themselves from their
ollution by bathing in it, and casting the clothes they had
orn into it. Having completed their ablutions they collected
p a few pieces of coral from the sea and returned to the
eceased, saying "with you may the pollution be", and threw
he coral on the top of the hole at the grave. The bodies, how-
ver, did not long remain intact, and by the end of a year the
ones had been collected and deposited either in secret caverns
r in their homes, lest in time of war they should be desecrated
y the victors.[36]

Images of the Dead

As in Ancient Egypt, desiccation and mummification often
ave been associated with the substitution of improvised por-
rait statues or images of the dead, either as the temporary abode
f the ghost for ritual purposes during the period of mourning,
r to become the surrogate of the body after the preserved tissues
ave decayed. Thus, in Mexico, for example, the image of a
ead king was arrayed with the royal insignia and honoured
vith addresses and presents as though it were the sovereign
imself. In the same district when a trader died away from
ome a figure of him was carved in wood, ornamented, and
fter the mourning ceremonies had been duly performed in

conjunction with it, was incinerated and the ashes wer interred.[37] After a battle an effigy representing the warrior slain was burned in front of the temple and the ashes wer sprinkled on the relatives while the actual bodies were burie where they died.[38]

Along the North-west Pacific coast in British Columbi portrait statues and posts have been found between the Skeen and Nass rivers, "made as life-like as possible". In one image which originally had been clothed and ornamented, th cremated remains of the body were concealed in the trunk. A Kitzegukela on the Skeena river, the image of a man who ha committed suicide was completely clothed and seated on th box containing his ashes. In his hands were the musket an bullets with which he had shot himself. In this district ther are traditions of similar statues at places where men who hav died on the trail were cremated and effigies have been erecte to personify or commemorate their corporeal presence.[39]

Three large wooden posts representing human figures, an several subordinate posts, occur at Tununuk village, Cap Vancouver, arrayed in a row parallel to the beach and acros the front of the central dwelling. These are said to symboliz people who have been lost at sea and their bodies neve recovered. The top of each post was carved in the form of human head and neck, and the one that was set up for woman who had been buried by a landslide was covered with a fur hood. The mouth and eyes were made of ivory inlai with wood, and walrus tusks were inserted for arms and legs.[4] The cemeteries of the villages in this district were full of carve images of this kind, some of which had wooden masks repre senting the human face with inlaid eyes and mouths, and votiv offerings in abundance hanging from various parts of the body

The Diegueño, who formerly lived in and around Sa Diego, California, at the *fiesta* of the images made effigies o eagle feathers, matting and cloth which were supposed to con tain the spirits of the dead. The face was carefully constructe and the characteristic features were reproduced as closely a possible in the image. The mouth was painted red outside an black within, the teeth were shaped in pearls, and the eyes were made of abalone shell with the pupils of black wax. Bunches of eagle and of yellow-hammer feathers were stuck on the shoulders, and strings of beads and other ornaments disposed upon it. Around the neck was hung a net containing two small vessels with food and drink for the ghost on its journey to the spirit-world. As soon as the image was completed it was thought to be occupied by the spirit of the deceased, and at the end of the *fiesta*, which occupied a week devoted to ceremonial dancing, it was burned, together with offerings of blankets, clothing and other articles, in order to free the indwelling soul.[41]

Thus an effigy may be regarded as a temporary substitute for the body, providing the spirit with a habitation while the funerary rites are in progress and then discarded when it is no longer required. But in the Diegueño *fiesta* it was made to represent the likeness of the person for whose mortal remains it was the surrogate, like the portrait-statue in Egypt. Therefore, it had a vital connexion with him and the physical integument. Consequently, if the image was the equivalent of the corpse, the fact that it was burned at the end of the rite to free the soul suggests an intimate relation between the preservation and cremation of the dead. Thus, the making of mortuary effigies as the counterpart of the mummy would seem to be an important link connecting the two modes of disposal. From the prehistoric evidence interment appears to have been the original form of burial in trench graves, very frequently in the flexed or contracted position. The motive may have been partly to prevent the return of the ghost to molest the living, but also to provide him with a permanent habitation in the hereafter; though, doubtless, once the rites had been duly performed little further thought or care was bestowed upon the departed. Nevertheless, the grave was made as secure and durable as possible, and as the technique of sepulture developed, tombs became increasingly elaborate in their construction, as is demonstrated in the Egyptian pyramids and the megalithic graves, while special methods were adopted for either preserving or disposing of the body.

Natural desiccation doubtless played an important part in concentrating attention upon the continuation of human exis-tence after death in the same physical body in which it had formerly functioned. This in Egypt led to an ever-increasing elaboration of the artificial methods of mummification to render the mortal remains imperishable, to preserve the likeness of the deceased and to restore the missing faculties by ritual devices. These attempts at preservation in a modified form have become a permanent heritage in the cult of the dead in primi-tive states of culture in areas as widely separated as Oceania and the New World from which regions and for this reason for the purposes of illustration most of our examples have been taken. But the labour and cost involved in the more complex processes of evisceration, embalmment and sepulture, restricted this type of burial to rulers and the privileged few who could afford the expense. For the rest of the community simpler and cheaper ways and means had to be found without materially affecting the underlying beliefs, except where two entirely dif-ferent funerary traditions were maintained for rulers and commoners. Natural desiccation in dry sand or saltpetre caves could only be resorted to where the right conditions pre-vailed. An alternative widely adopted both in prehistoric times and in modern primitive societies has been to dry the body over a fire, or to smoke a putrefying corpse. Sometimes only the head has been preserved, or the bones have been tied up in a bundle with preservative substances and kept by the near of kin until the secondary burial. Images also have been employed as substitutes for the body, and, therefore, have been treated as the real person. To transform the effigy into the human being, parts of the corpse or the ashes of the cremated relics have been transferred to it.

THE AFTER-LIFE

The Relation of Body and Soul

The provision of substitutes treated as surrogates of the physical organism no doubt has given emphasis to the idea of the existence of a spirit or soul separable from the mortal body.

Thus, like cremation with which, as we have seen, it has been very closely associated, it has facilitated the conception of man as a psycho-physical duality of body and soul, each independent of the other. As long as attention has been concentrated on the body, its burial and preservation in an "everlasting tomb" and imperishable mummy, the next life inevitably has been interpreted in terms of a continuation of the present existence. But if the life that survived the dissolution was capable of transference to some other object, of transmigration to another body, or of returning to the spirit-world whence it came in the smoke of its physical integument, the way was open for a less materialistic doctrine of immortality.

The primitive mind, however, being not prone to abstract thought, apparently has never been able to conceive of survival apart from a concrete entity of some kind, be it that of the human body, an animal, a spirit or a god. Hence the prevalence of the idea of reincarnation and transmigration, the cult of heroes, and of an after-life lived in a terrestrial paradise or on the isles of the blest, located often in the traditional home of the tribe, after a brief sojourn in the vicinity of the grave during the period of mourning and the performance of the transitional rites. The destruction of the corpse by fire no doubt has tended to foster the belief in the liberation of the spirit regarded as an independent entity only temporarily housed in the body, and of wafting it to the sky, as in the Tyrian version of the legend of Herakles in which the hero is said to have ascended in the smoke of his funeral pyre.[42]

Fire very frequently has been thought to be a spiritualizing agent, and for this reason sacrificial offerings have been burnt to liberate their vital essence. Thus, among the Semites children were "passed through the fire" to convert their material nature into an immaterial, just as Demeter at Eleusis endeavoured to render the infant son of Keleos immortal by bathing him in the fire.[43] In Brahmanic ritual in India three sacred fires were kindled to assist the soul in its ascent to the sky, each organ and attribute being conveyed by this means to the corresponding part of the universe.[44] In the New Hebrides the soul was believed to rise to the sun on the fire kindled at the grave,[45] and in California the ashes of the corpses were scattered in the air to give the disembodied spirit wings so that it mounts up to hover for ever in the upper air, very much as the Diegueño effigy was burnt to free the indwelling soul.

Burial and the After-life

Nevertheless, neither mummification nor cremation can be assigned a consistent eschatological significance. Broadly speaking, it may be true to say that the preservation of the dead normally has been associated with an after-life on, or below, or very closely connected with the earth. But even so in Egypt, the classical home of mummification, when Osiris from being the Lord of the underworld was celestialized, his abode was transferred to the heavenly realms. There those whom he pronounced justified continued their former life in its fullness in the delectable Fields of Aalu, watered by the heavenly Nile, or in the celestial abode of Re where the sun never set. But no attempt was made to substitute cremation for the preservation of the body.

Similarly, while cremation sometimes has been connected with the belief that the dead go to the sun or to some other part of the sky, the correlation is too sporadic to establish a definite association between the mode of disposal and a celestial after-life. Thus, in Melanesia, where Rivers tried to bring them into conjunctions,[46] the evidence is by no means convincing. For example, in Bougainville Malaita, Shortland Island and New Ireland, where cremation is most prevalent, there are very few indications of a belief in a sky-hereafter, while in the Society Islands and the Marquesa, where it occurs, cremation is absent. In the North Pacific coast of America and the surrounding district the notion of a celestial spirit-world is well established, but it is not connected with cremation, and the Hare Indians, who burnt their dead, placed the route to the land of the dead through a subterranean region.[47] In Peru in Inca times mummification was practised but nobles and good commoners were thought to pass to a happier state in the sun, whereas bad commoners lived after death in a state of hunger and misery within the earth.

There is, therefore, no hard and fast rule concerning the treatment of the body and the situation of the abode of the dead. Nevertheless, when modes of burial begin to be stereotyped by tradition they may tend to influence beliefs about the locality and nature of the next life. Once cremation has become the established procedure, for example, the place and function of the physical remains inevitably lose their earlier significance in and beyond the grave, as all that survives of the tissues are a few ashes and possibly some bones which may have been preserved in urns or ossuaries. With the movements of peoples from one district to another the tendency very often seems to have been to regard the original home as the land of the dead whither the ghost returned at death. The belief frequently has influenced not only the mode of disposal but also such aspects of funerary ritual as the orientation of the body in the grave, and the provision made for the journey to the ancestral spirit-world, until finally the actual abode of the dead may have lost its earlier character and locality and become a distant land, either beyond the sea or in a mythical island of the blest, in the palace of the sun in the western part of the sky where light perpetual shines, or in the more sombre nether regions, often regarded as dark and sad where everything is shadowy and unreal and enveloped always in a soft cloudy mist. As these ideas have become intermingled through culture contact and other causes, a confusion between doctrine and practice has arisen, the abode of the dead frequently being a combination of the upper and under worlds, and a western terrestrial paradise connected with the sun and the horizon.

Orientation

Thus, in Western Nuerland in the Nilotic Sudan a man is buried facing east and a woman facing west, but in Eastern Nuerland both sexes are buried facing west because the Eastern Nuer came originally from the west, and it was in Western Nuerland that their ancestors were created. But they also associate the passage from birth to death with the movement of the sun across the sky. "Death follows the setting sun", the Nuer say, and because "the west is the side of death, the east is the side of life".[48] These two beliefs find expression in the orientation of the corpse, which on no account should be buried facing north or south, and in the final mortuary ceremony, four or six months after burial, those taking part in the offering of an ox to liberate the soul of the deceased must sit with their backs to the rising sun and face the direction of the setting sun.[49] The purpose of the rites is to give the dead man the full status of a ghost, and by initiating him into the spirit-world to keep him and the taint of death away from the living and their haunts.

Orientation everywhere usually denotes the route which the dead must take on leaving the body, whether it be towards the final destination of the soul or away from its earthly abode and the dwellings of the living. Thus, those Indians west of the Mississippi who are in the habit of placing the dead with the head towards the south say that they do so in order that the spirit of the deceased may go south, the land from which they believe they originally came.[50] Graves with bodies orientated to the east may be those of Christians who have adopted the traditional Christian posture with feet towards Jerusalem ready to rise at the Judgment to meet Christ on His return to the Mount of Olives.

Orientation has been more particularly observed among people who have a definite conception of the location of the after-life in some specific territory in this world, or a hypothetical land of the rising or setting sun on the horizon, which may be underground since the sun appears to sink beneath the earth in the west in the evening and to emerge again in the morning. Thus, in Indonesia the corpse is often orientated to the west because it is believed that there the underworld is entered at the "hole" where the sun goes down on the horizon to give light to it at night.[51] Sometimes the burial takes place at sunset in order that the sun may take the soul thither as it descends. The Ousun in Borneo adopt the same orientation in the belief that the underworld is in the west, which, however, is also entered through a cave.[52] In the Malay peninsula the Jakun placed the feet towards the west, while the Mantra deposited the body in the tomb in either a sitting or standing position with the face to the west, but in the case of a child to the east.[53]

According to the Western Samang, the lay members of the tribe go to a land of screw-pines and thatch-pines across the sea where the hole is situated into which the sun falls at night, unless by reason of their evil deeds they are compelled to turn aside northwards across the sea to a less desirable abode.[54] But the normal mode of orientation among these Negritos is with the face towards the setting sun, the region towards which the ghost is thought to journey.[55] The Kensiu in Kedah, however, bury the body with the head to the east with the result that when the soul emerges from the head it does not know the direct way westwards to the kingdom of the dead. It first goes eastwards and then flies upwards until at length it reaches its destination in the west.[56]

In the south-western islands of the Malay Archipelago the usual custom seems to be to orientate the corpse in the direction of the original home of the tribe to which the dead are thought to return.[57] Thus, the Badoej adopt an east-west position with the head at the west end of the grave and the body lying on its right side so that it faces the land of the dead in the south.[58] Similarly, in British New Guinea in South Massim the body is placed on its side with the head in the direction of the legendary place of origin of the deceased's clan, while at Wamira the feet of the corpse are towards the direction whence came the clan to which it belonged.[59] In Borneo the Olo Ngadjoe lay the dead along the river in the direction of the spirit-world, Mambaroeh, which seems to be the traditional tribal home. Thus, the description of the journey made by the spirit recited by the priest at the funeral feast contains the names of various places to be passed *en route* which actually lie on the path to the cradleland of the tribe.[60] It is not improbable, therefore, that formerly the dead were taken back to the place of origin.

Status

Most of the more elaborate mortuary procedures in primitive societies are confined to the more important section of the community. The common people everywhere generally are buried immediately after death with little or no ceremony or delay. It is only the great ones who are subjected to prolonged funeral rites culminating in final or secondary burial, either at a distance in the real or assumed original home of the tribe, or in a secure and secret place, often associated with the ancestral history and land of the dead, be it in a cave, an ossuary, a remote island, or a sacred tree whence the founders of the community are thought to have emerged. The belief in human survival may be universal, but in primitive states of culture death produces no essential change in status, condition or character. Therefore, as in this life so beyond the grave only men of rank and position, or those who have shown conspicuous valour in battle, or rendered notable service to the community in some other manner, are accorded a blessed hereafter in a special paradise or Valhalla, since the next world is modelled on the pattern of existing society. The gibe "a pie in the sky when you die" as a sop for the less fortunate under mundane conditions, is certainly not applicable to the primitive conception of a future life where privileges enjoyed or denied on earth invariably are rigidly maintained in the mode of disposal of the body and in the final destination of the ghost.

Thus, in Southern Melanesia the underworld is said to be a poorer place, sad and dark, where everything is unreal and shadowy, and the dead are ethereal. It is this undesirable hereafter that is assigned to commoners in Polynesia who, according to Rivers, represent the earlier inhabitants.[61] But however it arose, a clear distinction is made in the nature and location of the after-life between commoners and rulers, the one infinitely inferior to the other. In San Cristoval the bodies of common people are cast into the sea while chiefs are interred, and some relic, such as a tooth or a skull, is preserved in a shrine in the village.[62] Sometimes the corpse of an important person is placed on a wooden platform surrounded by palisades until only the bones remain.[63] In the Shortland Islands commoners are interred or thrown into the sea while chiefs and their wives are burnt.[64] Among the Mafulu of British New Guinea chiefs and their families are laid in boxes or deposited in trees until the platform collapses. Then the skeleton is thrown away except the skull, and the larger bones of the arms and legs, which are interred below in a shallow grave covered with stones, kept in a box on the tree or hung up in the clubhouse (*emone*) till they are required for ritual purposes.[65] In Fiji the canoe that conveys the shades to the next life is thought to be divided in the middle, the one end (*vesi*) being reserved for chiefs, the other (*ndolou*) for commoners. On arrival at the river the shade announces his status and is thereupon assigned his proper position in the boat by the ferryman, Themba.[66]

That Fijian chiefs might be accompanied by their wives in the land of the dead, they (the wives) were often either strangled or buried alive at the funeral of their husbands, and laid at the bottom of the grave beneath the corpse. Sometimes the mother as well as the widow was sacrificed, but husbands were not killed at the death of their wives.[67] The same custom is recorded among the Sulka in New Britain.[68] In New Guinea a widow at her own request might be strangled and buried with her husband, and so acquired an honourable status in the next life,[69] very much as at the death of a Natchez chief there was considerable competition among his highest officers for the privilege of being killed at his obsequies and so to gain a place in his paradise.[70] Thus, the holocaust of wives in the royal tombs at Ur were part of a well-established tradition which has survived throughout the ages until restrictions have been placed upon the practice under the influence of higher civilizations and more humane ideas about the relations of the living and the dead.

For the vast mass of mankind, however, the spirit-world has been regarded as a mutilated existence determined by the status in the existing social structure. Sometimes bravery or cowardice has decided the fate of the soul, as, for example, among the

Haida of Queen Charlotte Islands off the North Pacific coast of America, where those who had not died as warriors went to a desolate region before they were admitted to the celestial realms of light.[71] Women guilty of infanticide and murderers of a kinsman were excluded from the Blackfeet paradise,[72] and cowards, adulterers, thieves and liars, and all who neglected their duties of life, found no admittance to the abode of bliss among the Ojibway, but were condemned to wander up and down among the rocks and morasses, and were stung by gnats as large as pigeons.[73] Only chiefs, hunters and warriors went to the Isles of the Blest reserved for this privileged section of the community,[74] just as the land of the dead beyond the mountains towards the setting sun was confined to chiefs and medicine-men among the Virginian tribes.[75]

The Ancient Mexicans maintained that men killed in war or offered as victims on the sacrificial stone, and women dying in childbirth (who were liable to become malevolent goddesses), joined the emperor and nobility in the Elysium of Huitzilopochtli in the eastern part of the sky where honeyed flowers and luscious fruits abounded in shady groves, and hunting was enjoyed in the parks. Dressed as warriors they accompanied the sun daily on its course and fought mock battles till it reached its zenith. Then it was transferred to the charge of the celestial women (e.g. those who had died in childbirth), who lived in the western part of the sun-house, where merchants who died on their journey also dwelt. After two years of this Elysium the souls of warriors were transmigrated into birds of golden plumage, and either returned to the earth or lived in the celestial gardens.[76] Those who were struck by lightning, drowned or died of contagious diseases went to a happy paradise (Calocan) on a mountain in the east. The rest of the people were destined to pass at death to the dreary subterranean region, Mictlan, "a most obscure land where light cometh not and whence none can ever return". There they were sunk in deep sleep, but class distinctions were maintained, the lords and nobles being separated from the commoners in the nine divisions into which it was divided.[77] At the end of the fourth year of residence in this cheerless abode the ninth division was reached, and in this its denizens were annihilated.

Duration

Although it is very rare to find no conception of a future life, endlessness is too abstract a concept for the primitive mind to grasp. Therefore, it is unable to conceive of an objective life for the dead for an indefinite period. Even when the fate of the soul is not an undesirable one and admits of a measure of idealization, it is only of temporary duration. The idea of an eternal and indestructible spirit or essence lies outside its range, which seldom extends beyond the few generations known to the individual, while the tomb is merely a habitation calculated to endure for many ages to come, as indeed it has in the case of Egyptian and megalithic monuments. But the land of the dead is the land of memory, as in Maeterlinck's fantasia, the inhabitants of which gradually pass into oblivion as the recollection of their existence becomes dim among the survivors. The holding of periodic festivals as a kind of "year's mind" has tended to prolong their survival by keeping the living in touch with them. Nevertheless, the feast of the dead and secondary burial usually mark the end of the funerary ritual, and with its termination the shades tend to pass into oblivion. In the case of commoners this is particularly apparent when mortuary rites are reduced to a minimum and the state of the hereafter is ill-defined and insecure. The distinguished and privileged classes, on the other hand, usually are assigned a position which secures for them some degree of permanence even though it may endure only for a limited period. Therefore, rank and status, together with the manner of death, determine the place in and the duration of the after-life.

Grave-goods

Closely associated with status in the spirit-world is the bestowal of grave-goods, which, as we have seen, has been a characteristic feature of funeral ritual from Palaeolithic times onwards. These gifts have generally been explained as the expression of the belief that the ghost has need of food, implements and the many and various articles lavished upon it. This doubtless is true, as is apparent, for example, in the personal necessities like rice, plates, betel-nut, money and similar articles that are laid in the ground with the Sea Dyaks in Borneo, and the baskets, swords, weaving materials, pots, jars and gongs which are placed on the surface. These unquestionably are believed to be carried into the other world "in some mystic way", as Ling Roth says, where they will be useful to the dead. The spirits of the wind, in fact, are invoked to invite the departed to come and feast on the food placed before them at the entrance of their former habitations.[78]

Similarly, the Kayans dress the corpse in its finest clothes and ornaments that he may appear to the best advantage in the next world, putting a bead of some value under each eyelid, apparently to pay for the passage of the ghost across the river of death. In the grave the body is surrounded by the most valuable personal property displayed in the most imposing manner, to indicate when possible that the deceased has been a man of wealth and position. Small packets of cooked rice and of tobacco are placed upon the coffin for the use of the soul, and hundreds of cigarettes sent by friends are hung in bundles about the low platform on which the coffin rests.[79] Among the coast Dusuns of North Borneo sometimes an open umbrella surmounts the grave to keep the spirit of the dead man dry on his last journey.[80]

In the Malay Peninsula the Sakai array their dead in their best garments, place a dagger or chopper on the breast, together with the betel-leaf wallet. As soon as the corpse is lowered into the grave tobacco and betel-nut are offered, and the furniture placed beside the body before the trench is covered up with earth. Rice and cakes are then laid on it, and these offerings are repeated on the third, seventh and hundredth days following. Sometimes, however, after leaving the body on a platform in front of the house for a day, they bury it and either burn or desert the house. Huts are constructed for the soul at the grave and filled with diminutive furniture consisting of models of various utensils and implements used by the deceased and placed in a soul-wallet made of fan-paten leaf.[81] This custom doubtless arose from the belief that the soul remained at the grave for a short time before journeying to its final abode and would seem to belong to the same tradition as that of the soul-chapel in Ancient Egypt. This temporary sojourn of the ghost at the place of the disposal of the body until it is dispatched at the feast of the dead coincides with the period of mourning during which the prescribed tabus have been carefully observed in respect of the grave-goods as well as of the behaviour of the survivors, since the gifts are solely for his own use. Any interference with the personal belongings of the deceased is calculated to call forth his vengeance, and, therefore, for safety's sake they should be buried with him or ritually destroyed. It is very probable, in fact, that the widespread custom of breaking grave-goods has been a precautionary measure rather than, as has been often supposed, a means of liberating their "souls".

This taboo at any rate avoids theft or disturbance inasmuch as it renders the articles useless to the living. Later it may have become interpreted in animistic terms, thereby making them of service to the dead in the hereafter. Primarily, however, it would seem more likely that the practice was associated with the sacredness of the possessions of the deceased upon which his well-being and status in the next life largely depended. As Codrington came to recognize in Melanesia, it was not just that grave-goods should accompany their former owners "in a ghostly manner", but that "they may be a memorial of him as a great and valued man, like the hatchment of old times". Similarly, his fruit-trees are cut down as a mark of respect and affection, not with any notion of these things serving him in the world of ghosts, but that they are sacred to him and so must not be enjoyed by anyone else.[82] Therefore, in Lepers' Island a man is buried with his bow and arrows and his best ornaments; but his pigs'-tusk bracelets are put on upside down. He will be known in the spirit-world to be a great man by his funerary equipment as it actually exists and not in its spiritual form as having "souls".[83] Such a belief may exist side by side

with the status value of tomb-furniture, but the value attached
to wealth is essentially the prestige it confers both here and
hereafter, and so it becomes "the reservoir of highest good", as
a sign of rank.[84] Consequently, in addition to food and drink
and life-giving amulets, a lavish display of grave-goods confers
status on the deceased.

Human Sacrifice

This also probably applies to the offering of human victims as
an integral element in funerary ritual, notably the wives and
slaves of rulers, constituting as they do an important part of
their possessions. Therefore, the widow in particular, but also
other members of the retinue of a chief, frequently have to
accompany him to the next life at his death. In Fiji, as we have
seen, the mother and wives were often strangled or buried alive
at the funeral of their husbands, and generally at their own
request, in the belief that both they and their husbands thereby
attained a higher status in the after-life. As an alternative to the
sacrifice of widows they may be treated as virtually dead, as, for
example, in Eddystone Island of the Solomons, where the wife
of a commoner instead of following her husband in death
discards all her ornaments and wears nothing but bark-cloth,
and is confined in a small enclosure inside the house. In the
case of the widow of a chief she must be quite invisible and sit
with her knees drawn up in the contracted position until a
successful head-hunter blows the conch in the house. Food is
prepared for her in another house, and she is no longer called
by her name. She is forbidden to take part in festivals, and to
all intents and purposes she is regarded as dead.[85] Therefore,
like the rest of the property and possessions of the deceased, she
has to be put out of action either permanently or temporarily
as part of the death taboo, her life being bound up with that
of her husband. The vigil of the widow by the grave, and the
many restrictions placed upon her movements and behaviour
henceforth, or for a specific period of mourning, would seem
to be survivals of the belief that in death as in life she is an
integral part of his personal equipment. Therefore, his status

and well-being in the hereafter is in great measure determined by his mortuary retinue and the conduct of his relatives and kinsfolk at and after his decease.

THE CULT OF THE DEAD

Thus, viewed in the light of the anthropological evidence, the cult of the dead appears to have been a fundamental element in man's spiritual culture, the roots of which are deeply laid in the archaeological record, and centre in the emotions aroused by the mysterious fact of death and the nature and destiny of human beings. These found expression in the first instance in ritual acts rather than in abstract ideas. Emotional situations arising out of recurrent crises such as death and the hope of immortality require perpetual satisfaction, and it has been around these events that the cult of the dead has taken shape.

From the cradle to the grave human existence has seemed to be in a state of flux, "never continuing in one stay", a dying to be born again, exemplified in the decay and regeneration in nature. This has called forth a series of *rites de passage* at the critical junctures to obtain a fresh outpouring of life and power. By the aid of this transitional ritual from life to death, or from death to life, the tension has been relieved. Death being the gateway to the hereafter the mortuary ritual has had for its purpose the liberation of the deceased from his terrestrial existence and its associations, human and material, and the means whereby he may pass successfully through the dark and dangerous portal and be safely and securely launched on his new career.

Thus, the idea of immortality appears not to have arisen from speculations about a separable soul and phantoms of the living, as was formerly supposed, but from this ritual organization, of which it is the natural corollary. Ever-renewing life is the normal sequence of everyday experience and observation in which death seems to be an intrusion caused by violence and vengeance usually of a supernatural character; this must be overcome by revitalizing energy and life-giving agents such as red ochre, amulets, and all the ritual devices and apparatus employed in the cult of the dead to overcome the fears and contagions with which death is surrounded, and to provide for the well-being of the departed in the spirit-world, however obscure, undefined and limited the state of the hereafter may have been. In all this fear and love have been inextricably intermingled, and the conflict between the mortality of the physical body and the immortality of the body politic has been resolved by the correct observance of the mortuary ceremonial connected with the disposal of the corpse and the eschatological beliefs. Since of all the mysterious disintegrating and critical situations with which man has been confronted death has been the most disturbing and devastating, the equilibrium of the social structure has been largely dependent on the due performance of the funerary ritual. It is not surprising, therefore, that the cult of the dead has occupied such a prominent position, and played an essential role in human society from its first emergence under Palaeolithic conditions.

The Mystery of Birth

TURNING now from the cultus that developed around the mystery of death and human survival to that associated with birth and fertility, the deepest emotions and most heartfelt needs, hopes and fears have been aroused by propagation and nutrition as the vital concern of man in all ages. As Frazer says, "to live and to cause to live, to eat food and to beget children, these were the primary wants of man in the past, and they will be the primary wants of man in the future so long as the world lasts".[1] Therefore, the promotion and conservation of life at all times has been a fundamental urge because an adequate supply of offspring and food is an essential need and a necessary condition of existence, and the production and maintenance of these two basic requirements have been the predominant concern of the human race from the Palaeolithic to the present day. But in the precarious environment in which Early Man had to engage in the struggle for survival the mysterious forces of propagation and nutrition acquired a sacred significance towards which a cautious and numinous attitude was adopted and a ritual technique developed in order to bring them under some measure of magico-religious control.

THE MYSTERY OF BIRTH IN PALAEOLITHIC TIMES
Sculptured "Venuses"

Thus, at the beginning of the Upper Palaeolithic female figurines in bone, ivory and stone, with the maternal organs grossly exaggerated, began to make their appearance in the Gravettian culture as part of the domestic equipment. The breasts are large and pendulous, the hips broad, the buttocks rotund, and excessive corpulency is suggestive of pregnancy. In these so-called "Venuses" of the squat type the face is seldom portrayed, and in that from Willendorf in Upper Austria the hair is braided like that of the head of a girl from Brassempouy in the Landes. The arms and legs are only very slightly indicated but the abdomen is prominent, and on the forearm dots seem to represent a necklace. Traces of red ochre occur in the porous limestone of which the nude figure was composed, and the emphasis clearly was on its sexual features, the rest being of little importance.

In the rock-shelter excavated by Dr Lalanne at Laussel on the Beaune near Les Eyzies in the Dordogne the remarkable relief of a nude female about 18 inches long carved on a block of stone holds in her right hand an object resembling the horn of a bison. The face is featureless, though the head is turned in profile, while the whole body had been coloured red, and all of it except the head had been polished. Two other fragmentary reliefs represent women, and a third may possibly depict the act of childbirth.[2] Another suggestion is that it represents a copulation and served an erotic purpose.[3] On this interpretation it is maintained that the emphasis was on the voluptuous character of the woman rather than on the generative maternal aspect. In support of this contention the engravings on the walls of an alcove in the cavern of Combarelles near Les Eyzies depicting male and female dancers clothed in skins and wearing tails,[4] with their faces obliterated by stalagmite, have been quoted as examples of erotic scenes in Palaeolithic art. But it would seem much more likely that they are portrayals of a masked fertility dance to control the chase like those on the walls of Marsoulas and Altamira, and on bone and reindeer horn from Abri-Murat, Abri-Mège, on a schist plaque at Lourdes, and on a pebble at La Madeleine. Moreover, it has yet to be established that the bas-relief represents a copulation. When the present writer inspected it some years ago at the house of Mme Lalanne at Bordeaux this seemed to be by no means a convincing interpretation. It may well be merely a female figure in outline resembling the other relief, or, as Miss Levy has suggested, the steatite statuette from Grimaldi.[5]

However the obscure figure is to be explained, these sculptured Venuses cannot be dismissed as "the characteristic products of unregenerated male imagination"[6] in view of their long history as an integral part of the cult of the Mother-goddess in more advanced stages of civilization. An erotic element may have been inherent in the tradition, but the main purpose has been that of the promotion and conservation of life in ever-increasing abundance mediated in and through the outward signs of maternal fecundity long before the urge of life was personified in the Earth-mother and her many and various counterparts in the composite figure of the Magna Mater of the Near and Middle East and in the Graeco-Roman world.

Like the rest of the Gravettian culture, it would seem that the Venus cult came into Europe from the east where in the valley of the Don numerous examples have been found, seven of which, skilfully carved in mammoth ivory, have come from Gagarino and one from Kostienki in the middle of Russia.[7] At Malta near Lake Baikal, Siberia, a highly conventionalized figure occurred, and not so very far to the north-east of Willendorf on the Danube Dr Absolon has discovered the Venus of Unter Wisternitz in Moravia and the portrait statue at Vistonice modelled in ground and burnt bones mixed with fat and mud. In the Apennines another conventionalized statuette occurred at Savignano sul Panàro in Emilia, and, as we have seen, two others in the Grimaldi graves on the Franco-Italian frontier. Those from Brassempouy and Sireuil in France are rather later in the Aurignacian, suggesting that the cult took a considerable time to move as far from its base as these sites in Western Europe. Since it is also to a late Aurignacian date that the conventionalized Venus engraved on ivory from Prĕdmost in Moravia has been assigned, the cult in Central Europe must have survived until the advent of the Solutreans.

In the light of recent evidence it would appear that it was among the hunting Gravettian communities of the South Russian steppe and Western Asia that female figurines were first fashioned as fertility charms with very considerable skill, giving excessive prominence to the sexual features. As they passed into Central and Western Europe they tended to become cruder and more conventionalized but continued to exercise the same function in relation to the mystery of birth and generation. There was also, however, a tall, more elegant, slim variety with the head clearly indicated, as, for example, in the ivory figure from Lespugne in Haute-Garonne, with a kind of loin-cloth concealing the sex organ.[8] Since some of these girdles have been decorated with cowrie and other shells as fertility amulets[9] the loin-cloth may have been depicted to stimulate fecundity.

Cowrie Shells

In addition to the squat Venuses, cowrie shells were used for amulets or ornaments by the Gravettians and in the middle Aurignacian.[10] Those at Grimaldi were associated with *cassio nufa* shell from the Indian Ocean, and, therefore, may have been brought to the Italian Riviera from India, or possibly obtained by barter since they also occur in graves in the Dordogne, where at Laugerie-Basse near Les Eyzies two sorts of Mediterranean cowries were scattered over the skeleton.[11] Shaped like the portal of birth, the cowrie was a life-giving agent which may have made its way into Europe from the East in association with the Venuses, and so was often associated with red ochre, the surrogate of blood, in the grave furniture.

Fertility Dances

It was not, however, only to revivify the dead and to make the human species fruitful and multiply and replenish the earth that the life-cult was practised. It was also employed by the Magdalenians to stimulate fecundity among the animals whereon the hunter subsisted. Thus, in a gallery of the inaccessible cavern of Tuc d'Audoubert near St Girons in Ariège, at the end of a long and narrow ascending passage, blocked by stalactite when it was first entered by the Count Bégouen and his son in 1912, two bisons modelled in clay were found, about two feet in length, leaning against a block of rock that had

Fig. 8. Dancing scene in the rock-shelter at Cogul, near Lérida, Spain

fallen from the roof. The female bison was represented as followed by the male, this suggesting a fertility motif. On the soft clay floor of the gallery were the impressions of human feet, and the incomplete model of a bison with some lumps of clay. To the right were a number of deep, rounded depressions which have been thought to be heel-marks made by dancers engaged in a fertility dance around a small hillock in the centre,[12] similar perhaps to that called the *duk-duk* in Melanesia.

Be this as it may, the numerous representations of persons dancing, apparently wearing animal masks or heads, such as the three figures masquerading in the skin of a chamois at Abri-Mège, Dordogne, and others with animal heads at Marsoulas, Hornos de la Pena, Altamira, and Lourdes, and most conclusively "the dancing sorcerer" in the case of Trois Frères near Tuc d'Audoubert, to be considered in the next chapter, show that the custom was firmly established in the Upper Palaeolithic. The practice of dancing round sacred objects, so prevalent in fertility ritual throughout the ages, and still surviving, for example, in the Maypole ceremonial, is revealed in the well-known fresco in the rock-shelter at Cogul near Lérida in Catalonia depicting a group of nine women, narrow-waisted, wearing skirts reaching to the knees, and caps but showing no facial features, dancing round a small naked male figure (Fig. 8).[13]

This celebrated scene has called forth a variety of conjectural interpretations ranging from that of a phallic cult to a gambol dance. As it now appears, incidentally in a very faded condition, a fecundity motif is suggested, though it is by no means established that the male figure has a phallic significance since the penis is not erect. The picture seems to have been the work of several Late Palaeolithic artists, executed perhaps at different times, the little dark brown male figure subsequently having been added to the representations of the black women. Even so, it is difficult to avoid the conclusion that its insertion was connected with a fertility rite in which the women were grouped round a male emblem to facilitate the production of life, however imperfectly the process of generation may have been understood.

The Aurignacians emphasized the maternal aspect of the mystery of birth and gave expression to it in their female figurines. The Magdalenians, concentrating on the magico-religious control of the chase, were mainly concerned with the cult of reproduction as it affected the maintenance of the means of subsistence,[14] and so they rarely fabricated human figurines.[15] The Eastern Spanish artists, on the other hand, at the end of the Upper Palaeolithic introduced both men and women into their vigorous and realistic schematic scenes in profusion. Thus, in the rock-shelter of La Vieja at Alpéra, between Alicante and Albacete, both male and female dancers are depicted in dark red resembling those at Cogul, and repainted at two successive epochs[16] (Fig. 9). This is essentially a hunting scene comprising some thirty goats or antelopes, twenty-six stags as well as cows, deer, moose, ibex, wild horses, wolves, and birds, combined with more than seventy human figures, mainly males, many of whom are shown with drawn bows shooting at the animals. Two of the men are quite unmistakably engaged in a dance, with legs apart showing the generative organ, and wearing a head-dress of plumes, while two of the three women are clad in skirts like those at Cogul, and one is nude and corpulent. The attitudes are those of a sacred dance rather than of the chase, though they are holding weapons. The bodily

Fig. 9. The "dancing chieftain" scene, a detail from a painting in the rock-shelter at Alpéra, Albacete, Spain (*after Breuil*)

proportions are fairly well preserved but the hands and faces are ovaloid and featureless. One of the women holds something in her left hand which it has been alleged is a statuette. But this is merely a conjecture as the object seemed to the present writer, when he visited Alpéra and inspected the representation, to be indecipherable.

If these eastern Spanish paintings are of Capsian origin as their technique might indicate, with possible African affinities, where similar designs occur so far south as Southern Rhodesia,[17] their precise purpose is no less obscure than their history. That they had a magico-religious significance is reasonably certain in view of their situation in rock-shelters which were shrines rather than habitations. But unlike the great caves of the Dordogne, the Pyrenees and Cantabria, where the decoration occurs in the most inaccessible recesses, they were not executed far from the profane gaze of all and sundry in mysterious darkness. Nevertheless, they must have been visited by successive generations of Upper Palaeolithic Man as some of the designs have been painted over and altered, as at Cantos de la Visera in Murcia. There a bull has been transformed into a stag, while at Minateda, between Chinchilla and Hellin, the Abbé Breuil has discovered the superposition of no less than thirteen layers of paintings. Among the reasons which took them to these unimpressive sacred places was, it would seem, the practice of a life-cult centred in the ritual dance in which men and women engaged to control the mysterious processes of birth and generation both in the human and animal species.

To the primitive mind the figure of a woman with her characteristic features given special prominence, and that of the phallus, represent the two poles of creative energy, the one feminine and receptive, the other masculine and procreative. Together they are conceived as one complete whole in the mystery of birth. The woman being the mother of the race, she is essentially the life-producer, as her male partner is the begetter. Therefore, their respective sex organs are thought to be endowed with generative power, and so they have become the symbols of fruitfulness and procreation, and employed to promote the fertility of the womb and its fecundation. In the complex process of birth, conception is the beginning and until this has been accomplished generation cannot ensue. This presupposes a union of the active and passive elements from which all life is derived, male and female, the father and the mother, brought together in a sacred conjunction in order to produce offspring.

But however essential in physiological reality the two partners may be in order to achieve procreation, the agent about whose maternal functions there can be no possibility of doubt is and always has been the woman. She is not only the symbol of generation but the actual producer of life. In the words of the writer of *The Book of Wisdom*, "all men have one entrance into life", and "in the womb of my mother was I moulded into flesh in time of ten months, being compacted in blood and the seed of man." While in primitive society there has been some

ncertainty about paternity,[18] this element of doubt cannot
btain in the case of the mother. Therefore, she and her organs
nd attributes have been the life-giving symbols *par excellence*
ver since their first appearance in the Middle East and in
Europe at the beginning of the Upper Palaeolithic. Her male
artner in all probability was at first supplementary because his
recise function in relation to conception and birth was less
bvious and less clearly understood.

NEOLITHIC AND CHALCOLITHIC FEMALE FIGURINES

With the transition from food-gathering to food-production
he female principle continued to predominate in the mysterious
rocesses of birth and generation. Thus, in the Neolithic period
lay and ivory figurines of the "Venus" type were in use,
ogether with the slim variety, in the Badarian and the Amratian
ultures in Egypt,[19] but elsewhere they have seldom been found
n the earlier sites. Recently two have come to light in the
re-Halaf levels at Hassuna, but west of Iran it is not until the
Halaf levels are reached that they become abundant.

Arpachiyah

At Arpachiyah near Nineveh at the height of the Halafian
ulture numerous headless clay female statuettes in the squatting
osture, suggestive of childbirth, and a painted type with bent
ead and pendulous breasts, occur in association with spindle-
whorls, cones and the bones of domestic animals. In all of
hem prominence is given to the maternal organs, and in some
state of pregnancy appears to have been represented. The
ainted examples are "steatopygous" with a garment indicated
n red pigment and braces crossed between the breasts. Some
ave a fiddle-shaped body flat or truncated and the protuberant
avel is suggestive of pregnancy. A tendency to conventionali-
ation is a marked feature, the body often having been reduced
o a peg or cone, though still showing the squatting position.
Many of them quite clearly are allied to the Gravettian Palaeo-
ithic prototypes, though often they are inferior in design and

technique to the earlier examples, but they constitute an impor
tant link with the Chalcolithic female figurines in Anatolia
Crete and Aegean in Europe, and those of the Middle East
Persia and Baluchistan.[20] In Palestine at Tell Beit Mirsom
Dr Albright found a group of five statuettes representing nud
women in what he describes as "the process of accouchement"
having an exaggerated protrusion of the vulva region which h
thinks was an attempt to suggest the descent of the infant's hea
at the time of delivery for the purpose of hastening parturitio
by magical means.[21]

Tepe Gawra

At Tepe Gawra in the Halaf deposits in the lower levels o
the mound the female figurines are of common occurrence an
those of males extremely rare, though the reverse is true o
painted human representations on pottery and in seal designs
Nearly all are of the same general type in the squatting position
the woman holding her breasts. The heads are crudely shaped
but the facial features are sometimes indicated in paint withou
any attempt at modelling. A highly conventionalized "fiddle"
type shows only the torso with prominent breasts and th
lower part of the body exaggerated, but the arms and legs ar
not shown. The head is merely a short projection while th
back is flat. If the stylization of this isolated example wa
intentional, it may have been intended to assist in parturition
as Tobler suggests.[22]

The stratified deposits of the mound have yielded an armles
type without pointed knees and having prominent breasts an
a painted skirt or kilt suspended from the shoulders by tw
straps between the breasts. There are also indications of tatto
marks or cicatrices. Fattening of the buttocks, distention of th
abdomen and protuberant navels are not characteristic feature
of the figurines at Gawra as elsewhere, and the erect type i
unknown in the mound. In the 'Ubaid period two are s
stylized as to be little more than cones, and except for the breast
they give little indication of being human figures at all. Mos
however, are either of the pointed knees, decorated variety wit

rms encircling the breasts, or without arms and showing a
kirt held by straps. Both belong to the lowest levels. Only the
fragment of one male statuette has been found with a spot of
aint at the end of the phallus.[23]

ell Hassuna and Al 'Ubaid

At Tell Hassuna near Mosul the clay figurines of the "Mother-
oddess" type conform to those found at Arpachiyah, though
he largest has an unexplained excrescence on the left thigh,
nd one of the truncated arms is missing.[24] The excavations
t Tell Chagar Bazar in North Syria have revealed naturalistic
rra-cotta figures wearing turbans and seated on circular stools,
s if in parturition. Several are painted with simple bands
round the neck, arms, and legs, or breasts. These marks
might represent tattooing, clothing or ornaments.[25] In the Tell
Al 'Ubaid settlements from below the flood deposit the earliest
f the Ur female figurines have been recovered. Some of them
re greenish as a result of the overfiring of the clay. Others are
much lighter, but both represent the slender type painted in
lack and red with wigs of bitumen applied to the head. The
eads are elongated and grotesque, but the bodies are well
modelled with feet together and hands at the waist, or holding
child to the breast, or sometimes resting their hands on their
ips. Bands and stripes are painted on the nude body to
ndicate ornaments or tattooing, and the pubes and division
etween the legs are depicted by linear incision.[26] Male counter-
arts have been found at Abu Shahrain, also with a monstrous
ead and having much the same posture though less skilfully
modelled with flattened shoulders.[27]

Varka

n the mound of Warka at Uruk the female figurines resemble
hose at Ur in form and ornamentation with black paint. One
as a cylindrical body, a splayed base with the division between
he legs marked by incision and wing-like arms. The heads are
gain monstrous with a snout and gashes in strips of clay for
yes, and wearing sometimes a peaked head-dress. Others in

contrast are equally small and devoid of features except for
large nose. Across the shoulder and under the right arm
a diagonal band has been painted in some of the examples.
Between the C and D levels of the Anu Ziqqurat a very small
nude female figure in translucent stone, excellently modelled
with arms bent at the elbows and clenched fists,[29] was doubtless employed for amuletic purposes.

Susa

In Iran similar painted figurines with conical heads have been
recovered from Juwi,[30] where on one of them what seem to be
cicatrices are shown as at Ur and Gawra.[31] In the earlier
settlements at Susa (A) figurines of women were modelled in
clay, the eyes and breasts were rendered by dabs, the nose and
brows by thick rolls struck on the flat slab, and an incised
triangle.[32] In the first Elamite period (c. 2800 B.C.) a statuette
was found on the Acropolis on which one of the splayed hands
is placed on the stomach and the other is shown holding the
breast.[33] In another figurine with a cylindrical body the hands
are clasped, the head appears to be covered with a turban, the
eyes are indicated by incised lines, and two bracelets are shown
on each wrist;[34] very much as in a later example, now in the
Ashmolean Museum in Oxford, in addition to a turban and
bracelets, a necklace of two strings of large beads is shown with
a rosette pendant in the middle. Another necklace passes across
the chest.[35] In the proto-Elamite period the use of necklaces in
this type of figurine was an established feature.[36]

Anau

At Anau in Transcaspia the terra-cotta figurines found by
Pumpelly were fragmentary, but in all those of females the
breasts were clearly marked, and in most of them also the navel.
A necklace ornament is represented on several torsos,[37] but
the head is indicated by a projection of the nose and by small
depressions of the eyes.[38] The hips are strongly developed, but
the legs are brought together in a point and the generative
organs are emphasized.[39] From the adjacent ruins now called

hiaur Kala, the ancient Merv, on the Acropolis naked
gures have been found painted in black, red and yellow, and
female relief standing in a long robe with neck ornaments,
olding a mirror in the right hand before the breast. The left
and is placed lower down but the head is missing.[40]

aluchistan

a South Baluchistan in the Kulli culture, established in
akran before 3000 B.C., a number of clay figurines of women
ave been discovered which finish at the waist in a splayed
edestal. The arms are bent with hands on the hips, and while
reasts are usually shown they are not unduly exaggerated. The
ces are grotesque caricatures with the eyes fashioned from
ellets, and the hair is elaborately dressed and kept in place by
fillet, or plaited. The ornaments which adorn the head include
val pendants resembling cowrie shells, while on the arms and
rists are bangles. Or, again, in the Zhob valley sites the same
pe of female figures recur with necklaces, large and beak-like
oses, hooded heads, exaggerated breasts, circular eye-holes,
d slit mouths and bangles.[41] These are so uniform in style
d features that Sir Aurel Stein conjectures that they "might
ave been intended to represent some tutelary goddess".[42] That
ey had a fertility significance is shown by the representation
 a phallus carved in stone at the mound of Mogul Ghundai
ar the left bank of the Zhob river south-west of Fort Sande-
an, and at the neighbouring mound of Periano-Ghundai on
e right bank of the river, where a vulva is depicted with
eat prominence.[43]

he Indus Valley

 the Indus valley terra-cotta female figurines have been dis-
overed in considerable numbers at Harappa and Mohenjo-
aro, the majority of which are nude except for a small skirt
cured by a girdle round the loins; they have a large fan-shaped
ead-dress and pannier-like side projections having a black
ain which seems to have been made by smoke. Therefore, the
ference is that they were used as lamps or incense-burners in

the practice of a cult connected with the Mother-goddess. A Mohenjo-daro they occurred at all levels, frequently in mutilated condition, in the streets and in the dwellings, painte over with a red slip or wash doubtless to enhance their lif giving potency, as in Ancient Egypt, Mesopotamia an Malta.[44] They were adorned with quantities of jewellery whic included bead necklaces with pendants, ornamental collar armlets, bracelets and anklets. Some in the higher levels we seated with hands clasped round the knees, roughly modelle and with no ornaments. Others were in postures which sugge that they were engaged in a ritual dance, such as is represente on a faience plaque.[45]

That they were sacred images is beyond doubt, and, a Sir John Marshall says, it is probable that "they represent goddess with attributes very similar to those of the gre Mother Goddess, 'the Lady of Heaven', and a special patrone of women, whose images are found in large numbers at s many sites in Elam, Mesopotamia, Egypt and the Easter Mediterranean area."[46] Dr Mackay may also be correct i thinking that they were household deities kept in a niche i the wall in almost every house in the Indus valley cities, ju as today in India the Mother-goddess is the guardian of th house and village, presiding over childbirth and daily needs.[4] If this be the correct interpretation of this type of figurin whether she was associated with a male partner—as in her lat developments both in India and elsewhere—is not clea Figures of male gods, frequently horned, recur in the Harapr culture,[48] but they are not prevalent and seldom are brougl into conjunction with those of goddesses. On pottery they a extremely rare and, unlike the skirted female statuettes, a entirely nude, though on one of the male figures red lines o the arms and neck probably represent bangles and a sca necklace.[49]

The three-faced male god from Mohenjo-daro sitting in th attitude of a *yogi* with arms outstretched and covered wit bangles, and the chest with triangular necklaces or torque like the figurines from Kulli and Zhob in Baluchistan,

irrounded by four animals—an elephant, tiger, rhinoceros and
uffalo—with two deer beneath his throne. A pair of horns
owns his head, and there is either a phallus or the end of a
aistband between the legs.[50] That this is a prototype of the
lindu god Shiva as Lord of the Beasts and Prince of *Yogis* is
nquestionably suggested by the form and symbolism.[51] More-
ver, on several seals a similar figure occurs associated with the
icred *pipal*, or fig-tree, and cult animals like the Lord of the
easts in Minoan Crete, and with Cybele the Anatolian
lother-goddess.[52]

Phallic Emblems

here is also evidence of phallic emblems, or *lingas*, in the form
f realistic models of the male generative organ, together with
ni, or female vulva,[53] used probably as life-bestowing
mulets, as among Saivites in India today. The more conven-
onalized resemble very closely *linga* from Mogul Ghundai
1 Baluchistan,[54] *yoni* bases having been used sometimes to
/mbolize the union of the two organs.[55] Some of the larger
nes, however, that have been found at Mohenjo-daro in
rdinary dwellings do not appear to have been *lingas*, their
nooth worn bases suggesting rather that they were grinders.
Jevertheless, there is every probability that many of the
nished cones showing no signs of polishing were in fact
hallic emblems.[56]

At Harappa a number of limestone conical *lingas* have been
ecorded, some of which are in the form of chessmen in
halcedony, carnelian, lapis lazuli, alabaster, faience, paste,
nell, ivory and terra-cotta, as well as in limestone.[57] A conven-
onalized example in yellow sandstone with finely cut coils
nd necklaces may have had a *yoni* base, and six occurred in
1 earthware jar with some small pieces of shell, a unicorn seal,
one pestles and a stone palette. Some miniature conical
aetyls have a sort of ring round the body which has been
egarded as a possible indication of a *yoni*.[58] Large undulating
ngs of stone are thought to symbolize the female principle,[59]
nd to these may be added miniature imitation carnelian

rings of the same class, and other small undulating ring of the same kind which fit exactly on a base taken to be *linga*.[60]

In the worship of Shiva today the *linga* is the most popula object of veneration, the pouring of libations over them an anointing them with butter being a universal practice through out India. It would seem that this phallic symbolism is ver deeply laid in the prehistoric substratum of Hinduism in th Indus valley civilization, going back to the third millenniun B.C. in the form of huge cone-shaped *linga* and *yoni* rings, ofter wavy along the edge like the modern Hindu counterparts, ane various much smaller varieties less than two inches high though some of these may have been used as "chessmen" is board-games. Behind this phallic cult was the mystery of birth and the predominance of female figurines over male in th earliest levels of all the cultures in which they occur in Ancient Middle East, from the Eastern Mediterranean to th Indus valley, shows that attention at first was concentrated of the feminine aspects of the process of generation.

There can be little doubt that they represent a deity respon sible for the bestowal of life, probably the Mother-goddess herself whose emblem, the dove, is of frequent occurrence in the Indus valley cities, though in this early Indian civilizatio her functions were confined apparently to this world, and not as elsewhere, also to the care and renewal of the dead. A Anau, for instance, the earliest figurines were found in th graves of children buried under the floor of the house,[6] suggesting that they were deposited there to facilitate thei rebirth. At Mohenjo-daro, Harappa and Chanhu-daro, a in Baluchistan, like the Hindu Mother-goddess, they wer connected essentially with household shrines. But they wer also emblems of the tutelary deity guarding the portal throug! which life emerges into this world as well as protectors of th house, village or city over which she presided. Whether or no she was associated with a male partner, such as the horned-goc depicted on the seals, cannot be determined with any degree o certainty. Be this as it may—and this will be considered later[6]

—she was by virtue of her functions destined to become the consort of the vegetation god.

Anatolia, Cyprus and the Cyclades

In western Anatolia, Cyprus and the Aegean, female figurines with marked genitalia and painted ornamentation occur in considerable numbers. Those in stone in Khirokitia sometimes afford no indication of their sex, but in the Erimi period in Cyprus the terra-cotta figures are true to type and they are frequent on the local red-ware, indicating the introduction of a life-giving cult in the Mother-goddess tradition in a fairly early phase of the Neolithic period.[63] Myres, in fact, suggested that Asia Minor and Syria constituted the cradleland of the emblems of the "Great Mother of Asia", which he described as "the earliest 'ideal type' in history, and the earliest cult of which we know the meaning as well as the symbol".[64] This, however, ignores the Palaeolithic "Venuses" as the prototype of the Neolithic comparable figurines, and until we know more precisely what lies behind the recent evidence from Arpachiyah, Samarra, and Tell Halaf in the fifth millennium B.C., the first civilization in Susa in Elam, and the latest discoveries at Mersin in Cilicia of an even greater antiquity, we are not in a position to determine the origin of the cult centred in the mystery of birth and the Earth-mother from whose womb all life proceeded and by whom it was nourished and sustained with the aid of the emblematic figurines modelled in clay or carved in stone, often highly conventionalized and worn as amulets.

At the first city of Troy (c. 3000 B.C.) she seems to have been portrayed sculptured in low relief flanking the gateway, her heart-shaped human face accentuated by the hair having been indicated by a series of small holes. To the left of the face is the haft of a staff or sceptre with a spherical head. Below the face to the right is further carving which may be that of an arm or hand.[65] At Thermi the clay figurines and phalli are later than the conventionalized stone statuettes, while in the Cyclades elegant figures in marble appear as importations from Asia

Minor, together with the "fiddle idol" type in the oldest
cemeteries (i.e. the Pelos group). In the poorer graves at
Antiparos the crudest and most conventionalized occurred,
but where any attempt had been made to fashion a figure in
the marble, special attention had been paid to the vulva
triangle, and in one figure the sitting posture was indicated.
From Amorgos came a female torso with the arm of another
person round her back, and in some of the graves were single
marble legs. The head invariably was "pointed like the blade
of a stone implement", and everywhere there was an excess of
female figures over male. From this it is concluded that it was
a goddess who was worshipped.[66]

Crete

That Neolithic Crete was an Anatolian province, as Evans
affirmed, is shown by the clay figurines from Knossos which
include all the principal types found in South-east Europe and
the Aegean basin—the so-called steatopygous variety of obese
females, those in the squatting attitude, and the flat fiddle-
shaped types, all of which, as we have seen, were so widespread
and recurrent throughout the Middle East, in Anatolia and
Northern Syria.[67] In the earliest Neolithic deposit at Knossos
with only one exception all were of the squatting or seated
"Venus" kind. In the succeeding period in Crete, Anatolia
and the Cyclades the extended stylized figures became prevalent as Western Asiatic and Anatolian influences increased,
bringing with them transitional forms, especially in Central
Crete, where attempts were made to reproduce facial features.

THE MOTHER-GODDESS

The Great Minoan Goddess

Since it is impossible to dissociate these figurines from those
that appear in the sanctuaries of the Great Minoan Goddess, it
can scarcely be mere coincidence, as Evans has pointed out,
that all the various centres in which the emblems occur eventually became seats of the Mother-goddess cult in its manifold
forms and nomenclatures.[68] But that Crete was its original

home, as has often been contended, is now less probable, however much it may have been its area of characterization. Thus, it seems to have flourished at Arpachiyah a thousand years before it was established in the Aegean. Moreover, the double axe, formerly supposed to have been a Cretan innovation, is now known to have been a cult object, together with the dove as a symbol of the Mother-goddess, among the Arpachiyahians and elsewhere in the Ancient Middle East in the Chalcolithic period. It was from Asia Minor that the earliest Neolithic influences were felt in Crete about 4000 B.C., and from this centre the Goddess symbolism almost certainly was introduced.

Once established on the island it soon became a dominating force, and the Cretan claim to have been the cradleland of the Phrygian Mysteries of the Great Mother cannot be lightly dismissed.[69] From Middle Minoan times she was worshipped as the Mistress of Trees and Mountains and Lady of the Wild Beasts. In association with her youthful male partner she represented the life-giving principle in nature and in man, until eventually on the Greek mainland her functions and attributes were assumed by a number of goddesses. Thus, Athena, once an Earth-divinity, acquired her snake and bird emblems;[70] Artemis her wild creatures, forests and streams,[71] while Aphrodite took over her doves who became her divine son and the dynamic embodiment of her own functions.

It was in her role of the Earth Mother, the Mountain Mother and the Goddess of Vegetation, that the Minoan Mother was represented in her figures in clay and porcelain with outstretched or uplifted arms, often holding or encircled by snakes, clad in a skirt with flounces and wearing a high crown, sometimes accompanied by a priestess or facsimile of herself, together with the double axe and horns of consecration and votive garments[72]. On some of the seals and signets she is represented as seated beneath her tree receiving offerings of the first-fruits of her bounty, or in later Minoan scenes (*c.* 1500 B.C.) as the hunting Goddess accompanied by lions and with a spear in her hand, or replaced by a pillar or mountain standing between rampant lions. At Knossos she is herself elevated on a mountain wearing the typical Minoan flounced skirt, holding a lance or sceptre and flanked by lions.[73] To the left is a shrine with "baetylic" pillars and horns of consecration—the symbols connecting her with plant and animal life. Before her stands a male divinity descending from the sky and accompanied by lions.[74] At Hagia Triada a female of gigantic stature is depicted between two smaller females before a shrine,[75] and everywhere the Goddess predominates in Cretan worship, the young male, when represented at all, always being subordinate and later in time than the Great Minoan Mother.

When the "Lady of the Mountain" made her way from Western Asia through the Eastern Mediterranean to the Aegean area she retained her position and life-giving functions which, as in Mesopotamia, extended to the land of the dead. Thus, the Temple Tomb in the glen above the Palace site at Knossos, which corresponds in essential details to the temple of Aphrodite, "the Lady of the Dove", described by Diodorus as the legendary tomb of Minos in Sicily,[76] was a temple of the Goddess with the double axe and horns of consecration in the upper sanctuary leading to the sepulchral chamber. This was a ritual pillar crypt used as a shrine in her honour as the guardian and reviver of the dead.[77] At Hagia Triada the sarcophagus in a kind of chamber-tomb ascribed to the Late Minoan II and III is ornamented with scenes depicting an altar with horns of consecration, an olive-tree with spreading branches, a pole painted pink with a double axe and a bird, a priestess with a vessel of offerings, a libation jug and a basket of fruit. Then follows the sacrifice of a bull; the blood, it seems, being collected in a pail while a priestess clad in the skin of a victim offers libations at an altar. Behind the bull is a figure playing the double pipes (Fig. 10).[78] Various interpretations of the pictures have been given, but the emblems suggest the cult of the Goddess in a funerary setting with her priestesses as the officiants in a sacrificial oblation on behalf of the deceased perhaps with the blood flowing down to the earth through

Fig. 10. Cult scene on the Hagia Triada sarcophagus in Crete

bottomless vessels as an offering to Mother-Earth as the ultimate source of rebirth.[79]

The Maltese Goddess Cult

In Malta obese female figurines of Western Asiatic type with Tell Halaf and Arpachiyah affinities are prevalent. Thus, from Hagia Kim have come a number of headless corpulent statuettes in the sitting posture with the legs folded towards the left and the hands resting on the thighs often showing traces of red pigment. The sex is not always at all easy to determine, but a woman clearly is indicated in the case of a figure with breasts, covered by a garment, resting on the upper part of the thighs, and clad in a flounced skirt which conceals what seems to be a stool. In another in a similar position the pigmented line of a necklace can be discerned, while in a standing naked female the breasts and abdomen are pendulous, the right hand resting on the right thigh, the left across the abdomen.[80]

At Tarxien a headless very corpulent statuette in the sitting posture has the hands resting on the thighs towards the genital organ,[81] and this attitude is repeated in a small clay model which is unmistakably female with the right hand pointing to the very clearly marked vulva.[82] In a small headless female sitting figure the knees are drawn up against the chest, and the pendulous breasts touch the thighs,[83] while on a fragment of a clay female figure found among the Neolithic debris the sexual triangle is shown by a deep incision.[84] A female torso of lightly baked red clay from Mnaidra has very large and protruding breasts resting on an immense projection from the abdomen which may suggest pregnancy.[85] The abdomen also is very prominent in another torso from this site, though the breasts are small in this case.[86]

The occurrence of a considerable number of both male and female figures suggests that in Malta the Goddess was associated with a partner in the guise of either a husband or son, as in the Eastern Mediterranean. This also may explain the temples having been built in pairs sometimes with a double shrine. Thus, outside the double chapel at Borg en Nadur a crude phallic figure was found in limestone with incised lines, probably of Neolithic Asiatic origin, and used to express the male procreative aspect of deity,[87] the female counterparts being employed as life-producing emblems. Therefore, in them emphasis was given to the maternal organs.

At the Hal-Saflieni Hypogeum near the Tarxien megalithic ruins, clay and alabaster figures of the naked steatopygous type, comparable to those from Hagiar Kim and the Tarxien temples, have been discovered, together with a perfectly baked clay model of a woman lying asleep on a couch on her right side with the head resting on her arm supported by a pillow.[88] As Zammit suggests, this may indicate that the Hypogeum was used for the practice of incubation in the consultation of oracles, with cubicles for devotees who slept there to have their dreams interpreted by the priests in the service of the Goddess, since emblems of her cult abound in the sanctuary. The breasts of the sleeping figure are large and prominent, the abdomen is transversely grooved and the hips are enormous. Above the flounced skirt the body is naked, and conforms in all essentials to the Tarxien and Hagia Kim type. With it was a similar terra-cotta model, very fat, naked to the waist and showing the remains of red pigment. It is lying on its face, and although the head is missing the pillow remains.[89]

Doubtless before it became an ossuary[90] this great sanctuary in the third millennium B.C. was the scene of a complex and composite cultus which included a variety of life-bestowing rites, sacrificial, votive and oracular, centred in the worship of the Asiatic Goddess. From the Near East came religious beliefs and practices deeply laid in the Tell Halaf culture which as they passed along the Mediterranean littoral and the hinterland of South-west Asia Minor and Thessaly developed the maternal features differentiating the Maltese Goddess cult from that of the Aegean, with its sepulchral emphasis. In the main court at Hal Tarxien she reigned supreme with her colossal statue standing over seven feet high, arrayed in a fluted skirt and having pear-shaped legs. In attendance were her priests in long skirts and short wigs like Chaldaean officials, offering before the statue burnt sacrifices on the near-by altar, and pouring the blood into a cylindrical stone vessel with a hollow base, decorated with pit marks on the outside and a deep cavity at the top to receive it, while incense was burnt in the cup-shaped cylindrical tops of pillars.[91]

The Iberian Goddess Cult

With the spread of Neolithic culture to the west, the cult of the Mother-goddess from its centre at Malta radiated its influence to the Iberian peninsula, where in Almeria it recurred and found expression in the hundreds of female figurines in the megalithic tombs and huts at Los Millares. So plentiful were they, in fact, that, as at Mohenjo-daro in the Indus valley, it would seem that they must have found a place as part of the regular equipment of every household. They are not as excessively corpulent as the Maltese figures, and often they are stylized almost beyond recognition. Some in Almeria and Portugal are mere outlines of human figures in stone without any faces, others are bone or ivory cylinders, schist plaques or bovine phalanges decorated with what have been described as "owl eyes" (Fig. 11). At El-Garcel in south-east Spain a small fiddle-shaped "idol" characteristic of the eastern Mediterranean Goddess tradition has been found, and similar examples have recurred at El Castillo near Pavia, Alemtejo, in

Portugal.[92] The schist plaque, however, is typical of the south-western province, and when it is not of common occurrence in Almeria a few incisions suffice for arms. The facial features are indicated by a few incised lines or carved knobs. In this area anthropomorphic designs for the most part are confined to figurines made from knuckle-bones or long-bones.[93]

Since El-Garcel with its slag of copper ores and the coastal Almerian province were colonized by Mediterranean mariners having Near East affinities, it is not surprising that the Goddess cult made its way into Western Europe by this route, probably about 2700 B.C. Thence it spread to the south-west of Spain and Portugal, where the marble cylindrical idols with incised face and eyes became a characteristic feature, distinct from the phalange figurines in Almeria. Flat stone and phalange examples recur in the collective tombs on the plateau of Granada in the neighbourhood of Guardix, Gor and Gorafe.[94] Similar designs appear incised on croziers and plaque idols in the Palmella graves in Portugal in addition to phalange and Almerian statuettes. On the Portuguese highlands schist and marble figurines are among the funerary furniture in the slab-cists,[95] and on the east coast of Spain phalanges recur sporadically in Catalonia.[96] But the farther from the great centres in the south the poorer the emblems of the Goddess become, suggesting that although the cult persisted in the hinterland and the north, only a few cherished symbols survived in the process of diffusion, thereby corresponding to the devolution of the megalithic monuments with which it was closely associated.

Statue-menhirs

That the worship of the Mother-goddess was an integral element in the megalithic culture is shown by the recurrence of its symbolism in menhir-statues in Brittany, the Paris Basin, the Marne and the Channel Islands, while the Abbé Breuil has claimed to have found the face and features of the Goddess in the highly conventionalized "buckler" and "octapus" patterns carved on the slabs of the tomb on Gavr'inis in Southern Morbihan. Be this as it may, the figures with breasts

Fig. 11. Owl-eyed female figurines, Almeria, Spain

nd necklaces discovered in Aveyron, the Tarn and Gard, and
a Guernsey, leave no doubt about their being emblems of the
ult. Thus, the Breton tomb designs conform to the Goddess
adition in respect of the maternal symbolism and schematic
epresentation of human features, the general affinity being with
he menhir-carvings of the south of France and Guernsey, the
eine-Oise-Marne (S.O.M.) cists, and the prehistoric tomb-
culptures and schist plaques of Spain and Portugal.[97]

In the Channel Islands the statue-menhirs appear to be an
ategral part of the earliest megalithic culture, the links being
.oser with the Iberian Atlantic littoral than with the south of
rance.[98] That known as "La Gran'mere du Chinquière", now
anding at the gates of the churchyard of St Martin's, Guernsey,
a rectangular granite pillar 5 feet 6 inches high, terminating
a a human head carved out of a block having a massive chin,
:ched eyebrows, oval eyes, a broad nose and deep upper lip.
wo slight elevations from the side of the statue suggest arms
d hands, and in the centre are two breasts close together in

high relief with a suggestion of nipples, surmounted by circular groove. Lower down is a girdle in the form of a hor zontal band running round the stone. The ornamentatio about the head and shoulders may have been intended depict a tightly fitting head-dress with a row of protrudir curls and a fringe across the forehead. Four bosses under th chin may be an ornament of some kind.[99] The predomina feature, however, are the breasts, as in other statue-menhir and the carved head reminiscent of the Corsican statuett with rudely carved facial features but no sexual organs.[100]

In the churchyard of S. Marie-du-Câtel in Guernsey the is a statue-menhir of local granite which formerly was buri within the chancel an equal distance from the north and sou walls, about a foot below the surface. It had been placed on i left side, lying east and west. The front was nearly flat exce for two projecting breasts close together, one of which has be broken. At the side of the boulder two shoulders are indicate and the portion corresponding with the head is dome-shape On each side of the head, extending from the forehead to th breasts, are two ridges raised a little above the surface of th stone, which may have been intended to represent a head-dre or tresses of hair. Whether or not it ever contained facial featur which have been destroyed deliberately can only be conjecture by signs of hammer and chisel marks on what should be th face.[101] In any case, it was an attempt to model a huma figure in the round with a collar above the breasts like th goddesses in the cists of the Seine and Oise valleys, as, f example, at Bellehaye, near Boury in the department of th Oise, where two hemispherical breasts occur only thre quarters of an inch apart with a collar above about 15 inch in length formed of three U-shaped bars.[102]

A similar statue-slab of a female divinity armed with an a was used as a lintel in a corbelled megalithic tomb at Collorgu in Gard on which, however, face, arms and fingers are scul tured in relief,[103] and in the chalk country of the Marne the walls of the artificial caves in the valley of Petit Orin, th conventionalized figure of the Goddess is carved or sketche in charcoal, bearing sometimes an axe, guarding the ante-chamber of the tomb.[104] But in these grottoes the face with eyebrows and wedge-shaped nose is emphasized at the expense of the breasts that appear only in one instance. In Brittany there is one long-cist with sculptured breasts at Tressé, Ille-et-Vilaine,[105] but the centre of the Goddess cult in Northern Europe was in the Paris Basin and the S.O.M. culture.

The Goddess Cult in Britain and Northern France

In England a fat figurine of a pregnant woman carved in chalk has been recovered from a ritual deposit at Grime's Graves in Norfolk with a chalk phallus carved on the left side, and an "altar" in front composed of blocks of flint in the form of a triangle with a chalk cup at the base opposite the Goddess. Upon the "altar" were seven deer-antler picks.[106] At Maiden Castle a headless conventionalized torso has been found, perhaps skirted, having two holes at the base for the insertion of legs, and from Windmill Hill a female figurine, together with phalli carved in chalk, have been recovered.[107] With the possible exception of alleged examples of phalli from Trundle, Whitehawk Camp, Blackpatch flint-mines and the Thickthorn long barrow,[108] and the employment of a phallic symbol in the central ceremony when the ashes of the dead were placed in an urn in Pond Cairn, Glamorgan, in the middle of the Bronze Age,[109] these generative symbols are unknown in the British Isles. Like clay female figurines, they are of very infrequent occurrence in the Neolithic culture in Western Europe, just as clay statuettes are confined to the fortified camp at Fort Harrouard on the downlands of northern France,[110] unless the example recovered by Déchelette from La Grotte Nicolas, Gard, be accepted as a genuine figurine.[111] The closest affinity of the Grime's Graves statuette is with the Palaeolithic "Venuses", and as the others from Britain and Northern France cannot be equated with the Iberian technique, they would seem to belong to the Eastern Mediterranean goddess tradition, where the mystery of birth appears to have most deeply impressed the mind and imagination of Early Man.

CHAPTER VII

Fertility and the Food Supply

So intimate appeared to be the relation between the processes of birth and generation and those of fertility in general that the two aspects of the same "mystery" found very similar modes of ritual expression under prehistoric conditions. As we have seen, food and offspring always have been the first need of the human species, as, indeed, of other organisms, and around these essential requirements a magico-religious cultus has developed to increase and control the supply.

PALAEOLITHIC HUNTING RITUAL

Thus, in the Upper Palaeolithic it has been estimated that four-fifths of the representations in the parietal art are of animals, presumably because they constituted the principal means of subsistence and so had a unique status and importance in the economy. Unlike an increase in the human population which raised the problem of providing an adequate food supply in a struggling Palaeolithic community, the greater the number of edible animals available the higher the standard of living for Early Man. Therefore, rites of increase, comparable to the Intichiuma ceremonies among the native tribes of Central Australia,[1] doubtless were of common occurrence in the cave sanctuaries, as is suggested by the representations of a male following a female in erotic fashion at Tuc d'Audoubert,[2] the numerous zoomorphic figures showing the conjunction of animals in various similar attitudes, often superimposed for magical purposes in the same style, as in the contemporary group of engraved animals at Teyjat in the Dordogne, or the stag's horn added to a hollow in the rock at Niaux near Tarascon-sur-Ariège, indicating that certain spots were considered to be charged especially with sacred potency which could be brought into operation by the masked dancers in animal disguises.

Increase Rites

In most instances the animal dances were connected with the designs executed on the walls of these deep and tortuous mysterious caves, often in nooks and corners, or in the most inaccessible or obscure positions, like the fine painting of a woolly rhinoceros high up on the left-hand wall at the end of a very narrow crevice at Font-de-Gaume, near Les Eyzies, drawn apparently by the artist standing on the shoulders of a companion. To reach the clay bisons 758 yards from the entrance at Tuc d'Audoubert the services of a boat, as has been pointed out, were required, while at the neighbouring cave of the Trois Frères, the three young sons of the Count Bégouen, when they first entered it, had to worm their way through a very small passage leading out of the little cave called Enlène until they reached an alcove on the right-hand side adorned with the engravings of a lion. Beyond this lay a small chamber covered with engravings of a great number of animals, and at the end of a winding passage opening out into a kind of window, about 12 feet above the ground, was the figure of a man with a human face and long beard, the eyes of an owl, the antlers of a stag, the ears of a wolf, the claws of a lion and the tail of a horse (Fig. 12) engraved on the rock wall just beside the window.[3] Whether or not this strange masked figure was the representation of the arch-sorcerer, or shaman, embodying the attributes and functions of the animals it portrayed, as Bégouen suggests,[4] a cult is indicated in which human beings and animals were brought together in a mystic communion with the source of providential bounty in a joint endeavour to conserve and promote the food supply. The emphasis clearly was on fecundity for the purpose of securing an abundance of the species on which man depended for his means of subsistence.

The mysterious forces of nutrition and propagation being sacred and the centres of emotional interest and concern, a reverent attitude was adopted towards them which found expression in a ritual technique to bring them under some measure of supernatural control. To eat is to live. Therefore, the main link between man and his environment was food; for, as Malinowski has said, "nature is his living larder".[5] Before the adoption of agriculture and herding, when a precarious existence was eked out on the chase and edible fruits, roots and berries, the animal and vegetable species which formed his staple diet acquired a sacred character and significance. With this he endeavoured to establish efficacious relations through a prescribed ritual procedure performed by experts in carefully secluded sanctuaries set apart for the purpose in awe-inspiring surroundings and conditions calculated to produce a sense of the numinous.

The Control of the Chase

Propagation was not, however, the only end in view in the practice of hunting magic. The animals had to be procured as well as to be rendered prolific. So to the cavern sanctuaries the Palaeolithic ritual experts repaired to set in motion powerful supernatural forces to control the fortunes of the chase. Thus, for example, in the great caves in the Garonne valley—those at Niaux, Portel, Montespan, Tuc d'Audoubert and Trois Frères—a very considerable number of the paintings and drawings of animals have spears and arrows drawn on their flanks in the region of the heart. At Niaux, just over half a mile from the entrance, three small cup-like hollows were cleverly utilized to represent wounds by drawing round them the outline of a bison and marking the cups with arrows in red ochre. In front of an outline figure of an expiring bison with its legs drawn up close to the body are circles and club-shaped designs depicting missiles (Fig. 13).

When in 1923 M. Casteret first explored the cave of Montespan near the château of the celebrated Marquise in the Haute Garonne, after swimming for nearly a mile in the icy water of a subterranean stream which filled part of the tunnel, and through a siphon, he found in the gallery over twenty clay models of wounded animals. These included the figures of a number of felines riddled with wounds, and raised on a platform in the centre a figure of a small headless bear $3\frac{1}{2}$ feet long

Fig. 12. "The Sorcerer" in Les Trois Frères, Ariège, France

and 2 feet high, holding the skull of a young bear between its paws. Against the walls, which are decorated with engravings, were three larger models, 5 feet long, apparently lionesses, and a model of a horse's head, while part of the body of a woman lay on a clay hillock. On the floor the design of a horse showed thrusts in the neck and marks made by spears were visible on the neck and chest of the bear, and on the breast of one of the lionesses. In another gallery having a very low roof is the representation of a small horse falling backwards covered with a coating of stalagmite. At the end of the passage there is a scene which Bégouen thinks depicts a corral surrounded with palisades into which wild horses are being driven by darts and stones.[6]

In this sanctuary the rites appear to have been concentrated on the killing of animals in the chase rather than on ensuring an ample supply of them. Thither the sorcerer resorted doubtless before a party set out on a hunting expedition and pierced the images with a spear as he uttered the magic spell that was destined to produce the reciprocal effect upon the prey. That the same model was used for this purpose time after time is shown by that of the headless bear and those of some of the felines being covered with spearmarks, though often fresh ones may have been made if and when the efficacy of the magic declined. At Marsoulas, also in Haute Garonne, a series of polychromes with spearmarkings have been painted one above the other as if they had been constantly renewed, an existing drawing having been modified according to the purpose required. In a small recess at Trois Frères the head of a lion engraved on stalactite had been redrawn three times in different positions, and the tail once shown as straight was subsequently rendered as curling. Judging from the number of arrows engraved or painted on it, it must have been in constant use as a magical effigy.

Sometimes—for example, at Tuc d'Audoubert—only particular parts of an animal, such as the head or horns, were depicted, as in the case of the conventionalized figurines discussed in the last chapter, since for the purposes of magical control these sufficed as efficacious symbols to convey the spell on the prey. In the cave known as PechMerle at Cabrerets in the valley of the Lot near Cahors in Corrèze, the Abbé Lemozi has detected representations of mammoth and cattle without eyes and ears, which he thinks have been deliberately portrayed in this manner for the purpose of depriving of sight and hearing their counterparts in the chase, thereby rendering them an easy prey to the hunters.[7] Whether or not this be the correct interpretation, that many of the animals do lack these organs was clear to the present writer after a recent visit to this very fine cave. But since headless figures of women also occur on the roof of the galleries at PechMerle, it may be that, like the female figurines lacking heads or faces, for purposes of the magic art these appendages were felt to be superfluous. In any

Fig. 13. Dying bison and claviform designs in Niaux, Ariège, France

ase, it was to control the chase that they were executed, some-
imes with consummate artistic skill, as at Altamira and Font-
le-Gaume; at other times merely in outline or in part, as at
Tuc d'Audoubert, Enlène and Cabrerets, or even in conven-
ionalized geometric patterns, as at Marsoulas and on bone
ools and Azilian pebbles.

In the hall and gallery at Lascaux near Montignac on the
Vézère, horses are represented with missiles directed towards
hem, striking them, or superimposed on them. There are no
ndications of actual wounds, however, except in the relatively
ate scene depicting a hunting tragedy, in the most secluded
ubterranean "crypt" reached by a hazardous descent of some
wenty-five feet. There occurs the stylized figure of a man with
bird-shaped head who apparently had been killed by a bison,
ortrayed with its flank transfixed by a spear exposing its
ntrails as it was about to fall to the ground, like a gored horse
n a bull-fight. To the left is a woolly rhinoceros, painted in
different style, which seems to be slowly moving away after
erhaps having ripped up the bison. A little lower down in
ont of the man is a bird on a pole, rather like an Egyptian
eremonial stave. Behind the rhinoceros below the tail are six
lack dots arranged in two rows.

In this remarkable fresco an accident in the chase appears to
ave been recorded. A Late Magdalenian hunter wearing a
ird-mask, and possibly carrying a bird-pole, is represented as

having been gored by a bison he had wounded; if the woolly rhinoceros has not been superimposed subsequently on the rest of the group, it then ripped open the bison with its horn.[8] The Abbé Breuil has conjectured that the scene is a votive painting to the deceased hunter who, he suggests, may have been buried in the cave.[9] This awaits confirmation. As Windels has pointed out, in view of the magical potency assigned to cave-paintings, it seems hardly likely that a tragedy of this kind would been given graphic portrayal.[10] An alternative interpretation would be that it has a more sinister motive, having been executed with malicious intent to bring about the destruction of the hunter. But against regarding it as a product of black magic is the fact that the death of the hunter is shown as having been avenged on his slayer by the rhinoceros. If, therefore, its original purpose and meaning remain obscure, there can be little doubt that the "problem picture" was delineated in this very difficult and dangerous "crypt" of the cave because for good or ill it was there that great potency could be put into operation in the control of the chase and the fortunes of the hunters.

More accessible on the left-hand side of the main hall is a mythical animal with a massive sagging body, oval rings on the flanks, and two long horns projecting from the forehead and terminating in a tuft. It is possible that it represents a masked sorcerer in a spotted skin of some *Bovidae* impersonating an ancestral spirit believed to be responsible for fertility and success in the chase. Since disguises and masks have been thought to confer supernatural power, Palaeolithic ritual experts appear to have clad themselves in the skins, horns and tails of animals to acquire the attributes and potency of the species they venerated and regarded as standing in a close relation with the food supply on which they depended for their subsistence. This strange figure, not very accurately described as of "unicorn" type, appears to be a mythical or sacred animal, resembling ancient Chinese paintings of horses with short legs and sagging barrel-like bodies, and does not correspond to any known species. Therefore, its reproduction, and possibly impersonation, was doubtless for the purpose either of veneration or

f destruction, if the large oval spots on the flank can be
nterpreted as wound marks. In another group at the end of
ne axial passage a horse is depicted falling over a precipice or
nto a pit, and the tectiform and other magical signs, which
equently appear on the paintings, may indicate traps, unless,
 Breuil suggests, they are local tribal marks.

Hunting Art and Ritual

n spite of the conjectural character of much of the symbolism,
nere can be little doubt that resort was made to these great
avern sanctuaries before setting out on hunting expeditions
nd for the performance of food-producing ceremonies analogous
 those known as Intichiuma among the Arunta tribe in
Central Australia. There at such sacred spots as Emily Gap
ear Alice Springs some of the rocks are believed to be full of
ne spirit-parts of animals awaiting reincarnation, and adorned
ith drawings of the totems.[11] Each local group has its own
totemic signs and paintings preserved in places which are taboo
 women, children and uninitiated men. Some are still painted
nd re-painted as part of the fertility ritual, and, as at Gargas,
astillo, Pech-Merle, Trois Frères and Altamira, in the
ranco-Cantabrian Palaeolithic caves, include designs of
encilled human hands, the meaning of which remains
oscure, though at Gargas mutilation suggests that the sacrifice
 fingers was practised as a propitiatory life-giving rite.
Many of the Australian zoomorphic and phytomorphic
aintings are merely outlines of animals and plants in charcoal
 red ochre, or conventionalized drawings, often very difficult
 decipher, and geometrical figures without apparently any
finite meaning, though probably they are derived from
omorphs of totemic origin.[12] Among the native tribes of
e north-west, realistic drawings of animals occur in the
ck-shelters in white pipe-clay, charcoal and red or yellow
hre, together with representations of mythical heroes con-
cted with rain and fertility; as, for example, Katuru or
ghtning man" at Kalurungari on the Calder river, and
ond'ina at the Kobudda shelter, Walcott Inlet—the ancestor

responsible for rain, the increase in nature and of spirit-children
Some are also mischievous spirits who are on the warpath a
night to lure away the souls of the unwary.[13] But, as in th
Palaeolithic cave ritual, the main purpose of the art is t
promote plenty by contributing towards the fertility of th
species on which the people depend for their food supply.

Among the Australian aborigines the performance of Int
chiuma is a collective responsibility and co-operative effor
Each totemic clan exercises its functions for the benefit of th
rest of the community since the sacred species is either taboo c
may be eaten only very sparingly by those who are responsibl
for its increase. The representation of so many different varieti
of animals in the same cave is not indicative of a totemi
organization of Palaeolithic society, as each totem presumabl
would have had its own sanctuary; even though, as Breuil ha
pointed out, the bones of the animals depicted in the caves ar
absent from the midden-heaps.[14] But whether or not anythin
that fairly can be described as totemism was practised i
connexion with the Palaeolithic designs,[15] it seems to hav
been the duty of ritual experts to carry out food-producing rit
in the seclusion of the remote sanctuaries on behalf of the grou
probably at set seasons and on specific occasions.

The figures of the masked dancers in animal disguises sugge
the existence of a cult in which the hunter would appear
have impersonated the "spirit" of the animals he embodied, an
to have dramatically represented in a series of ritual actions
rehearsal of that which it was earnestly desired should b
accomplished in the chase. The will to live as a prima
emotion was discharged by anticipatory rites as a pre-present
tion of a successful hunt. To these actions a magical effica
was given not because "like produces like" but because a ritu
that involved a more or less realistic reproduction of son
practical activity established the *ex post facto* idea of "symp
thetic" causation. Thus, the original re-enactment was giv
a secondary interpretation in magical terms. The prima
function, however, was to give expression to a vital impuls
the desire to act discharging itself on the symbol, the ritu

being the vent of pent-up emotions and activity.[16] The purpose of the actions performed and of their representation in visual form was to secure the prey, to gain control over the food supply, or to establish a "mystical union" with the source of bounty through ritual efficacy, and to relieve the tension in a precarious situation amid all the hazards of the chase and the vagaries of unpredictable events.

In a great sanctuary like Lascaux, Niaux or Les Trois Frères, the ceremonies must have involved an organized effort on the part of the community in a collective attempt to control natural forces and processes by supernatural means directed to the common good. The sacred tradition arose and functioned, it would appear, largely as an economic ritual to maintain the food supply. This became an integrating dynamic which afforded strength and power to the members of the group to enable them to cope with the perplexities and hazards of everyday life, and established a bond between man and his bewildering environment. Moreover, the community was thereby resolved into a co-operative fellowship in which each individual directly or indirectly played his part for the benefit of the whole under the leadership and direction of ritual experts who were responsible for the actual performance of the prescribed ceremonial at the appointed times and places in a representative capacity.

THE VEGETATION CULTUS IN THE ANCIENT NEAR EAST

With the transition from hunting and food-collecting to the cultivation of edible plants and/or the breeding of flocks and herds, the ritual control of fertility and food-production was concentrated on the crops, the sequence of the seasons and the breeding and rearing of cattle, sheep and goats rather than on the precarious conditions of the chase, even though hunting often lingered on side by side with husbandry and domestication. Nevertheless, under the influence of these new ceremonies, social structures and religious organizations began to emerge adapted to the requirements of an agricultural or pastoral mode of life, and those of "mixed farming" when cultivation was combined with stock-rearing and hunting.

In the Fertile Crescent this became apparent in the fifth millennium B.C. when food-production began to supplement and supplant food-gathering in Tells like Sialk on the western edge of the arid Iranian plateau, Qalat Jarmo on the Kurdish foothills to the east of the Tigris, Hassuna in Assyria, Merimde north of Cairo to the west of the Nile Delta, and at Badari and Deir Tasa in Middle Egypt, and in other similar favourable localities in the Ancient Near East. At first in the oases hunting and fishing usually were combined with tilling the land, growing grain and keeping a few sheep or cattle. But as the chase dropped more and more into the background, until finally it was abandoned as a means of subsistence in the agricultural or pastoral communities, the fertility of the soil and the succession of summer and winter, spring-time and harvest, together with the associated pursuits, became the centre of interest and of the ritual organization. Under these conditions the regular growth of the crops was a matter of no less vital concern than had been the hazards of the chase. Consequently, at the critical seasons an emotional reaction called forth a ritual response to ensure success in the food-producing activities at their several stages by overcoming the unpredictable elements in the situation which lay outside human control. Thus, when the ground was prepared and the crops were sown, and later when the harvest was gathered, a ritual technique was devised for the twofold purpose of overcoming sterility and promoting fertility in man, beast and the crops, around which a mythology developed in terms of a death and resurrection drama.

In prehistoric times the Nile valley was divided into a number of small city-states which before the beginning of the Dynastic period consisted of administrative nomes, each deriving its name from its ensign or standard. As these clan symbols often took the form of animals, such as the falcon or the ibis, and other sacred objects which were regarded as divine, sometimes they have been interpreted as totems. But in the Egyptian sources there are no indications that they stood actually in a totemic relationship to the clans or nomes, or were associated with such characteristic features as exogamy or rites of increase and tribal unity. They were essentially local gods who ruled the nomes and who gave to the nomarchs as the chief of the clans their authority, until at length when the nome became a kingdom and the nomarch a king, he was then regarded as the son of the god who exercised his rule and functions by virtue of his divine status.

The Divine Kingship in Egypt

The last of these primordial god-kings was "the Horus", a sky deity of the falcon clan in predynastic times who was alleged to have conquered the Delta and set up a single line of kings with a centralized administration. From the earliest times he was depicted as a bird, and Hierakonpolis in the third nome of Upper Egypt became the predynastic centre of his worship and clan. Other Falcon-gods, however, were identified with him, and when the Lower Kingdom conquered Upper Egypt his cult was established at Behdet (Edfu). Henceforth Horus often was called Behdety, "He of Behdet", and with the union of the country as a single nation the Behdetite was the predominant figure in the kingship accomplished by a ruler; this ruler may have been Narmer identified with the traditional Menes,[17] whose Falcon-god Horus was a sky-god who became incarnate in the person of the Upper Egyptian king and bestowed upon him his Horus-name.[18]

The Cult of Osiris

In the Eastern Delta at Busiris (Per-Usire or Djedu), the capital of the ninth nome, the cult of Osiris was established at an early date. It is possible that originally it was associated with a deified civilizing king who became the centre of a death and resurrection cultus before Osiris developed into a composite figure as the Lord of the dead, the God of vegetation and the personification of the fructifying waters of the Nile, and his sister-wife, Isis, personified his royal throne. Exactly how and under what circumstances Horus became identified with the son of Osiris is still a matter of debate, but however this is to be explained, very early in the Dynastic period the pharaohs reigned as the Osirian Horus conceived by Isis when she hovered over the mummy of her murdered husband. According to one interpretation, the struggle between Horus and his Uncle Seth, the perpetrator of the crime against his father (Osiris), was a re-enactment in myth and ritual of the conflicts of the pre-dynastic Horus kings before the nation was unified in a single ruler with divine prerogatives. Thus, Osiris, on this hypothesis, may have been a prehistoric nomadic chief or leader who introduced agriculture among the indigenous people in the Eastern Delta, and eventually came to blows with their ruler Seth when the intruders penetrated up the Nile as far south as Abydos. If Osiris was killed in this campaign, his son Horus may have rectified the position, and the episode eventually was immortalized in tradition in terms of a death and resurrection myth and ritual in which the culture hero, Osiris, played the leading role as the dead king, and his son Horus as the living king.[19] Alternatively, Osiris may have been the personification of the life-giving waters of the Nile and of the renewal of vegetation through the annual inundation rather than an historical character.

The Solar Theology

Both of these suggestions can claim support from the Pyramid Texts, which constitute the chief original sources of information on this complex problem, dating from the Fifth Dynasty (c. 2580 B.C.) when the solar theology had become predominant at Heliopolis. It was under the influence of the Heliopolitan priesthood that the solar line of kings was equated with Re, the Sun-god, and then associated with Osiris. Thus, in their Ennead, Osiris was represented as the son of Nut the Sky-goddess and Geb the Earth-god, and given a place in the sun by descent from Atum-Re, the head of the pantheon as the dead king, while the living pharaoh was Horus "the seed of Geb".[20] From prehistoric times Heliopolis had been a solar

ntre, and in the Fifth Dynasty it became the recognized home
the Re-cult with its temple, the "House of the Obelisk",
ected on the primordial hill—the "sandhill"—which was
pposed to have emerged out of the waters of Nun at the
eation, on the top of which Atum first appeared in the form
a phoenix.[21]

Under the influence of this Heliopolitan solar cult the
ctorious kings of Upper Egypt identified the Falcon-god
orus with Re in the composite deity Herakhite, "Horus of
e Horizon". This opened the way for them to be declared
e sons of Re. In the Second Dynasty the second king, Re-neb,
d been given a Horus-name, though it was not until the
ourth Dynasty that the Heliopolitan kings Khafre and
enkaure (the builders of the second and third pyramids)
tually assumed the title "son of Re". In the middle of the
xt century each king built a temple for the worship of the
n-god in conjunction with the royal residence on the margin
the desert. By the Sixth Dynasty (*c.* 2440–2250) the title
d become universally adopted, and with the Osirianization
the solar cult at Heliopolis the living king was equated with
orus, the posthumous son of Osiris. As a result of this
nthesis, as at death every pharaoh was Osiris, so he reigned
the guise of Horus who had been established in the throne
the decree of the gods when his father Osiris was vindicated
the Ennead.

By virtue of all these converging traditions and mythologies
nded down from remote prehistoric times, the pharaoh
came the epitome of all that was divine in the Nile valley,
d exercised his functions in relation to all the gods he
bodied. Foremost among these being Re, the personification
the all-enveloping glory and power of the Egyptian sun, and
siris, that of the life-giving waters of the inundation. As
easted has pointed out, these two great phenomena of nature,
e Sun and the Nile, made the most profound impression
on the ancient Egyptians, and the gods discerned in these
o insistent features of the country dominated religious and
ellectual development from the earliest times.[22] Upon both

of them, taken together, the remarkable fertility of the oa
depended.

It is hardly surprising, therefore, that the solar and Osiri
cults acquired a vegetation significance even though neith
Atum-Re nor Osiris was actually a vegetation god. Thus, t
Sun-god standing at the head of the Ennead, in his vario
aspects, manifestations and capacities was the creator an
begetter of life. Osiris, though not the personification of t
earth, was immanent in the annual sprouting of vegetation an
the growing grain and in the rising waters of the Nile, as w
as the bestower of life beyond the grave. In the Mystery pl
performed at the accession of Senusert I to the throne in t
Twelfth Dynasty about 1900 B.C. but containing much earl
material,[23] he is identified with the barley and the emmer th
nourishes the gods in heaven and man on earth, having ma
the corn from "the liquid that is in him".[24] This belief, like
many other prehistoric religious ideas and practices, lingered
until the Ptolemaic period and found expression in the wateri
of figures of Osiris made of earth and corn in order that t
grain might appear as sprouting from his body. These "Osi
gardens" were symbolical of his resurrection in the la
Mysteries, but, nevertheless, they suggest his association wi
the germination of the grain in a vegetation capacity whi
occupied such a prominent place in popular practice from ve
early times in the Nile valley.

In the official calendar, however, the Harvest Festival w
dedicated to Min, who as a sky- and fertility-god was esta
lished at the dawn of Egyptian civilization about 3500 B.C.,
and was regarded as the power immanent in the grain whi
was cut at this season. In the New Kingdom the ceremon
that culminated in the reaping of a sheaf of emmer by t
pharaoh were performed with all the signs of rejoicing rath
than of lamentation, such as would have been appropriate
the killing of the corn-spirit had been involved. The ithyphal
statue of Min was carried in procession on poles by prie
beneath a canopy preceded by a white bull, the sacred anim
of Min, and followed by bundles of lettuce, his plant. The ki

walked immediately behind the bull in front of the image, and on arriving at the temple of Min in the presence of the god and of his bull he reaped the sheaf of spelt "for his father".[26] Since in the Middle Kingdom Min was regarded as a form of Horus, the son of Osiris,[27] Gardiner is probably correct in assuming that the pharaoh in this ritual act impersonated Horus and in his capacity reaped the emmer for Osiris.[28] Therefore, as Min (whose generative powers were embodied in his sacred bull) personified the fertility of the fields, the beasts and vegetation, and was brought into relation with the reigning sovereign as the living Horus, the king exercised his functions at the Harvest Festival to secure a plentiful supply of crops in the ensuing year.

The Annual Festival

In the Spring Festival, celebrated during the latter part of the month of Khoiakh in honour of the death and resurrection of Osiris, an effigy of the dead god (Osiris) cast in a mould of gold in the form of a mummy was filled with a mixture of barley and sand, wrapped in rushes and laid in a shallow basin. For the next ten days (12th–21st) it was watered daily and then, on the 21st of Khoiakh, it was exposed to the sun just before sunset and sent on a voyage until on the 25th of the month it was buried in a coffin and laid in a grave.[29] On the last day of the festival (30th) the interment of Osiris was enacted, coinciding with the cessation of the inundation and the sprouting of the newly sown grain, symbolized later in the Ptolemaic temple of Isis at Philae by the representation of the stalks of wheat growing from the mummy of the dead god watered by a priest from a pitcher. Before the bier the *crux ansata* figured as the symbol of life, and the inscription records that "this is the form of him who may not be named, Osiris of the mysteries, who springs from the returning waters".[30] Moreover, it was on this last day of the rites that the *Djed*-column was raised by the king and the priests as a symbol of the god's resurrection,[31] thereby showing how very intimately the annual renewal in nature was related to the resuscitation of Osiris and the kingship, fertility and the food supply, both

of which were so dependent upon the rise and fall of th
Nile.

The Sacred Marriage of the King and the Goddess in Mesopotamia
In Mesopotamia, on the other hand, the unpredictable b
haviour of the Tigris and Euphrates in contrast to the uniformi
of the inundation in Egypt, and the variability of the climati
conditions, created a very different religious and social structu
and ritual order. The country was divided into a series of cit
states, as in Greece, loosely bound together to meet the needs
recurrent emergencies and governed by either a secular ruler
by the high priest of the city-god. Instead of being the co
solidating centre of the entire nation like the Egyptian thron
in Mesopotamia the royal office was confined to the local se
of administration and subordinate to that of the hierarch
Even after Hammurabi had unified the state in the empire
the second millennium B.C. and made Babylon the capit
with its chief god Marduk the head of the pantheon, the kin
had to deliver up the symbols of his office to the high prie
every year at the Annual Festival and be reinstated by hin
acting on behalf of Marduk.

Such an act of royal humiliation would have been unthink
able in Egypt, where the pharaohs reigned as gods incarnat
firmly established as the dynamic centre of the whole structu
of society and the bestowers of the vital forces of the earth
the annual flood of the Nile. In Mesopotamia kings we
human beings who had been chosen by the gods to act as the
servants on earth, and to be the instruments of the Mothe
goddess (Inanna or Ishtar), who chose the ruler to be h
bridegroom in a sacred marriage. In Egypt the queen w
visited by her royal husband in all his divine majesty and glo
to beget an heir to the throne. In Mesopotamia at the Annu
Festival the king in the guise of Tammuz, the generative for
in nature and the husband-son of Ishtar, engaged in a sacre
marriage with a priestess, personifying the Mother-goddess,
renew vegetation and fecundity in the spring. In this union sl
rather than the king was the active partner.

The Dying and Reviving Year-god in Western Asia

While Osiris was at once a dead king, the lord of the nether-world and the author and giver of the life of the grain personi-fied in the fructifying waters of the Nile, Tammuz, "the faithful son of the waters that came forth from the earth" (*Dumu-zi*), was a suffering god dependent upon the Goddess, Ishtar, his mother-consort. This youthful Dumu-zi, or "true son", died annually in the course of the normal rotation of the seasons, and passed into the land of darkness and death from which for ordinary mortals there was no return. From the Tammuz ritual texts it would seem that Ishtar descended into the under-world to seek her husband where he was held captive,[32] like Marduk in the "mountain",[33] invoking him by all his titles, and declaring that she had decked herself like a cedar to make glad the heart of him, her child, her beloved, who had passed over the river, so that "the noble cedar-tree was delivered from prison". It is possible, as Professor Hooke has suggested, that since the cedar-tree does not belong to the Mesopotamian plain, this is an ancient myth and ritual which the Sumerians brought with them when they migrated from the highlands lying to the north-west of Mesopotamia, before the theme was elaborated in the Babylonian New Year Festival.[34]

Be this as it may, throughout the ancient world, in Mesopo-tamia, Anatolia, Syria and Greece, the seasonal decline of nature was interpreted in terms of the vegetation year-god dying and reviving in the cycle of the crops as the child of the Mother-goddess who was the source of all life. The suffering and resurrected god in Mesopotamia though youthful was a mature figure, restored to fulfil his nuptial relations with the goddess in order that nature's prolific fertility might be insured. Adonis, the Syrian "Lord" (*Adon*), died at midsummer, and, unlike the vigorous youthful Tammuz, he personified the all too brief spring vegetation that passed away like a shadow 'dead ere his prime", when his virility was poured out under the pine-tree. Similarly, Kore, the daughter of the Earth-Mother Demeter, the maiden of the meadows whose abduction by Pluto caused the flowers in the fields to wilt, and man and beast to become sterile, symbolized the sudden end of the fleeting loveliness of a Levantine or Hellenic spring.

The Mesopotamian suffering and resurrected god, on the other hand, was the archetype of the recuperative powers of the Euphrates valley when it was flooded by the revitalizing waters of the two rivers in the later winter transforming the parched desert into a fertile oasis. But this inundation never inspired the dwellers in Mesopotamia with the same confidence in the cyclic sequence of the seasons that prevailed in Egypt, where the never-failing waters of the Nile gave a sense of assurance in a static cosmic order. The Babylonians were too much at the mercy of the vagaries of an uncertain rainfall and of the incalculable floods of the two great rivers.[35] Therefore, in this region it was not easy to harmonize in a stable ritual order the life of the community with that of the natural environment. Consequently, the suffering god who reflected these conditions was a complex figure with peculiarities of his own which differentiated him from the other comparable deities in the Fertile Crescent, Western Asia and the Aegean.

Thus, this figure did not fulfil Frazer's conception of the "dying god" as a generalized spirit of fertility dying to rise again. His relation to Inanna, or Ishtar, was quite different from that of Osiris to Isis. He was never a dead god who lived and reigned in a posthumous son like Horus and his earthly manifestation, the reigning pharaoh. Having been restored from the land of the dead in the fullness of his virile manhood, he was responsible for the revival of the new life springing forth from the parched ground in the spring and autumn. Therefore, his restoration as the "resurrected child" of the Goddess was celebrated annually with appropriate rejoicing, just as his descent was greeted with bitter lamentation and wailing.[36] The triumph, however precarious, was more enduring than in the Aegean, but it was never extended to man beyond the grave as in Egypt, where Osiris bestowed immortal life on those who were found to be "true of heart and voice" at the judgment. In Babylonia the renewal of life in nature did not carry any such implications in respect of the hereafter which remained a semi-conscious existence in a "land of no-return".

Therefore, whereas in Egypt the Osirian Festival was held in honour of the death and resurrection of the god personifying the emergence of life from death in all its ramifications, the Annual Festival, or *Akitu*, in Babylon in the month of Nisan centred in the liberation of the captive god, Marduk, the re-enactment of the creation Epic (the *Enuma elish*), the humiliation and reinstatement of the king, and his ritual marriage with the Goddess in his Tammuz capacity to renew the processes of vegetation, to secure the fertility of the land and to determine the destinies at the beginning of the New Year.[37] Although many of the details of this complex ritual are obscure, the central position of the king as the chief actor in the role of Marduk is clear. It might, therefore, seem paradoxical that at a crucial point on the fifth day of the Festival he was conducted to the shrine of the god and there before the statue of Marduk he was stripped of his royal insignia, struck on the cheek by the high priest, forced to his knees and made to declare that he had not been negligent regarding the divinity of the "Lord of the lands", or of having destroyed Babylon. He was then reinstated on the throne, the regalia were restored to him, and his face was again struck in the hope of drawing tears as a propitious omen, indicating that he was regarded with favour by Marduk, whose goodwill he enjoyed.

Precisely what happened after this humiliation of the king can only be conjectured, as the texts fail at this point. From a commentary, however, it appears that the suffering god (Marduk) having been confined in the mountain—that is to say, held captive by the forces of death—was liberated and resuscitated, apparently by the New Year rites then in progress of which the rehabilitation of the king was the crux. Thus, on the eighth day the restored sovereign, holding his sceptre in his hand, conducted the statue of Marduk in a triumphal procession to the *Bitakitu*, or Festival House, outside the city, to "fix the destinies" in a chapel dedicated to Nabu, the son of Marduk, who had rescued his father from the mountain.

There the victory of Marduk over Tiamat, the leader of the forces of Chaos in the creation story, was celebrated at a great banquet before a return was made to the city for the consummation of the sacred marriage in the *Esagila*, enacted by the king and the priestess in a chamber (*gigunu*) on one of the stages of the ziggurat—which may have been decorated with greenery[38] —in order to restore the fertility of the fields, the flocks and men after the blight of winter or summer.

Thus, the New Year Festival in Babylon was a ritual enactment of the death and resurrection of the god who was the embodiment of the conditions of fertility, even though Marduk was never conceived as a single cosmic power like Re in Egypt, any more than the monarch was the dynamic centre of the social structure in Mesopotamia. Neither the king, the government nor the gods had an assured and completely secure position in an immutable order with the same deity as the unchanging transcendental unifying principle, as in the Egyptian solar theology or in the Osirian Horus relationship of the pharaohs. Nevertheless, in the background of the New Year rites, long before the creation story had taken its later shape around the very ancient seasonal ritual going back to Neolithic times, *rites de passage* were held to effect the transition at the critical stages of each new season.[39]

That the sacral kingship played a significant part in these rites is beyond doubt, though exactly how it functioned and exercised supernatural control over the processes of fertility is by no means easily determined. We know that in the Ancient Near East the institution was regarded as the very basis of civilization, so that, for example, an ancient Sumerian epic affirmed that "kingship descended from heaven" as a gift of the gods, both before and after the Flood in the third millennium B.C.[40] Therefore, it was of divine origin just as in the Nile valley with the unification of Egypt under one pharaoh the throne acquired a sacred status as the dynamic centre of the nation by appointment of the gods who became incarnate in the reigning sovereign. Moreover, because he personified the fructifying waters of the inundation containing all the potentialities of life, the king was the god who brought fertility to Egypt. In this capacity he was the "herdsman of every one, without evil in his heart", whom the Sun-god "appointed to be shepherd of the land, to keep alive the people and the folk".[41] And the first responsibility of the herdsman was to maintain the food supply. Therefore, he produced the life-giving waters and at the Harvest Festival presented to the gods the sheaf of grain which symbolized the fruits of the earth and the fertility of the land.

In Mesopotamia, "mother earth" rather than the sun and the rivers was the inexhaustible source of new life. Consequently, the power manifest in fertility in all its forms was personified in the Goddess who was the incarnation of the reproductive forces in nature and the mother of the gods and of mankind. It was she who renewed vegetation, promoted the growth of the crops and the propagation of man and beast. In her Inanna-Ishtar guise her marriage with the shepherd-god Dumu-zi or Tammuz, who incarnated the creative powers of spring, was held to symbolize and effect the renewal of life at the turn of the year, delivering the earth from the blight of sterility.

In the prehistoric background of this death and resurrection drama the struggle between the two opposed forces in nature, those of fecundity and barrenness, was enacted by human beings with whom the conflicting powers were identified. From time immemorial the king or chieftain was believed to exercise supernatural control over the processes of fertility by virtue of his identification with the creative forces in nature. Thus, in Sumer the king was *Dumu-zi*, and his marriage with the priestess of Inanna was an act of renewal recreating "the life of all lands".[42] This beneficent gift, however, was only bestowed after the perennial struggle with the malevolent hosts of primeval chaos had been successfully accomplished, which involved the imprisonment of Marduk in the role of Dumu-zi-Tammuz in the mountain of death, the humiliation of his earthly counterpart, the king, and the descent of Inanna-Ishtar into the underworld, in which the populace joined at the New Year Festival in Babylon when the annual rescue and re-marriage were re-enacted in the *Akitu* drama. Thus, the suffering and reviving god theme was developed from a prehistoric *rite de passage* centred in and around the emotional situation arising out of the sequence of the seasons and the renewal of the life of nature in the spring.

Whether or not this involved the killing of the king to revivify the natural processes and promote the welfare of the community, as has been conjectured, the mysterious powers of fecundity were related to the virility of the occupant of the throne, which in ancient agricultural society often required the ritual renewal of the king, either annually or at stated periods.[43] In Egypt, for example, the very ancient *Sed*-festival was held periodically on the first day of spring (i.e. the season of "the Coming Forth"), either thirty years after the accession of the pharaoh, or at shorter intervals, to confirm the reigning sovereign in his kingdom by a ritual rejuvenescence.[44] This included his sitting alternately on each of two thrones to symbolize his rule over Upper and Lower Egypt, crossing the temple court ceremonially to assert his power over the entire land, and the reception of the sceptre, flail and crook of his office in the chapel of Horus of Libya. These insignia eventually he offered to the jackal-god Upuaut of Situ. While the symbolism is obscure, and it is by no means clear whether it was the death and resurrection of Osiris that was impersonated, as Gardiner maintains,[45] and Griffiths and Frankfort deny,[46] the festival in any case was closely associated with the periodic resuscitation of the king in his divine capacity.[47]

Similarly, from the Ras Shamra texts, it would seem that in Syria in the middle of the second millennium B.C. a fertility cult of the dying and rising vegetation-god was established in which a ritual renewal was held perhaps every seven years. Here, again, however, the evidence is very uncertain, the texts being fragmentary and their decipherment incomplete. Nevertheless, the central theme appears to have been the struggle between life and death in nature in which a number of gods and goddesses, such as Aleyan-Baal and his enemy Mot, lord of the underworld, play their familiar roles in a vegetation drama,[48] though it may not have been an annual death and revival of the god of fertility that was celebrated in the liturgical rituals.[49] In these texts drought and famine seem to have been represented as seven-year scourges rather than seasonal phenomena. It was, however, the death of the god that caused the languishing of the earth which lasted for seven years.[50] Therefore, apparently the Ugaritic Baal was a fertility but not a seasonal god who seems to have undergone considerable modification if the Ras Shamra ritual was a Canaanite version of the Tammuz-Adonis cult, having perhaps affinities with the Egyptian *Sed*-festival. That the theme was very deeply rooted and firmly established in Syria is shown by the persistence of the cult of Adonis with its germinating seeds sown in "gardens", coupled with wailings for the young god and the wilted plants, and all that these observances involved.

THE CULTUS IN THE AEGEAN

The Minoan-Mycenaean Goddess of Vegetation and the Young Male God

In the Eastern Mediterranean, as we have seen, the Mother-goddess became the principal object of worship, especially in Cyprus and Crete, where her emblems and adjuncts abounded —the snake, dove, double axe, horns of consecration, obese figurines, mountain, tree or pillar. While she was primarily concerned with birth and maternal functions, as the Earth-mother she was also the Goddess of vegetation, with or without a male partner. Thus, in a group of Minoan-Mycenaean signet rings the vegetation cycle is represented in a series of cult scenes portraying the Mother-goddess in a variety of settings. A Late Minoan ring now in the Ashmolean Museum at Oxford, which may have come from the Vapheio Tomb at Mycenae, shows a kneeling woman bending over a large jar with her left arm, bent at the elbow, resting on the rim. Her head is inclined forward supported by her left hand in an attitude of mourning. Above her are the eye and ear symbols, and a little to the left in the air is a small rigid male figure holding an oval object that looks like a bow. Below is a richly dressed female figure with wavy hair, thought by Evans to be the Mother-goddess, while the male figure he took to be the "boy-god" as a youthful archer (Fig. 14).[51] Professor Persson thinks the scene has a funerary significance, the vessel being of the type used in pithos burial, and the theme that of sorrow over death. The object next to the jar he interprets as an elliptically rounded stone with the leafless branches of a tree or bush behind it, symbolizing, as he suggests, the dying vegetation in winter and man's sorrow and lamentation "associated with the bleak world of nature gone dry and desiccate".[52]

On the Vapheio signet a mourning scene is represented in which the Goddess in a flounced skirt assumed apparently the role of the *Mater dolorosa* bowed in grief in the attitude of lamentation over a kind of miniature temenos. Within the sacred enclosure stands a narrow baetyl with a small Minoan shield hanging beside it; above, the Goddess is represented as a branch in leaf. To the right of her is a similar female figure, presumably the Goddess again in an upright position about to receive the fruit of a tree from a sanctuary containing a sacred pillar, and extended to her by a young male attendant whom Evans equates with the Cretan Zeus in a Tammuz role.[53] If the enclosure is a tomb containing a phallic stone, as is probable, the scene is brought into line with the grave of Attis in Phrygia and of Zeus at Knossos.[54] The mourning, therefore, may refer to a Minoan version of the suffering goddess theme in Western Asia and the vegetation cycle, the coming of spring being expressed in the budding leaves and ripening fruits. This is confirmed by the scene on a gold ring in the Museum of Candia, showing the sacred tree in an enclosure with scanty foliage. The stem is grasped by a woman with both hands, and on the left is an almost identical female figure in a flounced skirt with naked upper body and prominent breasts with her back to the tree and her arms extended to a third identical woman. In the fields are chevrons.[55]

Here the barrenness of winter gives place to the epiphany of the Goddess in its spring setting like that reproduced on a ring

Fig. 14. Minoan Goddess scene on a signet ring, Ashmolean Museum, Oxford

from a cist in a small tomb where an orgiastic dance in a field of lilies by four female votaries in typical Minoan garments is portrayed. Above the chief worshipper in the centre is a small female figure apparently rapidly descending, and to the left a human eye, which may symbolize the Goddess regarding the ecstatic dance being performed in her honour at the renewal of life in the spring, of which the snake by the side of the central figure below the eye is an emblem.[56] The bull which occupied such a conspicuous position in the Cretan "circus scenes"[57] may also have a fertility significance as a potent image of the reproductive force in nature in the spring festival[58] in which the king-god played the leading part, in conjunction with the Goddess as his consort, in the slaying of the Minotaur to overcome death and renew life.[59]

Zeus and Demeter

The function of the youthful male was to revive the life of vegetation in the annual cycle of the seasons, whereas that of the Goddess was to give birth to life of which she was the ultimate source and the generative force. Unlike her male partner she did not die to rise again, being the Earth-mother bringing forth vegetation as her offspring. With the development of agricultural society the "boy-god", however, became the Sky-father who fertilized the Earth-goddess by pouring upon her the fertilizing rain from heaven. Thus, in Greece, as will be considered in the next chapter,[60] the Indo-European sky-and-weather-god, Zeus, consorted with goddesses and mortal mistresses in his capacity as the head of the Olympian pantheon. Among these were the chthonian Demeter, the Earth-mother, whose daughter, Kore (Persephone) was the Corn-maiden embodying the ripe grain annually gathered at the time of harvest. That Demeter inherited the attributes of the Minoan Goddess can hardly be doubted. Whether or not it was her marriage with Zeus "to make the fields wave with yellow corn" that was celebrated in her mysteries at Eleusis, as Frazer maintains,[61] is less certain, though one of the purposes of the rites apparently was to secure the fertility of the crops and maintain the vegetation cycle, at any rate in the earlier developments of the cultus. Thus, it is not improbable that it arose from a very ancient agricultural festival which Nilsson suggests celebrated the bringing up of the threshold corn from the silos where after the harvest in June it had been stored to ripen until the seed-time in October. During the four months when it was below ground the fields were barren and desolate, withered by the scorching sun. Once the autumn rains began, ploughing started and the fields soon became green again in the mild winter with the crops ripening in early spring, about February or March. It was then that the annual commemoration of the dead, the Anthesteria, named after the flowers that appeared at that season, was held in Athens and the Lesser Mysteries of Demeter at Agrai, a suburb of the capital. Attendance at these rites was a preliminary to initiation at the Greater Mysteries at Eleusis in the autumn when the time of sowing was approaching and the seed corn was brought up from the silos, symbolizing the ascent of the Corn-maiden.[62]

This interpretation of the origin of the Mystery makes it essentially a corn festival and Demeter a corn-goddess. The precise meaning of *de* in her name is in dispute and could signify "corn" or "earth", but while at Eleusis she was primarily the giver of the grain, she was also the goddess of vegetation. As the personification of the fertile soil she was the Earth-mother whose daughter Kore later became confused with Persephone, queen of Hades and wife of Pluto, whose name connected her with Pluton, a god of the fruits of the fertile soil. Thus, Kore was transformed into Persephone and made responsible for sending up the new crops from below ground by her annual return from the nether regions. This gave the earlier agricultural rites a deeper meaning, associating them with the death and resurrection theme. But exactly how this was given ritual expression in the Mysteries can only be conjectured from the relatively late sources of information.

According to the post-Christian writer Hippolytus, the *mystae* in the Telesterion at Eleusis, at the supreme moment of initiation on the twenty-second day of Boedromion, sitting on stools covered with sheep-skins in darkness and complete silence, suddenly beheld the reaping of an ear of corn in a blaze of light, and heard the announcement of the birth of a divine child, Brimos.[63] Whether or not this had anything to do with a sacred marriage between Zeus and Demeter, symbolized by the union of the hierophant and the chief-priestess in their respective roles, is a matter of debate. While Hippolytus seems to have confused the Phrygian Attis rites with those of Demeter, if a corn-token was one of the sacred objects revealed it would be in accordance with the vegetation setting and circumstances of the Eleusinian Mysteries. The germinating ear was at once the symbol of the harvest of the grain and of the purpose of the Mysteries to secure a joyful resurrection of the initiates in the delectable meadows of Persephone, secured by means of a protracted series of purifications, processions, sacred utterances, the sacrifice of oxen and possibly a bull-fight.[64]

Furthermore, as the marriage of Zeus with goddesses in Greek tradition was an expression of the ancient belief in the union of heaven and earth whereby the earth was fertilized, a sacred alliance of this nature would be a normal and fitting conclusion of the Harvest Festival as in Mesopotamia and elsewhere in the Near East. This is confirmed by a passage in Proclus in the first century A.D., amended by Lobeck, in which the worshippers are said to have gazed up to the sky and cried aloud, "Rain (O Sky), Conceive (O Earth). Be fruitful."[65] This formula, as Farnell has pointed out, "savours of a very primitive liturgy that closely resembles the famous Dodonaean invocation to Zeus, the Sky-god, and Mother-earth; and it belongs to that part of the Eleusinian ritual *quod ad frumentum attinet*".[66]

Here, again, there are grounds for thinking that the same theme which prevails in the seasonal drama in the Ancient Near East recurred at Eleusis, and in combination with the more orgiastic Thraco-Phrygian Dionysiac,[67] the birth of a divine child (variously called Zagreus, Dionysos, Domophoon or Iacchos) appears to represent the fruit of a sacred marriage of the Sky-god (Zeus) and the Earth-goddess (Demeter), enacted by the hierophant in the capacity of the heavenly creator and the chief-priestess impersonating Demeter. The royal character of the ritual is suggested by the representation of the torch-bearers in the official robes of the high priests on a vase of the fifth century B.C. in the museum at Eleusis. The hair is wreathed with myrtle and tied at the forehead with a broad fillet, the *tout ensemble* giving the appearance of a king. The hierophant, the torch-bearer, the herald and the other principal officiants were members of the ancient Eleusinian families of the Eumolpidai and the Kerykes, to whom application had to be made for initiation. Therefore, while the Mysteries were open to all who could speak or understand Greek, and had not been polluted by blood-guilt or similar taboos, the rites were the hereditary possession of a priestly caste who may have been of royal descent.

Similarly, in the iconography on reliefs in the sacred precinct of Mycenaean origin, the mission of Triptolemus, the hero of agriculture and one of the princes of Eleusis, is depicted going about the earth in his chariot teaching men how to till the soil under instruction from the Goddess, reminiscent of the Osiris-Isis myth. In his raised left hand he is shown holding a sceptre and seated on a magnificently carved throne drawn by winged dragons. In his right hand he holds the ears of corn, and looks intently at Demeter in an attitude suggestive of listening to her instructions. On a later plaque, dedicated to the gods of Eleusis by the priest Lakrateides, he is represented seated on a throne transformed into a chariot and holding out his left hand to receive the corn from Demeter, who sits in front of him with Kore behind holding torches. Close to her is Pluto with the royal sceptre as king of the underworld, and to the right an unnamed god on a throne and a goddess with a sceptre. At the back is the upright figure of a young man carrying a torch, probably Eubouleus, one of the youthful Eleusinian king-gods to whom it is dedicated.[68]

On a red figured vase from Rhodes, now in the museum of Istanbul, the Earth-goddess is shown rising from the ground and lifting a cornucopia on the top of which sits a male child whom she presents to a goddess with a sceptre, standing to the right. To the left of Demeter is a figure, possibly that of Kore, and above her head is Triptolemus in his winged car.[69] Nilsson identifies the child with Ploutos,[70] the fruit of the fields and representative of vegetation, while Triptolemus was the revealer of the secrets of Demeter, the promoter of agriculture, and the bestower of beneficent bounty, who invariably stands by the side of the divine pair, the Corn-mother and Earth-goddess, and her daughter the Corn-maiden.

THE VEGETATION CULT IN NORTH-WEST EUROPE

As the Goddess cult was diffused from the Mediterranean through Spain and France to Brittany, Britain, the S.O.M. region and Scandinavia, to what extent the vegetation cycle was retained is progressively less apparent the farther it spread from its original cradleland in the Near East and the Aegean. Its chief emblems, as we have seen, unquestionably persisted throughout the megalithic region in such forms as the baetylic pillar, the sacred tree or pole, the snake, the dove, the bull, *Pectunculus* shells, female figurines sometimes in association with male statuettes, and representations and carvings on tombs of the tutelary divinity who presided over the occupants in the French graves. Professor Persson has compared with similar scenes on Minoan-Mycenaean gold rings two figures of a man and a woman beside a boat on a rock engraving in the province of Bohus in Sweden, and on another in the same area of a man and a woman embracing on a ship with a tree over them, possibly in process of marriage.[71] These, he maintains, are not isolated instances of such similarities in which can be detected the vegetation seasonal theme and its ritual expression. Thus, he equates with Aegean counterpart figures on Scandinavian rock engravings dressed in ancient skins with horns and, as he believes, with tails, and decapitated bodies, or bodies with amputated limbs.[72] Whether or not Nerthus, the Northern Goddess of vegetation, was associated with the seasonal ritual cycle, the magico-religious control of the processes of fertility in nature in its traditional Asiatic and Minoan-Mycenaean setting hardly can be excluded altogether in these more remote regions in North-west Europe. Thus, the procession of Nerthus in her wagon around the land, recorded by Tacitus,[73] is remarkably reminiscent of the progress of Cybele in her car drawn by oxen in the Roman ecstatic rites,[74] and of our own May Day revels.

Aegean Influences in Wessex

In the British Isles the vegetation cult of the Neolithic peasantry was overlaid by that of the sun and the heavens under Indo-European influence, introduced into the religion of the Beaker folk by their contact with the Battle-axe warriors in Central Europe. This becomes apparent in their great British sanctuaries at Avebury and Stonehenge in Wessex. As will be considered in the next chapter, both of these temples appear to have been dedicated to the worship of a sky-god. Nevertheless, the recent discovery at Stonehenge of engravings of a hilted dagger and a flanged axe with Mycenaean affinities on one of the horseshoe trilithons (No. 53), and similar axe-carvings on several of the sarsens of the outer circle, may indicate that the cult of the axe had penetrated to Britain from the Aegean not later than about 1470 B.C.[75] Indeed it is possible, as Mr Atkinson suggests, that between 1500 and 1400 B.C. the sarsens were erected and the blue stones rearranged by the Wessex chieftains under the inspiration of Mycenaean builders in a co-ordinate effort demanding great skill and ingenuity; of one of whom, he conjectures, Silbury Hill near Avebury may represent the cenotaph.[76] Whatever may be the precise significance of these latest discoveries at Stonehenge, they are another indication of a link between the Wessex culture and Mycenaean Greece from about 1500 to 1300 B.C.[77]

The source of the gold ornaments and the gold-mounted amber disks in Wessex graves would seem to have been the Aegean, just as the blue glazed beads worn by Wessex chieftains were of Eastern Mediterranean manufacture. That some of the British axes were inspired by metal Minoan *bipennes*, or their derivatives, is not improbable,[78] or that bronze axes with side-flanges were imported from the Eastern Mediterranean via Spain.[79] From about 1600 the amber route constituted another important highway between the Baltic, Central Europe and the Aegean, and along it, and the Atlantic maritime route, ideas and cult-practices as well as commodities passed to North-west Europe, which included the Goddess tradition. With it may have come the vegetation rites associated with the seasonal cycle. In Wessex, like cremation, they seem to have been an intrusive element in the Early Bronze Age, if the open sanctuaries were connected primarily with the worship of the Sky-god rather than with that of the Mother-goddess. Nevertheless, since the solar cult in its long and complex history was so intimately associated with fertility, it would not be difficult for rites of this character upon which the livelihood and prosperity of a pastoral community depended, to be resuscitated under Aegean influences at Stonehenge and elsewhere, in a seasonal ritual celebrated at the summer solstice to make its flocks and herds multiply and to renew the generative forces in nature.

The Sky-religion

If Early Man in his struggle for subsistence projected his religious consciousness primarily into the symbolic objects and emblems connected with the principle of fecundity, he also appears to have been aware of a transcendent power external to the world, directly or indirectly governing its processes, and having his abode in the sky.

THE IDEA OF GOD

Animism and Polytheism

Under the influence of the evolutionary thought that predominated at the end of the last century, a unilineal development of religion was postulated proceeding in an orderly sequence from animism through polytheism to monotheism. Thus, Tylor defined religion as "a belief in spiritual beings" arising, as he affirmed, from mistaken inferences from observation of such phenomena as dreams, trances, visions and death, transferred to the natural order. In this way, it was supposed, the sun, stars, trees, rivers, winds, clouds and mountains became animated by a soul or spirit and behaved like men or animals, the indwelling spiritual beings controlling the events of the material world and of man's life here and hereafter.[1] As human qualities were applied to them divine society and government were modelled on human society and its constitution with great gods and lesser spirits corresponding to chiefs and kings and their officers, and assigned their respective functions in a polytheistic pantheon of departmental deities.

The hierarchy of higher gods reigned in the sky in heavenly splendour and sent down rain to nourish the earth unless they were moved to wrath in which event they manifested their divine displeasure in the agonizing terror of the thunderstorm, the devastating hurricane, or the consuming fire. Rivalling in power and glory the all-encompassing Heavens was the Sun, rising anew every morning and passing into oblivion in the underworld in the evening, giving light and life to the living and the dead, and often becoming incarnate in the occupant of the throne on earth. Sometimes the Moon was his satellite, or the order might be reversed, the Moon taking precedence of the Sun. But whatever status was accorded to them, the various members of the polytheistic hierarchy were regarded as a development of animism, very much as in the world's assembly of great gods, chiefs, benefactors and other beneficent ancestors were among the deified heroes raised to divine rank and status after their death and duly venerated and propitiated as immortals.[2]

Therefore, from animism as "the minimum definition of religion" the development of the idea of deity proceeded in an orderly manner either, as Herbert Spencer stressed, from the deification and propitiation of the illustrious dead,[3] or, as Frazer maintained, by a supposed craving for simplification and unification reducing to a limited pantheon the gods believed to control the several departments, attributes and aspects of nature. "Instead of a separate spirit in every individual tree, they came to conceive of a god of the woods in general, a Silvanus or what not; instead of personifying all the winds as gods, each with his distinct character and features, they imagined a single god of the wind, an Aeolus, for example, who kept them shut up in a bag and could let them out at pleasure to lash the sea into fury." By a further generalization and abstraction "the instinctive craving of the mind after simplification and unification of its ideas" caused the many localized and departmentalized gods to be deposed in favour of one supreme creator and controller of all things. Thus, it was contended, as polytheism evolved out of animism, so monotheism emerged from polytheism when at length one solitary Deity was conceived as the sovereign lord and maker of heaven and earth.[4]

Supreme Beings

That such a neat and tidy theoretical interpretation of the development of theism was untenable became apparent when Andrew Lang called attention to the fact that so far from monotheism being the final product of an evolutionary process, among such very primitive people as the Australian aborigines tribal High Gods, or Supreme Beings, are neither spirits, ghosts of the dead nor departmental gods carried to the highest power.[5] While often they may stand aloof from everyday affairs, they are the personification and guardians of the tribal ethic. Having given the tribe its laws and instituted the initiation rites for the purpose of inculcating right conduct in society, the rules of which are handed on from generation to generation in these solemn assemblies over which they preside, they retired to dignified seclusion in the sky. So transcendent are these remote deities, in fact, representing the highest expression of supernatural power and will, primeval and beneficent, the guardians and givers of the social, ritual and moral orders, that Tylor and his followers dismissed them as importations by Christian missionaries. It has now been established, however, largely through the indefatigable researches of Pater Wilhelm Schmidt and his collaborators, that they constitute a genuine feature of uncontaminated primitive religion recurrent among such aboriginal people as the native tribes of Australia, the Fuegians in South America, the Californian tribes in North America, and certain negritos and other negroids in Africa and elsewhere.[6]

Whatever may have been their origin, these High Gods do in fact stand alone, head and shoulders above all secondary divinities, though certainly not to the exclusion of the lesser spiritual beings, totems, culture heroes and localized gods to whom popular worship is directed. Sometimes they have become so otiose that they are little more than a name, or, as in Central Australia, the personification of the bull-roarer, the thunderous booming of which is regarded as the voice of the god, at any rate by the women and uninitiated.[7] But although they are liable to become obscured in their lofty celestial seclusion, they stand on a plane by themselves, having greater and wider significance if a less clearly defined sphere of influence than that of the other divinities and spirits. Moreover, they seem to represent the ultimate moral value of the universe so far as the primitive mind conceives such a reality.

Thus, Professor Evans-Pritchard records that among the Nuer in Nilotic East Africa, God is *Kwoth*, a being of pure spirit, and because he is like wind or air "he is everywhere and being everywhere he is here now". He is far away in the sky yet present in the earth which he created and sustains. "Everything in nature, in culture, in society and in men is as it is because God made it so." Although he is ubiquitous and invisible he sees and hears all that happens, and being responsive to the supplications of those who call upon him, prayers are addressed to him and sacrifices offered to avoid misfortunes. Since God can be angry he can and does punish wrongdoing, and suffering is accepted with resignation because it is his will, and, therefore, beyond human control. But the consequences of wrongdoing can be stayed or mitigated by contrition and reparation, prayer and sacrifice.[8]

Such a conception of Deity, which is almost indistinguishable from that which obtains in the higher monotheisms like Christianity, Islam or Judaism,[9] is a religious response to the notion of divine Providence more fundamental than any gradual development from plurality to unity. It is a spontaneous, purposive functioning of an inherent type of thought and emotion; an evaluation of the *mysterium tremendum*, rather than speculation about souls or the universe. Indeed when the mind has reflected upon the animation of nature and arrived at conceptual ideas about spirits and organized pantheons the Supreme Being not infrequently has been left vaguely in the background. Therefore, so far from animism and polytheism passing into monotheism as a result of abstraction and generalization, simplification and unification, speculation about nature and its processes and man and his constitution appears to have led to the peopling of natural phenomena with a multiplicity of spirits, tutelary divinities, departmental gods and culture heroes in such profusion that the remote High God often has retired into the background.

The Universality and Antiquity of the Sky-god

This is not to suggest that a "primeval monotheism" once obtained, either as the result of a special divine revelation or of particular psychological processes and reactions which disappeared in the later stages of the development of any particular religion. The belief in High Gods among low races cannot be described as a true monotheism, since in addition to the transcendent Sky-god a number of particular lesser spirits of the air and of the earth, immanent in natural phenomena or growing out of the social, economic and cultural environment and the psychological concomitants of its organization, coexist with the Supreme Being and standardize behaviour by supernatural sanctions in which he is only remotely concerned. Pater Wilhelm Schmidt and his collaborators, it is true, have endeavoured to maintain that an exclusively monotheistic conception of Deity obtained in a hypothetical *Urkultur* at the threshold of human history, of which the Pygmy tribes, the Bushmen, the Ainus, the Tierra del Fuegians and the Kurnai, Kulin and Yin tribes of South-east Australia are modern representatives. But apart from the anthropological difficulties which the *Kulturkreise* method of ethnological analysis encounters in the determination of the origins and development of human institutions and beliefs, the available archaeological evidence affords little or no support for such a contention.

So far as the existence of Supreme Beings is concerned, the only possible indications of such a belief in Palaeolithic times are a few small oval pendants of bone and stone, perforated at one end, found at Laugerie-Basse and at Laugerie-Haute near Les Eyzies in the Dordogne,[10] identical in shape with the bull-roarer. Similar objects in bone have been discovered in a Magdalenian site at Saint Marcel, Indre, with markings not unlike those on Australian churinga,[11] and at Pin Hole cave at Cresswell Crags in Derbyshire in association with implements of a Mousterian type which apparently had survived in the

Gravettian phase at the beginning of the Upper Palaeolithic. Since the sacred bull-roarer and stone churinga figured prominently in the cult of the High God in Australia and elsewhere,[12] the occurrence of the mystic object in Upper Palaeolithic deposits could suggest that the belief in High Gods may have been a feature of the religion of the Gravettians and the Magdalenians in Western Europe. This is as far as the archaeological evidence takes us, and it must be recognized that a few very hypothetical pendants in a relatively late phase of the Palaeolithic is extremely insecure ground on which to build a far-reaching hypothesis concerning the beliefs that may have obtained at the emergence of the human race.

Nevertheless, the existence of a sky-god is so firmly established and deeply rooted in the history of religion from Neolithic times onwards, that this transcendental aspect of Deity may well go back to a very early period prior to the rise of the higher civilizations in the Near East. If in fact "bull-roarers" really were the outward and visible sign of the belief under Palaeolithic conditions, since they would have had to be made of wood to fulfil their functions in producing the weird thunderous noise which has been interpreted as the voice of the god, they could scarcely have survived the ravages of time any more than have other implements in wood. Thus, they cannot be expected to throw much light on the problem. The most that can be concluded from the pendants is that the sacred object may have existed and reproductions of it in more durable material were made and worn as amulets because of its sanctity, however and whenever the concept of Deity may have arisen in the religious consciousness of primeval man.

THE SKY-GOD IN THE NEAR EAST

The Sky-religion in Egypt

When the existence of an extra-mundane divine power was established and made the source of universal creative activity centred in the god of the sky, the various aspects and attributes of nature were related to him, directly or indirectly, as the head of the pantheon. Everywhere the same linguistic root connects the heavens, the clouds and the rain with their personifications in the Sky-god and his manifestations in the revivification of nature, the thunder and the storm. As Zeus, or Dyaus Pitar, among the Indo-Europeans was primarily the god of the sky and of the weather, known under a number of names, before he assumed the functions of the various gods whom he assimilated, so in Egypt the Falcon-god Horus is represented in the Pyramid Texts as the source of life and death, of rain and of celestial fire, thereby indirectly connecting the reigning pharaoh in his Horus capacity with an ancient predynastic Supreme Being[13] as well as with the son of Osiris, when the Sky-god had been replaced by the Sun-god as the Creator of the world.

The many forms in which the Sun-god was represented in the Egyptian texts are doubtless survivals of an earlier cult of the omnipresent Sky-god brought into conjunction with the all-prevailing solar worship in its many manifestations. As Breasted has pointed out, "the all-enveloping glory and power of the Egyptian sun is the most insistent fact in the Nile valley",[14] and it is hardly surprising that the ancient Egyptians saw the solar deity in different, doubtless originally local forms. Flying across the heavens like a falcon in his daily course, he was known as Harakhte, the "Horus of the Horizon", who with three other local Horuses constituted the Four Horuses of the eastern sky, represented as "four youths who sit on the east side of the sky, with curly hair".[15] In the morning he came forth as Khepera, a winged beetle rising in the east, and flying across the sky with outspread wings, the solar disk on his head, until he tottered down to the west as an aged man, Atum, as he appeared at Heliopolis, having run his daily course.

As head of the Egyptian pantheon, in his composite form Re combined all the forces of nature, and at Heliopolis before the First Dynasty he was conceived as the sun in the sky manifest in the solar disk. Horus became his son, and as the solar cult predominated after the unification of Egypt by the victorious Upper Egyptian kings (who personified the Sky-god Horus and came under Heliopolitan influence) Re became supreme among the gods, absolute in his control of the Nile valley, the ally and protector of the throne. Thus, in addition to his being the source of life and increase, he was a divine king, Re-Atum the self-created Creator, Re-Harakhte the youthful god on the eastern horizon, and eventually at Thebes, Amon-Re, the "king of the gods", worshipped in great magnificence at Karnak and Luxor. These aspects of deity, together with Ptah, the "Great One" of Memphis, in due course were blended not in a single monotheistic god but in three independent divinities with the same nature.

Thus, the Egyptians arrived at a conception of a universal God without abandoning their polytheistic tradition, except for the very short interlude in the Eighteenth Dynasty when Amenhotep IV (Ikhnaton) transferred his allegiance solely to Aton, an ancient god of the air and light, known also as Show, and set up a new hierarchy and temple organization. Karnak and the other temples of Amon-Re were closed, and the names of all the gods erased from the monuments. The capital having been removed from Thebes to Amarna in Middle Egypt and renamed Akhetaton, "the Horizon of Aton", the sole God of heaven and earth was there worshipped by his royal son and embodiment as the creator and sustainer of all things with altars in the open air. All anthropomorphic and theriomorphic images were rigidly excluded, the only symbol employed being that of the solar disk with emanating rays.[16] But although the monotheistic movement was in line with the new imperial power of the State, it made no permanent impression on the nation. Therefore, in the confusion that followed the death of Ikhnaton in 1350 B.C., the dispossessed Amonite priesthood regained its power, and the old régime was restored with a new line of kings.

In the ancient world the ephemeral Aton cult of Amenhotep IV was the only attempt to reduce a pantheon of polytheistic deities to a single all-embracing heavenly Creator. Thus, even Yahweh among the Hebrews, until the end of the Exile in the sixth century B.C. was primarily the God of Israel, an essentially exclusive God with a localized sovereignty in the land of his own choosing for the people with whom he stood in a covenant relationship. Indeed Ikhnaton, notwithstanding his fanatical zeal for the exclusiveness of Aton, apparently never tried to introduce the cult outside Egypt, except for erecting a temple in Nubia in a town he renamed Gematon. Where he differed from his immediate predecessors, who already had recognized the universality of Amon-Re, was in eliminating the syncretistic nature of Re as a blend of the deified sun, the horizon and the falcon, "Re-Harakhte of the two horizons rejoicing in his name of Show, who is the Aton". But, while the Aton was proclaimed to be the one and only God, for the Egyptians in general he was the actual heavenly orb as the ancient Sky-god was the falcon regarded as the manifestation of the power of the sun in the expanse of the sky.

Originally Horus was "the lofty one" (*Hrw*), and his association with the sun was subsidiary to his primary function in his Sky-god capacity.[17] Aton, on the other hand, was the material sun as it appears by day during its journey from the eastern to the western horizon, and his worship was so essentially centred in the solar disk that it was no more concerned with life on earth than with that in the hereafter.[18] Therefore, unlike that of Osiris, it made no popular appeal, having little or nothing to offer the toiling masses in this world or in the next life. It was confined to the pharaoh and his family, notwithstanding the universal supremacy of the Sun-god's dominion and his life-giving power emanating from his beneficent rays which shone upon the whole earth. For as Amenhotep IV declared, "there is no other that knoweth thee save thy son Ikhnaton". Thus, Atonism was destined to suffer the fate of the worship of all High Gods who became divorced from human affairs and the fundamental needs of mankind at large, expressed and made efficacious in an accessible cultus. To fulfil these requirements the Sky-gods and goddesses of the Egyptian solar cycle were brought into relation with the Earth-gods of the Osiris cycle and the cult of the dead so that the beneficence of the celestial realms through their agency might be bestowed on the earth in fruitful seasons with abundance of corn and wine, destroying the forces of evil and giving immortality and resurrection to the dead.

The Babylonian Triads

In Mesopotamia the assembly of gods in the sky was the highest authority in the universe determining the course of events on earth. Under the leadership of Anu, the god of heaven, the cosmic order as an organized whole was established out of chaos and anarchy. His name, in fact, in Sumerian was "the sky", and the high esteem in which he was held as the most potent force in the cosmos long after his cult had fallen into obscurity suggests his great antiquity going back to prehistoric times. He is not mentioned, however, in the Sumerian lists, and it is not until the time of Gudea, king of Lagash (c. 2060–2042 B.C.), that his supremacy is affirmed and maintained throughout the subsequent records of Babylonian religion. In the "An-Anum list" in which the Sumerian and Akkadian designations of the god of heaven are equated, his genealogy is given under a series of names, and "the twenty-one parents (i.e. ancestors) of Anu" accord with his descent from Apsu, the god of the subterranean ocean, and Tiamat, the primeval Chaos, in the Creation Epic.

Both he and the Storm-god, Enlil, the second member of the Great Triad of deities, were described as "king of the gods", and the kingship on earth was represented as a divine gift or invention with the royal insignia resting "before the throne of Anu".[19] But neither Anu nor Enlil nor the rulers (*lugal*) on earth, occupied the unique position of the Sun-god and the Pharaoh in Egypt. As in the heavenly pantheon the Triad were the leaders of the assembly, so in the Mesopotamian city-states the kings were their servants, rising and falling with the fortunes of the cities over which they ruled. Thus, although "kingship came down from heaven", it resided temporarily in five or six Sumerian centres with local dynasties subject to the vicissitudes of hegemonies established by conquest.[20] Even when Hammurabi unified the State into an Empire and made Babylon the capital with its chief god Marduk (who inherited the status and so many of the attributes and functions of Enlil) as the head of the pantheon, it was merely a temporary stability that was attained. The earlier Sumerian Triad (Anu, Enlil, and Ea, or Enki) with their respective priesthoods were only partially eclipsed, each continuing to rule over one of the three divisions of the universe, heaven, the air and the waters. Therefore, even Marduk was never regarded as the creator and source of all the other gods like Re or Ptah in Egypt.

Instead of the Creator emerging by a self-creative act from the primeval waters of Nun, in Mesopotamia, it was out of a state of chaos that the male and female progenitors, Apsu and Tiamat, brought forth their progeny, and, according to the original version, apparently the earth was created by Enlil before he was replaced by Marduk.[21] Eventually the kingship was established on the earth by the gods as an emergency measure before and after it had been destroyed by the Flood. The legendary "divine shepherd" *Dumu-zi* (Tammuz), under the designation of the "fisherman", alone continued the antediluvian régime in the Second Dynasty of Erech, between the god Lugal-banda and Gilgamesh in the traditional King-list. The Shepherd *par excellence* of Babylonia, however, was the historical Sumerian ruler Lugal-zaggesi, who claimed to exercise his sovereign rule over Mesopotamia under the sanction of Enlil, and when he was conquered by Sargon of Akkad the victor called himself "he who rules the Four Quarters". His son Naram-Sin assumed the title "king of the Four Quarters", which was also borne by the great gods, Anu, Enlil and Shamash (Uru), the Sun-god.[22] But it was not until Marduk was exalted over all the other gods by Anu and Enlil, and Babylon was declared to be the head of all the cities with Hammurabi as its ruler, that the kingship was brought into relation with a supreme deity at all comparable to Re and Osiris in Egypt. Even so, although Marduk was regarded as the Creator of mankind and king of the pantheon, it was only in a restricted sense that he had exercised his creative functions long after the universe had come into being when the gods were in conflict against Chaos.

Indeed in this pre-cosmic battle it was Ea, the god of water, originally Enki, the third of the Triad, who countered the threat to Tiamat and Apsu by casting a spell upon the waters and establishing a magical circle, before the gods conferred upon Marduk their collective power.[23] Moreover, he formed man from the blood of Kingu, the leader of the forces of Chaos,[24] and on the instructions of Ea Utnapishtim built his ship to save the human race from utter destruction during the Flood which Enlil had caused with that end in view.[25] Ea, in fact, was much more beneficent to mankind than either Anu or Enlil, and when Marduk attained supremacy he consulted his father (Ea) and sought his co-operation in the exercise of his office, as the source of wisdom and magical knowledge unrivalled among the gods. Upon his divinatory powers protection against the hostile supernatural forces depended, so that Ea became the patron of exorcists and was assigned his portion of the heavens whence he determined and controlled human destinies.

In a second Triad in the early god-lists Adad, or Hadad, the Storm-god of the air, is combined with Shamash, the Sun-god, and Sin, the Moon-god, also called Nannar in the Sumerian lists, the son of Enlil and the father of Shamash. It was Sin who both fixed the calendrical sequence of days, months and years and ordered the fertility of cattle. His son Shamash, the Utu or Babbar of the Sumerian lists, turned his "radiant face" upon kings and gave them the laws of good government. His special function being to uphold truth, order and justice, like that of Maat in Egypt, the daughter of Re, by whom the gods were said "to live", both he and Adad were concerned with oracular divination. They were, in fact, "lords of Oracles", and to their sanctuaries recourse was made to inspect the portents.

In his wider aspects, however, Adad was essentially an atmospheric High God whose cult extended throughout the Near East—in Mesopotamia, Syria and Palestine, and among the Hittites—under a variety of names (e.g. Addu, Resheph, Rammon and Teshub). Like Zeus, he was the god of the thunderstorms, and therefore his symbol was lightning, held in his right hand, and in his left hand an axe. In view of his destructive properties he was an object of fear, but combined with Shamash he was a god of justice whose sacred animal the bull was often associated with the sun in Syria.[26] This dual title was borne by some West Semitic kings who were said to give "his thunderings in the heaven as Adad so that the whole land trembles at his thunder".[27] Originally, however, Adad seems to have been primarily a sky-god connected with rain, the weather and the atmosphere, controlling the omens in the heavens, and as such readily acquired a solar relationship like most ancient deities of this nature.

Rain being the essential and most urgent need in parched arid regions, it was to those powers who controlled the elements that man turned in the first instance as the ultimate source of life and fertility. Therefore, it is not surprising that in the background of almost every prehistoric pantheon there is the figure of the Sky-god, however obscured it may have become in the process of solarization. Thus, Adad, like Horus and Min in Egypt, was a heavenly Being—the Power of the Sky—with his celestial bull, his thunderbolt and axe or hammer, who combined weather and fertility functions with those of the solar and storm divinities, and the attributes of the various gods associated with them.

THE INDO-EUROPEAN SKY-GODS

The Indo-Iranian Sky-gods

Amid all the vicissitudes of the Sky-god sometimes he retained his earlier supremacy in the physical universe and in the highest heaven, or he became incorporeal outside and independent of the world, as in the case of Varuna in India, whose name occurred with those of Mitra, Indra and the Nasatya twins, in a treaty between the Anatolian Hittites and the Mitanni in Syria about 1400 B.C.[28]

In prehistoric times the Aryans of India must have been very closely associated with those of Iran, even though they may not have been in actual historical contact with each other; the Indo-European cradleland towards the end of the third millennium B.C. having been somewhere between the Danube and the Oxus, not improbably on the steppes east of the Caspian Sea. This common home is reflected in the Iranian mythology but not in the hymns of the Rig-veda, the earliest Hindu texts which cannot be later than the middle of the second millennium B.C. (*c.* 1500), notwithstanding the recurrence of Iranian names in India and implied references to Persia in the Vedic literature.[29] This may have been an intentional repression, as the two sections appear to have been in a state of hostility for a very long time. Thus, in the earliest Indo-European religion only the gods of the sky, the wind and the sun, together with a sun-cult were recognized. To these the soma-cult was added by the Indo-Iranians. There was a tendency for an abstract quality to be associated with each god. Thus, Varuna was a heavenly god who upheld and regulated the moral cosmic order, like his Avestan counterpart, Ahura, who was also the supreme guardian of the moral law and of the cosmic order, symbolized in Rta. But when the Indian and Iranian groups broke asunder and developed their respective cultures the abstract deities, instead of being known as *daiva* gods as heretofore, were called in Iran *Asura*.[30]

In India, Varuna originally was the all-encompassing sky who supported heaven, earth and the air, bestowed rain, and whose Sanskrit name may be equated with the Greek *Ouranos* (sky).[31] In this capacity he was a heavenly monarch living in a golden abode in the sky, and became associated with Mitra, the solar god of light. The mighty warrior Indra, the god of thunder, had his headquarters in the atmosphere, between the sky and the earth, and Agni, the god of fire, was as all-pervading as the wind. Behind all these celestial gods was the old Indo-European Dyaus Pitar, identical with the Greek Zeus and the Roman Jupiter, the sky- and weather-god who eventually found a home on the Capitoline Hill at Rome in the temple in which an ancient boundary-stone open to the sky had been venerated from time immemorial. As the personification of the heavens Dyaus Pitar was the source of the fertilizing rain and also of the thunder, and in his paternal capacity he was united with Prithivi, the earth, as the universal parents. But he was only vaguely conceived in the Rig-veda, and very seldom appealed to, having been displaced by the nature gods and goddesses.

Thus, it was the all-encompassing Varuna taken in conjunction with Rta, "the right order", who in Iran eventually emerged as Ahura Mazda, the Wise-lord of the Avesta. But although in India the conception of Deity started from much the same presuppositions as those which prevailed in the Ancient Middle East, with the sky and the earth assuming their customary roles in the process of reproduction, the movement in Vedic tradition was towards a monistic unification of the universal cosmic order. When in due course the institution of sacrifice replaced Varuna and the nature gods under Brahmanic influence between 800 and 600 B.C., Prajapati became the Lord of Reproduction and the personification of the creative principle, at once creator and creation. As the ruler of the macrocosm and microcosm he pervaded all things, and through the universal cosmic and moral order (Rta) he fulfilled his operations as an immanent dynamic process permeating all things. By his primal sacrifice at the hands of the gods the phenomenal universe came into being as so many parts of his body, Prajapati having reproduced himself by means of a golden egg from which emerged the neuter impersonal creative principle Brahman operative in the sacred utterance (Veda) and in cosmic activity (Rta), generated by the sacrificial ritual. It was this creative process that was renewed by the priests, "the sacrifice being the god Prajapati at his own sacrifice", and by this offering the whole creation was resolved into a unity sustained by the rite.[32]

The merging of one divinity into another was the inevitable result of the cosmic principle expressed in terms of Rta and Varuna as the unifying element in nature and man, and of the various aspects of the universal order. When under Brahmanic influence the neuter Brahman emerged as the first-born of All, and in the Upanishads became the divine principle identified at once with the entire universe and the transcendent self

(Atman) of man, the ancient gods of the sky and of the earth were retained as aspects and attributes of the Absolute. Although the worship of the Vedic gods and the ritual order went on little changed in India among the masses, the One Ultimate Reality was resolved in Universal Being, expressed in the Upanishadic equation *tat tvam asi*, "That Thou art", centering in the unchanging, unknowable, actionless Brahman set over against yet pervading the unreal phenomenal world in a perpetual state of flux—the essence of all that is "unmoved, yet moving swifter than the mind", and like the air supporting all vital action.[33]

In Iran, on the other hand, against this monistic interpretation of the Ultimate Reality lying behind the world of phenomena and the desire to escape from the cycle of existences, the earlier polytheism moved in the direction of a monotheistic or dualistic totality of the one all-wise Lord Ahura Mazda, as the only God. To him the other *daevas* and *ahuras* were subordinated without losing all their primitive meaning and significance, since they became aspects of Ahura Mazda, modalities of his action. The struggle between good and evil, light and darkness, so fundamental in the magico-religious cult of Early Man, continued; but it was welded together into a single conflict in which God and man played their respective roles. Like Varuna, Ahura Mazda was the all-encompassing, all-wise, omniscient, governor of the universe and the actions of mankind, the embodiment of the "right law" (*Asha*). As Good Mind he was the Father of Reason, revealing himself to man and helping man to fulfil his proper vocation on earth, upholding the "Best Mind" (virtuous action), the Creator of Right, acting directly through the mind. In the Gathas he is the Eternal Being, who can be perceived only in thought, but his governance of the universe is apparent to all—the Good Architect whose sovereign righteous rule will be vindicated when the renovated world will be transformed at the end of the present age.[34]

When Mazdaeism began to spread throughout the Persian Empire, Ahura Mazda was represented on the royal

Achaemenian tombs and monuments at Persapolis by a winged disk out of which arose the head and shoulders of the Wise Lord, symbolizing how he reigned in the sky and enfolded and protected with his wings the earth and its ruler. Often he was surrounded by divine assistants who had been worshipped originally as polytheistic nature gods, and now engaged in the primeval struggle between the forces of good and evil under one or other of the twin spirits, Spenta Mainyu or Angra Mainyu.[35] As the oldest Avestan texts date back only to Zarathushtra, what lies behind his reform can only be conjectured. Nevertheless, this symbolism in Egyptian iconography belongs to the beginning of the monarchy in the fourth millennium B.C., where, as we have seen, the sky was represented by the outstretched wings of Horus. Indeed it seems that in some respects Zoroastrianism was not so much a break with the past as a determined effort to reassert the old Asura religion by ridding it of all *daivic* contaminations and pantheistic developments in order to restore the supreme Sky-god Varuna, now called Ahura Mazda, to his earlier position, and raising him to a unique level as an ethical monotheistic Deity. This would make him comparable to Yahweh in the neighbouring and contemporary post-exilic Jewish community which became part of the Persian Empire at the end of the sixth century B.C.

As Dumézil has shown, the structure of Indo-European society was reflected in its pantheons, and as an abstract entity tended to become associated with each god in the divine hierarchy, Zarathushtra succeeded in making Ahura Mazda the ethical Deity *par excellence* among the cattle-rearing farmers who were beset by the marauding Turanian nomads from the north, regarded as the followers of the forces of evil intent on capturing cattle for sacrifices to their *daevas*. Against them Zarathushtra fought his holy wars, and it was as a result of his victory over them that the new faith was established on firm foundations. The good life was identified with agriculture on earth and the reign of the Wise-Lord, the Father of Good Mind, in the heavenly realm, with the long history behind the tradition going back in all probability to prehistoric times and the worship of the Supreme Being as a tribal All-Father and guardian of the law of right conduct. Through Judaism it passed to the West and influenced Christian thought and theology, particularly in its eschatological aspects.

Zeus and the Olympian Divine Family

On the northern grasslands stretching from the Lower Danube eastwards along the north side of the Black Sea through southern Russia, and north and east of the Caspian Sea, the ancestors of the Indo-European peoples were still in the Stone Age, pasturing their herds on the steppe, before they separated in two groups about 2000 B.C. and dispersed into India and the Balkans, the pastures of Thessaly, and the verdant hills of Italy, where they became ancestors of the Greeks and Romans, speaking an Aryan type of language. Driving their herds before them, on the northern borders of Greece they settled under the shadow of Mount Olympus before they invaded the Aegean fortresses such as Tiryns and Mycenae. With them they brought their gods who were essentially the mountain deities of the Indo-European polytheistic tradition, as the Hebrews carried into Palestine Yahweh their god of the sacred mount, Horeb or Sinai.

At the head of their pantheon stood the great Sky-god whom they had worshipped on the grasslands under a variety of names, such as Dyaus Pitar, Varuna, and finally was known as Zeus, "the sky". On the summit of Mount Olympus he dwelt in his cloud palace with the lightning in his hand, ruling his *comitatus* like a Nordic chieftain. If in the Homeric tradition he reigned supreme in his heavenly kingdom organized on the model of a human clan, each of his retainers controlled as his own a realm of nature or of the affairs of men, though Zeus retained his position as their permanent overlord. But being primarily and originally the god of the sky and the weather, his proper home, and that of the rest of the Olympians, was in the heavens in contradistinction to the chthonians, whose domain was on and below the earth, being the gods of the indigenous population before the arrival of the Indo-European

and Achaean invaders in the second millennium B.C. In th
celestial realms with which Olympus was equated Zeus wa
the Supreme Deity ruling among the immortals as the "fathe
of gods and men", "of broad vision" (i.e. all-wise like Varun
and Ahura Mazda), and all-powerful over heaven and or
earth.

On the plains of Thessaly, however, the Homeric Olympian
mythology developed in a feudal society where feasting, fightin;
and hunting were prominent features of everyday life, especiall
among the Nordic chieftains and their vassals. Therefore, th
gods are represented as conquering chieftains, royal buccaneers
As Professor Gilbert Murray says, "they fight and feast, an
play, and make music; they drink deep, and roar with laughte
at the lame smith who waits on them. They are never afraid
except of their own king. They never tell lies, except in lov
and war."[36] In Greece they were conquerors rather tha
creators, and divided the spoils of war among themselves, an
lived on the revenues.

But the Homeric tradition was only one strand in th
complex Olympian pattern. Not only was the sky-and
weather-god endowed with the character of the society i
which he held dominion. But other legends grew up around
Zeus which had little to do with his original nature an
attributes, such as the Cretan story of his birth. In this myth
he is very unlike the Olympian heavenly chief. Rather than
being the Sky-god *par excellence* of the Homeric tradition h
was the son of Rhea, the consort of Kronos and the Cretan
counterpart of the Anatolian Mother-goddess, Cybele. Afte
his birth he was hidden in a cave in the mountain called
Aigaion and suckled by a goat, and, according to one curiou
tale, fire issued from it every year when the blood from th
birth of Zeus streamed forth, suggesting, as Nilsson says, tha
"this child is the year-god, the spirit of fertility, the new lif
of spring".[37]

This Cretan Zeus was a much more primitive figure tha
the Indo-European Sky-god, embodying the processes o
fecundity on earth rather than renewing them by sending th

vitalizing rain from the heavens. Nevertheless, as the Aryan-Achaean and Aegean aspects of Greek religion fused they found a common centre in "the father of gods and men" and the syncretistic Zeus came to occupy a position in the cultus as comprehensive as that of the Magna Mater in the Graeco-Roman world. It is hardly surprising that a deity equated with the sky and made responsible for the weather should be iden-tified with the god of fertility, ensuring abundant crops as well as the increase of flocks and herds. Such coalescence, as we have seen, had frequently occurred in the Near East, in Asia Minor, Egypt, and in the Indo-Iranian region, and it recurred in Greece when the cultus of the Indo-European invaders combined with that of the Aegean basin. Then without essen-tially changing his character and status the indigenous vegeta-tion deity became Zeus, but he continued to exercise his functions without any substantial change, while Zeus remained the head of the pantheon and took over a number of offices, aspects and attributes beyond the range of his original nature as sky-and-weather-god, the cloud-gatherer, the rain-giver, the thunderer, and the chief of the Olympians.

Thus, before he attained his exalted position, in the Hesiodic tradition he is represented as having had to overthrow the Titans, an earlier group of gods from whom he was himself descended through his father, Kronos. This may be a reflection of an historical situation when the Olympian Sky-religion defeated the chthonian indigenous cult of the soil but incor-porated much of the chthonian tradition, as the human race was thought to have imbibed a Titanic element in its essential ancestral history in combination with the divine nature derived from Zagreus-Dionysos. This dual character of the historic Zeus is revealed in his celestial aspects and attributes brought into relation with his connexion with the fertility of the earth and of vegetation the rain-producer when the invaders had to live on the produce of the soil on settling in Greece; very much as Yahweh acquired a vegetation cultus after the conquest of Palestine by the conglomeration of Hebrew tribes.

The Sky-father and the Earth-mother

The various unions of Zeus with Earth- and Corn-goddesse
—Hera, Dione, Demeter, Semele and Persephone—sugge
that in the background of these traditions lay the widesprea
conception of the marriage of Heaven and Earth in which h
played the role of the Sky-father. When the local legends wer
correlated in the Epic literature one of the brides was exalted t
the status of the official wife (i.e. Hera) of Zeus, while the re
were regarded as his mistresses, in accordance with the custor
that prevailed in the Greek States where such irregularitie
were generally accepted.[38] Thus, he was accredited with
considerable illegitimate offspring, partly divine when born c
goddesses, and partly human when their mothers were morta
women. But in prehistoric times it would seem that the Sky
father-Earth-mother fertility ritual was enacted, doubtless b
human instruments and agents of the respective god an
goddess, to enhance the fecundity of the soil and the reproduc
tive processes in nature generally.[39]

In the Aegean the youthful male god was subordinate to th
Mother-goddess who gave birth to all life, human, animal an
vegetable,[40] until with the fusion of the Olympian and th
chthonian cults the Sky-god became supreme as the chief dei
of the dominant invaders with their Indo-European back
ground. Henceforth Zeus played the leading role, and h
consorts were relatively minor figures, so that it is often difficu
to determine to what extent they were his wives. Even the cu
of Hera, concentrated on the life and function of women an
marriage, had little or nothing to do with that of Zeus, an
her union with him was merely the result of her having bee
the chief goddess and in consequence a fitting partner for th
chief god in spite of his previous nuptials with earth-goddesse
like Demeter, Semele and Themis.[41] But neither was Zeu
always the Sky-god, nor did he always marry an Earth-
Corn-goddess.[42] Taking over the functions of local less
divinities he was a syncretistic figure as he was much marrie
to a variety of subordinate wives, and had contracted unio
with innumerable concubines and mistresses. Nevertheless, l

retained his position of supremacy, paramount in nature, in the control of human life and its affairs, until in classical times he became for poets and philosophers the concept of deity in its abstract ethical and universal evaluation, either as a pantheistic principle or as the omnipotent and omniscient divine ruler of the universe.

The Scandinavian Heavenly Deities

The Indo-Europeans living originally in nomadic pastoral communities in a steppe country, unlike settled agriculturists, had always worshipped the Sky-father rather than the Earth-mother as their supreme god. Indeed as Childe has pointed out, no Earth-goddess is traceable in their language,[43] and female figurines were not prominent among them. But in Northern Europe, as in the Aegean, the Sky-god was often associated with the Earth-goddess as his consort, and the marriage of Zeus and Hera had its counterpart in Scandinavia. Thus, Othin (Woden), who in the early developments of Teutonic religion probably was a Sky-god, was the husband of Jörd, the Earth-goddess and mother of Thor, the thunder-god.

According to the Prose Edda, composed by Snorri in the twelfth century A.D., Othin was at once the All-Father, a divine king who came from the Black Sea, where as Asgard he was the chief of the city, a great warrior, conqueror, culture-hero and magician who taught by means of runes and spells. Among his children, Thor in addition to being the thunderer was a god of fertility who sent the showers to fertilize the ground and produce "the fair fruits of the earth", being the son of Jörd, the Earth-mother. When he blew into his red beard the thunder was heard, and his hammer was the lightning-bolt. To wield it with deadly consequences he put on iron gloves and clasped about him his "girdle of might", holding "the rod of power" wherein lay the magical strength of Othin. As he drove in the heavens in his wagon drawn by he-goats the thunder rolled, and such was his power and prestige that in Norway and Iceland he was worshipped as the beneficent Supreme God with aspects and attributes not unlike those of

Zeus. But like Indra he was the personification of strength and might, equipped with thunder-bolts as the thunder-god; the protector of mankind against his demonic adversaries. In fact, behind the two figures may stand a common hero of Indo-European tradition who has assumed a variety of forms in the process of diffusion from the transcaspian cradleland to India, the Eastern Mediterranean and Scandinavia, very much as Nerthus, the oldest Norse goddess of fertility, and the Phrygian Cybele, were local expressions of the universal Magna Mater.

The occurrence of small hammer-shaped amulets of amber, bone or stone, comparable to the almost identical hammers of Thor found in viking graves and to the symbols cut in runic stones, suggests that the lightning cult associated with Thor is of prehistoric origin, like the closely related cult of the double-axe in the Aegean and the Near East which recurs in Scandinavia. Thus, in Denmark frail ceremonial axes decorated with gold were used as votive offerings in the Bronze Age, and in a grave at Kivik in Skane two axes were engraved on each side of an altar, and in the scene of a procession men are depicted carrying axes of the same shape, together with solar symbols and pictures of ships.[44] In Iceland a bronze disk representing the sun was set on a chariot with six wheels and on the axles, doubtless depicting the horse-drawn chariot in which Sol, the sister of the Moon, drove across the sky by day. The Sun, however, was female in Old Norse mythology, and Snorri makes her one of the group of goddesses known as *asynja* who, although equal with the gods, were not in the same category as Othin the All-Father, Thor the Almighty and Frey the world's god. Sol, no doubt, was worshipped from very early times as the prehistoric solar symbolism indicates, but little or nothing of importance can be extracted from the mythological literature concerning the origins of the cult. The fire-festivals, however, which have been a prominent feature in Scandinavia and elsewhere in Europe at the summer solstice,[45] are probably relics of the magical rites performed at this season to assist the sun at the critical turning-point in its annual course along the heavenly road.

Sky-worship in Wessex

In the British Isles, as we have seen,[46] the Mediterranean megalithic cult so closely associated with the Earth-mother, death and rebirth, was fused with the Indo-European sky and solar religion at the beginning of the Bronze Age when the Beaker folk with their Battle-axe cultural affinities transformed the Avebury complex of monuments into sanctuaries open to the sky which culminated in the great stone circle on Salisbury Plain. Without endorsing the elaborate astronomical speculations which have been made in connexion with Stonehenge, that in this remarkable temple a celestial and solar ritual of some kind was practised can hardly be doubted, directed in all probability to a Sky-god comparable to Varuna, Zeus and Jupiter.

Thus, its orientation seems to have been aligned on the rising sun at midsummer, since on the summer solstice the sun rises so very near the peak of the Heelstone, even though the central line of the Avenue is not the point of sunrise, as Sir Norman Lockyer contended, because it is not visible from the centre of Stonehenge. Nevertheless, it seems that the monument has been intentionally arranged in relation to solar alignments connected with the solstices.[47] If this be so, it would appear to have been erected primarily for the performance of rites at seasonal festivals, probably associated with the rising and the setting of the sun in the north-east and the south-east respectively, as the alignments suggest, unless they were employed merely to fix the time of the festival.

In any case, whether or not Stonehenge was actually a Sun temple, unquestionably it was an open sanctuary characteristic of the Indo-European worship of the Sky-god, planned and erected in relation to celestial phenomena. Only a very intensive religious motive could have produced such uniquely elaborate and extensive cult-centres as Avebury and Stonehenge of which the simple stone circles were pale reflections. That these circular megalithic monuments are almost exclusively peculiar to Britain and Brittany, and in the case of Stonehenge underwent so many reconstructions from the Late Neolithic (*c.* 1900–1700 B.C.) to the end of the Bronze Age (*c.* 1300 B.C.), shows the vigour and vitality of the cultus in this region, under the supremacy of the Breton-Wessex chieftains who were largely responsible for the maintenance and development of Sky-worship in its central sanctuaries in Wiltshire.

CHAPTER IX

Prehistoric Religion

FROM the foregoing survey of the archaeological data it has become apparent that prehistoric religion centred in and developed around the three most critical and perplexing situations with which Early Man was confronted in his everyday experience—birth, death and the means of subsistence in a precarious environment. The pressure of events in the external world and in human affairs, the perpetual struggle for existence and survival here and hereafter, the innumerable frustrations and awe-inspiring experiences, often completely outside his control and comprehension, created, it would seem, a tension for the relief of which ways and means had to be found. When life depended largely on the hazards of the chase, the vagaries of the seasons and so many unpredictable and untoward circumstances and events, the emotional strain must have been endemic. And once a ritual technique had been devised to sublimate the stress, it became established and developed indefinitely to meet every new demand and maintain the equilibrium in an expanding social structure and religious organization.

THE RITUAL CONTROL OF NATURAL PROCESSES

Thus, the religious consciousness was projected into whatever natural force or process or object it identified with the sacred. A symbol as the image or mental reflex of instinct may arise spontaneously, as Jung maintains, independent of conscious volition, as in the realms of dreams, visions and hallucinations. This type of human experience has found expression in animistic and theistic interpretations of natural phenomena, so that the mysterious sacred power has been equated with particular species of animals and physical features such as mountains, rivers, the wind, the sun, the moon and the constellations. It has also been associated pre-eminently with life-giving processes—fecundity, maternity and everything connected with generation and birth—and with the disturbing and disintegrating phenomenon of death. Natural forces and events, in fact, have been so overwhelming that they have appeared as many different supernatural powers and principles at work in a variety of ways, good and bad, beneficent and malevolent. Consequently, as many symbolic images of divinity have been devised as different sacred identities have been established, each duly equipped with its appropriate ritual techniques in the form of a cultus designed to bring under control and to make efficacious the forces with which the symbols are associated.

In their several capacities these transcendental entities have been regarded as belonging essentially to the "other world" which mysteriously imposes itself on this world and its events. Therefore, the religious reaction is not just a mental reflex of instinct arising purely spontaneously as a product of a "psychological machine", as Durkheim contended; merely a product of society which has "all that is necessary to arouse the sensation of the Divine in minds by the power it has over them; so that to its members it is what a god is to its worshippers".[1] While it is true that religion has emerged within society and that it functions as an integral aspect of its structure enabling human beings to live together in an orderly arrangement of social relations, and to make their own life and characteristics explicit through a social medium,[2] it is very much more than the evaluation and personification of the organization of the community. The totem, for example, is not just "the clan itself personified and represented to the imagination under the visible form of the totemic animal or vegetable", as Durkheim contended, any more than religion is only "a unified system of beliefs and practices relative to sacred things" which "unite into one single community all those who adhere to them".[3]

That the discipline has arisen very largely in relation to such practical problems as the maintenance of the food supply has been demonstrated in this volume,[4] and unquestionably it has united individuals and groups into stable social structures in a higher unity to preserve a state of equilibrium; but behind and over and above the "collective representations" it has imposed on the members of a social group there has always been apparently the conception of a transcendental order external to man and society associated with abnormal, unpredictable, inexplicable and mysterious occurrences, objects and processes in the universe and in human experience. This is of the very essence of religion at all times and in all states of culture. Indeed, so far as this aspect of the discipline is concerned, religion may be described as the recognition of and the endeavour to establish and maintain beneficial relations with the supra-mundane sacred order manifesting itself in the universe and controlling its processes and human affairs, whether collective or personal. This found expression in a technique which aimed at establishing through ritual institutions an efficacious relationship with the source of life and power, of abundance and well-being at the heart of all existence, to overcome the disabilities of death, sterility and the ills to which mortal flesh is heir, as well as of producing stability and equilibrium in the body politic. By means of symbols, rites and dances human energies have been directed into new activities which have exercised an integrative function in society by enabling man individually and collectively to meet his crises with confidence, trust and hope by assimilating life-giving strength, allaying his fears and renewing his aspirations.

Thus, at critical junctures alike in the career of the individual from the cradle to the grave and its aftermath, and in the sequence of the seasons, especially at the turn of the year, the chances and changes of this mortal life have been unified, controlled and fortified by supernatural forces believed to govern the course of events and human destinies. Under Palaeolithic conditions, discharge of emotion and longing was centred on the food supply, birth and death. Therefore, it was in relation to these precarious phenomena that a ritual cultus developed to give effective expression to the most urgent needs of a tense situation fraught with such serious dangers, difficulties and consequences for all concerned. In respect of the food supply the position was complicated by the fact that a feeling of kinship existed between man and the animals which had to be hunted. Indeed, since they constituted a vital aspect of a providential bounty and beneficence of the world and its processes, they acquired a divine character and significance, being the primary source of the means of human subsistence. Consequently the necessity to kill and eat them was in conflict with the sense of kinship with them, and of dependence upon their goodwill and continuance. It was apparently out of this contradictory situation and its emotional tension that the cultus of the caves emerged.

The Nature and Function of Symbols

Thus, in the seclusion of these numinous and inaccessible Palaeolithic sanctuaries hunting magic to secure success in the chase was combined with fertility rites of increase and masked dances to establish and maintain a right relationship with the sacred species. To follow Lévy Bruhl and explain this behaviour as the result of a "prelogical mentality"[5] is a misconception of what he calls the "Law of Contradiction" and the "Law of Participation". On his hypothesis everything is permeated by forces, influences and actions which, though imperceptible to sense, are so real that all things are fused and no distinction is made between this world and the "other" world; "to what is actually present to sense, and what is beyond". Therefore, all the objects and entities of the natural order are not divided from one another, but are so united in a bond that each participates in the other, making it what it is not and enabling the same entity to be simultaneously in many places. Consequently, in totemic society a man imagines himself to be his totem, or under Palaeolithic conditions assumes animal disguises, as in the figure of "the Sorcerer" at Les Trois Frères, or in that of a masked dancer at Lourdes and elsewhere.

But while it is true that both primitive and prehistoric peoples not infrequently have regarded themselves as an animal or bird, or even an inanimate object, and equated natural phenomena with divine beings and activities, it cannot be maintained that "the law of contradiction" and the laws of magic are thereby excluded from their mentality. The identification of the symbol with the thing symbolized is the result of the introduction of a third term in the equation. In the case of the totemic relationship the union is achieved by the supposition that the human group participates in the spiritual nature of its sacred ally from whom it is descended, and it is this common element which effects the bond between them, making them what otherwise they would not be. Among the Nuer, in fact, the links between a lineage and its totem is the tutelary spirit of the lineage associated with the totem. The natural species is not identical with a spirit except in relation to its lineage. Similarly, when the relationship is represented by a material symbol the symbol is regarded and treated in the same way as the spiritual entity it symbolizes, not because it is thought to be other than it actually is but because it has acquired a spiritual quality which does not belong to it in its own nature without changing its outward and visible form and character.[6]

This sacramental conception of symbolism does not contravene either logic or the "law of contradiction". It merely presupposes the existence of an extra-mundane spiritual world standing against and in a particular relation with this world over which it exercises some measure of control. This is a fundamental religious assumption at all times and in all states of culture, however crudely and naively, or mystically and metaphysically, it may have been expressed and interpreted. In its prehistoric mode of expression it lay behind the ritual control of natural processes and events, the kinship with the animal creation and the mimetic dance in which animal disguises were a prominent feature. When a ritual expert arrayed himself in the skin and antlers of a stag, or in the feathers of a bird, and imitated the behaviour of the species he personified, he did so in the belief that for the time being, and for the prescribed purpose, he was what he represented himself to be, and in that capacity he did not imitate but he actually did what he set out to do. He caught and killed his prey; he made the copulation of male and female effective in the reproduction of offspring; he established a sacramental relationship between man and the providential source of his food supply.

Totemism and the Sacred Dance

That this involved the practice of totemism is not very probable since, apart from the archaeological objections that have been considered,[7] in its more developed forms the institution involves a social and religious structure which is not likely to have prevailed in Palaeolithic times. In practice it is a particular and specialized system of economics with its own technique for the supernatural control of the food supply and the elaborate kinship organization of society it entails, presupposing a long process of development. Although it is of frequent occurrence in primitive states of culture, its absence among such very rudimentary peoples as the Veddas of Ceylon, the Punan of Borneo, the Andaman Islanders, the Pygmies of the Congo, the Bushmen of South Africa, as well as the clanless inhabitants of the Northwest Pacific coast of America and the low Brazilian tribes in the southern half of the New World, shows that it is by no means universal in distribution or a constant feature in primitive society.

Nevertheless, it was from the sense of kinship with the animal order which the archaeological evidence establishes beyond reasonable doubt to have been a characteristic feature of Palaeolithic ritual and belief, that totemism in due course arose and developed as a dominant socioreligious institution in many parts of the world. This is most apparent in the sacred dances and their mimetic representations when those who took part in the rites, with the aid of masks, antlers, skins of animals and feathers of birds, and appropriate realistic gestures, identified themselves with the species they believed themselves to have become through a process of "participation". Thus, a realization of unity and kinship with the source of the food supply was attained, and the emotional desire for life in greater abundance given expression in mimetic actions to bring about the longed-for results, uniting in the closest bond of kinship those who took part in the rites by virtue of their all sharing in a common life-principle and the joint effort to secure the end in view. From such fundamental concepts as these, deeply laid in the cult of Early Man, totemism in all probability developed as a socio-religious institution.

In the Nile valley it would appear that Upper and Lower Egypt, unified as a theocratic State under a single divine ruler, emerged from a multiplicity of clans with their heraldic ensigns regarded as a sacred emblem and rallying sign, such as those of the falcon, the elephant, the cow, the serpent and the ibis. These survived in the Dynastic period after the clans and independent city-states had become administrative districts, or nomes, each having its own distinctive standards, towns and chief cities. In fact, some of the prehistoric ensigns which gave their name to the clan and the capital city remained in use until the end of Egyptian civilization, [8] having developed into local ancestral animal deities; later they sometimes occupied very prominent positions in the national pantheon. Thus, Amratian representations of a pole with cow's horns and a head on top may have had a quasi-totemic significance before they became the emblems of the fertility-goddess, later identified with Hathor and the other goddesses who subsequently were confused with their prototype the Mother-goddess, the nourisher and protector of the living and the dead, like the totemic supernatural ally. [9]

FERTILITY AND THE MYSTERY OF BIRTH AND GENERATION

Cow-symbolism

In the Late Predynastic Age in Egypt and at Al 'Ubaid on the Euphrates the Mother-goddess appears in a new guise identified with the cow. In this Hathor form her advent seems to have coincided with the rise to power of the Falcon clan, which eventually unified the "two lands" under its own ensign, and soon she became the predominant deity, assuming many and various roles. [10] It may have been under the influence of the peoples of the Western Desert who had domesticated cattle at a very early period that the Mother-goddess as Neith was first conceived as a cow,[11] or, as Hornblower believes, the symbolism may be of Mesopotamian origin.[12] In any case, Hathor emerged from the Stone Age as a female divinity with the solar disk on her head between two cow's horns, or as a cow wearing the solar disk and two plumes between her horns; the Hathor cow-head going back to the Gerzean period and recurring in Amratian rock-drawings in Upper Egypt.[13] Later her horns were worn by Isis in conjunction with the lunar disk, and in the Dynastic epoch she became the universal Mother-goddess worshipped throughout Egypt with Denderah as the centre of the cult. At Heliopolis she was made the wife of Re, and so became the mother of Horus, her name signifying "House of Horus". In this synthesis, typical of Egyptian mythology, her relation to Horus was at once that of mother and wife, while as Cow-goddess she was also his nurse. Thus, from a prehistoric zoomorphic origin a series of life-giving and life-sustaining deities emerged (especially in the seventh and twenty-second nomes of Upper Egypt and in the third nome of Lower Egypt) in which cow-symbolism was a dominant feature with shrines extending to Nubia, Syria and Sinai.

In Egypt, however, as we have seen, the function of the mother-goddesses was that of the reproduction of life. In Mesopotamia, on the other hand, they were regarded as the actual source of life to the living and the dead, exercising their creative operations in association with a male partner. At Al 'Ubaid, for instance, the goddess subsequently known as Nin-Khursag, "she who gives life to the dead", was the guardian of the fecundity of the fields and of the cattle they sustained, and from her was drawn the "holy milk" which nourished the sacred herd of the temple dairy at Lagash.[14] Not only was she the mother of the gods, but kings were "fashioned" in her womb, who pray to her that her gracious influence may be withdrawn from their enemies "so that birth may cease in their lands". Her usual symbol was the cow, and as is indicated on the seals, stone vases and limstone reliefs, she presided over the sacred farm at Al 'Ubaid, which provided the holy milk destined for the nourishment of kings and priests; very much as the members of a totemic clan were sustained by the totem, of which the cow and its symbolism seem to be a development adapted to the conditions of a pastoral society and brought into relation with the earlier cult centred in the mystery of birth and generation. If, as Gadd suggests, the hooped door-posts and lintel of the cow-byre in the form of a moon-crescent symbolized the fertility god of Ur, the Bull, upon whose union with the Goddess all increase depended, then it seems highly probable that the divine nuptials of the Cow-goddess Nin-Khursag and the Moon-god of Ur were celebrated annually in the customary manner and for the usual purposes of renewing the life of nature at its source.[15]

The cult of the cow which has occupied such a conspicuous place in Brahmanic Hinduism certainly was not introduced into India by the Aryan invasion in the second millennium B.C. since it is foreign to the Rig-veda. The first prohibition of cow-killing occurs in the comparatively Late Atharva-veda, which betrays signs of contact and admixture with non-Indo-European influences. In the earlier Vedas the sacrifice of cattle to Indra, Varuna and other deities was enjoined though it is said to be abhorrent to public opinion, suggesting that already they were regarded as sacred animals by the non-Aryan population as in Western Asia and Egypt, where, as we have seen, the bull and the cow were venerated as an integral element in the Goddess fertility cult. It would seem, therefore, that cow worship in India arose in the indigenous Dravidian civilization when with the development of agriculture the cow as the source of milk needed for sustenance became essentially the sacred emblem of fertility hedged round with taboos, so that even in the Rig-veda under pre-Aryan influences the epithet *aghnyax*, "not to be killed", was assigned to it.

While the Vedic Indians were meat-eaters and engaged in agriculture, like their predecessors they were primarily a pastoral people with milk and its products as a very important element in their staple diet. While the ox, the sheep and the goat were killed for food, and, like the horse, as sacrificial victims, the cow acquired an increasing sanctity by virtue of its being the source of the milk supply. In Indo-Iranian times it was treated with care and respect, milked three times daily and kept in a stall during the night and when the sun was at its height. Bulls and oxen used for ploughing fertilized the land by their droppings, and so played their part in the cultivation of the soil. The bull, therefore, became sacred to Shiva, a non-Vedic god, who before he acquired a destructive character when he was identified with Rudra, a minor Vedic storm-deity, may have had a fertility significance if the figure of the three-faced god at Mohenjo-daro with its horned head-dress was in fact his prototype, Pasupati,[16] the Lord of Beasts, and possibly a male partner of the Mother-goddess. Be this as it may, the cult of the bull is established beyond reasonable doubt as a feature of the Harappan civilization which in due course became a dominant element of non-Vedic origin in Brahmanism. Though no trace occurs of cow-worship in the Indus religions notwithstanding the numerous female figurines already reviewed,[17] bull-worship seems to indicate that some form of veneration of the Mother-goddess was an integral aspect of the Harappan household cult, similar to that which prevailed in Western Asia and in Palaeolithic Europe. The closely related phallic symbols were another pre-Aryan element destined to play an important role in post-Vedic Hinduism in the same context.

Generation and Maternity

Therefore, it may be concluded that in the prehistoric background of the ancient civilizations the religious preoccupation largely was concerned with fertility and the ever-present pressing problem of subsistence coupled with the mysterious phenomena connected with birth and generation, upon which the survival of the race also depended. The will to live finding expression in a variety of symbolic actions and objects—dances and mimetic rites, masks and other disguises, female figurines, phalli, realistic and stylized zoomorphic and anthropomorphic designs and tectiforms—is the most insistent and recurrent fact in prehistoric religion. The underlying principle in all and sundry is fecundity in its manifold forms conceived as a dynamic spiritual force and process manifest in the duality of male and female brought into conjunction for the procreation of life.

THE GODDESS CULT

At first it would seem to have been maternity that held the field. The life-producing mother was the central figure in reproduction in the human and animal world alike, and then extended to the vegetable kingdom when Mother-earth became the womb in which the crops were sown. With the establishment of husbandry and domestication, however, the function of the male in the process of generation became more apparent and vital, however dimly it may have been recognized in food-gathering communities. The Mother-goddess, therefore, was assigned a spouse to play his role as the begetter, even though, as in Mesopotamia, he remained the servant or son of the Goddess. But at length he became the co-equal, and eventually the predominant, partner in the sacred marriage, when the Sky-father contracted his alliance with the Earth-mother, or the pharaoh as the incarnate son of Re visited his queen to beget an heir to the throne.

In Crete, nevertheless, the Goddess retained her former position, for in the Minoan civilization she was clearly the chief anthropomorphic object of worship, either depicted alone or in association with her priestesses and her most characteristic emblems and accompaniments—doves, lions, snakes, the double axe, shells, horns of consecration, the sacred tree and the mountain on which she often stood. Indeed throughout the Eastern Mediterranean and the Aegean the cult of the Mother-goddess predominated, and to fertilize the Earth-mother the virility of the sacred bull may have been poured out sacrificially on the horned-altars in Minoan sanctuaries, especially at the spring festival. But she herself never was adorned with horns nor represented as suckling her offspring. In short, in Crete she did not assume the role of the divine cow and its symbolism.

On the mainland Zeus took the guise of a bull to carry off Europa to Crete, where she became the mother of Minos. His wife Pasiphae in her turn concealed herself in the effigy of a cow to have intercourse with the bull with which she had become infatuated and so conceived the Minotaur. Here there would appear to be a survival of a symbolic ritual marriage to a sacred bull and of the kind of mimetic dance portrayed in a Palaeolithic engraving of a man and woman clothed in skins with tails in the cave of Combarelles in the Dordogne.[18] The classical Moon-goddess Selene, the daughter of the Sun, with whom Pasiphae is connected by her name, was figured as a cow-goddess with horns, and in the legend the bull was the universal god of the sky and of fertility.[19] This association with the moon brings Pasiphae into line with the Goddess cult in the Near East, where the goddess of fertility was so often a lunar deity, perhaps because in arid districts the moon stimulates the dew and so promotes the growth of vegetation, just as the Earth-mother was thought to be fertilized by the rain bestowed upon her by the Sky-father. Therefore, to promote fertility in nature the life-giving forces had to be made operative through a ritual re-enactment of the act of copulation between the Goddess and her spouse symbolized by the cow and the bull, the earth and the sky, the moon and the sun.

Under this imagery the myth and ritual of the fertility and vegetation cult in Asia Minor, Syria, Babylonia, Egypt, the Eastern Mediterranean, Crete and the Aegean developed. In the Minoan-Mycenaean region the figures of gods are of very infrequent occurrence while those of goddesses abound. Indeed everywhere that of the universal Mother lying behind the various emblems and localizations of maternity predominates, representing the mystery of birth and generation in its manifold aspects and attributes. But closely associated with the Goddess was the young male god as her brother, spouse or son, brought together in a nuptial ritual in relation to the annual cycle of vegetation in the agricultural calendrical sequence in which the king and queen were cast to play the leading roles, either in a divine capacity, as in Egypt, or as servants of the Goddess, as in Mesopotamia.

With the concentration of creative energy in the male principle as the begetter, the Goddess tended to lose in some measure her dominance and prestige, but the Asiatic cult persisted in its diffusion from the Near East to Britain and Scandinavia, in association with the megalithic civilization. Centred in the sacred isle of Malta with its great temples and its colossal image of the obese Mother clad in a fluted skirt, it spread through Spain and along the Atlantic littoral to its Palaeolithic cradleland in Western Europe, to carry on and develop the ancient tradition of the "Venuses" and the decorated caves and rock-shelters under megalithic conditions. Thus, on cave walls and in adjacent shelters in the Iberian peninsula are to be seen paintings of ritual significance of wild animals and episodes of the chase which may be of Palaeolithic descent, combined with those of domestic cattle, sheep and goats, and pastoral scenes, while the owl-face of the Millares Goddess may be derived from Capsian conventionalized designs. In Brittany, the Paris Basin and the Channel Islands the statue-menhirs with their "cupolas" bear witness to the persistence of the cult in a relatively late stage of its diffusion in Northern France, where it had acquired essentially a funerary content.

THE CULT OF THE DEAD

Palaeolithic

The extension of the life-giving process to the dead which, as has been demonstrated, has been one of the earliest features of prehistoric religion, could hardly fail to bring the mystery of death into relation with that of birth and fertility. At first apparently it sufficed to lay the body to rest in a carefully prepared grave and to provide it with the implements and food offerings required in the after-life. The head seems to have been regarded as having special potency, and so was preserved for ritual purposes and the brain extracted and eaten to imbibe its magico-religious qualities. Usually, however, the body was

buried whole and entire in a position suggesting sleep, sometimes, as at La Ferrassie in the Dordogne, protected with slabs
of stone on which, in this case, were markings suggestive of
female symbols and heads of animals.[20] But the head of the
male corpse appears to have been severed after death.

In the Upper Palaeolithic, in addition to the extended
position and that of sleep, flexing was adopted, perhaps to
prevent the return of the ghost. But that the renewal of life was
the predominant motive is shown by the presence of such
vitalizing agents to reanimate the body as red ochre, shells and
occasionally horns or tusks. Dismemberment was rare, though
the nest of skulls at Ofnet shows that the practice of decapita-
tion survived in the Mesolithic period, coupled with the
ornamentation of the skulls with cowrie shells and burial in
red ochre, suggesting that they were honoured trophies preserved for veneration rather than cannibalistic relics. Whether
or not any such interpretation is to be placed on the painting of
the hunting tragedy at Lascaux remains to be determined. If the
mortal remains of the luckless hunter killed by the bison should
be revealed in the "crypt" of the cave, the Abbé Breuil's
suggestion that the scene represents a votive picture would be
substantiated in some measure.[21]

While the available data are still very incomplete, in the
Palaeolithic the veneration, revivification and fear of vengeance
of the dead appear to have constituted the general attitude
towards the mystery of death. The sacredness of the event
rendered it a taboo condition to be approached and treated
with the utmost caution and respect. That it was not the final
end of life seems to have been taken for granted, though
precisely what lay beyond the grave doubtless was as obscure
for Early Man as it is for many who foregather at the obsequies
of their relatives and friends in a modern community. That it
was a life like that to which the deceased had been accustomed
in the days of his flesh, where food and raiment, tools and
weapons and ornaments would be required, is indicated by
the grave-goods. But in addition to this material equipment the
body had to be restored to life by magical devices and adorned

with ornaments, partly as vitalizing agents but also as a mark of respect and of status here and hereafter. The horn of a bison hidden under a block of stone in the funerary trench at the entrance to the cave at La Chapelle-aux-Saints,[22] recalling the horn held by the woman in the bas-relief at Laussel,[23] and the large tusk of a mammoth at Brünn above the skeleton in a bed of ochre with an ivory male figure and shell ornaments,[24] together with the mammoth skull at Paviland in association with the ochreous burial,[25] may have been for the purpose of placing the dead under the protection of these mighty creatures so frequently depicted on the walls of the caves and in bas-reliefs.

With the transition from the precarious life of the chase to the cultivation of the soil and the keeping of flocks and herds under rather more secure Neolithic conditions, the sequence of the seasons and its ritual had its counterpart in the cult of the dead with a common symbolism. The "Venus" figures, which represent the earliest indications of a maternal cult in the Upper Palaeolithic, now began to find a place in the prehistoric graves at Badari, Arpachiyah, and throughout the Fertile Crescent and Western Asia, together with cowrie shells, red ochre and such closely related cult objects as the double axe, the dove, the bucrania and the serpent. Although female figurines have not been found in the earliest Neolithic sites, from the Halaf levels of Hassuna they occur everywhere west of Iran when the Goddess cult became the dominating influence, and eventually, as has been considered, she herself appeared in funerary architecture and its symbolism in her life-giving capacity to the dead.

Ancient Egypt

In Egypt, however, the desiccation of the bodies buried in the hot dry sand of the desert emphasized the continuation of life after death, and led to the elaborate efforts to preserve and reanimate the corpse and to erect the rectangular mastaba tombs of mud brick which developed through the palace façade mastaba into the vast royal pyramids at the beginning of the Dynastic period, when the divine kingship centred the cult of the dead in the throne. But while immortality then became the prerogative of the pharaohs who alone were destined to enter the realms of the gods after death as themselves gods, the royal tombs were, in fact, only a very complex development of the simple prehistoric Amratian and Gerzean trench-graves enlarged to contain an increasing number of food offerings and funerary gifts. At length a shaft was added and the superstructure erected over the series of chambers. Moreover, burial in mastabas was not confined to pharaohs. Therefore, although the nature of the continued existence of commoners in and before the Old Kingdom is not known, the prehistoric cemeteries in the desert graves on the margin of the alluvium disclose a relatively advanced belief in a future life from the fifth millennium B.C. in which all were destined to share. That it was centred in the tomb is shown by the increasing care bestowed upon its construction and furnishing, and the provision made for the comfort and well-being of those who "went down into the pit" lest they should molest the living. In fact, offerings to the dead were made in accordance with a prescribed ritual in the predynastic period long before the Pyramid Texts were drawn up.

From very early times each individual was believed to have an invisible immortal "soul" or ghost which often assumed the form of a bird with a human head, that either survived death or came into existence at the time of the dissolution. To this conception of the *ba* that of the *ka* eventually was added. Originally it was exclusively a royal attribute of divine creative power conceived as a beneficent and protective genius, or spiritual double, who guided the fortunes of the pharaoh primarily in the after-life when he went to his *ka* at death. Since, however, the king was a god, he held communion with his *ka* to some extent during his lifetime. In the Middle and New Kingdoms, when the *ka* became the possessions of commoners as well as of the pharaohs, it acquired a more impersonal character as the vital principle in this life, born with the individual, sustained through his life, and preceding him to the next world. It was symbolized by two raised arms with outspread hands, distinct from the bird-shaped *ba* with its ghostly attributes and functions in the grave and in relation to the mummy or portrait statue.

To what extent these highly complex interpretations of the constitution and survival of human personality can be regarded as of prehistoric origin and significance is difficult to say. The conception of the *ka* as a vital essence, a guardian spirit and an alter ego would seem to represent very ancient and primitive connotations, as does that of the ghostly *ba* of the dead man. The primitive mind, as we have seen, has always conceived of human survival in terms of some kind of concrete entity, and in Egypt attention was concentrated on the preservation and reanimation of the body and its burial in an "everlasting tomb", together with the portrait statue as its surrogate, after "life" had been imparted to them by the "Opening of the Mouth" ceremony—an extension of the Palaeolithic practice of revivification. While mummification became an elaborate re-enactment of the treatment of the body of Osiris, behind this myth and ritual lay a very long history of the preservation and restoration to life of the dead by magical and mechanical methods.

As Breasted has pointed out, although among no people ancient or modern has the idea of a life beyond the grave held so prominent a place as among the Egyptians, the belief in the immortal and imperishable soul cannot be attributed to them.[26] The purpose of their mortuary ritual was to reconstitute and resuscitate the deceased after the dissolution by magico-mechanical processes and ceremonies external to him, to enable him to continue his existence in the hereafter. And this is precisely what Early Man endeavoured to do in the cult of the dead. To achieve the resurrection of his predecessor the pharaoh erected the *Djed* column, which Frankfort suggests may have represented the Goddess Hathor,[27] thereby effecting his rebirth by an efficacious symbolic act in accordance with established primitive procedure. Or, again, all men could find a place in the everlasting kingdom of Osiris by undergoing the same rites of mummification that were performed on his dismembered and restored body, though eventually in the Middle Kingdom they had to be able to show that like him they were "true in heart and voice" when their hearts were weighed by Thoth against the feather of truth.

Mesopotamia

In Mesopotamia the cult of the dead never assumed the same proportions as in the Nile valley, where vast tombs, elaborate methods of mummification, judgment after death and resurrection dominated Egyptian religion. The Babylonian conception of the hereafter was that of a semi-conscious survival in the House of Darkness, a withering away like the generative force in nature in the devitalizing heat of a Mesopotamian summer. This mood of despair found expression in the lamentations for Tammuz or Marduk imprisoned in the "mountain" which symbolized the nether regions. Even though his liberation was celebrated at the New Year Festival with rejoicings when death appeared to have been vanquished in nature at the return of the rains, it was only life on earth that was renewed. For man, although the grave was not the absolute end of existence, beyond it lay the dreaded abode of Irkalla which none could leave once it was entered, for the gods had made immortality their own prerogative. Thus, Gilgamesh when he went in search of everlasting life failed in his quest, cheated by a serpent of the magic rejuvenating plant he had secured to renew his youth.[28] The gods, and heroes like Utnapishtim, his wife and daughter, alone could be revived and live for ever. This is confirmed in the myth of Adapa, where again mankind is represented as having lost immortality by a trick of the gods.[29] Therefore, the decline and restoration in nature is as near as the Babylonians ever got to the renewal of life emerging from death.

Nevertheless, behind this sinister conception of human destiny it seems that a prehistoric cult of the dead was sufficiently developed to require some equipment for the hereafter. Thus, apart from the elaborate ceremonial practised at the royal tombs at Ur, the normal Sumerian custom was to bury the dead in earth and brick graves with an adequate supply of food and drink, which sometimes appears to have been renewed by monthly offerings,[30] together with certain personal belongings.[31] Both extended and flexed burial were practised, the corpse frequently being clothed or wrapped in a mat or winding-sheet and interred, usually in the house under the floor of the court or of a room rather than in a cemetery. The grave-goods, though on the whole meagre, suggest a belief in survival, but individual immortality probably had not acquired a cultic significance except in the case of the royal obsequies with their galaxy of wealth and large-scale immolation of members of the king's household. These rites show that in contradistinction to the later notion of kings and commoners suffering the same fate in the nether regions, at the beginning of the Dynastic period at Ur great importance and significance was attached to status in the after-life. But for the rest of mankind survival readily became a static condition approached with resignation coupled with apprehension, and interpreted as a hopeless quest and divine deprivation arising from the jealousy of the gods who made themselves exclusively the partakers of a blessed immortality in their own realms.

The Indus Valley

Similarly, in India the cult of the dead in prehistoric times is very obscure. In the hill-villages adjacent to the Indus civilization the extensive cemetery at Nal in Southern Baluchistan has revealed, as we have seen,[32] that among the various methods of inhumation employed, "fractional" burial was the dominant practice in the third millennium B.C., suggestive of secondary interment after exposure elsewhere. No attempt was made to protect the bones beyond placing them in small rectangular chambers at Damb Buthi, and in similar brick constructions at Nal. But the pottery vessels, copper axes, beads and red pigment are indicative of a continued existence requiring provision for the well-being of the deceased.

At Mohenjo-daro scant attention appears to have been paid to the disposal of the dead, as the alleged fractional burials and the bones showing signs of incineration are probably relics of attacks by raiders rather than intentional interments. It was only in the cemetery discovered at Harappa in 1937 to the south of the citadel (R37) that definite evidence of ceremonial sepulture has come to light in the Indus valley. There personal ornaments worn by the dead included necklaces, shell bangles, steatite anklets, copper rings and mirrors, and in the thick wooden coffin found in one of the graves traces of a reed shroud reminiscent of similar burials in Sumer in the Early Dynastic period (*c*. 2800 B.C.),[33] suggesting a possible link with the Mesopotamian cult of the dead.

In the post-Harappan Cemetery H to the south of the citadel, the alleged mythological scenes depicting the journey of the soul to the next life, as described in the Rig-veda, painted as a frieze on a mortuary vat[34] might have a Vedic significance. The fate of the dead, however, in the early texts is very obscure, and in any case the paintings at Harappa are too late to be of much help in the elucidation of the prehistoric beliefs. Both cremation and inhumation were practised by the Indo-European invaders in the second millennium B.C.[35] and as the ashes were buried after incineration, interment probably was the original mode of disposal, though eventually cremation became the dominant rite in India. But at first it was to Mother-earth that the dead were committed and covered by her "as a mother wraps her skirt about her child". There they remained until they embarked on their journey across the rivers to the land of Yama, the king of the dead and the ruler of the abode of bliss, or wherever they might be destined to dwell ultimately. That cremation came to play some part in the process is suggested by the reference in the Rig-veda to the appeal to Agni, the fire-god, in a funeral hymn to bring the deceased to maturity and send him on his way to the Fathers but not consume him.[36]

The Mediterranean

In its western extension the cult of the dead increasingly came under the influence of that of the Mother-goddess in and after the Chalcolithic period, when her emblems are of frequent occurrence in the tombs and in the mortuary ritual. Burial in the contracted position was prevalent, and collective interment in tholoi was widely adopted in the Eastern Mediterranean, while rock-cut and chamber-tombs abounded in the Iberian megalithic region in the west. In Crete the vaulted tombs never reached the height of magnificence attained on the mainland by the great Mycenaean beehives, like the Treasury of Atreus at Mycenae and the Treasury of Munyas at Orchomenos. The Minoan funerary ritual appears to have been relatively simple, consisting in placing the body in the burial chamber unburnt, though fires were lighted in the tholoi for some ceremonial purpose and the offerings deposited in annexes to the circular tombs, unless they were votive deposits rather than offerings made at the time of the funeral. Sometimes libations were poured within a special enclosure, and at Knossos in the Tomb of the Double Axes vessels had been placed before a sacred pillar against the inner wall, evidently as an offering to the Minoan Mother-goddess on behalf of the dead.[37]

The scenes on the Late Minoan sarcophagus from Hagia Triada are very difficult to interpret, but, as has been pointed out,[38] they appear to have some relation to the Goddess cult in its funerary setting, connected probably with the journey of the soul to its final abode, and possibly with its deification. Dr Paribeni compares the figure with open eyes standing before a building, said to be a tomb, with the "Opening of the Mouth" ceremony in Egypt,[39] though there are no indications that actually it was a mummy. The scenes, he thinks, represent a series of episodes derived from the mortuary ritual and the current beliefs respecting the human destiny depicted to gain for the deceased the assistance of the gods in his transition to the next life. Sir Arthur Evans, however, regards the sacrificial scenes as the means whereby the dead hero was summoned back temporarily to the land of the living and the divinity charmed down into its material resting-place by the offerings and with the aid of music and ritual chants and the sacred symbols of the Minoan Goddess.[40] Miss Jane Harrison and Dr Petersen, on the other hand, interpret the picture in terms of the seasonal cycle myth and ritual.[41] But as the scenes decorate a tomb, the natural conclusion is that they had reference to the cult of the dead in the first instance, whatever secondary and subsidiary purposes they may have served. That they are of a composite character is suggested by the symbolism with its double axes, horns of consecration, imagery of bulls, sacred trees and pillars, votive boat, griffins, a hide-dress and the sacrificial scene. A combination of a mortuary ritual with the worship of the Minoan Goddess is indicated, coupled with the cult of the Double Axe as depicted on the walls of the palace at Knossos. Thus, Nilsson has been led to suppose that in Late Minoan times the dead were deified and worshipped in the form of a divine cult, perhaps under Egyptian influence. Therefore, he regards the scenes not as those of funeral ceremonies but of acts of worship consequent upon apotheosis when the deceased hero had been transported by griffins and accompanied by goddesses to the realms of the gods and there deified,[42] like the Roman emperors who were thought to be carried to the divine world on the back of an eagle.

The griffins, however, on the Ring of Nestor are associated with the Goddess seated in front of her companion and with tokens of her life-giving powers, representing apparently a rite of initiation into the halls of the blest in the underworld over which she presided.[43] And in Greece heroes were denizens of the nether regions however mighty and venerated they might be. But a composite cult along the lines indicated by Nilsson need not be incompatible with the conception of the illustrious dead acquiring from the Goddess a derived divine sanctity and exerting a beneficent influence with the deity on behalf of the living, and, therefore, the object of worship and the recipient of offerings in their magnificent tombs. In Malta, for instance, Evans has suggested that the baetylic worship in the megalithic sanctuaries of Hagiar Kim and Gigantea, in which the hero was represented by a pillar, developed out of the cult of the dead.[44] While the side-chambers in which it is alleged to have occurred may not have been dolmens in which deified heroes were buried, the worship may nevertheless have originated in a cult of the illustrious dead.

Western Europe

The baetylic tradition recurred in Minorca and in the great Spanish megalithic sepulchral structures at Los Millares, while the numerous stylized figurines, plaques and "idols" in Almerian and Portuguese graves show that the Mother-goddess continued to play a prominent part in the mortuary ritual, specially in the south-west of the peninsula and in the Balearic islands. In France the juxtaposition of the Goddess cult with that of the Axe was of frequent occurrence as it was in the Aegean, Sicily, Malta and the Iberian region. In Western Europe, Brittany, being one of the principal centres of religious activity, attracted apparently many "pilgrims" to worship at the megalithic sanctuaries, and perhaps to bring the remains of their powerful chiefs and venerated heroes to be interred within their sacred precincts. Thus, in addition to the vast array of dolmens and passage-tombs in Morbihan and the surrounding district, the alignments of menhirs at Carnac, covering 2,800 metres and divided into three distinct groups—the Field of Ménec with a cromlech to the north of the village, the Field of Kermario, and the Field of Kerlescan at the west also having a stone circle with rounded corners—and those of S. Pierre, Quiberon, are orientated in relation to the solstices. Therefore, they may have constituted the meeting-places for seasonal gatherings; those at Ménec and Quiberon for the celebration of the midsummer rites, and those at Kermario for the equinoxial ceremonies in the spring and autumn. But as the alignments so often end in tumuli (e.g. at Carnac, Mané-er-Hroeck, Locmariaquer, Clud-er-Yer and Kergo) they appear to have had a funerary origin and significance in which the worship of the dead was a conspicuous feature.

The construction, orientation and equipment of the sepulchral monuments in this area indicate a highly developed cult of the dead. This is clear from great dolmens like the Table des Marchands at Locmariaquer, or corridor-tombs such as that

on the island of Gavr'inis, Morbihan, covered by a tumulus
nearly 200 feet in diameter, the circular chamber 6 feet high
roofed by a huge block measuring 13 by 10 feet, approached
by a corridor 40 feet long, and having no less than twenty-two
upright blocks covered with engraved symbolic cult designs.
Sometimes, as at Mont S. Michel, the central burial chamber
was covered with a huge artificial mound, while at Calvados
no less than twelve circular corbelled chambers, each with its
own entrance passage, were concealed beneath a mound. As
in the case of the Palaeolithic decorated caves, it is only a very
profound religious motive that can explain either the sanctuaries
or tombs of this character and of these proportions.

This is confirmed by the contents of these megalithic tumuli
which include, besides necklace beads and the usual trinkets,
fine stone celts pierced at one end for amuletic uses and giving
every appearance of having been votive axes placed beside the
burial, perhaps as the emblem of or offering to the tutelary
spirit to whom the tomb was consecrated unless they were for
the benefit of the deceased in the next life. The bones of horse
and oxen in some of the monuments, and what seem to be the
bones or ashes of slaves and servants near by, suggest that both
animal and human sacrifices on occasions formed part of the
obsequies of chiefs and rulers in this region. Ritual urns
ornamented with sacred designs often have been ceremonially
broken, and show traces of incineration as if used for cooking
purposes. But the normal mode of disposal of the dead among
the megalithic folk being inhumation, cremation was only
adopted sporadically (e.g. in Finistère, Marne and Aisne)
doubtless as a result of a secondary intrusion from Central
Europe. Whether or not the contracted position, which was
freely adopted, had at this stage in cultural development any
reference to that of the embryo before birth and the idea of
rebirth beyond the grave, we do not know.

In the Early Bronze Age, as we have seen,[45] secondary
interment of cremations, sometimes later than the primary
inhumations, frequently occurred. When they are of the same
period as the original interments they may represent human

victims sacrificed at the death of a chieftain, but although this is a well-attested practice, especially in Mesopotamia as has been demonstrated, it has to be accepted with caution. When bones, burnt or unburnt, have been intentionally broken, as, for example, in the Cotswold Long Barrows in Britain, a ritual motive is indicated,[46] and when these are found in great tombs in association with a "royal" burial equipment the presumption is that they originally had a sacrificial significance, especially if the sepulchre was sealed at the end of the obsequies. Hemp has argued in favour of large rock-cut tombs having been monuments of individuals closed after the interment, which had included the sacrifice of relatives and servants, and were subsequently used by the deceased's descendants until eventually they became a tribal tomb.[47] In chamber-tombs, however, successive burial has been extensively practised, and the considerable number of skeletons in them (e.g. at Mesara in Crete, and Västergötaland and Troldhöj in Zealand, and Pant y Saer and Tinkinswood in Britain), ranging from a hundred to fifty bodies, is unquestionably the result of their having been used as ossuaries for several generations. The chaotic disorder in most of them is due to the older contents of the tomb having been disturbed by later additions of fresh burials or bones, sometimes after burial or exposure elsewhere.[48]

This doubtless explains some of the fragmentary and fractional burials which recur from the Indus valley to Britain. Thus, at the Pole's Wood South Barrow in Gloucestershire the rifling and destruction were most conspicuous, nine or ten skeletons having been packed away in a chamber measuring by 4 feet. In the entrance, however, one skeleton was in almost perfect condition. This suggests that the fragmentary state of the rest was the result of re-burial, and Crawford thinks that "the perfect skeleton in the entrance passage suggests the immolation of a victim",[49] a practice in his opinion that may have been in vogue also at Belas Knap. But if successive burial was practised it may have been merely the last addition to the ossuary, the bones of the rest having been broken either accidentally in re-interment, or intentionally for ritual purposes.

Against this, as Dr Daniel points out, is the fractional conditio
of some of the bones.[50]

What is clear, as he says, is that when skeletal and artifactu;
material is heaped up outside the passage-tomb, as in th
Scandinavian examples,[51] there must have been successiv
burial, and in Britain most of the chambers were collectiv
graves of this kind. It may also be agreed that intention;
breaking of the bones requires a ritual explanation, as do
fractional burial; even granting, as Keiller, Alexander an
Piggott have argued, that it could have been caused in son
instances by the seeping of water through part of the filling
the grave.[52] But whatever may have been the precise mode
disposal, the obsequies must have entailed an elabora
ceremonial involving a funeral feast, the equipment of the dea
with an adequate supply of grave-goods, sometimes includin
animal or human victims, to facilitate the journey to the ne;
life and to make every provision and comfort for the well-bein
of the deceased, and to guard against his return to molest th
living. These were the primary purposes and functions
the cult of the dead in prehistoric times.

THE SKY-RELIGION

The Celestial After-life

The widespread adoption of cremation in the Middle Bronz
Age was indirectly if not directly associated with an orientatio
in the conception of the hereafter in a celestial direction. It
true that the practice was only gradually adopted side by sic
with that of inhumation, often in the form of partial inciner;
tion. Nevertheless, once it was established and had become th
dominant mode of disposal of the dead, especially in Centr
and Northern Europe as an intrusion from the Near East,
could hardly fail to influence the conception of the location an
nature of the after-life and that of the constitution of man as
duality of body and soul. Moreover, as it coincided with th
development of the Sky-religion the way was open for a le
materialistic interpretation of the idea of immortality in tern
of the return of the soul or ghost to the spirit-world in th

smoke of its physical integument.[53] Here, however, extreme caution is needed in assuming a correlation between this mode of disposal of the body and an underlying belief about the destiny of the soul.

At death, it seems, the human organism was thought to undergo a process of dissolution in which the body lost its animating principle associated with the breath, blood and its mental and psychical attributes and functions. Ritual reanimation was an attempt to restore these vital elements, coupled sometimes with the preservation of the bones or the mummification of the corpse. What survived, or then came into being, was an independent shadowy entity—the shade or ghost—as a reflection or replica of the living person, which carried on an independent existence either in the grave or in the spirit-world, unless it returned to earth to be reborn in another body.

If in the first instance the Mother-goddess was the producer of life *par excellence*, when the dead were interred in "mother-earth" doubtless it appeared that they were returning whence they came. But in the background stood the obscure figure of the transcendent Supreme Being in the sky who as the Creator became the begetter, breathing into man the breath of life and, in union with the Earth-mother and personification of birth and generation, bestowing upon man and nature their fecundity. As a consequence, since, when the life left the body, it was frequently supposed to go back to the god from whom it came, in the Sky-religion normally it was to the celestial realms that it returned at death. Cremation was calculated to facilitate this transition, though the correlation of the practice with the belief in a heavenly hereafter is too sporadic to indicate that the one was dependent upon the other.

As an ancient funeral custom cremation was sometimes associated with the notion of a continued life in the grave or in the nether regions, as in Greece when after the Minoan-Mycenaean period it was introduced by the Dorians without any very marked change regarding the after-life for ordinary mortals. Nevertheless, it does appear to have been connected with a less concrete conception of the future life and of the grave as an "everlasting tomb" by placing the emphasis on the liberation of the human spirit, and of the immortal element even in the grave-goods, and so to have stressed the idea of a spiritual existence independent of a material matrix. Moreover, it frequent adoption as the mode of disposal of rulers, heroes and the more distinguished dead suggests that it was often related to an abode reserved for the privileged section of the community, and this tended to be located in the divine celestial realms

The Concept of the Universal Sky-god

The supreme God in the sky being the highest expression and evaluation of Deity, everything that was "above" was naturall associated with him, from celestial phenomena and spirits of the air to kings, chieftains and rulers on earth. But while he was, therefore, liable to become remote and detached from the world and its affairs, he was none the less as all-encompassing —like the sky itself, the air and the wind "blowing where it listeth", with which often he has been associated—as he was all-powerful and all-seeing. Consequently, although the archaeological evidence is very meagre prior to the rise of civilization, the idea of the Sky-god as the universal spirit becomes such a basic assumption that it has every appearance of having been one of the fundamental religious concepts of mankind.

In any case, once the Sky-religion was an established cult, was the celestial deity who was the Supreme Being responsible for sending rain and giving fertility to the soil (often in conjunction with the Mother-goddess) prior to the advent of the Sun-god with whom he became identified, or by whom he was obscured and even transplanted, as in Egypt. To meet all the requirements of such a celestial deity he was surrounded with a glorious company of gods and spirits with their sacred avocations in relation to the divine ordering of all things in heaven and on earth. Looked at from one angle he could be regarded as "monotheistic" in the sense of being wholly supreme and transcendent in his own domain and in respect of his divine attributes and functions. Conversely, the system could be described as polytheistic and animistic inasmuch as gods many and lords many unquestionably existed and played their allotted roles in the pantheon and in natural phenomena and human society, either for weal or for woe.

Under prehistoric conditions there are no indications that at any time or place, or in any cultural level, one single all-supreme Deity was believed to have existed to the exclusion of all other divine beings. That conception of monotheism is the prerogative of the higher religions (Zoroastrianism, Judaism, Christianity and Islam), but it has not evolved from polytheism or animism in the manner formerly supposed. Each and all of these different expressions of theistic faith and practice have arisen apparently within their own proper contexts and conditions, and at particular levels of thought and evaluation. Having coexisted for their specific purposes and functions they represent degrees of spiritual penetration and experience of the numinous, and different reactions to supernatural effects and relations in the phenomenal world, determined very largely by the religious and cultural environment and the social structure in which they function.

Thus, the Sky-religion cannot be assigned to any one phase or condition of religious development, monotheistic, polytheistic or animistic; or indeed to any type of society or geographical region. It has been a recurrent phenomenon, and, as we have seen,[54] to fulfil the needs of mankind it was brought into relation not only with the solar cult but also with that of the Earth-gods and goddesses. In this way the beneficence of the celestial realms was made accessible on earth providing fruitful seasons, destroying the forces of evil and giving immortal life to the dead. But notwithstanding this syncretism, the Sky-god in his own right normally was regarded as the ultimate source of the plenitude of divine power, omniscience and wisdom, even though the Sun-god was sometimes raised to the dignity of the Supreme Being, as, for example, by Ikhnaton in Egypt, among the Inca in Peru, and some of the Algonquian tribes in North America. Usually, however, he was originally in a subordinate position like Shamash in Mesopotamia, or Marti in the Vedic pantheon, where Dyaus Pitar held pre-eminence as the Sky-father and personification of the heavens, the giver of the fructifying rain to water the earth, until gradually he was displaced, first by the all-encompassing Varuna and then by the Vedic nature gods and goddesses. Later, after Varuna in conjunction with Rta had been resolved into a monistic unity as the universal cosmic and moral order immanent in all phenomena, and the neuter Brahman emerged as the Absolute, the ancient gods of the sky and of the earth were retained as the aspects and attributes of the One Ultimate Reality of universal Being.

In Iran, Zarathushtra having transformed and sublimated the ancient chief god of the vault of heaven into the All-wise Lord Ahura Mazda, and firmly established him as the one and only God of all the earth, he made the earlier polytheistic *daevas* and *ahuras* modalities of divine activity in the perennial struggle between good and evil, light and darkness. In so doing, he raised the prehistoric Sky-god Varuna, brought into relation with the celestial Mitra under the guise of Ahura Mazda, to the level of a genuine ethical monotheistic deity, comparable to Yahweh in post-exilic Judaism. Both of the ancient gods who lie behind the All-wise Lord of the Avesta were heavenly beings representing the all-encompassing sky in its complementary aspects, nocturnal and diurnal. Although Mitra was not the sun, as is clearly maintained in the Avesta,[55] his celestial origins and connexions with the light opened the way for him to acquire solar attributes and functions until in the Mithraic mystery cult the identification became complete. Therefore, Ahura Mazda before his transformation by Zarathushtra had behind him a long history going back to its prehistoric antecedents in the Sky tradition.

The universal Sky-god, in fact, in his divers forms and functions and syncretisms lies at the base of all the higher religions of the Orient and the Mediterranean deeply laid in their prehistoric foundations. Yahweh, the god of the sacred mountain whose voice was heard in the thunder, appears to have been a Western Semitic deity, Ya, or Yami, or Yahu, with celestial affinities before he became the consolidating centre of the Hebrew tribes, and eventually, under prophetic influence, the Creator of the universe and the Lord of history and of nature, controlling all things in accordance with his righteous will and purposes. Zeus, although a composite figure in the Olympian religion, was originally the prehistoric sky- and weather-god like Varuna and Ahura Mazda, long before he became the head of the mountain pantheon in Thessaly and then "the father of gods and men". In Crete, as we have seen,[56] he was brought into relation with the Minoan Goddess as the son of Rhea. In this capacity he was a more primitive figure than the Indo-European Sky-god, being concerned with the renewal of vegetation as a fertility deity. As the giver of fruitfulness and the divine farmer ($\gamma\varepsilon\omega\varrho\gamma\acute{o}\varsigma$) he was the vitalizing power in the soil ($\chi\theta\acuteo\nu\iota o\delta$). In fact, so close was his relationship with the Corn-goddess Demeter that he became virtually a chthonic god in his agricultural aspects.[57] But so comprehensive was his role that all natural phenomena fell within his domain. This universality of Zeus, which finds its roots in his celestial origins and control of the weather, is an indication of his fundamental nature as the Sky-god *par excellence* which could never be obliterated in the religious consciousness of the Greeks, notwithstanding his endless transformations and syncretisms.

The antiquity of this concept of the universal Sky-god going back to prehistoric times can be explained no doubt by a general inclination everywhere to look to the heavens as a seat of supernatural power. Therefore, the various aspects of celestial phenomena—the sky and its constellations, the sun, the moon, the air, the wind and the clouds—have acquired their places and functions in the ever-increasing pantheon of heavenly divine beings, together with their vital and arresting manifestations in the rain, the storm, the thunder and the tempest; beneficent or destructive, awe-inspiring or terrorizing.

Thus, in Egypt the four pairs of gods representing pre-cosmic disorder stood over against the Heliopolitan Ennead of cosmic order—the air and moisture, the sky and the earth, in their male and female forms—grouped round the self-created Sun-god Atum. From the union of Geb and Nut, the Earth and the Sky, Osiris and Isis, and Seth and Nephthys, were born; the posthumous son of Isis, Horus, being destined to engage in mortal combat with his Uncle Seth. Here the conflict in prehistoric times between the northern Horus invaders of the southern valley of the Nile and the indigenous inhabitants who were Seth worshippers may have been interpreted in terms of a more fundamental cosmic struggle in which the forces of "good" and "evil" were opposed, Horus and Seth playing the roles assigned to the Sky-god and the Storm-god in earlier cosmogonies.

Since the Supreme Being in the sky invariably has been regarded as the ultimate source of beneficence, sending the fructifying rain to fertilize the earth and bestowing upon mankind life and sustenance, very seldom has he been held responsible for malign and destructive influences. Nevertheless, while the archaeological evidence suggests that his primary function was the conservation and promotion of life and general well-being, often effected through his sacred marriage with the Earth-goddess, this aspect of the Sky-religion was only one of many manifestations of celestial divine power in connexion with natural phenomena. Thus, meteorites, thunder and lightning, constellations, sacred mountains and certain animals, rainbows, translucent stones, menhirs, and many other similar objects, have been emblems and expressions of the Sky-god in his manifold representations, attributes and functions, iconic and aniconic, in prehistoric religion.

Map showing the principal groups of painted caves and other Palaeolithic sites in France and northern Spain

262

Map showing Neolithic and Bronze Age cultures in Europe and the Near East

Anau

Hissar

SIALK CULTURES

Caspian Sea

Arpachiyah

Kurdistan Mts.

Susa

Uruk

Halaf Hassuna

Ur

Ras Shamra

FATTYANOVO CULTURE

STEPPE CULTURE

KUBAN CULTURE

Caucasus Mts.

Mersin

BATTLE AXE WARRIORS

Don

Tigris

Euphrates

Black Sea

TRIPOLYE CULTURE

Anatolia

Cyprus

NORTHERN CULTURES

Galicia

Carpathians

Iron Gates

Troy

DWELLING-PLACE CULTURES

BATTLE AXE WARRIORS

Moravia

DANUBIAN CULTURE

Vinca

Macedonia

CYCLADES

CISTS

Bohemia

Danube

Thessaly

Crete (MINOAN)

BEAKERS & FOOD-VESSELS

Mycenae

NEOLITHIC A & B

RÖSSEN CULTURE

Rhine

Alps

SICULAN

BEAKER & WINDMILL HILL CULTURES

S.O.M.

Rhône

TERRAMARE

Malta

Loire

Morbihan

Carnac

Dordogne

Sardinia

Pyrenees

Balearic Is.

Galicia

BELL BEAKERS

Palmella

ALMERIAN CULTURE

Algarve

Los Millares

Miles

0   500

•• Megalithic Culture

NOTES

CHAPTER I

1. Black, Teilhard du Chardin, Young, Pei, *Fossil Man in China*, Peiping, 1933, pp. 5 ff., 60.
2. *Dating the Past*, 3rd ed., 1953, pp. 274 ff.
3. D. Black, *Palaeotologia Sinica*, vol. ii, 1927, pp. 1 ff.; *Fossil Man in China*, pp. 83 ff.; Koenigswald, *Nature*, vol. cxliv, 1939, pp. 926 ff.; Weidernreich, *op. cit.*, vol. cxliii, 1938, p. 715.
4. J. H. Hutton, *J.R.A.I.*, vol. lviii, 1928, pp. 403 ff.; Hose and McDougall, *The Pagan Tribes of Borneo*, vol. i, 1912, pp. 114 f.; vol. ii, pp. 20 ff.; H. I. Marshall, *The Karen People of Borneo*, Ohio, 1922, p. 222.
5. Obermaier, *Fossil Man in Spain*, 1925, pp. 136 f., 339; P. Wernert, *Histoire Générale de Religion*, vol. i, p. 56.
6. Oppenoorth, *Early Man*, ed. MacCurdy, Philadephia, 1937, pp. 349 ff.
7. Breuil and Obermaier, *L'Anthropologie*, vol. xx, 1909, p. 523.
8. K. Gorjanovic-Kramberger, *Mittheilungen der Anthropologischer Gesellschaft in Wien*, vol. xxii, 1902, p. 189; vol. xxiv, 1904, pp. 187 f.
9. R. R. Schmidt, *Die diluviale Vorzeit Deutschlands*, Stuttgart, 1912.
10. Treat and Couturier, *L'Anthrop.*, vol. xxxviii, p. 235; Vernert, *op. cit.*, p. 65.
11. Kinyar, *Antiquity*, vol. xxvii, 1953, pp. 105 f.
12. O. Menghin, *Wienerprähistorische Zeitschrift*, vol. xiii, 1926, pp. 14 ff.; Wernert, *op. cit.*, p. 58.
13. Hauser, *Archiv. für Anthropologie*, vol. vii, 1909, p. 290.
14. Boule, *Annales de paléontologie*, 1911–13; A. and J. Bouyssonie and L. Bardon, *L'Anthrop.*, vol. xix, 1908, p. 513.
15. *L'Anthrop.*, 1913, pp. 616 ff.
16. Breuil, *L'Anthrop.*, vol. xxxi, 1921, pp. 343 ff.
17. Verneau, *Les Grottes de Grimaldi*, vol. ii, Monaco, 1906, pp. 23, 260, 277 ff.
18. Keith, *The Antiquity of Man*, vol. i, 1929, p. 99.
19. C. L. de Villeneuve, *Les Grottes de Grimaldi*, vol. i, p. 64; vol. ii, pl. ii; *L'Anthrop.*, vol. xiii, 1902, p. 561.
20. *Grimaldi*, vol. ii, pp. 298 ff.
21. *Op. cit.*, pp. 33, 298, fig. 4, p. 12.
22. Sollas, *J.R.A.I.*, vol. xliii, 1913, pp. 325 ff.
23. Obermaier, *Der Mensch der Vorzeit*, p. 298; Breuil, *L'Anthrop.*, 1924, pp. 549 ff.
24. L. Testut, *Bulletin de la société d'anthrop. de Lyon*, vol. viii, 1889; *L'Anthrop.*, vol. i, 1890, p. 716; Hardy, *La station quarternaire de Raymonden*, Paris, 1891, pp. 49 ff.; Sollas, *Ancient Hunters*, 1915, pp. 485 ff.
25. A. Arcelin, *L'Anthrop.*, vol. i, 1890, pp. 307 ff.

26. *Textbook of European Archaeology*, Cambridge, 1921, p. 502.

27. J. W. Jackson, *Shells as Evidence of the Migrations of Early Culture*, Manchester, 1917, pp. 138 ff.

28. *Comptes-Rendus de l'Acad. des Sciences*, vol. lxxiv, 1872, pp. 1060 f.

29. M. and St J. Péquart, *Arch. de l'Inst. de la Pal. Hum. Mémoires*, 19, 1937.

30. Mendes Correa, *Congrès Internat. d'anthrop. et d'archéol. préhistorique*, Paris, 1931, p. 362; Obermaier, *Fossil Man in Spain*, 1925, p. 324.

31. P. R. de Azua, *Bol. de la Soc. Española de hist. Nat.*, December 1918; cf. Burkitt, *Our Early Ancestors*, Cambridge, 1926, p. 22.

32. Dupont, *Mémoires de l'Academie royale des Sciences, des Lettres, et des Beaux-arts Belgiques*, vol. xix, 1867, pp. 1 ff.

33. E. Piette, *L'Anthrop.*, vol. vi, 1895, pp. 276 ff.; Zaborowsky, *Bull. et Mém. Soc. Anthrop. de Paris*, series v, vol. vii, 1906, p. 416.

34. Cf. *Fra Nationalmuseums Arbejdsmark*, 1945, p. 6.

35. Nordman, *Finskt Museum*, 4, 1929; *Acta Arch.*, vol. ii, p. 2651; Curwen, *Antiquity*, vol. xii, 1938, pp. 146 ff.

36. Childe, *Antiquity*, vol. xxiii, 1949, pp. 129 ff.

37. *A.A.*, N.S. vol. xxxiii, 1930, p. 39.

CHAPTER II

1. Brunton, *Mostagedda*, 1937, pp. 5 f., 7 f., 25 ff.

2. Baumgärtel, *The Cultures of Prehistoric Egypt*, Oxford, 1955, p. 20.

3. Brunton and Caton-Thompson, *The Badarian Civilization*, 1928, p. 18.

4. *Op. cit.*, pp. 181 ff.; Brunton, *Mostagedda*, pp. 26 ff.; Baumgärtel, *op. cit.*, pp. 21 ff.

5. *Mostagedda*, pp. 71 ff.

6. Cf. Caton-Thompson and E. W. Gardner, *The Desert Fayum*, 1934, p. 90.

7. J. E. Quibell and F. W. Green, *Hierakonpolis*, vol. ii, 1902, pp. 20 ff.; H. J. Kantor, *J.N.E.S.*, vol. iii, 1944, pp. 110 ff.

8. Breasted, *Religion and Thought in Ancient Egypt*, 1914, pp. 100 f.

9. Cf. Petrie, *The Royal Tombs of the First Dynasty*, 1900, pp. 8 ff.; *Abydos*, vol. i, 1902; vol. ii, 1903.

10. Petrie, *Pyramids and Temples at Gizeh*, 1885; C. M. Firth and J. E. Quibell, *The Step Pyramid*, 1936.

11. Watelin, *Kish*, vol. iv, Paris, 1934, pp. 17 ff.

12. Woolley, *The Sumerians*, Oxford, 1929, p. 36.

13. Seton Lloyd and Fuad Safar, *J.N.E.S.*, vol. iv; October 1945, pp. 267 f., figs. 17, 27, pl. iii, 1, 2, 3; A. L. Perkins, *The Comparative Archaeology of Early Mesopotamia*, Chicago, 1949, p. 5.

14. Perkins, *op. cit.*; E. E. Herzfeld, *Archaeologische Mitteilungen aus Iran*, vol. v, 1935, p. 29.

15. Tobler, *The Excavations at Tepe Gawra*, vol. ii, 1950, pp. 105, 124.

16. Cf. E. A. Speiser, *The Excavations at Tepe Gawra*, vol. i, Philadelphia, 1935, p. 177; Tobler, vol. ii, 1950, pp. 51 ff.

17. Perkins, *op. cit.*, pp. 22, 42.

18. Woolley, *The Antiquaries Journal*, vol. x, 1930, pl. xliv (a); Speiser, *Smith. Report*, 1939, p. 444.

19. Mallowan and C. Rose, *Iraq*, vol. ii, 1933, pp. 34 ff.; Perkins, *op. cit.*, pp. 74, 81.

20. *New Light on the Most Ancient East*, 1952, p. 115.

21. Lloyd and Safar, *Sumer*, vol. iv, no. 11, 1948, pp. 117 f.

22. Woolley, *The Antiquaries Journal*, vol. x, October 1930, pp. 327 ff.; cf. *Ur Excavations*, vol. ii, 1934, pp. 35 ff.

23. *Excavations at Ur*, 1954, pp. 16 ff.; *Ur of the Chaldees*, 1950, pp. 29, 68.

24. *Ur Excavations*, vol. ii, 1934, pp. 33 ff.; *Ur of the Chaldees*, pp. 35 ff.; cf. Parrot, *Syria*, vol. xviii, 1937, p. 60.

25. Woolley, *Ur Excavations*, vol. ii, pp. 33 ff.

26. *Op. cit.*, p. 51.

27. Cf. Jacobsen, *The Sumerian King List*, Chicago, 1939, p. 58.

28. *Mémoires de la Mission Archéologique en Iran*, vol. xxx, Paris, 1947, pp. 177 ff.

29. D. E. McCown, *The Comparative Stratigraphy of Early Iran*, Chicago, 1942, pp. 43 ff.

30. *Mémoires*, vol. xxix, 1943, pp. 5 ff.

31. R. de Mecquenem, *Fouilles préhistoriques en Asie occidentale*, 1934, p. 190; *L'Anthrop.*, vol. xlviii, 1938, pp. 67 ff.

32. E. Pottier, *Délégation en Perse, Mémoires*, vol. xiii, 1912, fig. 168, pl. xxx, 7.

33. De Mecquenem, *Mémoires*, vol. xxv, 1934, figs. 60, 3, 12; 61, 1; 62, 1–2.

34. Piggott, *Antiquity*, vol. xvii, 1943, pp. 162 ff.; *Ancient India*, no. i, 1946, pp. 8–26; no. iv, 1948, pp. 162 ff.

35. Piggott, *Prehistoric India*, 1950, pp. 72 ff.; *Ancient India*, no. 1, 1946, pp. 8 ff.; no. 3, 1947, pp. 113 ff.

36. *Annual Survey of India*, 1904–5, p. 105, pl. xxxiii, xxxiv.

37. H. Hargreaves, *Excavations in Baluchistan*, 1925; *Memoirs Arch. Survey of India*, no. 35, Calcutta, 1929, pp. 17 ff.

38. Mockler, *J.R.A.S.*, vol. ix, 1877, pp. 121 ff.

39. E. J. H. Mackay, *Further Excavations at Mohenjo-daro*, vol. i, 1938, pp. 116 ff., 615, 648 ff.

40. *Op. cit.*, p. 117.

41. Marshall, *Mohenjo-daro and the Indus Civilization*, vol. i, 1931, pp. 79 ff.

42. Mackay, *op. cit.*, pp. 94 f.

43. Mackay, *Chanhu-daro Excavations*, New Haven, 1943, pp. 137 ff.

44. Vats, *Excavations at Harappa*, vol. i, 1940, pp. 198 ff.

45. *Op. cit.*, p. 161 f.

46. *The Cambridge History of India*, "The Indus Civilization", Cambridge, 1953, pp. 24 f.

47. Cf. p. 53.

48. Wheeler, *op. cit.*, pp. 48 f.; *Ancient India*, no. 3, 1947, pp. 85 ff.

49. Vats, *op. cit.*, vol. i, pp. 203 ff.

50. R. E. M. Wheeler, *Ancient India*, no. 3, 1947, pp. 76 ff.; *Cambridge History of India*, 1954, pp. 23, 33.

CHAPTER III

1. Cf. chap. ii, pp. 46 f.

2. Dikaios, *Syria*, 1932, pp. 345 ff.

3. Dikaios, *Iraq*, vol. vii, 1940, pp. 72 ff.

4. *Op. cit.*, pp. 77 ff.

5. Dikaios, *Archaeologia*, vol. lxxxviii, 1938, pp. 4 ff., 95 ff.

6. S. Xanthoudides, *The Vaulted Tombs of Mesara*, 1924, pp. 4 ff.

7. Petrie, *Royal Tombs*, vol. i, p. 18; vol. ii, p. 38.

8. Evans, *The Palace of Minos*, vol. i, 1921, pp. 125 ff.; vol. ii, p. 45.

9. R. B. Seager, *Explorations in Mochlos*, Boston, 1912, pp. 13 ff.; *The Cemetery of Pachyammos*, Crete, Univ. of Penn. Anthrop. Pub. VII, no. 1, Philadelphia, 1916, pp. 9 ff.

10. C. C. Edgar, *B.S.A.*, vol. iii, 1896, pp. 35 ff.

11. Cf. Bent, *J.H.S.*, vol. v, 1884, pp. 48 ff.

12. C. C. Edgar, *Excavations at Phylakopi*, Society Hellenic Studies, no. 4, 1904, pp. 234 ff.

13. T. E. Peet, *The Stone and Bronze Ages in Italy and Sicily*, Oxford, 1909, pp. 223 ff.

14. F. von Duhn, *Italische Grabenkunde*, Heidelberg, 1924, pp. 71 ff.

15. *Op. cit.*, p. 76

16. D. Mackenzie, *British School of Rome*, vol. v, no. 2, 1910, pp. 101 ff.

17. *Op. cit.*, pp. 89 ff.

18. Pallottino, *La Sardegna nuragica*, 1950, pp. 29 ff., 41 f.

19. Hemp, *The Antiquaries Journal*, vol. xii, 1932, pp. 127 ff.

20. Hemp, *Archaeologia*, vol. lxxvi, 1927, pp. 121 ff.

21. *The Antiquaries Journal*, vol. xii, 1932, p. 134.

22. *Malta: Origini della civilta mediterranea*, Rome, 1934.

23. *Prehistoric Malta*, Oxford, 1930, p. 44.

24. Cf. Hawkes, *The Prehistoric Foundations of Europe*, pp. 153 f.

25. J. B. Ward-Perkins, *Antiquity*, vol. xvi, 1942, pp. 30 ff.

26. Zammit, *The Neolithic Temples at Hajar Kin and Mnaidra*, Valetta, 1927, pp. 9, 28.

27. Zammit, *Prehistoric Malta*, "The Tarxien Temples", Oxford, 1930, pp. 7 ff.

28. Zammit, *Antiquity*, 1930, p. 26.

29. *Op. cit.*, p. 17.

30. Chap. vi, pp. 166 f.

31. *The Antiquaries Journal*, vol. viii, 1928, p. 483.

32. L. Siret, *Revue préhistorique*, 1908, nos, 7, 8; *L'Anthrop.*, 1892, no. 4, pp. 391 ff.; Leisner, *Arqueologia e Historia*, vol. i, Lisbon, 1945, pp. 13 ff.; Siret, *Les premiers Ages du métal dans le sud-est de l'Espagne*, 1888.

33. Siret, *Revue des questions scientifiques*, Bruxelles, 1893, pp. 522 ff.

34. Leisner, *Die Megalithgräber der iberischen Halbinsel. i. Der Süden*, Berlin, 1943, pp. 59, 63, 73.

35. *Op. cit.*, pp. 174 ff.; C. de Mergelina, *Actas y Memorias Sociedad Española de Antropologia Etnografis y Prehistoria*, Madrid, 1921–2; Hemp, *The Antiquaries Journal*, vol. xiv, 1934, pp. 404 ff.

36. Siret, *Proceedings Congress Prehistoric and Protohistoric Sciences*, 1932, pp. 250 ff.; Obermaier, *El Dolmen de Matarrubilla Sevilla, Comisión de Investigaciones paleontológicas y prehistóricas*, Madrid, 1919, 21, no. 267.

37. Estacio de Veiga, *Antiguidades monumentaes do Algarve*, Lisbon, 1886–91, pp. 248 ff.; no. 3, p. 137.

38. *O Archaeologo Português*, vol. xii, Lisbon, 1907, pp. 210, 320; Cartailhac, *Les Ages préhistoriques de l'Espagne et du Portugal*, Paris, 1886, p. 119.

39. Cf. Hawkes, *The Prehistoric Foundations of Europe*, pp. 166 f., 169 ff.

40. Cf. Forde, *A.A.*, vol. xxxii, 1930, p. 39.

41. Cf. pp. 74 f.

42. Cf. Forde, *op. cit.*, pp. 70 ff.; Le Rouzic, *L'Anthrop.*, vol. xliii, 1933, pp. 233 ff.

43. Forde, *P.P.S.*, 1940, pp. 170 ff.; Piggott, *Antiquity*, 1937, pp. 441 ff.; Fleure, *Corridors of Time*, vol. vi, Oxford, 1929, pp. 81 ff.; *Arch. Camb.*, 1924, pp. 249.

44. *P.P.S.*, 1939, pp. 159 ff.; *The Antiquaries Journal*, vol. xix, 1939, pp. 157 ff.

45. Piggott, *op. cit.*, pp. 447 f.

46. Daniel, *P.P.S.*, 1939, pp. 161 ff.

47. Forde, *op. cit.*, pp. 77 f.

48. Le Rouzig, *L'Anthrop.*, vol. xliii, pp. 251 ff.

49. *Mém. Soc. académique d'Archéol. du Dép. de l'Oise*, vol. iv, Beauvais, 1860, p. 465; *Bulletin de la Société préhistorique française*, vol. viii, Paris, 1911, p. 669; Forde, *op. cit.*, pp. 63 ff.

50. E. C. Curwen, *Antiquity*, vol. iv, 1930, pp. 32 ff.; Piggott, *The Neolithic Cultures of the British Isles*, Cambridge, 1954, pp. 17 ff.

51. G. E. Daniel, *The Prehistoric Chamber Tombs of England and Wales*, Cambridge, 1950, pp. 38 ff.

52. Hawkes, *The Prehistoric Foundations of Europe*, pp. 175 ff.; Piggott, *op. cit.*, pp. 50 ff.

53. Hemp, *Trans. Bristol and Gloucester Archaeol. Society*, vol. li, 1929, pp. 261 ff.; Berry, *op. cit.*, vol. lii, 1930, pp. 123, 295; Crawford, *The Long Barrows of the Cotswolds*, Gloucester, 1925, pp. 67 ff.; Daniel, *op. cit.*, pp. 73 ff.

54. Cf. chap. i, pp. 18 ff.

55. J. Ward, *Archaeologia Cambrensis*, 1915, p. 79.

56. *Proceedings of the Cotteswold Naturalists Field Club*, vol. v, p. 340.

57. Hemp, *Archaeologia*, vol. 80, 1930, pp. 183 ff.; vol. 76, 1926, pp. 126, 128.

58. Hemp, *op. cit.*, vol. 85, 1935, p. 253.

59. Daniel, *Prehistoric Chamber Tombs of England and Wales*, p. 57; *Antiquity*, vol. xi, 1936, p. 190.

60. G. Coffey, *New Grange and other Incised Tumuli of Ireland*, 1912; T. G. E. Powell, *P.P.S.*, vol. iv, 1938, pp. 243 ff.

61. Macalister, *The Archaeology of Ireland*, 1928, p. 127.

62. Breuil and Macalister, *Proc. Royal Irish Academy*, vol. xxxvi, p. 1; Coffey, *Trans. R.I.A.*, vol. xxx, 1891, pp. 1 ff.

63. *The Antiquaries Journal*, vol. xiv, 1934, p. 204.

64. Powell, *P.P.S.*, vol. iv, 1938, pp. 239 ff.; Piggott, *Neolithic Cultures of the British Isles*, pp. 193 ff.

65. *Co. Louth Archaeological Journal*, vol. ix, 1939, pp. 1–18.

66. Breuil, *P.P.S.(A.)*, vol. vii, 1934, pp. 293 ff.

67. Childe, *Prehistoric Communities of the British Isles*, 1940, p. 53.

68. Childe, *The Prehistory of Scotland*, 1935, pp. 41 ff.

69. Cf. p. 87.

70. Childe, *The Prehistory of Scotland*, p. 34.

71. Cf. Crawford, *Ordinance Survey Professional Papers*, N.S., no. 8, p. 3; R. F. Jessup, *The Archaeology of Kent*, 1930, pp. 70 ff.; Daniel, *op. cit.*, pp. 80 f.

72. Piggott, *P.P.S.*, N.S., vol. i, 1935, p. 122.

73. Coon, *The Races of Europe*, New York, 1939, p. 111.

74. Daniel and Powell, *P.P.S.*, vol. xv, 1949, p. 178.

75. Chap. i, pp. 33 f.

76. Childe, *Antiquity*, vol. xxiii, 1949, p. 134.

77. The passage-grave at Karleby near Falköping has a chamber 16·65 metres long and a passage 12 metres in length.

78. Cf. C. A. Nordman, *Jaettestuer i Danmark nya fynd, Nordisker Fortisminder*, vol. ii, 1918, p. 118; H. Shetslig and Falk, *Scandinavian Archaeology*, E.T. by E. V. Gordon, Oxford, 1937, pp. 56 f.

79. Nordman, "Megalithic Culture in Northern Europe", *Suomen Muinais-muistohydistyksen Aikakauskirja*, Helsinki, 1935, xxxix, 3, p. 28.

80. Childe, *Dawn of Civilization*, pp. 162 f.

CHAPTER IV

1. Greenwell, *British Barrows*, 1878, pp. 506 f.

2. *Op. cit.*, p. 19.

3. Hogg, *P.P.S.*, vol. iv, 1938, pp. 335 f.

4. S. Rudder, *A New History of Gloucestershire*, 1779, p. 306.

5. J. R. Mortimer, *Forty Years' Researches in British and Saxon Burial Mounds of East Yorkshire*, 1905, pp. 298 ff.; cf. p. 240.

6. *Prehistoric Communities of the British Isles*, 1940, p. 63.

7. Cf. chap. v, p. 123.

8. J. F. S. Stone, *P.P.S.*, vol. xv, 1949, pp. 122 ff.

9. M. E. Cunnington, *Woodhenge*, Devizes, 1929, p. 88; Piggott, *Antiquity*, vol. x, 1936, pp. 221 f.

10. Piggott, *Aspects of Archaeology*, 1951, pp. 274 ff.

11. Piggott, *Antiquity*, vol. iv, 1938, pp. 58 ff.

12. Cf. R. C. C. Clay, *Wilts. Archaeological Magazine*, vol. xliv, 1928, p. 103; R. S. Newall, *op. cit.*, vol. xlv, 1931, pp. 432 ff.; Piggott, *Neolithic Cultures in Britain*, 1954, pp. 355 ff.; L. V. Grinsell, *Ancient Burial-Mounds of England*. 1953, pp. 17 ff.

13. Childe, *The Danube in Prehistory*, Oxford, 1929, p. 295.

14. Cf. Hawkes, *The Prehistoric Foundations of Europe*, pp. 343 f.

15. *Villanovans and Early Etruscans*, Oxford, 1924, pp. 5 ff., 267 f.

16. Pigorini, *Bulletina di Palalnologia Italiana*, vol. xxix, 1903, pp. 76, 169.

17. Childe, *The Bronze Age*, 1930, p. 202.

18. Childe, *op. cit.*, p. 204; Randall-MacIver, *op. cit.*, pp. 35 ff.

19. Gozzadini, *La nécropole de Villanova découverte et décrite*, Bologna, 1870, p. 14.

20. Childe, *Antiquity*, vol. ii, 1928, pp. 37 ff.

21. Childe, *The Danube in Prehistory*, p. 334.

22. Peake, *The Bronze Age and the Celtic World*, 1922, pp. 81 ff.

23. Hawkes, *P.P.S.*, vol. xiv, 1948, p. 199.

24. Woolley, *Annals of Archaeology and Anthropology*, vol. vi, Liverpool, 1914, pp. 95 ff.; *Antiquaries Journal*, vol. xviii, 1938, p. 4.

25. Childe, *P.P.S.*, vol. xiv, 1948, p. 183.

26. Cf. chap. v, pp. 122 f.

27. Cf. chap. v, pp. 123 f.

28. Elliot Smith, *The Migrations of Early Culture*, Manchester, 1915, pp. 32 ff.; Elliot Smith and W. R. Dawson, *Egyptian Mummies*, 1924, pp. 23 f., 73.

29. Quibell, *Report of Brit. Assoc.*, Dundee, 1912, p. 612.

30. Garstang, *Burial Customs of Ancient Egypt*, 1907, p. 30.

31. Petrie, *Medum*, 1892, pp. 17 ff.

32. Petrie, *Deshasheh*, 1898, p. 15.

33. *J.E.A.*, vol. i, 1914, pp. 252 f.

34. Cf. Blackman, *op. cit.*, vol. iii, 1916, pp. 253 f.

35. N. G. Davies and A. H. Gardiner, *The Tomb of Amenembet*, 1915, pp. 57 f.

36. Gardiner, *E.R.E.*, vol. viii, p. 23; Breasted, *Religion and Thought in Ancient Egypt*, p. 54.

37. Cf. chap. ii, pp. 40 f.

38. Sethe, *Urkunden*, vol. i, p. 114; *Palermo Stone*, vol. i, no. 3, p. 4.

39. Budge, *The Book of Opening the Mouth*, 1909, 2 vols.

40. Lepsius, *Denkmäler*, vol. ii, p. 4; *Pyramid Texts*, 1929, E.T. by Mercer, vol. iv, pp. 36ff.

41. Budge, *op. cit.*, vol. i, p. vii.

42. Blackman, *J.E.A.*, vol. xxi, 1935, pp. 6f.

43. *The Tomb of Amenemhet*, pp. 56ff.; Moret, *Le Rituel du Culte divin journalier en Egypte*, Paris, 1902, pp. 147ff.; Wilson, *J.N.E.S.*, Chicago, 1944, vol. iii, pp. 201ff.; Schiaparelli, *Il libro dei Funerali*, Turin, 1882–90, 3 vols.; Baly, *J.E.A.*, vol. xvi, 1930, pp. 176ff.; Blackman and Fairman, *op. cit.*, vol. xxxii, 1946, pp. 75ff. For a parallel rite in connexion with the statue of a god in Babylonia, cf. Blackman, *op. cit.*, vol. v, 1918, pp. 117ff.; vol. x, 1924, pp. 47ff.; S. Smith, *J.R.A.S.*, 1925, pp. 37ff.

44. Cf. W. R. Dawson, *J.E.A.*, vol. xiii, 1927, pp. 40ff.; *Egyptian Mummies*, 1924, pp. 45ff.; T. J. Pettigrew, *History of Egyptian Mummies*, 1834, pp. 44ff.

45. Wilson, *Journal of Near Eastern Studies*, 1944, pp. 201ff.; Davies, *The Tomb of Rekh-mi-Re at Thebes*, 1943, pp. 70ff.

CHAPTER V

1. *Het Animisme in der Indischen Archipel*, 1906, p. 372.

2. J. G. F. Riedel, *De Sluik en Kroeshaarige rassen tussehen Selebes en Papua*, 1886, pp. 410f., 460, 466.

3. Routledge, *The Mystery of Easter Island*, 1919, pp. 231f.

4. G. Brown, *Melanesians and Polynesians*, 1910, p. 396.

5. Codrington, *The Melanesians*, Oxford, 1891, p. 272.

6. Rivers, *History of Melanesian Society*, vol. ii, Cambridge, 1914, pp. 264ff., 530ff.; Seligman, *The Melanesians of British New Guinea*, Cambridge, 1910, pp. 715ff.; Codrington, *op. cit.*, p. 288, n. 1.

7. Cf. chap. i, pp. 17ff.

8. Cf. chap. iii, p. 75.

9. Codrington, *op. cit.*, pp. 261ff.

10. Riedel, *op. cit.*, p. 483.

11. Seligman, *op. cit.*, pp. 728f.

12. B. Spencer, *Wanderings in Wild Australia*, vol. ii, 1928, pp. 489ff.

13. H. Basedow, *The Australian Aboriginal*, 1925, p. 214.

14. J. Dawson, *Australian Aborigines*, Melbourne, 1881, p. 67.

15. W. E. Roth, *Bull. of Records of the Australian Museum*, vol. vi, 1907, p. 393; A. P. Elkin, *The Australian Aborigines*, Sydney, 1938, p. 249.

16. Codrington, *op. cit.*, p. 267.

17. *Contrib. to N. Amer. Ethnol.*, vol. iv, 1881, pp. 218, 220f.

18. Reutter, *De L'embaumement avant et après J. Xt.*, Paris, 1912, p. 142.

19. Gann, *64th Bull. B.A.E.*, Washington, 1918, p. 127.

20. H. C. Mercer, *Public. Univ. Penn.* no. 6, 1897, pp. 93 ff.; Bushnell, *71st Bull. B.A.E.*, 1920, pp. 58 f.

21. *12th Report B.A.E.*, 1894, p. 379; J. W. Foster, *Prehistoric Races*, 1878, pp. 149 ff.; Willcox, *Proc. Acad. Nat. Sci.*, 1874, pp. 165 ff.

22. Le Plongeon, *Queen Moo and the Egyptian Sphinx*, 1896, p. 138.

23. Pepper, *Amer. Mus. Nat. Hist. Anunal Report*, 2, 1902, no. 44; Guernsey and Kidder, *Papers of Peabody Mus.*, 1921, pp. 13 ff.; 19 f.; Z. Nuttall, *The Book of the Life of the American Mexicans*, Berkeley, 1903, pp. 54 ff.; Duc de Loubat, *Codex Magliabecchiano*, 3, Rome, 1904, p. 13.

24. *65th Bull. B.A.E.*, 1919, p. 83.

25. J. W. Fawkes, *Smith. Misc. Collections*, no. 63, 1914, pp. 50 ff.; C. L. Webster, *Archaeol. Bulletin*, no. 3, pp. 70, 73.

26. Chap. iv, p. 104.

27. Lumholtz, *Unknown Mexico*, vol. i, 1903, pp. 71 ff.

28. *Trans. & Coll. Amer. Antiq. Soc.*, vol. i, 1820, pp. 318 ff., 359 f., 362.

29. *Contrib. to N. Amer. Ethnology*, vol. i, 1887, pp. 90 f.

30. *Billings Expedition*, 1802, p. 161.

31. Dall, *Smithsonian Contributions*, 1878, pp. 31, 84 ff.

32. R. Beverley, *History of Virginia*, 1772, p. 185.

33. Turner, *Samoa*, 1884, pp. 148 f.; *Nineteen Years in Samoa*, 1861, p. 232.

34. Hare Hongi, *Journal of the Polynesian Society*, vol. xxv, 1916, pp. 169 ff.

35. *Op. cit.*, p. 172.

36. W. Ellis, *Polynesian Researches*, vol. i, 1829, pp. 520 ff.

37. G. de Mendieta, *Historia eclesiastica Indiana*, Mexico, 1870, p. 358.

38. Brasseur de Bourbourg, *Histoire des nations civilisées du Mexique et de l'Amérique*, vol. iv, Paris, 1859, 3, pp. 239 ff., 407 ff.

39. *A.A.*, N.S. vol. 16, 1914, pp. 62 ff.

40. *18th Report B.A.E.*, 1899, pp. 317 ff.

41. *Contrib. Mus. Amer. Ind.; Heye Foundation*, vol. v, 1919, pp. 9 ff.; *A.A.*, N.S. vol. 7, 1905, pp. 625 f.

42. Sophocles, *Trachiniae*, pp. 1191 f.; Hyginus, *Fab.*, p. 36.

43. Iamblicus, *De Mysteriis*, p. 12.

44. Monier-Williams, *Brahmanism and Hinduism*, 1887, pp. 283 f.

45. Turner, *Samoa*, p. 335; *Contrib. to N. Amer. Ethnol.*, vol. iii, 1877, pp. 181 f.

46. *History of Melanesian Society*, vol. ii, pp. 546, 549 ff.

47. Hill-Tout, *British North America*, 1907, pp. 178 ff.

48. Evans-Pritchard, *African Affairs*, vol. xlviii, no. 190, January 1949, pp. 56 ff.

49. *Op. cit.*, p. 59.

50. Bushnell, *83rd Bull. B.A.E.*, 1927, p. 25.

51. Kruijt, *Het Animisme in der Indischen Archipel*, 1906, pp. 369 ff., 380.

52. *Op. cit.*, pp. 371, 381.

53. Skeat and Blagden, *Pagan Races of the Malay Peninsula*, vol. ii, 1906, pp. 103, 110, 114.

54. *Op. cit.*, pp. 208 ff.

55. I. H. N. Evans, *Ethnology and Archaeology of the Malay Peninsula*, Cambridge, 1927, pp. 18 ff.

56. P. Schebesta, *Among the Forest Dwarfs of Malaya*, 1929, p. 255.

57. Cf. Perry, *J.R.A.I.*, vol. xliv, 1914, pp. 281 ff.; *Folk-Lore*, vol. xxvi, 1915, pp. 138 ff.; Riedel, *De sluik en Kroeshaarige rassen tussehen Selebes en Papua*, 1886, pp. 334 ff., 360.

58. Kruijt, *op. cit.*, p. 373.

59. Seligman, *The Melanesians of British New Guinea*, Cambridge, 1910, p. 616.

60. Kruijt, *op. cit.*, pp. 345 f.

61. *Op. cit.*, vol. ii, pp. 262 f.

62. Codrington, *The Melanesians*, p. 258.

63. Rivers, *op. cit.*, p. 267.

64. Wheeler, *Archiv. für Religionwissenschaft*, vol. xvii, 1914, p. 64.

65. R. W. Williamson, *The Mafulu Mountain People in British New Guinea*, 1912, pp. 258 ff., pls. 87, 88, 89.

66. B. Thomson, *The Fijians*, 1908, pp. 120 ff.

67. *Op. cit.*, p. 132; Fison, *Tales of Old Fiji*, 1904, p. 168; J. J. Williams, *Fiji and the Fijians*, vol. i, 1870, pp. 200 ff.; Frazer, *Belief in Immortality*, vol. i, 1913, pp. 424 f.

68. Frazer, *op. cit.*, p. 399.

69. Keysser, Neuhauss, *Deutsch New Guinea*, vol. iii, Berlin, 1911, pp. 82 f., 143.

70. Brinton, *Myths of the New World*, Philadelphia, 1896, p. 280.

71. *J.A.I.*, vol. xxi, 1891, pp. 18 f.; Bancroft, *Native States of North America*, vol. iii, New York, 1883, p. 520.

72. J. Franklin, *Second Expedition*, 1828, pp. 291 ff.

73. A. Henry, *Travels and Adventures in Canada*, Toronto, 1901, p. 144; *71st Report B.A.E.*, 1920, p. 30.

74. Copeway, *Ojibway Nation*, 1847, p. 32; Schoolcraft, *Indian Tribes*, Philadelphia, 1853, vol. i, p. 321.

75. Pinkerton, *Voyages and Travels*, vol. xiii, 1812, p. 41.

76. Sahagun, *Hist. Gen. de las cosas de Nueva España*, vol. i, Mexico, 1829, lib. ii, p. 164; Brasseur de Bourbourg, *Histoire Nat. Civ.*, vol. iii, p. 497.

77. Sahagun, *op. cit.*, vols. II, vii, pp. 253 ff.

78. H. Ling Roth, *Natives of Sarawak and British North Borneo*, vol. i, 1896, pp. 204 ff.

79. Hose and McDougall, *The Pagan Tribes of Borneo*, vol. ii, 1912, pp. 32 ff.

80. O. Rutter, *The Pagans of North Borneo*, 1929, p. 216.

81. Skeat and Blagden, *Pagan Races of the Malay Peninsula*, vol. ii, 1906, pp. 99 ff., 106 ff.

82. *Melanesians*, p. 255.

83. *Op. cit.*, p. 285.

84. Malinowski, *Argonauts of the Western Pacific*, p. 513.

85. Hocart, *J.R.A.I.*, vol. lii, 1922, p. 84.

CHAPTER VI

1. *Golden Bough,* vol. iv, part I (Adonis), p. 5.
2. *L'Anthrop.,* vol. xx, 1911, pp. 257ff.; vol. xxiii, 1912, pp. 129, 143; *Revue préhistorique,* vol. v, 1910, p. 33; Capitan, *Rev. de l'Ecole d'anthrop.,* vol. xxii, 1912, pp. 316ff.
3. L. Passemard, *Les statuettes féminines dites Vénus stéatopyges,* Nîmes, 1938, pp. 121f; Luquet, *The Art and Religion of Fossil Man,* Oxford, 1930, pp. 85, 110.
4. Capitan, *Peintures et gravures murales des cavernes paléolithiques. Les Combarelles aux Eyzies,* 1924, pl. vi.
5. *The Gate of Horn,* 1948, p. 57.
6. G. Clark, *Savagery to Civilization,* 1946, p. 56.
7. E. A. Golomshtok, *L'Anthrop.,* vol. xliii, 1933, pp. 334ff.; S. N. Zamiatnine, *Paleolit. S.S.S.R.,* Moscow, 1935, pp. 26ff.
8. Burkitt, *Eurosia Septentrionalis Antiqua,* ix. Helsinki, 1934, p. 113.
9. J. W. Jackson, *Shells as Evidence of the Migration of Early Culture,* Manchester, 1917, pp. 135ff.
10. Cf. Didon, "L'Abri Blanchard, Périgueux, 1911", extract from *Bull. de la Soc. Hist. et Archéol. du Périgord,* pl. vi, no. 28; Mortillet, *Musée Préhistorique,* 2nd ed., no. 189.
11. Boule, *Les Hommes Fossiles,* Paris, 1923, p. 266.
12. *L'Anthrop.,* vol. xxiii, 1912, p. 657; *C.R. Acad. Inscrip. et Belles-Lettres,* 1912, pp. 532ff.
13. Breuil and Calve Aguilo, *L'Anthrop.,* vol. xx, 1909, p. 1.
14. Cf. chap. vii, pp. 172f.
15. Only four Magdalenian figurines have been discovered, all of them in France.
16. Breuil, *L'Anthrop.,* vol. xxiii, 1912, p. 529.
17. Cf. Obermaier, *Fossil Man in Spain,* 1925, pp. 257ff.; *L'Anthrop.,* vol. xxxvi, 1926, pp. 5–6.
18. Cf. E. S. Hartland, *Primitive Paternity,* 1909–10; Malinowski, *The Father in Primitive Psychology,* 1927, pp. 28ff., 43ff.; *Sexual Life of Savages in North-Western Melanesia,* 1929, pp. 146ff.
19. Petrie, *Prehistoric Egypt,* 1920, pp. 8f.; Brunton and Caton-Thompson, *The Bedarian Civilization,* 1928, p. 29.
20. M. E. I. Mallowan and J. Cruikshank Rose, *Iraq,* vol. ii, 1935, pp. 79ff.
21. *The Archaeology of Palestine and the Bible,* New York, 1932, p. 109.
22. *Excavations at Tepe Gawra,* Philadelphia, 1950, p. 163.
23. *Op. cit.,* p. 165.
24. Seton Lloyd and Fuad Safar, *J.N.E.S.,* vol. iv, 1945, p. 270.
25. Mallowan, *Iraq,* vol. iii, 1936, pp. 19f.
26. Woolley, *The Development of Sumerian Art,* 1935, pp. 37f., pls. 6a–e, f, h; *Antiq. Journal,* vol. x, no 4, 1930, p. 338, pl. xcviii.
27. *J.E.A.,* vol. ix, 1923, pp. 191f.

28. *Deutsche Forschungsgemeinschaft in Uruk-Warka*, vol. vii, Berlin, 1936, pl. 47; cf. vol. viii, p. 50.

29. *Op. cit.*, vol. viii, p. 52, pl. 49e.

30. R. de Mecquenem, *L'Anthrop.*, vol. xlv, 1935, pp. 93ff., pls. 1–2.

31. *Op. cit.*, pls. 7 i.

32. Contenau, *Syria*, vol. viii, 1927, p. 198, figs. 2, 3; *La Déesse nue babylonienne*, Paris, 1914, p. 59, fig. 58; cf. p. 62, fig. 59; *Délégation en Perse, Mémoires*, vol. i, p. 125, fig. 276; cf. p. 130, pls. vii, 14, viii, 19.

33. Pézard et Pottier, *Les Antiquités de la Susiane*, Paris, 1913, p. 129.

34. *Op. cit.*, p. 149.

35. *De Morgan Collection*, no. 276.

36. Cf. *Délégation en Perse*, vol. i, p. 130, pls. vii, 10; Pézard, *op. cit.*, p. 129; Contenau, fig. 60.

37. *Explorations in Turkestan*, 1904; Pumpelly, vol. i, 1908, p. 171, pl. 46, figs. 13, 14.

38. *Op. cit.*, pl. 46, fig. 11.

39. *Op. cit.*, figs. 10a, 10b.

40. *Op. cit.*, pls. 4, 55.

41. Piggott, *Prehistoric India*, 1950, p. 127; Stein, *Memoirs Arch. Survey of India*, no. 37, 1925, pp. 38, 42, 60, 75, pls. ix, P.W. 9, P. 262; xii, K. 14; xvi, D.N. d. 9, S.J. 68; Piggott, *Ancient India*, 1950, pp. 107f., 126ff.

42. Stein, *op. cit.*, p. 60.

43. *Op. cit.*, pl. ix, P.C. 17.

44. Cf. Brunton and Cater-Thompson, *Badarian Civilization*, p. 29; Woolley, *Antiq. Journal*, vol. xi, p. 368; Zammit, *Archaeologia*, vol. lxx, p. 197.

45. Mackay, *Further Excavations at Mohenjo-daro*, vol. ii, 1937, pls. xci, 12; xcii, i, a; vol. i, pp. 257ff.; Marshall, *Mohenjo-daro and the Indus Valley Civilization*, vol. i, 1931, pp. 338ff.; Vats, *Excavations at Harappa*, vol. i, 1940, pp. 292ff.; Piggott, *Ancient India*, no. 3, 1946, pp. 126ff.

46. Marshall, *op. cit.*, vol. i, p. 339.

47. Mackay, *op. cit.*, p. 259; *The Indus Civilization*, 1948, pp. 53f.

48. Marshall, *op. cit.*, pl. xciv, 11; Mackay, *op. cit.*, vol. ii, pl. lxxii, 7; pl. lxxvi, 5; Vats, *op. cit.*, pls. lxxvi, lxxvii.

49. Marshall, *op. cit.*, pl. xciv, no. 11.

50. *Op. cit.*, pl. xii, no. 17.

51. Marshall, *op. cit.*, vol. i, pp. 53ff.

52. Mackay, *Further Excavations at Mohenjo-daro*, vol. i, pp. 335ff.

53. Marshall, *op. cit.*, pls. xiii, 1, 7; xiv, 2, 4.

54. *Op. cit.*, pls. xiii, 1, 2, 8.

55. *Op. cit.*, pls. cxxx, 21, 23.

56. Mackay, *op. cit.*, pp. 407f.

57. Vats, *Excavations at Harappa*, 1940, pp. 51, 53, 55ff.

58. *Op. cit.*, p. 370.   59. Cf. p. 140.   60. p. 371.

61. Pumpelly, *Exploration in Turkestan*, vol. i, 1908, p. 47.

62. Cf. chap. ix, pp. 237f.

63. Oikaios, *Iraq*, vol. vii, 1940, p. 78.

64. *Cambridge Ancient History*, vol. i, 1923, p. 91.

65. C. W. Blegen, *American Journal of Archaeology*, vol. xli, 1937, p. 569, pl. xx.

66. J. T. Bent, *J.H.S.*, vol. v, 1884, pp. 49 ff.

67. Cf. Evans, *The Palace of Minos*, vol. i, 1921, p. 49, figs. 12, 13.

68. *Op. cit.*, p. 52.

69. Cf. Homer, *Odyssey*, pp. 125–7; Hesiod, *Theogony*, p. 969; *Diodorus*, vol. v, pp. 25 ff.; J. E. Harrison, *Themis*, Cambridge, 1912, pp. 54 n. 7, 164; *Prolegomena to Study of Greek Religion*, 1903, p. 456.

70. Harrison, *Prolegomena*, fig. 86.

71. Solinus, vol. xi, p. 8; Nilsson, *The Minoan-Mycenaean Religion*, 1927, p. 439.

72. Evans, *op. cit.*, pp. 500 ff., figs. 359, 362, 377; Nilsson, *op. cit.*, pp. 268 ff.; B. E. Williams, *Gournia*, Philadelphia, 1908, pp. 47 ff., pl. xi.

73. Evans, *op. cit.*, vol. iv, p. 559, figs. 522 a, b; *B.S.A.*, vol. vii, 1900, p. 29, fig. 9.

74. *B.S.A.*, *op. cit.*, p. 101; vol. ix, fig. 38.

75. *J.H.S.*, vol. xxii, p. 77, fig. 2.

76. Diodorus, I, iv, c. 79, 3.

77. Evans, *op. cit.*, vol. iv, pp. 959 ff.

78. Evans, *op. cit.*, vol. i, pp. 438 f.; Nilsson, *op. cit.*, pp. 368 ff.; Paribeni, *Mon. ant.*, vol. xix, pp. 1 ff.

79. Evans, *B.S.A.* vol. viii, pp. 101 ff.; *op. cit.*, vol. i, p. 447.

80. Zammit and Singer, *J.R.A.I.*, vol. liv, 1924, pp. 79 ff.; pls. v, 6, 7, 9; vol. xix, pl. 10.

81. Zammit, *Prehistoric Malta*, Oxford, 1930, p. 80, pl. xxii.

82. *J.R.A.I.*, *op. cit.*, pl. xv, 49.

83. *Op. cit.*, pl. xviii, 53.

84. *Op. cit.*, pl. xviii, 54.

85. *Op cit.*, pl. xi, 29.

86. *Op. cit.*, pl. xx, 30.

87. M. A. Murray, *Excavations in Malta*, 1929, pp. 11, 29.

88. Zammit, *The Hal-Saflieni Prehistoric Hypogeum*, Malta, 1910, p. 40; *J.R.A.I.*, *op. cit.*, pl. ix, 22.

89. *J.R.A.I.*, pl. x, 23.

90. Cf. chap. iii, pp. 70f.

91. Zammit, *Prehistoric Malta*, pp. 13, 15, 84, 96.

92. Siret, *Revue préhistorique*, 1908, pp. 10, 21.

93. Correia, *Comisión de investigaciones paleontológicas y prehistóricas*, Madrid, 1921, pp. 27, 63 ff., figs. 50, 56, 58.

94. Cf. chap. iii, pp. 76 f.   95. Correia, *op. cit.*, p. 75.

96. *Junta superior para excavaciones archeologicas*, Madrid, 1930, *Mems.*, p. 112.

97. Z. le Rouzic, *Carnac, Menhir-Statues avec signes figuratifs et Amulettes ou Idoles des Dolmens du Morbihan*, Nantes, 1931, pp. 13 ff.

98. Kendrick, *The Archaeology of the Channel Islands*, vol. i, 1928, p. 32.

99. *Op. cit.*, pp. 21 ff.; *Antiq. Journal*, vol. v, 1925, pp. 429 f.

00. Et Michon, *Rés. des mém. Soc. de Antiq. de France*, Centenaire, 1904, p. 299.

01. E. MacCulloch, *Proc. Soc. Antiq.*, vol. viii, 1881, p. 32.

02. A. de Mortillet, *Bull. Soc. d'Anthrop.*, Paris, 1893, p. 664.

03. *Association Française pour l'avancement des Sciences*, Paris, 1890, p. 629.

04. *Bull. Soc. préhistorique française*, vol. viii, Paris, 1911, p. 669.

05. V. C. C. Collum, *The Tressé Iron-Age Megalithic Monument*, Oxford, 1935.

06. Piggott, *The Neolithic Cultures of the British Isles*, 1954, p. 42; Childe, *Prehistoric Communities of the British Isles*, 1949, 3rd ed., p. 40.

07. Piggott, *op. cit.*, p. 88, figs. 14, 1–4, 10.

08. Piggott, *P.P.S.*, N.S. vol. ii, 1936, p. 87.

09. C. Fox, *The Early Cultures of North-west Europe*, Cambridge, 1950, pp. 59 f.

10. Philippe, "Cinq Années de Fouilles au Fort-Harrouard, 1921–5", *Société normande d'études préhistoriques*, vol. xxv, bis Rouen, 1927.

11. *Manuel d'archéologie préhistorique*, Paris, 1908, p. 603.

CHAPTER VII

1. Spencer and Gillen, *Native Tribes of Central Australia*, 1938, pp. 167 ff.

2. Cf. chap. iv, p. 148.

3. Breuil, *Quatre cents siècles d'art pariétal*, Montignac, 1954, pp. 166, 176 f.

4. *Antiquity*, vol. iii, no. 9, 1929, p. 17.

5. *Science, Religion and Reality*, 1926, p. 44.

6. Bégouen, *C. r. Ac. Inscrip.*, 1923, p. 14; Breuil, *op. cit.*, pp. 236 ff.

7. A. Lemozi, *La Grotte-Temple du Pech-Merle*, Paris, 1929; Breuil, *op. cit.*, pp. 266 ff.

8. F. Windels, *The Lascaux Cave Paintings*, 1949, pp. 27 ff.; A. H. Brodrick, *Lascaux: A Commentary*, 1948, pp. 81 ff.

9. Breuil, *op. cit.*, pp. 131, 134 f.

0. Windels, *op. cit.*, p. 63; Levy, *The Gate of Horn*, 1948, p. 21.

1. Spencer and Gillen, *op. cit.*, pp. 171 ff.

2. *Op. cit.*, pp. 614 ff.

3. Spencer and Gillen, *Northern Tribes of Central Australia*, pp. 436 ff.

4. *La Caverne d'Altamira*, Monaco, 1909, p. 139.

5. Cf. chap. ix, pp. 23 f.

6. Cf. Marett, *The Threshold of Religion*, 1914, pp. 40 ff.; J. E. Harrison, *Ancient Art Ritual*, 1913, p. 26.

17. Driston, *L'Egypte*, Paris, 1938, p. 597.

18. Cf. chap. viii, pp. 210f.

19. Frazer, *Golden Bough*, part IV (Adonis II), p. 219.

20. Pyr. Texts, 466b, Sethe, *Urgeschichte und älteste Religion der Aegypter*, Leipzig, 1930, p. 99.

21. Frankfort, *Kingship and the Gods*, Chicago, 1947, pp. 150ff.; *The Birth of Civilization in the Near East*, 1951, p. 54.

22. *Religion and Thought in Ancient Egypt*, 1914, pp. 8f.

23. Cf. Frankfort, *Kingship and the Gods*, pp. 123ff.

24. Blackman, *Studia Aegyptiaca*, "Analecta Orientalia", vol. xvii, 1938, p. 2.

25. Wainwright, *The Sky-Religion in Egypt*, Cambridge, 1938, pp. 11f.

26. Blackman, *Luxor and its Temples*, 1923, pp. 179ff.

27. A. Erman and A. M. Blackman, *The Literature of the Ancient Egyptians*, 1927, p. 137.

28. *J.E.A.*, vol. ii, 1915, p. 125.

29. Brugsch, *Zeitschrift für aegypt. Sprache und Altertumskunde*, vol. xix, 1881, pp. 71–111; Loret, *Recueil de travaux relatifs à la Philologie et à l'archéol. Egyptiennes et Assyriennes*, vol. iii, 1882, pp. 43ff.; vol. iv, 1883, pp. 21ff.; vol. v, 1884, pp. 85ff.

30. Brugsch, *Religion und Mythologie der alten Aegypter*, Leipzig, 1885–8, p. 621.

31. Gardiner, *op. cit.*, p. 123; Brugsch, *Zeitschrift*, pp. 84, 94; *Rel. und Myth.*, p. 618.

32. S. N. Kramer, *Sumerian Mythology*, Philadelphia, 1944, pp. 83ff.

33. Langdon, *The Babylonian Epic of Creation*, Oxford, 1923, p. 37, line 14.

34. *Folk-lore*, 1939, p. 140.

35. Cf. T. Jacobsen, *The Intellectual Adventure of Ancient Man*, Chicago, 1946, pp. 126ff.; Frankfort, *Ancient Egyptian Religion*, Chicago, 1948, pp. 54ff.

36. Ezek. viii. 14.

37. Pallis, *The Babylonian Akitu Festival*, Copenhagen, 1926, pp. 193ff., 252ff.; Langdon, *The Babylonian Epic of Creation*, Oxford, 1923, pp. 34ff.

38. S. Smith, *J.R.A.S.*, 1928, pp. 849ff.; Pallis, *op. cit.*, p. 109; Tallquist, *Sumerisch-akkadische Namen der Totenwelt*, Helsingfors, 1934, p. 26, n. 4.

39. A. J. Wensinck, *Acta Orientalia*, vol. i, pp. 169ff.

40. Jacobsen, *The Sumerian King List*, Chicago, 1939; Assyr. Studies, no. 11, p. 58.

41. Admon., 12, 1; Cairo, 34501.

42. E. Chiera, *Sumerian Ritual Texts*, vol. xxxi, Upland Pa., 1924, 24, i, 22–5.

43. Frazer, *Golden Bough*, part IV, pp. 9ff.; B. Z. and C. G. Seligman, *The Pagan Tribes of the Nilotic Sudan*, 1932, pp. 90ff.; *Egypt and Negro Africa*, 1934, pp. 28ff.; Meek, *The Northern Tribes of Nigeria*, vol. i, 1925, pp. 255ff.; vol. ii, pp. 58ff.; Evans-Pritchard, *The Divine Kingship of the Shilluk of the Nilotic Sudan*, Cambridge, 1948, pp. 18f., 21, 36f.

44. Moret, *Du caractère religieux de la royauté Pharaonique*, Paris, 1902, pp. 256ff.

Breasted, *Religion and Thought in Ancient Egypt*, p. 39; Murray, *Ancient Egypt*, vol. ii, 1926, pp. 33 ff.; Seligman, *Egypt and Negro Africa*, p. 2; Frankfort, *Kingship and the Gods*, 1948, pp. 79 ff.

45. *J.E.A.*, vol. ii, 1915, p. 134.

46. *J.E.A.*, vol. xxviii, 1942, p. 71; *Kingship and the Gods*, p. 79.

47. Sethe, *Untersuchungen zur Geschichte und Altertumskunde aegyptens*, vol. iii, 1905, pp. 134 ff.

48. T. H. Gaster, *Thespis*, New York, 1950, pp. 57 ff.; R. de Langhe, *Les textes de Ras Shamra-Ugarit*, Paris, 1945.

49. Cf. C. H. Gordon, *Ugaritic Literature*, Rome, 1949, pp. 3 ff.

50. *Baal-'Anat Cycle*, p. 67; vol. ii, pp. 5-6.

51. *Palace of Minos*, vol. ii, p. 842; vol. iii, p. 142; cf. Nilsson, *Minoan-Mycenaean Religion*, pp. 296 f.

52. A. W. Persson, *The Religion of Greece in Prehistoric Times*, California, 1942, p. 34.

53. Evans, *op. cit.*, vol. i, pp. 161 f.

54. *Op. cit.*, vol. ii, pp. 838 ff.

55. Nilsson, *op. cit.*, p. 230, pl. i, 4.

56. Cf. Evans, *Archaeologia*, vol. xv, 1914, pp. 10 f., fig. 16; Persson, *op. cit.*, p. 49.

57. Evans, *op. cit.*, vol. i, p. 432, fig. 310a; vol. iii, pp. 220, 225, figs. 154, 158.

58. Cf. Persson, *op. cit.*, pp. 91 ff.; Malten, *Archäologisches Jahrbuch*, 1928, pp. 90 ff.

59. Cf. Deedes, *The Labyrinth*, 1935, pp. 27 ff.

60. Chap. viii, pp. 221 ff.

61. *The Golden Bough*, part ii, p. 140.

62. Nilsson, *Greek Popular Religion*, New York, 1940, pp. 51 ff.

63. *Refutatio omnium haeresium*, vol. v, p. 8; cf. Farnell, *Cult of the Greek States*, vol. iii, pp. 177, 183.

64. Artemidorus, vol. i, p. 8.

65. Proclus ad Plato, *Timaeus*, p. 293 (Lobeck).

66. Farnell, *op. cit.*, vol. iii, p. 184.

67. Euripides, *Bacchae*, pp. 20 ff.; Farnell, *op. cit.*, vol. v, pp. 86 ff.; Rhode, *Psyche*, 1925, pp. 250 ff.

68. These examples are quoted from notes made by the author during a visit to the museum at Eleusis.

69. Farnell, *op. cit.*, vol. iii, pl. xxi b, p. 256.

70. *Minoan-Mycenaean Religion*, p. 490.

71. *Op. cit.*, pp. 153 f., figs. 28, 29.

72. *Op. cit.*, p. 155.

73. Tacitus, *Germania*, 40.

74. Lucretius, vol. ii, pp. 600-43.

75. Cf. Crawford, *Antiquity*, 1954, pp. 25 ff.; R. J. C. Atkinson, *P.P.S.*, vol. xviii, part ii, 1952, p. 236; *Stonehenge*, 1956, pp. 33 f., 84 f., 163 f.

76. *Stonehenge*, p. 165.
77. Hawkes, *P.P.S.*, 1948, pp. 196 ff.; Navarro, *The Early Cultures of North-west Europe*, Cambridge, 1950, pp. 77 ff.; Atkinson, *op. cit.*, pp. 162 ff.
78. Cf. Childe, *Prehistoric Communities of the British Isles*, p. 122, n. 14.
79. Piggott, *P.P.S.*, 1938, pp. 58 ff.

CHAPTER VIII

1. *Primitive Culture*, 4th ed., vol. i, 1903, pp. 426 ff.
2. *Op. cit.*, vol. ii, pp. 113 f., 247 ff., 311 f.
3. *Principles of Sociology*, vol. i, 1885, p. 411.
4. Frazer, *The Worship of Nature*, 1926, pp. 9 f.
5. *The Making of Religion*, 1898, pp. 160 ff.; cf. Howitt, *Native Tribes of South-east Australia*, 1904, pp. 488 ff.
6. Cf. Schmidt, *Der Ursprung der Gottesidee*, Munster, 1912–54.
7. Spencer and Gillen, *Native Tribes of Central Australia*, 1938, p. 246, n. 1
8. *Nuer Religion*, Oxford, 1956, pp. 2 ff., 118, 124, 200 ff.
9. *Op. cit.*, p. 316.
10. *Bulletin Société préhistorique française*, vol. iv, 1907, p. 215.
11. A. B. Cook, *L'Anthrop.*, vol. xiv, 1903, pp. 34 ff.
12. Cf. A. C. Haddon, *The Study of Man*, 1898, pp. 277 ff.; Marett, *The Threshold of Religion*, 1914, pp. 17 f., 145 f.; Howitt, *op. cit.*, pp. 578 f. Spencer and Gillen, *Native Tribes of Central Australia*, pp. 246 n., 634
13. Cf. Wainwright, *The Sky-Religion in Egypt*, Cambridge, 1938.
14. *Religion and Thought in Ancient Egypt*, 1914, p. 9.
15. Pyr. Texts, p. 1105.
16. Budge, *Tutankhamon, Amenism, Atonism and Egyptian Monotheism*, 1923, p. 79.
17. Frankfort, *Kingship and the Gods*, 1948, p. 38.
18. Cf. Davies, *J.E.A.*, vol. ix, 1923, pp. 133 ff.; *Journal of the Society of Oriental Research*, vol. x, Chicago, 1926, pp. 25 ff.
19. Langdon, *Babyloniaca*, vol. xii, Paris, 1931, p. 11, lines 11–12.
20. Gadd, *The Idea of Divine Rule in the Ancient East*, Oxford, 1948, p. 34.
21. Cf. F. Nötscher, *Ellil in Sumer und Akkad*, pp. 56, 66.
22. Cf. Frankfort, *op. cit.*, p. 228; F. Thureau-Dangin, *Sumerische und Akkadische Königschriften*, Leipzig, 1907, pp. 156 f.
23. Heidel, *The Babylonian Genesis*, Chicago, 1950, pp. 20 ff.; vol. ii, pp. 60 ff
24. *Op. cit.*, p. 47; vol. ii, pp. 31 ff.
25. Heidel, *The Gilgamesh Epic*, Chicago, 1951, p. 229.
26. Cf. Cook, *Zeus*, vol. i, pp. 577 ff., 635; Garstang, *The Hittite Empire* 1929, pp. 204 f.
27. S. Mercer, *The Tell El Amarna Tablets*, vol. ii, Toronto, 1939, pp. 48? (13 f.).

28. Konow, *The Aryan Gods of the Mitanni People*, Kristiana, 1921, pp. 1f.

29. *Rig-veda*, vi, 27, 8; x, 33, 2; *Atharvaveda*, v, 22, 5, 7, 9.

30. The Sanskrit form of the Avestan *Ahura* adopted by Zarathushtra as the designation of the All-wise Lord, Ahura Mazda, the Supreme Being of Zoroastrian monotheism, whose power was limited only by the spirit of evil, Angra Mainyu or the Druj. The Avesta, *Yasna*, xxx.

31. Cf. Keith, *Indian Culture*, vol. iii, p. 421.

32. *Satapatha Brahmana*, v, 1, 1, 2; iii, 2, 2, 4.

33. *Chandogya-Upanishad*, vi, 8, 7f.; *Brihadaranyaki*, i, 4, 10; *Isa Upanishad*, 1 ff.

34. *Yasna*, 34, 44, 45, 48.

35. *Yasna*, 30.

36. *Five Stages of Greek Religion*, Oxford, 1925, p. 65.

37. Nilsson, *History of Greek Religion*, Oxford, 1925, p. 31.

38. Cf. Rose, *Handbook of Greek Mythology*, 1933, pp. 49f.

39. Cf. Aeschylus, *Danaids, Tragg. Graec.*, Fr. ed., Nauck, p. 44; Euripides, Fr. 898, pp. 7ff.; Cook, *Zeus*, vol. iii, pp. 456ff.; Farnell, *Cult of the Greek States*, vol. i, pp. 244ff.

40. Chap. vii, p. 197.

41. Rose, *op. cit.*, pp. 102ff.

42. Frazer, *The Golden Bough*, part II, p. 140.

43. *The Aryans*, 1926, p. 81.

44. Shetelig and Falk, *Scandinavian Archaeology*, Oxford, 1937, pp. 156f.

45. *The Golden Bough*, part X, pp. 160ff.

46. Chap. vii, p. 203.

47. Cf. Atkinson, *Stonehenge*, 1956, p. 172.

CHAPTER IX

1. *Elementary Forms of the Religious Life*, 1913, p. 206.

2. A. R. Radcliffe-Brown, *A.A.*, 1935, pp. 394ff.; *J.R.A.I.*, vol. lxxv, 1945, p. 33.

3. *Op. cit.*, pp. 47, 206.   4. Cf. chaps. v, vi.

5. *Les fonctions dans les Sociétés Inférieures*, Paris, 1915; *La Mentalité primitive*, Paris, 1921; *L'Expérience mystique et les symboles chez les primitifs*, Paris, 1938.

6. Evans-Pritchard, *Nuer Religion*, Oxford, 1956, pp. 77, 82, 132f., 140f.

7. Chap. vii, p. 180.

8. Newberry, *Annals of Archaeology and Anthropology*, vol. v, Liverpool, 1913, p. 136.

9. Baumgärtel, *The Cultures of Prehistoric Egypt*, Oxford, 1955, p. 31.

10. Hornblower, *J.E.A.*, vol. xv, 1929, p. 39.

11. Levy, *The Gate of Horn*, 1948, p. 116.

12. *Op. cit.*, pp. 38, 43.

13. Winckler, *Rock-Drawings of Southern Upper Egypt*, 1938, p. 22.

14. Gadd, in Hall and Woolley, *Ur Excavations*, vol. i; *Al 'Ubaid*, Oxford, 1927, pp. 142 f.

15. *Op. cit.*, p. 143.

16. Cf. chap. vi, p. 159.

17. Chap. vi, p. 158.

18. Capitan, *Les Combarelles aux Eyzies*, 1924, pl. vi; Picard, *Revue de Philologie* 1933, pp. 344 ff.

19. Cf. Malton, *Archäologisches Jahrbuch*, 1928, pp. 90 ff.

20. Capitan and Peyrony, *Revue anthropologique*, vol. xxxi, 1921, pp. 92 ff.

21. Chap. vii, p. 178.

22. *L'Anthrop.*, vol. xxiv, 1913, pp. 627 ff.

23. Cf. chap. vi, p. 146.

24. A. Makowski, *Mittheilungen der Anthropologischen Gesellschaft in Wien*, 1892 p. 73; Obermaier, *Der Mensch der Vorzeit*, p. 298; Breuil, *L'Anthrop.*, 1924 pp. 549 ff.

25. Buckland, *Reliquiae Diluvianae*, 1823, pp. 82 ff.

26. *Religion and Thought in Ancient Egypt*, p. 61.

27. Frankfort, *Kingship and the Gods*, p. 178.

28. Tablet XI.

29. Cf. Heidel, *The Gilgamesh Epic and the Old Testament Parallels*, Chicago 1949, pp. 207 ff.

30. F. Thureau-Dangin, *Hilprecht Anniversary Volume*, Leipzig, 1909, p. 161

31. Chap. ii, p. 43.

32. Chap. ii, p. 53.

33. Chap. ii, pp. 48 f. Also, Woolley, *Ur Excavations, The Royal Cemeteries* vol. ii, 1934, pp. 135 ff.; Mackay, *Report on the Excavations of the "A" Cemetery at Kish*, vol. i, Chicago, 1925, pp. 13 f.

34. Vats, *Excavations at Harappa*, vol. i, 1940, pp. 207 ff.

35. *Rig-veda*, x, 18.

36. *Rig-veda*, x, 1, 4, 16.

37. Evans, *Palace of Minos*, vol. ii, p. 279.

38. Chap. vi, p. 164.

39. *Monumenti Antichi*, vol. xix, pp. 5–86, pls. i–iii.

40. *Palace of Minos*, vol. i, pp. 439, 447.

41. Harrison, *Themis*, 1912, p. 178; Petersen, *Arch. Jahrbuch*, vol. xxiv, 1909 p. 162.

42. *Minoan-Mycenaean Religion*, pp. 378 ff.

43. Evans, *J.H.S.*, vol. xlv, 1925, pp. 68 ff.

44. *Mycenaean Tree and Pillar Cult*, 1901, pp. 98 ff.

45. Chap. iv, p. 108.

46. Cf. Crawford, *The Long Barrows of the Cotswolds*, 1925, p. 14.

47. *P.P.S.*, N.S. i, vol. ii, 1935, p. 108.

48. C. A. Nordman, *The Megalithic Culture in Northern Europe*, Helsinki, 1935 p. 28; Crawford, *op. cit.*, p. 13.

49. *Op. cit.*, p. 127.
50. *Prehistoric Chamber Tombs of England and Wales*, 1950, p. 110.
51. Nordman, *op. cit.*, p. 29.
52. *P.P.S.*, N.S. IV, 1938, p. 128.
53. Chap. v, p. 133.
54. Chap. viii, p. 224.
55. *Yasht.*, x, 13.
56. Chap. viii, p. 222.
57. Cf. Nilsson, *History of Greek Religion*, pp. 121 f.

ABBREVIATIONS

A.A.	American Anthropologist.
L'ANTHROP.	L'Anthropologie.
B.A.E.	Bureau of American Ethnology.
B.S.A.	British School of Athens, Annual of.
E.R.E.	Encyclopaedia of Religion and Ethics.
J.E.A.	Journal of Egyptian Archaeology.
J.H.S.	Journal of Hellenic Studies.
J.N.E.S.	Journal of Near Eastern Studies.
J.R.A.I.	Journal of the Royal Anthropological Institute.
J.R.A.S.	Journal of the Royal Asiatic Society.
P.P.S.	Proceedings of the Prehistoric Society.

BIBLIOGRAPHY

CHAPTER I

Black, D., *Fossil Man in China,* Peiping, 1933.

Boule, H., *Les Hommes Fossiles,* 3rd ed., Paris, 1946.

Broderick, A. H., *Early Man,* 1946.

Burkitt, M. C., *Prehistory,* 2nd ed., Cambridge, 1927; *Our Early Ancestors,* Cambridge, 1926; *The Old Stone Age,* 3rd ed., 1955.

Clark, J. G. D., *The Mesolithic Settlements of Northern Europe,* Cambridge, 1936.

Hose, C., and McDougall, W., *The Pagan Tribes of Borneo,* 1912.

Jackson, J. W., *Shells as Evidence of the Migrations of Early Culture,* 1917.

Keith, A., *The Antiquity of Man,* 2 vols., 2nd ed., 1929.

Luquet, G. H., *The Art and Religion of Fossil Man,* 1930.

Macalister, R. A. S., *Textbook of European Archaeology,* Cambridge, 1921.

Marshall, H. I., *The Karen People of Borneo,* Ohio, 1922.

Obermaier, H., *Fossil Man in Spain,* New Haven, Yale Press, 1925.

Oppenoorth, W. F. F., *Early Man,* edited by MacCurdy, Philadelphia, 1937.

Osborn, H., *Men of the Old Stone Age,* 1918.

Sollas, W. J., *Ancient Hunters,* 3rd ed., 1924.

Teilhard de Chardin, *Early Man in China,* Peiping, 1941.

Verneau, R., *Les Grottes de Grimaldi,* Monaco, 1906.

Zeuner, F. E., *Dating the Past,* 1952; *The Pleistocene Period,* 1945.

CHAPTER II

Baumgärtel, E. J., *The Cultures of Prehistoric Egypt,* Oxford, 1955.

Breasted, J. H., *Religion and Thought in Ancient Egypt,* 1914.

Brunton, G., *Mostagedda,* 1937.

Brunton, G., and Caton-Thompson, G., *The Badarian Civilization,* 1928.

Caton-Thompson, G., and Gardner, E. W., *The Desert Fayum,* 1934.

Childe, V. G., *New Light on the Most Ancient East,* new edition, 1952.

Hargreaves, H., *Excavations in Baluchistan,* 1925.

Jacobsen, T., *The Sumerian King Lists,* Chicago, 1939.

Lloyd, Seton, *Mesopotamia,* 1936.

Mackay, E. J. H., *Further Excavations at Mohenjo-daro,* 1938; *The Indus Civilization,* 1935; *Chanhu-daro Excavations,* New Haven, 1943.

Marshall, Sir J., *Mohenjo-daro and the Indus Civilization*, 2 vols., 1931.

McCown, D. E., *The Comparative Stratigraphy of Early Iran*, Chicago, 1942.

Perkins, A. L., *The Comparative Archaeology of Early Mesopotamia*, Chicago, 1949.

Petrie, Sir Flinders W. M., *Prehistoric Egypt*, 1920; *The Royal Tombs of the First Dynasty*, 1900; *Abydos*, vol. i, 1902; vol. ii, 1903; *Pyramids and Temples at Gizeh*, 1885.

Piggott, S., *Prehistoric India*, 1950; *Some Ancient Cities of India*, 1945.

Pumpelly, R., *Explorations in Turkestan*, Carnegie Institute, 1906–8.

Quibell, J. E., and Green, F. W., *Hierakonpolis*, vol. ii, 1902.

Speiser, E. A., *The Excavations at Tepe Gawra*, vol. i, Philadelphia, 1935.

Tobler, A. J., *The Excavations at Tepe Gawra*, vol. ii, Philadelphia, 1950.

Vats, M. S., *Excavations at Harappa*, New Delhi, 1940.

Watelin, L. C., *Kish*, vol. iv, Paris, 1934.

Wheeler, Sir Mortimer R. E., *The Cambridge History of India; The Indus Civilization*, Cambridge, 1953.

Woolley, Sir Leonard, *The Sumerians*, Oxford, 1929; *Ur of the Chaldees*, 1950.

Woolley, L., and Hall, H. R., *Ur Excavations*, vol. i, Al 'Ubaid, 1927; *The Royal Cemetery*, 1934.

CHAPTER III

Crawford, O. G. S., *The Long Barrows of the Cotswolds*, Gloucester, 1925.

Childe, V. G., *The Dawn of European Civilization*, 3rd ed., 1950; *Prehistoric Communities of the British Isles*, 1940; *The Prehistory of Scotland*, 1935; *Skara Brae*, 1931.

Curwen, E. C., *The Archaeology of Sussex*, 2nd ed., 1954.

Daniel, G. E., *The Prehistoric Chamber Tombs of England and Wales*, Cambridge, 1950; "The Dual Nature of the Megalithic Colonisation of Prehistoric Europe", *Proceedings of the Prehistoric Society*, vol. vii, 1941.

Evans, Sir Arthur, *The Palace of Minos*, vols. i–iv, 1922–35.

Forde, C. D., "Early Culture of Atlantic Europe", *American Anthropologist*, 32, pp. 19–100, 1930.

Hawkes, C. F. C., *The Prehistoric Foundations of Europe*, 1940.

Jessup, R. F., *The Archaeology of Kent*, 1930.

Macalister, R. A. S., *The Archaeology of Ireland*, 1928.

Nordman, C. A., *The Megalithic Culture in Northern Europe*, 1935.

Peet, T. E., *The Stone and Bronze Ages in Italy and Sicily*, Oxford, 1909.

Petrie, Sir Flinders, *Royal Tombs of the First Dynasty*, 1900–1.

Piggott, S., *The Neolithic Cultures of the British Isles*, Cambridge, 1954.

Seager, R. B., *Explorations in Mochlos*, Boston, 1912.

Siret, L., *Les premiers Ages du metal dans le sud-est de l'Espagne*, Paris, 1888.

Xanthoudides, S., *The Vaulted Tombs of Mesara*, 1924.

Zammit, T., *Prehistoric Malta;* "The Tarxien Temples", Oxford, 1930; *The Neolithic Temples at Hajar Kin and Mnaidra*, Valetta, 1927.

CHAPTER IV

Breasted, J. H., *Religion and Thought in Ancient Egypt*, 1914.

Budge, Sir Ernest A. W., *The Book of the Opening of the Mouth*, 2 vols., 1909.

Childe, V. G., *Prehistoric Communities of the British Isles*, 1940; *The Danube in Prehistory*, Oxford, 1929.

Davies, N. G., and Gardiner, A. H., *The Tomb of Amenembet*, 1915.

Elliot Smith, Sir Grafton, and Dawson, W. R., *Egyptian Mummies*, 1924.

Garstang, J., *Burial Customs of Ancient Egypt*, 1907.

Greenwell, W., *British Barrows*, 1877.

Grinsell, L. V., *Ancient Burial-Mounds of England*, 1953.

Hawkes, C. F. C., *The Prehistoric Foundations of Europe*, 1940.

Mercer, S., *The Pyramid Texts*, 1929.

Moret, A., *Le Rituel du Culte divin journalier en Egypte*, Paris, 1902.

Peake, H. J. E., *The Bronze Age and the Celtic World*, 1922.

Petrie, Sir Flinders, *Medum*, 1892; *Deshasheh*, 1898.

Piggott, S., *Aspects of Archaeology*, 1951.

Randall-MacIver, *Villanovans and Early Etruscans*, Oxford, 1924.

CHAPTER V

Basedown, H., *The Australian Aboriginal*, 1925.

Brasseur de Bourbourg, *Histoire des nations civilisée du Mexique et de l'Amérique*, vol. iv, Paris, 1859.

Brown, A. R., *The Andaman Islanders*, Cambridge, 1922.

Brown, G., *Melanesians and Polynesians*, 1910.

Codrington, R. H., *The Melanesians, their Anthropology and Folklore*, Oxford, 1891.

Dawson, J., *Australian Aborigines*, Melbourne, 1881.

Ellis, W., *Polynesian Researches,* 1829.

Elkin, A. P., *The Australian Aborigines,* Sydney, 1938.

Evans-Pritchard, E. E., *Nuer Religion,* Oxford, 1956.

Evans, I. H. N., *Ethnology and Archaeology of the Malay Peninsula,* Cambridge, 1927.

Frazer, Sir J. G., *Belief in Immortality,* vol. i, 1913.

Hose, C., and McDougall, W., *The Pagan Tribes of Borneo,* 2 vols., 1912.

Lumholtz, C., *Unknown Mexico,* 1903.

Malinowski, B., *Argonauts of the Western Pacific,* 1922.

Rivers, W. H. R., *History of Melanesian Society,* vol. i, Cambridge, 1914.

Routledge, W. S., *The Mystery of Easter Island,* 1919.

Rutter, O., *The Pagans of North Borneo,* 1929.

Schebesta, P., *Among the Forest Dwarfs of Malaya,* 1929.

Seligman, C. G., *The Melanesians of British New Guinea,* Cambridge, 1910.

Skeat, W. W., and Blagden, C. O., *Pagan Races of the Malay Peninsula,* 2 vols., 1906.

Spencer, B., *Wanderings in Wild Australia,* 2 vols., 1928.

Turner, G., *Samoa,* 1884; *Nineteen Years in Samoa,* 1861.

Williamson, R. W., *The Mafulu Mountain People in British New Guinea,* 1912.

CHAPTER VI

Brunton, G., and Caton-Thompson, G., *The Bedarian Civilization,* 1928.

Childe, V. G., *Prehistoric Communities of the British Isles,* 1949.

Evans, Sir A. J., *The Palace of Minos,* vols. i and iv, 1922–35.

Harrison, J. E., *Prolegomena to the Study of Greek Religion,* Cambridge, 1903; *Themis,* Cambridge, 1912.

Kendrick, T. D., *The Archaeology of the Channel Islands,* 1928.

Levy, G. R., *The Gate of Horn,* 1948.

Luquet, G. H., *The Art and Religion of Fossil Man,* Oxford, 1930.

Mackay, E. J. H., *Further Excavations at Mohenjo-daro,* 1937.

Malinowski B., *The Father in Primitive Psychology,* 1927; *Sexual Life of Savages in North-western Melanesia,* 1929.

Marshall, Sir John, *Mohenjo-daro and the Indus Valley Civilization,* 1931.

Obermaier, H., *Fossil Man in Spain,* Yale Press, 1925.

Petrie, Sir Flinders, *Prehistoric Egypt,* 1920.

Piggott, S., *Prehistoric India,* 1950; *The Neolithic Cultures of the British Isles,* 1954.

Pumpelly, R., *Explorations in Turkestan,* Carnegie Institute, 1906–8.

Stein, Sir A., *Memoirs Arch. Survey of India*, No. 37, 1925.

Tobler, A. J., *Excavations at Tepe Gawra*, Philadelphia, 1950.

Vats, M. S., *Excavations at Harappa*, 1940.

Woolley, Sir L., *The Development of Sumerian Art*, 1935.

Zammit, T., *Prehistoric Malta*, Oxford, 1930; *The Hal-Saflieni Prehistoric Hypogeum*, Malta, 1910.

CHAPTER VII

Atkinson, R. J. C., *Stonehenge*, 1956.

Blackman, A. M., *Luxor and its Temples*, 1923.

Breasted, J. H., *Religion and Thought in Ancient Egypt*, 1914.

Breuil, H., *Quatre cents siècles d'art pariétal*, Montignac, 1954; *La Caverne d'Altamira*, Monaco, 1909.

Brodrick, A. H., *Lascaux: A Commentary*, 1948.

Erman, A., and Blackman, A. M., *The Literature of the Ancient Egyptians*, 1927.

Evans, Sir A. J., *The Palace of Minos*, vols. ii and iii, 1928–30.

Farnell, L. R., *Cult of the Greek States*, vol. iii, Oxford, 1907.

Frankfort, H., *Kingship and the Gods*, Chicago, 1947; *Ancient Egyptian Religion*, Chicago, 1948; *The Intellectual Adventure of Ancient Man*, Chicago, 1946.

Frazer, Sir J. G., *The Golden Bough*, part iv, 1914.

Gaster, T., *Thespis*, New York, 1950.

Harrison, J. E., *Ancient Art and Ritual*, 1913.

Kramer, S. N., *Sumerian Mythology*, Philadelphia, 1944.

Langdon, S., *The Babylonian Epic of Creation*, Oxford, 1923.

Lemozi, A., *La Grotte-Temple du Pech-Merle*, Paris, 1929.

Levy, G. R., *The Gate of Horn*, 1948.

Marett, R. R., *The Threshold of Religion*, 1914.

Moret, A., *Du caractère religieux de la royauté Pharaonique*, Paris, 1909.

Nilsson, M. P., *Minoan-Mycenaean Religion*, Oxford, 1927; *Greek Popular Religion*, New York, 1940.

Pallis, S. A., *The Babylonian Akitu Festival*, Kobenhavn, 1926.

Persson, A. W., *The Religion of Greece in Prehistoric Times*, California, 1942.

Spencer, W. B., and Gillen, F. J., *The Native Tribes of Central Australia*, 1938; *Northern Tribes of Central Australia*, 1904.

Wainwright, G. A., *The Sky-Religion in Egypt*, Cambridge, 1938.

Windels, F., *The Lascaux Cave Paintings*, 1949.

CHAPTER VIII

Breasted, J. H., *Religion and Thought in Ancient Egypt,* 1914.

Budge, Sir E. A. W., *Tutankhamon, Amenism, Atonism and Egyptian Monotheism,* 1923.

Childe, V. G., *The Aryans,* 1926.

Cook, A. B., *Zeus,* 3 vols., Cambridge, 1914–38.

Evans-Pritchard, E. E., *Nuer Religion,* Oxford, 1956.

Farnell, L. R., *The Cult of the Greek States,* vol. i, Oxford, 1896.

Frankfort, H., *Kingship and the Gods,* Chicago, 1948.

Frazer, Sir J. G., *The Worship of Nature,* 1926; *The Golden Bough,* parts ii and x, 1914.

Gadd, C. J., *The Idea of Divine Rule in the Ancient East,* Oxford, 1948.

Haddon, A. C., *The Study of Man,* 1898.

Heidel, A., *The Babylonian Genesis,* Chicago, 1950; *The Gilgamesh Epic,* Chicago, 1951.

Howitt, A. W., *Native Tribes of South-east Australia,* 1904.

Lang, A., *The Making of Religion,* 1898.

Murray, G., *Five Stages of Greek Religion,* Oxford, 1925.

Nilsson, M. P., *History of Greek Religion,* Oxford, 1925.

Rose, H. J., *Handbook of Greek Mythology,* 1933.

Schmidt, P. W., *Der Ursprung, der Gottesidee,* Munster, 1912–54.

Shetelig, H., and Falk, H., *Scandinavian Archaeology,* Oxford, 1937.

Spencer, W. B., and Gillen, F. J., *Native Tribes of Central Australia,* 1938.

Tylor, Sir E. B., *Primitive Culture,* 4th ed., 2 vols., 1903.

Wainwright, G. A., *The Sky-Religion in Egypt,* Cambridge, 1938.

Chart of the Pleistocene and Palaeolithic Periods

DIVISIONS OF PLEISTOCENE	GLACIATIONS AND INTERGLACIALS	FLINT INDUSTRIES	HUMAN TYPES	CULT PRACTICES
Lower . 1000000– 00000 years	Pre-glacial and Günz glaciation Günz-Mindel Interglacial	Pre-Crag Abbevillian Clactonian Cromerian		
Middle .50000 years . 200000	Mindel glaciation Mindel-Riss Interglacial Riss glaciation	Clactonian Abbevillian Lower Acheulian Late Clactonian Lower Tayacian Levalloisian I, II, and III Upper Acheulian	Pithecanthropus Sinanthropus Heidelberg Swanscombe Mount Carmel	Cult of skulls
Upper . 150000	Riss-Würm Interglacial Würm I glaciation (maximum)	Levalloisian III, IV Latest Acheulian Mousterian Levalloisian V–VII Châtelperron	Neanderthal Man	Ceremonial interments
72000 25000– 10000	*The Upper Palaeolithic* Interstadial Würm II Würm III	Aurignacian Gravettian Solutrean Magdalenian and Grimaldian	*Homo sapiens* Crô-Magnons Combe Capelle Grimaldi	Venuses, Ochre-burials, Hunting ritual, Increase rites, sacred dance

The provisional time-scale is based on Prof. E. F. Zeuner's estimates.
cf. *Dating the Past*, 3rd edition, 1952, pp. 286, 299.

The Mesolithic Period

0000 B.C.	Late Glacial and Pre-Boreal	Capsian, Azilian- Tardenoisian	Upper Palaeo- lithic survivors and precursors of the modern races of Europe	Cult of skulls (Ofnet ritual burial) Sacred dance Ossuaries (Téviec) Danish *Dyssers*
7000 B.C.	Boreal	Maglemosean Ertebølle (Denmark) Asturian (Spain) Natufian (Palestine)		
2500 B.C.	Sub-Boreal			

Sequence of Cultures in Western Europe

B.C.	SICILY	IBERIA	FRANCE	BRITAIN	SCANDINAVIA	CENTRAL EUROPE
3000	Neolithic (Stentinello)	Mesolithic	Mesolithic	Mesolithic	Mesolithic Ertebølle	Danubian I
2500	Siculan I (Chalcolithic)	Almerian (El Garcel)	Neolithic I	Neolithic A Windmill Hill Barrows	Neolithic II	Rössen Lengyel
2100	Siculan I	Los Millares Portuguese megaliths	Chalcolithic Cists, Passage-graves Chassy S.O.M. Channelard	Clyde-Carlingford		Early Saxo-Thuringian
2000	Siculan I	Beakers, Palmella Alcala		Galleries Neolithic B Peterborough	Passage-graves	Jordansmühl Beakers
1900	Siculan I	Early Bronze Age	Chalcolithic II Beakers	Neolithic Beakers B Round barrows	Single graves Stone cists culture	Corded-ware warrior-cultures Globular ware Altheim Early Bronze Age
1800	Siculan I	Viejo	Megalithic culture Breton Early Bronze Age	Avebury Stonehenge		
1700	Siculan I	El Argar	Barrow cult	Wessex Early Bronze Age		Aunjetitz West Alpine Lake dwellings
1600	Siculan I		Corded ware Bronze Age III	Food-vessels Wessex warrior-culture	Early Bronze Age Stone cists	Apennine I Middle Bronze Age
1500	Siculan II (Middle Bronze Age)					Terremare Apennine II Tumulus culture Lausitz
1400				Middle Bronze Age Urnfields	Bronze Age II	
1000			Tumulus culture	Late Bronze Age		Urnfields Villanovan B Hallstatt A

Sequence of Cultures in the Eastern Mediterranean

B.C.	CRETE	THESSALY	GREECE	TROAD	DANUBE
3000	Neolithic				Danubian I
c. 2600	Early Minoan I	Dimini, Vardar	Early Helladic I	Troy I	Vinča
					Butmir
2400	Early Minoan II	Early Macedonian	Early Helladic II	Troy II	Danubian II
2200	Early Minoan III		Early Helladic III	Troy III and IV	Tripolye, Tordos
2000	Middle Minoan I	Middle Macedonian	Middle Helladic I	Troy V	Danubian III
1800	Middle Minoan II		Middle Helladic II	Troy VI	Bronze Age
			Minyan		
1600	Late Minoan I	Late Macedonian	Late Helladic I		Baden
					Perjamos
1400	Late Minoan II	Mycenaean	Late Helladic II		
1300	Fall of Knossos	Mycenaean	Late Helladic III	Troy VIIa, VIIb	

Sequence of Cultures in the Near East

B.C.	EGYPT	MESOPO-TAMIA	SUSA AND IRAN	SIND AND PUNJAB
From c. 4000	Tasian Fayum Badarian Merimdian Amratian Naqada I Gerzean Naqada II	Qalat Jarmo Hassuna Samarra, Halaf Gawra Arpachiyah Nineveh I Ubaid Uruk Gawra XII Nineveh II Hassuna V Uruk Jemdet Nasr.	Sialk I Sialk II Hissar I Sialk III Susa I. Anau I Susa B Sialk IV Anau II Susa C	Harappa I
c. 3000	1st Dynasty	Ur I–III	Hissar III Susa D	Mohenjo-daro Harappa II (R.37)
c. 2800	Old Kingdom	Sargon (c. 2300)	Hissar III Anau III	Chanhu-daro I
c. 2000	Middle Kingdom	Hammurabi		Harappa III (H) Chanhu-daro II

INDEX